THE MULTILINGUAL COMPUTER DICTIONARY

THE MULTILINGUAL COMPUTER DICTIONARY

Dr. Alan Isaacs, editor

Facts On File, Inc.
460 Park Avenue South, New York, N.Y. 10016

THE MULTILINGUAL COMPUTER DICTIONARY

First published in 1981 by Facts On File, Inc.,
460 Park Avenue South, New York, N.Y. 10016

Library of Congress Cataloging in Publication Data

Isaacs, Alan, 1925–
The multilingual computer dictionary.

English, French, German, Italian, Portuguese, and Spanish.
1. Computers—Dictionaries—Polyglot.
2. Electronic data processing—Dictionaries—Polyglot.
3. Dictionaries, Polyglot. I. Title.
QA76.15.I78 001.64'03 80-39587
ISBN 0-87196-431-7
ISBN 0-87196-822-3 pbk

10 9 8 7 6 5 4 3 2

Printed in the United States of America

A

abändern *vb* De
En modify
Es modificar
Fr modifier
It modificare
Pt modificar

Abänderung *(f) n* De
En modification
Es modificación *(f)*
Fr modification *(f)*
It modificazione *(f)*
Pt modificação *(f)*

abbrechen *vb* De
En abort
Es malograrse
Fr suspendre
It abortire
Pt abortar

abertura de entrada-sair *(f)* Pt
De Eingangs-Ausgangsanschluβ *(m)*
En input-output port
Es puerta de entrada-salida *(f)*
Fr point d'accès entrée-sortie *(m)*
It porto entrata-uscita *(m)*

Abfragestation *(f) n* De
En inquiry terminal
Es terminal de interrogación *(m)*
Fr poste d'interrogation *(m)*
It terminale per informazioni *(m)*
Pt terminal de indagação *(m)*

abgehen *vb* De
En go down
Es tener una avería
Fr tomber en panne
It avere una panna
Pt avariar

abgeschlossenes Programm *(n)* De
En closed routine
Es rutina cerrada *(f)*
Fr routine fermée *(f)*
It routine chiusa *(f)*
Pt rotina fechada *(f)*

Ablauf *(m) n* De
En computer run
Es pasada de ordenador *(f)*
Fr phase de traitement *(f)*
It esecuzione di elaboratore *(f)*
Pt passagem de computador *(f)*

Ablaufende *(n) n* De
En end of run (EOR)
Es fin de pasada *(m)*
Fr fin de passage *(f)*
It fine dell'elaborazione *(f)*
Pt fim da passagem *(m)*

Abnahmeprüfung *(f) n* De
En acceptance test
Es ensayo de aceptación *(m)*
Fr essai de réception *(m)*
It test di accettazione *(m)*
Pt teste de aceitação *(m)*

abnormal termination En
De Programmabbruch *(m)*
Es terminación anormal *(f)*
Fr terminaison anormale *(f)*
It conclusione anormale *(f)*
Pt terminação anormal *(f)*

abort *n* En
De Blockabbruch *(m)*
Es suspensión *(f)*
Fr suspension d'exécution *(f)*
It insuccesso *(m)*
Pt aborto *(m)*

abort *vb* En
De abbrechen
Es malograrse
Fr suspendre
It abortire
Pt abortar

abortar *vb* Pt
De abbrechen
En abort
Es malograrse
Fr suspendre
It abortire

abortire *vb* It
De abbrechen
En abort
Es malograrse
Fr suspendre
Pt abortar

aborto *(m) n* Pt
De Blockabbruch *(m)*
En abort
Es suspensión *(f)*
Fr suspension d'exécution *(f)*
It insuccesso *(m)*

abrechenbare Zeit *(f)* De
En accountable time
Es tiempo contable *(m)*
Fr temps comptable *(m)*
It tempo responsabile *(m)*
Pt tempo justificável *(m)*

Abruflesen *(n) n* De
En demand reading
Es lectura inmediata *(f)*
Fr lecture immédiate *(f)*
It lettura a domanda *(f)*
Pt leitura de procura *(f)*

Abrufschreiben *(n) n* De
En demand writing
Es escritura inmediata *(f)*
Fr écriture immédiate *(f)*
It scrittura a domanda *(f)*
Pt escrita de procura *(f)*

Abrufverarbeitung *(f)* De
En demand processing
Es tratamiento inmediato *(m)*
Fr traitement immédiat *(m)*
It elaborazione a domanda *(f)*
Pt processamento de procura *(m)*

Absatz *(m) n* De
En chapter
Es capítulo *(m)*
Fr chapitre *(m)*
It capitolo *(m)*
Pt capítulo *(m)*

Abschneidefehler *(m) n* De
En truncation error
Es error de truncamiento *(m)*
Fr erreur par troncation *(f)*
It errore di troncamento *(m)*
Pt erro de truncamento *(m)*

abschneiden *vb* De
En truncate
Es truncar
Fr tronquer
It troncare
Pt truncar

abschreiben *vb* De
En transcribe
Es transcribir
Fr transcrire
It trascrivere
Pt transcrever

absolute address En
De absolute Adresse *(f)*
Es dirección absoluta *(f)*
Fr adresse absolue *(f)*
It indirizzo assoluto *(m)*
Pt direcção absoluta *(f)*

absolute Adresse *(f)* De
En absolute address
Es dirección absoluta *(f)*
Fr adresse absolue *(f)*
It indirizzo assoluto *(m)*
Pt direcção absoluta *(f)*

absolute code En
De absoluter Code *(m)*
Es código absoluto *(m)*
Fr code absolu *(m)*
It codice assoluto *(m)*
Pt código absoluto *(m)*

absoluter Code *(m)* De
En absolute code
Es código absoluto *(m)*
Fr code absolu *(m)*
It codice assoluto *(m)*
Pt código absoluto *(m)*

Abstimmung *(f) n* De
En tuning
Es sintonización *(f)*

Fr mise au point *(f)*
It sintonizzazione *(f)*
Pt afinação *(f)*

abtasten *vb* De
En scan
Es explorar
Fr explorer
It scrutare
Pt explorar

Abtaster *(m) n* De
En scanner
Es explorador *(m)*
Fr explorateur *(m)*
It analizzatore per scansione *(m)*
Pt dispositivo de exploração *(m)*

Abtastfrequenz *(f) n* De
En sampling rate
Es frecuencia de muestreo *(f)*
Fr vitesse d'échantillonnage *(f)*
It volume di campionamento *(m)*
Pt índice de amostragem *(m)*

Abtastung *(f) n* De
En scan
Es exploración *(f)*
Fr exploration *(f)*
It esplorazione *(f)*
Pt exploracão *(f)*

Abwechslung *(f) n* De
En alternation
Es alternancia *(f)*
Fr alternance *(f)*
It alternanza *(f)*
Pt alternância *(f)*

abwickeln *vb* De
En unwind
Es desovillar
Fr dérouler
It svolgere
Pt desenrolar

abzweigen *vb* De
En branch
Es bifurcar
Fr brancher
It diramarsi
Pt ligar

acceder *vb* Es
De zugreifen
En access
Fr accéder
It accedere
Pt aceder

accéder *vb* Fr
De zugreifen
En access
Es acceder
It accedere
Pt aceder

accedere *vb* It
De zugreifen
En access
Es acceder
Fr accéder
Pt aceder

accélération *(f) n* Fr
De Durchschlag *(m)*
En crash
Es choque *(m)*
It urto *(m)*
Pt colisão *(f)*

acceleration time En
De Beschleunigungszeit *(f)*
Es tiempo de aceleración *(m)*
Fr temps d'accélération *(m)*
It tempo di accelerazione *(m)*
Pt tempo de aceleração *(m)*

accélérer *vb* Fr
De durchschlagen
En crash
Es quebrar
It urtare
Pt colidir

acceptance test En
De Abnahmeprüfung *(f)*
Es ensayo de aceptación *(m)*
Fr essai de réception *(m)*
It test di accettazione *(m)*
Pt teste de aceitação *(m)*

accès *(m) n* Fr
De Zugriff *(m)*
En access
Es acceso *(m)*
It accesso *(m)*
Pt acesso *(m)*

accès direct *(m)* Fr
De direkter Zugriff *(m)*
En direct access
Es acceso directo *(m)*
It accesso diretto *(m)*
Pt acesso directo *(m)*

accès en parallèle *(m)* Fr
De Parallelzugriff *(m)*
En parallel access
Es acceso en paralelo *(m)*
It accesso parallelo *(m)*
Pt acesso paralelo *(m)*

accès en serie *(m)* Fr
De sequenzieller Zugriff *(m)*
En serial access
Es acceso en serie *(m)*
It accesso in serie *(m)*
Pt acesso em série *(m)*

accès immédiat *(m)* Fr
De unmittelbarer Zugriff *(m)*
En immediate access
Es acceso inmediato *(m)*
It accesso immediato *(m)*
Pt acesso imediato *(m)*

accès-multiples *adj* Fr
De Mehrfachzugriff
En multi-access
Es acceso-múltiple
It accesso-multiplo
Pt multi-acesso

acceso *(m) n* Es
De Zugriff *(m)*
En access
Fr accès *(m)*
It accesso *(m)*
Pt acesso *(m)*

acceso al azar *(m)* Es
De direkter Zugriff *(m)*
En random access
Fr accès sélectif *(m)*
It accesso casuale *(m)*
Pt acesso aleatório *(m)*

acceso directo *(m)* Es
De direkter Zugriff *(m)*
En direct access
Fr accès direct *(m)*
It accesso diretto *(m)*
Pt acesso directo *(m)*

acceso en paralelo *(m)* Es
De Parallelzugriff *(m)*
En parallel access
Fr accès en parallèle *(m)*
It accesso parallelo *(m)*
Pt acesso paralelo *(m)*

acceso en serie *(m)* Es
De sequenzieller Zugriff *(m)*
En serial access
Fr accès en série *(m)*
It accesso in serie *(m)*
Pt acesso em série *(m)*

acceso inmediato *(m)* Es
De unmittelbarer Zugriff *(m)*
En immediate access
Fr accès immédiat *(m)*
It accesso immediato *(m)*
Pt acesso imediato *(m)*

acceso-múltiple *adj* Es
De Mehrfachzugriff
En multi-access
Fr accès-multiples
It accesso-multiplo
Pt multi-acesso

acceso secuencial *(m)* Es
De Folgezugriff *(m)*
En sequential access
Fr accès séquentiel *(m)*
It accesso sequenziale *(m)*
Pt acesso sequencial *(m)*

acceso simultáneo *(m)* Es
De gleichzeitiger Zugriff *(m)*
En simultaneous access
Fr accès simultané *(m)*
It accesso simultaneo *(m)*
Pt acesso simultâneo *(m)*

access *n* En
De Zugriff *(m)*
Es acceso *(m)*
Fr accès *(m)*

It accesso *(m)*
Pt acesso *(m)*

access *vb* En
De zugreifen
Es acceder
Fr accéder
It accedere
Pt aceder

accès sélectif *(m)* Fr
De direkter Zugriff *(m)*
En random access
Es acceso al azar *(m)*
It accesso casuale *(m)*
Pt acesso aleatório *(m)*

accès séquentiel *(m)* Fr
De Folgezugriff *(m)*
En sequential access
Es acceso secuencial *(m)*
It accesso sequenziale *(m)*
Pt acesso sequencial *(m)*

accès simultané *(m)* Fr
De gleichzeitiger Zugriff *(m)*
En simultaneous access
Es acceso simultáneo *(m)*
It accesso simultaneo *(m)*
Pt acesso simultâneo *(m)*

access level En
De Zugriffsstufe *(f)*
Es nivel de acceso *(m)*
Fr niveau d'accès *(m)*
It livello di accesso *(m)*
Pt nível de acesso *(m)*

accesso *(m) n* It
De Zugriff *(m)*
En access
Es acceso *(m)*
Fr accès *(m)*
Pt acesso *(m)*

accesso casuale *(m)* It
De direkter Zugriff *(m)*
En random access
Es acceso al azar *(m)*
Fr accès sélectif *(m)*
Pt acesso aleatório *(m)*

accesso diretto *(m)* It
De direkter Zugriff *(m)*
En direct access
Es acceso directo *(m)*
Fr accès direct *(m)*
Pt acesso directo *(m)*

accesso immediato *(m)* It
De unmittelbarer Zugriff *(m)*
En immediate access
Es acceso inmediato *(m)*
Fr accès immédiat *(m)*
Pt acesso imediato *(m)*

accesso in serie *(m)* It
De sequenzieller Zugriff *(m)*
En serial access
Es acceso en serie *(m)*
Fr accès en série *(m)*
Pt acesso em série *(m)*

accesso-multiplo *adj* It
De Mehrfachzugriff
En multi-access
Es acceso-múltiple
Fr accès-multiples
Pt multi-acesso

accesso parallelo *(m)* It
De Parallelzugriff *(m)*
En parallel access
Es acceso en paralelo *(m)*
Fr accès en parallèle *(m)*
Pt acesso paralelo *(m)*

accesso sequenziale *(m)* It
De Folgezugriff *(m)*
En sequential access
Es acceso secuencial *(m)*
Fr accès séquentiel *(m)*
Pt acesso sequencial *(m)*

accesso simultaneo *(m)* It
De gleichzeitiger Zugriff *(m)*
En simultaneous access
Es acceso simultáneo *(m)*
Fr accès simultané *(m)*
Pt acesso simultâneo *(m)*

access time En
De Zugriffszeit *(f)*
Es tiempo de acceso *(m)*
Fr temps d'accès *(m)*
It tempo di accesso *(m)*
Pt tempo de acesso *(m)*

accionamento da fita *(m)* Pt
De Bandantrieb *(m)*
En tape drive
Es impulsor de cinta *(m)*
Fr dérouleur de bande *(m)*
It guida del nastro *(f)*

accionamento de acesso duplo *(m)* Pt
De Doppelzugriffsantrieb *(m)*
En dual-access drive
Es unidad de doble acceso *(f)*
Fr entraînement d'accès double *(m)*
It unità ad accesso duplice *(f)*

accionamento de disco *(m)* Pt
De Plattenantrieb *(m)*
En disk drive
Es unidad de discos *(f)*
Fr unité de disque(s) *(f)*
It unità a dischi *(f)*

accionamento do disco floppy *(m)* Pt
De Floppy-Disk-Antrieb *(m)*
En floppy-disk drive
Es unidad de discos flexibles *(f)*
Fr unité de disque souple *(f)*
It unità floppy disk *(f)*

accionar *vb* Pt
De antreiben
En drive
Es impulsar
Fr entraîner
It azionare

acción de archivar *(f)* Es
De Archivierung *(f)*
En archiving
Fr archivage *(m)*
It archiviazione *(f)*
Pt acto de arquivar *(m)*

accoppiado fortemente It
De eng gekoppelt
En tightly coupled
Es fuertemente acoplado
Fr à couplage serré
Pt firmemente acoplado

accoppiado lentamente It
De lose gekoppelt
En loosely coupled
Es débilmente acoplado
Fr lâchement couplé
Pt acoplado de forma solta

accoppiamento *(m) n* It
De Ubereinstimmung *(f)*
En match
Es correspondencia *(f)*
Fr assortiment *(m)*
Pt equiparação *(f)*

accoppiatore acustico *(m)* It
De akustischer Koppler *(m)*
En acoustic coupler
Es acoplador acústico *(m)*
Fr coupleur acoustique *(m)*
Pt acoplador acústico *(m)*

accountable time En
De abrechenbare Zeit *(f)*
Es tiempo contable *(m)*
Fr temps comptable *(m)*
It tempo responsabile *(m)*
Pt tempo justificável *(m)*

accumulateur *(m) n* Fr
De Kontroll-Summenfeld *(n)*
En accumulator
Es acumulador *(m)*
It accumulatore *(m)*
Pt acumulador *(m)*

accumulator *n* En
De Kontroll-Summenfeld *(n)*
Es acumulador *(m)*
Fr accumulateur *(m)*
It accumulatore *(m)*
Pt acumulador *(m)*

accumulatore *(m) n* It
De Kontroll-Summenfeld *(n)*
En accumulator
Es acumulador *(m)*
Fr accumulateur *(m)*
Pt acumulador *(m)*

accusé de réception *(m)* Fr
De Rückmeldung *(f)*
En acknowledgment
Es admisión confirmación *(f)*
It riconoscimento *(m)*
Pt confirmação de recepção *(f)*

accusé de réception négatif *(m)* Fr
De negative Rückmeldung *(f)*
En negative acknowledgment
Es confirmación negativa *(f)*
It riconoscimento negativo *(m)*
Pt confirmação negativa *(f)*

aceder *vb* Pt
De zugreifen
En access
Es acceder
Fr accéder
It accedere

acesso *(m) n* Pt
De Zugriff *(m)*
En access
Es acceso *(m)*
Fr accès *(m)*
It accesso *(m)*

acesso aleatório *(m)* Pt
De direkter Zugriff *(m)*
En random access
Es acceso al azar *(m)*
Fr accès sélectif *(m)*
It accesso casuale *(m)*

acesso directo *(m)* Pt
De direkter Zugriff *(m)*
En direct access
Es acceso directo *(m)*
Fr accès direct *(m)*
It accesso diretto *(m)*

acesso em série *(m)* Pt
De sequenzieller Zugriff *(m)*
En serial access
Es acceso en serie *(m)*
Fr accès en série *(m)*
It accesso in serie *(m)*

acesso imediato *(m)* Pt
De unmittelbarer Zugriff *(m)*
En immediate access
Es acceso inmediato *(m)*
Fr accès immédiat *(m)*
It accesso immediato *(m)*

acesso paralelo *(m)* Pt
De Parallelzugriff *(m)*
En parallel access
Es acceso en paralelo *(m)*
Fr accès en parallèle *(m)*
It accesso parallelo *(m)*

acesso sequencial *(m)* Pt
De Folgezugriff *(m)*
En sequential access
Es acceso secuencial *(m)*
Fr accès séquentiel *(m)*
It accesso sequenziale *(m)*

acesso simultâneo *(m)* Pt
De gleichzeitiger Zugriff *(m)*
En simultaneous access
Es acceso simultáneo *(m)*
Fr accès simultané *(m)*
It accesso simultaneo *(m)*

acheminar *vb* Fr
De führen
En route
Es encaminar
It incanalare
Pt encaminhar

acheminement des messages *(m)* Fr
De Nachrichten-vermittlung *(f)*
En message routing
Es encaminamiento de mensajes *(m)*
It incanalazione dei messaggi *(f)*
Pt encaminhamento de mensagens *(m)*

achtzig-Spalten-Karte *(f)* De
En eighty-column card
Es tarjeta de ochenta columnas *(f)*
Fr carte de quatre-vingt colonnes *(f)*
It scheda ad ottanta colonne *(f)*
Pt ficha de oitenta colunas *(f)*

acknowledgment *n* En
De Rückmeldung *(f)*
Es admisión confirmación *(f)*
Fr accusé de réception *(m)*
It riconoscimento *(m)*
Pt confirmação de recepção *(f)*

acoplado de forma solta Pt
De lose gekoppelt
En loosely coupled
Es débilmente acoplado
Fr lâchement couplé
It accoppiado lentamente

acoplador acústico *(m)* Es, Pt
De akustischer Koppler *(m)*
En acoustic coupler
Fr coupleur acoustique *(m)*
It accoppiatore acustico *(m)*

acoplamiento hombre-máquina *(m)* Es
De Personal-Maschinen Schnittstelle *(f)*
En man-machine interface
Fr interface homme-machine *(f)*
It interfaccia uomo-macchina *(f)*
Pt interface homem-máquina *(f)*

acoplamiento mutuo *(m)* Es
De Schnittstelle *(f)*
En interface
Fr interface *(f)*
It interfaccia *(f)*
Pt interface *(f)*

acoplamiento mutuo por bucle de corriente *(m)* Es
De Stromschleifen-Schnittstelle *(f)*
En current-loop interface
Fr interface boucle courant *(f)*
It interfaccia del ciclo corrente *(f)*
Pt interface de circuito de corrente *(f)*

à couplage serré Fr
De eng gekoppelt
En tightly coupled
Es fuertemente acoplado
It accoppiado fortemente
Pt firmemente acoplado

acoustic coupler En
De akustischer Koppler *(m)*
Es acoplador acústico *(m)*
Fr coupleur acoustique *(m)*
It accoppiatore acustico *(m)*
Pt acoplador acústico *(m)*

acquisto automatico dei dati *(m)* It
De automatische Datenerwerbung *(f)*
En automatic data acquisition (ADA)
Es adquisición automatica de datos *(f)*
Fr saisie de donneés automatique *(f)*
Pt adquisição automática de dados *(f)*

acto de arquivar *(m)* Pt
De Archivierung *(f)*
En archiving
Es acción de archivar *(f)*
Fr archivage *(m)*
It archiviazione *(f)*

actual address En
De echte Adresse *(f)*
Es dirección real *(f)*
Fr adresse réelle *(f)*
It indirizzo effettivo *(m)*
Pt direcção real *(f)*

actualização atrasada *(f)* Pt
De verzögerte Aktualisierung *(f)*
En delayed updating
Es actualización diferida *(f)*
Fr mise à jour temporisée *(f)*
It aggiornamento ritardato *(m)*

actualización diferida *(f)* Es
De verzögerte Aktualisierung *(f)*
En delayed updating
Fr mise à jour temporisée *(f)*
It aggiornamento ritardato *(m)*
Pt actualização atrasada *(f)*

actualizar *vb* Es, Pt
De auf den neuesten Stand bringen
En update
Fr mettre à jour
It aggiornare

acumulador *(m) n* Es, Pt
De Kontroll-Summenfeld *(n)*
En accumulator
Fr accumulateur *(m)*
It accumulatore *(m)*

adaptive-control system En
De adaptives Steuersystem *(n)*
Es sistema de control autoadaptable *(m)*
Fr système de commande adaptatif *(m)*
It sistema a controllo adattivo *(m)*
Pt sistema de controlo adaptável *(m)*

adaptives Steuersystem *(n)* De
En adaptive-control system
Es sistema de control autoadaptable *(m)*
Fr système de commande adaptatif *(m)*
It sistema a controllo adattivo *(m)*
Pt sistema de controlo adaptável *(m)*

adder *n* En
De Addierglied *(n)*
Es sumador *(m)*
Fr additionneur *(m)*
It addizionatore *(m)*
Pt somador *(m)*

adder-subtracter *n* En
De Addier-Subtrahierglied *(n)*
Es sumador-sustractor *(m)*
Fr additionneur-soustracteur *(m)*
It addizionatore-sottrattore *(m)*
Pt somador-subtractor *(m)*

Addierglied *(n) n* De
En adder
Es sumador *(m)*
Fr additionneur *(m)*
It addizionatore *(m)*
Pt somador *(m)*

Addier- Subtrahierglied *(n)* De
En adder-subtracter
Es sumador-sustractor *(m)*
Fr additionneur-soustracteur *(m)*
It addizionatore-sottrattore *(m)*
Pt somador-subtractor *(m)*

Addier-Subtrahierzeit *(f)* De
En add-subtract time
Es tiempo de suma-resta *(m)*
Fr temps d'addition-soustraction *(m)*
It tempo di addizione-sottrazione *(m)*
Pt tempo de soma-subtracção *(m)*

addition destructive *(f)* Fr
De Löschen der Addition *(n)*
En destructive addition
Es suma destructiva *(f)*
It addizione distruttiva *(f)*
Pt adição destrutiva *(f)*

additionneur *(m) n* Fr
De Addierglied *(n)*
En adder
Es sumador *(m)*
It addizionatore *(m)*
Pt somador *(m)*

additionneur complet *(m)* Fr
De Feldaddierer *(m)*
En full adder
Es adicionador completo *(m)*
It addizionatore totale *(m)*
Pt somador total *(m)*

additionneur-soustracteur *(m)* Fr
De Addier-Subtrahierglied *(n)*
En adder-subtracter
Es sumador-sustractor *(m)*
It addizionatore-sottrattore *(m)*
Pt somador-subtractor *(m)*

addizionatore *(m) n* It
De Addierglied *(n)*
En adder
Es sumador *(m)*
Fr additionneur *(m)*
Pt somador *(m)*

addizionatore-sottrattore *(m)* It
De Addier-Subtrahierglied *(n)*
En adder-subtracter
Es sumador-sustractor *(m)*
Fr additionneur-soustracteur *(m)*
Pt somador-subtractor *(m)*

addizionatore totale *(m)* It
De Feldaddierer *(m)*
En full adder
Es adicionador completo *(m)*
Fr additionneur complet *(m)*
Pt somador total *(m)*

addizione distruttiva *(f)* It
De Löschen der Addition *(n)*
En destructive addition
Es suma destructiva *(f)*
Fr addition destructive *(f)*
Pt adição destrutiva *(f)*

address *n* En
De Adresse *(f)*
Es dirección *(f)*
Fr adresse *(f)*
It indirizzo *(m)*
Pt endereço *(m)*

address *vb* En
De adressieren
Es direccionar
Fr adresser
It indirizzare
Pt endereçar

address part En
De Adressenteil *(n)*
Es parte de la dirección *(f)*
Fr partie d'adresse *(f)*
It indirizzo parziale *(m)*
Pt parte de endereço *(f)*

add-subtract time En
De Addier-Subtrahierzeit *(f)*
Es tiempo de suma-resta *(m)*
Fr temps d'addition-soustraction *(m)*
It tempo di addizione-sottrazione *(m)*
Pt tempo de soma-subtracção *(m)*

adição destrutiva *(f)* Pt
De Löschen der Addition *(n)*
En destructive addition
Es suma destructiva *(f)*
Fr addition destructive *(f)*
It addizione distruttiva *(f)*

adicionador completo *(m)* Es
De Feldaddierer *(m)*
En full adder
Fr additionneur complet *(m)*
It addizionatore totale *(m)*
Pt somador total *(m)*

admisión confirmación *(f)* Es
De Rückmeldung *(f)*
En acknowledgment
Fr accusé de réception *(m)*
It riconoscimento *(m)*
Pt confirmação de recepção *(f)*

ad orientamento di voce It
De wortorientiert
En word-orientated
Es orientado a la palabra
Fr à mots
Pt orientado por palavras

adquisição automática de dados *(f)* Pt
De automatische Datenerwerbung *(f)*
En automatic data acquisition (ADA)
Es adquisición automatica de datos *(f)*
Fr saisie de donneés automatique *(f)*
It acquisto automatico dei dati *(m)*

adquisición automatica de datos *(f)* Es
De automatische Datenerwerbung *(f)*
En automatic data acquisition (ADA)
Fr saisie de donneés automatique *(f)*
It acquisto automatico dei dati *(m)*
Pt adquisição automática de dados *(f)*

adressage direct *(m)* Fr
De direkte Adressierung *(f)*
En direct addressing
Es direccionamiento directo *(m)*
It indirizzamento diretto *(m)*
Pt enderaçamento directo *(m)*

adressage relatif *(m)* Fr
De relative Adressierung *(f)*
En relative addressing
Es direccionado relativo *(m)*
It indirizzamento relativo *(m)*
Pt endereçamento relativo *(m)*

adressage sous-entendu *(m)* Fr
De wiederholte Adressierung *(f)*
En repetitive addressing
Es direccionado repetitivo *(m)*
It indirizzamento ripetitivo *(m)*
Pt endereçamento repetitivo *(m)*

adresse *(f)* *n* Fr
De Adresse *(f)*
En address
Es dirección *(f)*
It indirizzo *(m)*
Pt endereço *(m)*

Adresse *(f)* *n* De
En address
Es dirección *(f)*
Fr adresse *(f)*
It indirizzo *(m)*
Pt endereço *(m)*

adresse absolue *(f)* Fr
De absolute Adresse; Maschinenadresse *(f)*
En absolute address; machine address
Es dirección absoluta; dirección de máquina *(f)*
It indirizzo assoluto; indirizzo di macchina *(m)*
Pt direcção absoluta; endereço da máquina *(f m)*

adresse à deuxième niveau *(f)* Fr
De Adresse der zweiten Stufe *(f)*
En second-level address
Es dirección de segundo nivel *(f)*
It indirizzo del secondo livello *(m)*
Pt endereço de segundo nível *(m)*

adresse de base *(f)* Fr
De Basisadresse *(f)*
En base address
Es dirección de base *(f)*
It indirizzo base *(m)*
Pt direcção de base *(f)*

Adresse der zweiten Stufe *(f)* De
En second-level address
Es dirección de segundo nivel *(f)*
Fr adresse à deuxième niveau *(f)*
It indirizzo del secondo livello *(m)*
Pt endereço de segundo nível *(m)*

adresse immédiate *(f)* Fr
De unmittelbare Adresse *(f)*
En immediate address
Es dirección inmediata *(f)*
It indirizzo immediato *(m)*
Pt endereço imediato *(m)*

adresse indirecte *(f)* Fr
De indirekte Adresse *(f)*
En indirect address
Es dirección indirecta *(f)*
It indirizzo indiretto *(m)*
Pt endereço indirecto *(m)*

Adressenteil *(n)* *n* De
En address part
Es parte de la dirección *(f)*
Fr partie d'adresse *(f)*
It indirizzo parziale *(m)*
Pt parte de endereço *(f)*

adresse primitive *(f)* Fr
De Bezugsadresse *(f)*
En reference address
Es dirección de referencia *(f)*
It indirizzo di riferimento *(m)*
Pt endereço de referência *(m)*

adresser *vb* Fr
De adressieren
En address
Es direccionar
It indirizzare
Pt endereçar

adresse réelle *(f)* Fr
De echte Adresse; effektive Adresse *(f)*
En actual address; effective address
Es dirección efectiva; dirección real *(f)*
It indirizzo effettivo; indirizzo efficace *(m)*
Pt direcção real; endereço real *(f m)*

adresse relative *(f)* Fr
De relative Adresse *(f)*
En relative address
Es dirección relativa *(f)*
It indirizzo relativo *(m)*
Pt endereço relativo *(m)*

adresse symbolique *(f)* Fr
De symbolische Adresse *(f)*
En symbolic address
Es dirección simbólica *(f)*
It indirizzo simbolico *(m)*
Pt endereço simbólico *(m)*

adresse translatable *(f)* Fr
De verschiebliche Adresse *(f)*
En relocatable address
Es dirección reubicable *(f)*
It indirizzo rilocabile *(m)*
Pt endereço relocalizável *(m)*

adresse virtuelle *(f)* Fr
De virtuelle Adresse *(f)*
En virtual address
Es dirección virtual *(f)*
It indirizzo virtuale *(m)*
Pt endereço virtual *(m)*

adressieren *vb* De
En address
Es direccionar
Fr adresser
It indirizzare
Pt endereçar

advance-feed tape En
De Bandvorausvorschub *(m)*
Es cinta de alimentación por arrastre *(f)*
Fr défilement-avancement bande *(m)*
It avanzare-alimentare nastro *(m)*
Pt fita de alimentação por avanço *(f)*

affectation *(f) n* Fr
De Zuweisung *(f)*
En allocation
Es asignación *(f)*
It allocazione *(f)*
Pt atribuição *(f)*

affectation de la mémoire *(f)* Fr
De Speicherzuweisung *(f)*
En storage allocation
Es asignación de almacenamiento *(f)*
It assegnazione in memoria *(f)*
Pt atribuição de armazenamento *(f)*

affectation des ressources *(f)* Fr
De Betriebsmittel-zuweisung *(f)*
En resource allocation
Es asignación de recursos *(f)*
It allocazione delle risorse *(f)*
Pt atribuição de recursos *(f)*

affectation dynamique *(f)* Fr
De dynamische Zuweisung *(f)*
En dynamic allocation
Es asignación dinámica *(f)*
It allocazione dinamica *(f)*
Pt designação dinâmica *(f)*

affecter *vb* Fr
De zuweisen
En allocate
Es asignar
It allocare
Pt atribuir

affichage *(m) n* Fr
De Anzeige *(f)*
En display
Es representación visual *(f)*
It visualizzatore *(m)*
Pt representação visual *(f)*

affichage d'enregistrement *(m)* Fr
De Speicheranzeige *(f)*
En storage display
Es presentación de almacenamiento *(f)*
It visualizzazione di memoria *(f)*
Pt visualização de armazenamento *(f)*

affichage mode point par point *(m)* Fr
De punktweise Darstellung *(f)*
En point-mode display
Es representación de modo puntual *(f)*
It mostra di modo punto a punto *(f)*
Pt display de modo pontual *(m)*

affichage mode vectoriel *(m)* Fr
De Vektorbetriebs-artanzeige *(f)*
En vector-mode display
Es representación en modo vectorial *(f)*
It visualizzazione di modo vettore *(f)*
Pt visualização de modo vector *(f)*

affichage-régénération *(m)* Fr
De Auffrischungsanzeige *(f)*
En refresh display
Es representación regenerada *(f)*
It visualizzazione di aggiornamento *(f)*
Pt apresentação de refrescamento *(f)*

affichage tabulaire *(m)* Fr
De tabellarische Anzeige *(f)*
En tabular display
Es representación tabular *(f)*
It visualizzazione tabulare *(f)*
Pt visualização tabelar *(f)*

affichage tramé *(m)* Fr
De Rasteranzeige *(f)*
En raster display
Es presentación de trama *(f)*
It visualizzazione trama *(f)*
Pt apresentação quadriculada *(f)*

afficher *vb* Fr
De anzeigen
En display
Es presentar
It visualizzare
Pt mostrar

affidabilita *(f) n* It
De Zuverlässigkeit *(f)*
En reliability
Es fiabilidad *(f)*
Fr fiabilité *(f)*
Pt confiança *(f)*

afinação *(f) n* Pt
De Abstimmung *(f)*
En tuning
Es sintonización *(f)*
Fr mise au point *(f)*
It sintonizzazione *(f)*

afirmação *(f) n* Pt
De Anweisung *(f)*
En statement
Es sentencia *(f)*
Fr instructions *(f pl)*
It statement *(m)*

afirmação declarativa *(f)* Pt
De Prozeduranweisung *(f)*
En declarative statement
Es sentencia de declaración *(f)*
Fr instruction déclarative *(f)*
It statement di dichiarazione *(m)*

afirmação de controlo *(f)* Pt
De Steueranweisung *(f)*
En control statement
Es sentencia de control *(f)*
Fr ordre de contrôle *(m)*
It statement di controllo *(m)*

agenda *n* En; Es, It, Pt *(f)*
De Agende *(f)*
Fr ordre du jour *(m)*

Agende *(f) n* De
En agenda
Es agenda *(f)*
Fr ordre du jour *(m)*
It agenda *(f)*
Pt agenda *(f)*

aggiornamento ritardato *(m)* It
De verzögerte Aktualisierung *(f)*
En delayed updating
Es actualización diferida *(f)*
Fr mise à jour temporisée *(f)*
Pt actualização atrasada *(f)*

aggiornare *vb* It
De auf den neuesten Stand bringen
En update
Es actualizar
Fr mettre à jour
Pt actualizar

aire constante *(f)* Fr
De Konstantbereich *(m)*
En constant area
Es área constante *(f)*
It area costante *(f)*
Pt área constante *(f)*

ajuda de desparasitação *(f)* Pt
De Fehlersuchhilfe *(f)*
En debugging aid
Es ayuda a la depuración *(f)*
Fr outil de mise au point *(m)*

It strumento di messa a punto (di un programma) *(m)*

ajustar *vb* Es
De setzen
En set
Fr régler
It disporre
Pt colocar

aktivieren *vb* De
En execute
Es ejecutar
Fr exécuter
It eseguire
Pt executar

Aktivierpuls *(m) n* De
En enable pulse
Es impulso de activación *(m)*
Fr impulsion de validation *(f)*
It impulso di abilitazione *(m)*
Pt impulso de capacitação *(m)*

Aktiviersignal *(n) n* De
En enabling signal
Es señal de activación *(f)*
Fr signal de validation *(m)*
It segnale di abilitazione *(m)*
Pt sinal de capacitação *(m)*

Aktivierungsphase *(f) n* De
En execute phase
Es fase de ejecución *(f)*
Fr phase opératoire *(f)*
It fase di esecuzione *(f)*
Pt fase de execução *(f)*

Aktivierungsprogramm *(n) n* De
En executive program
Es programa ejecutivo *(m)*
Fr programme superviseur *(m)*
It programma esecutivo *(m)*
Pt programa de execução *(m)*

Aktivierungszeit *(f) n* De
En execution time
Es tiempo de ejecución *(m)*
Fr durée d'exécution *(f)*
It tempo di esecuzione *(m)*
Pt tempo de execução *(m)*

akustischer Koppler *(m)* De
En acoustic coupler
Es acoplador acústico *(m)*
Fr coupleur acoustique *(m)*
It accoppiatore acustico *(m)*
Pt acoplador acústico *(m)*

albero *(m) n* It
De Überlagerungsbaum *(m)*
En tree
Es árbol *(m)*
Fr arbre *(m)*
Pt árvore *(f)*

alcance *(m) n* Pt
De Bereich *(m)*
En range
Es margen *(m)*
Fr gamme *(f)*
It gamma *(f)*

alfabeto *(m) n* Es, It, Pt
De Alphabet *(n)*
En alphabet
Fr alphabet *(m)*

alfanumerico *adj* It
De alphanumerisch
En alphanumeric
Es alfanumérico
Fr alphanumérique
Pt alfanumérico

alfanumérico *adj* Es, Pt
De alphanumerisch
En alphanumeric
Fr alphanumérique
It alfanumerico

algebra booleana *(f)* It
De Boolesche Algebra *(f)*
En Boolean algebra
Es álgebra de Boole *(f)*
Fr algèbre de Boole *(f)*
Pt algebra de Boole *(f)*

algebra de Boole *(f)* Pt
De Boolesche Algebra *(f)*
En Boolean algebra
Es álgebra de Boole *(f)*
Fr algèbre de Boole *(f)*
It algebra booleana *(f)*

álgebra de Boole *(f)* Es
De Boolesche Algebra *(f)*
En Boolean algebra
Fr algèbre de Boole *(f)*
It algebra booleana *(f)*
Pt algebra de Boole *(f)*

algèbre de Boole *(f)* Fr
De Boolesche Algebra *(f)*
En Boolean algebra
Es álgebra de Boole *(f)*
It algebra booleana *(f)*
Pt algebra de Boole *(f)*

algorithm *n* En
De Algorithmus *(m)*
Es algoritmo *(m)*
Fr algorithme *(m)*
It algoritmo *(m)*
Pt algoritmo *(m)*

algorithme *(m) n* Fr
De Algorithmus *(m)*
En algorithm
Es algoritmo *(m)*
It algoritmo *(m)*
Pt algoritmo *(m)*

algorithme ligne cachée *(m)* Fr
De Verstecktzeilen-algorithmus *(m)*
En hidden-line algorithm
Es algoritmo de línea oculta *(m)*
It algoritmo a linea nascosta *(m)*
Pt algoritmo de linha oculta *(m)*

Algorithmus *(m) n* De
En algorithm
Es algoritmo *(m)*
Fr algorithme *(m)*
It algoritmo *(m)*
Pt algoritmo *(m)*

algoritmo *(m) n* Es, It, Pt
De Algorithmus *(m)*
En algorithm
Fr algorithme *(m)*

algoritmo a linea nascosta *(m)* It
De Verstecktzeilen-algorithmus *(m)*
En hidden-line algorithm
Es algoritmo de línea oculta *(m)*
Fr algorithme ligne cachée *(m)*
Pt algoritmo de linha oculta *(m)*

algoritmo de línea oculta *(m)* Es
De Verstecktzeilen-algorithmus *(m)*
En hidden-line algorithm
Fr algorithme ligne cachée *(m)*
It algoritmo a linea nascosta *(m)*
Pt algoritmo de linha oculta *(m)*

algoritmo de linha oculta *(m)* Pt
De Verstecktzeilen-algorithmus *(m)*
En hidden-line algorithm
Es algoritmo de línea oculta *(m)*
Fr algorithme ligne cachée *(m)*
It algoritmo a linea nascosta *(m)*

alimentação *(f) n* Pt
De Vorschub *(m)*
En feed
Es alimentación *(f)*
Fr avance *(f)*
It alimentazione *(f)*

alimentação de fita *(f)* Pt
De Bandvorschub *(m)*
En tape feed
Es alimentador de cinta *(m)*
Fr entraînement du ruban *(m)*
It alimentazione del nastro *(f)*

alimentação de formulários *(f)* Pt
De Formularvorschub *(m)*
En form feed
Es alimentación del papel *(f)*
Fr alimentation en papier *(f)*

It alimentazione del modulo *(f)*

alimentação horizontal *(f)* Pt
De Horizontalvorschub *(m)*
En horizontal feed
Es alimentación horizontal *(f)*
Fr avance horizontale *(f)*
It alimentazione orizzontale *(f)*

alimentación *(f) n* Es
De Vorschub *(m)*
En feed
Fr avance *(f)*
It alimentazione *(f)*
Pt alimentação *(f)*

alimentación del papel *(f)* Es
De Formularvorschub *(m)*
En form feed
Fr alimentation en papier *(f)*
It alimentazione del modulo *(f)*
Pt alimentação de formulários *(f)*

alimentación horizontal *(f)* Es
De Horizontalvorschub *(m)*
En horizontal feed
Fr avance horizontale *(f)*
It alimentazione crizzontale *(f)*
Pt alimentação horizontal *(f)*

alimentador de cinta *(m)* Es
De Bandvorschub *(m)*
En tape feed
Fr entraînement du ruban *(m)*
It alimentazione del nastro *(f)*
Pt alimentação de fita *(f)*

alimentar *vb* Es, Pt
De vorschieben
En feed
Fr faire avancer
It alimentare

alimentare *vb* It
De vorschieben
En feed
Es alimentar
Fr faire avancer
Pt alimentar

alimentation en papier *(f)* Fr
De Formularvorschub *(m)*
En form feed
Es alimentación del papel *(f)*
It alimentazione del modulo *(f)*
Pt alimentação de formulários *(f)*

alimentazione *(f) n* It
De Vorschub *(m)*
En feed
Es alimentación *(f)*
Fr avance *(f)*
Pt alimentação *(f)*

alimentazione del modulo *(f)* It
De Formularvorschub *(m)*
En form feed
Es alimentación del papel *(f)*
Fr alimentation en papier *(f)*
Pt alimentação de formulários *(f)*

alimentazione del nastro *(f)* It
De Bandvorschub *(m)*
En tape feed
Es alimentador de cinta *(m)*
Fr entraînement du ruban *(m)*
Pt alimentação de fita *(f)*

alimentazione orizzontale *(f)* It
De Horizontalvorschub *(m)*
En horizontal feed
Es alimentación horizontal *(f)*
Fr avance horizontale *(f)*
Pt alimentação horizontal *(f)*

Allgemeinzweck-computer *(m) n* De
En general-purpose computer
Es ordenador universal *(m)*
Fr calculateur universel *(m)*
It elaboratore a scopo generale *(m)*
Pt computador para todos os fins *(m)*

allocare *vb* It
De zuweisen
En allocate
Es asignar
Fr affecter
Pt atribuir

allocate *vb* En
De zuweisen
Es asignar
Fr affecter
It allocare
Pt atribuir

allocation *n* En
De Zuweisung *(f)*
Es asignación *(f)*
Fr affectation *(f)*
It allocazione *(f)*
Pt atribuição *(f)*

allocazione *(f) n* It
De Zuweisung *(f)*
En allocation
Es asignación *(f)*
Fr affectation *(f)*
Pt atribuição *(f)*

allocazione delle risorse *(f)* It
De Betriebsmittel-zuweisung *(f)*
En resource allocation
Es asignación de recursos *(f)*
Fr affectation des ressources *(f)*
Pt atribuição de recursos *(f)*

allocazione dinamica *(f)* It
De dynamische Zuweisung *(f)*
En dynamic allocation
Es asignación dinámica *(f)*
Fr affectation dynamique *(f)*
Pt designação dinâmica *(f)*

almacén *(m) n* Es
De Magazin *(n)*
En magazine
Fr magasin *(m)*
It caricatore *(m)*
Pt armazém *(m)*

almacenamiento *(m) n* Es
De Speicherung *(f)*
En storage
Fr stockage *(m)*
It immagazzinamento *(m)*
Pt armazenamento *(m)*

almacenamiento principal *(m)* Es
De Hauptspeicherung *(f)*
En main storage
Fr stockage central *(m)*
It immagazzinamento principale *(m)*
Pt armazenagem principal *(f)*

almacenar *vb* Es
De speichern
En store
Fr mémoriser
It memorizzare
Pt armazenar

almacenar previamente Es
De vorspeichern
En pre-store
Fr pré-enregistrer
It preregistrare
Pt pré-amazenar

almofada de raspar *(f)* Pt
De Arbeitspuffer *(m)*
En scratch pad
Es bloc de notas *(m)*
Fr mémoire de travail *(f)*
It bloc-notes *(m)*

alphabet *n* En; Fr *(m)*
De Alphabet *(n)*
Es alfabeto *(m)*
It alfabeto *(m)*
Pt alfabeto *(m)*

Alphabet *(n) n* De
En alphabet
Es alfabeto *(m)*
Fr alphabet *(m)*
It alfabeto *(m)*
Pt alfabeto *(m)*

alphanumeric (or **alphameric)** *adj* En
De alphanumerisch
Es alfanumérico
Fr alphanumérique
It alfanumerico
Pt alfanumérico

alphanumérique *adj* Fr
De alphanumerisch
En alphanumeric
Es alfanumérico
It alfanumerico
Pt alfanumérico

alphanumerisch *adj* De
En alphanumeric
Es alfanumérico
Fr alphanumérique
It alfanumerico
Pt alfanumérico

alternance *(f) n* Fr
De Abwechslung *(f)*
En alternation
Es alternancia *(f)*
It alternanza *(f)*
Pt alternância *(f)*

alternancia *(f) n* Es
De Abwechslung *(f)*
En alternation
Fr alternance *(f)*
It alternanza *(f)*
Pt alternância *(f)*

alternância *(f) n* Pt
De Abwechslung *(f)*
En alternation
Es alternancia *(f)*
Fr alternance *(f)*
It alternanza *(f)*

alternanza *(f) n* It
De Abwechslung *(f)*
En alternation
Es alternancia *(f)*
Fr alternance *(f)*
Pt alternância *(f)*

alternation *n* En
De Abwechslung *(f)*
Es alternancia *(f)*
Fr alternance *(f)*
It alternanza *(f)*
Pt alternância *(f)*

ambiance *(f) n* Fr
De Umgebung *(f)*
En environment
Es ambiente *(m)*
It ambiente *(m)*
Pt ambiente *(m)*

ambiente *(m) n* Es, It, Pt
De Umgebung *(f)*
En environment
Fr ambiance *(f)*

ambiguity error En
De Zweideutigkeitsfehler *(m)*
Es error de ambigüedad *(m)*
Fr erreur d'ambiguité *(f)*
It errore di ambiguità *(m)*
Pt erro de ambiguidade *(m)*

amorce *(f) n* Fr
De Startroutine *(f)*
En bootstrap
Es autocargador *(m)*
It istruzioni di avviamento *(f)*
Pt bootstrap *(m)*

amortecimento *(m) n* Pt
De Dämpfung *(f)*
En damping
Es amortiguamiento *(m)*
Fr amortissement *(m)*
It smorzamento *(m)*

amortiguamiento *(m) n* Es
De Dämpfung *(f)*
En damping
Fr amortissement *(m)*
It smorzamento *(m)*
Pt amortecimento *(m)*

amortissement *(m) n* Fr
De Dämpfung *(f)*
En damping
Es amortiguamiento *(m)*
It smorzamento *(m)*
Pt amortecimento *(m)*

à mots Fr
De wortorientiert
En word-orientated
Es orientado a la palabra
It ad orientamento di voce
Pt orientado por palavras

analisador *(m) n* Pt
Am analyzer
De Analysator *(m)*
En analyser
Es analizador *(m)*
Fr analyseur *(m)*
It analizzatore *(m)*

analisador diferencial *(m)* Pt
Am differential analyzer
De Differenzialanalysator *(m)*
En differential analyser
Es analizador diferencial *(m)*
Fr analyseur différentiel *(m)*
It analizzatore differenziale *(m)*

análise de rede *(f)* Pt
De Netzanalyse *(f)*
En network analysis
Es análisis de redes *(m)*
Fr analyse de réseau *(f)*
It analisi delle reti *(f)*

análise de sistemas *(f)* Pt
De Systemanalyse *(f)*
En systems analysis
Es análisis de sistemas *(m)*
Fr analyse fonctionnelle *(f)*
It analisi dei sistemi *(f)*

análise numérica *(f)* Pt
De numerische Analyse *(f)*
En numerical analysis
Es análisis numérico *(m)*
Fr analyse numérique *(f)*
It analisi numerica *(f)*

analisi dei sistemi *(f)* It
De Systemanalyse *(f)*
En systems analysis
Es análisis de sistemas *(m)*
Fr analyse fonctionnelle *(f)*
Pt análise de sistemas *(f)*

analisi delle reti *(f)* It
De Netzanalyse *(f)*
En network analysis
Es análisis de redes *(m)*
Fr analyse de réseau *(f)*
Pt análise de rede *(f)*

analisi numerica *(f)* It
De numerische Analyse *(f)*
En numerical analysis
Es análisis numérico *(m)*
Fr analyse numérique *(f)*
Pt análise numérica *(f)*

análisis de redes *(m)* Es
De Netzanalyse *(f)*
En network analysis
Fr analyse de réseau *(f)*
It analisi delle reti *(f)*
Pt análise de rede *(f)*

análisis de sistemas *(m)* Es
De Systemanalyse *(f)*
En systems analysis
Fr analyse fonctionnelle *(f)*
It analisi dei sistemi *(f)*
Pt análise de sistemas *(f)*

análisis numérico *(m)* Es
De numerische Analyse *(f)*
En numerical analysis
Fr analyse numérique *(f)*
It analisi numerica *(f)*
Pt análise numérica *(f)*

analista *(m) n* Es, It, Pt
De Analysierer *(m)*
En analyst
Fr analyste *(m)*

analista de sistemas *(m)* Es, Pt
De Systemanalyst *(m)*
En systems analyst
Fr analyste fonctionnel *(m)*
It analista di sistemi *(m)*

analista di sistemi *(m)* It
De Systemanalyst *(m)*
En systems analyst
Es analista de sistemas *(m)*
Fr analyste fonctionnel *(m)*
Pt analista de sistemas *(m)*

analizador *(m) n* Es
Am analyzer
De Analysator *(m)*
En analyser
Fr analyseur *(m)*

It analizzatore *(m)*
Pt analisador *(m)*

analizador diferencial *(m)* Es
Am differential analyzer
De Differenzialanalysator *(m)*
En differential analyser
Fr analyseur différentiel *(m)*
It analizzatore differenziale *(m)*
Pt analisador diferencial *(m)*

analizzatore *(m) n* It
Am analyzer
De Analysator *(m)*
En analyser
Es analizador *(m)*
Fr analyseur *(m)*
Pt analisador *(m)*

analizzatore differenziale *(m)* It
Am differential analyzer
De Differenzialanalysator *(m)*
En differential analyser
Es analizador diferencial *(m)*
Fr analyseur différentiel *(m)*
Pt analisador diferencial *(m)*

analizzatore per scansione *(m)* It
De Abtaster *(m)*
En scanner
Es explorador *(m)*
Fr explorateur *(m)*
Pt dispositivo de exploração *(m)*

analizzatore per scansione di caratteri ottici *(m)* It
De optischer Abtaster *(m)*
En optical scanner
Es explorador óptico *(m)*
Fr lecteur optique *(m)*
Pt explorador óptico *(m)*

analog *adj* De, En
Es analógico
Fr analogique
It analogico
Pt análogo

analog computer En
De Analogrechner *(m)*
Es ordenador analógico *(m)*
Fr calculateur analogique *(m)*
It elaboratore analogico *(m)*
Pt computador de analogia *(m)*

analog-digital converter En
De Analog-Digitalumwandler *(m)*
Es convertidor analógico-digital *(m)*
Fr convertisseur analogique-numérique *(m)*
It convertitore analogico-digitale *(m)*
Pt conversor análogo-digital *(m)*

Analog-Digitalumwandler *(m)* De
En analog-digital converter
Es convertidor analógico-digital *(m)*
Fr convertisseur analogique-numérique *(m)*
It convertitore analogico-digitale *(m)*
Pt conversor análogo-digital *(m)*

analogico *adj* It
De analog
En analog
Es analógico
Fr analogique
Pt análogo

analógico *adj* Es
De analog
En analog
Fr analogique
It analogico
Pt análogo

analogique *adj* Fr
De analog
En analog
Es analógico
It analogico
Pt análogo

análogo *adj* Pt
De analog
En analog
Es analógico
Fr analogique
It analogico

Analogrechner *(m) n* De
En analog computer
Es ordenador analógico *(m)*
Fr calculateur analogique *(m)*
It elaboratore analogico *(m)*
Pt computador de analogia *(m)*

Analysator *(m) n* De
Am analyzer
En analyser
Es analizador *(m)*
Fr analyseur *(m)*
It analizzatore *(m)*
Pt analisador *(m)*

analyse de réseau *(f)* Fr
De Netzanalyse *(f)*
En network analysis
Es análisis de redes *(m)*
It analisi delle reti *(f)*
Pt análise de rede *(f)*

analyse fonctionnelle *(f)* Fr
De Systemanalyse *(f)*
En systems analysis
Es análisis de sistemas *(m)*
It analisi dei sistemi *(f)*
Pt análise de sistemas *(f)*

analyse numérique *(f)* Fr
De numerische Analyse *(f)*
En numerical analysis
Es análisis numérico *(m)*
It analisi numerica *(f)*
Pt análise numérica *(f)*

analyser *n* En
Am analyzer
De Analysator *(m)*
Es analizador *(m)*
Fr analyseur *(m)*
It analizzatore *(m)*
Pt analisador *(m)*

analyseur *(m) n* Fr
Am analyzer
De Analysator *(m)*
En analyser
Es analizador *(m)*
It analizzatore *(m)*
Pt analisador *(m)*

analyseur différentiel *(m)* Fr
Am differential analyzer
De Differenzialanalysator *(m)*
En differential analyser
Es analizador diferencial *(m)*
It analizzatore differenziale *(m)*
Pt analisador diferencial *(m)*

Analysierer *(m) n* De
En analyst
Es analista *(m)*
Fr analyste *(m)*
It analista *(m)*
Pt analista *(m)*

analyst *n* En
De Analysierer *(m)*
Es analista *(m)*
Fr analyste *(m)*
It analista *(m)*
Pt analista *(m)*

analyste *(m) n* Fr
De Analysierer *(m)*
En analyst
Es analista *(m)*
It analista *(m)*
Pt analista *(m)*

analyste fonctionnel *(m)* Fr
De Systemanalyst *(m)*
En systems analyst
Es analista de sistemas *(m)*
It analista di sistemi *(m)*
Pt analista de sistemas *(m)*

analyzer *n* Am
De Analysator *(m)*
En analyser
Es analizador *(m)*
Fr analyseur *(m)*
It analizzatore *(m)*
Pt analisador *(m)*

anchura de banda *(f)* Es
De Bandbreite *(f)*
En bandwidth
Fr largeur de bande *(f)*
It larghezza di banda *(f)*
Pt largura de banda *(f)*

Änderungssatz *(m) n* De
En change record
Es registro de cambio *(m)*
Fr record de modification *(m)*
It record di cambiamento *(m)*
Pt registo de mudança *(m)*

AND-gate *n* En
De UND-Schaltung *(f)*
Es puerta Y *(f)*
Fr porte ET *(f)*
It porta E *(f)*
Pt porta AND *(f)*

AND-operation *n* En
De UND-Verknüpfung *(f)*
Es operación Y *(f)*
Fr opération ET *(f)*
It operazione E *(f)*
Pt operação AND *(f)*

Anfangskennsatz *(m) n* De
En header label
Es etiqueta de cabecera *(f)*
Fr label début *(m)*
It etichetta della testata *(f)*
Pt rótulo de porta-cabeças *(m)*

anhalten *vb* De
En hold
Es mantener
Fr tenir
It mantenere
Pt manter

aninhar *vb* Pt
De schachteln
En nest
Es jerarquizar
Fr emboîter
It nidificare

Anschlußsystem *(n) n* De
En tandem system
Es sistema en tandem *(m)*
Fr système en tandem *(m)*
It sistema abbinato *(m)*
Pt sistema em tandem *(m)*

Ansprechzeit *(f) n* De
En response time
Es tiempo de respuesta *(m)*
Fr temps de réponse *(m)*
It tempo di risposta *(m)*
Pt tempo de resposta *(m)*

anticoincidence gate En
De Antizusammentreffensschaltung *(f)*
Es puerta de anticoincidencia *(f)*
Fr porte anti-coïncidence *(f)*
It porta di anticoincidenza *(f)*
Pt porta de anticoincidência *(f)*

Antivalenzfunktion *(f)* De
En exclusive-or operation
Es operación O exclusivo *(f)*
Fr opération OU exclusif *(f)*
It operazione o-esclusivo *(f)*
Pt operação exclusiva-ou *(f)*

Antizusammentreffensschaltung *(f)*
En anticoincidence gate
Es puerta de anticoincidencia *(f)*
Fr porte anti-coïncidence *(f)*
It porta di anticoincidenza *(f)*
Pt porta de anticoincidência *(f)*

antreiben *vb* De
En drive
Es impulsar
Fr entraîner
It azionare
Pt accionar

anuário *(m) n* Pt
De Inhaltsverzeichnis *(n)*
En directory
Es directorio *(m)*
Fr répertoire d'adresses *(m)*
It elenco *(m)*

Anweisung *(f) n* De
En statement
Es sentencia *(f)*
Fr instructions *(f pl)*
It statement *(m)*
Pt afirmação *(f)*

Anweisungscode *(m) n* De
En order code
Es código de orden *(m)*
Fr code d'ordre *(m)*
It codice di ordine *(m)*
Pt código de ordens *(m)*

Anwendung *(f) n* De
En application
Es aplicación *(f)*
Fr application *(f)*
It applicazione *(f)*
Pt aplicação *(f)*

Anwendungsprogramm *(n) n* De
En application program
Es programa de aplicación *(m)*
Fr programme d'application *(m)*
It programma applicativo *(m)*
Pt programa de aplicação *(m)*

Anzeige *(f) n* De
En display
Es representación visual *(f)*
Fr affichage *(m)*
It visualizzatore *(m)*
Pt representação visual *(f)*

Anzeigeendstation *(f) n* De
En display terminal
Es terminal de visualización *(m)*
Fr terminal à écran de visualisation *(m)*
It terminale di visualizzazione *(m)*
Pt terminal de visualização *(m)*

Anzeigekonsole *(f) n* De
En display console
Es consola de visualización *(f)*
Fr console de visualisation *(f)*
It console di visualizzazione *(f)*
Pt consola de visualização *(f)*

anzeigen *vb* De
En display
Es presentar
Fr afficher
It visualizzare
Pt mostrar

Anzeigeröhre *(f) n* De
En display tube
Es tubo de representación visual *(m)*
Fr tube cathodique de visualisation *(m)*
It tubo visualizzatore *(m)*
Pt válvula de visualização *(f)*

Anzeigestation *(f) n* De
En display station
Es estación de visualización *(f)*
Fr poste de visualisation *(m)*
It posto di visualizzazione *(m)*
Pt estação de visualização *(f)*

apagado *(m) n* Pt
De Löschung *(f)*
En deletion
Es eliminación *(f)*
Fr effacement *(m)*
It cancellazione *(f)*

apagamento de dados *(m)* Pt
De Datenlöschung *(f)*
En data cleaning
Es limpieza de los datos *(f)*
Fr nettoyage de données *(f)*
It pulizia dei dati *(f)*

apagar *vb* Pt
De löschen
En delete; erase
Es suprimir; borrar

Fr éliminer; effacer
It cancellare

apanhar *vb* Pt
De fangen
En trap
Es entrampar
Fr piéger
It intrappolare

aplicação *(f) n* Pt
De Anwendung *(f)*
En application
Es aplicación *(f)*
Fr application *(f)*
It applicazione *(f)*

aplicación *(f) n* Es
De Anwendung *(f)*
En application
Fr application *(f)*
It applicazione *(f)*
Pt aplicação *(f)*

apoio *(m) n* Pt
De Ausweichbetrieb *(m)*
En backup
Es reserva *(f)*
Fr sauvegarde *(f)*
It riserva *(f)*

appareil de visualisation (AV) *(m)* Fr
De Sichtgerät *(n)*
En visual-display unit (VDU)
Es unidad de visualización *(f)*
It unitá di visualizzazione *(f)*
Pt unidade de visualização *(f)*

appel *(m) n* Fr
De Aufruf *(m)*
En call
Es llamada *(f)*
It chiamata *(f)*
Pt chamada *(f)*

appeler *vb* Fr
De aufrufen
En call
Es llamar
It chiamare
Pt chamar

application *n* En; Fr *(f)*
De Anwendung *(f)*
Es aplicación *(f)*
It applicazione *(f)*
Pt aplicação *(f)*

application program En
De Anwendungsprogramm *(n)*
Es programa de aplicación *(m)*
Fr programme d'application *(m)*
It programma applicativo *(m)*
Pt programa de aplicação *(m)*

application programs library (APL) En
De Bibliothek der Anwendungsprogramme *(f)*
Es biblioteca de programas de aplicación *(f)*
Fr bibliothèque des programmes d'application *(f)*
It libreria dei programmi applicativi *(f)*
Pt biblioteca de programas de aplicação *(f)*

applicazione *(f) n* It
De Anwendung *(f)*
En application
Es aplicación *(f)*
Fr application *(f)*
Pt aplicação *(f)*

apprendimento basato sull'elaboratore *(m)* It
De computerbasiertes Lernen *(n)*
En computer-based learning
Es enseñanza automatizada *(f)*
Fr enseignement automatisé *(m)*
Pt aprendizagem baseada em computador *(f)*

aprendizagem baseada em computador *(f)* Pt
De computerbasiertes Lernen *(n)*
En computer-based learning
Es enseñanza automatizada *(f)*
Fr enseignement automatisé *(m)*
It apprendimento basato sull'elaboratore *(m)*

apresentação de refrescamento *(f)* Pt
De Auffrischungsanzeige *(f)*
En refresh display
Es representación regenerada *(f)*
Fr affichageré-génération *(m)*
It visualizzazione di aggiornamento *(f)*

apresentação quadriculada *(f)* Pt
De Rasteranzeige *(f)*
En raster display
Es presentación de trama *(f)*
Fr affichage tramé *(m)*
It visualizzazione trama *(f)*

aptidão a ser utilizado *(f)* Pt
De Betriebsfähigkeit *(f)*
En serviceability
Es utilidad *(f)*
Fr aptitude au service *(f)*
It utilità *(f)*

aptitude au service *(f)* Fr
De Betriebsfähigkeit *(f)*
En serviceability
Es utilidad *(f)*
It utilità *(f)*
Pt aptidão a ser utilizado *(f)*

Äquivalenzschaltung *(f)* De
En equality unit
Es unidad de igualdad *(f)*
Fr unité d'égalité *(f)*
It unità di uguaglianza *(f)*
Pt unidade de igualdade *(f)*

Arbeitsband *(n) n* De
En work tape
Es cinta de maniobra *(f)*
Fr bande de travail *(f)*
It nastro di lavoro *(m)*
Pt fita de trabalho *(f)*

Arbeitsbereich *(m) n* De
En work area
Es zona de maniobra *(f)*
Fr zone de travail *(f)*
It area di lavoro *(f)*
Pt área de trabalho *(f)*

Arbeitsplanung *(f) n* De
En scheduling
Es planificación *(f)*
Fr planification *(f)*
It pianificazione *(f)*
Pt planificação *(f)*

Arbeitspuffer *(m) n* De
En scratch pad
Es bloc de notas *(m)*
Fr mémoire de travail *(f)*
It bloc-notes *(m)*
Pt almofada de raspar *(f)*

Arbeitsstation *(f) n* De
En operating station
Es estación operativa *(f)*
Fr poste d'exploitation *(m)*
It posto funzionante *(m)*
Pt estação de operação *(f)*

Arbeitsverhältnis *(n) n* De
En operating ratio
Es relación de utilización *(f)*
Fr rapport de disponibilité *(m)*
It rapporto di operazione *(m)*
Pt ratio de operação *(f)*

árbol *(m) n* Es
De Überlagerungsbaum *(m)*
En tree
Fr arbre *(m)*
It albero *(m)*
Pt árvore *(f)*

arbre *(m) n* Fr
De Überlagerungsbaum *(m)*
En tree

Es árbol *(m)*
It albero *(m)*
Pt árvore *(f)*

architectural protection En
De Aufbauschutz *(m)*
Es protección estructural *(f)*
Fr protection architecturale *(f)*
It protezione dell'architettura *(f)*
Pt protecção arquitectónica *(f)*

architecture *n* En; Fr *(f)*
De Aufbau *(m)*
Es arquitectura *(f)*
It architettura *(f)*
Pt arquitectura *(f)*

architecture unifiée de réseau (AUR) *(f)* Fr
De Systemnetzaufbau *(m)*
En systems network architecture (SNA)
Es estructura de redes de sistemas *(f)*
It architettura della rete di sistemi *(f)*
Pt arquitectura de rede de sistemas *(f)*

architettura *(f) n* It
De Aufbau *(m)*
En architecture
Es arquitectura *(f)*
Fr architecture *(f)*
Pt arquitectura *(f)*

architettura della rete di sistemi *(f)* It
De Systemnetzaufbau *(m)*
En systems network architecture (SNA)
Es estructura de redes de sistemas *(f)*
Fr architecture unifiée de réseau (AUR) *(f)*
Pt arquitectura de rede de sistemas *(f)*

archivage *(m) n* Fr
De Archivierung *(f)*
En archiving
Es acción de archivar *(f)*
It archiviazione *(f)*
Pt acto de arquivar *(m)*

archived file En
De archivierte Datei *(f)*
Es fichero archivado *(m)*
Fr fichier archivé *(m)*
It file archiviato *(m)*
Pt dossier arquivado *(m)*

archiviazione *(f) n* It
De Archivierung *(f)*
En archiving
Es acción de archivar *(f)*
Fr archivage *(m)*
Pt acto de arquivar *(m)*

archivierte Datei *(f)* De
En archived file
Es fichero archivado *(m)*
Fr fichier archivé *(m)*
It file archiviato *(m)*
Pt dossier arquivado *(m)*

Archivierung *(f) n* De
En archiving
Es acción de archivar *(f)*
Fr archivage *(m)*
It archiviazione *(f)*
Pt acto de arquivar *(m)*

archiving *n* En
De Archivierung *(f)*
Es acción de archivar *(f)*
Fr archivage *(m)*
It archiviazione *(f)*
Pt acto de arquivar *(m)*

área constante *(f)* Es, Pt
De Konstantbereich *(m)*
En constant area
Fr aire constante *(f)*
It area costante *(f)*

area costante *(f)* It
De Konstantbereich *(m)*
En constant area
Es área constante *(f)*
Fr aire constante *(f)*
Pt área constante *(f)*

área de output *(f)* Pt
De Ausgangsbereich *(m)*
En output area
Es área de salida *(f)*
Fr zone de sortie *(f)*
It area di uscita *(f)*

área de salida *(f)* Es
De Ausgangsbereich *(m)*
En output area
Fr zone de sortie *(f)*
It area di uscita *(f)*
Pt área de output *(f)*

área de trabalho *(f)* Pt
De Arbeitsbereich *(m)*
En work area
Es zona de maniobra *(f)*
Fr zone de travail *(f)*
It area di lavoro *(f)*

area di lavoro *(f)* It
De Arbeitsbereich *(m)*
En work area
Es zona de maniobra *(f)*
Fr zone de travail *(f)*
Pt área de trabalho *(f)*

area di uscita *(f)* It
De Ausgangsbereich *(m)*
En output area
Es área de salida *(f)*
Fr zone de sortie *(f)*
Pt área de output *(f)*

argomento *(m) n* It
De Argument *(n)*
En argument
Es argumento *(m)*
Fr argument *(m)*
Pt argumento *(m)*

argument *n* En; Fr *(m)*
De Argument *(n)*
Es argumento *(m)*
It argomento *(m)*
Pt argumento *(m)*

Argument *(n) n* De
En argument
Es argumento *(m)*
Fr argument *(m)*
It argomento *(m)*
Pt argumento *(m)*

argumento *(m) n* Es, Pt
De Argument *(n)*
En argument
Fr argument *(m)*
It argomento *(m)*

arithmetic and logic unit (ALU) En
De arithmetische und logische Einheit *(f)*
Es unidad aritmética y lógica (UAL) *(f)*
Fr unité arithmétique et logique (UAL) *(f)*
It unità logica ed aritmetica *(f)*
Pt unidade aritmética e lógica *(f)*

arithmetic instruction En
De arithmetische Anweisung *(f)*
Es instrucción aritmética *(f)*
Fr instruction arithmétique *(f)*
It istruzione aritmetica *(f)*
Pt instrução aritmética *(f)*

arithmetic operation En
De arithmetische Funktion *(f)*
Es operación aritmética *(f)*
Fr opération arithmétique *(f)*
It operazione aritmetica *(f)*
Pt operação aritmética *(f)*

arithmetic shift En
De arithmetische Stellen- verschiebung *(f)*
Es desplazamiento aritmético *(m)*
Fr décalage arithmétique *(m)*
It spostamento aritmetico *(m)*
Pt mudança aritmética *(f)*

arithmetic unit (AU) En
De Rechenwerk *(n)*
Es unidad aritmética (UA) *(f)*
Fr unité de calcul (UC) *(f)*
It unità aritmetica *(f)*
Pt unidade aritmética *(f)*

Arithmetik mit mehrfacher Wortlänge *(f)* De
En multiple-length arithmetic
Es aritmética de longitud múltiple *(f)*
Fr calcul à précision multiple *(m)*
It aritmetica a lunghezza multipla *(f)*
Pt aritmética de

comprimento múltiplo *(f)*

arithmétique en fixe *(f)* Fr
De Festpunktarithmetik *(f)*
En fixed-point arithmetic
Es aritmética de coma fija *(f)*
It aritmetica a virgola fissa *(f)*
Pt aritmética de ponto fixo *(f)*

arithmétique matricielle *(f)* Fr
De Matrixarithmetik *(f)*
En matrix arithmetic
Es aritmética matricial *(f)*
It aritmetica delle matrici *(f)*
Pt aritmética de matriz *(f)*

arithmétique vectorielle *(f)* Fr
De Vektorarithmetik *(f)*
En vector arithmetic
Es aritmética vectorial *(f)*
It aritmetica dei vettori *(f)*
Pt aritmética de vectores *(f)*

arithmetische Anweisung *(f)* De
En arithmetic instruction
Es instrucción aritmética *(f)*
Fr instruction arithmétique *(f)*
It istruzione aritmetica *(f)*
Pt instrução aritmética *(f)*

arithmetische Funktion *(f)* De
En arithmetic operation
Es operación aritmética *(f)*
Fr opération arithmétique *(f)*
It operazione aritmetica *(f)*
Pt operação aritmética *(f)*

arithmetische Stellenverschiebung *(f)* De
En arithmetic shift
Es desplazamiento aritmético *(m)*
Fr décalage arithmétique *(m)*
It spostamento aritmetico *(m)*
Pt mudança aritmética *(f)*

arithmetische und logische Einheit *(f)* De
En arithmetic and logic unit (ALU)
Es unidad aritmética y lógica (UAL) *(f)*
Fr unité arithmétique et logique (UAL) *(f)*
It unità logica ed aritmetica *(f)*
Pt unidade aritmética e lógica *(f)*

aritmetica a lunghezza multipla *(f)* It
De Arithmetik mit mehrfacher Wortlänge *(f)*
En multiple-length arithmetic
Es aritmética de longitud múltiple *(f)*
Fr calcul à précision multiple *(m)*
Pt aritmética de comprimento múltiplo *(f)*

aritmetica a virgola fissa *(f)* It
De Festpunktarithmetik *(f)*
En fixed-point arithmetic
Es aritmética de coma fija *(f)*
Fr arithmétique en fixe *(f)*
Pt aritmética de ponto fixo *(f)*

aritmetica a virgola mobile *(f)* It
De Flüssigpunkt-arithmetik *(f)*
En floating-point arithmetic
Es aritmética de coma flotante *(f)*
Fr calcul en virgule flottante *(m)*
Pt aritmética de ponto flutuante *(f)*

aritmética de coma fija *(f)* Es
De Festpunktarithmetik *(f)*
En fixed-point arithmetic
Fr arithmétique en fixe *(f)*
It aritmetica a virgola fissa *(f)*
Pt aritmética de ponto fixo *(f)*

aritmética de coma flotante *(f)* Es
De Flüssigpunkt-arithmetik *(f)*
En floating-point arithmetic
Fr calcul en virgule flottante *(m)*
It aritmetica a virgola mobile *(f)*
Pt aritmética de ponto flutuante *(f)*

aritmética de comprimento múltiplo *(f)* Pt
De Arithmetik mit mehrfacher Wortlänge *(f)*
En multiple-length arithmetic
Es aritmética de longitud múltiple *(f)*
Fr calcul à précision multiple *(m)*
It aritmetica a lunghezza multipla *(f)*

aritmetica dei vettori *(f)* It
De Vektorarithmetik *(f)*
En vector arithmetic
Es aritmética vectorial *(f)*
Fr arithmétique vectorielle *(f)*
Pt aritmética de vectores *(f)*

aritmetica delle matrici *(f)* It
De Matrixarithmetik *(f)*
En matrix arithmetic
Es aritmética matricial *(f)*
Fr arithmétique matricielle *(f)*
Pt aritmética de matriz *(f)*

aritmética de longitud múltiple *(f)* Es
De Arithmetik mit mehrfacher Wortlänge *(f)*
En multiple-length arithmetic
Fr calcul à précision multiple *(m)*
It aritmetica a lunghezza multipla *(f)*
Pt aritmética de comprimento múltiplo *(f)*

aritmética de matriz *(f)* Pt
De Matrixarithmetik *(f)*
En matrix arithmetic
Es aritmética matricial *(f)*
Fr arithmétique matricielle *(f)*
It aritmetica delle matrici *(f)*

aritmética de ponto fixo *(f)* Pt
De Festpunktarithmetik *(f)*
En fixed-point arithmetic
Es aritmética de coma fija *(f)*
Fr arithmétique en fixe *(f)*
It aritmetica a virgola fissa *(f)*

aritmética de ponto flutuante *(f)* Pt
De Flüssigpunkt-arithmetik *(f)*
En floating-point arithmetic
Es aritmética de coma flotante *(f)*
Fr calcul en virgule flottante *(m)*
It aritmetica a virgola mobile *(f)*

aritmética de vectores *(f)* Pt
De Vektorarithmetik *(f)*
En vector arithmetic
Es aritmética vectorial *(f)*

Fr arithmétique vectorielle *(f)*
It aritmetica dei vettori *(f)*

aritmética matricial *(f)* Es
De Matrixarithmetik *(f)*
En matrix arithmetic
Fr arithmétique matricielle *(f)*
It aritmetica delle matrici *(f)*
Pt aritmética de matriz *(f)*

aritmética vectorial *(f)* Es
De Vektorarithmetik *(f)*
En vector arithmetic
Fr arithmétique vectorielle *(f)*
It aritmetica dei vettori *(f)*
Pt aritmética de vectores *(f)*

armadilha *(f)* *n* Pt
De Haftstelle *(f)*
En trap
Es trampa *(f)*
Fr piège *(m)*
It trappola *(f)*

armadio *(m)* *n* It
De Stapel *(m)*
En stack
Es pila *(f)*
Fr pile *(f)*
Pt pilha *(f)*

armazém *(m)* *n* Pt
De Speicher; Magazin *(m n)*
En store; magazine
Es memoria; almacén *(f m)*
Fr mémoire; magasin *(f m)*
It memoria; caricatore *(f m)*

armazém de apoio *(m)* Pt
De Hilfsspeicher *(m)*
En backing store
Es memoria auxiliar *(f)*
Fr mémoire auxiliaire *(f)*
It memoria ausiliaria *(f)*

armazém de arquivo *(m)* Pt
De Dateispeicher *(m)*
En file store
Es memoria fichero *(f)*
Fr mémoire fichier *(f)*
It memoria dei file *(f)*

armazém de discos intercambiáveis *(m)* Pt
De auswechselbarer Plattenspeicher *(m)*
En exchangeable disk store (EDS)
Es unidad de discos móviles *(f)*
Fr unité de disques à chargeur (UTC) *(f)*
It memoria a dischi inseribili *(f)*

armazém de emergência *(m)* Pt
De Wiedereinstiegs-speicherauszug *(m)*
En rescue dump
Es vaciado de rescate *(m)*
Fr vidage de secours *(m)*
It dump di salvataggio *(m)*

armazém de massa *(m)* Pt
De Massenspeicher *(m)*
En mass store
Es memoria de gran capacidad *(f)*
Fr mémoire de grande capacité *(f)*
It memoria di massa *(f)*

armazém de matriz *(m)* Pt
De Matrizenspeicher *(m)*
En matrix store
Es memoria matricial *(f)*
Fr mémoire matricielle *(f)*
It memoria a matrice *(f)*

armazém de raio *(m)* Pt
De Strahlenspeicher *(m)*
En beam store
Es memoria a rayos *(f)*
Fr mémoire à faisceau *(f)*
It memoria a fascio *(f)*

armazém de um só nível *(m)* Pt
De Einstufenspeicher *(m)*
En one-level store
Es memoria de un solo nivel *(f)*
Fr mémoire à un niveau *(f)*
It memoria ad un livello *(f)*

armazém escravo *(m)* Pt
De Nebenspeicher *(m)*
En slave store
Es memoria sin parte residente *(f)*
Fr mémoire asservie *(f)*
It memoria satellite *(f)*

armazém estático *(m)* Pt
De statischer Speicher *(m)*
En static store
Es memoria estática *(f)*
Fr mémoire statique *(f)*
It memoria statica *(f)*

armazém exterior *(m)* Pt
De Außenspeicher *(m)*
En external store
Es memoria externa *(f)*
Fr mémoire externe *(f)*
It memoria esterna *(f)*

armazém interno *(m)* Pt
De Innenspeicher *(m)*
En internal store
Es memoria interna *(f)*
Fr mémoire interne *(f)*
It memoria interna *(f)*

armazém não apagável *(m)* Pt
De nicht löschbarer Speicher *(m)*
En nonerasable store
Es memoria imborrable *(f)*
Fr mémoire non effaçable *(f)*
It memoria non cancellabile *(f)*

armazém primária *(m)* Pt
De Primärspeicher *(m)*
En primary store
Es memoria principal *(f)*
Fr mémoire centrale *(f)*
It memoria centrale *(f)*

armazém real *(m)* Pt
De Realspeicher *(m)*
En real store
Es memoria real *(f)*
Fr mémoire réelle *(f)*
It memoria reale *(f)*

armazém regenerativo *(m)* Pt
De regenerativer Speicher *(m)*
En regenerative store
Es memoria regenerativa *(f)*
Fr mémoire à régénération *(f)*
It memoria rigenerativa *(f)*

armazenagem intermediária *(m)* Pt
De Zwischens-peicherung *(f)*
En intermediate storage
Es memoria intermedia *(f)*
Fr mémoire intermédiaire *(f)*
It memoria intermedia *(f)*

armazenagem principal *(f)* Pt
De Hauptspeicherung *(f)*
En main storage
Es almacenamiento principal *(m)*
Fr stockage central *(m)*
It immagazzinamento principale *(m)*

armazenamento *(m)* *n* Pt
De Speicherung *(f)*
En storage
Es almacenamiento *(m)*
Fr stockage *(m)*
It immagazzinamento *(m)*

armazénamento bidimensional *(m)* Pt
De zweidimensionale Speicherung *(f)*
En two-dimensional storage
Es memoria bidimensional *(f)*
Fr stockage à double entrée *(m)*
It memoria

armazenamento temporário *(m)* Pt
De vorübergehende Speicherung *(f)*
En temporary storage
Es memoria temporal *(f)*
Fr mémoire intermédiaire *(f)*
It memoria temporanea *(f)*

armazenar *vb* Pt
De speichern
En store
Es almacenar
Fr mémoriser
It memorizzare

arquitectura *(f) n* Es, Pt
De Aufbau *(m)*
En architecture
Fr architecture *(f)*
It architettura *(f)*

arquitectura de rede de sistemas *(f)* Pt
De Systemnetzaufbau *(m)*
En systems network architecture (SNA)
Es estructura de redes de sistemas *(f)*
Fr architecture unifiée de réseau (AUR) *(f)*
It architettura della rete di sistemi *(f)*

arquivo *(m) n* Pt
De Datei *(f)*
En file
Es fichero *(m)*
Fr fichier *(m)*
It file *(m)*

arquivo de discos *(m)* Pt
De Plattendatei *(f)*
En disk file
Es fichero de discos *(m)*
Fr fichier sur disque *(m)*
It file su disco *(m)*

arquivo de discos fixos *(m)* Pt
De Festplattendatei *(f)*
En fixed-disk file
Es fichero de discos fijos *(m)*
Fr fichier de disques fixes *(m)*
It file del disco fisso *(m)*

arquivo envolvido *(m)* Pt
De Hülldatei *(f)*
En enveloped file
Es fichero envuelto *(m)*
Fr dossier sous enveloppe *(m)*
It file inviluppato *(m)*

arquivo físico *(m)* Pt
De physische Datei *(f)*
En physical file
Es fichero físico *(m)*
Fr fichier physique *(m)*
It file fisico *(m)*

arquivo principal *(m)* Pt
De Stammdatei *(f)*
En master file
Es fichero maestro *(m)*
Fr fichier principal *(m)*
It file principale *(m)*

arquivos compartidos *(m pl)* Pt
De gemeinsam benutzte Datei *(f)*
En shared files
Es ficheros compartidos *(m pl)*
Fr fichiers partagés *(m pl)*
It file in comune *(f pl)*

arquivo sequencial *(f)* Pt
De Folgedatei *(f)*
En sequential file
Es fichero secuencial *(m)*
Fr fichier séquentiel *(m)*
It file sequenziale *(m)*

arrastre parcial *(m)* Es
De Teilübertrag *(m)*
En partial carry
Fr report partiel *(m)*
It riporto parziale *(m)*
Pt transporte parcial *(m)*

arredondar *vb* Pt
De runden
En round off
Es redondear
Fr arrondir
It arrotondare

arresto *(m) n* It
De Stopp *(m)*
En halt
Es parada *(f)*
Fr arrêt *(m)*
Pt paragem *(f)*

arresto automatico *(m)* It
De automatischer Stopp *(m)*
En automatic stop
Es parada automática *(f)*
Fr arrêt automatique *(m)*
Pt paragem automática *(f)*

arresto del modulo *(m)* It
De Formularanschlag *(m)*
En form stop
Es parada del papel *(f)*
Fr arrêt de papier *(m)*
Pt paragem de formulários *(f)*

arrêt *(m) n* Fr
De Stopp *(m)*
En halt
Es parada *(f)*
It arresto *(m)*
Pt paragem *(f)*

arrêt automatique *(m)* Fr
De automatischer Stopp *(m)*
En automatic stop
Es parada automática *(f)*
It arresto automatico *(m)*
Pt paragem automática *(f)*

arrêt de papier *(m)* Fr
De Formularanschlag *(m)*
En form stop
Es parada del papel *(f)*
It arresto del modulo *(m)*
Pt paragem de formulários *(f)*

arrondir *vb* Fr
De runden
En round off
Es redondear
It arrotondare
Pt arredondar

arrotondare *vb* It
De runden
En round off
Es redondear
Fr arrondir
Pt arredondar

article du fichier permanent *(m)* Fr
De Hauptsatz *(m)*
En master record
Es registro maestro *(m)*
It record principale *(m)*
Pt registo principal *(m)*

article fin *(m)* Fr
De Beisatz *(m)*
En trailer record
Es registro de cola *(m)*
It record di fine *(m)*
Pt registo de trailer *(m)*

artificial intelligence (AI) En
De künstliche Intelligenz *(f)*
Es inteligencia artificial *(f)*
Fr intelligence artificielle (IA) *(f)*
It intelligenza artificiale *(f)*
Pt inteligência artificial *(f)*

árvore *(f) n* Pt
De Überlagerungsbaum *(m)*
En tree
Es árbol *(m)*
Fr arbre *(m)*
It albero *(m)*

ascendant *adj* Fr
De kieloben
En bottom-up
Es boca-abajo
It sottosopra
Pt fundo para cima

à sécurité intégrée Fr
De eigensicher
En fail-safe
Es sin riesgo de fallo
It sicuro contro guasti
Pt seguro contra falhas

asignación *(f) n* Es
De Zuweisung *(f)*
En allocation
Fr affectation *(f)*
It allocazione *(f)*
Pt atribuição *(f)*

asignación de almacenamiento *(f)* Es

De Speicherzuweisung *(f)*
En storage allocation
Fr affectation de la mémoire *(f)*
It assegnazione in memoria *(f)*
Pt atribuição de armazenamento *(f)*

asignación de recursos *(f)* Es
De Betriebsmittelzuweisung *(f)*
En resource allocation
Fr affectation des ressources *(f)*
It allocazione delle risorse *(f)*
Pt atribuição de recursos *(f)*

asignación dinámica *(f)* Es
De dynamische Zuweisung *(f)*
En dynamic allocation
Fr affectation dynamique *(f)*
It allocazione dinamica *(f)*
Pt designação dinâmica *(f)*

asignar *vb* Es
De zuweisen
En allocate
Fr affecter
It allocare
Pt atribuir

aspecto confidencial *(m)* Es, Pt
De Vertraulichkeit *(f)*
En privacy
Fr confidentialité *(f)*
It riservatezza *(f)*

assegnazione in memoria *(f)* It
De Speicherzuweisung *(f)*
En storage allocation
Es asignación de almacenamiento *(f)*
Fr affectation de la mémoire *(f)*
Pt atribuição de armazenamento *(f)*

assemblare *vb* It
De assemblieren
En assemble
Es ensamblar
Fr assembler
Pt montar

assemblatore *(m) n* It
De Assemblierer *(m)*
En assembler
Es ensamblador *(m)*
Fr assembleur *(m)*
Pt montador *(m)*

assemble *vb* En
De assemblieren
Es ensamblar
Fr assembler
It assemblare
Pt montar

assembler *n* En
De Assemblierer *(m)*
Es ensamblador *(m)*
Fr assembleur *(m)*
It assemblatore *(m)*
Pt montador *(m)*

assembler *vb* Fr
De assemblieren
En assemble
Es ensamblar
It assemblare
Pt montar

assembleur *(m) n* Fr
De Assemblierer *(m)*
En assembler
Es ensamblador *(m)*
It assemblatore *(m)*
Pt montador *(m)*

assemblieren *vb* De
En assemble
Es ensamblar
Fr assembler
It assemblare
Pt montar

Assemblierer *(m) n* De
En assembler
Es ensamblador *(m)*
Fr assembleur *(m)*
It assemblatore *(m)*
Pt montador *(m)*

Assembliersprache *(f) n* De
En assembly language
Es lenguaje ensamblador *(m)*
Fr langage d'assemblage *(m)*
It linguaggio assemblatore *(m)*
Pt linguagem de montagem *(f)*

assembly language En
De Assembliersprache *(f)*
Es lenguaje ensamblador *(m)*
Fr langage d'assemblage *(m)*
It linguaggio assemblatore *(m)*
Pt linguagem de montagem *(f)*

associative memory En
De Assoziativspeicher *(m)*
Es memoria asociativa *(f)*
Fr mémoire associative *(f)*
It memoria associativa *(f)*
Pt memória associativa *(f)*

assortiment *(m) n* Fr
De Übereinstimmung *(f)*
En match
Es correspondencia *(f)*
It accoppiamento *(m)*
Pt equiparação *(f)*

Assoziativspeicher *(m)* De
En associative memory
Es memoria asociativa *(f)*
Fr mémoire associative *(f)*
It memoria associativa *(f)*
Pt memória associativa *(f)*

asynchronous communication En
De Start-Stopp-Steuerung *(f)*
Es comunicación asíncrona *(f)*
Fr transmission asynchrone *(f)*
It comunicazione asincrona *(f)*
Pt comunicação assíncrona *(f)*

atascamiento *(m) n* Es
De Verklemmung *(f)*
En jam
Fr bourrage *(m)*
It inceppamento *(m)*
Pt congestionamento *(m)*

atraso rotacional *(m)* Pt
De Umdrehungswartezeit *(f)*
En rotational delay
Es retraso rotacional *(m)*
Fr délai d'attente *(m)*
It ritardo rotazionale *(m)*

atribuição *(f) n* Pt
De Zuweisung *(f)*
En allocation
Es asignación *(f)*
Fr affectation *(f)*
It allocazione *(f)*

atribuição de armazenamento *(f)* Pt
De Speicherzuweisung *(f)*
En storage allocation
Es asignación de almacenamiento *(f)*
Fr affectation de la mémoire *(f)*
It assegnazione in memoria *(f)*

atribuição de recursos *(f)* Pt
De Betriebsmittelzuweisung *(f)*
En resource allocation
Es asignación de recursos *(f)*
Fr affectation des ressources *(f)*
It allocazione delle risorse *(f)*

atribuir *vb* Pt
De zuweisen
En allocate
Es asignar
Fr affecter
It allocare

audio response unit En
De Sprachausgabe *(f)*
Es unidad de respuesta de audio *(f)*
Fr répondeur vocal *(m)*
It unità della risposta audio *(f)*
Pt unidade de audio-resposta *(f)*

audit trail En
De Prüfliste *(f)*
Es pista de auditoría *(f)*
Fr vérification à rebours *(f)*
It lista di verifica *(f)*
Pt trilho de verificação *(m)*

Aufbau *(m) n* De
En architecture
Es arquitectura *(f)*
Fr architecture *(f)*
It architettura *(f)*
Pt arquitectura *(f)*

Aufbauschutz *(m) n* De
En architectural protection
Es protección estructural *(f)*
Fr protection architecturale *(f)*
It protezione dell'architettura *(f)*
Pt protecção arquitectónica *(f)*

auf den neuesten Stand bringen De
En update
Es actualizar
Fr mettre à jour
It aggiornare
Pt actualizar

auffrischen *vb* De
En refresh
Es regenerar
Fr régénérer
It rinfrescare
Pt refrescar

Auffrischungsanzeige *(f)* De
En refresh display
Es representación regenerada *(f)*
Fr affichageré-génération *(m)*
It visualizzazione di aggiornamento *(f)*
Pt apresentação de refrescamento *(f)*

Auffüllen *(n) n* De
En padding
Es relleno *(m)*
Fr remplissage *(m)*
It ricaricamento *(m)*
Pt enchimento *(m)*

Aufgabe *(f) n* De
En task
Es tarea *(f)*
Fr tâche *(f)*
It compito *(m)*
Pt tarefa *(f)*

auflisten *vb* De
En list
Es listar
Fr lister
It listare
Pt enumerar em lista

Aufruf *(m) n* De
En call
Es llamada *(f)*
Fr appel *(m)*
It chiamata *(f)*
Pt chamada *(f)*

aufrufen *vb* De
En call
Es llamar
Fr appeler
It chiamare
Pt chamar

Aufruffolge *(f) n* De
En calling sequence
Es secuencia de llamada *(f)*
Fr séquence d'appel *(f)*
It sequenza di richiamo *(f)*
Pt sequência de chamada *(f)*

Aufspulen *(n) n* De
En spooling
Es bobinado *(m)*
Fr bobinage *(m)*
It bobinaggio *(m)*
Pt embobinagem *(f)*

Aufspulgerät *(n) n* De
En spooler
Es bobinadora *(f)*
Fr enrouleur *(m)*
It avvolgitore *(m)*
Pt embobinador *(m)*

aufsuchen *vb* De
En look up
Es consultar
Fr consulter
It consultare
Pt consultar

Auftrag *(m) n* De
En order
Es orden *(f)*
Fr ordre *(m)*
It ordine *(f)*
Pt ordem *(f)*

aufzeichnen *vb* De
En record
Es registrar
Fr enregistrer
It registrare
Pt registar

Aufzeichnungskopf *(m) n* De
En record head
Es cabeza de registro *(f)*
Fr tête d'enregistrement *(f)*
It testina del record *(f)*
Pt cabeça de registo *(f)*

Aufzeichnungslinie *(f) n* De
En trace
Es traza *(f)*
Fr trace *(f)*
It traccia *(f)*
Pt decalque *(m)*

augmented content-addressed memory (ACAM) En
De erweiterter inhaltsadressierter Speicher *(m)*
Es memoria asociativa ampliada *(f)*
Fr mémoire associative complétée *(f)*
It memoria a contenuto indirizzato aumentato *(f)*
Pt memória de direcção de conteúdo aumentada *(f)*

à une plus une adresse *(f)* Fr
De Eins-plus-Eins-Adresse *(f)*
En one-plus-one address
Es dirección uno más uno *(f)*
It indirizzo uno-più-uno *(m)*
Pt endereço um mais um *(m)*

Ausdruck *(m) n* De
En expression; printout
Es expresión; vaciado a la impresora *(f m)*
Fr expression; sortie sur imprimante *(f)*
It espressione; stampato *(f m)*
Pt expressão; impressão *(f)*

Ausfallhäufigkeit *(f) n* De
En failure rate
Es frecuencia de fallos *(f)*
Fr taux de défaillance *(m)*
It numero di guasti *(m)*
Pt índice de falhas *(m)*

Ausfallrückgängigkeit *(f) n* De
En failure recovery
Es reparación de fallo *(f)*
Fr redressement de défaillance *(m)*
It recupero di fallimento *(m)*
Pt recuperação de falha *(f)*

Ausfallzeit *(f) n* De
En downtime
Es tiempo de pana *(m)*
Fr temps de panne *(m)*
It tempo di panna *(m)*
Pt tempo de paragem *(m)*

Ausgang *(m) n* De
En exit; output
Es salida *(f)*
Fr sortie *(f)*
It uscita *(f)*
Pt output; saída *(m f)*

Ausgangsbereich *(m) n* De
En output area
Es área de salida *(f)*
Fr zone de sortie *(f)*

It area di uscita *(f)*
Pt área de output *(f)*

Ausgangsvorrichtung *(m) n* De
En output device
Es dispositivo de salida *(m)*
Fr unité périphérique de sortie *(f)*
It organo di uscita *(m)*
Pt dispositivo de output *(m)*

ausgeben *vb* De
En output
Es extraer
Fr sortir
It output
Pt sair

ausgehen *vb* De
En exit
Es salir
Fr sortir
It uscire
Pt sair

Ausgleichspunkt *(m) n* De
En breakpoint
Es punto de interrupción *(m)*
Fr point de rupture *(m)*
It punto di arresto *(m)*
Pt ponto de rotura *(m)*

Ausgleichspunktbefehl *(m) n* De
En breakpoint instruction
Es instrucción de punto de interrupción *(f)*
Fr instruction de point de rupture *(f)*
It istruzione del punto di arresto *(f)*
Pt instruções de ponto de rotura *(f)*

Auslese-geschwindigkeit *(f) n* De
En read rate
Es velocidad de lectura *(f)*
Fr vitesse de lecture *(f)*
It volume di lettura *(m)*
Pt velocidade de leitura *(f)*

auslesen *vb* De
En read out
Es leer en salida
Fr extraire de la memoire
It leggere dalla memoria
Pt ler em saida

Ausleser *(m) n* De
En read-out
Es lectura de salida *(f)*
Fr sortie de lecture *(f)*
It lettura dalla memoria *(f)*
Pt leitura de saida *(f)*

Auslesezeit *(f) n* De
En read time
Es tiempo de lectura *(m)*
Fr durée de lecture *(f)*
It tempo di lettura *(m)*
Pt tempo de leitura *(m)*

auslösen *vb* De
En release
Es liberar
Fr libérer
It rilasciare
Pt libertar

Ausnahmeprinzip-system *(n) n* De
En exception principle system
Es control por excepción *(m)*
Fr gestion par exception *(f)*
It sistema a principio di eccezione *(m)*
Pt sistema de princípio de excepção *(m)*

auspacken *vb* De
En unpack
Es desempaquetar
Fr décondenser
It separare
Pt desembalar

ausschließlich zugeordnet De
En dedicated
Es dedicado
Fr spécialisé
It dedicato
Pt dedicado

Außenkonsole *(f) n* De
En remote console
Es consola remota *(f)*
Fr pupitre à distance *(m)*
It console a distanza *(f)*
Pt consola remota *(f)*

Außenspeicher *(m) n* De
En external store
Es memoria externa *(f)*
Fr mémoire externe *(f)*
It memoria esterna *(f)*
Pt armazém exterior *(m)*

auswählen *vb* De
En select
Es seleccionar
Fr sélectionner
It selezionare
Pt seleccionar

auswechselbarer Plattenspeicher *(m)* De
En exchangeable disk store (EDS)
Es unidad de discos móviles *(f)*
Fr unité de disques à chargeur (UTC) *(f)*
It memoria a dischi inseribili *(f)*
Pt armazém de discos intercambiáveis *(m)*

Ausweichbetrieb *(m) n* De
En backup
Es reserva *(f)*
Fr sauvegarde *(f)*
It riserva *(f)*
Pt apoio *(m)*

autocargador *(m) n* Es
De Startroutine *(f)*
En bootstrap
Fr amorce *(f)*
It istruzioni di avviamento *(f)*
Pt bootstrap *(m)*

autoestructurador *adj* Es
De selbstorganisierend
En self-organizing
Fr auto-organisant
It auto-organizzante
Pt auto-organizante

automa *(m) n* It
De Automat *(m)*
En automaton
Es autómata *(m)*
Fr automate *(m)*
Pt autómato *(m)*

automação *(f) n* Pt
De Automatisierung *(f)*
En automation
Es automación *(f)*
Fr automation *(f)*
It automazione *(f)*

automación *(f) n* Es
De Automatisierung *(f)*
En automation
Fr automation *(f)*
It automazione *(f)*
Pt automação *(f)*

Automat *(m) n* De
En automaton
Es autómata *(m)*
Fr automate *(m)*
It automa *(m)*
Pt autómato *(m)*

autómata *(m) n* Es
De Automat *(m)*
En automaton
Fr automate *(m)*
It automa *(m)*
Pt autómato *(m)*

automate *(m) n* Fr
De Automat *(m)*
En automaton
Es autómata *(m)*
It automa *(m)*
Pt autómato *(m)*

automated engineering design (AED) En
De automatisierte Maschinen-konstruktion *(f)*
Es diseño técnico automatizado *(m)*
Fr étude technique automatisée (ETA) *(f)*
It disegno di ingegneria automatizzata *(m)*
Pt desenho de engenharia automatizado *(m)*

automatically programmed tools (APT) *n pl* En
De automatisch

programmierte Werkzeuge *(pl)*
Es herramientas programadas automáticamente *(f pl)*
Fr machines-outils programmées automatiquement *(f pl)*
It strumenti programmati automaticamente *(m pl)*
Pt ferramentas programadas automaticamente *(f pl)*

automatic check En
De automatische Prüfung *(f)*
Es verificación automática *(f)*
Fr contrôle automatique *(m)*
It controllo automatico *(m)*
Pt verificação automática *(f)*

automatic coding En
De automatische Kodierung *(f)*
Es codificación automática *(f)*
Fr codage automatique *(m)*
It codificazione automatica *(f)*
Pt codificação automática *(f)*

automatic data acquisition (ADA) En
De automatische Datenerwerbung *(f)*
Es adquisición automatica de datos *(f)*
Fr saisie de donneés automatique *(f)*
It acquisto automatico dei dati *(m)*
Pt adquisição automática de dados *(f)*

automatic data conversion En
De automatische Datenumwandlung *(f)*
Es conversión automática de datos *(f)*
Fr conversion de données automatique *(f)*
It conversione automatica dei dati *(f)*
Pt conversão automática de dados *(f)*

automatic data processing En
De automatische Datenverarbeitung *(f)*
Es proceso automático de datos *(m)*
Fr traitement automatique de l'information (TAI) *(m)*
It elaborazione automatica dei dati *(f)*
Pt tratamento automático de dados *(m)*

automatic interrupt En
De automatische Unterbrechung *(f)*
Es interrupción automática *(f)*
Fr interruption automatique *(f)*
It interruzione automatica *(f)*
Pt interrupção automática *(f)*

automatic stop En
De automatischer Stopp *(m)*
Es parada automática *(f)*
Fr arrêt automatique *(m)*
It arresto automatico *(m)*
Pt paragem automática *(f)*

automatic system design En
De automatische System- konstruktion *(f)*
Es diseño automático de sistemas *(m)*
Fr conception de système automatique *(f)*
It progettazione automatica del sistema *(f)*
Pt desenho de sistema automático *(m)*

automation *n* En; Fr *(f)*
De Automatisierung *(f)*
Es automación *(f)*
It automazione *(f)*
Pt automação *(f)*

automatische Datenerwerbung *(f)* De
En automatic data acquisition (ADA)
Es adquisición automatica de datos *(f)*
Fr saisie de donneés automatique *(f)*
It acquisto automatico dei dati *(m)*
Pt adquisição automática de dados *(f)*

automatische Datenumwandlung *(f)* De
En automatic data conversion
Es conversión automática de datos *(f)*
Fr conversion de données automatique *(f)*
It conversione automatica dei dati *(f)*
Pt conversão automática de dados *(f)*

automatische Datenverarbeitung *(f)* De
En automatic data processing
Es proceso automático de datos *(m)*
Fr traitement automatique de l'information (TAI) *(m)*
It elaborazione automatica dei dati *(f)*
Pt tratamento automático de dados *(m)*

automatische Kodierung *(f)* De
En automatic coding
Es codificación automática *(f)*
Fr codage automatique *(m)*
It codificazione automatica *(f)*
Pt codificação automática *(f)*

automatische Prüfung *(f)* De
En automatic check
Es verificación automática *(f)*
Fr contrôle automatique *(m)*
It controllo automatico *(m)*
Pt verificação automática *(f)*

automatischer Stopp *(m)* De
En automatic stop
Es parada automática *(f)*
Fr arrêt automatique *(m)*
It arresto automatico *(m)*
Pt paragem automática *(f)*

automatische System-konstruction *(f)* De
En automatic system design
Es diseño automático de sistemas *(m)*
Fr conception de système automatique *(f)*
It progettazione automatica del sistema *(f)*
Pt desenho de sistema automático *(m)*

automatische Unterbrechung *(f)* De
En automatic interrupt
Es interrupción automática *(f)*

Fr interruption automatique *(f)*
It interruzione automatica *(f)*
Pt interrupção automática *(f)*

automatisch programmierte Werkzeuge *(pl)* De
En automatically programmed tools (APT)
Es herramientas programadas automáticamente *(f pl)*
Fr machines-outils programmées automatiquement *(f pl)*
It strumenti programmati automaticamente *(m pl)*
Pt ferramentas programadas automaticamente *(f pl)*

automatisierte Maschinen-konstruktion *(f)* De
En automated engineering design (AED)
Es diseño técnico automatizado *(m)*
Fr étude technique automatisée (ETA) *(f)*
It disegno di ingegneria automatizzata *(m)*
Pt desenho de engenharia automatizado *(m)*

Automatisierung *(f) n* De
En automation
Es automación *(f)*
Fr automation *(f)*
It automazione *(f)*
Pt automação *(f)*

autómato *(m) n* Pt
De Automat *(m)*
En automaton
Es autómata *(m)*
Fr automate *(m)*
It automa *(m)*

automaton *n* En
De Automat *(m)*
Es autómata *(m)*
Fr automate *(m)*
It automa *(m)*
Pt autómato *(m)*

automazione *(f) n* It
De Automatisierung *(f)*
En automation
Es automación *(f)*
Fr automation *(f)*
Pt automação *(f)*

auto-organisant *adj* Fr
De selbstorganisierend
En self-organizing
Es autoestructurador
It auto-organizzante
Pt auto-organizante

auto-organizante *adj* Pt
De selbstorganisierend
En self-organizing
Es autoestructurador
Fr auto-organisant
It auto-organizzante

auto-organizzante *adj* It
De selbstorganisierend
En self-organizing
Es autoestructurador
Fr auto-organisant
Pt auto-organizante

available time En
De verfügbare Zeit *(f)*
Es tiempo disponible *(m)*
Fr temps disponible *(m)*
It tempo disponibile *(m)*
Pt tempo disponível *(m)*

avance *(f) n* Fr
De Vorschub *(m)*
En feed
Es alimentación *(f)*
It alimentazione *(f)*
Pt alimentação *(f)*

avance horizontale *(f)* Fr
De Horizontalvorschub *(m)*
En horizontal feed
Es alimentación horizontal *(f)*
It alimentazione orizzontale *(f)*
Pt alimentação horizontal *(f)*

avanzare-alimentare nastro *(m)* It
De Bandvorausvorschub *(m)*
En advance-feed tape
Es cinta de alimentación por arrastre *(f)*
Fr défilement-avancement bande *(m)*
Pt fita de alimentação por avanço *(f)*

avariar *vb* Pt
De abgehen
En go down
Es tener una avería
Fr tomber en panne
It avere una panna

avere una panna It
De abgehen
En go down
Es tener una avería
Fr tomber en panne
Pt avariar

avvolgitore *(m) n* It
De Aufspulgerät *(n)*
En spooler
Es bobinadora *(f)*
Fr enrouleur *(m)*
Pt embobinador *(m)*

ayuda a la depuración *(f)* Es
De Fehlersuchhilfe *(f)*
En debugging aid
Fr outil de mise au point *(m)*
It strumento di messa a punto (di un programma) *(m)*
Pt ajuda de desparasitação *(f)*

azionare *vb* It
De antreiben
En drive
Es impulsar
Fr entraîner
Pt accionar

B

background processing En
De Hintergrundverarbeitung *(f)*
Es proceso de programas subordinados *(m)*
Fr traitement non prioritaire *(m)*
It elaborazione non precedenza *(f)*
Pt tratamento de plano de fundo *(m)*

background program En
De Hintergrund-programm *(n)*
Es programa subordinado *(m)*
Fr programme non prioritaire *(m)*
It programma non precedenza *(m)*
Pt programa de plano de fundo *(m)*

backing store En
De Hilfsspeicher *(m)*
Es memoria auxiliar *(f)*
Fr mémoire auxiliaire *(f)*
It memoria ausiliaria *(f)*
Pt armazém de apoio *(m)*

backspace *vb* En
De rückwärtsschreiten
Es retroceder
Fr rappeler le chariot
It tornare indietro
Pt retroceder

backup *n* En
De Ausweichbetrieb *(m)*
Es reserva *(f)*
Fr sauvegarde *(f)*
It riserva *(f)*
Pt apoio *(m)*

Balkencode *(m) n* De
En bar code
Es código de trazos *(m)*
Fr code à bâtonnets *(m)*
It codice a barra *(m)*
Pt código de barra *(m)*

bancada de prueba *(f)* Es
De Prüfstand *(m)*
En test-bed
Fr piste d'entraînement de test *(f)*
It banco di prova *(m)*
Pt mesa de ensaio *(f)*

banca dei dati *(f)* It
De Datenbank *(f)*
En data bank
Es banco de datos *(m)*
Fr banque de données *(f)*
Pt banco de dados *(m)*

banco de dados *(m)* Pt
De Datenbank *(f)*
En data bank
Es banco de datos *(m)*
Fr banque de données *(f)*
It banca dei dati *(f)*

banco de datos *(m)* Es
De Datenbank *(f)*
En data bank
Fr banque de données *(f)*
It banca dei dati *(f)*
Pt banco de dados *(m)*

banco di prova *(m)* It
De Prüfstand *(m)*
En test-bed
Es bancada de prueba *(f)*
Fr piste d'entraînement de test *(f)*
Pt mesa de ensaio *(f)*

band *n* En
De Band *(n)*
Es banda *(f)*
Fr bande *(f)*
It banda *(f)*
Pt banda *(f)*

Band *(n) n* De
En band; tape
Es banda; cinta *(f)*
Fr bande *(f)*
It banda; nastro *(f m)*
Pt banda; fita *(f)*

banda *(f) n* Es, It, Pt
De Band *(n)*
En band
Fr bande *(f)*

banda ancha *(f)* Es
De Breitband *(n)*
En broadband
Fr bande large *(f)*
It banda larga *(f)*
Pt banda larga *(f)*

banda de guardia *(f)* Es
De Schutzband *(n)*
En guard band
Fr bande protection *(f)*
It banda di guardia *(f)*
Pt banda de protecção *(f)*

banda de protecção *(f)* Pt
De Schutzband *(n)*
En guard band
Es banda de guardia *(f)*
Fr bande protection *(f)*
It banda di guardia *(f)*

banda di guardia *(f)* It
De Schutzband *(n)*
En guard band
Es banda de guardia *(f)*
Fr bande protection *(f)*
Pt banda de protecção *(f)*

banda larga *(f)* It, Pt
De Breitband *(n)*
En broadband
Es banda ancha *(f)*
Fr bande large *(f)*

Bandantrieb *(m) n* De
En tape drive
Es impulsor de cinta *(m)*
Fr dérouleur de bande *(m)*
It guida del nastro *(f)*
Pt accionamento da fita *(m)*

Bandbibliothek *(f) n* De
En tape library
Es biblioteca de cintas *(f)*
Fr bandothèque *(f)*
It libreria dei nastri *(f)*
Pt biblioteca de fitas *(f)*

Bandbreite *(f) n* De
En bandwidth
Es anchura de banda *(f)*
Fr largeur de bande *(f)*
It larghezza di banda *(f)*
Pt largura de banda *(f)*

bande *(f) n* Fr
De Band *(n)*
En band; tape
Es banda; cinta *(f)*
It banda; nastro *(f m)*
Pt banda; fita *(f)*

bande à entraînement central *(f)* Fr
Am center-feed tape
De Band mit Zentralvorschub *(n)*
En centre-feed tape
Es cinta de alimentación central *(f)*
It nastro ad alimentazione centrale *(m)*
Pt fita de alimentação central *(f)*

bande à perforations complètes *(f)* Fr
De geschuppter Streifen *(m)*
En chadded tape
Es cinta de perforación completa *(f)*
It nastro con perforazioni totali *(m)*
Pt fita recortada *(f)*

bande créatrice *(f)* Fr
De Urband *n*
En father tape
Es cinta creadora *(f)*
It nastro padre *(m)*
Pt fita pai *(f)*

bande de papier *(f)* Fr
De Papierstreifen *(m)*
En paper tape
Es cinta de papel *(f)*
It nastro di carta *(m)*
Pt fita de papel *(f)*

bande de programme d'exploitation (BPE) *(f)* Fr
De Hauptbefehlsband *(n)*
En master-instruction tape (MIT)
Es cinta programa de explotación *(f)*
It nastro dell'istruzioni principali *(m)*
Pt fita de instruções principais *(f)*

bande de travail *(f)* Fr
De Arbeitsband *(n)*
En work tape
Es cinta de maniobra *(f)*
It nastro di lavoro *(m)*
Pt fita de trabalho *(f)*

bandeira *(f) n* Pt
De Markierung *(f)*
En flag
Es señalizador *(m)*
Fr drapeau *(m)*
It indicatore *(m)*

bande large *(f)* Fr
De Breitband *(n)*
En broadband
Es banda ancha *(f)*
It banda larga *(f)*
Pt banda larga *(f)*

bande magnétique *(f)* Fr
De Magnetband *(n)*
En magnetic tape
Es cinta magnética *(f)*
It nastro magnetico *(m)*
Pt fita magnética *(f)*

bande maîtresse *(f)* Fr
De Stammband *(n)*
En master tape
Es bobina emisora *(f)*
It nastro principale *(m)*
Pt fita principal *(f)*

Bandende *(n) n* De
En end of tape (EOT)
Es fin de cinta *(m)*
Fr fin de bande *(f)*
It fine del nastro *(f)*
Pt fim da fita *(m)*

bande perforée *(f)* Fr
De Lochstreifen *(m)*
En perforated tape; punched tape
Es cinta perforada *(f)*
It nastro perforato *(m)*
Pt fita perfurada *(f)*

bande pilote *(f)* Fr
De Wagensteuerband *(n)*
En carriage-control tape
Es cinta de control del carro *(f)*
It nastrino di controllo del carrello *(m)*
Pt fita com controle de carro *(f)*

bande première génération *(f)* Fr

De Erstgenerationsband *(n)*
En grandfather tape
Es cinta primera generación *(f)*
It nastro nonno *(m)*
Pt fita avó *(f)*

bande protection *(f)* Fr
De Schutzband *(n)*
En guard band
Es banda de guardia *(f)*
It banda di guardia *(f)*
Pt banda de protecção *(f)*

bande semi-perforée *(f)* Fr
De Schuppenstreifen *(m)*
En chadless tape
Es cinta semiperforada *(f)*
It nastro semiperforato *(m)*
Pt fita sem recorte *(f)*

bande vierge *(f)* Fr
De Neuband *(n)*
En virgin tape
Es cint a virgen *(f)*
It nastro vergine *(m)*
Pt fita virgem *(f)*

Bandgerät *(n)* *n* De
En tape unit
Es unidad de cinta *(f)*
Fr unité de ruban magnétique *(f)*
It unità a nastri *(f)*
Pt unidade de fita *(f)*

Bandkennzeichen *(n)* *n* De
En tape mark
Es marca de cinta *(f)*
Fr marque de bande *(f)*
It segno del nastro *(m)*
Pt marca de fita *(f)*

Bandleser *(m)* *n* De
En tape reader
Es lectora de cinta *(f)*
Fr lecteur de bande *(m)*
It lettore di nastri *(m)*
Pt leitor de fita *(m)*

Bandlocher *(m)* *n* De
En tape punch
Es perforadora de cinta *(f)*
Fr perforatrice de bande *(f)*
It perforatrice di nastri *(f)*
Pt perfuradora de fita *(f)*

Band mit Zentralvorschub *(n)* De
Am center-feed tape
En centre-feed tape
Es cinta de alimentación central *(f)*
Fr bande à entraînement central *(f)*
It nastro ad alimentazione centrale *(m)*
Pt fita de alimentação central *(f)*

bandothèque *(f)* *n* Fr
De Bandbibliothek *(f)*
En tape library
Es biblioteca de cintas *(f)*
It libreria dei nastri *(f)*
Pt biblioteca de fitas *(f)*

Bandprüfgerät *(n)* *n* De
En tape verifier
Es verificadora de cinta *(f)*
Fr vérificatrice de bande *(f)*
It verificatrice di nastri *(f)*
Pt verificador de fita *(m)*

Bandtransport *(m)* *n* De
En tape transport
Es transporte de cinta *(m)*
Fr transport de la bande *(m)*
It trasporto del nastro *(m)*
Pt transporte de fita *(m)*

Bandvorausvorschub *(m)* *n* De
En advance-feed tape
Es cinta de alimentación por arrastre *(f)*
Fr défilement-avancement bande *(m)*
It avanzare-alimentare nastro *(m)*
Pt fita de alimentação por avanço *(f)*

Bandvorschub *(m)* *n* De
En tape feed
Es alimentador de cinta *(m)*
Fr entraînement du ruban *(m)*
It alimentazione del nastro *(f)*
Pt alimentação de fita *(f)*

bandwidth *n* En
De Bandbreite *(f)*
Es anchura de banda *(f)*
Fr largeur de bande *(f)*
It larghezza di banda *(f)*
Pt largura de banda *(f)*

banque de données *(f)* Fr
De Datenbank *(f)*
En data bank
Es banco de datos *(m)*
It banca dei dati *(f)*
Pt banco de dados *(m)*

baraja *(f)* *n* Es
Am deck (of cards)
De Kartensatz *(m)*
En pack (of cards)
Fr paquet de cartes *(m)*
It mazzo *(m)*
Pt baralho (de cartas) *(m)*

baralho (de cartas) *(m)* Pt
Am deck (of cards)
De Kartensatz *(m)*
En pack (of cards)
Es baraja *(f)*
Fr paquet de cartes *(m)*
It mazzo *(m)*

bar code En
De Balkencode *(m)*
Es código de trazos *(m)*
Fr code à bâtonnets *(m)*
It codice a barra *(m)*
Pt código de barra *(m)*

barra *(f)* *n* It
De Hauptverbindung *(f)*
En bus
Es conductor común *(m)*
Fr bus *(m)*
Pt condutor *(m)*

barra de tipos *(f)* Es, Pt
De Typenstange *(f)*
En type bar
Fr barre d'impression *(f)*
It sbarra di caratteri *(f)*

barre d'impression *(f)* Fr
De Typenstange *(f)*
En type bar
Es barra de tipos *(f)*
It sbarra di caratteri *(f)*
Pt barra de tipos *(f)*

barrel printer En
De Trommeldrucker *(m)*
Es impresora de rodillo *(f)*
Fr imprimante à tambour *(f)*
It stampatrice a tamburo *(f)*
Pt impressora de tambor *(f)*

bascule électronique *(f)* Fr
De elektronischer Schalter *(m)*
En electronic switch
Es conmutador electrónico *(m)*
It interruttore elettronico *(m)*
Pt comutador electrónico *(m)*

base *n* En
De Basis *(f)*
Es base *(f)*
Fr base *(f)*
It base *(f)*
Pt base *(f)*

base *(f)* *n* Es, Fr, It
De Basis *(f)*
En base; radix
Pt base; raiz *(f)*

base *(f)* *n* Pt
De Basis *(f)*
En base
Es base *(f)*
Fr base *(f)*
It base *(f)*

base address En
De Basisadresse *(f)*
Es dirección de base *(f)*
Fr adresse de base *(f)*
It indirizzo base *(m)*
Pt direcção de base *(f)*

base de dados *(f)* Pt
De Datenbasis *(f)*
En database
Es base de datos *(f)*
Fr base de données *(f)*
It base dei dati *(f)*

base de datos *(f)* Es
De Datenbasis *(f)*
En database
Fr base de données *(f)*
It base dei dati *(f)*
Pt base de dados *(f)*

base de données *(f)* Fr
De Datenbasis *(f)*
En database
Es base de datos *(f)*
It base dei dati *(f)*
Pt base de dados *(f)*

base dei dati *(f)* It
De Datenbasis *(f)*
En database
Es base de datos *(f)*
Fr base de données *(f)*
Pt base de dados *(f)*

base register En
De Basisregister *(n)*
Es registro de base *(m)*
Fr registre de base *(m)*
It registro base *(m)*
Pt registo de base *(m)*

Basis *(f)* *n* De
En base; radix
Es base *(f)*
Fr base *(f)*
It base *(f)*
Pt base; raiz *(f)*

Basisadresse *(f)* *n* De
En base address
Es dirección de base *(f)*
Fr adresse de base *(f)*
It indirizzo base *(m)*
Pt direcção de base *(f)*

Basiskomplement *(n)* *n* De
En radix complement
Es complemento de la base *(m)*
Fr complément à la base *(m)*
It complemento di base *(m)*
Pt complemento de raiz *(m)*

Basispunkt *(m)* *n* De
En radix point
Es coma de la base *(f)*
Fr point à la base *(m)*
It punto di base *(m)*
Pt ponto de raiz *(m)*

Basisregister *(n)* *n* De
En base register
Es registro de base *(m)*
Fr registre de base *(m)*
It registro base *(m)*
Pt registo de base *(m)*

batch job En
De Stapelarbeit *(f)*
Es trabajo por lotes *(m)*
Fr travail en traitement par lots *(m)*
It lavoro a lotti *(m)*
Pt trabalho por lotes *(m)*

batch processing En
De Stapelverarbeitung *(f)*
Es proceso por lotes *(m)*
Fr traitement par lot *(m)*
It elaborazione a lotti *(f)*
Pt tratamento por lotes *(m)*

baud *n* En, Fr, It, Pt *(m)*
De Baud *(n)*
Es baudio *(m)*

Baud *(n)* *n* De
En baud
Es baudio *(m)*
Fr baud *(m)*
It baud *(m)*
Pt baud *(m)*

Baudgeschwindigkeit *(f)* *n* De
En baud rate
Es velocidad en baudios *(f)*
Fr débit en bauds *(m)*
It numero di baud *(m)*
Pt taxa de baud *(f)*

baudio *(m)* *n* Es
De Baud *(n)*
En baud
Fr baud *(m)*
It baud *(m)*
Pt baud *(m)*

baud rate En
De Baudgeschwindigkeit *(f)*
Es velocidad en baudios *(f)*
Fr débit en bauds *(m)*
It numero di baud *(m)*
Pt taxa de baud *(f)*

Baukastensystem *(n)* *n* De
En modular system
Es sistema modular *(m)*
Fr système modulaire *(m)*
It sistema modulare *(m)*
Pt sistema modular *(m)*

bead *n* En
De Kugel *(f)*
Es perla *(f)*
Fr perle *(f)*
It perla *(f)*
Pt boleado *(m)*

beam store En
De Strahlenspeicher *(m)*
Es memoria a rayos *(f)*
Fr mémoire à faisceau *(f)*
It memoria a fascio *(f)*
Pt armazém de raio *(m)*

bearbeiten *vb* De
En process
Es procesar
Fr traiter
It elaborare
Pt processar

beat frequency En
De Schwebungsfrequenz *(f)*
Es frecuencia de pulsación *(f)*
Fr fréquence de battement *(f)*
It frequenza di battimento *(f)*
Pt frequência de pulso *(f)*

beauftragen *vb* De
En order
Es ordenar
Fr ordonner
It ordinare
Pt ordenar

Bediener *(m)* *n* De
En operator
Es operador *(m)*
Fr opérateur *(m)*
It operatore *(m)*
Pt operador *(m)*

bedingte Funktion *(f)* De
En conditional implication
Es implicación condicional *(f)*
Fr implication conditionnelle *(f)*
It implicazione condizionale *(f)*
Pt implicação condicional *(f)*

bedingter Betrieb *(m)* De
En conditional operation
Es operación condicional *(f)*
Fr opération conditionnelle *(f)*
It operazione condizionale *(f)*
Pt operação condicional *(f)*

bedingter Verzweigungsbefehl *(m)* De
En conditional branch instruction
Es instrucción de bifurcación condicional *(f)*
Fr instruction de branchement conditionnelle *(f)*
It istruzione di diramazione condizionale *(f)*
Pt instrução de ramificação condicional *(f)*

bedingte Übergabe *(f)* De
En conditional transfer
Es transferencia condicional *(f)*
Fr transfert conditionnel *(m)*
It trasferimento condizionale *(m)*
Pt transferência condicional *(f)*

Befehl *(m)* *n* De
En command; instruction
Es instrucción; orden *(f)*
Fr commande; instruction *(f)*

It comando; istruzione (m f)
Pt ordem; instrução (f)

Befehlsadressen-register (n) n De
En instruction-address register
Es registro de instrucciòndirección (m)
Fr registre d'adresse de l'instruction (m)
It registro dell'indirizzo dell'istruzione (m)
Pt registo de endereço de instrução (m)

Befehlscode (m) n De
En instruction code
Es código de instrucción (m)
Fr code d'instruction (m)
It codice dell'istruzione (m)
Pt código de instruções (m)

Befehlsformat (n) n De
En instruction format
Es formato de la instrucción (m)
Fr structure de l'instruction (f)
It formato dell'istruzione (m)
Pt formato de instruções (m)

Befehlsmnemonik (f) n De
En instruction mnemonic
Es instrucción mnemotécnica (f)
Fr mnémonique d'instruction (f)
It mnemonica dell'istruzione (f)
Pt mnemónica de instruções (f)

Befehlssprache (f) n De
En command language
Es lenguaje de orden (m)
Fr langage de commande (m)
It linguaggio del comando (m)
Pt linguagem de ordem (f)

Befehlsvorrat (m) n De
En instruction set
Es juego de instrucciones (m)
Fr jeu d'instructions (m)
It gruppo di istruzioni (m)
Pt conjunto de instruções (m)

Befehlszeit (f) n De
En instruction time
Es tiempo de una instrucción (m)
Fr temps d'exécution d'une instruction (m)
It tempo per l'istruzione (m)
Pt tempo de instruções (m)

begrenzen vb De
En delimit
Es delimitar
Fr délimiter
It delimitare
Pt delimitar

Begrenzer (m) n De
En delimiter
Es delimitador (m)
Fr delimitateur (m)
It delimitatore (m)
Pt delimitador (m)

Beisatz (m) n De
En trailer record
Es registro de cola (m)
Fr article fin (m)
It record di fine (m)
Pt registo de trailer (m)

Beisatzkennzeichen (n) n De
En trailer label
Es etiqueta de cola (f)
Fr label fin (m)
It etichetta di fine (f)
Pt rótulo de trailer (m)

benchmark n En
De Fixpunkt (m)
Es referencia (f)
Fr repère (m)
It riferimento (m)
Pt referência de nível (f)

Benutzer (m) n De
En user
Es usuario (m)
Fr utilisateur (m)
It utente (m)
Pt utente (m)

Benutzergruppe (f) n De
En user group
Es grupo de usuarios (m)
Fr groupement d'utilisateurs (m)
It gruppo di utenti (m)
Pt group utente (m)

Benutzerzeit (f) n De
En uptime
Es tiempo productivo (m)
Fr temps de bon fonctionnement (m)
It tempo di utilizzazione (m)
Pt tempo terminado (m)

Benutzungsverhältnis (n) n De
En utilization ratio
Es relación de utilización (f)
Fr rapport d'utilisation (m)
It rapporto di utilizzazione (m)
Pt ratio de utilização (f)

Bereich (m) n De
En range
Es margen (m)
Fr gamme (f)
It gamma (f)
Pt alcance (m)

Bereichs-unabhängigkeit (f) n De
En range independence
Es independencia del margen (f)
Fr indépendance de gamme (f)
It indipendenza di gamma (f)
Pt independência do alcance (f)

Beschleunigungszeit (f) n De
En acceleration time
Es tiempo de aceleración (m)
Fr temps d'accélération (m)
It tempo di accelerazione (m)
Pt tempo de aceleração (m)

Beschreiber (m) n De
En descriptor
Es descriptor (m)
Fr descripteur (m)
It descrittore (m)
Pt descritor (m)

beschriften vb De
En inscribe
Es marcar
Fr marquer
It inscrivere
Pt inscrever

Betriebsart (f) n De
En mode
Es modo (m)
Fr mode (m)
It modalità (f)
Pt modo (m)

Betriebsfähigkeit (f) n De
En serviceability
Es utilidad (f)
Fr aptitude au service (f)
It utilità (f)
Pt aptidão a ser utilizado (f)

Betriebsmittel (n) n De
En resource
Es recurso (m)
Fr ressource (f)
It risorsa (f)
Pt recurso (m)

Betriebsmittel-zuweisung (f) n De
En resource allocation
Es asignación de recursos (f)
Fr affectation des ressources (f)
It allocazione delle risorse (f)
Pt atribuição de recursos (f)

Betriebssystem (n) n De
En operating system (OS)
Es sistema operativo (m)

Fr système d'exploitation *(m)*
It sistema operativo *(m)*
Pt sistema de operação *(m)*

Bezeichner *(m) n* De
En identifier
Es identificador *(m)*
Fr identificateur *(m)*
It identificatore *(m)*
Pt identificador *(m)*

Bezugsadresse *(f) n* De
En reference address
Es dirección de referencia *(f)*
Fr adresse primitive *(f)*
It indirizzo di riferimento *(m)*
Pt endereço de referência *(m)*

Bezugsliste *(f) n* De
En reference listing
Es lista de referencias *(f)*
Fr listage primitif *(m)*
It listato di riferimento *(m)*
Pt listagem de referência *(f)*

bianco *(m) n* It
De Leerstelle *(f)*
En blank
Es blanco *(m)*
Fr espace *(m)*
Pt espaço *(m)*

bias *n* En
De Vorspannung *(f)*
Es polarización *(f)*
Fr polarisation *(f)*
It polarizzazione *(f)*
Pt polarisação *(f)*

bias *vb* En
De vorspannen
Es polarizar
Fr polariser
It polarizzare
Pt polarizar

biblioteca *(f) n* Es, Pt
De Bibliothek *(f)*
En library
Fr bibliothèque *(f)*
It libreria *(f)*

biblioteca de cintas *(f)* Es
De Bandbibliothek *(f)*
En tape library
Fr bandothèque *(f)*
It libreria dei nastri *(f)*
Pt biblioteca de fitas *(f)*

biblioteca de fitas *(f)* Pt
De Bandbibliothek *(f)*
En tape library
Es biblioteca de cintas *(f)*
Fr bandothèque *(f)*
It libreria dei nastri *(f)*

biblioteca de programas *(f)* Es, Pt
De Programmbibliothek *(f)*
En program library
Fr bibliothèque de programmes *(f)*
It libreria dei programmi *(f)*

biblioteca de programas de aplicação *(f)* Pt
De Bibliothek der Anwendungs-programme *(f)*
En application programs library (APL)
Es biblioteca de programas de aplicación *(f)*
Fr bibliothèque des programmes d'application *(f)*
It libreria dei programmi applicativi *(f)*

biblioteca de programas de aplicación *(f)* Es
De Bibliothek der Anwendungs-programme *(f)*
En application programs library (APL)
Fr bibliothèque des programmes d'application *(f)*
It libreria dei programmi applicativi *(f)*
Pt biblioteca de programas de aplicação *(f)*

Bibliothek *(f) n* De
En library
Es biblioteca *(f)*
Fr bibliothèque *(f)*
It libreria *(f)*
Pt biblioteca *(f)*

Bibliothek der Anwendungs-programme *(f)* De
En application programs library (APL)
Es biblioteca de programas de aplicación *(f)*
Fr bibliothèque des programmes d'application *(f)*
It libreria dei programmi applicativi *(f)*
Pt biblioteca de programas de aplicação *(f)*

bibliothèque *(f) n* Fr
De Bibliothek *(f)*
En library
Es biblioteca *(f)*
It libreria *(f)*
Pt biblioteca *(f)*

bibliothèque de programmes *(f)* Fr
De Programmbibliothek *(f)*
En program library
Es biblioteca de programas *(f)*
It libreria dei programmi *(f)*
Pt biblioteca de programas *(f)*

bibliothèque des programmes d'application *(f)* Fr
De Bibliothek der Anwendungs-programme *(f)*
En application programs library (APL)
Es biblioteca de programas de aplicación *(f)*
It libreria dei programmi applicativi *(f)*
Pt biblioteca de programas de aplicação *(f)*

bicha de mensagens *(f)* Pt
De Nachrichten-schlangestehen *(n)*
En message queuing
Es formación de colas de mensajes *(f)*
Fr mise en file d'attente de message *(f)*
It messa in coda dei messaggi *(f)*

bifurcación *(f) n* Es
De Zweig *(m)*
En branch
Fr branchement *(m)*
It diramazione *(f)*
Pt ramo *(m)*

bifurcar *vb* Es
De abzweigen
En branch
Fr brancher
It diramarsi
Pt ligar

Bildschirmformat *(n) n* De
En map
Es mapa *(m)*
Fr carte *(f)*
It mappa *(f)*
Pt mapa *(m)*

binaire *adj* Fr
De binär
En binary
Es binario
It binario
Pt binário

binär *adj* De
En binary
Es binario
Fr binaire
It binario
Pt binário

Binärcode *(m) n* De
En binary code
Es código binario *(m)*
Fr code binaire *(m)*
It codice binario *(m)*
Pt código binário *(m)*

binärcodierte Dezimal-darstellung *(f)* De
En binary-coded decimal (BCD)
Es decimal codificado en binario (DCB) *(m)*

Fr décimale codée en binaire (DCB) *(f)*
It decimale codificato in binario (DCB) *(m)*
Pt decimal de código binário (DCB) *(m)*

Binärdarstellung *(f) n* De
En binary notation
Es notación binaria *(f)*
Fr notation binaire *(f)*
It notazione binaria *(f)*
Pt notação binária *(f)*

Binär-Dezimal-umwandlung *(f)* De
En binary-to-decimal conversion
Es conversión de binario a decimal *(f)*
Fr conversion de binaire en décimal *(f)*
It conversione da decimale a binario *(f)*
Pt conversão de binário em decimal *(f)*

binäres Suchen *(n)* De
En binary search
Es búsqueda binaria *(f)*
Fr recherche dichotomique *(f)*
It ricerca binaria *(f)*
Pt busca binária *(f)*

Binärfunktion *(f) n* De
En binary operation
Es operación binaria *(f)*
Fr opération binaire *(f)*
It operazione binaria *(f)*
Pt operação binário *(f)*

Binärinverter *(m) n* De
En inverter
Es inversor *(m)*
Fr inverseur *(m)*
It invertitore *(m)*
Pt inversor *(m)*

binario *adj* Es, It
De binär
En binary
Fr binaire
Pt binário

binário *adj* Pt
De binär
En binary
Es binario
Fr binaire
It binario

binary *adj* En
De binär
Es binario
Fr binaire
It binario
Pt binário

binary code En
De Binärcode *(m)*
Es código binario *(m)*
Fr code binaire *(m)*
It codice binario *(m)*
Pt código binário *(m)*

binary-coded decimal (BCD) En
De binärcodierte Dezimaldarstellung *(f)*
Es decimal codificado en binario (DCB) *(m)*
Fr décimale codée en binaire (DCB) *(f)*
It decimale codificato in binario (DCB) *(m)*
Pt decimal de código binário (DCB) *(m)*

binary notation En
De Binärdarstellung *(f)*
Es notación binaria *(f)*
Fr notation binaire *(f)*
It notazione binaria *(f)*
Pt notação binária *(f)*

binary operation En
De Binärfunktion *(f)*
Es operación binaria *(f)*
Fr opération binaire *(f)*
It operazione binaria *(f)*
Pt operação binário *(f)*

binary search En
De binäres Suchen *(n)*
Es búsqueda binaria *(f)*
Fr recherche dichotomique *(f)*
It ricerca binaria *(f)*
Pt busca binária *(f)*

binary-to-decimal conversion En
De Binär-Dezimal-umwandlung *(f)*
Es conversión de binario a decimal *(f)*
Fr conversion de binaire en décimal *(f)*
It conversione da decimale a binario *(f)*
Pt conversão de binário em decimal *(f)*

Binärzeichen *(n) n* De
En bit
Es bit *(m)*
Fr bit *(m)*
It bit *(m)*
Pt bit *(m)*

Binärzeichendichte *(f) n* De
En bit density
Es densidad de bits *(f)*
Fr densité de bits *(f)*
It densità di bit *(f)*
Pt densidade de bit *(f)*

Binärzeichenfolge *(f) n* De
En bit string
Es serie de bits *(f)*
Fr chaîne de bits *(f)*
It stringa di bit *(f)*
Pt fila de bits *(f)*

Binärzeichen-geschwindigkeit *(f) n* De
En bit rate
Es tasa en bits *(f)*
Fr débit de bits *(m)*
It volume di bit *(m)*
Pt taxa de bit *(f)*

Binärzeichenmuster *(n) n* De
En bit pattern
Es configuración de bits *(f)*
Fr configuration de bits *(f)*
It configurazione dei bit *(f)*
Pt padrão de bit *(m)*

Binärzeichenortung *(f) n* De
En bit location
Es posición de bit *(f)*
Fr position de bits *(f)*
It locazione del bit *(f)*
Pt localização de bit *(f)*

Binärzeichen pro Sekunde *(pl)* De
En bits per second (bps)
Es bits por segundo *(m pl)*
Fr bits par seconde *(m pl)*
It bits al secondo *(m pl)*
Pt bits por segundo *(m pl)*

bionica *(f) n* It
De Bionie *(f)*
En bionics
Es biónica *(f)*
Fr bionique *(f)*
Pt biónica *(f)*

biónica *(f) n* Es, Pt
De Bionie *(f)*
En bionics
Fr bionique *(f)*
It bionica *(f)*

bionics *n* En
De Bionie *(f)*
Es biónica *(f)*
Fr bionique *(f)*
It bionica *(f)*
Pt biónica *(f)*

Bionie *(f) n* De
En bionics
Es biónica *(f)*
Fr bionique *(f)*
It bionica *(f)*
Pt biónica *(f)*

bionique *(f) n* Fr
De Bionie *(f)*
En bionics
Es biónica *(f)*
It bionica *(f)*
Pt biónica *(f)*

bipolaire *adj* Fr
De bipolar
En bipolar
Es bipolar
It bipolare
Pt bipolar

bipolar *adj* De, En, Es, Pt
Fr bipolaire
It bipolare

bipolare *adj* It
De bipolar
En bipolar
Es bipolar
Fr bipolaire
Pt bipolar

biprocesador *(m) n* Es
De Parallelverarbeiter *(m)*
En dual processor
Fr biprocesseur *(m)*
It elaboratore duplice *(m)*

Pt processador duplo *(m)*

biprocesseur *(m) n* Fr
De Parallelverarbeiter *(m)*
En dual processor
Es biprocesador *(m)*
It elaboratore duplice *(m)*
Pt processador duplo *(m)*

biquinärer Code *(m)* De
En biquinary code
Es código biquinario *(m)*
Fr code biquinaire *(m)*
It codice biquinario *(m)*
Pt código biquinário *(m)*

biquinary code En
De biquinärer Code *(m)*
Es código biquinario *(m)*
Fr code biquinaire *(m)*
It codice biquinario *(m)*
Pt código biquinário *(m)*

bistabile Kippschaltung *(f)* De
En bistable circuit
Es circuito biestable *(m)*
Fr circuit bistable *(m)*
It circuito bistabile *(m)*
Pt circuito biestável *(m)*

bistable circuit En
De bistabile Kippschaltung *(f)*
Es circuito biestable *(m)*
Fr circuit bistable *(m)*
It circuito bistabile *(m)*
Pt circuito biestável *(m)*

bit *n* En, Es, Fr, It, Pt *(m)*
De Binärzeichen *(n)*

bit de contrôle *(m)* Fr
De Prüfbit *(m)*
En check bit
Es bit de verificación *(m)*
It bit di controllo *(m)*
Pt bit de verificação *(m)*

bit del segno *(m)* It
De Vorzeichenbit *(m)*
En sign bit
Es bit de signo *(m)*
Fr bit de signe *(m)*
Pt bit de sinal *(m)*

bit density En
De Binärzeichendichte *(f)*
Es densidad de bits *(f)*
Fr densité de bits *(f)*
It densità di bit *(f)*
Pt densidade de bit *(f)*

bit de paridad *(m)* Es
De Paritätsbit *(m)*
En parity bit
Fr bit de parité *(m)*
It bit di parità *(m)*
Pt bit de paridade *(m)*

bit de paridade *(m)* Pt
De Paritätsbit *(m)*
En parity bit
Es bit de paridad *(m)*
Fr bit de parité *(m)*
It bit di parità *(m)*

bit de parité *(m)* Fr
De Paritätsbit *(m)*
En parity bit
Es bit de paridad *(m)*
It bit di parità *(m)*
Pt bit de paridade *(m)*

bit de service *(m)* Fr
De Dienstbit *(m)*
En service bit
Es bit de servicio *(m)*
It bit di servizio *(m)*
Pt bit de serviço *(m)*

bit de servicio *(m)* Es
De Dienstbit *(m)*
En service bit
Fr bit de service *(m)*
It bit di servizio *(m)*
Pt bit de serviço *(m)*

bit de serviço *(m)* Pt
De Dienstbit *(m)*
En service bit
Es bit de servicio *(m)*
Fr bit de service *(m)*
It bit di servizio *(m)*

bit de signe *(m)* Fr
De Vorzeichenbit *(m)*
En sign bit
Es bit de signo *(m)*
It bit del segno *(m)*
Pt bit de sinal *(m)*

bit de signo *(m)* Es
De Vorzeichenbit *(m)*
En sign bit
Fr bit de signe *(m)*
It bit del segno *(m)*
Pt bit de sinal *(m)*

bit de sinal *(m)* Pt
De Vorzeichenbit *(m)*
En sign bit
Es bit de signo *(m)*
Fr bit de signe *(m)*
It bit del segno *(m)*

bit de verificação *(m)* Pt
De Prüfbit *(m)*
En check bit
Es bit de verificación *(m)*
Fr bit de contrôle *(m)*
It bit di controllo *(m)*

bit de verificación *(m)* Es
De Prüfbit *(m)*
En check bit
Fr bit de contrôle *(m)*
It bit di controllo *(m)*
Pt bit de verificação *(m)*

bit de zona *(m)* Es, Pt
De Zonenbit *(m)*
En zone bit
Fr bit de zone *(m)*
It bit di zonatura *(m)*

bit de zone *(m)* Fr
De Zonenbit *(m)*
En zone bit
Es bit de zona *(m)*
It bit di zonatura *(m)*
Pt bit de zona *(m)*

bit di controllo *(m)* It
De Prüfbit *(m)*
En check bit
Es bit de verificación *(m)*
Fr bit de contrôle *(m)*
Pt bit de verificação *(m)*

bit di parità *(m)* It
De Paritätsbit *(m)*
En parity bit
Es bit de paridad *(m)*
Fr bit de parité *(m)*
Pt bit de paridade *(m)*

bit di servizio *(m)* It
De Dienstbit *(m)*
En service bit
Es bit de servicio *(m)*
Fr bit de service *(m)*
Pt bit de serviço *(m)*

bit di zonatura *(m)* It
De Zonenbit *(m)*
En zone bit
Es bit de zona *(m)*
Fr bit de zone *(m)*
Pt bit de zona *(m)*

bit location En
De Binärzeichenortung *(f)*
Es posición de bit *(f)*
Fr position de bits *(f)*
It locazione del bit *(f)*
Pt localização de bit *(f)*

bit pattern En
De Binärzeichenmuster *(n)*
Es configuración de bits *(f)*
Fr configuration de bits *(f)*
It configurazione dei bit *(f)*
Pt padrão de bit *(m)*

bit rate En
De Binärzeichengeschwindigkeit *(f)*
Es tasa en bits *(f)*
Fr débit de bits *(m)*
It volume di bit *(m)*
Pt taxa de bit *(f)*

bits al secondo *(m pl)* It
De Binärzeichen pro Sekunde *(pl)*
En bits per second (bps)
Es bits por segundo *(m pl)*
Fr bits par seconde *(m pl)*
Pt bits por segundo *(m pl)*

bits par seconde *(m pl)* Fr
De Binärzeichen pro Sekunde *(pl)*
En bits per second (bps)
Es bits por segundo *(m pl)*
It bits al secondo *(m pl)*
Pt bits por segundo *(m pl)*

bits per second (bps) En
De Binärzeichen pro Sekunde *(pl)*
Es bits por segundo *(m pl)*

Fr bits par seconde *(m pl)*
It bits al secondo *(m pl)*
Pt bits por segundo *(m pl)*

bits por segundo *(m pl)* Es, Pt
De Binärzeichen pro Sekunde *(pl)*
En bits per second (bps)
Fr bits par seconde *(m pl)*
It bits al secondo *(m pl)*

bit string En
De Binärzeichenfolge *(f)*
Es serie de bits *(f)*
Fr chaîne de bits *(f)*
It stringa di bit *(f)*
Pt fila de bits *(f)*

blanco *(m) n* Es
De Leerstelle *(f)*
En blank
Fr espace *(m)*
It bianco *(m)*
Pt espaço *(m)*

blank *n* En
De Leerstelle *(f)*
Es blanco *(m)*
Fr espace *(m)*
It bianco *(m)*
Pt espaço *(m)*

Blindbefehl *(m) n* De
En dummy instruction
Es instrucción ficticia *(f)*
Fr instruction fictive *(f)*
It istruzione fittizia *(f)*
Pt instrução simulada *(f)*

bloc *(m) n* Fr
De Datenblock *(m)*
En block
Es bloque *(m)*
It blocco *(m)*
Pt bloco *(m)*

bloccaggio di record *(m)* It
De Satzblockierung *(f)*
En record blocking
Es bloqueo de registro *(m)*
Fr groupage enregistrement *(m)*
Pt bloqueio de registo *(m)*

blocco *(m) n* It
De Datenblock *(m)*
En block
Es bloque *(m)*
Fr bloc *(m)*
Pt bloco *(m)*

bloc de longueur fixe *(m)* Fr
De feste Blocklänge *(f)*
En fixed block length
Es longitud de bloque fija *(f)*
It lunghezza del blocco fisso *(f)*
Pt comprimento de bloco fixo *(m)*

bloc de notas *(m)* Es
De Arbeitspuffer *(m)*
En scratch pad
Fr mémoire de travail *(f)*
It bloc-notes *(m)*
Pt almofada de raspar *(f)*

block *n* En
De Datenblock *(m)*
Es bloque *(m)*
Fr bloc *(m)*
It blocco *(m)*
Pt bloco *(m)*

Block *(m) n* De
En tablet
Es tableta *(f)*
Fr tablette *(f)*
It tavoletta *(f)*
Pt bloco *(m)*

Blockabbruch *(m) n* De
En abort
Es suspensión *(f)*
Fr suspension d'exécution *(f)*
It insuccesso *(m)*
Pt aborto *(m)*

block diagram En
De Blockschaltung *(f)*
Es diagrama por bloques *(m)*
Fr schéma fonctionnel *(m)*
It diagramma a blocchi *(m)*
Pt diagrama de bloco *(m)*

Blockdiagrammsymbol-Entscheidung *(f)* De
En decision box
Es símbolo de decisión *(m)*
Fr symbole de décision *(m)*
It casella di decisione *(f)*
Pt caixa de decisão *(f)*

Blocklänge *(f) n* De
En block length
Es longitud de bloque *(f)*
Fr longueur de bloc *(f)*
It lunghezza del blocco *(m)*
Pt comprimento de bloco *(m)*

block length En
De Blocklänge *(f)*
Es longitud de bloque *(f)*
Fr longueur de bloc *(f)*
It lunghezza del blocco *(m)*
Pt comprimento de bloco *(m)*

Blockschalten *(n) n* De
En block switching
Es conmutación del bloque *(f)*
Fr commutation par blocs *(f)*
It commutazione di blocco *(f)*
Pt comutação de bloco *(f)*

Blockschaltung *(f) n* De
En block diagram
Es diagrama por bloques *(m)*
Fr schéma fonctionnel *(m)*
It diagramma a blocchi *(m)*
Pt diagrama de bloco *(m)*

block switching En
De Blockschalten *(n)*
Es conmutación del bloque *(f)*
Fr commutation par blocs *(f)*
It commutazione di blocco *(f)*
Pt comutação de bloco *(f)*

block transfer En
De Blockübergabe *(f)*
Es transferencia del bloque *(f)*
Fr transfert par blocs *(m)*
It trasferimento di blocco *(m)*
Pt transferência de bloco *(f)*

Blockübergabe *(f) n* De
En block transfer
Es transferencia del bloque *(f)*
Fr transfert par blocs *(m)*
It trasferimento di blocco *(m)*
Pt transferência de bloco *(f)*

bloc-notes *(m) n* It
De Arbeitspuffer *(m)*
En scratch pad
Es bloc de notas *(m)*
Fr mémoire de travail *(f)*
Pt almofada de raspar *(f)*

bloco *(m) n* Pt
De Block; Datenblock *(m)*
En block, tablet
Es bloque; tableta *(m f)*
Fr bloc; tablette *(m f)*
It blocco; tavoletta *(m f)*

bloque *(m) n* Es
De Datenblock *(m)*
En block
Fr bloc *(m)*
It blocco *(m)*
Pt bloco *(m)*

bloquear *vb* Es, Pt
De sperren
En lock out
Fr bloquer
It chiudere fuori

bloqueio de registo *(m)* Pt
De Satzblockierung *(f)*
En record blocking
Es bloqueo de registro *(m)*
Fr groupage enregistrement *(m)*
It bloccaggio di record *(m)*

bloqueo de registro *(m)* Es
De Satzblockierung *(f)*
En record blocking
Fr groupage enregistrement *(m)*
It bloccaggio di record *(m)*
Pt bloqueio de registo *(m)*

bloquer *vb* Fr
De sperren
En lock out
Es bloquear
It chiudere fuori
Pt bloquear

bobina *(f) n* It, Pt
De Spule *(f)*
En reel; spool
Es bobina; carrete *(f m)*
Fr bobine *(f)*

bobina *(f) n* Es
De Spule *(f)*
En spool
Fr bobine *(f)*
It bobina *(f)*
Pt bobina *(f)*

bobinado *(m) n* Es
De Aufspulen *(n)*
En spooling
Fr bobinage *(m)*
It bobinaggio *(m)*
Pt embobinagem *(f)*

bobinadora *(f) n* Es
De Aufspulgerät *(n)*
En spooler
Fr enrouleur *(m)*
It avvolgitore *(m)*
Pt embobinador *(m)*

bobina emisora *(f)* Es
De Stammband *(n)*
En master tape
Fr bande maîtresse *(f)*
It nastro principale *(m)*
Pt fita principal *(f)*

bobinage *(m) n* Fr
De Aufspulen *(n)*
En spooling
Es bobinado *(m)*
It bobinaggio *(m)*
Pt embobinagem *(f)*

bobinaggio *(m) n* It
De Aufspulen *(n)*
En spooling
Es bobinado *(m)*
Fr bobinage *(m)*
Pt embobinagem *(f)*

bobinar *vb* Es
De spulen
En spool
Fr bobiner
It bobinare
Pt embobinar

bobinare *vb* It
De spulen
En spool
Es bobinar
Fr bobiner
Pt embobinar

bobine *(f) n* Fr
De Spule *(f)*
En reel; spool
Es bobina; carrete *(f m)*
It bobina *(f)*
Pt bobina *(f)*

bobiner *vb* Fr
De spulen
En spool
Es bobinar
It bobinare
Pt embobinar

boca *(f) n* Es
De Nabe *(f)*
En hub
Fr moyeu porte-bobine *(m)*
It mozzo *(m)*
Pt cubo *(m)*

boca-abajo *adj* Es
De kieloben
En bottom-up
Fr ascendant
It sottosopra
Pt fundo para cima

boleado *(m) n* Pt
De Kugel *(f)*
En bead
Es perla *(f)*
Fr perle *(f)*
It perla *(f)*

Boolean algebra En
De Boolesche Algebra *(f)*
Es álgebra de Boole *(f)*
Fr algèbre de Boole *(f)*
It algebra booleana *(f)*
Pt algebra de Boole *(f)*

Boolesche Algebra *(f)* De
En Boolean algebra
Es álgebra de Boole *(f)*
Fr algèbre de Boole *(f)*
It algebra booleana *(f)*
Pt algebra de Boole *(f)*

Boolescher Operator *(m)* De
En logic(al) operator
Es operador lógico *(m)*
Fr opérateur logique *(m)*
It operatore logico *(m)*
Pt operador lógico *(m)*

bootstrap *n* En, Pt *(m)*
De Startroutine *(f)*
Es autocargador *(m)*
Fr amorce *(f)*
It istruzioni di avviamento *(f)*

borrado *(m) n* Es
De Löschung *(f)*
En erase
Fr effacement *(m)*
It cancellazione *(f)*
Pt eliminação *(f)*

borrar *vb* Es
De löschen
En erase
Fr effacer
It cancellare
Pt apagar

bottom-up *adj* En
De kieloben
Es boca-abajo
Fr ascendant
It sottosopra
Pt fundo para cima

boucle *(f) n* Fr
De Schleife *(f)*
En loop
Es bucle *(m)*
It ciclo *(m)*
Pt circuito *(m)*

boucle d'accès rapide *(f)* Fr
De Schnellzugriffs-schleife *(f)*
En rapid-access loop
Es bucle de acceso rápido *(m)*
It ciclo ad accesso rapido *(m)*
Pt circuito de acesso rápido *(m)*

boucle fermée *(f)* Fr
De geschlossene Schleife *(f)*
En closed loop
Es circuito cerrado *(m)*
It ciclo chiuso *(m)*
Pt circuito fechado *(m)*

boucle ouverte *(f)* Fr
De offene Schleife *(f)*
En open loop
Es circuito abierto *(m)*
It ciclo aperto *(m)*
Pt circuito aberto *(m)*

bourrage *(m) n* Fr
De Verklemmung *(f)*
En jam
Es atascamiento *(m)*
It inceppamento *(m)*
Pt congestionamento *(m)*

branch *n* En
De Zweig *(m)*
Es bifurcación *(f)*
Fr branchement *(m)*
It diramazione *(f)*
Pt ramo *(m)*

branch *vb* En
De abzweigen
Es bifurcar
Fr brancher
It diramarsi
Pt ligar

branchement *(m) n* Fr
De Zugriffspfad; Zweig *(m)*
En branch; path
Es bifurcación; curso *(f m)*
It diramazione; percorso *(f m)*
Pt caminho; ramo *(m)*

brancher *vb* Fr
De abzweigen
En branch
Es bifurcar
It diramarsi
Pt ligar

branch instruction En
De Verzweigungsbefehl *(m)*
Es instrucción de bifurcación *(f)*
Fr instruction de branchement *(f)*
It istruzione di diramazione *(f)*
Pt instruções para ligar *(f)*

breakpoint *n* En
De Ausgleichspunkt *(m)*
Es punto de interrupción *(m)*
Fr point de rupture *(m)*
It punto di arresto *(m)*
Pt ponto de rotura *(m)*

breakpoint instruction En
De Ausgleichspunkt-befehl *(m)*
Es instrucción de punto de interrupción *(f)*
Fr instruction de point de rupture *(f)*
It istruzione del punto di arresto *(f)*
Pt instruções de ponto de rotura *(f)*

Breitband *(n) n* De
En broadband
Es banda ancha *(f)*
Fr bande large *(f)*
It banda larga *(f)*
Pt banda larga *(f)*

Breitbandübertragung *(f) n* De
En broadband transmission
Es transmisión en banda ancha *(f)*
Fr transmission bande large *(f)*
It trasmissione a banda larga *(f)*
Pt transmissão de banda larga *(f)*

broadband *n* En
De Breitband *(n)*
Es banda ancha *(f)*
Fr bande large *(f)*
It banda larga *(f)*
Pt banda larga *(f)*

broadband transmission En
De Breitband-übertragung *(f)*
Es transmisión en banda ancha *(f)*
Fr transmission bande large *(f)*
It trasmissione a banda larga *(f)*
Pt transmissão de banda larga *(f)*

bruit *(m) n* Fr
De Rauschen *(n)*
En noise
Es ruido *(m)*
It rumore *(m)*
Pt ruído *(m)*

bubble memory En
De Perlspeicher *(m)*
Es memoria de burbuja *(f)*
Fr mémoire à bulles *(f)*
It memoria a bolle *(f)*
Pt memória de bolha *(f)*

bucle *(m) n* Es
De Schleife *(f)*
En loop
Fr boucle *(f)*
It ciclo *(m)*
Pt circuito *(m)*

bucle de acceso rápido *(m)* Es
De Schnellzugriffs-schleife *(f)*
En rapid-access loop
Fr boucle d'accès rapide *(f)*
It ciclo ad accesso rapido *(m)*
Pt circuito de acesso rápido *(m)*

buffer store En
De Pufferspeicher *(m)*
Es registro intermedio *(m)*
Fr mémoire tampon *(f)*
It memoria di transito *(f)*
Pt memória buffer *(f)*

bug *n* En
De Defekt *(m)*
Es defecto *(m)*
Fr défaut *(m)*
It difetto *(m)*
Pt perturbação *(f)*

bulk store En
De Groβspeicher *(m)*
Es memoria de gran capacidad *(f)*
Fr mémoire de masse *(f)*
It memoria di massa *(f)*
Pt memória global *(f)*

bündig machen De
En justify
Es justificar
Fr justifier
It giustificare
Pt justificar

burster *n* En
De Reiβer *(m)*
Es separadora de hojas *(f)*
Fr rupteuse *(f)*
It impulsore *(m)*
Pt separador de folha *(m)*

bus *n* En, Fr *(m)*
De Hauptverbindung *(f)*
Es conductor común *(m)*
It barra *(f)*
Pt condutor *(m)*

busca *(f) n* Pt
De Suche *(f)*
En search
Es búsqueda sistemática *(f)*
Fr recherche *(f)*
It ricerca *(f)*

busca binária *(f)* Pt
De binäres Suchen *(n)*
En binary search
Es búsqueda binaria *(f)*
Fr recherche dichotomique *(f)*
It ricerca binaria *(f)*

busca de cadeia *(f)* Pt
De Kettensuche *(f)*
En chaining search
Es búsqueda de la cadena *(f)*
Fr recherche par chaînage *(f)*
It ricerca concatenata *(f)*

busca dicotomizante *(f)* Pt
De dichotomizierendes Suchen *(n)*
En dichotomizing search
Es búsqueda dicotómica *(f)*
Fr recherche dichotomique *(f)*
It ricerca dicotoma *(f)*

búsqueda binaria *(f)* Es
De binäres Suchen *(n)*
En binary search
Fr recherche dichotomique *(f)*
It ricerca binaria *(f)*
Pt busca binária *(f)*

búsqueda de la cadena *(f)* Es
De Kettensuche *(f)*
En chaining search
Fr recherche par chaînage *(f)*
It ricerca concatenata *(f)*
Pt busca de cadeia *(f)*

búsqueda dicotómica *(f)* Es
De dichotomizierendes Suchen *(n)*
En dichotomizing search
Fr recherche dichotomique *(f)*
It ricerca dicotoma *(f)*
Pt busca dicotomizante *(f)*

búsqueda sistemática *(f)* Es
De Suche *(f)*
En search
Fr recherche *(f)*
It ricerca *(f)*
Pt busca *(f)*

byte *n* En, Es, It, Pt *(m)*
De Byte *(m)*
Fr multiplet *(m)*

Byte *(m) n* De
En byte
Es byte *(m)*
Fr multiplet *(m)*
It byte *(m)*
Pt byte *(m)*

C

cabeça *(f) n* Pt
De Magnetkopf *(m)*
En head
Es cabeza *(f)*
Fr tête *(f)*
It testina *(f)*

cabeça apagadora *(f)* Pt
De Löschkopf *(m)*
En erase head
Es cabeza de borrado *(f)*
Fr tête d'effacement *(f)*
It testina di cancellazione *(f)*

cabeça de leitura-escrita *(f)* Pt
De Les-Schreibkopf *(m)*
En read-write head
Es cabeza de lectura-escritura *(f)*
Fr tête lecture-écriture *(f)*
It testina di lettura-scrittura *(f)*

cabeça de playback *(f)* Pt
De Wiedergabekopf *(m)*
En playback head
Es cabeza reproductora *(f)*
Fr tête de lecture *(f)*
It testina di lettura *(f)*

cabeça de pré-leitura *(f)* Pt
De Vorlesekopf *(m)*
En pre-read head
Es cabeza de lectura previa *(f)*
Fr tête de première lecture *(f)*
It testina di pre-lettura *(f)*

cabeça de registo *(f)* Pt
De Aufzeichnungskopf *(m)*
En record head
Es cabeza de registro *(f)*
Fr tête d'enregistrement *(f)*
It testina del record *(f)*

cabeça escritora *(f)* Pt
De Schreibkopf *(m)*
En write head
Es cabeza de excritura *(f)*
Fr tête d'écriture *(f)*
It testina di scrittura *(f)*

cabeça leitora *(f)* Pt
De Lesekopf *(m)*
En read head
Es cabeza de lectura *(f)*
Fr tête de lecture *(f)*
It testina di lettura *(f)*

cabecera *(f) n* Es
De Kennsatz *(m)*
En header
Fr en-tête *(f)*
It testata *(f)*
Pt porta-cabeças *(m)*

cabeza *(f) n* Es
De Magnetkopf *(m)*
En head
Fr tête *(f)*
It testina *(f)*
Pt cabeça *(f)*

cabeza de borrado *(f)* Es
De Löschkopf *(m)*
En erase head
Fr tête d'effacement *(f)*
It testina di cancellazione *(f)*
Pt cabeça apagadora *(f)*

cabeza de excritura *(f)* Es
De Schreibkopf *(m)*
En write head
Fr tête d'écriture *(f)*
It testina di scrittura *(f)*
Pt cabeça escritora *(f)*

cabeza de lectura *(f)* Es
De Lesekopf *(m)*
En read head
Fr tête de lecture *(f)*
It testina di lettura *(f)*
Pt cabeça leitora *(f)*

cabeza de lectura-escritura *(f)* Es
De Les-Schreibkopf *(m)*
En read-write head
Fr tête lecture-écriture *(f)*
It testina di lettura-scrittura *(f)*
Pt cabeça de leitura-escrita *(f)*

cabeza de lectura previa *(f)* Es
De Vorlesekopf *(m)*
En pre-read head
Fr tête de première lecture *(f)*
It testina di pre-lettura *(f)*
Pt cabeça de pré-leitura *(f)*

cabeza de registro *(f)* Es
De Aufzeichnungskopf *(m)*
En record head
Fr tête d'enregistrement *(f)*
It testina del record *(f)*
Pt cabeça de registo *(f)*

cabeza reproductora *(f)* Es
De Wiedergabekopf *(m)*
En playback head
Fr tête de lecture *(f)*
It testina di lettura *(f)*
Pt cabeça de playback *(f)*

cable de conexión *(m)* Es
De Schaltschnur *(f)*
En patchcord
Fr fiche de connexion *(f)*
It cordone di connessione *(m)*
Pt cabo de concerto *(m)*

cabo de concerto *(m)* Pt
De Schaltschnur *(f)*
En patchcord
Es cable de conexión *(m)*
Fr fiche de connexion *(f)*
It cordone di connessione *(m)*

cadeia *(f) n* Pt
De Kette *(f)*
En chain
Es cadena *(f)*
Fr chaîne *(f)*
It catena *(f)*

cadena *(f) n* Es
De Kette *(f)*
En chain
Fr chaîne *(f)*
It catena *(f)*
Pt cadeia *(f)*

cadré à droite Fr
De rechtsbündig
En right-justified
Es justificado a la derecha
It giustificato a destra
Pt justificado à direita

cadré à gauche Fr
De linksbündig
En left-justified
Es justificado a la izquierda
It giustificato a sinistra
Pt justificado à esquerda

cadre *(m) n* Fr
De Rahmen *(m)*
En frame
Es encuadre *(m)*
It telaio *(m)*
Pt quadro *(m)*

cadrer *vb* Fr
De skalieren
En scale
Es pasar a escala
It scalare
Pt fazer concordar com a escala

caixa de decisão *(f)* Pt
De Blockdiagramm-symbol-Entscheidung *(f)*
En decision box
Es símbolo de decisión *(m)*
Fr symbole de décision *(m)*
It casella di decisione *(f)*

caja de fichas *(f)* Es
De Kartenkorb *(m)*
En card cage
Fr porte-carte *(m)*
It scatola schede *(f)*
Pt gaiola de ficha *(f)*

calcolatore *(m) n* It
De Rechner *(m)*
En calculator
Es calculadora *(f)*
Fr calculateur *(m)*
Pt calculador *(m)*

calcolatore a programmi memorizzati *(m)* It
De Computer für gespeicherte Programme *(m)*
En stored-program computer
Es ordenador en programa almacenado *(m)*
Fr ordinateur à programme enregistré *(m)*
Pt computador com programa armazenado *(m)*

calcolatore personale *(m)* It
De persönlicher Rechner *(m)*
En personal computer
Es ordenador personal *(m)*
Fr ordinateur privé *(m)*
Pt computador pessoal *(m)*

calcolatore portabile *(m)* It
De tragbarer Computer *(m)*
En portable computer
Es ordenador portátil *(m)*
Fr ordinateur portatif *(m)*
Pt computador portátil *(m)*

calcolatore principale *(m)* It
De Hauptrechner *(m)*
En mainframe computer
Es computador principal *(m)*
Fr ordinateur principal *(m)*
Pt computador principal *(m)*

calcolatore satellite *(m)* It
De Satellitenrechner *(m)*
En satellite (computer)
Es ordenador satélite *(m)*
Fr calculateur satellite *(m)*
Pt computador satélite *(m)*

calcoli interattivi *(m)* It
De Dialogbetrieb *(m)*
En interactive computing
Es cálculo interactivo *(m)*
Fr traitement interactif *(m)*
Pt computação interactiva *(f)*

calcolo ad accesso multiplo *(m)* It
De Mehrfachzugriffs-rechnen *(n)*
En multi-access computing (MAC)
Es cálculo de acceso múltiple *(m)*
Fr traitement à accès multiple (TAM) *(m)*
Pt computação de multi-acesso *(f)*

calculador *(m)* *n* Pt
De Rechner *(m)*
En calculator
Es calculadora *(f)*
Fr calculateur *(m)*
It calcolatore *(m)*

calculadora *(f)* *n* Es
De Rechner *(m)*
En calculator
Fr calculateur *(m)*
It calcolatore *(m)*
Pt calculador *(m)*

calcul à précision multiple *(m)* Fr
De Arithmetik mit mehrfacher Wortlänge *(f)*
En multiple-length arithmetic
Es aritmética de longitud múltiple *(f)*
It aritmetica a lunghezza multipla *(f)*
Pt aritmética de comprimento múltiplo *(f)*

calculateur *(m)* *n* Fr
De Rechner *(m)*
En calculator
Es calculadora *(f)*
It calcolatore *(m)*
Pt calculador *(m)*

calculateur analogique *(m)* Fr
De Analogrechner *(m)*
En analog computer
Es ordenador analógico *(m)*
It elaboratore analogico *(m)*
Pt computador de analogia *(m)*

calculateur hybride *(m)* Fr
De Hybridrechner *(m)*
En hybrid computer
Es ordenador híbrido *(m)*
It elaboratore ibrido *(m)*
Pt computador híbrido *(m)*

calculateur numérique *(m)* Fr
De Digitalrechner *(m)*
En digital computer
Es ordenador digital *(m)*
It elaboratore digitale *(m)*
Pt computador digital *(m)*

calculateur satellite *(m)* Fr
De Satellitenrechner *(m)*
En satellite (computer)
Es ordenador satélite *(m)*
It calcolatore satellite *(m)*
Pt computador satélite *(m)*

calculateur spécialisé *(m)* Fr
De Spezialrechner *(m)*
En special-purpose computer
Es ordenador especializado *(m)*
It elaboratore a scopo speciale *(m)*
Pt computador para fins especiais *(m)*

calculateur synchrone *(m)* Fr
De Synchronisierrechner *(m)*
En synchronous computer
Es ordenador síncrono *(m)*
It elaboratore sincrono *(m)*
Pt computador sincronizado *(m)*

calculateur universel *(m)* Fr
De Allgemeinzweck-computer *(m)*
En general-purpose computer
Es ordenador universal *(m)*
It elaboratore a scopo generale *(m)*
Pt computador para todos os fins *(m)*

calculator *n* En
De Rechner *(m)*
Es calculadora *(f)*
Fr calculateur *(m)*
It calcolatore *(m)*
Pt calculador *(m)*

calcul en virgule flottante *(m)* Fr
De Flüssigpunkt-arithmetik *(f)*
En floating-point arithmetic
Es aritmética de coma flotante *(f)*
It aritmetica a virgola mobile *(f)*
Pt aritmética de ponto flutuante *(f)*

cálculo de acceso múltiple *(m)* Es
De Mehrfachzugriffs-rechnen *(n)*
En multi-access computing (MAC)
Fr traitement à accès multiple (TAM) *(m)*
It calcolo ad accesso multiplo *(m)*
Pt computação de multi-acesso *(f)*

cálculo inicial *(m)* Es
De Lokalrechnung *(f)*
En home computing
Fr traitement domestique *(m)*
It elaborazione in proprio *(f)*
Pt computação doméstica *(f)*

cálculo interactivo *(m)* Es
De Dialogbetrieb *(m)*
En interactive computing
Fr traitement interactif *(m)*
It calcoli interattivi *(m)*
Pt computação interactiva *(f)*

call *n* En
De Aufruf *(m)*
Es llamada *(f)*
Fr appel *(m)*
It chiamata *(f)*
Pt chamada *(f)*

call *vb* En
De aufrufen
Es llamar
Fr appeler
It chiamare
Pt chamar

calling sequence En
De Aufruffolge *(f)*
Es secuencia de llamada *(f)*
Fr séquence d'appel *(f)*
It sequenza di richiamo *(f)*
Pt sequência de chamada *(f)*

call number En
De Rufnummer *(f)*
Es número de llamada *(m)*
Fr numéro d'appel *(m)*
It numero di richiamo *(m)*
Pt número de chamada *(m)*

cambiar *vb* Es
De vermitteln
En exchange
Fr intervenir
It scambiare
Pt intercambiar

cambio de paso *(m)* Es
De Schrittwechsel *(m)*
En step change
Fr changement de phase *(m)*
It cambio di passo *(m)*
Pt mudança de passo *(f)*

cambio di passo *(m)* It
De Schrittwechsel *(m)*
En step change
Es cambio de paso *(m)*
Fr changement de phase *(m)*
Pt mudança de passo *(f)*

caminho *(m) n* Pt
De Leitweg; Zugriffspfad *(m)*
En path; route
Es curso; ruta *(m f)*
Fr branchement; itinéraire *(m)*
It percorso; pista *(m f)*

campo *(m) n* Es, It, Pt
De Feld *(n)*
En field
Fr champ *(m)*

campo fijo *(m)* Es
De festes Feld *(n)*
En fixed field
Fr zone fixe *(f)*
It campo fisso *(m)*
Pt campo fixo *(m)*

campo fisso *(m)* It
De festes Feld *(n)*
En fixed field
Es campo fijo *(m)*
Fr zone fixe *(f)*
Pt campo fixo *(m)*

campo fixo *(m)* Pt
De festes Feld *(n)*
En fixed field
Es campo fijo *(m)*
Fr zone fixe *(f)*
It campo fisso *(m)*

campo libero *(m)* It
De Freifeld *(n)*
En free field
Es campo libre *(m)*
Fr champ libre *(m)*
Pt campo livre *(m)*

campo libre *(m)* Es
De Freifeld *(n)*
En free field
Fr champ libre *(m)*
It campo libero *(m)*
Pt campo livre *(m)*

campo livre *(m)* Pt
De Freifeld *(n)*
En free field
Es campo libre *(m)*
Fr champ libre *(m)*
It campo libero *(m)*

campo variabile *(m)* It
De veränderliches Feld *(n)*
En variable field
Es campo variable *(m)*
Fr champ variable *(m)*
Pt campo variável *(m)*

campo variable *(m)* Es
De veränderliches Feld *(n)*
En variable field
Fr champ variable *(m)*
It campo variabile *(m)*
Pt campo variável *(m)*

campo variável *(m)* Pt
De veränderliches Feld *(n)*
En variable field
Es campo variable *(m)*
Fr champ variable *(m)*
It campo variabile *(m)*

canal *(m) n* Es, Fr, Pt
De Kanal *(m)*
En channel
It canale *(m)*

canal de comunicação *(m)* Pt
De Kommunikations-kanal *(m)*
En communication channel
Es canal de comunicación *(m)*
Fr voie de communication *(f)*
It canale di comunicazione *(m)*

canal de comunicación *(m)* Es
De Kommunikations kanal *(m)*
En communication channel
Fr voie de communication *(f)*
It canale di comunicazione *(m)*
Pt canal de comunicação *(m)*

canal de lectura-escritura *(m)* Es
De Lesen-Schreiben-Kanal *(m)*
En read-write channel
Fr voie lecture-écriture *(f)*
It canale di lettura-scrittura *(m)*
Pt canal de leitura-escrita *(m)*

canal de leitura-escrita *(m)* Pt
De Lesen-Schreiben-Kanal *(m)*
En read-write channel
Es canal de lectura-escritura *(m)*
Fr voie lecture-écriture *(f)*
It canale di lettura-scrittura *(m)*

canal de rango vocal *(m)* Es
De Telefonleitung *(f)*
En voice-grade channel
Fr voie téléphonique *(f)*
It canale a frequenze vocali *(m)*
Pt canal para fonia *(m)*

canale *(m) n* It
De Kanal *(m)*
En channel
Es canal *(m)*
Fr canal *(m)*
Pt canal *(m)*

canale a frequenze vocali *(m)* It
De Telefonleitung *(f)*
En voice-grade channel
Es canal de rango vocal *(m)*
Fr voie téléphonique *(f)*
Pt canal para fonia *(m)*

canale del selettore *(m)* It
De Wählkanal *(m)*
En selector channel
Es canal selector *(m)*
Fr canal sélecteur *(m)*
Pt canal selector *(m)*

canale di comunicazione *(m)* It

De Kommunikations-kanal *(m)*
En communication channel
Es canal de comunicación *(m)*
Fr voie de communication *(f)*
Pt canal de comunicação *(m)*

canale di lettura-scrittura *(m)* It
De Lesen-Schreiben-Kanal *(m)*
En read-write channel
Es canal de lectura-escritura *(m)*
Fr voie lecture-écriture *(f)*
Pt canal de leitura-escrita *(m)*

canal para fonia *(m)* Pt
De Telefonleitung *(f)*
En voice-grade channel
Es canal de rango vocal *(m)*
Fr voie téléphonique *(f)*
It canale a frequenze vocali *(m)*

canal sélecteur *(m)* Fr
De Wählkanal *(m)*
En selector channel
Es canal selector *(m)*
It canale del selettore *(m)*
Pt canal selector *(m)*

canal selector *(m)* Es, Pt
De Wählkanal *(m)*
En selector channel
Fr canal sélecteur *(m)*
It canale del selettore *(m)*

cancellare *vb* It
De löschen
En delete; erase
Es borrar; suprimir
Fr effacer; éliminer
Pt apagar

cancellazione *(f) n* It
De Löschung *(f)*
En deletion; erase
Es borrado; eliminación *(m f)*
Fr effacement *(m)*
Pt apagado; eliminação *(m f)*

caneta de luz *(f)* Pt
De Lichtschreiber *(m)*
En light pen
Es lápiz fotosensible *(f)*
Fr photo-style *(f)*
It penna luminosa *(f)*

capacidad *(f) n* Es
De Kapazität *(f)*
En capacity
Fr capacité *(f)*
It capacità *(f)*
Pt capacidade *(f)*

capacidad de almacenamiento *(f)* Es
De Speicherkapazität *(f)*
En storage capacity
Fr capacité de mémoire *(f)*
It capacità di memoria *(f)*
Pt capacidade de armazenamento *(f)*

capacidad de tratamiento *(f)* Es
De Durchfluβ *(m)*
En throughput
Fr débit *(m)*
It capacità di trattamento *(f)*
Pt capacidade de tratamento *(f)*

capacidade *(f) n* Pt
De Kapazität *(f)*
En capacity
Es capacidad *(f)*
Fr capacité *(f)*
It capacità *(f)*

capacidade de armazenamento *(f)* Pt
De Speicherkapazität *(f)*
En storage capacity
Es capacidad de almacenamiento *(f)*
Fr capacité de mémoire *(f)*
It capacità di memoria *(f)*

capacidade de tratamento *(f)* Pt
De Durchfluβ *(m)*
En throughput
Es capacidad de tratamiento *(f)*
Fr débit *(m)*
It capacità di trattamento *(f)*

capacità *(f) n* It
De Kapazität *(f)*
En capacity
Es capacidad *(f)*
Fr capacité *(f)*
Pt capacidade *(f)*

capacità di memoria *(f)* It
De Speicherkapazität *(f)*
En storage capacity
Es capacidad de almacenamiento *(f)*
Fr capacité de mémoire *(f)*
Pt capacidade de armazenamento *(f)*

capacità di trattamento *(f)* It
De Durchfluβ *(m)*
En throughput
Es capacidad de tratamiento *(f)*
Fr débit *(m)*
Pt capacidade de tratamento *(f)*

capacité *(f) n* Fr
De Kapazität *(f)*
En capacity
Es capacidad *(f)*
It capacità *(f)*
Pt capacidade *(f)*

capacité de mémoire *(f)* Fr
De Speicherkapazität *(f)*
En storage capacity
Es capacidad de almacenamiento *(f)*
It capacità di memoria *(f)*
Pt capacidade de armazenamento *(f)*

capacity *n* En
De Kapazität *(f)*
Es capacidad *(f)*
Fr capacité *(f)*
It capacità *(f)*
Pt capacidade *(f)*

capitolo *(m) n* It
De Absatz *(m)*
En chapter
Es capítulo *(m)*
Fr chapitre *(m)*
Pt capítulo *(m)*

capítulo *(m) n* Es, Pt
De Absatz *(m)*
En chapter
Fr chapitre *(m)*
It capitolo *(m)*

captação de dados de origem *(f)* Pt
De Quelldatenfang *(m)*
En source data capture
Es captura de datos fuente *(f)*
Fr saisie des données à la source *(f)*
It cattura di dati all'origine *(f)*

captura de datos fuente *(f)* Es
De Quelldatenfang *(m)*
En source data capture
Fr saisie des données à la source *(f)*
It cattura di dati all'origine *(f)*
Pt captação de dados de origem *(f)*

carácter *(m) n* Es, Pt
De Schriftzeichen *(n)*
En character
Fr caractère *(m)*
It carattere *(m)*

carácter blanco *(m)* Es
De Leerstellenzeichen *(n)*
En space character
Fr caractère blanc *(m)*
It carattere di spazio *(m)*
Pt carácter de espaço *(m)*

carácter de escape *(m)* Es, Pt
De Datenübertragungs-umschaltung *(f)*
En escape character
Fr caractère échappatoire *(m)*
It carattere di uscita *(m)*

carácter de espaço *(m)* Pt
De Leerstellenzeichen *(n)*
En space character
Es carácter blanco *(m)*
Fr caractère blanc *(m)*
It carattere di spazio *(m)*

carácter de supresión *(m)* Es
De Übergehenzeichen *(n)*
En ignore character
Fr caractère d'omission *(m)*
It carattere di ignorare *(m)*
Pt carácter ignore *(m)*

caractère *(m) n* Fr
De Schriftzeichen *(n)*
En character
Es carácter *(m)*
It carattere *(m)*
Pt carácter *(m)*

caractère blanc *(m)* Fr
De Leerstellenzeichen *(n)*
En space character
Es carácter blanco *(m)*
It carattere di spazio *(m)*
Pt carácter de espaço *(m)*

caractère de contrôle *(m)* Fr
De Prüfziffer *(f)*
En check digit
Es dígito de verificación *(m)*
It digit di controllo *(m)*
Pt número digital de verificação *(m)*

caractère de signe *(m)* Fr
De Vorzeichenziffer *(f)*
En sign digit
Es dígito de signo *(m)*
It digit del segno *(m)*
Pt número digital de sinal *(m)*

caractère d'omission *(m)* Fr
De Übergehenzeichen *(n)*
En ignore character
Es carácter de supresión *(m)*
It carattere di ignorare *(m)*
Pt carácter ignore *(m)*

caractère échappatoire *(m)* Fr
De Datenübertragungs-umschaltung *(f)*
En escape character
Es carácter de escape *(m)*
It carattere di uscita *(m)*
Pt carácter de escape *(m)*

caractère interdit *(m)* Fr
De unzulässiges Zeichen *(n)*
En illegal character
Es carácter no válido *(m)*
It carattere illegale *(m)*
Pt carácter ilegal *(m)*

caractères par seconde *(m pl)* Fr
De Zeichen pro Sekunde *(pl)*
En characters per second (cps)
Es caracteres por segundo *(m pl)*
It caratteri al secondo *(m pl)*
Pt caracteres por segundo *(m pl)*

carácter especial *(m)* Es, Pt
De Sonderzeichen *(n)*
En special character
Fr caractère spécial *(m)*
It carattere speciale *(m)*

caractère spécial *(m)* Fr
De Sonderzeichen *(n)*
En special character
Es carácter especial *(m)*
It carattere speciale *(m)*
Pt carácter especial *(m)*

caracteres por segundo *(m pl)* Es, Pt
De Zeichen pro Sekunde *(pl)*
En characters per second (cps)
Fr caractères par seconde *(m pl)*
It caratteri al secondo *(m pl)*

carácter ignore *(m)* Pt
De Übergehenzeichen *(n)*
En ignore character
Es carácter de supresión *(m)*
Fr caractère d'omission *(m)*
It carattere di ignorare *(m)*

carácter ilegal *(m)* Pt
De unzulässiges Zeichen *(n)*
En illegal character
Es carácter no válido *(m)*
Fr caractère interdit *(m)*
It carattere illegale *(m)*

carácter no válido *(m)* Es
De unzulässiges Zeichen *(n)*
En illegal character
Fr caractère interdit *(m)*
It carattere illegale *(m)*
Pt carácter ilegal *(m)*

carattere *(m) n* It
De Schriftzeichen *(n)*
En character
Es carácter *(m)*
Fr caractère *(m)*
Pt carácter *(m)*

carattere di ignorare *(m)* It
De Übergehenzeichen *(n)*
En ignore character
Es carácter de supresión *(m)*
Fr caractère d'omission *(m)*
Pt carácter ignore *(m)*

carattere di spazio *(m)* It
De Leerstellenzeichen *(n)*
En space character
Es carácter blanco *(m)*
Fr caractère blanc *(m)*
Pt carácter de espaço *(m)*

carattere di uscita *(m)* It
De Datenübertragungs-umschaltung *(f)*
En escape character
Es carácter de escape *(m)*
Fr caractère échappatoire *(m)*
Pt carácter de escape *(m)*

carattere illegale *(m)* It
De unzulässiges Zeichen *(n)*
En illegal character
Es carácter no válido *(m)*
Fr caractère interdit *(m)*
Pt carácter ilegal *(m)*

carattere speciale *(m)* It
De Sonderzeichen *(n)*
En special character
Es carácter especial *(m)*
Fr caractère spécial *(m)*
Pt carácter especial *(m)*

caratteri al secondo *(m pl)* It
De Zeichen pro Sekunde *(pl)*
En characters per second (cps)
Es caracteres por segundo *(m pl)*
Fr caractères par seconde *(m pl)*
Pt caracteres por segundo *(m pl)*

card *n* En
De Karte *(f)*
Es ficha *(f)*
Fr carte *(f)*
It scheda *(f)*
Pt ficha *(f)*

card cage En
De Kartenkorb *(m)*
Es caja de fichas *(f)*
Fr porte-carte *(m)*
It scatola schede *(f)*
Pt gaiola de ficha *(f)*

card column En
De Lochkartenspalte *(f)*
Es columna de ficha *(f)*
Fr colonne de carte *(f)*
It colonna della scheda *(f)*
Pt coluna de ficha *(f)*

card punch En
De Kartenlocher *(m)*
Es perforadora de fichas *(f)*
Fr perforatrice de cartes *(f)*
It perforatrice di schede *(f)*

Pt perfuradora de ficha *(f)*

card reader En
De Kartenleser *(m)*
Es lectora de fichas *(f)*
Fr lecteur de cartes *(m)*
It lettore di schede *(m)*
Pt leitor de fichas *(m)*

card verifying En
De Kartenprüfung *(f)*
Es verificación de fichas *(f)*
Fr vérification de cartes *(f)*
It verifica delle schede *(f)*
Pt verificação de fichas *(f)*

carga *(f) n* Pt
De Patrone *(f)*
En cartridge
Es cartucho *(m)*
Fr cartouche *(f)*
It cartuccia *(f)*

carga de dados *(f)* Pt
De Datenpatrone *(f)*
En data cartridge
Es cartucho de datos *(m)*
Fr cartouche de données *(f)*
It cartuccia di dati *(f)*

cargador *(m) n* Es
De Lader *(m)*
En loader
Fr chargeur *(m)*
It caricatore *(m)*
Pt carregador *(m)*

cargar *vb* Es
De laden
En load
Fr charger
It caricare
Pt carregar

cargar y ejecutar Es
De umwandeln und ausführen
En load and go
Fr charger et exécuter
It caricare e eseguire
Pt carregar e seguir

caricare *vb* It
De laden
En load
Es cargar
Fr charger
Pt carregar

caricare e eseguire It
De umwandeln und ausführen
En load and go
Es cargar y ejecutar
Fr charger et exécuter
Pt carregar e seguir

caricatore *(m) n* It
De Lader; Magazin *(m n)*
En loader; magazine
Es almacén; cargador *(m)*
Fr chargeur; magasin *(m)*
Pt armazém; carregador *(m)*

carregador *(m) n* Pt
De Lader *(m)*
En loader
Es cargador *(m)*
Fr chargeur *(m)*
It caricatore *(m)*

carregar *vb* Pt
De laden
En load
Es cargar
Fr charger
It caricare

carregar e seguir Pt
De umwandeln und ausführen
En load and go
Es cargar y ejecutar
Fr charger et exécuter
It caricare e eseguire

carrello elevatore *(m)* It
De Stapler *(m)*
En stacker
Es casillero receptor *(m)*
Fr case de réception *(f)*
Pt empilhadora *(f)*

carrete *(m) n* Es
De Spule *(f)*
En reel
Fr bobine *(f)*
It bobina *(f)*
Pt bobina *(f)*

carriage-control tape En
De Wagensteuerband *(n)*
Es cinta de control del carro *(f)*
Fr bande pilote *(f)*
It nastrino di controllo del carrello *(m)*
Pt fita com controle de carro *(f)*

carriage return En
De Wagenrücklauf *(m)*
Es retorno del carro *(m)*
Fr retour chariot *(m)*
It ritorno del carrello *(m)*
Pt retrocesso do carro *(m)*

carrier *n* En
De Ladungsträger *(m)*
Es portador *(m)*
Fr courant porteur *(m)*
It supporto *(m)*
Pt portador *(m)*

carta da tabulati a fisarmonica *(f)* It
De Endlosvordrucke *(pl)*
En continuous stationery
Es papel continuo *(m)*
Fr papier en continu *(m)*
Pt continuo-estacionário *(m)*

carte *(f) n* Fr
De Bildschirmformat; Karte *(n f)*
En card; map
Es ficha; mapa *(f m)*
It mappa; scheda *(f)*
Pt ficha; mapa *(f m)*

carte de quatre-vingt colonnes *(f)* Fr
De achtzig-Spalten-Karte *(f)*
En eighty-column card
Es tarjets de ochenta columnas *(f)*
It scheda ad ottanta colonne *(f)*
Pt ficha de oitenta colunas *(f)*

carte magnétique *(f)* Fr
De Magnetkarte *(f)*
En magnetic card
Es ficha magnética *(f)*
It scheda magnetica *(f)*
Pt ficha magnética *(f)*

carte mécanographique *(f)* Fr
Am punch card
De Lochkarte *(f)*
En punched card
Es ficha perforada *(f)*
It scheda perforata *(f)*
Pt ficha perfurada *(f)*

cartouche *(f) n* Fr
De Patrone *(f)*
En cartridge
Es cartucho *(m)*
It cartuccia *(f)*
Pt carga *(f)*

cartouche de données *(f)* Fr
De Datenpatrone *(f)*
En data cartridge
Es cartucho de datos *(m)*
It cartuccia di dati *(f)*
Pt carga de dados *(f)*

cartridge *n* En
De Patrone *(f)*
Es cartucho *(m)*
Fr cartouche *(f)*
It cartuccia *(f)*
Pt carga *(f)*

cartridge disk En
De Patronenplatte *(f)*
Es disco de cartucho *(m)*
Fr disque à cartouche *(m)*
It disco a cartuccia *(m)*
Pt disco de carga *(m)*

cartuccia *(f) n* It
De Patrone *(f)*
En cartridge
Es cartucho *(m)*
Fr cartouche *(f)*
Pt carga *(f)*

cartuccia di dati *(f)* It
De Datenpatrone *(f)*
En data cartridge
Es cartucho de datos *(m)*
Fr cartouche de données *(f)*
Pt carga de dados *(f)*

cartucho *(m) n* Es
De Patrone *(f)*
En cartridge
Fr cartouche *(f)*

It cartuccia *(f)*
Pt carga *(f)*

cartucho de datos *(m)* Es
De Datenpatrone *(f)*
En data cartridge
Fr cartouche de données *(f)*
It cartuccia di dati *(f)*
Pt carga de dados *(f)*

casa de software *(f)* Pt
De Softwarehaus *(n)*
Es sociedad especializada en programación *(f)*
En software house
Fr société de services et de conseils en informatique (SSCI) *(f)*
It ditta specializzata nel fare programmi per conto terzi *(f)*

cascaded programs En
De Kaskadenprogramme *(pl)*
Es programas en cascada *(m pl)*
Fr programmes en cascade *(m pl)*
It programmi in cascata *(m pl)*
Pt programas em cascada *(m pl)*

case de réception *(f)* Fr
De Stapler *(m)*
En stacker
Es casillero receptor *(m)*
It carrello elevatore *(m)*
Pt empilhadora *(f)*

casella di decisione *(f)* It
De Blockdiagramm-symbol-Entscheidung *(f)*
En decision box
Es símbolo de decisión *(m)*
Fr symbole de décision *(m)*
Pt caixa de decisão *(f)*

casillero receptor *(m)* Es
De Stapler *(m)*
En stacker
Fr case de réception *(f)*
It carrello elevatore *(m)*
Pt empilhadora *(f)*

cassetta *(f) n* It
De Kassette *(f)*
En cassette
Es cassette *(f)*
Fr cassette *(f)*
Pt cassette *(f)*

cassette *n* En, Es, Fr, Pt
De Kassette *(f)*
It cassetta *(f)*

catena *(f) n* It
De Kette *(f)*
En chain
Es cadena *(f)*
Fr chaîne *(f)*
Pt cadeia *(f)*

cathode-ray tube (CRT) En
De Kathodenstrahlröhre *(f)*
Es tubo de rayos catódicos (TRC) *(m)*
Fr tube à rayons cathodiques *(m)*
It tubo a raggi catodici *(m)*
Pt válvula catódica *(f)*

cattura di dati all'origine *(f)* It
De Quelldatenfang *(m)*
En source data capture
Es captura de datos fuente *(f)*
Fr saisie des données à la source *(f)*
Pt captação de dados de origem *(f)*

celda magnética *(f)* Es
De Magnetelement *(n)*
En magnetic cell
Fr cellule magnétique *(f)*
It cellula magnetica *(f)*
Pt célula magnética *(f)*

cell *n* En
De Zelle *(f)*
Es célula *(f)*
Fr cellule *(f)*
It cellula *(f)*
Pt célula *(f)*

cellula *(f) n* It
De Zelle *(f)*
En cell
Es célula *(f)*
Fr cellule *(f)*
Pt célula *(f)*

cellula magnetica *(f)* It
De Magnetelement *(n)*
En magnetic cell
Es celda magnética *(f)*
Fr cellule magnétique *(f)*
Pt célula magnética *(f)*

cellule *(f) n* Fr
De Zelle *(f)*
En cell
Es célula *(f)*
It cellula *(f)*
Pt célula *(f)*

cellule magnétique *(f)* Fr
De Magnetelement *(n)*
En magnetic cell
Es celda magnética *(f)*
It cellula magnetica *(f)*
Pt célula magnética *(f)*

célula *(f) n* Es, Pt
De Zelle *(f)*
En cell
Fr cellule *(f)*
It cellula *(f)*

célula magnética *(f)* Pt
De Magnetelement *(n)*
En magnetic cell
Es celda magnética *(f)*
Fr cellule magnétique *(f)*
It cellula magnetica *(f)*

center-feed tape Am
De Band mit Zentralvorschub *(n)*
En centre-feed tape
Es cinta de alimentación central *(f)*
Fr bande à entraînement central *(f)*
It nastro ad alimentazione centrale *(m)*
Pt fita de alimentação central *(f)*

central processing unit En
De Zentraleinheit *(f)*
Es unidad central de proceso *(f)*
Fr unité de traitement centrale *(f)*
It unità centrale di elaborazione *(f)*
Pt unidade de processamento central *(f)*

centre de commutation *(m)* Fr
De Relaiszentrale *(f)*
En relay centre
Es reemisor *(m)*
It centro di relè *(m)*
Pt centro de relé *(m)*

centre de commutation *(m)* Fr
De Schaltzentrum *(n)*
En switching centre
Es centro de conmutación *(m)*
It centro di commutazione *(m)*
Pt centro de comutação *(m)*

centre-feed tape En
Am center-feed tape
De Band mit Zentralvorschub *(n)*
Es cinta de alimentación central *(f)*
Fr bande à entraînement central *(f)*
It nastro ad alimentazione centrale *(m)*
Pt fita de alimentação central *(f)*

centro de comutação *(m)* Pt
De Schaltzentrum *(n)*
En switching centre
Es centro de conmutación *(m)*
Fr centre de commutation *(m)*
It centro di commutazione *(m)*

centro de conmutación *(m)* Es
De Schaltzentrum *(n)*
En switching centre
Fr centre de commutation *(m)*
It centro di commutazione *(m)*
Pt centro de comutação *(m)*

centro de relé *(m)* Pt
De Relaiszentrale *(f)*
En relay centre
Es reemisor *(m)*

Fr centre de commutation *(m)*
It centro di relè *(m)*

centro di commutazione *(m)* It
De Schaltzentrum *(n)*
En switching centre
Es centro de conmutación *(m)*
Fr centre de commutation *(m)*
Pt centro de comutação *(m)*

centro di relè *(m)* It
De Relaiszentrale *(f)*
En relay centre
Es reemisor *(m)*
Fr centre de commutation *(m)*
Pt centro de relé *(m)*

chad *n* En
De Stanzrückstand *(m)*
Es confeti *(m)*
Fr confetti *(m)*
It coriandoli di perforazione *(m)*
Pt recorte *(m)*

chadded tape En
De geschuppter Streifen *(m)*
Es cinta de perforación completa *(f)*
Fr bande à perforations complètes *(f)*
It nastro con perforazioni totali *(m)*
Pt fita recortada *(f)*

chadless tape En
De Schuppenstreifen *(m)*
Es cinta semiperforada *(f)*
Fr bande semi-perforée *(f)*
It nastro semiperforato *(m)*
Pt fita sem recorte *(f)*

chain *n* En
De Kette *(f)*
Es cadena *(f)*
Fr chaîne *(f)*
It catena *(f)*
Pt cadeia *(f)*

chain code En
De Kettencode *(m)*
Es código en cadena *(m)*
Fr code à enchaînement *(m)*
It codice di catena *(m)*
Pt código de cadeia *(m)*

chaîne *(f) n* Fr
De Folge; Kette *(f)*
En chain; string
Es cadena; serie *(f)*
It catena; stringa *(f)*
Pt cadeia; fileira *(f)*

chaîne de bits *(f)* Fr
De Binärzeichenfolge *(f)*
En bit string
Es serie de bits *(f)*
It stringa di bit *(f)*
Pt fila de bits *(f)*

chained list En
De gekettete Liste *(f)*
Es lista en cadena *(f)*
Fr liste en chaîne *(f)*
It lista concatenata *(f)*
Pt lista com cadeia *(f)*

chained record En
De Kettensatz *(m)*
Es registro en cadena *(m)*
Fr enregistrement en chaîne *(m)*
It record concatenato *(m)*
Pt registo com cadeia *(m)*

chaining search En
De Kettensuche *(f)*
Es búsqueda de la cadena *(f)*
Fr recherche par chaînage *(f)*
It ricerca concatenata *(f)*
Pt busca de cadeia *(f)*

chain printer En
De Kettendrucker *(m)*
Es impresora de cadena *(f)*
Fr imprimante à chaîne *(f)*
It stampatrice a catena *(f)*
Pt impressora de cadeia *(f)*

chamada *(f) n* Pt
De Aufruf *(m)*
En call
Es llamada *(f)*
Fr appel *(m)*
It chiamata *(f)*

chamar *vb* Pt
De aufrufen
En call
Es llamar
Fr appeler
It chiamare

champ *(m) n* Fr
De Feld *(n)*
En field
Es campo *(m)*
It campo *(m)*
Pt campo *(m)*

champ libre *(m)* Fr
De Freifeld *(n)*
En free field
Es campo libre *(m)*
It campo libero *(m)*
Pt campo livre *(m)*

champ variable *(m)* Fr
De veränderliches Feld *(n)*
En variable field
Es campo variable *(m)*
It campo variabile *(m)*
Pt campo variável *(m)*

changement de page *(m)* Fr
De Seitenwechsel *(m)*
En page turning
Es transferencia de página *(f)*
It trasferimento di pagina *(m)*
Pt mudança de páginas *(f)*

changement de phase *(m)* Fr
De Schrittwechsel *(m)*
En step change
Es cambio de paso *(m)*
It cambio di passo *(m)*
Pt mudança de passo *(f)*

change record En
De Änderungssatz *(m)*
Es registro de cambio *(m)*
Fr record de modification *(m)*
It record di cambiamento *(m)*
Pt registo de mudança *(m)*

channel *n* En
De Kanal *(m)*
Es canal *(m)*
Fr canal *(m)*
It canale *(m)*
Pt canal *(m)*

chapitre *(m) n* Fr
De Absatz *(m)*
En chapter
Es capítulo *(m)*
It capitolo *(m)*
Pt capítulo *(m)*

chapter *n* En
De Absatz *(m)*
Es capítulo *(m)*
Fr chapitre *(m)*
It capitolo *(m)*
Pt capítulo *(m)*

character *n* En
De Schriftzeichen *(n)*
Es carácter *(m)*
Fr caractère *(m)*
It carattere *(m)*
Pt carácter *(m)*

character code En
De Zeichencode *(m)*
Es código de caracteres *(m)*
Fr code de caractère *(m)*
It codice del carattere *(m)*
Pt código de caracteres *(m)*

character density En
De Zeichendichte *(f)*
Es densidad de caracteres *(f)*
Fr densité de caractères *(f)*
It densità di caratteri *(f)*
Pt densidade de caracteres *(f)*

character-orientated *adj* En
De zeichenmäßig ausgerichtet
Es orientado a los caracteres

Fr fonctionnement à caractères
It orientato a carattere
Pt orientado por caracteres

character reader En
De Zeichenleser *(m)*
Es lectora de caracteres *(f)*
Fr lecteur de caractères *(m)*
It lettore di caratteri *(m)*
Pt leitor de caracteres *(m)*

character recognition En
De Zeichenerkennung *(f)*
Es reconocimiento de caracteres *(m)*
Fr reconnaissance de caractères *(f)*
It riconoscimento di carattere *(m)*
Pt reconhecimento de caracteres *(m)*

character set En
De Zeichensatz *(m)*
Es juego de caracteres *(m)*
Fr jeu de caractères *(m)*
It gruppo di caratteri *(m)*
Pt jogo de caracteres *(m)*

characters per second (cps) En
De Zeichen pro Sekunde *(pl)*
Es caracteres por segundo *(m pl)*
Fr caractères par seconde *(m pl)*
It caratteri al secondo *(m pl)*
Pt caracteres por segundo *(m pl)*

charge-coupled device (CCD) En
De ladungsgekoppelte Vorrichtung *(f)*
Es dispositivo acoplado por carga *(m)*
Fr dispositif à couplage de charge (DCC) *(m)*
It dispositivo accoppiato a carica *(m)*
Pt dispositivo de acoplamento por carga *(m)*

charger *vb* Fr
De laden
En load
Es cargar
It caricare
Pt carregar

charger et exécuter Fr
De umwandeln und ausführen
En load and go
Es cargar y ejecutar
It caricare e eseguire
Pt carregar e seguir

chargeur *(m) n* Fr
De Lader *(m)*
En loader
Es cargador *(m)*
It caricatore *(m)*
Pt carregador *(m)*

check *n* En
De Prüfung *(f)*
Es verificación *(f)*
Fr contrôle *(m)*
It controllo *(m)*
Pt verificação *(f)*

check bit En
De Prüfbit *(m)*
Es bit de verificación *(m)*
Fr bit de contrôle *(m)*
It bit di controllo *(m)*
Pt bit de verificação *(m)*

check digit En
De Prüfziffer *(f)*
Es dígito de verificación *(m)*
Fr caractère de contrôle *(m)*
It digit di controllo *(m)*
Pt número digital de verificação *(m)*

check indicator En
De Prüfanzeiger *(m)*
Es indicador de verificación *(m)*
Fr indicateur de contrôle *(m)*
It indicatore di controllo *(m)*
Pt indicador de verificação *(m)*

checking program En
De Prüfprogramm *(n)*
Es programa de verificación *(m)*
Fr programme de contrôle *(m)*
It programma di controllo *(m)*
Pt programa de verificação *(m)*

checkpoint *n* En
De Kontrollpunkt *(m)*
Es punto de control *(m)*
Fr point de contrôle *(m)*
It punto di controllo *(m)*
Pt ponto de verificação *(m)*

check sum *n* En
De Summenprüfung *(f)*
Es suma de verificación *(f)*
Fr somme de contrôle *(f)*
It somma di controllo *(f)*
Pt soma de verificação *(f)*

chercher *vb* Fr
De suchen
En search
Es investigar
It ricercare
Pt procurar

chevaucher *vb* Fr
De überlappen
En overlap
Es solapar
It sovrapporre
Pt sobrepor-se

chiamare *vb* It
De aufrufen
En call
Es llamar
Fr appeler
Pt chamar

chiamata *(f) n* It
De Aufruf *(m)*
En call
Es llamada *(f)*
Fr appel *(m)*
Pt chamada *(f)*

chiffre *(m) n* Fr
De Ziffer *(f)*
En digit
Es dígito *(m)*
It digit *(m)*
Pt número digital *(m)*

chiffre d'auto-vérification *(m)* Fr
De Prüfnummer *(f)*
En self-checking number
Es número autoverificador *(m)*
It numero autocontrollante *(m)*
Pt número autoverificante *(m)*

chiffre de zone *(m)* Fr
De Zonenziffer *(f)*
En zone digit
Es dígito de zona *(m)*
It digit di zonatura *(m)*
Pt número digital de zona *(m)*

chiffres binaires équivalents *(m pl)* Fr
De gleichwertige Binärziffern *(pl)*
En equivalent binary digits
Es dígitos binarios equivalentes *(m pl)*
It digiti binari equivalenti *(m pl)*
Pt números digitais binários equivalentes *(m pl)*

chiffres significatifs *(m pl)* Fr
De wesentliche Ziffern *(pl)*
En significant digits
Es dígitos significativos *(m pl)*
It digiti significativi *(m pl)*
Pt números digitais significativos *(m pl)*

chilobit *(m) n* It
De Kilobit *(m)*
En kilobit
Es kilobit *(m)*
Fr kilobit *(m)*
Pt kilobit *(m)*

chilobyte *(m) n* It
De Kilobyte *(m)*
En kilobyte
Es kilo-octeto *(m)*

Fr kilomultiplet *(m)*
Pt kilobyte *(m)*

chilo secondi di memoria *(m pl)* It
De Kilokern Sekunden *(pl)*
En kilo core seconds (KCS)
Es kilonúcleo segundos *(m pl)*
Fr kilo tores secondes (KTS) *(f pl)*
Pt kilo core segundos *(m pl)*

chip *n* En, It *(m)*
De Chip *(m)*
Es plaqueta *(f)*
Fr puce *(f)*
Pt lasca *(f)*

Chip *(m) n* De
En chip
Es plaqueta *(f)*
Fr puce *(f)*
It chip *(m)*
Pt lasca *(f)*

chiudere fuori It
De sperren
En lock out
Es bloquear
Fr bloquer
Pt bloquear

choque *(m) n* Es
De Durchschlag *(m)*
En crash
Fr accélération *(f)*
It urto *(m)*
Pt colisão *(f)*

cibernetica *(f) n* It
De Kybernetik *(f)*
En cybernetics
Es cibernética *(f)*
Fr cybernétique *(f)*
Pt cibernética *(f)*

cibernética *(f) n* Es, Pt
De Kybernetik *(f)*
En cybernetics
Fr cybernétique *(f)*
It cibernetica *(f)*

ciclo *(m) n* Es, Pt
De Gang *(m)*
En cycle
Fr cycle *(m)*
It ciclo *(m)*

ciclo *(m) n* It
De Gang; Schleife *(m f)*
En cycle; loop
Es bucle; ciclo *(m)*
Fr boucle; cycle *(f m)*
Pt ciclo; circuito *(m)*

ciclo ad accesso rapido *(m)* It
De Schnellzugriffs-schleife *(f)*
En rapid-access loop
Es bucle de acceso rápido *(m)*
Fr boucle d'accès rapide *(f)*
Pt circuito de acesso rápido *(m)*

ciclo aperto *(m)* It
De offene Schleife *(f)*
En open loop
Es circuito abierto *(m)*
Fr boucle ouverte *(f)*
Pt circuito aberto *(m)*

ciclo chiuso *(m)* It
De geschlossene Schleife *(f)*
En closed loop
Es circuito cerrado *(m)*
Fr boucle fermée *(f)*
Pt circuito fechado *(m)*

ciclo de funcionamiento en paralelo *(m)* Es
De Parallellauf *(m)*
En parallel running
Fr exploitation en parallèle *(f)*
It esecuzione parallela *(f)*
Pt passagens paralelas *(f)*

ciência de computadores *(f)* Pt
De Computer-wissenschaft *(f)*
En computer science
Es ciencia de ordenador *(f)*
Fr ordinatique *(f)*
It scienza degli elaboratoria elettronici *(f)*

ciencia de ordenador *(f)* Es
De Computer-wissenschaft *(f)*
En computer science
Fr ordinatique *(f)*
It scienza degli elaboratoria elettronici *(f)*
Pt ciência de computadores *(f)*

cilindro *(m) n* Es, It, Pt
De Zylinder *(m)*
En cylinder
Fr cylindre *(m)*

cilindro impresor *(m)* Es
De Trommeldrucker *(m)*
En print barrel
Fr tambour d'impression *(m)*
It tamburo di stampa *(m)*
Pt cilindro impressor *(m)*

cilindro impressor *(m)* Pt
De Trommeldruckerfaβ *(n)*
En print barrel
Es cilindro impresor *(m)*
Fr tambour d'impression *(m)*
It tamburo di stampa *(m)*

cincuenta excedente *(f)* Es
De Fünfzig-Überschuβ *(m)*
En excess fifty
Fr code plus cinquante *(m)*
It cinquanta di eccesso *(f)*
Pt cinquenta em excesso *(f)*

cinquanta di eccesso *(f)* It
De Fünfzig-Überschuβ *(m)*
En excess fifty
Es cincuenta excedente *(f)*
Fr code plus cinquante *(m)*
Pt cinquenta em excesso *(f)*

cinquenta em excesso *(f)* Pt
De Fünfzig-Überschuβ *(m)*
En excess fifty
Es cincuenta excedente *(f)*
Fr code plus cinquante *(m)*
It cinquanta di eccesso *(f)*

cinta *(f) n* Es
De Band *(n)*
En tape
Fr bande *(f)*
It nastro *(m)*
Pt fita *(f)*

cinta creadora *(f)* Es
De Urband *n*
En father tape
Fr bande créatrice *(f)*
It nastro padre *(m)*
Pt fita pai *(f)*

cinta de alimentación central *(f)* Es
Am center-feed tape
De Band mit Zentralvorschub *(n)*
En centre-feed tape
Fr bande à entraînement central *(f)*
It nastro ad alimentazione centrale *(m)*
Pt fita de alimentação central *(f)*

cinta de alimentación por arrastre *(f)* Es
De Bandvorausvorschub *(m)*
En advance-feed tape
Fr défilement-avancement bande *(m)*
It avanzare-alimentare nastro *(m)*
Pt fita de alimentação por avanço *(f)*

cinta de control del carro *(f)* Es
De Wagensteuerband *(n)*
En carriage-control tape
Fr bande pilote *(f)*
It nastrino di controllo del carrello *(m)*
Pt fita com controle de carro *(f)*

cinta de maniobra *(f)* Es
De Arbeitsband *(n)*
En work tape

Fr bande de travail *(f)*
It nastro di lavoro *(m)*
Pt fita de trabalho *(f)*

cinta de papel *(f)* Es
De Papierstreifen *(m)*
En paper tape
Fr bande de papier *(f)*
It nastro di carta *(m)*
Pt fita de papel *(f)*

cinta de perforación completa *(f)* Es
De geschuppter Streifen *(m)*
En chadded tape
Fr bande à perforations complètes *(f)*
It nastro con perforazioni totali *(m)*
Pt fita recortada *(f)*

cinta entintada *(f)* Es
De Farbband *(n)*
En ink ribbon
Fr ruban à encre *(m)*
It nastro ad inchiostro *(m)*
Pt fita de tinta *(f)*

cinta magnética *(f)* Es
De Magnetband *(n)*
En magnetic tape
Fr bande magnétique *(f)*
It nastro magnetico *(m)*
Pt fita magnética *(f)*

cinta perforada *(f)* Es
De Lochstreifen *(m)*
En perforated tape; punched tape
Fr bande perforée *(f)*
It nastro perforato *(m)*
Pt fita perfurada *(f)*

cinta primera generación *(f)* Es
De Erstgenerationsband *(n)*
En grandfather tape
Fr bande première génération *(f)*
It nastro nonno *(m)*
Pt fita avó *(f)*

cinta programa de explotación *(f)* Es
De Hauptbefehlsband *(n)*
En master-instruction tape (MIT)
Fr bande de programme d'exploitation (BPE) *(f)*
It nastro dell'istruzioni principali *(m)*
Pt fita de instruções principais *(f)*

cinta semiperforada *(f)* Es
De Schuppenstreifen *(m)*
En chadless tape
Fr bande semi-perforée *(f)*
It nastro semiperforato *(m)*
Pt fita sem recorte *(f)*

cint a virgen *(f)* Es
De Neuband *(n)*
En virgin tape
Fr bande vierge *(f)*
It nastro vergine *(m)*
Pt fita virgem *(f)*

circuit *n* En; Fr *(m)*
De Schaltung *(f)*
Es circuito *(m)*
It circuito *(m)*
Pt circuito *(m)*

circuit bistable *(m)* Fr
De bistabile Kippschaltung *(f)*
En bistable circuit
Es circuito biestable *(m)*
It circuito bistabile *(m)*
Pt circuito biestável *(m)*

circuit de déclenchement *(m)* Fr
De Triggerschaltung *(f)*
En trigger circuit
Es circuito de disparo *(m)*
It circuito di scatto *(m)*
Pt circuito de disparo *(m)*

circuit intégré *(m)* Fr
De integrierte Schaltung *(f)*
En integrated circuit
Es circuito integrado *(m)*
It circuito integrato *(m)*
Pt circuito integrado *(m)*

circuit interurbain *(m)* Fr
De Sammelschaltung *(f)*
En trunk circuit
Es circuito común *(m)*
It rete interurbana *(f)*
Pt circuito principal *(m)*

circuit logique *(m)* Fr
De Verknüpfungs-schaltung *(f)*
En logic circuit
Es circuito lógico *(m)*
It circuito logico *(m)*
Pt circuito lógico *(m)*

circuito *(m) n* Es, It
De Schaltung *(f)*
En circuit
Fr circuit *(m)*
Pt circuito *(m)*

circuito *(m) n* Pt
De Schaltung; Schleife *(f)*
En circuit; loop
Es bucle; circuito *(m)*
Fr boucle; circuit *(f m)*
It ciclo; circuito *(m)*

circuito aberto *(m)* Pt
De offene Schleife *(f)*
En open loop
Es circuito abierto *(m)*
Fr boucle ouverte *(f)*
It ciclo aperto *(m)*

circuito abierto *(m)* Es
De offene Schleife *(f)*
En open loop
Fr boucle ouverte *(f)*
It ciclo aperto *(m)*
Pt circuito aberto *(m)*

circuito a quattro fili *(m)* It
De Vierdrahtschaltung *(f)*
En four-wire circuit
Es circuito de cuatro hilos *(m)*
Fr circuit quatre fils *(m)*
Pt circuito de quatro fios *(m)*

circuito biestable *(m)* Es
De bistabile Kippschaltung *(f)*
En bistable circuit
Fr circuit bistable *(m)*
It circuito bistabile *(m)*
Pt circuito biestável *(m)*

circuito biestável *(m)* Pt
De bistabile Kippschaltung *(f)*
En bistable circuit
Es circuito biestable *(m)*
Fr circuit bistable *(m)*
It circuito bistabile *(m)*

circuito bistabile *(m)* It
De bistabile Kippschaltung *(f)*
En bistable circuit
Es circuito biestable *(m)*
Fr circuit bistable *(m)*
Pt circuito biestável *(m)*

circuito cerrado *(m)* Es
De geschlossene Schleife *(f)*
En closed loop
Fr boucle fermée *(f)*
It ciclo chiuso *(m)*
Pt circuito fechado *(m)*

circuito común *(m)* Es
De Sammelschaltung *(f)*
En trunk circuit
Fr circuit interurbain *(m)*
It rete interurbana *(f)*
Pt circuito principal *(m)*

circuito de acesso rápido *(m)* Pt
De Schnellzugriffs-schleife *(f)*
En rapid-access loop
Es bucle de acceso rápido *(m)*
Fr boucle d'accès rapide *(f)*
It ciclo ad accesso rapido *(m)*

circuito de cuatro hilos *(m)* Es
De Vierdrahtschaltung *(f)*
En four-wire circuit
Fr circuit quatre fils *(m)*
It circuito a quattro fili *(m)*
Pt circuito de quatro fios *(m)*

circuito de disparo *(m)* Es, Pt
De Triggerschaltung *(f)*
En trigger circuit
Fr circuit de déclenchement *(m)*
It circuito di scatto *(m)*

circuito de quatro fios *(m)* Pt
De Vierdrahtschaltung *(f)*

En four-wire circuit
Es circuito de cuatro hilos *(m)*
Fr circuit quatre fils *(m)*
It circuito a quattro fili *(m)*

circuito di scatto *(m)* It
De Triggerschaltung *(f)*
En trigger circuit
Es circuito de disparo *(m)*
Fr circuit de déclenchement *(m)*
Pt circuito de disparo *(m)*

circuito fechado *(m)* Pt
De geschlossene Schleife *(f)*
En closed loop
Es circuito cerrado *(m)*
Fr boucle fermée *(f)*
It ciclo chiuso *(m)*

circuito integrado *(m)* Es, Pt
De integrierte Schaltung *(f)*
En integrated circuit
Fr circuit intégré *(m)*
It circuito integrato *(m)*

circuito integrato *(m)* It
De integrierte Schaltung *(f)*
En integrated circuit
Es circuito integrado *(m)*
Fr circuit intégré *(m)*
Pt circuito integrado *(m)*

circuito logico *(m)* It
De Verknüpfungsschaltung *(f)*
En logic circuit
Es circuito lógico *(m)*
Fr circuit logique *(m)*
Pt circuito lógico *(m)*

circuito lógico *(m)* Es, Pt
De Verknüpfungsschaltung *(f)*
En logic circuit
Fr circuit logique *(m)*
It circuito logico *(m)*

circuito principal *(m)* Pt
De Sammelschaltung *(f)*
En trunk circuit
Es circuito común *(m)*
Fr circuit interurbain *(m)*
It rete interurbana *(f)*

circuit quatre fils *(m)* Fr
De Vierdrahtschaltung *(f)*
En four-wire circuit
Es circuito de cuatro hilos *(m)*
It circuito a quattro fili *(m)*
Pt circuito de quatro fios *(m)*

circulating register En
De Umlaufregister *(n)*
Es registro circulante *(m)*
Fr registre circulant *(m)*
It registro circolante *(m)*
Pt registo de circulação *(m)*

clasificación *(f)* *n* Es
De Sortierung *(f)*
En sort
Fr tri *(m)*
It selezione *(f)*
Pt espécie *(f)*

clasificación-fusión *(f)* *n* Es
De Sortierungfusion *(f)*
En sort-merge
Fr tri-fusion *(m)*
It selezione-inserimento *(f)*
Pt classificação-fusão *(f)*

clasificadora *(f)* *n* Es
De Sortierer *(m)*
En sorter
Fr trieuse *(f)*
It selezionatrice *(f)*
Pt classificador *(m)*

clasificadora de documentos *(f)* Es
De Schriftstücksortierer *(m)*
En document sorter
Fr trieuse de documents *(f)*
It selezionatrice di documenti *(f)*
Pt classificador de documentação *(m)*

clasificar *vb* Es
De sortieren
En sort
Fr trier
It classificare
Pt classificar

classificação-fusão *(f)* *n* Pt
De Sortierungfusion *(f)*
En sort-merge
Es clasificación-fusión *(f)*
Fr tri-fusion *(m)*
It selezione-inserimento *(f)*

classificador *(m)* *n* Pt
De Sortierer *(m)*
En sorter
Es clasificadora *(f)*
Fr trieuse *(f)*
It selezionatrice *(f)*

classificador de documentação *(m)* Pt
De Schriftstücksortierer *(m)*
En document sorter
Es clasificadora de documentos *(f)*
Fr trieuse de documents *(f)*
It selezionatrice di documenti *(f)*

classificar *vb* Pt
De sortieren
En sort
Es clasificar
Fr trier
It classificare

classificare *vb* It
De sortieren
En sort
Es clasificar
Fr trier
Pt classificar

clavier *(m)* *n* Fr
De Tastatur *(m)*
En keyboard
Es teclado *(m)*
It tastiera *(f)*
Pt teclado *(m)*

clavija *(f)* *n* Es
De Stecker *(m)*
En plug
Fr fiche *(f)*
It spina *(f)*
Pt ficha eléctrica *(f)*

clear *vb* En
De löschen
Es despejar
Fr remettre à zéro
It rimettere a zero
Pt limpar

clock *n* En
De Taktgeber *(m)*
Es reloj *(m)*
Fr horloge *(f)*
It orologio *(m)*
Pt relógio *(m)*

clock pulses *n pl* En
De Taktimpulse *(pl)*
Es impulsos de reloj *(m pl)*
Fr impulsions d'horloge *(f pl)*
It impulsi dell'orologio *(m pl)*
Pt impulsos de relógio *(m pl)*

clock rate En
De Taktgeschwindigkeit *(f)*
Es velocidad de impulsos de reloj *(f)*
Fr fréquence des impulsions d'horloge *(f)*
It frequenza degli impulsi dell'orologio *(f)*
Pt taxa de impulsos de relógio *(f)*

closed loop En
De geschlossene Schleife *(f)*
Es circuito cerrado *(m)*
Fr boucle fermée *(f)*
It ciclo chiuso *(m)*
Pt circuito fechado *(m)*

closed routine En
De abgeschlossenes Programm *(n)*
Es rutina cerrada *(f)*
Fr routine fermée *(f)*
It routine chiusa *(f)*
Pt rotina fechada *(f)*

codage *(m) n* Fr
De Kodierung *(f)*
En coding
Es codificación *(f)*
It codificazione *(f)*
Pt codificação *(f)*

codage automatique *(m)* Fr
De automatische Kodierung *(f)*
En automatic coding
Es codificación automática *(f)*
It codificazione automatica *(f)*
Pt codificação automática *(f)*

code *n* En; Fr *(m)*
De Code *(m)*
Es código *(m)*
It codice *(m)*
Pt código *(m)*

code *vb* En
De kodieren
Es codificar
Fr coder
It codificare
Pt pôr em código

Code *(m) n* De
En code
Es código *(m)*
Fr code *(m)*
It codice *(m)*
Pt código *(m)*

code à bâtonnets *(m)* Fr
De Balkencode *(m)*
En bar code
Es código de trazos *(m)*
It codice a barra *(m)*
Pt código de barra *(m)*

code absolu *(m)* Fr
De absoluter Code *(m)*
En absolute code
Es código absoluto *(m)*
It codice assoluto *(m)*
Pt código absoluto *(m)*

code à enchaînement *(m)* Fr
De Kettencode *(m)*
En chain code
Es código en cadena *(m)*
It codice di catena *(m)*
Pt código de cadeia *(m)*

code binaire *(m)* Fr
De Binärcode *(m)*
En binary code
Es código binario *(m)*
It codice binario *(m)*
Pt código binário *(m)*

code biquinaire *(m)* Fr
De biquinärer Code *(m)*
En biquinary code
Es código biquinario *(m)*
It codice biquinario *(m)*
Pt código biquinário *(m)*

code correcteur d'erreurs *(m)* Fr
De Fehlerkorrekturcode *(m)*
En error-correcting code
Es código de corrección de errores *(m)*
It codice di correzione errore *(m)*
Pt código de correcção de erros *(m)*

code cyclique *(m)* Fr
De zyklischer Code *(m)*
En cyclic code
Es código cíclico *(m)*
It codice ciclico *(m)*
Pt código cíclico *(m)*

code d'accès minimal *(m)* Fr
De Minimum-zugriffscode *(m)*
En minimum-access code
Es código de mínimo acceso *(m)*
It codice di accesso minimo *(m)*
Pt código de acesso mínimo *(m)*

code de caractère *(m)* Fr
De Zeichencode *(m)*
En character code
Es código de caracteres *(m)*
It codice del carattere *(m)*
Pt código de caracteres *(m)*

code détecteur d'erreurs *(m)* Fr
De Fehlerer-kennungscode *(m)*
En error-detecting code
Es código de detección de errores *(m)*
It codice di individuazione errore *(m)*
Pt código de detecção de erros *(m)*

code d'exploitation mnémonique *(m)* Fr
De Mnemonik-Betriebscode *(m)*
En mnemonic operation code
Es código de operación mnemotécnico *(m)*
It codice dell'operazione mnemonico *(m)*
Pt código de operação mnemónico *(m)*

code d'instruction *(m)* Fr
De Befehlscode *(m)*
En instruction code
Es código de instrucción *(m)*
It codice dell'istruzione *(m)*
Pt código de instruções *(m)*

code d'ordre *(m)* Fr
De Anweisungscode *(m)*
En order code
Es código de orden *(m)*
It codice di ordine *(m)*
Pt código de ordens *(m)*

code Gray *(m)* Fr
De Gray-Code *(n)*
En Gray code
Es código Gray *(m)*
It codice Gray *(m)*
Pt código Gray *(m)*

code Hollerith *(m)* Fr
De Hollerith-Code *(m)*
En Hollerith code
Es código Hollerith *(m)*
It codice di Hollerith *(m)*
Pt código Hollerith *(m)*

code machine *(m)* Fr
De Maschinencode *(m)*
En machine code
Es código de máquina *(m)*
It codice macchina *(m)*
Pt código da máquina *(m)*

code objet *(m)* Fr
De Objektcode *(m)*
En object code
Es código objeto *(m)*
It codice oggetto *(m)*
Pt código de objecto *(m)*

code plus cinquante *(m)* Fr
De Fünfzig-Überschuß *(m)*
En excess fifty
Es cincuenta excedente *(f)*
It cinquanta di eccesso *(f)*
Pt cinquenta em excesso *(f)*

code plus trois *(m)* Fr
De Drei-Überschuß *(m)*
En excess three
Es tres excedente *(m)*
It tre di eccesso *(m)*
Pt três em excesso *(m)*

coder *vb* Fr
De kodieren
En code; encode
Es codificar
It codificare
Pt codificar

code redondant *(m)* Fr
De redundanter Code *(m)*
En redundant code
Es código redundante *(m)*
It codice ridondante *(m)*
Pt código redundante *(m)*

code relative *(m)* Fr
De relativer Code *(m)*
En relative code
Es código relativo *(m)*
It codice relativo *(m)*
Pt código relativo *(m)*

code translatable *(m)* Fr
De verschieblicher Code *(m)*
En relocatable code
Es código reubicable *(m)*
It codice rilocabile *(m)*
Pt código relocalizável *(m)*

codeur *(m) n* Fr
De Verschlüssler *(m)*
En encoder
Es codificador *(m)*
It codificatore *(m)*
Pt codificador *(m)*

codice *(m) n* It
De Code *(m)*
En code
Es código *(m)*
Fr code *(m)*
Pt código *(m)*

codice a barra *(m)* It
De Balkencode *(m)*
En bar code
Es código de trazos *(m)*
Fr code à bâtonnets *(m)*
Pt código de barra *(m)*

codice assoluto *(m)* It
De absoluter Code *(m)*
En absolute code
Es código absoluto *(m)*
Fr code absolu *(m)*
Pt código absoluto *(m)*

codice binario *(m)* It
De Binärcode *(m)*
En binary code
Es código binario *(m)*
Fr code binaire *(m)*
Pt código binário *(m)*

codice biquinario *(m)* It
De biquinärer Code *(m)*
En biquinary code
Es código biquinario *(m)*
Fr code biquinaire *(m)*
Pt código biquinário *(m)*

codice ciclico *(m)* It
De zyklischer Code *(m)*
En cyclic code
Es código cíclico *(m)*
Fr code cyclique *(m)*
Pt código cíclico *(m)*

codice del carattere *(m)* It
De Zeichencode *(m)*
En character code
Es código de caracteres *(m)*
Fr code de caractère *(m)*
Pt código de caracteres *(m)*

codice dell'istruzione *(m)* It
De Befehlscode *(m)*
En instruction code
Es código de instrucción *(m)*
Fr code d'instruction *(m)*
Pt código de instruções *(m)*

codice dell'operazione mnemonico *(m)* It
De Mnemonik-Betriebscode *(m)*
En mnemonic operation code
Es código de operación mnemotécnico *(m)*
Fr code d'exploitation mnémonique *(m)*
Pt código de operação mnemónico *(m)*

codice di accesso minimo *(m)* It
De Minimum-zugriffscode *(m)*
En minimum-access code
Es código de mínimo acceso *(m)*
Fr code d'accès minimal *(m)*
Pt código de acesso mínimo *(m)*

codice di catena *(m)* It
De Kettencode *(m)*
En chain code
Es código en cadena *(m)*
Fr code à enchaînement *(m)*
Pt código de cadeia *(m)*

codice di correzione errore *(m)* It
De Fehlerkorrekturcode *(m)*
En error-correcting code
Es código de corrección de errores *(m)*
Fr code correcteur d'erreurs *(m)*
Pt código de correcção de erros *(m)*

codice di Hollerith *(m)* It
De Hollerith-Code *(m)*
En Hollerith code
Es código Hollerith *(m)*
Fr code Hollerith *(m)*
Pt código Hollerith *(m)*

codice di individuazione errore *(m)* It
De Fehlerer-kennungscode *(m)*
En error-detecting code
Es código de detección de errores *(m)*
Fr code détecteur d'erreurs *(m)*
Pt código de detecção de erros *(m)*

codice di ordine *(m)* It
De Anweisungscode *(m)*
En order code
Es código de orden *(m)*
Fr code d'ordre *(m)*
Pt código de ordens *(m)*

codice Gray *(m)* It
De Gray-Code *(n)*
En Gray code
Es código Gray *(m)*
Fr code Gray *(m)*
Pt código Gray *(m)*

codice macchina *(m)* It
De Maschinencode *(m)*
En machine code
Es código de máquina *(m)*
Fr code machine *(m)*
Pt código da máquina *(m)*

codice oggetto *(m)* It
De Objektcode *(m)*
En object code
Es código objeto *(m)*
Fr code objet *(m)*
Pt código de objecto *(m)*

codice origine *(m)* It
De Quellcode *(m)*
En source code
Es código fuente *(m)*
Fr séquence en langage source *(f)*
Pt código de origem *(m)*

codice relativo *(m)* It
De relativer Code *(m)*
En relative code
Es código relativo *(m)*
Fr code relative *(m)*
Pt código relativo *(m)*

codice ridondante *(m)* It
De redundanter Code *(m)*
En redundant code
Es código redundante *(m)*
Fr code redondant *(m)*
Pt código redundante *(m)*

codice rilocabile *(m)* It
De verschieblicher Code *(m)*
En relocatable code
Es código reubicable *(m)*
Fr code translatable *(m)*
Pt código relocalizável *(m)*

codice schematico *(m)* It
De Skelettcode *(m)*
En skeletal code
Es código esquemático *(m)*
Fr séquence paramétrable *(f)*
Pt código reduzido *(m)*

codificação *(f) n* Pt
De Kodierung *(f)*
En coding
Es codificación *(f)*
Fr codage *(m)*
It codificazione *(f)*

codificação automática *(f)* Pt
De automatische Kodierung *(f)*
En automatic coding
Es codificación automática *(f)*
Fr codage automatique *(m)*
It codificazione automatica *(f)*

codificación *(f) n* Es
De Kodierung *(f)*
En coding
Fr codage *(m)*
It codificazione *(f)*
Pt codificação *(f)*

codificación automática *(f)* Es
De automatische Kodierung *(f)*
En automatic coding
Fr codage automatique *(m)*

It codificazione automatica *(f)*
Pt codificação automática *(f)*

codificador *(m) n* Es, Pt
De Verschlüssler *(m)*
En encoder
Fr codeur *(m)*
It codificatore *(m)*

codificar *vb* Es, Pt
De kodieren
En code; encode
Fr coder
It codificare

codificare *vb* It
De kodieren
En code; encode
Es codificar
Fr coder
Pt codificar

codificatore *(m) n* It
De Verschlüssler *(m)*
En encoder
Es codificador *(m)*
Fr codeur *(m)*
Pt codificador *(m)*

codificazione *(f) n* It
De Kodierung *(f)*
En coding
Es codificación *(f)*
Fr codage *(m)*
Pt codificação *(f)*

codificazione automatica *(f)* It
De automatische Kodierung *(f)*
En automatic coding
Es codificación automática *(f)*
Fr codage automatique *(m)*
Pt codificação automática *(f)*

código *(m) n* Es, Pt
De Code *(m)*
En code
Fr code *(m)*
It codice *(m)*

código absoluto *(m)* Es, Pt
De absoluter Code *(m)*
En absolute code
Fr code absolu *(m)*
It codice assoluto *(m)*

código binario *(m)* Es
De Binärcode *(m)*
En binary code
Fr code binaire *(m)*
It codice binario *(m)*
Pt código binário *(m)*

código binário *(m)* Pt
De Binärcode *(m)*
En binary code
Es código binario *(m)*
Fr code binaire *(m)*
It codice binario *(m)*

código biquinario *(m)* Es
De biquinärer Code *(m)*
En biquinary code
Fr code biquinaire *(m)*
It codice biquinario *(m)*
Pt código biquinário *(m)*

código biquinário *(m)* Pt
De biquinärer Code *(m)*
En biquinary code
Es código biquinario *(m)*
Fr code biquinaire *(m)*
It codice biquinario *(m)*

código cíclico *(m)* Es, Pt
De zyklischer Code *(m)*
En cyclic code
Fr code cyclique *(m)*
It codice ciclico *(m)*

código da máquina *(m)* Pt
De Maschinencode *(m)*
En machine code
Es código de máquina *(m)*
Fr code machine *(m)*
It codice macchina *(m)*

código de acesso mínimo *(m)* Pt
De Minimum-zugriffscode *(m)*
En minimum-access code
Es código de mínimo acceso *(m)*
Fr code d'accès minimal *(m)*
It codice di accesso minimo *(m)*

código de barra *(m)* Pt
De Balkencode *(m)*
En bar code
Es código de trazos *(m)*
Fr code à bâtonnets *(m)*
It codice a barra *(m)*

código de cadeia *(m)* Pt
De Kettencode *(m)*
En chain code
Es código en cadena *(m)*
Fr code à enchaînement *(m)*
It codice di catena *(m)*

código de caracteres *(m)* Es, Pt
De Zeichencode *(m)*
En character code
Fr code de caractère *(m)*
It codice del carattere *(m)*

código de correcção de erros *(m)* Pt
De Fehlerkorrekturcode *(m)*
En error-correcting code
Es código de corrección de errores *(m)*
Fr code correcteur d'erreurs *(m)*
It codice di correzione errore *(m)*

código de corrección de errores *(m)* Es
De Fehlerkorrekturcode *(m)*
En error-correcting code
Fr code correcteur d'erreurs *(m)*
It codice di correzione errore *(m)*
Pt código de correcção de erros *(m)*

código de detecção de erros *(m)* Pt
De Fehlerer-kennungscode *(m)*
En error-detecting code
Es código de detección de errores *(m)*
Fr code détecteur d'erreurs *(m)*
It codice di individuazione errore *(m)*

código de detección de errores *(m)* Es
De Fehlerer-kennungscode *(m)*
En error-detecting code
Fr code détecteur d'erreurs *(m)*
It codice di individuazione errore *(m)*
Pt código de detecção de erros *(m)*

código de instrucción *(m)* Es
De Befehlscode *(m)*
En instruction code
Fr code d'instruction *(m)*
It codice dell'istruzione *(m)*
Pt código de instruções *(m)*

código de instruções *(m)* Pt
De Befehlscode *(m)*
En instruction code
Es código de instrucción *(m)*
Fr code d'instruction *(m)*
It codice dell'istruzione *(m)*

código de máquina *(m)* Es
De Maschinencode *(m)*
En machine code
Fr code machine *(m)*
It codice macchina *(m)*
Pt código da máquina *(m)*

código de mínimo acceso *(m)* Es
De Minimum-zugriffscode *(m)*
En minimum-access code
Fr code d'accès minimal *(m)*
It codice di accesso minimo *(m)*
Pt código de acesso mínimo *(m)*

código de objecto *(m)* Pt
De Objektcode *(m)*
En object code
Es código objeto *(m)*

Fr code objet *(m)*
It codice oggetto *(m)*

código de operação mnemónico *(m)* Pt
De Mnemonik-Betriebscode *(m)*
En mnemonic operation code
Es código de operación mnemotécnico *(m)*
Fr code d'exploitation mnémonique *(m)*
It codice dell'operazione mnemonico *(m)*

código de operación mnemotécnico *(m)* Es
De Mnemonik-Betriebscode *(m)*
En mnemonic operation code
Fr code d'exploitation mnémonique *(m)*
It codice dell'operazione mnemonico *(m)*
Pt código de operação mnemónico *(m)*

código de orden *(m)* Es
De Anweisungscode *(m)*
En order code
Fr code d'ordre *(m)*
It codice di ordine *(m)*
Pt código de ordens *(m)*

código de ordens *(m)* Pt
De Anweisungscode *(m)*
En order code
Es código de orden *(m)*
Fr code d'ordre *(m)*
It codice di ordine *(m)*

código de origem *(m)* Pt
De Quellcode *(m)*
En source code
Es código fuente *(m)*
Fr séquence en langage source *(f)*
It codice origine *(m)*

código de trazos *(m)* Es
De Balkencode *(m)*
En bar code
Fr code à bâtonnets *(m)*
It codice a barra *(m)*
Pt código de barra *(m)*

código en cadena *(m)* Es
De Kettencode *(m)*
En chain code
Fr code à enchaînement *(m)*
It codice di catena *(m)*
Pt código de cadeia *(m)*

código esquemático *(m)* Es
De Skelettcode *(m)*
En skeletal code
Fr séquence paramétrable *(f)*
It codice schematico *(m)*
Pt código reduzido *(m)*

código fuente *(m)* Es
De Quellcode *(m)*
En source code
Fr séquence en langage source *(f)*
It codice origine *(m)*
Pt código de origem *(m)*

código Gray *(m)* Es, Pt
De Gray-Code *(n)*
En Gray code
Fr code Gray *(m)*
It codice Gray *(m)*

código Hollerith *(m)* Es, Pt
De Hollerith-Code *(m)*
En Hollerith code
Fr code Hollerith *(m)*
It codice di Hollerith *(m)*

código objeto *(m)* Es
De Objektcode *(m)*
En object code
Fr code objet *(m)*
It codice oggetto *(m)*
Pt código de objecto *(m)*

código redundante *(m)* Es, Pt
De redundanter Code *(m)*
En redundant code
Fr code redondant *(m)*
It codice ridondante *(m)*

código reduzido *(m)* Pt
De Skelettcode *(m)*
En skeletal code
Es código esquemático *(m)*
Fr séquence paramétrable *(f)*
It codice schematico *(m)*

código relativo *(m)* Es, Pt
De relativer Code *(m)*
En relative code
Fr code relative *(m)*
It codice relativo *(m)*

código relocalizável *(m)* Pt
De verschieblicher Code *(m)*
En relocatable code
Es código reubicable *(m)*
Fr code translatable *(m)*
It codice rilocabile *(m)*

código reubicable *(m)* Es
De verschieblicher Code *(m)*
En relocatable code
Fr code translatable *(m)*
It codice rilocabile *(m)*
Pt código relocalizável *(m)*

coding *n* En
De Kodierung *(f)*
Es codificación *(f)*
Fr codage *(m)*
It codificazione *(f)*
Pt codificação *(f)*

coding check En
De Kodierungsprüfung *(f)*
Es verificación de la codificación *(f)*
Fr contrôle de codage *(m)*
It controllo di codificazione *(m)*
Pt verificação de codificação *(f)*

coeficiente de errores *(m)* Es
De Fehlerhäufigkeit *(f)*
En error rate
Fr taux d'erreurs *(m)*
It tasso di errori *(m)*
Pt índice de erros *(m)*

coincidence gate En
De Zusammentreffens-Schaltung *(f)*
Es puerta de coincidencia *(f)*
Fr porte à coïncidence *(f)*
It porta di coincidenza *(f)*
Pt porta de coincidência *(f)*

colecção de dados *(f)* Pt
De Datenerfassung *(f)*
En data collection
Es ecopilación de datos *(f)*
Fr collecte de données *(f)*
It raccolta dei dati *(f)*

colección de programas *(f)* Es
De Programmpaket *(n)*
En program package
Fr programme-produit *(m)*
It serie di programmi *(f)*
Pt pacote de programa *(m)*

colidir *vb* Pt
De durchschlagen
En crash
Es quebrar
Fr accélérer
It urtare

colisão *(f)* *n* Pt
De Durchschlag *(m)*
En crash
Es choque *(m)*
Fr accélération *(f)*
It urto *(m)*

collate *vb* En
De kollationieren
Es intercalar
Fr interclasser
It inserire
Pt conferir

collator *n* En
De Kollationierer *(m)*
Es intercaladora *(f)*
Fr interclasseuse *(f)*
It inseritrice *(f)*
Pt conferidor *(m)*

collaudo a distanza *(m)* It
De Fernprüfung *(f)*
En remote testing
Es ensayo a distancia *(m)*
Fr contrôle à distance *(m)*
Pt tele-ensaio *(m)*

collaudo del programma *(m)* It
De Programmprüfung *(f)*
En program testing
Es ensayo de programa *(m)*
Fr contrôle de programme *(m)*
Pt ensaio do programa *(m)*

collecte de données *(f)* Fr
De Datenerfassung *(f)*
En data collection
Es recopilación de datos *(f)*
It raccolta dei dati *(f)*
Pt colecção de dados *(f)*

collegamento di dati *(m)* It
De Datenübermittlungsabschnitt *(m)*
En data link
Es enlace para transmisión de datos *(m)*
Fr liaison de transmission *(f)*
Pt elemento de ligação de dados *(m)*

collegamento digitale *(m)* It
De Digitalverbindung *(f)*
En digital link
Es enlace digital *(m)*
Fr liaison numérique *(f)*
Pt elemento de ligação digital *(m)*

colleuse de bandes *(f)* Fr
De Klebegerät *(n)*
En splicer
Es empalmadora *(f)*
It incollatrice *(f)*
Pt emendador *(m)*

colocar *vb* Pt
De setzen
En set
Es ajustar
Fr régler
It disporre

colonna *(f) n* It
De Pfeiler *(m)*
En column
Es columna *(f)*
Fr colonne *(f)*
Pt coluna *(f)*

colonna della scheda *(f)* It
De Lochkartenspalte *(f)*
En card column
Es columna de ficha *(f)*
Fr colonne de carte *(f)*
Pt coluna de ficha *(f)*

colonne *(f) n* Fr
De Pfeiler *(m)*
En column
Es columna *(f)*
It colonna *(f)*
Pt coluna *(f)*

colonne de carte *(f)* Fr
De Lochkartenspalte *(f)*
En card column
Es columna de ficha *(f)*
It colonna della scheda *(f)*
Pt coluna de ficha *(f)*

column *n* En
De Pfeiler *(m)*
Es columna *(f)*
Fr colonne *(f)*
It colonna *(f)*
Pt coluna *(f)*

columna *(f) n* Es
De Pfeiler *(m)*
En column
Fr colonne *(f)*
It colonna *(f)*
Pt coluna *(f)*

columna de ficha *(f)* Es
De Lochkartenspalte *(f)*
En card column
Fr colonne de carte *(f)*
It colonna della scheda *(f)*
Pt coluna de ficha *(f)*

coluna *(f) n* Pt
De Pfeiler *(m)*
En column
Es columna *(f)*
Fr colonne *(f)*
It colonna *(f)*

coluna de ficha *(f)* Pt
De Lochkartenspalte *(f)*
En card column
Es columna de ficha *(f)*
Fr colonne de carte *(f)*
It colonna della scheda *(f)*

coma de la base *(f)* Es
De Basispunkt *(m)*
En radix point
Fr point à la base *(m)*
It punto di base *(m)*
Pt ponto de raiz *(m)*

comando *(m) n* It
De Befehl *(m)*
En command
Es orden *(f)*
Fr commande *(f)*
Pt ordem *(f)*

comentario *(m) n* Es
De Kommentar *(m)*
En comment
Fr commentaire *(m)*
It commento *(m)*
Pt comentário *(m)*

comentário *(m) n* Pt
De Kommentar *(m)*
En comment
Es comentario *(m)*
Fr commentaire *(m)*
It commento *(m)*

command *n* En
De Befehl *(m)*
Es orden *(f)*
Fr commande *(f)*
It comando *(m)*
Pt ordem *(f)*

commande *(f) n* Fr
De Befehl *(m)*
En command
Es orden *(f)*
It comando *(m)*
Pt ordem *(f)*

commande de processus *(f)* Fr
De Verfahrenssteuerung *(f)*
En process control
Es control de procesos *(m)*
It controllo di processo *(m)*
Pt controle de processo *(m)*

commande de rétroaction *(f)* Fr
De rückgekoppeltes Regelungssystem *(n)*
En feedback control
Es control de realimentación *(m)*
It controllo di retroazione *(m)*
Pt controle de realimentação *(m)*

commande de superviseur *(f)* Fr
De Überwachungssteuerung *(f)*
En supervisory control
Es control supervisor *(m)*
It controllo di supervisione *(m)*
Pt controle de supervisão *(m)*

commande manuelle *(f)* Fr
De Handsteuerung *(f)*
En manual control
Es control manual *(m)*
It controllo manuale *(m)*
Pt controle manual *(m)*

commande numérique *(f)* Fr
De numerische Steuerung *(f)*
En numerical control
Es control numérico *(m)*
It controllo numerico *(m)*
Pt controle numérico *(m)*

command language En
De Befehlssprache *(f)*
Es lenguaje de orden *(m)*
Fr langage de commande *(m)*
It linguaggio del comando *(m)*
Pt linguagem de ordem *(f)*

comment *n* En
De Kommentar *(m)*
Es comentario *(m)*
Fr commentaire *(m)*
It commento *(m)*
Pt comentário *(m)*

commentaire *(m) n* Fr
De Kommentar *(m)*
En comment
Es comentario *(m)*
It commento *(m)*
Pt comentário *(m)*

commento *(m) n* It
De Kommentar *(m)*
En comment
Es comentario *(m)*
Fr commentaire *(m)*
Pt comentário *(m)*

communication *n* En, Fr *(f)*
De Kommunikation *(f)*
Es comunicación *(f)*
It comunicazione *(f)*
Pt comunicação *(f)*

communication channel En
De Kommunikations-kanal *(m)*
Es canal de comunicación *(m)*
Fr voie de communication *(f)*
It canale di comunicazione *(m)*
Pt canal de comunicação *(m)*

communication network En
De Kommunikationsnetz *(n)*
Es red de comunicaciones *(f)*
Fr réseau de communication *(m)*
It rete di comunicazione *(f)*
Pt rede de comunicação *(f)*

communication system En
De Kommunikations-system *(n)*
Es sistema de comunicaciones *(m)*
Fr système de communication *(m)*
It sistema di comunicazione *(m)*
Pt sistema de comunicação *(m)*

communication téléphonique *(f)* Fr
De telefonische Verbindung *(f)*
En telephonic communication
Es comunicación telefónica *(f)*
It comunicazione telefonica *(f)*
Pt comunicação telefónica *(f)*

commutare *vb* It
De schalten
En switch
Es conmutar
Fr commuter
Pt comutar

commutation de lignes *(f)* Fr
De Leitungsschalten *(n)*
En line switching
Es conmutación de líneas *(f)*
It commutazione di linea *(f)*
Pt comutação de linha *(f)*

commutation de messages *(f)* Fr
De Nachrichten-verteilung *(f)*
En message switching
Es conmutación de mensajes *(f)*
It commutazione di messaggi *(f)*
Pt comutação de mensagem *(f)*

commutation numérique *(f)* Fr
De digitales Schalten *(n)*
En digital switching
Es conmutación digital *(f)*
It commutazione digitale *(f)*
Pt comutação digital *(f)*

commutation par blocs *(f)* Fr
De Blockschalten *(n)*
En block switching
Es conmutación del bloque *(f)*
It commutazione di blocco *(f)*
Pt comutação de bloco *(f)*

commutation par paquets *(f)* Fr
De Paketschalten *(n)*
En packet switching
Es conmutación de paquetes *(f)*
It commutazione di pacci *(f)*
Pt comutação de pacotes *(f)*

commutation téléphonique *(f)* Fr
De telefonische Vermittlung *(f)*
En telephone switching
Es conmutación telefónica *(f)*
It commutazione telefonica *(f)*
Pt comutação telefónica *(f)*

commutazione di blocco *(f)* It
De Blockschalten *(n)*
En block switching
Es conmutación del bloque *(f)*
Fr commutation par blocs *(f)*
Pt comutação de bloco *(f)*

commutazione digitale *(f)* It
De digitales Schalten *(n)*
En digital switching
Es conmutación digital *(f)*
Fr commutation numérique *(f)*
Pt comutação digital *(f)*

commutazione di linea *(f)* It
De Leitungsschalten *(n)*
En line switching
Es conmutación de líneas *(f)*
Fr commutation de lignes *(f)*
Pt comutação de linha *(f)*

commutazione di messaggi *(f)* It
De Nachrichten-verteilung *(f)*
En message switching
Es conmutación de mensajes *(f)*
Fr commutation de messages *(f)*
Pt comutação de mensagem *(f)*

commutazione di pacci *(f)* It
De Paketschalten *(n)*
En packet switching
Es conmutación de paquetes *(f)*
Fr commutation par paquets *(f)*
Pt comutação de pacotes *(f)*

commutazione telefonica *(f)* It
De telefonische Vermittlung *(f)*
En telephone switching
Es conmutación telefónica *(f)*
Fr commutation téléphonique *(f)*
Pt comutação telefónica *(f)*

commuter *vb* Fr
De schalten
En switch
Es conmutar
It commutare
Pt comutar

comparador *(m) n* Es, Pt
De Grenzwertvergleicher *(m)*
En comparator
Fr comparateur *(m)*
It comparatore *(m)*

comparar *vb* Es, Pt
De vergleichen
En compare
Fr comparer
It comparare

comparare *vb* It
De vergleichen
En compare
Es comparar
Fr comparer
Pt comparar

comparateur *(m) n* Fr
De Grenzwertvergleicher *(m)*
En comparator
Es comparador *(m)*
It comparatore *(m)*
Pt comparador *(m)*

comparator *n* En
De Grenzwertvergleicher *(m)*
Es comparador *(m)*
Fr comparateur *(m)*
It comparatore *(m)*
Pt comparador *(m)*

comparatore *(m) n* It
De Grenzwertvergleicher *(m)*
En comparator
Es comparador *(m)*
Fr comparateur *(m)*
Pt comparador *(m)*

compare *vb* En
De vergleichen
Es comparar
Fr comparer
It comparare
Pt comparar

comparer *vb* Fr
De vergleichen
En compare
Es comparar
It comparare
Pt comparar

compartido tempo *(m)* Pt
De Zeitteilung *(f)*
En time sharing
Es tiempo compartido *(m)*
Fr utilisation en temps partagé *(f)*
It lavoro di multi-programmazione *(m)*

compatibilidad *(f) n* Es
De Verträglichkeit *(f)*
En compatibility
Fr compatibilité *(f)*
It compatibilità *(f)*
Pt compatibilidade *(f)*

compatibilidad de programas *(f)* Es
De Programm-verträglichkeit *(f)*
En program compatibility
Fr compatibilité-programme *(f)*
It compatibilità di programma *(f)*
Pt compatibilidade de programas *(f)*

compatibilidade *(f) n* Pt
De Verträglichkeit *(f)*
En compatibility
Es compatibilidad *(f)*
Fr compatibilité *(f)*
It compatibilità *(f)*

compatibilidade de programas *(f)* Pt
De Programm-verträglichkeit *(f)*
En program compatibility
Es compatibilidad de programas *(f)*
Fr compatibilité-programme *(f)*
Pt compatibilità di programma *(f)*

compatibilidade do equipamento *(f)* Pt
De Maschinen-verträglichkeit *(f)*
En equipment compatibility
Es compatibilidad entre equipos *(f)*
Fr compatibilité de matériels *(f)*
It compatibilità delle apparecchiature *(f)*

compatibilidad entre equipos *(f)* Es
De Maschinen-verträglichkeit *(f)*
En equipment compatibility
Fr compatibilité de matériels *(f)*
It compatibilità delle apparecchiature *(f)*
Pt compatibilidade do equipamento *(f)*

compatibilità *(f) n* It
De Verträglichkeit *(f)*
En compatibility
Es compatibilidad *(f)*
Fr compatibilité *(f)*
Pt compatibilidade *(f)*

compatibilità delle apparecchiature *(f)* It
De Maschinen-verträglichkeit *(f)*
En equipment compatibility
Es compatibilidad entre equipos *(f)*
Fr compatibilité de matériels *(f)*
Pt compatibilidade do equipamento *(f)*

compatibilità di programma *(f)* It
De Programm-verträglichkeit *(f)*
En program compatibility
Es compatibilidad de programas *(f)*
Fr compatibilité-programme *(f)*
Pt compatibilidade de programas *(f)*

compatibilité *(f) n* Fr
De Verträglichkeit *(f)*
En compatibility
Es compatibilidad *(f)*
It compatibilità *(f)*
Pt compatibilidade *(f)*

compatibilité de matériels *(f)* Fr
De Maschinen-verträglichkeit *(f)*
En equipment compatibility
Es compatibilidad entre equipos *(f)*
It compatibilità delle apparecchiature *(f)*
Pt compatibilidade do equipamento *(f)*

compatibilité-programme *(f)* Fr
De Programm-verträglichkeit *(f)*
En program compatibility
Es compatibilidad de programas *(f)*
It compatibilità di programma *(f)*
Pt compatibilidade de programas *(f)*

compatibility *n* En
De Verträglichkeit *(f)*
Es compatibilidad *(f)*
Fr compatibilité *(f)*
It compatibilità *(f)*
Pt compatibilidade *(f)*

compilação *(f) n* Pt
De Kompilierung *(f)*
En compilation
Es compilación *(f)*
Fr compilation *(f)*
It compilazione *(f)*

compilación *(f) n* Es
De Kompilierung *(f)*
En compilation
Fr compilation *(f)*
It compilazione *(f)*
Pt compilação *(f)*

compilador *(m) n* Es, Pt
De Kompilierer *(m)*
En compiler
Fr compilateur *(m)*
It compilatore *(m)*

compilador cruzado *(m)* Es, Pt
De Gegenkompilierer *(m)*
En cross compiler
Fr compilateur croisé *(m)*
It compilatore incrociato *(m)*

compilar *vb* Es, Pt
De kompilieren
En compile
Fr compiler
It compilare

compilare *vb* It
De kompilieren
En compile
Es compilar
Fr compiler
Pt compilar

compilateur *(m) n* Fr
De Kompilierer *(m)*
En compiler
Es compilador *(m)*
It compilatore *(m)*
Pt compilador *(m)*

compilateur croisé *(m)* Fr
De Gegenkompilierer *(m)*
En cross compiler

Es compilador cruzado *(m)*
It compilatore incrociato *(m)*
Pt compilador cruzado *(m)*

compilation *n* En, Fr *(f)*
De Kompilierung *(f)*
Es compilación *(f)*
It compilazione *(f)*
Pt compilação *(f)*

compilatore *(m) n* It
De Kompilierer *(m)*
En compiler
Es compilador *(m)*
Fr compilateur *(m)*
Pt compilador *(m)*

compilatore incrociato *(m)* It
De Gegenkompilierer *(m)*
En cross compiler
Es compilador cruzado *(m)*
Fr compilateur croisé *(m)*
Pt compilador cruzado *(m)*

compilazione *(f) n* It
De Kompilierung *(f)*
En compilation
Es compilación *(f)*
Fr compilation *(f)*
Pt compilação *(f)*

compile *vb* En
De kompilieren
Es compilar
Fr compiler
It compilare
Pt compilar

compiler *n* En
De Kompilierer *(m)*
Es compilador *(m)*
Fr compilateur *(m)*
It compilatore *(m)*
Pt compilador *(m)*

compiler *vb* Fr
De kompilieren
En compile
Es compilar
It compilare
Pt compilar

compito *(m) n* It
De Aufgabe *(f)*
En task
Es tarea *(f)*
Fr tâche *(f)*
Pt tarefa *(f)*

complement *n* En
De Ergänzung *(f)*
Es complemento *(m)*
Fr complément *(m)*
It complemento *(m)*
Pt complemento *(m)*

complement *vb* En
De ergänzen
Es complementar
Fr prendre le complément de
It complementare
Pt complementar

complément *(m) n* Fr
De Ergänzung *(f)*
En complement
Es complemento *(m)*
It complemento *(m)*
Pt complemento *(m)*

complément à dix *(m)* Fr
De Zehnerkomplement *(n)*
En tens complement
Es complemento a diez *(m)*
It complemento di decine *(m)*
Pt complemento de dezenas *(m)*

complément à la base *(m)* Fr
De Basiskomplement *(n)*
En radix complement
Es complemento de la base *(m)*
It complemento di base *(m)*
Pt complemento de raiz *(m)*

complément à neuf *(m)* Fr
De Neunerkomplement *(n)*
En nines complement
Es complemento a nueves *(m)*
It complemento al nove *(m)*
Pt complemento de noves *(m)*

complementar *vb* Es, Pt
De ergänzen
En complement
Fr prendre le complément de
It complementare

complementare *vb* It
De ergänzen
En complement
Es complementar
Fr prendre le complément de
Pt complementar

complementary MOS En
De komplementäres MOS *(n)*
Es MOS suplementario *(m)*
Fr MOS complémentaire *(m)*
It MOS complementare *(m)*
Pt MOS complementar *(m)*

complementary operation En
De komplementäre Funktion *(f)*
Es operación complementaria *(f)*
Fr opération complémentaire *(f)*
It operazione complementare *(f)*
Pt operação complementar *(f)*

complément à un *(m)* Fr
De Einerkomplement *(n)*
En ones complement
Es complemento a uno *(m)*
It complemento all'uno *(m)*
Pt complemento de unidades *(m)*

complément deux *(m)* Fr
De Zweierkomplement *(n)*
En twos complement
Es complemento a dos *(m)*
It complemento al due *(m)*
Pt complemento de dois *(m)*

complemento *(m) n* Es, It, Pt
De Ergänzung *(f)*
En complement
Fr complément *(m)*

complemento a diez *(m)* Es
De Zehnerkomplement *(n)*
En tens complement
Fr complément à dix *(m)*
It complemento di decine *(m)*
Pt complemento de dezenas *(m)*

complemento a dos *(m)* Es
De Zweierkomplement *(n)*
En twos complement
Fr complément deux *(m)*
It complemento al due *(m)*
Pt complemento de dois *(m)*

complemento al due *(m)* It
De Zweierkomplement *(n)*
En twos complement
Es complemento a dos *(m)*
Fr complément deux *(m)*
Pt complemento de dois *(m)*

complemento all'uno *(m)* It
De Einerkomplement *(n)*
En ones complement
Es complemento a uno *(m)*
Fr complément à un *(m)*
Pt complemento de unidades *(m)*

complemento al nove *(m)* It
De Neunerkomplement *(n)*
En nines complement
Es complemento a nueves *(m)*
Fr complément à neuf *(m)*
Pt complemento de noves *(m)*

complemento a nueves *(m)* Es
De Neunerkomplement *(n)*
En nines complement
Fr complément à neuf *(m)*
It complemento al nove *(m)*
Pt complemento de noves *(m)*

complemento a uno *(m)* Es
De Einerkomplement *(n)*
En ones complement
Fr complément à un *(m)*
It complemento all'uno *(m)*
Pt complemento de unidades *(m)*

complemento de dezenas *(m)* Pt
De Zehnerkomplement *(n)*
En tens complement
Es complemento a diez *(m)*
Fr complément à dix *(m)*
It complemento di decine *(m)*

complemento de dois *(m)* Pt
De Zweierkomplement *(n)*
En twos complement
Es complemento a dos *(m)*
Fr complément deux *(m)*
It complemento al due *(m)*

complemento de la base *(m)* Es
De Basiskomplement *(n)*
En radix complement
Fr complément à la base *(m)*
It complemento di base *(m)*
Pt complemento de raiz *(m)*

complemento de noves *(m)* Pt
De Neunerkomplement *(n)*
En nines complement
Es complemento a nueves *(m)*
Fr complément à neuf *(m)*
It complemento al nove *(m)*

complemento de raiz *(m)* Pt
De Basiskomplement *(n)*
En radix complement
Es complemento de la base *(m)*
Fr complément à la base *(m)*
It complemento di base *(m)*

complemento de unidades *(m)* Pt
De Einerkomplement *(n)*
En ones complement
Es complemento a uno *(m)*
Fr complément à un *(m)*
It complemento all'uno *(m)*

complemento di base *(m)* It
De Basiskomplement *(n)*
En radix complement
Es complemento de la base *(m)*
Fr complément à la base *(m)*
Pt complemento de raiz *(m)*

complemento di decine *(m)* It
De Zehnerkomplement *(n)*
En tens complement
Es complemento a diez *(m)*
Fr complément à dix *(m)*
Pt complemento de dezenas *(m)*

compréhensible par une machine Fr
De maschinenlesbar
En machine-readable
Es legible por la máquina
It leggibile dalla macchina
Pt legível pela máquina

comprimento de bloco *(m)* Pt
De Blocklänge *(f)*
En block length
Es longitud de bloque *(f)*
Fr longueur de bloc *(f)*
It lunghezza del blocco *(m)*

comprimento de bloco fixo *(m)* Pt
De feste Blocklänge *(f)*
En fixed block length
Es longitud de bloque fija *(f)*
Fr bloc de longueur fixe *(m)*
It lunghezza del blocco fisso *(f)*

comprimento de campo *(m)* Pt
De Feldlänge *(f)*
En field length
Es longitud de campo *(f)*
Fr longueur de zone *(f)*
It lunghezza del campo *(f)*

comprimento de palavra *(m)* Pt
De Wortlänge *(f)*
En word length
Es longitud de palabra *(f)*
Fr longueur de mot *(f)*
It lunghezza della voce *(f)*

comprimento de registo *(m)* Pt
De Satzlänge *(f)*
En record length
Es longitud de registro *(f)*
Fr longueur d'enregistrement *(f)*
It lunghezza del record *(f)*

comprimento duplo *(m)* Pt
De Doppellänge *(f)*
En double-length
Es doble longitud *(f)*
Fr longueur double *(f)*
It lunghezza doppia *(f)*

comprimer *vb* Fr
De stapeln
En pack
Es empaquetar
It impaccare
Pt empacotar

comprobación de suma *(f)* Es
De Summenprüfung *(f)*
En summation check
Fr contrôle par totalisation *(m)*
It controllo di addizione *(m)*
Pt verificação de soma *(f)*

comptage de cycles *(m)* Fr
De Gangzählung *(f)*
En cycle count
Es cuenta de ciclos *(f)*
It conteggio dei cicli *(m)*
Pt contagem de ciclos *(f)*

compteur *(m) n* Fr
De Zähler *(m)*
En counter
Es contador *(m)*
It contatore *(m)*
Pt contador *(m)*

compteur annulaire *(m)* Fr
De Ringzähler *(m)*
En ring counter
Es contador en anillo *(m)*
It contatore ad anello *(m)*
Pt contador anular *(m)*

compteur-décompteur *(m)* Fr
De umkehrbarer Zähler *(m)*
En reversible counter
Es contador reversible *(m)*
It contatore reversibile *(m)*
Pt contador reversível *(m)*

compteur d'emplacement *(m)* Fr
De Dateilagezähler *(m)*
En location counter
Es contador de posiciones *(m)*
It contatore di locazioni *(m)*

Pt contador de localização *(m)*

computação de multi-acesso *(f)* Pt
De Mehrfachzugriffs-rechnen *(n)*
En multi-access computing (MAC)
Es cálculo de acceso múltiple *(m)*
Fr traitement à accès multiple (TAM) *(m)*
It calcolo ad accesso multiplo *(m)*

computação doméstica *(f)* Pt
De Lokalrechnung *(f)*
En home computing
Es cálculo inicial *(m)*
Fr traitement domestique *(m)*
It elaborazione in proprio *(f)*

computação interactiva *(f)* Pt
De Dialogbetrieb *(m)*
En interactive computing
Es cálculo interactivo *(m)*
Fr traitement interactif *(m)*
It calcoli interattivi *(m)*

computador *(m)* *n* Pt
De Computer; Rechner *(m)*
En computer
Es ordenador *(m)*
Fr ordinateur *(m)*
It elaboratore *(m)*

computador com programa armazenado *(m)* Pt
De Computer für gespeicherte Programme *(m)*
En stored-program computer
Es ordenador en programa almacenado *(m)*
Fr ordinateur à programme enregistré *(m)*
It calcolatore a programmi memorizzati *(m)*

computador de analogia *(m)* Pt
De Analogrechner *(m)*
En analog computer
Es ordenador analógico *(m)*
Fr calculateur analogique *(m)*
It elaboratore analogico *(m)*

computador de mesa *(m)* Pt
De Tischrechner *(m)*
En desk-top computer
Es ordenador de mesa *(m)*
Fr petit ordinateur de bureau *(m)*
It elaboratore da tavolo *(m)*

computador digital *(m)* Pt
De Digitalrechner *(m)*
En digital computer
Es ordenador digital *(m)*
Fr calculateur numérique *(m)*
It elaboratore digitale *(m)*

computador híbrido *(m)* Pt
De Hybridrechner *(m)*
En hybrid computer
Es ordenador híbrido *(m)*
Fr calculateur hybride *(m)*
It elaboratore ibrido *(m)*

computador hospedeiro *(m)* Pt
De Wirtsrechner *(m)*
En host computer
Es ordenador anfitrión *(m)*
Fr ordinateur central *(m)*
It elaboratore per conto terzi *(m)*

computador para fins especiais *(m)* Pt
De Spezialrechner *(m)*
En special-purpose computer
Es ordenador especializado *(m)*
Fr calculateur spécialisé *(m)*
It elaboratore a scopo speciale *(m)*

computador para todos os fins *(m)* Pt
De Allgemeinzweck-computer *(m)*
En general-purpose computer
Es ordenador universal *(m)*
Fr calculateur universel *(m)*
It elaboratore a scopo generale *(m)*

computador pessoal *(m)* Pt
De persönlicher Rechner *(m)*
En personal computer
Es ordenador personal *(m)*
Fr ordinateur privé *(m)*
It calcolatore personale *(m)*

computador pneumático *(m)* Pt
De pneumatischer Computer *(m)*
En pneumatic computer
Es ordenador neumático *(m)*
Fr ordinateur pneumatique *(m)*
It elaboratore pneumatico *(m)*

computador portátil *(m)* Pt
De tragbarer Computer *(m)*
En portable computer
Es ordenador portátil *(m)*
Fr ordinateur portatif *(m)*
It calcolatore portabile *(m)*

computador principal *(m)* Es, Pt
De Hauptrechner *(m)*
En mainframe computer
Fr ordinateur principal *(m)*
It calcolatore principale *(m)*

computador satélite *(m)* Pt
De Satellitenrechner *(m)*
En satellite (computer)
Es ordenador satélite *(m)*
Fr calculateur satellite *(m)*
It calcolatore satellite *(m)*

computador sincronizado *(m)* Pt
De Synchronisierrechner *(m)*
En synchronous computer
Es ordenador síncrono *(m)*
Fr calculateur synchrone *(m)*
It elaboratore sincrono *(m)*

computer *n* En
De Computer; Rechner *(m)*
Es ordenador *(m)*
Fr ordinateur *(m)*
It elaboratore *(m)*
Pt computador *(m)*

Computer *(m)* *n* De
En computer
Es ordenador *(m)*
Fr ordinateur *(m)*
It elaboratore *(m)*
Pt computador *(m)*

computer-aided design (CAD) En
De computer-unterstützte Konstruktion *(f)*
Es diseño con la ayuda de ordenador *(m)*
Fr conception assistée par ordinateur (CAO) *(f)*
It progettazione basata sull'elaboratore *(f)*
Pt desenho com auxílio de computador (CAD) *(m)*

computer-aided instruction En
De computer-unterstützter Unterricht *(m)*
Es instrucción com la

ayuda de ordenador *(f)*
Fr enseignement assisté par ordinateur *(m)*
It istruzione basata sull'elaboratore *(f)*
Pt instrução auxiliada por computador *(f)*

computer-aided manufacture (CAM) En
De computer-unterstützte Herstellung *(f)*
Es fabricación con la ayuda de ordenador *(f)*
Fr fabrication assistée par ordinateur (FAO) *(f)*
It produzione basata sull'elaboratore *(f)*
Pt manufactura com auxílio de computador *(f)*

Computerausgang auf Mikrofilm *(m)* De
En computer output on microfilm (COM)
Es salida de ordenador en microfilm *(f)*
Fr impression sur microfilm *(f)*
It output del elaboratore su microfilm *(m)*
Pt output de computador em microfilme *(m)*

computer-based learning En
De computerbasiertes Lernen *(n)*
Es enseñanza automatizada *(f)*
Fr enseignement automatisé *(m)*
It apprendimento basato sull'elaboratore *(m)*
Pt aprendizagem baseada em computador *(f)*

computerbasiertes Lernen *(n)* De
En computer-based learning
Es enseñanza automatizada *(f)*
Fr enseignement automatisé *(m)*
It apprendimento basato sull'elaboratore *(m)*
Pt aprendizagem baseada em computador *(f)*

Computer für gespeicherte Programme *(m)* De
En stored-program computer
Es ordenador en programa almacenado *(m)*
Fr ordinateur à programme enregistré *(m)*
It calcolatore a programmi memorizzati *(m)*
Pt computador com programa armazenado *(m)*

computer output on microfilm (COM) En
De Computerausgang auf Mikrofilm *(m)*
Es salida de ordenador en microfilm *(f)*
Fr impression sur microfilm *(f)*
It output del elaboratore su microfilm *(m)*
Pt output de computador em microfilme *(m)*

computer program En
De Programm *(n)*
Es programa de ordenador *(m)*
Fr programme machine *(m)*
It programma dell'elaboratore *(m)*
Pt programa de computador *(m)*

computer programmer En
De Programmierer *(m)*
Es programador de ordenador *(m)*
Fr programmateur *(m)*
It programmatore di elaboratori *(m)*
Pt programador de computador *(m)*

computer run En
De Ablauf *(m)*
Es pasada de ordenador *(f)*
Fr phase de traitement *(f)*
It esecuzione di elaboratore *(f)*
Pt passagem de computador *(f)*

computer science En
De Computer-wissenschaft *(f)*
Es ciencia de ordenador *(f)*
Fr ordinatique *(f)*
It scienza degli elaboratoria elettronici *(f)*
Pt ciência de computadores *(f)*

computerunterstützte Herstellung *(f)* De
En computer-aided manufacture (CAM)
Es fabricación con la ayuda de ordenador *(f)*
Fr fabrication assistée par ordinateur (FAO) *(f)*
It produzione basata sull'elaboratore *(f)*
Pt manufactura com auxílio de computador *(f)*

computerunterstützte Konstruktion *(f)* De
En computer-aided design (CAD)
Es diseño con la ayuda de ordenador *(m)*
Fr conception assistée par ordinateur (CAO) *(f)*
It progettazione basata sull'elaboratore *(f)*
Pt desenho com auxílio de computador (CAD) *(m)*

computerunterstützter Unterricht *(m)* De
En computer-aided instruction
Es instrucción com la ayuda de ordenador *(f)*
Fr enseignement assisté par ordinateur *(m)*
It istruzione basata sull'elaboratore *(f)*
Pt instrução auxiliada por computador *(f)*

Computerwissenschaft *(f) n* De
En computer science
Es ciencia de ordenador *(f)*
Fr ordinatique *(f)*
It scienza degli elaboratoria elettronici *(f)*
Pt ciência de computadores *(f)*

comunicação *(f) n* Pt
De Kommunikation *(f)*
En communication
Es comunicación *(f)*
Fr communication *(f)*
It comunicazione *(f)*

comunicação assíncrona *(f)* Pt
De Start-Stopp-Steuerung *(f)*
En asynchronous communication
Es comunicación asíncrona *(f)*
Fr transmission asynchrone *(f)*
It comunicazione asincrona *(f)*

comunicação telefónica *(f)* Pt
De telefonische Verbindung *(f)*
En telephonic communication
Es comunicación telefónica *(f)*
Fr communication téléphonique *(f)*
It comunicazione telefonica *(f)*

comunicación *(f) n* Es
De Kommunikation *(f)*
En communication
Fr communication *(f)*
It comunicazione *(f)*
Pt comunicação *(f)*

comunicación asíncrona *(f)* Es
De Start-Stopp-Steuerung *(f)*
En asynchronous communication
Fr transmission asynchrone *(f)*
It comunicazione asincrona *(f)*
Pt comunicação assíncrona *(f)*

comunicaciones entre sistemas *(f pl)* Es
De Zwischensystem-Verbindungswege *(pl)*
En intersystem communications
Fr transmission inter-système *(f)*
It comunicazioni tra sistemi *(f pl)*
Pt comunicações entre sistemas *(f pl)*

comunicaciones ópticas *(f)* Es
De optische Fernmeldung *(f)*
En optical communications
Fr transmission optique *(f)*
It comunicazioni ottiche *(f)*
Pt comunicações ópticas *(f)*

comunicación telefónica *(f)* Es
De telefonische Verbindung *(f)*
En telephonic communication
Fr communication téléphonique *(f)*
It comunicazione telefonica *(f)*
Pt comunicação telefónica *(f)*

comunicações entre sistemas *(f pl)* Pt
De Zwischensystem-Verbindungswege *(pl)*
En intersystem communications
Es comunicaciones entre sistemas *(f pl)*
Fr transmission inter-système *(f)*
It comunicazioni tra sistemi *(f pl)*

comunicações ópticas *(f)* Pt
De optische Fernmeldung *(f)*
En optical communications
Es comunicaciones ópticas *(f)*
Fr transmission optique *(f)*
It comunicazioni ottiche *(f)*

comunicazione *(f)* *n* It
De Kommunikation *(f)*
En communication
Es comunicación *(f)*
Fr communication *(f)*
Pt comunicação *(f)*

comunicazione asincrona *(f)* It
De Start-Stopp-Steuerung *(f)*
En asynchronous communication
Es comunicación asíncrona *(f)*
Fr transmission asynchrone *(f)*
Pt comunicação assíncrona *(f)*

comunicazione telefonica *(f)* It
De telefonische Verbindung *(f)*
En telephonic communication
Es comunicación telefónica *(f)*
Fr communication téléphonique *(f)*
Pt comunicação telefónica *(f)*

comunicazioni ottiche *(f)* It
De optische Fernmeldung *(f)*
En optical communications
Es comunicaciones ópticas *(f)*
Fr transmission optique *(f)*
Pt comunicações ópticas *(f)*

comunicazioni tra sistemi *(f pl)* It
De Zwischensystem-Verbindungswege *(pl)*
En intersystem communications
Es comunicaciones entre sistemas *(f pl)*
Fr transmission inter-système *(f)*
Pt comunicações entre sistemas *(f pl)*

comutação de bloco *(f)* Pt
De Blockschalten *(n)*
En block switching
Es conmutación del bloque *(f)*
Fr commutation par blocs *(f)*
It commutazione di blocco *(f)*

comutação de linha *(f)* Pt
De Leitungsschalten *(n)*
En line switching
Es conmutación de líneas *(f)*
Fr commutation de lignes *(f)*
It commutazione di linea *(f)*

comutação de mensagem *(f)* Pt
De Nachrichten-verteilung *(f)*
En message switching
Es conmutación de mensajes *(f)*
Fr commutation de messages *(f)*
It commutazione di messaggi *(f)*

comutação de pacotes *(f)* Pt
De Paketschalten *(n)*
En packet switching
Es conmutación de paquetes *(f)*
Fr commutation par paquets *(f)*
It commutazione di pacci *(f)*

comutação digital *(f)* Pt
De digitales Schalten *(n)*
En digital switching
Es conmutación digital *(f)*
Fr commutation numérique *(f)*
It commutazione digitale *(f)*

comutação telefónica *(f)* Pt
De telefonische Vermittlung *(f)*
En telephone switching
Es conmutación telefónica *(f)*
Fr commutation téléphonique *(f)*
It commutazione telefonica *(f)*

comutador *(m)* *n* Pt
De Schalter *(m)*
En switch
Es conmutador *(m)*
Fr interrupteur *(m)*
It interruttore *(m)*

comutador electrónico *(m)* Pt
De elektronischer Schalter *(m)*
En electronic switch
Es conmutador electrónico *(m)*
Fr bascule électronique *(f)*
It interruttore elettronico *(m)*

comutar *vb* Pt
De schalten
En switch
Es conmutar
Fr commuter
It commutare

conception assistée par ordinateur (CAO) *(f)* Fr
De computer-unterstützte Konstruktion *(f)*
En computer-aided design (CAD)
Es diseño con la ayuda de ordenador *(m)*
It progettazione basata sull'elaboratore *(f)*
Pt desenho com auxílio

de computador (CAD) *(m)*

conception de système automatique *(f)* Fr
De automatische Systemkonstruktion *(f)*
En automatic system design
Es diseño automático de sistemas *(m)*
It progettazione automatica del sistema *(f)*
Pt desenho de sistema automático *(m)*

conception fonctionnelle *(f)* Fr
De funktionsmäßige Konstruktion *(f)*
En functional design
Es diseño funcional *(m)*
It disegno funzionale *(m)*
Pt desenho funcional *(m)*

conclusione *(f) n* It
De Endstelle *(f)*
En termination
Es terminación *(f)*
Fr fin *(f)*
Pt terminação *(f)*

conclusione anormale *(f)* It
De Programmabbruch *(m)*
En abnormal termination
Es terminación anormal *(f)*
Fr terminaison anormale *(f)*
Pt terminação anormal *(f)*

concurrent processing En
De verzahnt ablaufende Verarbeitung *(f)*
Es proceso concurrente *(m)*
Fr traitement en simultané *(m)*
It elaborazione concorrente *(f)*
Pt processamento concorrente *(m)*

conditional branch instruction En
De bedingter Verzweigungsbefehl *(m)*
Es instrucción de bifurcación condicional *(f)*
Fr instruction de branchement conditionnelle *(f)*
It istruzione di diramazione condizionale *(f)*
Pt instrução de ramificação condicional *(f)*

conditional implication En
De bedingte Funktion *(f)*
Es implicación condicional *(f)*
Fr implication conditionnelle *(f)*
It implicazione condizionale *(f)*
Pt implicação condicional *(f)*

conditional operation En
De bedingter Betrieb *(m)*
Es operación condicional *(f)*
Fr opération conditionnelle *(f)*
It operazione condizionale *(f)*
Pt operação condicional *(f)*

conditional transfer En
De bedingte Übergabe *(f)*
Es transferencia condicional *(f)*
Fr transfert conditionnel *(m)*
It trasferimento condizionale *(m)*
Pt transferência condicional *(f)*

conductor común *(m)* Es
De Hauptverbindung *(f)*
En bus
Fr bus *(m)*
It barra *(f)*
Pt condutor *(m)*

condutor *(m) n* Pt
De Hauptverbindung *(f)*
En bus
Es conductor común *(m)*
Fr bus *(m)*
It barra *(f)*

conector *(m) n* Es, Pt
De Verbinder *(m)*
En connector
Fr connecteur *(m)*
It connettore *(m)*

conferidor *(m) n* Pt
De Kollationierer *(m)*
En collator
Es intercaladora *(f)*
Fr interclasseuse *(f)*
It inseritrice *(f)*

conferir *vb* Pt
De kollationieren
En collate
Es intercalar
Fr interclasser
It inserire

confeti *(m) n* Es
De Stanzrückstand *(m)*
En chad
Fr confetti *(m)*
It coriandoli di perforazione *(m)*
Pt recorte *(m)*

confetti *(m) n* Fr
De Stanzrückstand *(m)*
En chad
Es confeti *(m)*
It coriandoli di perforazione *(m)*
Pt recorte *(m)*

confiança *(f) n* Pt
De Zuverlässigkeit *(f)*
En reliability
Es fiabilidad *(f)*
Fr fiabilité *(f)*
It affidabilita *(f)*

confidentialité *(f) n* Fr
De Vertraulichkeit *(f)*
En privacy
Es aspecto confidencial *(m)*
It riservatezza *(f)*
Pt aspecto confidencial *(m)*

configuração *(f) n* Pt
De Konfiguration *(f)*
En configuration
Es configuración *(f)*
Fr configuration *(f)*
It configurazione *(f)*

configuración *(f) n* Es
De Konfiguration *(f)*
En configuration
Fr configuration *(f)*
It configurazione *(f)*
Pt configuração *(f)*

configuración de bits *(f)* Es
De Binärzeichenmuster *(n)*
En bit pattern
Fr configuration de bits *(f)*
It configurazione dei bit *(f)*
Pt padrão de bit *(m)*

configuration *n* En, Fr *(f)*
De Konfiguration *(f)*
Es configuración *(f)*
It configurazione *(f)*
Pt configuração *(f)*

configuration de bits *(f)* Fr
De Binärzeichenmuster *(n)*
En bit pattern
Es configuración de bits *(f)*
It configurazione dei bit *(f)*
Pt padrão de bit *(m)*

configurazione *(f) n* It
De Konfiguration *(f)*
En configuration
Es configuración *(f)*
Fr configuration *(f)*
Pt configuração *(f)*

configurazione dei bit *(f)* It
De Binärzeichenmuster *(n)*
En bit pattern
Es configuración de bits *(f)*
Fr configuration de bits *(f)*
Pt padrão de bit *(m)*

confirmação de recepção *(f)* Pt
De Rückmeldung *(f)*
En acknowledgment
Es admisión confirmación *(f)*
Fr accusé de réception *(m)*
It riconoscimento *(m)*

confirmação negativa *(f)* Pt
De negative Rückmeldung *(f)*
En negative acknowledgment
Es confirmación negativa *(f)*
Fr accusé de réception négatif *(m)*
It riconoscimento negativo *(m)*

confirmación negativa *(f)* Es
De negative Rückmeldung *(f)*
En negative acknowledgment
Fr accusé de réception négatif *(m)*
It riconoscimento negativo *(m)*
Pt confirmação negativa *(f)*

confondere *vb* It
De fusionieren
En merge
Es fusionar
Fr fusionner
Pt misturar

congestionamento *(m) n* Pt
De Verklemmung *(f)*
En jam
Es atascamiento *(m)*
Fr bourrage *(m)*
It inceppamento *(m)*

congiunzione *(f) n* It
De Konjunktion *(f)*
En conjunction
Es conjunción *(f)*
Fr conjonction *(f)*
Pt conjunção *(f)*

conjonction *(f) n* Fr
De Konjunktion *(f)*
En conjunction
Es conjunción *(f)*
It congiunzione *(f)*
Pt conjunção *(f)*

conjunção *(f) n* Pt
De Konjunktion *(f)*
En conjunction
Es conjunción *(f)*
Fr conjonction *(f)*
It congiunzione *(f)*

conjunción *(f) n* Es
De Konjunktion *(f)*
En conjunction
Fr conjonction *(f)*
It congiunzione *(f)*
Pt conjunção *(f)*

conjunction *n* En
De Konjunktion *(f)*
Es conjunción *(f)*
Fr conjonction *(f)*
It congiunzione *(f)*
Pt conjunção *(f)*

conjunto *(m) n* Es, Pt
De Menge *(f)*
En set
Fr ensemble *(m)*
It insieme *(m)*

conjunto de dados telefónicos *(m)* Pt
De Telefondatensatz *(m)*
En telephone data set
Es equipo de datos telefónicos *(m)*
Fr ensemble de données téléphoniques *(m)*
It gruppo di dati telefonici *(m)*

conjunto de instruções *(m)* Pt
De Befehlsvorrat *(m)*
En instruction set
Es juego de instrucciones *(m)*
Fr jeu d'instructions *(m)*
It gruppo di istruzioni *(m)*

conmutación del bloque *(f)* Es
De Blockschalten *(n)*
En block switching
Fr commutation par blocs *(f)*
It commutazione di blocco *(f)*
Pt comutação de bloco *(f)*

conmutación de líneas *(f)* Es
De Leitungsschalten *(n)*
En line switching
Fr commutation de lignes *(f)*
It commutazione di linea *(f)*
Pt comutação de linha *(f)*

conmutación de mensajes *(f)* Es
De Nachrichtenverteilung *(f)*
En message switching
Fr commutation de messages *(f)*
It commutazione di messaggi *(f)*
Pt comutação de mensagem *(f)*

conmutación de paquetes *(f)* Es
De Paketschalten *(n)*
En packet switching
Fr commutation par paquets *(f)*
It commutazione di pacci *(f)*
Pt comutação de pacotes *(f)*

conmutación digital *(f)* Es
De digitales Schalten *(n)*
En digital switching
Fr commutation numérique *(f)*
It commutazione digitale *(f)*
Pt comutação digital *(f)*

conmutación telefónica *(f)* Es
De telefonische Vermittlung *(f)*
En telephone switching
Fr commutation téléphonique *(f)*
It commutazione telefonica *(f)*
Pt comutação telefónica *(f)*

conmutador *(m) n* Es
De Schalter *(m)*
En switch
Fr interrupteur *(m)*
It interruttore *(m)*
Pt comutador *(m)*

conmutador electrónico *(m)* Es
De elektronischer Schalter *(m)*
En electronic switch
Fr bascule électronique *(f)*
It interruttore elettronico *(m)*
Pt comutador electrónico *(m)*

conmutar *vb* Es
De schalten
En switch
Fr commuter
It commutare
Pt comutar

connecteur *(m) n* Fr
De Verbinder *(m)*
En connector
Es conector *(m)*
It connettore *(m)*
Pt conector *(m)*

connector *n* En
De Verbinder *(m)*
Es conector *(m)*
Fr connecteur *(m)*
It connettore *(m)*
Pt conector *(m)*

connessione *(f) n* It
De Korrektur *(f)*
En patch
Es parche *(m)*
Fr correction *(f)*
Pt remendo *(m)*

connettore *(m) n* It
De Verbinder *(m)*
En connector
Es conector *(m)*
Fr connecteur *(m)*
Pt conector *(m)*

consignation *(f) n* Fr
De Journal *(n)*
En log
Es registro *(m)*
It registro *(m)*
Pt diário *(m)*

consigner *vb* Fr
De senden
En log
Es registrar
It registrare
Pt registar em diário

consistency check En
De Kontrolle der Konsistenz *(f)*
Es control de uniformidad *(m)*
Fr contrôle de cohérence *(m)*
It controllo di consistenza *(m)*
Pt verificação de congruência *(f)*

consola *(f) n* Es, Pt
De Systemkonsole *(f)*
En console
Fr pupitre de commande *(m)*
It console *(f)*

consola de visualização *(f)* Pt
De Anzeigekonsole *(f)*
En display console
Es consola de visualización *(f)*
Fr console de visualisation *(f)*
It console di visualizzazione *(f)*

consola de visualización *(f)* Es
De Anzeigekonsole *(f)*
En display console
Fr console de visualisation *(f)*
It console di visualizzazione *(f)*
Pt consola de visualização *(f)*

consola remota *(f)* Es, Pt
De Auβenkonsole *(f)*
En remote console
Fr pupitre à distance *(m)*
It console a distanza *(f)*

console *n* En, It *(f)*
De Systemkonsole *(f)*
Es consola *(f)*
Fr pupitre de commande *(m)*
Pt consola *(f)*

console a distanza *(f)* It
De Auβenkonsole *(f)*
En remote console
Es consola remota *(f)*
Fr pupitre à distance *(m)*
Pt consola remota *(f)*

console de visualisation *(f)* Fr
De Anzeigekonsole *(f)*
En display console
Es consola de visualización *(f)*
It console di visualizzazione *(f)*
Pt consola de visualização *(f)*

console di visualizzazione *(f)* It
De Anzeigekonsole *(f)*
En display console
Es consola de visualización *(f)*
Fr console de visualisation *(f)*
Pt consola de visualização *(f)*

console typewriter En
De Konsolenschreibmaschine *(f)*
Es máquina de escribir de consola *(f)*
Fr machine à écrire de pupitre *(f)*
It macchina da scrivere a console *(f)*
Pt máquina de escrever de consola *(f)*

constant area En
De Konstantbereich *(m)*
Es área constante *(f)*
Fr aire constante *(f)*
It area costante *(f)*
Pt área constante *(f)*

constantes *(f pl) n* Es, Fr, Pt
De Konstante *(pl)*
En constants
It costanti *(m pl)*

constants *n pl* En
De Konstante *(pl)*
Es constantes *(f pl)*
Fr constantes *(f pl)*
It costanti *(m pl)*
Pt constantes *(f pl)*

construção de modelo *(f)* Pt
De Modellaufbau *(m)*
En model building
Es construcción de modelos *(f)*
Fr construction de modèles *(f)*
It costruzione di modelli *(f)*

construcción de modelos *(f)* Es
De Modellaufbau *(m)*
En model building
Fr construction de modèles *(f)*
It costruzione di modelli *(f)*
Pt construção de modelo *(f)*

construction de modèles *(f)* Fr
De Modellaufbau *(m)*
En model building
Es construcción de modelos *(f)*
It costruzione di modelli *(f)*
Pt construção de modelo *(f)*

consulta de tabela *(f)* Pt
De Tabellenaufsuchung *(f)*
En table look up (TLU)
Es consulta de tablas *(f)*
Fr consultation de table *(f)*
It consulta di tavola *(f)*

consulta de tablas *(f)* Es
De Tabellenaufsuchung *(f)*
En table look up (TLU)
Fr consultation de table *(f)*
It consulta di tavola *(f)*
Pt consulta de tabela *(f)*

consulta di tavola *(f)* It
De Tabellenaufsuchung *(f)*
En table look up (TLU)
Es consulta de tablas *(f)*
Fr consultation de table *(f)*
Pt consulta de tabela *(f)*

consultar *vb* Es, Pt
De aufsuchen
En look up
Fr consulter
It consultare

consultare *vb* It
De aufsuchen
En look up
Es consultar
Fr consulter
Pt consultar

consultation de table *(f)* Fr
De Tabellenaufsuchung *(f)*
En table look up (TLU)
Es consulta de tablas *(f)*
It consulta di tavola *(f)*
Pt consulta de tabela *(f)*

consulter *vb* Fr
De aufsuchen
En look up
Es consultar
It consultare
Pt consultar

contador *(m) n* Es, Pt
De Zähler *(m)*
En counter
Fr compteur *(m)*
It contatore *(m)*

contador anular *(m)* Pt
De Ringzähler *(m)*
En ring counter
Es contador en anillo *(m)*
Fr compteur annulaire *(m)*
It contatore ad anello *(m)*

contador de localização *(m)* Pt
De Dateilagezähler *(m)*
En location counter
Es contador de posiciones *(m)*
Fr compteur d'emplacement *(m)*
It contatore di locazioni *(m)*

contador de posiciones *(m)* Es
De Dateilagezähler *(m)*
En location counter

Fr compteur d'emplacement *(m)*
It contatore di locazioni *(m)*
Pt contador de localização *(m)*

contador en anillo *(m)* Es
De Ringzähler *(m)*
En ring counter
Fr compteur annulaire *(m)*
It contatore ad anello *(m)*
Pt contador anular *(m)*

contador reversible *(m)* Es
De umkehrbarer Zähler *(m)*
En reversible counter
Fr compteur-décompteur *(m)*
It contatore reversibile *(m)*
Pt contador reversível *(m)*

contador reversível *(m)* Pt
De umkehrbarer Zähler *(m)*
En reversible counter
Es contador reversible *(m)*
Fr compteur-décompteur *(m)*
It contatore reversibile *(m)*

contagem de ciclos *(f)* Pt
De Gangzählung *(f)*
En cycle count
Es cuenta de ciclos *(f)*
Fr comptage de cycles *(m)*
It conteggio dei cicli *(m)*

contatore *(m) n* It
De Zähler *(m)*
En counter
Es contador *(m)*
Fr compteur *(m)*
Pt contador *(m)*

contatore ad anello *(m)* It
De Ringzähler *(m)*
En ring counter
Es contador en anillo *(m)*
Fr compteur annulaire *(m)*
Pt contador anular *(m)*

contatore di locazioni *(m)* It
De Dateilagezähler *(m)*
En location counter
Es contador de posiciones *(m)*
Fr compteur d'emplacement *(m)*
Pt contador de localização *(m)*

contatore reversibile *(m)* It
De umkehrbarer Zähler *(m)*
En reversible counter
Es contador reversible *(m)*
Fr compteur-décompteur *(m)*
Pt contador reversível *(m)*

conteggio dei cicli *(m)* It
De Gangzählung *(f)*
En cycle count
Es cuenta de ciclos *(f)*
Fr comptage de cycles *(m)*
Pt contagem de ciclos *(f)*

contenido *(m) n* Es
De Inhalt *(m)*
En content
Fr contenu *(m)*
It contenuto *(m)*
Pt conteúdo *(m)*

contenido direccionable Es
De inhaltsadressierbar
En content-addressable
Fr contenu adressable
It contenuto indirizzabile
Pt endereçável ao conteúdo

content *n* En
De Inhalt *(m)*
Es contenido *(m)*
Fr contenu *(m)*
It contenuto *(m)*
Pt conteúdo *(m)*

content-addressable *adj* En
De inhaltsadressierbar
Es contenido direccionable
Fr contenu adressable
It contenuto indirizzabile
Pt endereçável ao conteúdo

contenu *(m) n* Fr
De Inhalt *(m)*
En content
Es contenido *(m)*
It contenuto *(m)*
Pt conteúdo *(m)*

contenu adressable Fr
De inhaltsadressierbar
En content-addressable
Es contenido direccionable
It contenuto indirizzabile
Pt endereçável ao conteúdo

contenuto *(m) n* It
De Inhalt *(m)*
En content
Es contenido *(m)*
Fr contenu *(m)*
Pt conteúdo *(m)*

contenuto indirizzabile It
De inhaltsadressierbar
En content-addressable
Es contenido direccionable
Fr contenu adressable
Pt endereçável ao conteúdo

conteúdo *(m) n* Pt
De Inhalt *(m)*
En content
Es contenido *(m)*
Fr contenu *(m)*
It contenuto *(m)*

continuo-estacionário *(m) n* Pt
De Endlosvordrucke *(pl)*
En continuous stationery
Es papel continuo *(m)*
Fr papier en continu *(m)*
It carta da tabulati a fisarmonica *(f)*

continuous stationery En
De Endlosvordrucke *(pl)*
Es papel continuo *(m)*
Fr papier en continu *(m)*
It carta da tabulati a fisarmonica *(f)*
Pt continuo-estacionário *(m)*

contraseña *(f) n* Es
De Kennwort *(n)*
En password
Fr mot de passe *(m)*
It parola d'ordine *(f)*
Pt contra-senha *(f)*

contra-senha *(f) n* Pt
De Kennwort *(n)*
En password
Es contraseña *(f)*
Fr mot de passe *(m)*
It parola d'ordine *(f)*

contra-verificar *vb* Pt
De gegenprüfen
En cross check
Es verificar por comparación
Fr contre-vérifier
It contra-verificare

contra-verificare *vb* It
De gegenprüfen
En cross check
Es verificar por comparación
Fr contre-vérifier
Pt contra-verificar

contre-vérification *(f) n* Fr
De Gegenprüfung *(f)*
En cross check
Es verificación cruzada *(f)*
It verifica generale completa *(f)*
Pt verificação cruzada *(f)*

contre-vérifier *vb* Fr
De gegenprüfen
En cross check
Es verificar por comparación
It contra-verificare
Pt contra-verificar

control *n* En, Es *(m)*
De Steuerung *(f)*
Es control *(m)*

Fr contrôle *(m)*
It controllo *(m)*
Pt controlo *(m)*

control *vb* En
De steuern
Es controlar
Fr contrôler
It controllare
Pt controlar

controlador periférico *(m)* Es, Pt
De peripheres Steuergerät *(n)*
En peripheral controller
Fr contrôleur de périphérique(s) *(m)*
It unità di controllo satellite *(f)*

controlar *vb* Es, Pt
De steuern
En control
Fr contrôler
It controllare

control data En
De Steuerungsdaten *(pl)*
Es datos de control *(m pl)*
Fr données de contrôle *(f pl)*
It dati di controllo *(m pl)*
Pt dados de controlo *(m pl)*

control de paridad *(m)* Es
De Paritätsprüfung *(f)*
En parity check
Fr contrôle de parité *(m)*
It controllo di parità *(m)*
Pt verificação de paridade *(f)*

control de paridad par-impar *(m)* Es
De gerade-ungerade Paritätsprüfung *(f)*
En odd-even check
Fr contrôle de parité pair-impair *(m)*
It controllo pari-dispari *(m)*
Pt verificação par-impar *(f)*

control de procesos *(m)* Es
De Verfahrenssteuerung *(f)*
En process control
Fr commande de processus *(f)*
It controllo di processo *(m)*
Pt controle de processo *(m)*

control de realimentación *(m)* Es
De rückgekoppeltes Regelungssystem *(n)*
En feedback control
Fr commande de rétroaction *(f)*
It controllo di retroazione *(m)*
Pt controle de realimentação *(m)*

control de uniformidad *(m)* Es
De Kontrolle der Konsistenz *(f)*
En consistency check
Fr contrôle de cohérence *(m)*
It controllo di consistenza *(m)*
Pt verificação de congruência *(f)*

contrôle *(m) n* Fr
De Prüfung; Steuerung *(f)*
En check; control
Es control; verificación *(m f)*
It controllo *(m)*
Pt controlo; verificação *(m f)*

contrôle à distance *(m)* Fr
De Fernprüfung *(f)*
En remote testing
Es ensayo a distancia *(m)*
It collaudo a distanza *(m)*
Pt tele-ensaio *(m)*

contrôle automatique *(m)* Fr
De automatische Prüfung *(f)*
En automatic check
Es verificación automática *(f)*
It controllo automatico *(m)*
Pt verificação automática *(f)*

contrôle de codage *(m)* Fr
De Kodierungsprüfung *(f)*
En coding check
Es verificación de la codificación *(f)*
It controllo di codificazione *(m)*
Pt verificação de codificação *(f)*

contrôle de cohérence *(m)* Fr
De Kontrolle der Konsistenz *(f)*
En consistency check
Es control de uniformidad *(m)*
It controllo di consistenza *(m)*
Pt verificação de congruência *(f)*

contrôle de parité *(m)* Fr
De Paritätsprüfung *(f)*
En parity check
Es control de paridad *(m)*
It controllo di parità *(m)*
Pt verificação de paridade *(f)*

contrôle de parité pair-impair *(m)* Fr
De gerade-ungerade Paritätsprüfung *(f)*
En odd-even check
Es control de paridad par-impar *(m)*
It controllo pari-dispari *(m)*
Pt verificação par-impar *(f)*

controle de processo *(m)* Pt
De Verfahrenssteuerung *(f)*
En process control
Es control de procesos *(m)*
Fr commande de processus *(f)*
It controllo di processo *(m)*

contrôle de programme *(m)* Fr
De Programmprüfung *(f)*
En program testing
Es ensayo de programa *(m)*
It collaudo del programma *(m)*
Pt ensaio do programa *(m)*

controle de realimentação *(m)* Pt
De rückgekoppeltes Regelungssystem *(n)*
En feedback control
Es control de realimentación *(m)*
Fr commande de rétroaction *(f)*
It controllo di retroazione *(m)*

contrôle de résidu *(m)* Fr
De Restprüfung *(f)*
En residue check
Es verificación por residuo *(f)*
It controllo residuo *(m)*
Pt verificação de resíduos *(f)*

contrôle de séquence *(m)* Fr
De Folgeprüfung *(f)*
En sequence check
Es verificación de secuencia *(f)*
It controllo di sequenza *(m)*
Pt verificação de sequência *(f)*

controle de supervisão *(m)* Pt
De Überwachungs-steuerung *(f)*
En supervisory control
Es control supervisor *(m)*
Fr commande de superviseur *(f)*
It controllo di supervisione *(m)*

contrôle de vraisemblance *(m)* Fr

De Gültigkeitsprüfung *(f)*
En validity check
Es verificación de validez *(f)*
It controllo di validità *(m)*
Pt verificação de validez *(f)*

controle manual *(m)* Pt
De Handsteuerung *(f)*
En manual control
Es control manual *(m)*
Fr commande manuelle *(f)*
It controllo manuale *(m)*

contrôle module-n *(m)* Fr
De Modulo-N-Kontrolle *(f)*
En modulo-n check
Es verificación de módulo N *(f)*
It controllo modulo-n *(m)*
Pt verificação modulo-n *(f)*

controle numérico *(m)* Pt
De numerische Steuerung *(f)*
En numerical control
Es control numérico *(m)*
Fr commande numérique *(f)*
It controllo numerico *(m)*

contrôle par écho *(m)* Fr
De Echoprüfung *(f)*
En echo check
Es verificación por eco *(f)*
It controllo dell'eco *(m)*
Pt verificação de eco *(f)*

contrôle par redondance *(m)* Fr
De Redundanzkontrolle *(f)*
En redundancy check
Es verificación por redundancia *(f)*
It controllo di ridondanza *(m)*
Pt verificação de redundância *(f)*

contrôle par répétition *(m)* Fr
De Übertragungsprüfung *(f)*
En transfer check
Es verificación de transferencia *(f)*
It controllo di trasferimento *(m)*
Pt verificação de transferência *(f)*

contrôle par totalisation *(m)* Fr
De Summenprüfung *(f)*
En summation check
Es comprobación de suma *(f)*
It controllo di addizione *(m)*
Pt verificação de soma *(f)*

contrôle par vidage *(m)* Fr
De Speicherauszugsprüfung *(f)*
En dump check
Es control por vaciado *(m)*
It controllo del dump *(m)*
Pt verificação de descarga *(f)*

controle proporcional *(m)* Pt
De Proportionalsteuerung *(f)*
En proportional control
Es control proporcional *(m)*
Fr contrôle proportionnel *(m)*
It controllo proporzionale *(m)*

contrôle proportionnel *(m)* Fr
De Proportionalsteuerung *(f)*
En proportional control
Es control proporcional *(m)*
It controllo proporzionale *(m)*
Pt controle proporcional *(m)*

contrôler *vb* Fr
De steuern
En control
Es controlar
It controllare
Pt controlar

contrôleur de périphérique(s) *(m)* Fr
De peripheres Steuergerät *(n)*
En peripheral controller
Es controlador periférico *(m)*
It unità di controllo satellite *(f)*
Pt controlador periférico *(m)*

control language En
De Steuersprache *(f)*
Es lenguaje de control *(m)*
Fr langage de contrôle *(m)*
It linguaggio di controllo *(m)*
Pt linguagem de controlo *(f)*

controllare *vb* It
De steuern
En control
Es controlar
Fr contrôler
Pt controlar

controllo *(m) n* It
De Prüfung; Steuerung *(f)*
En check; control
Es control; verificación *(m f)*
Fr contrôle *(m)*
Pt controlo; verificação *(m f)*

controllo accettazione clienti *(m)* It
De Kundenabnahmeprüfung *(f)*
En customer-acceptance test
Es ensayo de aceptación por el cliente *(m)*
Fr test de réception en clientèle *(m)*
Pt teste de aceitação de cliente *(m)*

controllo automatico *(m)* It
De automatische Prüfung *(f)*
En automatic check
Es verificación automática *(f)*
Fr contrôle automatique *(m)*
Pt verificação automática *(f)*

controllo del dump *(m)* It
De Speicherauszugsprüfung *(f)*
En dump check
Es control por vaciado *(m)*
Fr contrôle par vidage *(m)*
Pt verificação de descarga *(f)*

controllo dell'eco *(m)* It
De Echoprüfung *(f)*
En echo check
Es verificación por eco *(f)*
Fr contrôle par écho *(m)*
Pt verificação de eco *(f)*

controllo di addizione *(m)* It
De Summenprüfung *(f)*
En summation check
Es comprobación de suma *(f)*
Fr contrôle par totalisation *(m)*
Pt verificação de soma *(f)*

controllo di codificazione *(m)* It
De Kodierungsprüfung *(f)*
En coding check
Es verificación de la codificación *(f)*
Fr contrôle de codage *(m)*
Pt verificação de codificação *(f)*

controllo di consistenza *(m)* It
De Kontrolle der Konsistenz *(f)*
En consistency check
Es control de uniformidad *(m)*
Fr contrôle de cohérence *(m)*
Pt verificação de congruência *(f)*

controllo di parità *(m)* It
De Paritätsprüfung *(f)*
En parity check
Es control de paridad *(m)*
Fr contrôle de parité *(m)*
Pt verificação de paridade *(f)*

controllo di processo *(m)* It
De Verfahrenssteuerung *(f)*
En process control
Es control de procesos *(m)*
Fr commande de processus *(f)*
Pt controle de processo *(m)*

controllo di retroazione *(m)* It
De rückgekoppeltes Regelungssystem *(n)*
En feedback control
Es control de realimentación *(m)*
Fr commande de rétroaction *(f)*
Pt controle de realimentação *(m)*

controllo di ridondanza *(m)* It
De Redundanzkontrolle *(f)*
En redundancy check
Es verificación por redundancia *(f)*
Fr contrôle par redondance *(m)*
Pt verificação de redundância *(f)*

controllo di sequenza *(m)* It
De Folgeprüfung *(f)*
En sequence check
Es verificación de secuencia *(f)*
Fr contrôle de séquence *(m)*
Pt verificação de sequência *(f)*

controllo di supervisione *(m)* It
De Überwachungssteuerung *(f)*
En supervisory control
Es control supervisor *(m)*
Fr commande de superviseur *(f)*
Pt controle de supervisão *(m)*

controllo di trasferimento *(m)* It
De Übertragungsprüfung *(f)*
En transfer check
Es verificación de transferencia *(f)*
Fr contrôle par répétition *(m)*
Pt verificação de transferência *(f)*

controllo di validità *(m)* It
De Gültigkeitsprüfung *(f)*
En validity check
Es verificación de validez *(f)*
Fr contrôle de vraisemblance *(m)*
Pt verificação de validez *(f)*

controllo manuale *(m)* It
De Handsteuerung *(f)*
En manual control
Es control manual *(m)*
Fr commande manuelle *(f)*
Pt controle manual *(m)*

controllo modulo-n *(m)* It
De Modulo-N-Kontrolle *(f)*
En modulo-n check
Es verificación de módulo N *(f)*
Fr contrôle module-n *(m)*
Pt verificação modulo-n *(f)*

controllo numerico *(m)* It
De numerische Steuerung *(f)*
En numerical control
Es control numérico *(m)*
Fr commande numérique *(f)*
Pt controle numérico *(m)*

controllo pari-dispari *(m)* It
De gerade-ungerade Paritätsprüfung *(f)*
En odd-even check
Es control de paridad par-impar *(m)*
Fr contrôle de parité pair-impair *(m)*
Pt verificação par-impar *(f)*

controllo proporzionale *(m)* It
De Proportionalsteuerung *(f)*
En proportional control
Es control proporcional *(m)*
Fr contrôle proportionnel *(m)*
Pt controle proporcional *(m)*

controllo residuo *(m)* It
De Restprüfung *(f)*
En residue check
Es verificación por residuo *(f)*
Fr contrôle de résidu *(m)*
Pt verificação de resíduos *(f)*

control manual *(m)* Es
De Handsteuerung *(f)*
En manual control
Fr commande manuelle *(f)*
It controllo manuale *(m)*
Pt controle manual *(m)*

control numérico *(m)* Es
De numerische Steuerung *(f)*
En numerical control
Fr commande numérique *(f)*
It controllo numerico *(m)*
Pt controle numérico *(m)*

controlo *(m) n* Pt
De Steuerung *(f)*
En control
Es control *(m)*
Fr contrôle *(m)*
It controllo *(m)*

control panel En
De Steuertafel *(f)*
Es panel de control *(m)*
Fr panneau de contrôle *(m)*
It pannello di comando *(m)*
Pt painel de controlo *(m)*

control por excepción *(m)* Es
De Ausnahmeprinzipsystem *(n)*
En exception principle system
Fr gestion par exception *(f)*
It sistema a principio di eccezione *(m)*
Pt sistema de princípio de excepção *(m)*

control por vaciado *(m)* Es
De Speicherauszugsprüfung *(f)*
En dump check
Fr contrôle par vidage *(m)*
It controllo del dump *(m)*
Pt verificação de descarga *(f)*

control proporcional *(m)* Es
De Proportionalsteuerung *(f)*
En proportional control
Fr contrôle proportionnel *(m)*
It controllo proporzionale *(m)*
Pt controle proporcional *(m)*

control register En
De Steuerregister *(n)*
Es registro de control *(m)*
Fr registre de contrôle *(m)*
It registro di controllo *(m)*
Pt registo de controlo *(m)*

control sequence En
De Steuerfolge *(f)*
Es secuencia de control *(f)*

Fr séquence de contrôle *(f)*
It sequenza di controllo *(f)*
Pt sequência de controlo *(f)*

control statement En
De Steueranweisung *(f)*
Es sentencia de control *(f)*
Fr ordre de contrôle *(m)*
It statement di controllo *(m)*
Pt afirmação de controlo *(f)*

control supervisor *(m)* Es
De Überwachungs-steuerung *(f)*
En supervisory control
Fr commande de superviseur *(f)*
It controllo di supervisione *(m)*
Pt controle de supervisão *(m)*

control theory En
De Steuertheorie *(f)*
Es teoría de control *(f)*
Fr théorie de contrôle *(f)*
It teoria del controllo *(f)*
Pt teoria de controlo *(f)*

control total En
De Kontrollsumme *(f)*
Es total de control *(m)*
Fr total de contrôle *(m)*
It totale di controllo *(m)*
Pt total de controlo *(m)*

control unit En
De Leitwerk *(n)*
Es unidad de control *(f)*
Fr unité de contrôle *(f)*
It unità di controllo *(f)*
Pt unidade de controlo *(f)*

control word En
De Schablone *(f)*
Es palabra de control *(f)*
Fr mot de contrôle *(m)*
It voce di controllo *(f)*
Pt palavra de controlo *(f)*

conversão *(f) n* Pt
De Umwandlung *(f)*
En conversion
Es conversión *(f)*
Fr conversion *(f)*
It conversione *(f)*

conversão automática de dados *(f)* Pt
De automatische Datenumwandlung *(f)*
En automatic data conversion
Es conversión automática de datos *(f)*
Fr conversion de données automatique *(f)*
It conversione automatica dei dati *(f)*

conversão de arquivo *(f)* Pt
De Dateiumwandlung *(f)*
En file conversion
Es conversión de ficheros *(f)*
Fr conversion de fichiers *(f)*
It conversione del file *(f)*

conversão de binário em decimal *(f)* Pt
De Binär-Dezimal-umwandlung *(f)*
En binary-to-decimal conversion
Es conversión de binario a decimal *(f)*
Fr conversion de binaire en décimal *(f)*
It conversione da decimale a binario *(f)*

conversational mode En
De Dialogbetriebsart *(f)*
Es modo diálogo *(m)*
Fr mode dialogué *(m)*
It modalità conversazionale *(f)*
Pt modo conversacional *(m)*

conversion *n* En, Fr
De Umwandlung *(f)*
Es conversión *(f)*
It conversione *(f)*
Pt conversão *(f)*

conversión *(f) n* Es
De Umwandlung *(f)*
En conversion
Fr conversion *(f)*
It conversione *(f)*
Pt conversão *(f)*

conversión automática de datos *(f)* Es
De automatische Datenumwandlung *(f)*
En automatic data conversion
Fr conversion de données automatique *(f)*
It conversione automatica dei dati *(f)*
Pt conversão automática de dados *(f)*

conversion de binaire en décimal *(f)* Fr
De Binär-Dezimal-umwandlung *(f)*
En binary-to-decimal conversion
Es conversión de binario a decimal *(f)*
It conversione da decimale a binario *(f)*
Pt conversão de binário em decimal *(f)*

conversión de binario a decimal *(f)* Es
De Binär-Dezimal-umwandlung *(f)*
En binary-to-decimal conversion
Fr conversion de binaire en décimal *(f)*
It conversione da decimale a binario *(f)*
Pt conversão de binário em decimal *(f)*

conversion de données automatique *(f)* Fr
De automatische Datenumwandlung *(f)*
En automatic data conversion
Es conversión automática de datos *(f)*
It conversione automatica dei dati *(f)*
Pt conversão automática de dados *(f)*

conversión de ficheros *(f)* Es
De Dateiumwandlung *(f)*
En file conversion
Fr conversion de fichiers *(f)*
It conversione del file *(f)*
Pt conversão de arquivo *(f)*

conversion de fichiers *(f)* Fr
De Dateiumwandlung *(f)*
En file conversion
Es conversión de ficheros *(f)*
It conversione del file *(f)*
Pt conversão de arquivo *(f)*

conversione *(f) n* It
De Umwandlung *(f)*
En conversion
Es conversión *(f)*
Fr conversion *(f)*
Pt conversão *(f)*

conversione automatica dei dati *(f)* It
De automatische Datenumwandlung *(f)*
En automatic data conversion
Es conversión automática de datos *(f)*
Fr conversion de données automatique *(f)*
Pt conversão automática de dados *(f)*

conversione da decimale a binario *(f)* It
De Binär-Dezimal-umwandlung *(f)*
En binary-to-decimal conversion
Es conversión de binario a decimal *(f)*
Fr conversion de binaire en décimal *(f)*
Pt conversão de binário em decimal *(f)*

conversione del file *(f)* It
De Dateiumwandlung *(f)*
En file conversion

Es conversión de ficheros *(f)*
Fr conversion de fichiers *(f)*
Pt conversão de arquivo *(f)*

conversor *(m) n* Pt
De Umwandler *(m)*
En converter
Es convertidor *(m)*
Fr convertisseur *(m)*
It convertitore *(m)*

conversor análogo-digital *(m)* Pt
De Analog-Digital-umwandler *(m)*
En analog-digital converter
Es convertidor analógico-digital *(m)*
Fr convertisseur analogique-numérique *(m)*
It convertitore analogico-digitale *(m)*

conversor de série em paralelo *(m)* Pt
De Reihen-Parallelumwandler *(m)*
En serial-parallel converter
Es convertidor serie-paralelo *(m)*
Fr convertisseur série-parallèle *(m)*
It convertitore serie-parallelo *(m)*

conversor digital-análogo *(m)* Pt
De Digital-Analogumwandler *(m)*
En digital-analog converter
Es convertidor de digital-analógico *(m)*
Fr convertisseur numérique-analogique *(m)*
It convertitore digitale-analogico *(m)*

convert *vb* En
De umwandeln
Es convertir
Fr convertir
It convertire
Pt converter

converter *n* En
De Umwandler *(m)*
Es convertidor *(m)*
Fr convertisseur *(m)*
It convertitore *(m)*
Pt conversor *(m)*

converter *vb* Pt
De umwandeln
En convert
Es convertir
Fr convertir
It convertire

convertidor *(m) n* Es
De Umwandler *(m)*
En converter
Fr convertisseur *(m)*
It convertitore *(m)*
Pt conversor *(m)*

convertidor analógico-digital *(m)* Es
De Analog-Digitalumwandler *(m)*
En analog-digital converter
Fr convertisseur analogique-numérique *(m)*
It convertitore analogico-digitale *(m)*
Pt conversor análogo-digital *(m)*

convertidor de digital-analógico *(m)* Es
De Digital-Analogumwandler *(m)*
En digital-analog converter
Fr convertisseur numérique-analogique *(m)*
It convertitore digitale-analogico *(m)*
Pt conversor digital-análogo *(m)*

convertidor serie-paralelo *(m)* Es
De Reihen-Parallelumwandler *(m)*
En serial-parallel converter
Fr convertisseur série-parallèle *(m)*
It convertitore serie-parallelo *(m)*
Pt conversor de série em paralelo *(m)*

convertir *vb* Es, Fr
De umwandeln
En convert
It convertire
Pt converter

convertire *vb* It
De umwandeln
En convert
Es convertir
Fr convertir
Pt converter

convertisseur *(m) n* Fr
De Umwandler *(m)*
En converter
Es convertidor *(m)*
It convertitore *(m)*
Pt conversor *(m)*

convertisseur analogique-numérique *(m)* Fr
De Analog-Digitalumwandler *(m)*
En analog-digital converter
Es convertidor analógico-digital *(m)*
It convertitore analogico-digitale *(m)*
Pt conversor análogo-digital *(m)*

convertisseur numérique-analogique *(m)* Fr
De Digital-Analogumwandler *(m)*
En digital-analog converter
Es convertidor de digital-analógico *(m)*
It convertitore digitale-analogico *(m)*
Pt conversor digital-análogo *(m)*

convertisseur série-parallèle *(m)* Fr
De Reihen-Parallelumwandler *(m)*
En serial-parallel converter
Es convertidor serie-paralelo *(m)*
It convertitore serie-parallelo *(m)*
Pt conversor de série em paralelo *(m)*

convertitore *(m) n* It
De Umwandler *(m)*
En converter
Es convertidor *(m)*
Fr convertisseur *(m)*
Pt conversor *(m)*

convertitore analogico-digitale *(m)* It
De Analog-Digitalumwandler *(m)*
En analog-digital converter
Es convertidor analógico-digital *(m)*
Fr convertisseur analogique-numérique *(m)*
Pt conversor análogo-digital *(m)*

convertitore digitale-analogico *(m)* It
De Digital-Analogumwandler *(m)*
En digital-analog converter
Es convertidor de digital-analógico *(m)*
Fr convertisseur numérique-analogique *(m)*
Pt conversor digital-análogo *(m)*

convertitore serie-parallelo *(m)* It
De Reihen-Parallelumwandler *(m)*
En serial-parallel converter
Es convertidor serie-paralelo *(m)*
Fr convertisseur série-parallèle *(m)*
Pt conversor de série em paralelo *(m)*

cópia dura *(f)* Pt
De dauerhafter Text *(m)*
En hard copy
Es salida impresa *(f)*
Fr document en clair *(m)*
It copia stampata *(f)*

copiage *(m) n* Fr
De Replikation *(f)*
En replication
Es respuesta *(f)*
It ripetizione *(f)*
Pt resposta *(f)*

copiar *vb* Es, Pt
De kopieren
En copy
Fr copier
It copiare

copiare *vb* It
De kopieren
En copy
Es copiar
Fr copier
Pt copiar

copia stampata *(f)* It
De dauerhafter Text *(m)*
En hard copy
Es salida impresa *(f)*
Fr document en clair *(m)*
Pt cópia dura *(f)*

copier *vb* Fr
De kopieren
En copy
Es copiar
It copiare
Pt copiar

copy *vb* En
De kopieren
Es copiar
Fr copier
It copiare
Pt copiar

cordone di connessione *(m)* It
De Schaltschnur *(f)*
En patchcord
Es cable de conexión *(m)*
Fr fiche de connexion *(f)*
Pt cabo de concerto *(m)*

core *n* En
De Kern *(m)*
Es núcleo *(m)*
Fr mémoire centrale *(f)*
It memoria centrale *(f)*
Pt núcleo *(m)*

core memory (or **store**) En
De Kernspeicher *(m)*
Es memoria de núcleos *(f)*
Fr mémoire à tores *(f)*
It memoria a nuclei *(f)*
Pt memória de núcleo *(f)*

coriandoli di perforazione *(m)* It
De Stanzrückstand *(m)*
En chad
Es confeti *(m)*
Fr confetti *(m)*
Pt recorte *(m)*

correction *(f) n* Fr
De Korrektur *(f)*
En patch
Es parche *(m)*
It connessione *(f)*
Pt remendo *(m)*

corrective maintenance En
De Verbesserungs-wartung *(f)*
Es mantenimiento correctivo *(m)*
Fr entretien correctif *(m)*
It manutenzione correttiva *(f)*
Pt manutenção correctiva *(f)*

correggere un programma It
De korrigieren (ein Programm)
En patch
Es parchear un programa
Fr corriger un programme
Pt remendar uma programa

correspondencia *(f) n* Es
De Übereinstimmung *(f)*
En match
Fr assortiment *(m)*
It accoppiamento *(m)*
Pt equiparação *(f)*

corriger un programme Fr
De korrigieren (ein Programm)
En patch
Es parchear un programa
It correggere un programma
Pt remendar uma programa

corrupção *(f) n* Pt
De Entstellung *(f)*
En corruption
Es corrupción *(f)*
Fr corruption *(f)*
It corruzione *(f)*

corrupción *(f) n* Es
De Entstellung *(f)*
En corruption
Fr corruption *(f)*
It corruzione *(f)*
Pt corrupção *(f)*

corruption *n* En, Fr *(f)*
De Entstellung *(f)*
Es corrupción *(f)*
It corruzione *(f)*
Pt corrupção *(f)*

corruzione *(f) n* It
De Entstellung *(f)*
En corruption
Es corrupción *(f)*
Fr corruption *(f)*
Pt corrupção *(f)*

costanti *(m pl) n* It
De Konstante *(pl)*
En constants
Es constantes *(f pl)*
Fr constantes *(f pl)*
Pt constantes *(f pl)*

costruzione di modelli *(f)* It
De Modellaufbau *(m)*
En model building
Es construcción de modelos *(f)*
Fr construction de modèles *(f)*
Pt construção de modelo *(f)*

counter *n* En
De Zähler *(m)*
Es contador *(m)*
Fr compteur *(m)*
It contatore *(m)*
Pt contador *(m)*

coup d'essai *(m)* Fr
De Versuchslauf *(m)*
En dry run
Es pasada en seco *(f)*
It passo a prova *(m)*
Pt passagem a seco *(f)*

coupleur acoustique *(m)* Fr
De akustischer Koppler *(m)*
En acoustic coupler
Es acoplador acústico *(m)*
It accoppiatore acustico *(m)*
Pt acoplador acústico *(m)*

courant porteur *(m)* Fr
De Ladungsträger *(m)*
En carrier
Es portador *(m)*
It supporto *(m)*
Pt portador *(m)*

crash *n* En
De Durchschlag *(m)*
Es choque *(m)*
Fr accélération *(f)*
It urto *(m)*
Pt colisão *(f)*

crash *vb* En
De durchschlagen
Es quebrar
Fr accélérer
It urtare
Pt colidir

creación de monotonías *(f)* Es
De Vorsortierung *(f)*
En pre-sort
Fr tri préalable *(m)*
It pre-selezione *(f)*
Pt pré-classificação *(f)*

crear monotonías Es
De vorsortieren
En pre-sort
Fr trier préalablement
It pre-selezionare
Pt pré-classificado

cribar *vb* Es
De schirmen
En screen
Fr sélectionner
It schermare
Pt mascarar

cross check En
De Gegenprüfung *(f)*
Es verificación cruzada *(f)*
Fr contre-vérification *(f)*
It verifica generale completa *(f)*
Pt verificação cruzada *(f)*

cross check En
De gegenprüfen
Es verificar por comparación
Fr contre-vérifier
It contra-verificare
Pt contra-verificar

cross compiler En
De Gegenkompilierer *(m)*
Es compilador cruzado *(m)*
Fr compilateur croisé *(m)*
It compilatore incrociato *(m)*
Pt compilador cruzado *(m)*

cross talk En
De Nebensprechen *(n)*
Es diafonía *(f)*
Fr diaphonie *(f)*
It diafonia *(f)*
Pt diafonia *(f)*

cryogenic memory En
De kryogenischer Speicher *(m)*
Es memoria criogénica *(f)*
Fr mémoire cryogénique *(f)*
It memoria criogenica *(f)*
Pt memória criogénica *(f)*

cuadro de alfileres *(m)* Es
De Steckplatte *(f)*
En pinboard
Fr tableau à aiguilles *(m)*
It pannello a spine *(m)*
Pt prancheta de alfinetes *(f)*

cuadro de conexión *(m)* Es
De Steckerbrett *(n)*
En plugboard
Fr tableau de connexions *(m)*
It pannello di connessioni *(m)*
Pt placa de conexões eléctricas *(f)*

cuadro de control *(m)* Es
De Schalttafel *(f)*
En patchboard
Fr tableau de connexions *(m)*
It pannello di connessione *(m)*
Pt placa de concerto *(f)*

cuantificación *(f) n* Es
De Quantisierung *(f)*
En quantization
Fr quantification *(f)*
It quantizzazione *(f)*
Pt quantização *(f)*

cuantificador *(m) n* Es
De Quantisierer *(m)*
En quantizer
Fr quantificateur *(m)*
It quantizzatore *(f)*
Pt quantizador *(m)*

cuarta-generación *adj* Es
De viertgeneration
En fourth-generation
Fr quatrième-génération
It quarta-generazione
Pt quarta-geração

cuasi-instrucción *(f) n* Es
De Quasianweisung *(f)*
En quasi instruction
Fr quasi-instruction *(f)*
It quasi istruzione *(f)*
Pt quase-instrução *(f)*

cubo *(m) n* Pt
De Nabe *(f)*
En hub
Es boca *(f)*
Fr moyeu porte-bobine *(m)*
It mozzo *(m)*

cuenta de ciclos *(f)* Es
De Gangzählung *(f)*
En cycle count
Fr comptage de cycles *(m)*
It conteggio dei cicli *(m)*
Pt contagem de ciclos *(f)*

current-loop interface En
De Stromschleifen-Schnittstelle *(f)*
Es acoplamiento mutuo por bucle de corriente *(m)*
Fr interface boucle courant *(f)*
It interfaccia del ciclo corrente *(f)*
Pt interface de circuito de corrente *(f)*

curso *(m) n* Es
De Zugriffspfad *(m)*
En path
Fr branchement *(m)*
It percorso *(m)*
Pt caminho *(m)*

curso do papel *(m)* Pt
De Papiervorschub *(m)*
En paper throw
Es salto del papel *(m)*
Fr saut de papier *(m)*
It salto di pagina (di un modulo) *(m)*

customer-acceptance test En
De Kundenabnahme-prüfung *(f)*
Es ensayo de aceptación por el cliente *(m)*
Fr test de réception en clientèle *(m)*
It controllo accettazione clienti *(m)*
Pt teste de aceitação de cliente *(m)*

cybernetics *n* En
De Kybernetik *(f)*
Es cibernética *(f)*
Fr cybernétique *(f)*
It cibernetica *(f)*
Pt cibernética *(f)*

cybernétique *(f) n* Fr
De Kybernetik *(f)*
En cybernetics
Es cibernética *(f)*
It cibernetica *(f)*
Pt cibernética *(f)*

cycle *n* En, Fr *(m)*
De Gang *(m)*
Es ciclo *(m)*
It ciclo *(m)*
Pt ciclo *(m)*

cycle count En
De Gangzählung *(f)*
Es cuenta de ciclos *(f)*
Fr comptage de cycles *(m)*
It conteggio dei cicli *(m)*
Pt contagem de ciclos *(f)*

cyclic code En
De zyklischer Code *(m)*
Es código cíclico *(m)*
Fr code cyclique *(m)*
It codice ciclico *(m)*
Pt código cíclico *(m)*

cylinder *n* En
De Zylinder *(m)*
Es cilindro *(m)*
Fr cylindre *(m)*
It cilindro *(m)*
Pt cilindro *(m)*

cylindre *(m) n* Fr
De Zylinder *(m)*
En cylinder
Es cilindro *(m)*
It cilindro *(m)*
Pt cilindro *(m)*

D

dados *(m pl) n* Pt
De Daten *(pl)*
En data
Es datos *(m pl)*
Fr données *(f pl)*
It dati *(m pl)*

dados de controlo *(m pl)* Pt
De Steuerungsdaten *(pl)*
En control data
Es datos de control *(m pl)*
Fr données de contrôle *(f pl)*
It dati di controllo *(m pl)*

dados de ensaio *(m pl)* Pt
De Prüfdaten *(pl)*
En test data
Es datos para ensayo *(m pl)*
Fr donnée d'essai *(f)*
It dati di prova *(m pl)*

dados de transacção *(m pl)* Pt
De Transaktionsdaten *(pl)*
En transaction data
Es datos de transacciones *(m pl)*
Fr mouvements *(m pl)*
It dati della transazione *(m pl)*

dados em bruto *(m pl)* Pt
De Ursprungsdaten *(pl)*
En raw data
Es datos sin procesar *(m pl)*
Fr données brutes *(f pl)*
It dati crudi *(m pl)*

daisywheel printer En
De Gänseblümchen-Typenraddrucker *(m)*
Es impresora de ruedas de mariposa *(f)*
Fr imprimante à marguerite *(f)*
It stampatrice daisywheel *(f)*
Pt impressora margarida *(f)*

Dämpfung *(f) n* De
En damping
Es amortiguamiento *(m)*
Fr amortissement *(m)*
It smorzamento *(m)*
Pt amortecimento *(m)*

damping *n* En
De Dämpfung *(f)*
Es amortiguamiento *(m)*
Fr amortissement *(m)*
It smorzamento *(m)*
Pt amortecimento *(m)*

data *n* En
De Daten *(pl)*
Es datos *(m pl)*
Fr données *(f pl)*
It dati *(m pl)*
Pt dados *(m pl)*

data bank En
De Datenbank *(f)*
Es banco de datos *(m)*
Fr banque de données *(f)*
It banca dei dati *(f)*
Pt banco de dados *(m)*

database *n* En
De Datenbasis *(f)*
Es base de datos *(f)*
Fr base de données *(f)*
It base dei dati *(f)*
Pt base de dados *(f)*

database management system (DBMS) En
De Datenverwaltungs-system *(n)*
Es sistema de gestión del banco de datos *(m)*
Fr système de gestion de base de données (SGBD) *(m)*
It sistema di gestione della banca dei dati *(m)*
Pt sistema de management de base de dados *(m)*

data cartridge En
De Datenpatrone *(f)*
Es cartucho de datos *(m)*
Fr cartouche de données *(f)*
It cartuccia di dati *(f)*
Pt carga de dados *(f)*

data cleaning En
De Datenlöschung *(f)*
Es limpieza de los datos *(f)*
Fr nettoyage de données *(f)*
It pulizia dei dati *(f)*
Pt apagamento de dados *(m)*

data collection En
De Datenerfassung *(f)*
Es recopilación de datos *(f)*
Fr collecte de données *(f)*
It raccolta dei dati *(f)*
Pt colecção de dados *(f)*

data description language (DDL) En
De Datenbeschreib-ungssprache *(f)*
Es lenguaje de descripción de datos *(m)*
Fr langage de description des données *(m)*
It linguaggio di descrizione dei dati *(m)*
Pt linguagem de descrição de dados *(f)*

data entry En
De Dateneingabe *(f)*
Es entrada de datos *(f)*
Fr saisie de données *(f)*
It ingresso dei dati *(m)*
Pt entrada de dados *(f)*

data item En
De Datenfeld *(n)*
Es unidad de información *(f)*
Fr donnée élémentaire *(f)*
It voce di dato *(f)*
Pt item de dados *(m)*

data link En
De Datenübermitt-lungsabschnitt *(m)*
Es enlace para transmisión de datos *(m)*
Fr liaison de transmission *(f)*
It collegamento di dati *(m)*
Pt elemento de ligação de dados *(m)*

data name En
De Datenname *(m)*
Es nombre de datos *(m)*
Fr nom des données *(m)*
It nome dei dati *(m)*
Pt nome de dados *(m)*

data network En
De Datennetz *(n)*
Es red para transmisión de datos *(f)*
Fr réseau de transmission de données *(m)*
It rete di dati *(f)*
Pt rede de dados *(f)*

data preparation En
De Datenvorbereitung *(f)*
Es preparación de los datos *(f)*
Fr préparation des données *(f)*
It preparazione dei dati *(f)*
Pt preparação de dados *(f)*

data processing (DP) En
De Datenverarbeitung *(f)*
Es proceso de datos *(m)*
Fr traitement de l'information *(m)*
It elaborazione dei dati *(f)*
Pt tratamento de dados *(m)*

data protection En
De Datenschutz *(m)*
Es protección de los datos *(f)*
Fr protection des données *(f)*
It protezione dei dati *(f)*
Pt protecção de dados *(f)*

data reduction En
De Datenverdichtung *(f)*
Es reducción de datos *(f)*
Fr réduction de données *(f)*
It riduzione dei dati *(f)*
Pt redução de dados *(f)*

data transmission En
De Datenübertragung *(f)*
Es transmisión de datos *(f)*
Fr transmission de données *(f)*
It trasmissione dei dati *(f)*
Pt transmissão de dados *(f)*

Datei *(f) n* De
En file
Es fichero *(m)*
Fr fichier *(m)*
It file *(m)*
Pt arquivo *(m)*

Dateiende *(n) n* De
En end of file (EOF)
Es fin de fichero *(m)*
Fr fin de fichier *(f)*
It fine del file *(f)*
Pt fim de arquivo *(m)*

Dateikennsatz *(m) n* De
En file label
Es etiqueta de fichero *(f)*
Fr étiquette de fichier *(f)*
It etichetta del file *(f)*
Pt rótulo de arquivo *(m)*

Dateikennzeichnung *(f) n* De
En file identification
Es identificación del fichero *(f)*
Fr identification de fichier *(f)*
It identificazione del file *(f)*
Pt identificação de arquivo *(f)*

Dateilage *(f) n* De
En location
Es posición *(f)*
Fr emplacement *(m)*
It locazione *(f)*
Pt localização *(f)*

Dateilagezähler *(m) n* De
En location counter
Es contador de posiciones *(m)*
Fr compteur d'emplacement *(m)*
It contatore di locazioni *(m)*
Pt contador de localização *(m)*

Dateischutz *(m) n* De
En file protection
Es protección de fichero *(f)*
Fr protection de fichier *(f)*
It protezione del file *(f)*
Pt protecção de arquivo *(f)*

Dateispeicher *(m) n* De
En file store
Es memoria fichero *(f)*
Fr mémoire fichier *(f)*
It memoria dei file *(f)*
Pt armazém de arquivo *(m)*

Dateiumwandlung *(f) n* De
En file conversion
Es conversión de ficheros *(f)*
Fr conversion de fichiers *(f)*
It conversione del file *(f)*
Pt conversão de arquivo *(f)*

Dateiwartung *(f) n* De
En file maintenance
Es mantenimiento de ficheros *(m)*
Fr tenue à jour de fichier *(f)*
It manutenzione del file *(f)*
Pt manutenção de arquivo *(f)*

Daten *(pl) n* De
En data
Es datos *(m pl)*
Fr données *(f pl)*
It dati *(m pl)*
Pt dados *(m pl)*

Datenaustauschbarkeit *(f) n* De
En portability
Es facultad de ser portátil *(f)*
Fr portabilité *(f)*
It portabilità *(f)*
Pt portatilidade *(f)*

Datenbank *(f) n* De
En data bank
Es banco de datos *(m)*
Fr banque de données *(f)*
It banca dei dati *(f)*
Pt banco de dados *(m)*

Datenbank-verwaltungs-system *(n) n* De
En database management system
Es sistema de gestión del banco de datos *(m)*
Fr système de gestion de base de données *(m)*
It sistema di gestione della banca dei dati *(m)*
Pt sistema de management de base de dados *(m)*

Datenbasis *(f) n* De
En database
Es base de datos *(f)*
Fr base de données *(f)*
It base dei dati *(f)*
Pt base de dados *(f)*

Datenbeschreib-ungssprache *(f) n* De
En data description language (DDL)
Es lenguaje de descripción de datos *(m)*
Fr langage de description des données *(m)*
It linguaggio di descrizione dei dati *(m)*
Pt linguagem de descrição de dados *(f)*

Datenblock *(m) n* De
En block
Es bloque *(m)*
Fr bloc *(m)*
It blocco *(m)*
Pt bloco *(m)*

Dateneingabe *(f) n* De
En data entry
Es entrada de datos *(f)*
Fr saisie de données *(f)*
It ingresso dei dati *(m)*
Pt entrada de dados *(f)*

Datenerfassung *(f) n* De
En data collection
Es recopilación de datos *(f)*
Fr collecte de données *(f)*
It raccolta dei dati *(f)*
Pt colecção de dados *(f)*

Datenfeld *(n) n* De
En data item
Es unidad de información *(f)*
Fr donnée élémentaire *(f)*
It voce di dato *(f)*
Pt item de dados *(m)*

Datenfeldkonstruktion *(f) n* De
En item design
Es diseño de elementos *(m)*
Fr définition du découpage des articles *(f)*
It disegno delle voci *(m)*
Pt desenho de ítem *(m)*

Datenlöschung *(f) n* De
En data cleaning
Es limpieza de los datos *(f)*
Fr nettoyage de données *(f)*
It pulizia dei dati *(f)*
Pt apagamento de dados *(m)*

Datenname *(m) n* De
En data name
Es nombre de datos *(m)*
Fr nom des données *(m)*
It nome dei dati *(m)*
Pt nome de dados *(m)*

Datennetz *(n) n* De
En data network
Es red para transmisión de datos *(f)*
Fr réseau de transmission de données *(m)*
It rete di dati *(f)*
Pt rede de dados *(f)*

Datenpatrone *(f) n* De
En data cartridge
Es cartucho de datos *(m)*
Fr cartouche de données *(f)*
It cartuccia di dati *(f)*
Pt carga de dados *(f)*

Datenschutz *(m) n* De
En data protection
Es protección de los datos *(f)*

Fr protection des données *(f)*
It protezione dei dati *(f)*
Pt protecção de dados *(f)*

Datenübermittlungsabschnitt *(m)* *n* De
En data link
Es enlace para transmisión de datos *(m)*
Fr liaison de transmission *(f)*
It collegamento di dati *(m)*
Pt elemento de ligação de dados *(m)*

Datenübertragung *(f)* *n* De
En data transmission
Es transmisión de datos *(f)*
Fr transmission de données *(f)*
It trasmissione dei dati *(f)*
Pt transmissão de dados *(f)*

Datenübertragungsumschaltung *(f)* *n* De
En escape character
Es carácter de escape *(m)*
Fr caractère échappatoire *(m)*
It carattere di uscita *(m)*
Pt carácter de escape *(m)*

Datenverarbeitung *(f)* *n* De
En data processing (DP)
Es proceso de datos *(m)*
Fr traitement de l'information *(m)*
It elaborazione dei dati *(f)*
Pt tratamento de dados *(m)*

Datenverdichtung *(f)* *n* De
En data reduction
Es reducción de datos *(f)*
Fr réduction de données *(f)*
It riduzione dei dati *(f)*
Pt redução de dados *(f)*

Datenverwaltungssystem *(n)* *n* De
En database management system (DBMS)
Es sistema de gestión del banco de datos *(m)*
Fr système de gestion de base de données (SGBD) *(m)*
It sistema di gestione della banca dei dati *(m)*
Pt sistema de management de base de dados *(m)*

Datenvorbereitung *(f)* *n* De
En data preparation
Es preparación de los datos *(f)*
Fr préparation des données *(f)*
It preparazione dei dati *(f)*
Pt preparação de dados *(f)*

dati *(m pl)* *n* It
De Daten *(pl)*
En data
Es datos *(m pl)*
Fr données *(f pl)*
Pt dados *(m pl)*

dati crudi *(m pl)* It
De Ursprungsdaten *(pl)*
En raw data
Es datos sin procesar *(m pl)*
Fr données brutes *(f pl)*
Pt dados em bruto *(m pl)*

dati della transazione *(m pl)* It
De Transaktionsdaten *(pl)*
En transaction data
Es datos de transacciones *(m pl)*
Fr mouvements *(m pl)*
Pt dados de transacção *(m pl)*

dati di controllo *(m pl)* It
De Steuerungsdaten *(pl)*
En control data
Es datos de control *(m pl)*
Fr données de contrôle *(f pl)*
Pt dados de controlo *(m pl)*

dati di prova *(m pl)* It
De Prüfdaten *(pl)*
En test data
Es datos para ensayo *(m pl)*
Fr donnée d'essai *(f)*
Pt dados de ensaio *(m pl)*

datos *(m pl)* *n* Es
De Daten *(pl)*
En data
Fr données *(f pl)*
It dati *(m pl)*
Pt dados *(m pl)*

datos de control *(m pl)* Es
De Steuerungsdaten *(pl)*
En control data
Fr données de contrôle *(f pl)*
It dati di controllo *(m pl)*
Pt dados de controlo *(m pl)*

datos de transacciones *(m pl)* Es
De Transaktionsdaten *(pl)*
En transaction data
Fr mouvements *(m pl)*
It dati della transazione *(m pl)*
Pt dados de transacção *(m pl)*

datos para ensayo *(m pl)* Es
De Prüfdaten *(pl)*
En test data
Fr donnée d'essai *(f)*
It dati di prova *(m pl)*
Pt dados de ensaio *(m pl)*

datos sin procesar *(m pl)* Es
De Ursprungsdaten *(pl)*
En raw data
Fr données brutes *(f pl)*
It dati crudi *(m pl)*
Pt dados em bruto *(m pl)*

dauerhafter Text *(m)* De
En hard copy
Es salida impresa *(f)*
Fr document en clair *(m)*
It copia stampata *(f)*
Pt cópia dura *(f)*

Dauerspeicher *(m)* *n* De
En permanent memory
Es memoria permanente *(f)*
Fr mémoire permanente *(f)*
It memoria permanente *(f)*
Pt memória permanente *(f)*

dead time En
De Totzeit *(f)*
Es tiempo muerto *(m)*
Fr temps mort *(m)*
It tempo morto *(m)*
Pt tempo morto *(m)*

débilmente acoplado Es
De lose gekoppelt
En loosely coupled
Fr lâchement couplé
It accoppiado lentamente
Pt acoplado de forma solta

débit *(m)* *n* Fr
De Durchfluß *(m)*
En throughput
Es capacidad de tratamiento *(f)*
It capacità di trattamento *(f)*
Pt capacidade de tratamento *(f)*

débit de bits *(m)* Fr
De Binärzeichengeschwindigkeit *(f)*
En bit rate
Es tasa en bits *(f)*
It volume di bit *(m)*
Pt taxa de bit *(f)*

débit en bauds *(m)* Fr
De Baudgeschwindigkeit *(f)*
En baud rate

Es velocidad en baudios *(f)*
It numero di baud *(m)*
Pt taxa de baud *(f)*

debug *vb* En
De fehlersuchen
Es depurar
Fr mettre au point
It mettere a punto un programma
Pt desparasitar

debugging aid En
De Fehlersuchhilfe *(f)*
Es ayuda a la depuración *(f)*
Fr outil de mise au point *(m)*
It strumento di messa a punto (di un programma) *(m)*
Pt ajuda de desparasitação *(f)*

década *(f) n* Es, Pt
De Dekade *(f)*
En decade
Fr décade *(f)*
It decade *(f)*

decade *n* En; It *(f)*
De Dekade *(f)*
Es década *(f)*
Fr décade *(f)*
Pt década *(f)*

décade *(f) n* Fr
De Dekade *(f)*
En decade
Es década *(f)*
It decade *(f)*
Pt década *(f)*

décalage *(m) n* Fr
De Stellenverschiebung *(f)*
En shift
Es desplazamiento *(m)*
It riporto *(m)*
Pt mudança *(f)*

décalage à droite *(m)* Fr
De Rechtsschiebung *(f)*
En right shift
Es desplazamiento a la derecha *(m)*
It spostamento a destra *(m)*
Pt mudança à direita *(f)*

décalage à gauche *(m)* Fr
De Linksverschiebung *(f)*
En left shift
Es desplazamiento a la izquierda *(m)*
It spostamento a sinistra *(m)*
Pt mudança à esquerda *(f)*

décalage arithmétique *(m)* Fr
De arithmetische Stellenverschiebung *(f)*
En arithmetic shift
Es desplazamiento aritmético *(m)*
It spostamento aritmetico *(m)*
Pt mudança aritmética *(f)*

décalage logique *(m)* Fr
De logische Verschiebung *(f)*
En logic(al) shift
Es desplazamiento lógico *(m)*
It spostamento logico *(m)*
Pt mudança lógica *(f)*

décaler *vb* Fr
De versetzen
En shift
Es desplazar
It spostare (dati)
Pt mudar

decalque *(m) n* Pt
De Aufzeichnungslinie *(f)*
En trace
Es traza *(f)*
Fr trace *(f)*
It traccia *(f)*

deceleration time En
De Verzögerungszeit *(f)*
Es tiempo de deceleración *(m)*
Fr temps de décélération *(m)*
It tempo di decelerazione *(m)*
Pt tempo de desaceleração *(m)*

decimal *adj* En, Es, Pt
De dezimal
Fr décimal
It decimale

décimal *adj* Fr
De dezimal
En decimal
Es decimal
It decimale
Pt decimal

decimal codificado en binario (DCB) *(m)* Es
De binärcodierte Dezimaldarstellung *(f)*
En binary-coded decimal (BCD)
Fr décimale codée en binaire (DCB) *(f)*
It decimale codificato in binario (DCB) *(m)*
Pt decimal de código binário (DCB) *(m)*

decimal de código binário (DCB) *(m)* Pt
De binärcodierte Dezimaldarstellung *(f)*
En binary-coded decimal (BCD)
Es decimal codificado en binario (DCB) *(m)*
Fr décimale codée en binaire (DCB) *(f)*
It decimale codificato in binario (DCB) *(m)*

decimale *adj* It
De dezimal
En decimal
Es decimal
Fr décimal
Pt decimal

décimale codée en binaire (DCB) *(f)* Fr
De binärcodierte Dezimaldarstellung *(f)*
En binary-coded decimal (BCD)
Es decimal codificado en binario (DCB) *(m)*
It decimale codificato in binario (DCB) *(m)*
Pt decimal de código binário (DCB) *(m)*

decimale codificato in binario (DCB) *(m)* It
De binärcodierte Dezimaldarstellung *(f)*
En binary-coded decimal (BCD)
Es decimal codificado en binario (DCB) *(m)*
Fr décimale codée en binaire (DCB) *(f)*
Pt decimal de código binário (DCB) *(m)*

decimal notation En
De Dezimaldarstellung *(f)*
Es notación decimal *(f)*
Fr notation décimale *(f)*
It notazione decimale *(f)*
Pt notação decimal *(f)*

decimal-to-binary notation En
De Dezimal-Binär-darstellung *(f)*
Es notación de decimal a binario *(f)*
Fr notation décimale-binaire *(f)*
It notazione da decimale a binario *(f)*
Pt notação decimal-a-binária *(f)*

decision box En
De Blockdiagramm-symbol-Entscheidung *(f)*
Es símbolo de decisión *(m)*
Fr symbole de décision *(m)*
It casella di decisione *(f)*
Pt caixa de decisão *(f)*

decision table En
De Entscheidungstabelle *(f)*
Es tabla de decisión *(f)*
Fr table de décision *(f)*
It tavola di decisione *(f)*
Pt tabela de decisão *(f)*

deck (of cards) *n* Am
De Kartensatz *(m)*
En pack (of cards)
Es baraja *(f)*
Fr paquet de cartes *(m)*
It mazzo *(m)*
Pt baralho (de cartas) *(m)*

declarative statement En
De Prozeduranweisung *(f)*
Es sentencia de declaración *(f)*
Fr instruction déclarative *(f)*
It statement di dichiarazione *(m)*
Pt afirmação declarativa *(f)*

declencher *vb* Fr
De triggern
En trigger
Es disparar
It innescare
Pt disparar

decode *vb* En
De entschlüsseln
Es decodificar
Fr décoder
It decodificare
Pt descodificar

decoder *n* En
De Entschlüssler *(m)*
Es decodificador *(m)*
Fr décodeur *(m)*
It decodificatore *(m)*
Pt descodificador *(m)*

décoder *vb* Fr
De entschlüsseln
En decode
Es decodificar
It decodificare
Pt descodificar

décodeur *(m) n* Fr
De Entschlüssler *(m)*
En decoder
Es decodificador *(m)*
It decodificatore *(m)*
Pt descodificador *(m)*

decodificador *(m) n* Es
De Entschlüssler *(m)*
En decoder
Fr décodeur *(m)*
It decodificatore *(m)*
Pt descodificador *(m)*

decodificar *vb* Es
De entschlüsseln
En decode
Fr décoder
It decodificare
Pt descodificar

decodificare *vb* It
De entschlüsseln
En decode
Es decodificar
Fr décoder
Pt descodificar

decodificatore *(m) n* It
De Entschlüssler *(m)*
En decoder
Es decodificador *(m)*
Fr décodeur *(m)*
Pt descodificador *(m)*

décollateur *(m) n* Fr
De Dekollationierer *(m)*
En decollator
Es desglosador *(m)*
It decollatore *(m)*
Pt degolador *(m)*

decollator *n* En
De Dekollationierer *(m)*
Es desglosador *(m)*
Fr décollateur *(m)*
It decollatore *(m)*
Pt degolador *(m)*

decollatore *(m) n* It
De Dekollationierer *(m)*
En decollator
Es desglosador *(m)*
Fr décollateur *(m)*
Pt degolador *(m)*

décondenser *vb* Fr
De auspacken
En unpack
Es desempaquetar
It separare
Pt desembalar

découpage du temps *(m)* Fr
De Zeitscheiben-verfahren *(n)*
En time slice
Es fracción de tiempo *(f)*
It ripartizione di tempo *(f)*
Pt fatia de tempo *(f)*

decrement *n* En
De Dekrement *(n)*
Es decremento *(m)*
Fr décrément *(m)*
It decremento *(m)*
Pt decremento *(m)*

décrément *(m) n* Fr
De Dekrement *(n)*
En decrement
Es decremento *(m)*
It decremento *(m)*
Pt decremento *(m)*

decremento *(m) n* Es, It, Pt
De Dekrement *(n)*
En decrement
Fr décrément *(m)*

dedicado *adj* Es, Pt
De ausschließlich zugeordnet
En dedicated
Fr spécialisé
It dedicato

dedicated *adj* En
De ausschließlich zugeordnet
Es dedicado
Fr spécialisé
It dedicato
Pt dedicado

dedicato *adj* It
De ausschließlich zugeordnet
En dedicated
Es dedicado
Fr spécialisé
Pt dedicado

défaut *(m) n* Fr
De Defekt *(m)*
En bug
Es defecto *(m)*
It difetto *(m)*
Pt perturbação *(f)*

defecto *(m) n* Es
De Defekt *(m)*
En bug
Fr défaut *(m)*
It difetto *(m)*
Pt perturbação *(f)*

defeito *(m) n* Pt
De Defekt *(m)*
En fault
Es fallo *(m)*
Fr faute *(f)*
It guasto *(m)*

Defekt *(m) n* De
En bug; fault
Es defecto; fallo *(m)*
Fr défaut; faute *(m f)*
It difetto; guasto *(m)*
Pt defeito; perturbação *(m f)*

defekttolerant *adj* De
En fault-tolerant
Es tolerante con las averías
Fr insensible aux défaillances
It tollerante di guasto
Pt tolerante relativamente a erros

défilement-avancement bande *(m)* Fr
De Bandvorausvorschub *(m)*
En advance-feed tape
Es cinta de alimentación por arrastre *(f)*
It avanzarealimentare nastro *(m)*
Pt fita de alimentação por avanço *(f)*

definição do problema *(f)* Pt
De Problembestimmung *(f)*
En problem definition
Es definición del problema *(f)*
Fr définition des problèmes *(f)*
It definizione del problema *(f)*

definición del problema *(f)* Es
De Problembestimmung *(f)*
En problem definition
Fr définition des problèmes *(f)*
It definizione del problema *(f)*
Pt definição do problema *(f)*

définition des problèmes *(f)* Fr
De Problembestimmung *(f)*
En problem definition
Es definición del problema *(f)*
It definizione del problema *(f)*
Pt definição do problema *(f)*

définition du découpage des articles *(f)* Fr
De Datenfeld-konstruktion *(f)*
En item design
Es diseño de elementos *(m)*
It disegno delle voci *(m)*
Pt desenho de ítem *(m)*

definizione del problema *(f)* It
De Problembestimmung *(f)*
En problem definition
Es definición del problema *(f)*
Fr définition des problèmes *(f)*
Pt definição do problema *(f)*

degolador *(m) n* Pt
De Dekollationierer *(m)*
En decollator
Es desglosador *(m)*
Fr décollateur *(m)*
It decollatore *(m)*

degré de précision *(m)* Fr
De Präzision *(f)*
En precision
Es precisión *(f)*
It precisione *(f)*
Pt precisão *(f)*

Dekade *(f) n* De
En decade
Es década *(f)*
Fr décade *(f)*
It decade *(f)*
Pt década *(f)*

Dekollationierer *(m) n* De
En decollator
Es desglosador *(m)*
Fr décollateur *(m)*
It decollatore *(m)*
Pt degolador *(m)*

Dekrement *(n) n* De
En decrement
Es decremento *(m)*
Fr décrément *(m)*
It decremento *(m)*
Pt decremento *(m)*

délai d'attente *(m)* Fr
De Umdrehungs-wartezeit *(f)*
En rotational delay
Es retraso rotacional *(m)*
It ritardo rotazionale *(m)*
Pt atraso rotacional *(m)*

delayed updating En
De verzögerte Aktualisierung *(f)*
Es actualización diferida *(f)*
Fr mise à jour temporisée *(f)*
It aggiornamento ritardato *(m)*
Pt actualização atrasada *(f)*

delay line En
De Verzögerungsleitung *(f)*
Es línea de retardo *(f)*
Fr ligne à retard *(f)*
It linea di ritardo *(f)*
Pt linha de atraso *(f)*

delete *vb* En
De löschen
Es suprimir
Fr éliminer
It cancellare
Pt apagar

deletion *n* En
De Löschung *(f)*
Es eliminación *(f)*
Fr effacement *(m)*
It cancellazione *(f)*
Pt apagado *(m)*

deletion record En
De Löschungssatz *(m)*
Es registro de eliminación *(m)*
Fr enregistrement d'effacement *(m)*
It record di cancellazione *(m)*
Pt registo de apagamento *(m)*

delimit *vb* En
De begrenzen
Es delimitar
Fr délimiter
It delimitare
Pt delimitar

delimitador *(m) n* Es, Pt
De Begrenzer *(m)*
En delimiter
Fr delimitateur *(m)*
It delimitatore *(m)*

delimitar *vb* Es, Pt
De begrenzen
En delimit
Fr délimiter
It delimitare

delimitare *vb* It
De begrenzen
En delimit
Es delimitar
Fr délimiter
Pt delimitar

delimitateur *(m) n* Fr
De Begrenzer *(m)*
En delimiter
Es delimitador *(m)*
It delimitatore *(m)*
Pt delimitador *(m)*

delimitatore *(m) n* It
De Begrenzer *(m)*
En delimiter
Es delimitador *(m)*
Fr delimitateur *(m)*
Pt delimitador *(m)*

delimiter *n* En
De Begrenzer *(m)*
Es delimitador *(m)*
Fr delimitateur *(m)*
It delimitatore *(m)*
Pt delimitador *(m)*

délimiter *vb* Fr
De begrenzen
En delimit
Es delimitar
It delimitare
Pt delimitar

demand processing En
De Abrufverarbeitung *(f)*
Es tratamiento inmediato *(m)*
Fr traitement immédiat *(m)*
It elaborazione a domanda *(f)*
Pt processamento de procura *(m)*

demand reading En
De Abruflesen *(n)*
Es lectura inmediata *(f)*
Fr lecture immédiate *(f)*
It lettura a domanda *(f)*
Pt leitura de procura *(f)*

demand writing En
De Abrufschreiben *(n)*
Es escritura inmediata *(f)*
Fr écriture immédiate *(f)*
It scrittura a domanda *(f)*
Pt escrita de procura *(f)*

demi-additionneur *(m) n* Fr
De Halbaddierglied *(n)*
En half adder
Es semi-sumador *(m)*
It metà addizionatore *(m)*
Pt semi-somador *(m)*

demi-mot *(m) n* Fr
De Halbwort *(n)*
En half word
Es media palabra *(f)*
It metà voce *(f)*
Pt meia-palavra *(f)*

demodulador *(m) n* Es
De Demodulator *(m)*
En demodulator
Fr démodulateur *(m)*
It demodulatore *(m)*
Pt desmodulador *(m)*

démodulateur *(m) n* Fr
De Demodulator *(m)*
En demodulator
Es demodulador *(m)*
It demodulatore *(m)*
Pt desmodulador *(m)*

demodulator *n* En
De Demodulator *(m)*
Es demodulador *(m)*
Fr démodulateur *(m)*
It demodulatore *(m)*
Pt desmodulador *(m)*

Demodulator *(m) n* De
En demodulator
Es demodulador *(m)*
Fr démodulateur *(m)*
It demodulatore *(m)*
Pt desmodulador *(m)*

demodulatore *(m) n* It
De Demodulator *(m)*
En demodulator
Es demodulador *(m)*
Fr démodulateur *(m)*
Pt desmodulador *(m)*

densidad de almacenamiento *(f)* Es
De Speicherdichte *(f)*
En storage density
Fr densité de stockage *(f)*
It densità di memoria *(f)*
Pt densidade de armazenamento *(f)*

densidad de bits *(f)* Es
De Binärzeichendichte *(f)*
En bit density
Fr densité de bits *(f)*
It densità di bit *(f)*
Pt densidade de bit *(f)*

densidad de caracteres *(f)* Es
De Zeichendichte *(f)*
En character density
Fr densité de caractères *(f)*
It densità di caratteri *(f)*
Pt densidade de caracteres *(f)*

densidad de empaquetamiento *(f)* Es
De Fluβwechseldichte *(f)*
En packing density
Fr densité d'implantation *(f)*
It densita di compattezza *(f)*
Pt densidade de acumulação *(f)*

densidad de registro *(f)* Es
De Schreibdichte *(f)*
En recording density
Fr densité d'enregistrement *(f)*
It densità di registrazione *(f)*
Pt densidade de registo *(f)*

densidade de acumulação *(f)* Pt
De Fluβwechseldichte *(f)*
En packing density
Es densidad de empaquetamiento *(f)*
Fr densité d'implantation *(f)*
It densita di compattezza *(f)*

densidade de armazenamento *(f)* Pt
De Speicherdichte *(f)*
En storage density
Es donsidad de almacenamiento *(f)*
Fr densité de stockage *(f)*
It densità di memoria *(f)*

densidade de bit *(f)* Pt
De Binärzeichendichte *(f)*
En bit density
Es densidad de bits *(f)*
Fr densité de bits *(f)*
It densità di bit *(f)*

densidade de caracteres *(f)* Pt
De Zeichendichte *(f)*
En character density
Es densidad de caracteres *(f)*
Fr densité de caractères *(f)*
It densità di caratteri *(f)*

densidade de registo *(f)* Pt
De Schreibdichte *(f)*
En recording density
Es densidad de registro *(f)*
Fr densité d'enregistrement *(f)*
It densità di registrazione *(f)*

densità di bit *(f)* It
De Binärzeichendichte *(f)*
En bit density
Es densidad de bits *(f)*
Fr densité de bits *(f)*
Pt densidade de bit *(f)*

densità di caratteri *(f)* It
De Zeichendichte *(f)*
En character density
Es densidad de caracteres *(f)*
Fr densité de caractères *(f)*
Pt densidade de caracteres *(f)*

densita di compattezza *(f)* It
De Fluβwechseldichte *(f)*
En packing density
Es densidad de empaquetamiento *(f)*
Fr densité d'implantation *(f)*
Pt densidade de acumulação *(f)*

densità di memoria *(f)* It
De Speicherdichte *(f)*
En storage density
Es densidad de almacenamiento *(f)*
Fr densité de stockage *(f)*
Pt densidade de armazenamento *(f)*

densità di registrazione *(f)* It
De Schreibdichte *(f)*
En recording density
Es densidad de registro *(f)*
Fr densité d'enregistrement *(f)*
Pt densidade de registo *(f)*

densité de bits *(f)* Fr
De Binärzeichendichte *(f)*
En bit density
Es densidad de bits *(f)*
It densità di bit *(f)*
Pt densidade de bit *(f)*

densité de caractères *(f)* Fr
De Zeichendichte *(f)*
En character density
Es densidad de caracteres *(f)*
It densità di caratteri *(f)*
Pt densidade de caracteres *(f)*

densité d'enregistrement *(f)* Fr
De Schreibdichte *(f)*
En recording density
Es densidad de registro *(f)*
It densità di registrazione *(f)*
Pt densidade de registo *(f)*

densité de stockage *(f)* Fr
De Speicherdichte *(f)*
En storage density
Es densidad de almacenamiento *(f)*
It densità di memoria *(f)*
Pt densidade de armazenamento *(f)*

densité d'implantation *(f)* Fr
De Fluswechseldichte *(f)*
En packing density
Es densidad de empaquetamiento *(f)*
It densita di compattezza *(f)*
Pt densidade de acumulação *(f)*

dentro il primo, fuori il primo *(m)* It
De Prioritätssteuerung *(f)*
En first in, first out (FIFO)
Es primero a llegar, primero que sale *(m)*
Fr premier entré, premier sorti *(m)*
Pt primeiro a entrar, primeiro a sair *(m)*

dépannage *(m) n* Fr
De Fehlersuchen *(n)*
En trouble shooting
Es localización de errores *(f)*
It risoluzione dei problemi organizzativi *(f)*
Pt detecção de avarias *(f)*

dépassement de capacité *(m)* Fr
De Überlauf *(m)*
En overflow
Es desbordamiento *(m)*
It superamento della capacità di memoria *(m)*
Pt trasbordamento *(m)*

dépassement de capacité inférieur *(m)* Fr

De Unterlauf *(m)*
En underflow
Es subdesbordamiento *(m)*
It sottoflusso *(m)*
Pt subfluxo *(m)*

deposit *n* En
De Einlage *(f)*
Es depósito *(m)*
Fr dépôt *(m)*
It deposito *(m)*
Pt depósito *(m)*

deposito *(m) n* It
De Einlage *(f)*
En deposit
Es depósito *(m)*
Fr dépôt *(m)*
Pt depósito *(m)*

depósito *(m) n* Es, Pt
De Einlage *(f)*
En deposit
Fr dépôt *(m)*
It deposito *(m)*

depósito de alimentación *(m)* Es
De Magazin *(n)*
En hopper
Fr magasin d'alimentation *(m)*
It serbatoio di alimentazione (schede) *(m)*
Pt tremonha *(f)*

dépôt *(m) n* Fr
De Einlage *(f)*
En deposit
Es depósito *(m)*
It deposito *(m)*
Pt depósito *(m)*

depurar *vb* Es
De fehlersuchen
En debug
Fr mettre au point
It mettere a punto un programma
Pt desparasitar

dérouler *vb* Fr
De abwickeln
En unwind
Es desovillar
It svolgere
Pt desenrolar

dérouleur de bande *(m)* Fr
De Bandantrieb *(m)*
En tape drive
Es impulsor de cinta *(m)*
It guida del nastro *(f)*
Pt accionamento da fita *(m)*

desbordamiento *(m) n* Es
De Überlauf *(m)*
En overflow
Fr dépassement de capacité *(m)*
It superamento della capacità di memoria *(m)*
Pt trasbordamento *(m)*

descarregador *(m) n* Pt
De Speicherauszug *(m)*
En dump
Es vuelco de la memoria *(m)*
Fr vidage *(m)*
It dump *(m)*

descarregador de autópsia *(m)* Pt
De Speicherauszug nach dem Tode *(m)*
En post-mortem dump
Es vaciado póstumo *(m)*
Fr vidage d'autopsie *(m)*
It dump di autopsia *(m)*

descarregador de memória *(m)* Pt
De Speicherauszug *(m)*
En memory dump
Es vuelco de la memoria *(m)*
Fr vidage de la mémoire *(m)*
It dump della memoria *(m)*

descarregador estático *(m)* Pt
De statischer Speicherauszug *(m)*
En static dump
Es vuelco estático de la memoria *(m)*
Fr vidage en un point fixe du programme *(m)*
It dump statico *(m)*

descarregar *vb* Pt
De speicherausziehen
En dump
Es volcar
Fr vider
It fare un dump

descodificador *(m) n* Pt
De Entschlüssler *(m)*
En decoder
Es decodificador *(m)*
Fr décodeur *(m)*
It decodificatore *(m)*

descodificar *vb* Pt
De entschlüsseln
En decode
Es decodificar
Fr décoder
It decodificare

descripteur *(m) n* Fr
De Beschreiber *(m)*
En descriptor
Es descriptor *(m)*
It descrittore *(m)*
Pt descritor *(m)*

descriptor *n* En; Es *(m)*
De Beschreiber *(m)*
Fr descripteur *(m)*
It descrittore *(m)*
Pt descritor *(m)*

descritor *(m) n* Pt
De Beschreiber *(m)*
En descriptor
Es descriptor *(m)*
Fr descripteur *(m)*
It descrittore *(m)*

descrittore *(m) n* It
De Beschreiber *(m)*
En descriptor
Es descriptor *(m)*
Fr descripteur *(m)*
Pt descritor *(m)*

desembalar *vb* Pt
De auspacken
En unpack
Es desempaquetar
Fr décondenser
It separare

desempaquetar *vb* Es
De auspacken
En unpack
Fr décondenser
It separare
Pt desembalar

desenho com auxílio de computador (CAD) *(m)* Pt
De computer-unterstützte Konstruktion *(f)*
En computer-aided design (CAD)
Es diseño con la ayuda de ordenador *(m)*
Fr conception assistée par ordinateur (CAO) *(f)*
It progettazione basata sull'elaboratore *(f)*

desenho de engenharia automatizado *(m)* Pt
De automatisierte Maschinen-konstruktion *(f)*
En automated engineering design (AED)
Es diseño técnico automatizado *(m)*
Fr étude technique automatisée (ETA) *(f)*
It disegno di ingegneria automatizzata *(m)*

desenho de ítem *(m)* Pt
De Datenfeld-konstruktion *(f)*
En item design
Es diseño de elementos *(m)*
Fr définition du découpage des articles *(f)*
It disegno delle voci *(m)*

desenho de sistema automático *(m)* Pt
De automatische Systemkonstruktion *(f)*
En automatic system design
Es diseño automático de sistemas *(m)*
Fr conception de système automatique *(f)*
It progettazione automatica del sistema *(f)*

desenho funcional *(m)* Pt

De funktionsmäβige Konstruktion *(f)*
En functional design
Es diseño funcional *(m)*
Fr conception fonctionnelle *(f)*
It disegno funzionale *(m)*

desenrolar *vb* Pt
De abwickeln
En unwind
Es desovillar
Fr dérouler
It svolgere

desglosador *(m) n* Es
De Dekollationierer *(m)*
En decollator
Fr décollateur *(m)*
It decollatore *(m)*
Pt degolador *(m)*

designação *(f) n* Pt
De Kennzeichnung *(f)*
En designation
E. indicación *(f)*
Fr indication *(f)*
It designazione *(f)*

designação dinâmica *(f)* Pt
De dynamische Zuweisung *(f)*
En dynamic allocation
Es asignación dinámica *(f)*
Fr affectation dynamique *(f)*
It allocazione dinamica *(f)*

designation *n* En
De Kennzeichnung *(f)*
Es indicación *(f)*
Fr indication *(f)*
It designazione *(f)*
Pt designação *(f)*

designazione *(f) n* It
De Kennzeichnung *(f)*
En designation
Es indicación *(f)*
Fr indication *(f)*
Pt designação *(f)*

desk-top computer En
De Tischrechner *(m)*
Es ordenador de mesa *(m)*
Fr petit ordinateur de bureau *(m)*
It elaboratore da tavolo *(m)*
Pt computador de mesa *(m)*

desmodulador *(m) n* Pt
De Demodulator *(m)*
En demodulator
Es demodulador *(m)*
Fr démodulateur *(m)*
It demodulatore *(m)*

desovillar *vb* Es
De abwickeln
En unwind
Fr dérouler
It svolgere
Pt desenrolar

desparasitar *vb* Pt
De fehlersuchen
En debug
Es depurar
Fr mettre au point
It mettere a punto un programma

despejar *vb* Es
De löschen
En clear
Fr remettre à zéro
It rimettere a zero
Pt limpar

desplazamiento *(m) n* Es
De Stellenverschiebung *(f)*
En shift
Fr décalage *(m)*
It riporto *(m)*
Pt mudança *(f)*

desplazamiento a la derecha *(m)* Es
De Rechtsschiebung *(f)*
En right shift
Fr décalage à droite *(m)*
It spostamento a destra *(m)*
Pt mudança à direita *(f)*

desplazamiento a la izquierda *(m)* Es
De Linksverschiebung *(f)*
En left shift
Fr décalage à gauche *(m)*
It spostamento a sinistra *(m)*
Pt mudança à esquerda *(f)*

desplazamiento aritmético *(m)* Es
De arithmetische Stellenverschiebung *(f)*
En arithmetic shift
Fr décalage arithmétique *(m)*
It spostamento aritmetico *(m)*
Pt mudança aritmética *(f)*

desplazamiento en anillo *(m)* Es
De Ringschiebung *(f)*
En ring shift
Fr permutation circulaire *(f)*
It dislocamento ad anello *(m)*
Pt mudança anular *(f)*

desplazamiento lógico *(m)* Es
De logische Verschiebung *(f)*
En logic(al) shift
Fr décalage logique *(m)*
It spostamento logico *(m)*
Pt mudança lógica *(f)*

desplazar *vb* Es
De versetzen
En shift
Fr décaler
It spostare (dati)
Pt mudar

destructive addition En
De Löschen der Addition *(n)*
Es suma destructiva *(f)*
Fr addition destructive *(f)*
It addizione distruttiva *(f)*
Pt adição destrutiva *(f)*

destructive read-out En
De Löschen der Auslesung *(n)*
Es lectura destructiva *(f)*
Fr lecture destructive *(f)*
It lettura distruttiva *(f)*
Pt leitura destrutiva *(f)*

detecção de avarias *(f)* Pt
De Fehlersuchen *(n)*
En trouble shooting
Es localización de errores *(f)*
Fr dépannage *(m)*
It risoluzione dei problemi organizzativi *(f)*

detectar *vb* Es
De fühlen
En sense
Fr détecter
It rilevare
Pt pesquisar

détecter *vb* Fr
De fühlen
En sense
Es detectar
It rilevare
Pt pesquisar

détente *(f) n* Fr
De Trigger (m)
En trigger
Es disparador *(m)*
It scatto *(m)*
Pt gatilho *(m)*

determinação da marca *(f)* Pt
De Kennzeichenfühlung *(f)*
En mark sensing
Es lectura de marcas *(f)*
Fr lecture de marques *(f)*
It lettura di marcature *(f)*

deuxième-génération Fr
De zweitgeneration
En second-generation
Es segunda-generación
It seconda-generazione
Pt segunda-geração

dezimal *adj* De
En decimal
Es decimal
Fr décimal
It decimale
Pt decimal

Dezimal-Binär-darstellung *(f)* De
En decimal-to-binary notation

Es notación de decimal a binario *(f)*
Fr notation décimale-binaire *(f)*
It notazione da decimale a binario *(f)*
Pt notação decimal-a-binária *(f)*

Dezimaldarstellung *(f)* *n* De
En decimal notation
Es notación decimal *(f)*
Fr notation décimale *(f)*
It notazione decimale *(f)*
Pt notação decimal *(f)*

diafonia *(f)* *n* It, Pt
De Nebensprechen *(n)*
En cross talk
Es diafonía *(f)*
Fr diaphonie *(f)*

diafonía *(f)* *n* Es
De Nebensprechen *(n)*
En cross talk
Fr diaphonie *(f)*
It diafonia *(f)*
Pt diafonia *(f)*

diagnosis de errores *(f)* Es
De Fehlerdiagnostik *(f)*
En error diagnostics
Fr diagnostics d'erreurs *(m)*
It diagnostica degli errori *(f)*
Pt diagnóstico de erros *(m)*

diagnostica degli errori *(f)* It
De Fehlerdiagnostik *(f)*
En error diagnostics
Es diagnosis de errores *(f)*
Fr diagnostics d'erreurs *(m)*
Pt diagnóstico de erros *(m)*

diagnóstico de erros *(m)* Pt
De Fehlerdiagnostik *(f)*
En error diagnostics
Es diagnosis de errores *(f)*
Fr diagnostics d'erreurs *(m)*
It diagnostica degli errori *(f)*

diagnostic routine En
De Diagnostikprogramm *(n)*
Es rutina de diagnóstico *(f)*
Fr programme de diagnostic *(m)*
It routine diagnostica *(f)*
Pt rotina de diagnóstico *(f)*

diagnostics d'erreurs *(m)* Fr
De Fehlerdiagnostik *(f)*
En error diagnostics
Es diagnosis de errores *(f)*
It diagnostica degli errori *(f)*
Pt diagnóstico de erros *(m)*

diagnostic test En
De diagnostische Prüfung *(f)*
Es prueba de diagnóstico *(f)*
Fr test de diagnostic *(m)*
It test diagnostico *(m)*
Pt teste de diagnóstico *(m)*

Diagnostikprogramm *(n)* *n* De
En diagnostic routine
Es rutina de diagnóstico *(f)*
Fr programme de diagnostic *(m)*
It routine diagnostica *(f)*
Pt rotina de diagnóstico *(f)*

diagnostische Prüfung *(f)* De
En diagnostic test
Es prueba de diagnóstico *(f)*
Fr test de diagnostic *(m)*
It test diagnostico *(m)*
Pt teste de diagnóstico *(m)*

diagrama de bloco *(m)* Pt
De Blockschaltung *(f)*
En block diagram
Es diagrama por bloques *(m)*
Fr schéma fonctionnel *(m)*
It diagramma a blocchi *(m)*

diagrama lógico *(m)* Es, Pt
De Verknüpfungs-diagramm *(n)*
En logic diagram
Fr schéma logique *(m)*
It diagramma logico *(m)*

diagrama por bloques *(m)* Es
De Blockschaltung *(f)*
En block diagram
Fr schéma fonctionnel *(m)*
It diagramma a blocchi *(m)*
Pt diagrama de bloco *(m)*

diagramma a blocchi *(m)* It
De Blockschaltung *(f)*
En block diagram
Es diagrama por bloques *(m)*
Fr schéma fonctionnel *(m)*
Pt diagrama de bloco *(m)*

diagramma di flusso *(m)* It
De Flußdiagramm *(n)*
En flowchart
Es ordinograma *(m)*
Fr organigramme *(m)*
Pt gráfico de fluxo *(m)*

diagramma logico *(m)* It
De Verknüpfungs-diagramm *(n)*
En logic diagram
Es diagrama lógico *(m)*
Fr schéma logique *(m)*
Pt diagrama lógico *(m)*

Dialoganzeige *(f)* *n* De
En interactive display
Es representación interactiva *(f)*
Fr visualisation interactive *(f)*
It visualizzatore interattivo *(m)*
Pt visualização interactiva *(f)*

Dialogbetrieb *(m)* *n* De
En interactive computing
Es cálculo interactivo *(m)*
Fr traitement interactif *(m)*
It calcoli interattivi *(m)*
Pt computação interactiva *(f)*

Dialogbetriebsart *(f)* *n* De
En conversational mode
Es modo diálogo *(m)*
Fr mode dialogué *(m)*
It modalità conversazionale *(f)*
Pt modo conversacional *(m)*

Dialogdatenstation *(f)* *n* De
En interactive terminal
Es terminal interactivo *(m)*
Fr terminal interactif *(m)*
It terminale interattivo *(m)*
Pt terminal interactivo *(m)*

diaphonie *(f)* *n* Fr
De Nebensprechen *(n)*
En cross talk
Es diafonía *(f)*
It diafonia *(f)*
Pt diafonia *(f)*

diário *(m)* *n* Pt
De Journal *(n)*
En log
Es registro *(m)*
Fr consignation *(f)*
It registro *(m)*

diccionario *(m)* *n* Es
De Wörterbuch *(n)*
En dictionary
Fr dictionnaire *(m)*
It dizionario *(m)*
Pt dicionário *(m)*

dichotomizierendes Suchen *(n)* De
En dichotomizing search
Es búsqueda dicotómica *(f)*

Fr recherche dichotomique *(f)*
It ricerca dicotoma *(f)*
Pt busca dicotomizante *(f)*

dichotomizing search En
De dichotomizierendes Suchen *(n)*
Es búsqueda dicotómica *(f)*
Fr recherche dichotomique *(f)*
It ricerca dicotoma *(f)*
Pt busca dicotomizante *(f)*

dicionário *(m) n* Pt
De Wörterbuch *(n)*
En dictionary
Es diccionario *(m)*
Fr dictionnaire *(m)*
It dizionario *(m)*

dictionary *n* En
De Wörterbuch *(n)*
Es diccionario *(m)*
Fr dictionnaire *(m)*
It dizionario *(m)*
Pt dicionário *(m)*

dictionnaire *(m) n* Fr
De Wörterbuch *(n)*
En dictionary
Es diccionario *(m)*
It dizionario *(m)*
Pt dicionário *(m)*

Dienstbit *(m) n* De
En service bit
Es bit de servicio *(m)*
Fr bit de service *(m)*
It bit di servizio *(m)*
Pt bit de serviço *(m)*

Dienstprogramm *(n) n* De
En service routine
Es rutina de servicio *(f)*
Fr programme de service *(m)*
It routine di servizio *(f)*
Pt rotina de serviço *(f)*

diferenciador *(m) n* Es, Pt
De differenzierendes Netz *(n)*
En differentiator
Fr différentiateur *(m)*
It differenziatore *(m)*

difetto *(m) n* It
De Defekt *(m)*
En bug
Es defecto *(m)*
Fr défaut *(m)*
Pt perturbação *(f)*

differential analyser En
Am differential analyzer
De Differenzialanalysator *(m)*
Es analizador diferencial *(m)*
Fr analyseur différentiel *(m)*
It analizzatore differenziale *(m)*
Pt analisador diferencial *(m)*

differential analyzer Am
De Differenzialanalysator *(m)*
En differential analyser
Es analizador diferencial *(m)*
Fr analyseur différentiel *(m)*
It analizzatore differenziale *(m)*
Pt analisador diferencial *(m)*

différentiateur *(m) n* Fr
De differenzierendes Netz *(n)*
En differentiator
Es diferenciador *(m)*
It differenziatore *(m)*
Pt diferenciador *(m)*

differentiator *n* En
De differenzierendes Netz *(n)*
Es diferenciador *(m)*
Fr différentiateur *(m)*
It differenziatore *(m)*
Pt diferenciador *(m)*

Differenzialanalysator *(m) n* De
Am differential analyzer
En differential analyser
Es analizador diferencial *(m)*
Fr analyseur différentiel *(m)*
It analizzatore differenziale *(m)*
Pt analisador diferencial *(m)*

differenziatore *(m) n* It
De differenzierendes Netz *(n)*
En differentiator
Es diferenciador *(m)*
Fr différentiateur *(m)*
Pt diferenciador *(m)*

differenzierendes Netz *(n)* De
En differentiator
Es diferenciador *(m)*
Fr différentiateur *(m)*
It differenziatore *(m)*
Pt diferenciador *(m)*

digit *n* En; It *(m)*
De Ziffer *(f)*
Es dígito *(m)*
Fr chiffre *(m)*
Pt número digital *(m)*

digital *adj* De, En, Es, Fr, Pt
It digitale

digital-analog converter En
De Digital-Analogumwandler *(m)*
Es convertidor de digital-analógico *(m)*
Fr convertisseur numérique-analogique *(m)*
It convertitore digitale-analogico *(m)*
Pt conversor digital-análogo *(m)*

Digital-Analogumwandler *(m)* De
En digital-analog converter
Es convertidor de digital-analógico *(m)*
Fr convertisseur numérique-analogique *(m)*
It convertitore digitale-analogico *(m)*
Pt conversor digital-análogo *(m)*

digital clock En
De Digitalzeitgeber *(m)*
Es reloj digital *(m)*
Fr horloge numérique *(f)*
It orologio digitale *(m)*
Pt relógio digital *(m)*

digital computer En
De Digitalrechner *(m)*
Es ordenador digital *(m)*
Fr calculateur numérique *(m)*
It elaboratore digitale *(m)*
Pt computador digital *(m)*

digitale *adj* It
De digital
En digital
Es digital
Fr digital
Pt digital

digitales Schalten *(n)* De
En digital switching
Es conmutación digital *(f)*
Fr commutation numérique *(f)*
It commutazione digitale *(f)*
Pt comutação digital *(f)*

digitale Übertragung *(f)* De
En digital transmission
Es transmisión digital *(f)*
Fr transmission numérique *(f)*
It trasmissione digitale *(f)*
Pt transmissão digital *(f)*

digitalizador *(m) n* Es, Pt
De Verzifferer *(m)*
En digitizer
Fr numériseur *(m)*
It digitalizzatore *(m)*

digitalizar *vb* Es, Pt
De verziffern
En digitize
Fr numériser
It digitalizzare

digitalizzare *vb* It
De verziffern
En digitize
Es digitalizar

Fr numériser
Pt digitalizar

digitalizzatore *(m) n* It
De Verzifferer *(m)*
En digitizer
Es digitalizador *(m)*
Fr numériseur *(m)*
Pt digitalizador *(m)*

digital link En
De Digitalverbindung *(f)*
Es enlace digital *(m)*
Fr liaison numérique *(f)*
It collegamento digitale *(m)*
Pt elemento de ligação digital *(m)*

digital network En
De Digitalnetz *(n)*
Es red digital *(f)*
Fr réseau numérique *(m)*
It rete digitale *(f)*
Pt rede digital *(f)*

Digitalnetz *(n) n* De
En digital network
Es red digital *(f)*
Fr réseau numérique *(m)*
It rete digitale *(f)*
Pt rede digital *(f)*

Digitalrechner *(m) n* De
En digital computer
Es ordenador digital *(m)*
Fr calculateur numérique *(m)*
It elaboratore digitale *(m)*
Pt computador digital *(m)*

digital switching En
De digitales Schalten *(n)*
Es conmutación digital *(f)*
Fr commutation numérique *(f)*
It commutazione digitale *(f)*
Pt comutação digital *(f)*

digital transmission En
De digitale Übertragung *(f)*
Es transmisión digital *(f)*
Fr transmission numérique *(f)*
It trasmissione digitale *(f)*
Pt transmissão digital *(f)*

Digitalverbindung *(f) n* De
En digital link
Es enlace digital *(m)*
Fr liaison numérique *(f)*
It collegamento digitale *(m)*
Pt elemento de ligação digital *(m)*

Digitalzeitgeber *(m) n* De
En digital clock
Es reloj digital *(m)*
Fr horloge numérique *(f)*
It orologio digitale *(m)*
Pt relógio digital *(m)*

digit del segno *(m)* It
De Vorzeichenziffer *(f)*
En sign digit
Es dígito de signo *(m)*
Fr caractère de signe *(m)*
Pt número digital de sinal *(m)*

digit di controllo *(m)* It
De Prüfziffer *(f)*
En check digit
Es dígito de verificación *(m)*
Fr caractère de contrôle *(m)*
Pt número digital de verificação *(m)*

digit di zonatura *(m)* It
De Zonenziffer *(f)*
En zone digit
Es dígito de zona *(m)*
Fr chiffre de zone *(m)*
Pt número digital de zona *(m)*

digiti binari equivalenti *(m pl)* It
De gleichwertige Binärziffern *(pl)*
En equivalent binary digits
Es dígitos binarios equivalentes *(m pl)*
Fr chiffres binaires équivalents *(m pl)*
Pt números digitais binários equivalentes *(m pl)*

digiti significativi *(m pl)* It
De wesentliche Ziffern *(pl)*
En significant digits
Es dígitos significativos *(m pl)*
Fr chiffres significatifs *(m pl)*
Pt números digitais significativos *(m pl)*

digitize *vb* En
De verziffern
Es digitalizar
Fr numériser
It digitalizzare
Pt digitalizar

digitizer *n* En
De Verzifferer *(m)*
Es digitalizador *(m)*
Fr numériseur *(m)*
It digitalizzatore *(m)*
Pt digitalizador *(m)*

dígito *(m) n* Es
De Ziffer *(f)*
En digit
Fr chiffre *(m)*
It digit *(m)*
Pt número digital *(m)*

dígito de signo *(m)* Es
De Vorzeichenziffer *(f)*
En sign digit
Fr caractère de signe *(m)*
It digit del segno *(m)*
Pt número digital de sinal *(m)*

dígito de verificación *(m)* Es
De Prüfziffer *(f)*
En check digit
Fr caractère de contrôle *(m)*
It digit di controllo *(m)*
Pt número digital de verificação *(m)*

dígito de zona *(m)* Es
De Zonenziffer *(f)*
En zone digit
Fr chiffre de zone *(m)*
It digit di zonatura *(m)*
Pt número digital de zona *(m)*

dígitos binarios equivalentes *(m pl)* Es
De gleichwertige Binärziffern *(pl)*
En equivalent binary digits
Fr chiffres binaires équivalents *(m pl)*
It digiti binari equivalenti *(m pl)*
Pt números digitais binários equivalentes *(m pl)*

dígitos significativos *(m pl)* Es
De wesentliche Ziffern *(pl)*
En significant digits
Fr chiffres significatifs *(m pl)*
It digiti significativi *(m pl)*
Pt números digitais significativos *(m pl)*

diode *n* En; Fr *(f)*
De Diode *(f)*
Es diodo *(m)*
It diodo *(m)*
Pt díodo *(m)*

Diode *(f) n* De
En diode
Es diodo *(m)*
Fr diode *(f)*
It diodo *(m)*
Pt díodo *(m)*

diode électro-luminescente *(f)* Fr
De Leuchtdiode *(f)*
En light-emitting diode (LED)
Es diodo luminoso *(m)*
It diodo emittente luce *(m)*
Pt díodo emissor de luz *(m)*

Diodentransistor-verknüpfung *(f) n* De
En diode transistor logic (DTL)
Es lógica diodo-transistor *(f)*
Fr logique à diodes et transistors *(f)*
It logica diodo-transistore *(f)*

Pt lógica de transistor de díodo *(f)*

diode-transistor logic (DTL) En
De Diodentransistorverknüpfung *(f)*
Es lógica diodo-transistor *(f)*
Fr logique à diodes et transistors *(f)*
It logica diodo-transistore *(f)*
Pt lógica de transistor de díodo *(f)*

diodo *(m) n* Es, It
De Diode *(f)*
En diode
Fr diode *(f)*
Pt díodo *(m)*

díodo *(m) n* Pt
De Diode *(f)*
En diode
Es diodo *(m)*
Fr diode *(f)*
It diodo *(m)*

díodo emissor de luz *(m)* Pt
De Leuchtdiode *(f)*
En light-emitting diode (LED)
Es diodo luminoso *(m)*
Fr diode électro-luminescente *(f)*
It diodo emittente luce *(m)*

diodo emittente luce *(m)* It
De Leuchtdiode *(f)*
En light-emitting diode (LED)
Es diodo luminoso *(m)*
Fr diode électro-luminescente *(f)*
Pt díodo emissor de luz *(m)*

diodo luminoso *(m)* Es
De Leuchtdiode *(f)*
En light-emitting diode (LED)
Fr diode électro-luminescente *(f)*
It diodo emittente luce *(m)*
Pt díodo emissor de luz *(m)*

diramarsi *vb* It
De abzweigen
En branch
Es bifurcar
Fr brancher
Pt ligar

diramazione *(f) n* It
De Zweig *(m)*
En branch
Es bifurcación *(f)*
Fr branchement *(m)*
Pt ramo *(m)*

direcção absoluta *(f)* Pt
De absolute Adresse *(f)*
En absolute address
Es dirección absoluta *(f)*
Fr adresse absolue *(f)*
It indirizzo assoluto *(m)*

direcção de base *(f)* Pt
De Basisadresse *(f)*
En base address
Es dirección de base *(f)*
Fr adresse de base *(f)*
It indirizzo base *(m)*

direcção real *(f)* Pt
De echte Adresse *(f)*
En actual address
Es dirección real *(f)*
Fr adresse réelle *(f)*
It indirizzo effettivo *(m)*

dirección *(f) n* Es
De Adresse *(f)*
En address
Fr adresse *(f)*
It indirizzo *(m)*
Pt endereço *(m)*

dirección absoluta *(f)* Es
De absolute Adresse *(f)*
En absolute address
Fr adresse absolue *(f)*
It indirizzo assoluto *(m)*
Pt direcção absoluta *(f)*

direccionado relativo *(m)* Es
De relative Adressierung *(f)*
En relative addressing
Fr adressage relatif *(m)*
It indirizzamento relativo *(m)*
Pt endereçamento relativo *(m)*

direccionado repetitivo *(m)* Es
De wiederholte Adressierung *(f)*
En repetitive addressing
Fr adressage sous-entendu *(m)*
It indirizzamento ripetitivo *(m)*
Pt endereçamento repetitivo *(m)*

direccionamiento directo *(m)* Es
De direkte Adressierung *(f)*
En direct addressing
Fr adressage direct *(m)*
It indirizzamento diretto *(m)*
Pt endereçamento directo *(m)*

direccionar *vb* Es
De adressieren
En address
Fr adresser
It indirizzare
Pt endereçar

dirección de base *(f)* Es
De Basisadresse *(f)*
En base address
Fr adresse de base *(f)*
It indirizzo base *(m)*
Pt direcção de base *(f)*

dirección de máquina *(f)* Es
De Maschinenadresse *(f)*
En machine address
Fr adresse absolue *(f)*
It indirizzo di macchina *(m)*
Pt endereço da máquina *(m)*

dirección de referencia *(f)* Es
De Bezugsadresse *(f)*
En reference address
Fr adresse primitive *(f)*
It indirizzo di riferimento *(m)*
Pt endereço de referência *(m)*

dirección de segundo nivel *(f)* Es
De Adresse der zweiten Stufe *(f)*
En second-level address
Fr adresse à deuxième niveau *(f)*
It indirizzo del secondo livello *(m)*
Pt endereço de segundo nível *(m)*

dirección efectiva *(f)* Es
De effektive Adresse *(f)*
En effective address
Fr adresse réelle *(f)*
It indirizzo efficace *(m)*
Pt endereço real *(m)*

dirección indirecta *(f)* Es
De indirekte Adresse *(f)*
En indirect address
Fr adresse indirecte *(f)*
It indirizzo indiretto *(m)*
Pt endereço indirecto *(m)*

dirección inmediata *(f)* Es
De unmittelbare Adresse *(f)*
En immediate address
Fr adresse immédiate *(f)*
It indirizzo immediato *(m)*
Pt endereço imediato *(m)*

dirección real *(f)* Es
De echte Adresse *(f)*
En actual address
Fr adresse réelle *(f)*
It indirizzo effettivo *(m)*
Pt direcção real *(f)*

dirección relativa *(f)* Es
De relative Adresse *(f)*
En relative address
Fr adresse relative *(f)*
It indirizzo relativo *(m)*
Pt endereço relativo *(m)*

dirección reubicable *(f)* Es
De verschiebliche Adresse *(f)*
En relocatable address
Fr adresse translatable *(f)*
It indirizzo rilocabile *(m)*
Pt endereço relocalizável *(m)*

dirección simbólica *(f)* Es
De symbolische Adresse *(f)*
En symbolic address
Fr adresse symbolique *(f)*
It indirizzo simbolico *(m)*
Pt endereço simbólico *(m)*

dirección uno más uno *(f)* Es
De Eins-plus-Eins-Adresse *(f)*
En one-plus-one address
Fr à une plus une adresse *(f)*
It indirizzo uno-più-uno *(m)*
Pt endereço um mais um *(m)*

dirección virtual *(f)* Es
De virtuelle Adresse *(f)*
En virtual address
Fr adresse virtuelle *(f)*
It indirizzo virtuale *(m)*
Pt endereço virtual *(m)*

direct *adj* Fr
De direkt
En on-line
Es en línea
It in linea
Pt sobre a linha

direct access En
De direkter Zugriff *(m)*
Es acceso directo *(m)*
Fr accès direct *(m)*
It accesso diretto *(m)*
Pt acesso directo *(m)*

direct-access storage device (DASD) En
De Direktzugriffsspeicher *(m)*
Es dispositivo de almacenamiento de acceso directo *(m)*
Fr unité à mémoire à accès direct *(f)*
It dispositivo con memoria ad accesso diretto *(m)*
Pt dispositivo de armazenagem de acesso directo *(m)*

direct addressing En
De direkte Adressierung *(f)*
Es direccionamiento directo *(m)*
Fr adressage direct *(m)*
It indirizzamento diretto *(m)*
Pt endereçamento directo *(m)*

directiva *(f) n* Es, Pt
De Vereinbarung *(f)*
En directive
Fr directive *(f)*
It direttiva *(f)*

directive *n* En; Fr *(f)*
De Vereinbarung *(f)*
Es directiva *(f)*
It direttiva *(f)*
Pt directiva *(f)*

directorio *(m) n* Es
De Inhaltsverzeichnis *(n)*
En directory
Fr répertoire d'adresses *(m)*
It elenco *(m)*
Pt anuário *(m)*

directory *n* En
De Inhaltsverzeichnis *(n)*
Es directorio *(m)*
Fr répertoire d'adresses *(m)*
It elenco *(m)*
Pt anuário *(m)*

direkt *adj* De
En on-line
Es en línea
Fr direct
It in linea
Pt sobre a linha

direkte Adressierung *(f)* De
En direct addressing
Es direccionamiento directo *(m)*
Fr adressage direct *(m)*
It indirizzamento diretto *(m)*
Pt endereçamento directo *(m)*

direkte Datenverdichtung *(f)* De
En on-line data reduction
Es reducción de datos en línea *(f)*
Fr réduction des données en exploitation continue *(f)*
It riduzione in linea dei dati *(f)*
Pt redução de dados sobre a linha *(f)*

direkter Zugriff *(m)* De
En direct access
Es acceso directo *(m)*
Fr accès direct *(m)*
It accesso diretto *(m)*
Pt acesso directo *(m)*

direkter Zugriff *(m)* De
En random access
Es acceso al azar *(m)*
Fr accès sélectif *(m)*
It accesso casuale *(m)*
Pt acesso aleatório *(m)*

Direktzugriffsspeicher *(m)* De
En direct-access storage device (DASD)
Es dispositivo de almacenamiento de acceso directo *(m)*
Fr unité à mémoire à accès direct *(f)*
It dispositivo con memoria ad accesso diretto *(m)*
Pt dispositivo de armazenagem de acesso directo *(m)*

Direktzugriffsspeicher *(m)* De
En random-access memory (RAM)
Es memoria de acceso al azar *(f)*
Fr mémoire à accès sélectif *(f)*
It memoria ad accesso casuale *(f)*
Pt memória de acesso aleatório *(f)*

direttiva *(f) n* It
De Vereinbarung *(f)*
En directive
Es directiva *(f)*
Fr directive *(f)*
Pt directiva *(f)*

dirottare *vb* It
De wiederführen
En reroute
Es reencaminar
Fr réacheminer
Pt reencaminhar

discho duro *(m)* It
De Hartplatte *(f)*
En hard disk
Es disco duro *(m)*
Fr disque dur *(m)*
Pt disco duro *(m)*

disco *(m) n* Es, It, Pt
De Platte *(f)*
En disc; disk
Fr disque *(m)*

disco a cartuccia *(m)* It
De Patronenplatte *(f)*
En cartridge disk
Es disco de cartucho *(m)*
Fr disque à cartouche *(m)*
Pt disco de carga *(m)*

disco blando *(m)* Es
De Floppy Disk *(m)*
En floppy disk
Fr disque souple *(m)*
It floppy disk *(m)*
Pt disco floppy *(m)*

disco de carga *(m)* Pt
De Patronenplatte *(f)*
En cartridge disk
Es disco de cartucho *(m)*
Fr disque à cartouche *(m)*
It disco a cartuccia *(m)*

disco de cartucho *(m)* Es
De Patronenplatte *(f)*
En cartridge disk
Fr disque à cartouche *(m)*
It disco a cartuccia *(m)*
Pt disco de carga *(m)*

disco duro *(m)* Es, Pt
De Hartplatte *(f)*
En hard disk
Fr disque dur *(m)*
It discho duro *(m)*

disco flexible *(m)* Es
De Diskette *(f)*
En diskette
Fr minidisque *(m)*
It diskette *(m)*
Pt disqueta *(f)*

disco floppy *(m)* Pt
De Floppy Disk *(m)*
En floppy disk
Es disco blando *(m)*
Fr disque souple *(m)*
It floppy disk *(m)*

disco magnetico *(m)* It
De Magnetplatte *(f)*
En magnetic disk
Es disco magnético *(m)*
Fr disque magnétique *(m)*
Pt disco magnético *(m)*

disco magnético *(m)* Es
De Magnetplatte *(f)*
En magnetic disk
Fr disque magnétique *(m)*
It disco magnetico *(m)*
Pt disco magnético *(m)*

disco magnético *(m)* Pt
De Magnetplatte *(f)*
En magnetic disk
Es disco magnético *(m)*
Fr disque magnétique *(m)*
It disco magnetico *(m)*

disco minifloppy *(m)* Pt
De Mini-Floppy-Disk *(m)*
En minifloppy disk
Es minidisco flexible *(m)*
Fr mini-disque souple *(m)*
It mini floppy disk *(m)*

disegno delle voci *(m)* It
De Datenfeld-konstruktion *(f)*
En item design
Es diseño de elementos *(m)*
Fr définition du découpage des articles *(f)*
Pt desenho de ítem *(m)*

disegno di ingegneria automatizzata *(m)* It
De automatisierte Maschinen-konstruktion *(f)*
En automated engineering design (AED)
Es diseño técnico automatizado *(m)*
Fr étude technique automatisée (ETA) *(f)*
Pt desenho de engenharia automatizado *(m)*

disegno funzionale *(m)* It
De funktionsmäßige Konstruktion *(f)*
En functional design
Es diseño funcional *(m)*
Fr conception fonctionnelle *(f)*
Pt desenho funcional *(m)*

diseñar *vb* Es
De modellieren
En model
Fr modeler
It modellare
Pt modelar

diseño automático de sistemas *(m)* Es
De automatische Systemkonstruktion *(f)*
En automatic system design
Fr conception de système automatique *(f)*
It progettazione automatica del sistema *(f)*
Pt desenho de sistema automático *(m)*

diseño con la ayuda de ordenador *(m)* Es
De computer-unterstützte Konstruktion *(f)*
En computer-aided design (CAD)
Fr conception assistée par ordinateur (CAO) *(f)*
It progettazione basata sull'elaboratore *(f)*
Pt desenho com auxílio de computador (CAD) *(m)*

diseño de elementos *(m)* Es
De Datenfeld-konstruktion *(f)*
En item design
Fr définition du découpage des articles *(f)*
It disegno delle voci *(m)*
Pt desenho de ítem *(m)*

diseño funcional *(m)* Es
De funktionsmäßige Konstruktion *(f)*
En functional design
Fr conception fonctionnelle *(f)*
It disegno funzionale *(m)*
Pt desenho funcional *(m)*

diseño técnico automatizado *(m)* Es
De automatisierte Maschinen-konstruktion *(f)*
En automated engineering design (AED)
Fr étude technique automatisée (ETA) *(f)*
It disegno di ingegneria automatizzata *(m)*
Pt desenho de engenharia automatizado *(m)*

disjunction (or **inclusive-or operation**) *n* En
De Inklusiv-ODER-Verknüpfung *(f)*
Es opéración O inclusivo *(f)*
Fr opération OU inclusif *(f)*
It operazione inclusivo-o *(f)*
Pt operação inclusivé-ou *(f)*

disk (or **disc**) *n* En
De Platte *(f)*
Es disco *(m)*
Fr disque *(m)*
It disco *(m)*
Pt disco *(m)*

disk-based operating system (DOS) En
De Plattenbetriebsystem *(n)*
Es sistema operativo en discos *(m)*
Fr système d'exploitation à disques *(m)*
It sistema operativo su disco *(m)*
Pt sistema de operação baseado em discos *(m)*

disk drive En
De Plattenantrieb *(m)*
Es unidad de discos *(f)*
Fr unité de disque(s) *(f)*
It unità a dischi *(f)*
Pt accionamento de disco *(m)*

diskette *n* En, It *(m)*
De Diskette *(f)*
Es disco flexible *(m)*
Fr minidisque *(m)*
Pt disqueta *(f)*

Diskette *(f) n* De
En diskette
Es disco flexible *(m)*
Fr minidisque *(m)*
It diskette *(m)*
Pt disqueta *(f)*

disk file En
De Plattendatei *(f)*
Es fichero de discos *(m)*
Fr fichier sur disque *(m)*
It file su disco *(m)*
Pt arquivo de discos *(m)*

disk pack En
De Magnetplatten-installation *(f)*
Es pila de discos *(f)*
Fr dispac *(m)*
It pacco di dischi *(m)*
Pt pacote de discos *(m)*

dislocamento ad anello *(m)* It
De Ringschiebung *(f)*
En ring shift
Es desplazamiento en anillo *(m)*
Fr permutation circulaire *(f)*
Pt mudança anular *(f)*

dispac *(m) n* Fr
De Magnetplatten-installation *(f)*
En disk pack
Es pila de discos *(f)*
It pacco di dischi *(m)*
Pt pacote de discos *(m)*

disparador *(m) n* Es
De Trigger *(m)*
En trigger
Fr détente *(f)*
It scatto *(m)*
Pt gatilho *(m)*

disparar *vb* Es, Pt
De triggern
En trigger
Fr declencher
It innescare

display *n* En
De Anzeige *(f)*
Es representación visual *(f)*
Fr affichage *(m)*
It visualizzatore *(m)*
Pt representação visual *(f)*

display *vb* En
De anzeigen
Es presentar
Fr afficher
It visualizzare
Pt mostrar

display console En
De Anzeigekonsole *(f)*
Es consola de visualización *(f)*
Fr console de visualisation *(f)*
It console di visualizzazione *(f)*
Pt consola de visualização *(f)*

display de modo pontual *(m)* Pt
De punktweise Darstellung *(f)*
En point-mode display
Es representación de modo puntual *(f)*
Fr affichage mode point par point *(m)*
It mostra di modo punto a punto *(f)*

display station En
De Anzeigestation *(f)*
Es estación de visualización *(f)*
Fr poste de visualisation *(m)*
It posto di visualizzazione *(m)*
Pt estação de visualização *(f)*

display terminal En
De Anzeigeendstation *(f)*
Es terminal de visualización *(m)*
Fr terminal à écran de visualisation *(m)*
It terminale di visualizzazione *(m)*
Pt terminal de visualização *(m)*

display tube En
De Anzeigeröhre *(f)*
Es tubo de representación visual *(m)*
Fr tube cathodique de visualisation *(m)*
It tubo visualizzatore *(m)*
Pt válvula de visualização *(f)*

disporre *vb* It
De setzen
En set
Es ajustar
Fr régler
Pt colocar

disposição semicondutora *(f)* Pt
De Halbleiterfeld *(n)*
En semiconductor array
Es matriz de semiconductores *(f)*
Fr ensemble à semiconducteurs *(m)*
It rete semiconduttori *(f)*

dispositif à couplage de charge (DCC) *(m)* Fr
De ladungsgekoppelte Vorrichtung *(f)*
En charge-coupled device (CCD)
Es dispositivo acoplado por carga *(m)*
It dispositivo accoppiato a carica *(m)*
Pt dispositivo de acoplamento por carga *(m)*

dispositivo accoppiato a carica *(m)* It
De ladungsgekoppelte Vorrichtung *(f)*
En charge-coupled device (CCD)
Es dispositivo acoplado por carga *(m)*
Fr dispositif à couplage de charge (DCC) *(m)*
Pt dispositivo de acoplamento por carga *(m)*

dispositivo acoplado por carga *(m)* Es
De ladungsgekoppelte Vorrichtung *(f)*
En charge-coupled device (CCD)
Fr dispositif à couplage de charge (DCC) *(m)*
It dispositivo accoppiato a carica *(m)*
Pt dispositivo de acoplamento por carga *(m)*

dispositivo con memoria ad accesso diretto *(m)* It
De Direktzugriffsspeicher *(m)*
En direct-access storage device (DASD)
Es dispositivo de almacenamiento de acceso directo *(m)*
Fr unité à mémoire à accès direct *(f)*
Pt dispositivo de armazenagem de acesso directo *(m)*

dispositivo de acoplamento por carga *(m)* Pt
De ladungsgekoppelte Vorrichtung *(f)*
En charge-coupled device (CCD)
Es dispositivo acoplado por carga *(m)*
Fr dispositif à couplage de charge (DCC) *(m)*
It dispositivo accoppiato a carica *(m)*

dispositivo de almacenamiento *(m)* Es
De Speichergerät *(n)*
En storage device
Fr unité de stockage *(f)*
It organo di memoria *(m)*
Pt dispositivo de armazenamento *(m)*

dispositivo de almacenamiento de acceso directo *(m)* Es
De Direktzugriffsspeicher *(m)*
En direct-access storage device (DASD)
Fr unité à mémoire à accès direct *(f)*
It dispositivo con memoria ad accesso diretto *(m)*
Pt dispositivo de armazenagem de acesso directo *(m)*

dispositivo de armazenagem de acesso directo *(m)* Pt
De Direktzugriffsspeicher *(m)*
En direct-access storage device (DASD)
Es dispositivo de almacenamiento de acceso directo *(m)*
Fr unité à mémoire à accès direct *(f)*
It dispositivo con memoria ad accesso diretto *(m)*

dispositivo de armazenamento *(m)* Pt
De Speichergerät *(n)*
En storage device
Es dispositivo de almacenamiento *(m)*
Fr unité de stockage *(f)*
It organo di memoria *(m)*

dispositivo de entrada *(m)* Pt
De Eingangsvorrichtung *(f)*
En input device
Es dispositivo de entrada *(m)*
Fr périphérique d'entrée *(m)*
It organo di entrata *(m)*

dispositivo de entrada-sair *(m)* Pt
De Eingangs-Ausgangs-vorrichtung *(f)*
En input-output device
Es dispositivo de entrada-salida *(m)*
Fr périphérique entrée-sortie *(m)*
It organo di entrata-uscita *(m)*

dispositivo de entrada-salida *(m)* Es
De Eingangs-Ausgangs-vorrichtung *(f)*
En input-output device
Fr périphérique entrée-sortie *(m)*
It organo di entrata-uscita *(m)*
Pt dispositivo de entrada-sair *(m)*

dispositivo de exploração *(m)* Pt
De Abtaster *(m)*
En scanner
Es explorador *(m)*
Fr explorateur *(m)*
It analizzatore per scansione *(m)*

dispositivo de output *(m)* Pt
De Ausgangsvorrichtung *(m)*
En output device
Es dispositivo de salida *(m)*
Fr unité périphérique de sortie *(f)*
It organo di uscita *(m)*

dispositivo de salida *(m)* Es
De Ausgangsvorrichtung *(m)*
En output device
Fr unité périphérique de sortie *(f)*
It organo di uscita *(m)*
Pt dispositivo de output *(m)*

disque *(m) n* Fr
De Platte *(f)*
En disc; disk
Es disco *(m)*
It disco *(m)*
Pt disco *(m)*

disque à cartouche *(m)* Fr
De Patronenplatte *(f)*
En cartridge disk
Es disco de cartucho *(m)*
It disco a cartuccia *(m)*
Pt disco de carga *(m)*

disque dur *(m)* Fr
De Hartplatte *(f)*
En hard disk
Es disco duro *(m)*
It discho duro *(m)*
Pt disco duro *(m)*

disque magnétique *(m)* Fr
De Magnetplatte *(f)*
En magnetic disk
Es disco magnético *(m)*
It disco magnetico *(m)*
Pt disco magnético *(m)*

disque souple *(m)* Fr
De Floppy Disk *(m)*
En floppy disk
Es disco blando *(m)*
It floppy disk *(m)*
Pt disco floppy *(m)*

disqueta *(f) n* Pt
De Diskette *(f)*
En diskette
Es disco flexible *(m)*
Fr minidisque *(m)*
It diskette *(m)*

distance de signalisation *(f)* Fr
De Signalabstand *(m)*
En signal distance
Es distancia de señal *(f)*
It distanza del segnale *(f)*
Pt distância de sinal *(f)*

distancia de señal *(f)* Es
De Signalabstand *(m)*
En signal distance
Fr distance de signalisation *(f)*
It distanza del segnale *(f)*
Pt distância de sinal *(f)*

distância de sinal *(f)* Pt
De Signalabstand *(m)*
En signal distance
Es distancia de señal *(f)*
Fr distance de signalisation *(f)*
It distanza del segnale *(f)*

distanza dalla testina *(f)* It
De Magnetkopfspalt *(m)*
En head gap
Es entrehierro *(m)*
Fr entrefer *(m)*
Pt intervalo de cabeça *(m)*

distanza del segnale *(f)* It
De Signalabstand *(m)*
En signal distance
Es distancia de señal *(f)*
Fr distance de signalisation *(f)*
Pt distância de sinal *(f)*

distanza tra i record *(f)* It
De Satzzwischenraum *(m)*
En inter-record gap
Es separación entre registros *(f)*
Fr espace interbloc *(m)*
Pt intervalo entre registos *(m)*

distributed processing En
De verteilte Verarbeitung *(f)*
Es proceso distribuido *(m)*
Fr informatique répartie *(f)*
It elaborazione ripartita *(f)*
Pt tratamento distribuido *(m)*

ditta specializzata nel fare programmi per conto terzi *(f)* It
De Softwarehaus *(n)*
Es sociedad especializada en programación *(f)*
En software house
Fr société de services et de conseils en informatique (SSCI) *(f)*
Pt casa de software *(f)*

divider *n* En
De Teiler *(m)*
Es divisor *(m)*
Fr diviseur *(m)*
It divisore *(m)*
Pt divisor *(m)*

diviseur *(m) n* Fr
De Teiler *(m)*
En divider
Es divisor *(m)*
It divisore *(m)*
Pt divisor *(m)*

divisor *(m) n* Es, Pt
De Teiler *(m)*
En divider
Fr diviseur *(m)*
It divisore *(m)*

divisore *(m) n* It
De Teiler *(m)*
En divider
Es divisor *(m)*
Fr diviseur *(m)*
Pt divisor *(m)*

dizionario *(m) n* It
De Wörterbuch *(n)*
En dictionary
Es diccionario *(m)*
Fr dictionnaire *(m)*
Pt dicionário *(m)*

doble control *(m)* Es
De Doppelprüfung *(f)*
En twin check
Fr double contrôle *(m)*
It doppio controllo *(m)*
Pt verificação dupla paralela *(f)*

doble longitud *(f)* Es
De Doppellänge *(f)*
En double-length
Fr longueur double *(f)*
It lunghezza doppia *(f)*
Pt comprimento duplo *(m)*

doble precisión *(f)* Es
De Doppelgenauigkeit *(f)*
En double precision
Fr double précision *(f)*
It precisione doppia *(f)*
Pt precisão dupla *(f)*

document *n* En; Fr *(m)*
De Schriftstück *(m)*
Es documento *(m)*
It documento *(m)*
Pt documento *(m)*

documentação *(f) n* Pt
De Programmunterlagen *(pl)*
En documentation
Es documentación *(f)*
Fr documentation *(f)*
It documentazione *(f)*

documentación *(f) n* Es
De Programmunterlagen *(pl)*
En documentation
Fr documentation *(f)*
It documentazione *(f)*
Pt documentação *(f)*

documentation *n* En; Fr *(f)*
De Programmunterlagen *(pl)*
Es documentación *(f)*
It documentazione *(f)*
Pt documentação *(f)*

documentazione *(f) n* It
De Programmunterlagen *(pl)*
En documentation
Es documentación *(f)*
Fr documentation *(f)*
Pt documentação *(f)*

document de base *(m)* Fr
De Quelldokument *(n)*
En source document
Es documento fuente *(m)*
It documento origine *(m)*
Pt documento de origem *(m)*

document en clair *(m)* Fr
De dauerhafter Text *(m)*
En hard copy
Es salida impresa *(f)*
It copia stampata *(f)*
Pt cópia dura *(f)*

documento *(m) n* Es, It, Pt
De Schriftstück *(m)*
En document
Fr document *(m)*

documento de origem *(m)* Pt
De Quelldokument *(n)*
En source document
Es documento fuente *(m)*
Fr document de base *(m)*
It documento origine *(m)*

documento fuente *(m)* Es
De Quelldokument *(n)*
En source document
Fr document de base *(m)*
It documento origine *(m)*
Pt documento de origem *(m)*

documento origine *(m)* It
De Quelldokument *(n)*
En source document
Es documento fuente *(m)*
Fr document de base *(m)*
Pt documento de origem *(m)*

document sorter En
De Schriftstücksortierer *(m)*
Es clasificadora de documentos *(f)*
Fr trieuse de documents *(f)*
It selezionatrice di documenti *(f)*
Pt classificador de documentação *(m)*

donnée d'essai *(f)* Fr
De Prüfdaten *(pl)*
En test data
Es datos para ensayo *(m pl)*
It dati di prova *(m pl)*
Pt dados de ensaio *(m pl)*

donnée élémentaire *(f)* Fr
De Datenfeld *(n)*
En data item
Es unidad de información *(f)*
It voce di dato *(f)*
Pt item de dados *(m)*

données *(f pl) n* Fr
De Daten *(pl)*
En data
Es datos *(m pl)*
It dati *(m pl)*
Pt dados *(m pl)*

données brutes *(f pl)* Fr
De Ursprungsdaten *(pl)*
En raw data
Es datos sin procesar *(m pl)*
It dati crudi *(m pl)*
Pt dados em bruto *(m pl)*

données de contrôle *(f pl)* Fr
De Steuerungsdaten *(pl)*
En control data
Es datos de control *(m pl)*
It dati di controllo *(m pl)*
Pt dados de controlo *(m pl)*

Doppelbetrieb *(m) n* De
En dual operation
Es operación dual *(f)*
Fr double opération *(f)*
It operazione duplice *(f)*
Pt operação dupla *(f)*

Doppelgenauigkeit *(f) n* De
En double precision
Es doble precisión *(f)*
Fr double précision *(f)*
It precisione doppia *(f)*
Pt precisão dupla *(f)*

Doppellänge *(f) n* De
En double-length
Es doble longitud *(f)*
Fr longueur double *(f)*
It lunghezza doppia *(f)*
Pt comprimento duplo *(m)*

doppeln *vb* De
En duplicate
Es duplicar
Fr faire le double
It duplicare
Pt duplicar

Doppelprüfung *(f) n* De
En twin check
Es doble control *(m)*
Fr double contrôle *(m)*
It doppio controllo *(m)*
Pt verificação dupla paralela *(f)*

Doppelzugriffsantrieb *(m) n* De
En dual-access drive
Es unidad de doble acceso *(f)*
Fr entraînement d'accès double *(m)*
It unità ad accesso duplice *(f)*
Pt accionamento de acesso duplo *(m)*

doppio controllo *(m)* It
De Doppelprüfung *(f)*
En twin check
Es doble control *(m)*
Fr double contrôle *(m)*
Pt verificação dupla paralela *(f)*

dossier arquivado *(m)* Pt
De archivierte Datei *(f)*
En archived file
Es fichero archivado *(m)*
Fr fichier archivé *(m)*
It file archiviato *(m)*

dossier sous enveloppe *(m)* Fr
De Hülldatei *(f)*
En enveloped file
Es fichero envuelto *(m)*
It file inviluppato *(m)*
Pt arquivo envolvido *(m)*

dot matrix En
De Punktmatrix *(f)*
Es matriz de puntos *(f)*
Fr matrice par points *(f)*
It matrice di punti *(f)*
Pt matriz de pontos *(f)*

dot printer En
De Punktdrucker *(m)*
Es impresora por puntos *(f)*

Fr imprimante par points *(f)*
It stampatrice a punti *(f)*
Pt impressora de pontos *(f)*

double contrôle *(m)* Fr
De Doppelprüfung *(f)*
En twin check
Es doble control *(m)*
It doppio controllo *(m)*
Pt verificação dupla paralela *(f)*

double-length En
De Doppellänge *(f)*
Es doble longitud *(f)*
Fr longueur double *(f)*
It lunghezza doppia *(f)*
Pt comprimento duplo *(m)*

double opération *(f)* Fr
De Doppelbetrieb *(m)*
En dual operation
Es operación dual *(f)*
It operazione duplice *(f)*
Pt operação dupla *(f)*

double precision En
De Doppelgenauigkeit *(f)*
Es doble precisión *(f)*
Fr double précision *(f)*
It precisione doppia *(f)*
Pt precisão dupla *(f)*

double précision *(f)* Fr
De Doppelgenauigkeit *(f)*
En double precision
Es doble precisión *(f)*
It precisione doppia *(f)*
Pt precisão dupla *(f)*

downtime *n* En
De Ausfallzeit *(f)*
Es tiempo de pana *(m)*
Fr temps de panne *(m)*
It tempo di panna *(m)*
Pt tempo de paragem *(m)*

drapeau *(m) n* Fr
De Markierung *(f)*
En flag
Es señalizador *(m)*
It indicatore *(m)*
Pt bandeira *(f)*

drapeau groupe *(m)* Fr
De Trennmarke *(f)*
En group mark
Es marca de grupo *(f)*
It segno di gruppo *(m)*
Pt marca de grupo *(f)*

drapeau indicateur *(m)* Fr
De Endezeichen *(n)*
En end mark
Es marca final *(f)*
It marcatura di fine *(f)*
Pt marca final *(f)*

Dreiadressen-anweisung *(f) n* De
En three-address instruction
Es instrucción con tres direcciones *(f)*
Fr instruction à trois adresses *(f)*
It istruzione a tre indirizzi *(f)*
Pt instrução de três endereços *(f)*

Dreieingangs-datenelement *(n) n* De
En three-input element
Es elemento con tres entradas *(m)*
Fr élément à trois entrées *(m)*
It elemento a tre entrati *(m)*
Pt elemento de três entradas *(m)*

dreifache Präzision *(f)* De
En triple precision
Es precisión triple *(f)*
Fr précision triple *(f)*
It precisione tripla *(f)*
Pt precisão tripla *(f)*

Drei-Überschuß *(m) n* De
En excess three
Es tres excedente *(m)*
Fr code plus trois *(m)*
It tre di eccesso *(m)*
Pt três em excesso *(m)*

drittgeneration *adj* De
En third-generation
Es tercera-generación
Fr troisième-génération
It terza-generazione
Pt terceira-geração

drive *vb* En
De antreiben
Es impulsar
Fr entraîner
It azionare
Pt accionar

Drucker *(m) n* De
En printer
Es impresora *(f)*
Fr imprimante *(f)*
It stampatrice *(f)*
Pt impressora *(f)*

Druckformat *(n) n* De
En print format
Es formato de impresión *(m)*
Fr présentation de l'impression *(f)*
It formato di stampa *(m)*
Pt formato de impressão *(m)*

Drucklocher *(m) n* De
En printing punch
Es perforadora impresora *(f)*
Fr perforatrice imprimante *(f)*
It perforatrice di stampa *(f)*
Pt perfuradora de impressão *(f)*

drum *n* En
De Trommel *(f)*
Es tambor *(m)*
Fr tambour *(m)*
It tamburo *(m)*
Pt tambor *(m)*

drum plotter En
De Trommelkurven-zeichner *(m)*
Es trazador a tambor *(m)*
Fr traceur à tambour *(m)*
It tracciatore a tamburo *(m)*
Pt plotador de tambor *(m)*

drum printer En
De Trommeldrucker *(m)*
Es impresora a tambor *(f)*
Fr imprimante à tambour *(f)*
It stampatrice a tamburo *(f)*
Pt impressora de tambor *(f)*

dry run En
De Versuchslauf *(m)*
Es pasada en seco *(f)*
Fr coup d'essai *(m)*
It passo a prova *(m)*
Pt passagem a seco *(f)*

dual-access drive En
De Doppelzugriffsantrieb *(m)*
Es unidad de doble acceso *(f)*
Fr entraînement d'accès double *(m)*
It unità ad accesso duplice *(f)*
Pt accionamento de acesso duplo *(m)*

dual operation En
De Doppelbetrieb *(m)*
Es operación dual *(f)*
Fr double opération *(f)*
It operazione duplice *(f)*
Pt operação dupla *(f)*

dual processor En
De Parallelverarbeiter *(m)*
Es biprocesador *(m)*
Fr biprocesseur *(m)*
It elaboratore duplice *(m)*
Pt processador duplo *(m)*

dual recording En
De Parallelaufzeichnung *(f)*
Es registro en paralelo *(m)*
Fr enregistrement double *(m)*
It registrazione duplice *(f)*
Pt registo duplo *(m)*

dummy *adj* En
De Schein-
Es ficticio
Fr fictif
It fittizio
Pt simulado

dummy instruction En
De Blindbefehl *(m)*
Es instrucción ficticia *(f)*
Fr instruction fictive *(f)*

It istruzione fittizia *(f)*
Pt instrução simulada *(f)*

dummy variable En
De Scheinvariable *(f)*
Es variable ficticia *(f)*
Fr variable fictive *(f)*
It variabile fittizia *(f)*
Pt variável simulada *(f)*

dump *n* En; It *(m)*
De Speicherauszug *(m)*
Es vuelco de la memoria *(m)*
Fr vidage *(m)*
Pt descarregador *(m)*

dump *vb* En
De speicherausziehen
Es volcar
Fr vider
It fare un dump
Pt descarregar

dump check En
De Speicherauszugs-prüfung *(f)*
Es control por vaciado *(m)*
Fr contrôle par vidage *(m)*
It controllo del dump *(m)*
Pt verificação de descarga *(f)*

dump della memoria *(m)* It
De Speicherauszug *(m)*
En memory dump
Es vuelco de la memoria *(m)*
Fr vidage de la mémoire *(m)*
Pt descarregador de memória *(m)*

dump di autopsia *(m)* It
De Speicherauszug nach dem Tode *(m)*
En post-mortem dump
Es vaciado póstumo *(m)*
Fr vidage d'autopsie *(m)*
Pt descarregador de autópsia *(m)*

dump di salvataggio *(m)* It
De Wiedereinstiegs-speicherauszug *(m)*
En rescue dump
Es vaciado de rescate *(m)*
Fr vidage de secours *(m)*
Pt armazém de emergência *(m)*

dump point En
De Speichauszugspunkt *(m)*
Es punto de vaciado *(m)*
Fr point de vidage *(m)*
It punto di dump *(m)*
Pt ponto de descarga *(m)*

dump statico *(m)* It
De statischer Speicherauszug *(m)*
En static dump
Es vuelco estático de la memoria *(m)*
Fr vidage en un point fixe du programme *(m)*
Pt descarregador estático *(m)*

Dünnfilmspeicher *(m) n* De
En thin-film memory
Es memoria de película delgada *(f)*
Fr mémoire à couche mince *(f)*
It memoria a pellicola sottile *(f)*
Pt memória de película fina *(f)*

duplex computer system En
De Duplex-Rechnersystem *(n)*
Es sistema de ordenador duplex *(m)*
Fr système informatique en duplex *(m)*
It sistema di calcolatore doppio *(m)*
Pt sistema de computador duplex *(m)*

Duplex-Rechnersystem *(n)* De
En duplex computer system
Es sistema de ordenador duplex *(m)*
Fr système informatique en duplex *(m)*
It sistema di calcolatore doppio *(m)*
Pt sistema de computador duplex *(m)*

duplicação *(f) n* Pt
De Verdopplung *(f)*
En duplication
Es duplicación *(f)*
Fr duplication *(f)*
It duplicazione *(f)*

duplicación *(f) n* Es
De Verdopplung *(f)*
En duplication
Fr duplication *(f)*
It duplicazione *(f)*
Pt duplicação *(f)*

duplicar *vb* Es, Pt
De doppeln
En duplicate
Fr faire le double
It duplicare

duplicare *vb* It
De doppeln
En duplicate
Es duplicar
Fr faire le double
Pt duplicar

duplicate *vb* En
De doppeln
Es duplicar
Fr faire le double
It duplicare
Pt duplicar

duplication *n* En; Fr *(f)*
De Verdopplung *(f)*
Es duplicación *(f)*
It duplicazione *(f)*
Pt duplicação *(f)*

duplicazione *(f) n* It
De Verdopplung *(f)*
En duplication
Es duplicación *(f)*
Fr duplication *(f)*
Pt duplicação *(f)*

Durchfluß *(m) n* De
En throughput
Es capacidad de tratamiento *(f)*
Fr débit *(m)*
It capacità di trattamento *(f)*
Pt capacidade de tratamento *(f)*

Durchführung *(f) n* De
En implementation
Es realización *(f)*
Fr mise en application *(f)*
It implementazione *(f)*
Pt implementação *(f)*

Durchlauf *(m) n* De
En run
Es pasada *(f)*
Fr passage *(m)*
It esecuzione *(f)*
Pt passagem *(f)*

durchlaufen *vb* De
En run
Es pasar
Fr exécuter
It passare
Pt passar

Durchlaufzeit *(f) n* De
En run time
Es tiempo de pasada *(m)*
Fr temps d'exécution *(m)*
It tempo di esecuzione *(m)*
Pt tempo de passagem *(m)*

Durchschlag *(m) n* De
En crash
Es choque *(m)*
Fr accélération *(f)*
It urto *(m)*
Pt colisão *(f)*

durchschlagen *vb* De
En crash
Es quebrar
Fr accélérer
It urtare
Pt colidir

durchsichtig *adj* De
En transparent
Es transparente
Fr transparent
It trasparente
Pt transparente

Durchsichtigkeit *(f) n* De
En transparency
Es transparencia *(f)*
Fr transparence *(f)*
It trasparenza *(f)*
Pt transparência *(f)*

durée de lecture *(f)* Fr
De Auslesezeit *(f)*
En read time
Es tiempo de lectura *(m)*
It tempo di lettura *(m)*
Pt tempo de leitura *(m)*

durée d'essai de fonctionnement *(f)* Fr
De Kontrollzeit *(f)*
En proving time
Es tiempo de ensayo *(m)*
It tempo di prova *(m)*
Pt tempo de prova *(m)*

durée d'exécution *(f)* Fr
De Aktivierungszeit *(f)*
En execution time
Es tiempo de ejecución *(m)*
It tempo di esecuzione *(m)*
Pt tempo de execução *(m)*

dyadic operation En
De zweistellige Funktion *(f)*
Es operación diádica *(f)*
Fr opération dvadique *(f)*
It operazione diadica *(f)*
Pt operação diádica *(f)*

dynamic allocation En
De dynamische Zuweisung *(f)*
Es asignación dinámica *(f)*
Fr affectation dynamique *(f)*
It allocazione dinamica *(f)*
Pt designação dinâmica *(f)*

dynamic debugging technique (DDT) En
De dynamische Fehlerbeseitigung *(f)*
Es técnica dinámica de depuración *(f)*
Fr technique de mise au point dynamique *(f)*
It tecnica di messa a punto di un programma dinamica *(f)*
Pt técnica de desparatização dinâmica *(f)*

dynamic memory En
De dynamischer Speicher *(m)*
Es memoria dinámica *(f)*
Fr mémoire dynamique *(f)*
It memoria dinamica *(f)*
Pt memória dinâmico *(f)*

dynamische Fehlerbeseitigung *(f)* De
En dynamic debugging technique (DDT)
Es técnica dinámica de depuración *(f)*
Fr technique de mise au point dynamique *(f)*
It tecnica di messa a punto di un programma dinamica *(f)*
Pt técnica de desparatização dinâmica *(f)*

dynamischer Speicher *(m)* De
En dynamic memory
Es memoria dinámica *(f)*
Fr mémoire dynamique *(f)*
It memoria dinamica *(f)*
Pt memória dinâmico *(f)*

dynamische Zuweisung *(f)* De
En dynamic allocation
Es asignación dinámica *(f)*
Fr affectation dynamique *(f)*
It allocazione dinamica *(f)*
Pt designação dinâmica *(f)*

E

échange *(m) n* Fr
De Vermittlung *(f)*
En exchange
Es intercambio *(m)*
It scambio *(m)*
Pt intercâmbio *(m)*

échelle *(f) n* Fr
De Skala *(f)*
En scale
Es escala *(f)*
It scala *(f)*
Pt escala *(f)*

échelle des temps *(f)* Fr
De Zeitskala *(f)*
En time scale
Es escala de tiempos *(f)*
It scala di tempo *(f)*
Pt escala de tempo *(f)*

echo check En
De Echoprüfung *(f)*
Es verificación por eco *(f)*
Fr contrôle par écho *(m)*
It controllo dell'eco *(m)*
Pt verificação de eco *(f)*

Echoprüfung *(f) n* De
En echo check
Es verificación por eco *(f)*
Fr contrôle par écho *(m)*
It controllo dell'eco *(m)*
Pt verificação de eco *(f)*

echte Adresse *(f)* De
En actual address
Es dirección real *(f)*
Fr adresse réelle *(f)*
It indirizzo effettivo *(m)*
Pt direcção real *(f)*

Echtheitstabelle *(f) n* De
En truth table
Es tabla de decisión lógica *(f)*
Fr table de vérité *(f)*
It tavola della verità *(f)*
Pt tabela de valores verdadeiros *(f)*

Echtzeit *(f) n* De
En real time
Es tiempo real *(m)*
Fr temps réel *(m)*
It tempo reale *(m)*
Pt tempo real *(m)*

econometria *(f) n* It
De Ökonometrik *(f)*
En econometrics
Es econométrica *(f)*
Fr économétrie *(f)*
Pt econométrica *(f)*

econométrica *(f) n* Es, Pt
De Ökonometrik *(f)*
En econometrics
Fr économétrie *(f)*
It econometria *(f)*

econometrics *n* En
De Ökonometrik *(f)*
Es econométrica *(f)*
Fr économétrie *(f)*
It econometria *(f)*
Pt econométrica *(f)*

économétrie *(f) n* Fr
De Ökonometrik *(f)*
En econometrics
Es econométrica *(f)*
It econometria *(f)*
Pt econométrica *(f)*

écran *(m) n* Fr, Pt
De Schirm *(m)*
En screen
Es pantalla *(f)*
It schermo *(m)*

écrêtage polygone *(m)* Fr
De Vieleckbegrenzung *(f)*
En polygon clipping
Es recorte poligonal *(m)*
It limitazione poligonale *(f)*
Pt recorte poligonal *(m)*

écrire *vb* Fr
De schreiben
En write
Es escribir
It scrivere
Pt escrever

écrire à la machine Fr
De maschinenschreiben
En type
Es escribir a máquina

It scrivere a macchina
Pt escrever à máquina

écrire en regroupant Fr
De sammelnbeschreiben
En gather write
Es escribir agrupada
It scrivere di raccolta
Pt escrever em condensado

écriture immédiate *(f)* Fr
De Abrufschreiben *(n)*
En demand writing
Es escritura inmediata *(f)*
It scrittura a domanda *(f)*
Pt escrita de procura *(f)*

edieren *vb* De
En edit
Es editar
Fr mettre en forme
It manipolare
Pt editar

edit *vb* En
De edieren
Es editar
Fr mettre en forme
It manipolare
Pt editar

editar *vb* Es, Pt
De edieren
En edit
Fr mettre en forme
It manipolare

éditeur de textes *(m)* Fr
De Textredakteur *(m)*
En text editor
Es editor de texto *(m)*
It programma di manipolazione di testo *(m)*
Pt editor de textos *(m)*

editor *n* En
De Redakteur *(m)*
Es programa de edición *(m)*
Fr programme d'édition *(m)*
It programma di manipolazione *(m)*
Pt programa de edição *(m)*

editor de texto *(m)* Es
De Textredakteur *(m)*
En text editor
Fr éditeur de textes *(m)*
It programma di manipolazione di testo *(m)*
Pt editor de textos *(m)*

editor de textos *(m)* Pt
De Textredakteur *(m)*
En text editor
Es editor de texto *(m)*
Fr éditeur de textes *(m)*
It programma di manipolazione di testo *(m)*

effacement *(m) n* Fr
De Löschung *(f)*
En deletion; erase
Es borrado; eliminación *(m f)*
It cancellazione *(f)*
Pt apagado; eliminação *(m f)*

effacer *vb* Fr
De löschen
En erase
Es borrar
It cancellare
Pt apagar

effective address En
De effektive Adresse *(f)*
Es dirección efectiva *(f)*
Fr adresse réelle *(f)*
It indirizzo efficace *(m)*
Pt endereço real *(m)*

effective time En
De effektive Zeit *(f)*
Es tiempo efectivo *(m)*
Fr temps utile *(m)*
It tempo efficace *(m)*
Pt tempo efectivo *(m)*

effektive Adresse *(f)* De
En effective address
Es dirección efectiva *(f)*
Fr adresse réelle *(f)*
It indirizzo efficace *(m)*
Pt endereço real *(m)*

effektive Reparaturzeit *(f)* De
En mean repair time
Es tiempo medio para reparación *(m)*
Fr temps moyen de réparation *(m)*
It tempo di riparazione medio *(m)*
Pt tempo médio de reparação *(m)*

effektive Zeit *(f)* De
En effective time
Es tiempo efectivo *(m)*
Fr temps utile *(m)*
It tempo efficace *(m)*
Pt tempo efectivo *(m)*

Effektivzeit zwischen Ausfällen *(f)* De
En mean time between failures
Es tiempo medio entre fallos *(m)*
Fr moyenne des temps de bon fonctionnement *(f)*
It tempo medio tra i guasti *(m)*
Pt tempo médio entre falhas *(m)*

eigensicher *adj* De
En fail-safe
Es sin riesgo de fallo
Fr à sécurité intégrée
It sicuro contro guasti
Pt seguro contra falhas

eighty-column card En
De achtzig-Spalten-Karte *(f)*
Es tarjeta de ochenta columnas *(f)*
Fr carte de quatre-vingt colonnes *(f)*
It scheda ad ottanta colonne *(f)*
Pt ficha de oitenta colunas *(f)*

Einerkomplement *(n) n* De
En ones complement
Es complemento a uno *(m)*
Fr complément à un *(m)*
It complemento all'uno *(m)*
Pt complemento de unidades *(m)*

Eingang *(m) n* De
En entry; input
Es entrada *(f)*
Fr entrée *(f)*
It entrata *(f)*
Pt entrada *(f)*

Eingang-Ausgang De
En input-output
Es entrada-salida
Fr entrée-sortie
It entrata-uscita
Pt entrada-sair

Eingangs-Ausgangsanschluß *(m)* De
En input-output port
Es puerta de entrada-salida *(f)*
Fr point d'accès entrée-sortie *(m)*
It porto entrata-uscita *(m)*
Pt abertura de entrada-sair *(f)*

Eingangs-Ausgangspuffer *(m)* De
En input-output buffer
Es memoria intermedia de entrada-salida *(f)*
Fr tampon entrée-sortie *(m)*
It memoria di transito entrata-uscita *(f)*
Pt separador de entrada-sair *(m)*

Eingangs-Ausgangs-vorrichtung *(f)* De
En input-output device
Es dispositivo de entrada-salida *(m)*
Fr périphérique entrée-sortie *(m)*
It organo di entrata-uscita *(m)*
Pt dispositivo de entrada-sair *(m)*

Eingangspuffer *(m) n* De
En input buffer
Es memoria intermedia de entrada *(f)*
Fr tampon d'entrée *(m)*
It memoria di transito dell'entrata *(f)*
Pt separador de entrada *(m)*

Eingangspunkt *(m) n* De
En entry point
Es punto de entrada *(m)*
Fr point d'entrée *(m)*

It punto di entrata *(m)*
Pt ponto de entrada *(m)*

Eingangsvorrichtung *(f)* *n* De
En input device
Es dispositivo de entrada *(m)*
Fr périphérique d'entrée *(m)*
It organo di entrata *(m)*
Pt dispositivo de entrada *(m)*

eingeben *vb* De
En input
Es introducir
Fr entrer
It immettere
Pt entrar

Einheit *(f)* *n* De
En unit
Es unidad *(f)*
Fr unité *(f)*
It unità *(f)*
Pt unidade *(f)*

Einheitssatz *(m)* *n* De
En unit record
Es registro unitario *(m)*
Fr enregistrement unitaire *(m)*
It record di unitá *(m)*
Pt registo de unidades *(m)*

Einlage *(f)* *n* De
En deposit
Es depósito *(m)*
Fr dépôt *(m)*
It deposito *(m)*
Pt depósito *(m)*

einrichten *vb* De
En set up
Es montar
Fr mettre en place
It mettere a punto
Pt instalar

Einrichtezeit *(f)* *n* De
En set-up time
Es tiempo de preparación *(m)*
Fr temps de préparation *(m)*
It tempo messa a punto *(m)*
Pt tempo de instalação *(m)*

Eins-plus-Eins-Adresse *(f)* De
En one-plus-one address
Es dirección uno más uno *(f)*
Fr à une plus une adresse *(f)*
It indirizzo uno-più-uno *(m)*
Pt endereço um mais um *(m)*

Einstufenspeicher *(m)* *n* De
En one-level store
Es memoria de un solo nivel *(f)*
Fr mémoire à un niveau *(f)*
It memoria ad un livello *(f)*
Pt armazém de um só nível *(m)*

eintasten *vb* De
En keyboard
Es introducir desde teclado
Fr introduire par clavier
It introdurre (dati) mediante la tastiera
Pt introduzir desde teclado

Einzeladressanweisung *(f)* *n* De
En single-address instruction
Es instrucción de una sola dirección *(f)*
Fr instruction à une adresse *(f)*
It istruzione ad indirizzo singolo *(f)*
Pt instrução de endereço único *(f)*

Einzeleinheit *(f)* *n* De
En identity unit
Es unidad de identidad *(f)*
Fr unité d'identification *(f)*
It unità di identità *(f)*
Pt unidade de identidade *(f)*

Einzelelement *(n)* *n* De
En identity element
Es elemento de identidad *(m)*
Fr élément d'identification *(m)*
It elemento di identità *(m)*
Pt elemento de identidade *(m)*

Einzelschrittfunktion *(f)* *n* De
En single-step operation
Es operación de paso único *(f)*
Fr opération en pas à pas *(f)*
It operazione a fase singola *(f)*
Pt operação de uma só fase *(f)*

Einzustand *(m)* *n* De
En one state
Es estado uno *(m)*
Fr état un *(m)*
It stato uno *(m)*
Pt estado de unidade *(m)*

either-or operation En
De Entweder-oder-Funktion *(f)*
Es operación ambos o uno *(f)*
Fr opération soit-ou *(f)*
It operazione sia-o *(f)*
Pt operação de ou-ou *(f)*

ejecutar *vb* Es
De aktivieren
En execute
Fr exécuter
It eseguire
Pt executar

elaborare *vb* It
De bearbeiten
En process
Es procesar
Fr traiter
Pt processar

elaboratore *(m)* *n* It
De Computer; Verarbeiter *(m)*
En computer; processor
Es ordenador; procesador *(m)*
Fr ordinateur *(m)*
Pt computador; processor *(m)*

elaboratore analogico *(m)* It
De Analogrechner *(m)*
En analog computer
Es ordenador analógico *(m)*
Fr calculateur analogique *(m)*
Pt computador de analogia *(m)*

elaboratore a scopo generale *(m)* It
De Allgemeinzweck-computer *(m)*
En general-purpose computer
Es ordenador universal *(m)*
Fr calculateur universel *(m)*
Pt computador para todos os fins *(m)*

elaboratore a scopo speciale *(m)* It
De Spezialrechner *(m)*
En special-purpose computer
Es ordenador especializado *(m)*
Fr calculateur spécialisé *(m)*
Pt computador para fins especiais *(m)*

elaboratore da tavolo *(m)* It
De Tischrechner *(m)*
En desk-top computer
Es ordenador de mesa *(m)*
Fr petit ordinateur de bureau *(m)*
Pt computador de mesa *(m)*

elaboratore digitale *(m)* It
De Digitalrechner *(m)*
En digital computer
Es ordenador digital *(m)*
Fr calculateur numérique *(m)*
Pt computador digital *(m)*

elaboratore duplice *(m)* It
De Parallelverarbeiter *(m)*
En dual processor

Es biprocesador *(m)*
Fr biprocesseur *(m)*
Pt processador duplo *(m)*

elaboratore ibrido *(m)* It
De Hybridrechner *(m)*
En hybrid computer
Es ordenador híbrido *(m)*
Fr calculateur hybride *(m)*
Pt computador híbrido *(m)*

elaboratore multiplo *(m)* It
De Mehrprozessor-system *(n)*
En multiprocessor
Es procesador múltiple *(m)*
Fr multicalculateur *(m)*
Pt multiprocessador *(m)*

elaboratore per conto terzi *(m)* It
De Wirtsrechner *(m)*
En host computer
Es ordenador anfitrión *(m)*
Fr ordinateur central *(m)*
Pt computador hospedeiro *(m)*

elaboratore pneumatico *(m)* It
De pneumatischer Computer *(m)*
En pneumatic computer
Es ordenador neumático *(m)*
Fr ordinateur pneumatique *(m)*
Pt computador pneumático *(m)*

elaboratore sincrono *(m)* It
De Synchronisierrechner *(m)*
En synchronous computer
Es ordenador síncrono *(m)*
Fr calculateur synchrone *(m)*
Pt computador sincronizado *(m)*

elaborazione *(f)* *n* It
De Verarbeitung *(f)*
En processing
Es tratamiento *(m)*
Fr traitement *(m)*
Pt processamento *(m)*

elaborazione a distanza *(f)* It
De Fernverarbeitung *(f)*
En remote processing
Es proceso a distancia *(m)*
Fr télétraitement *(m)*
Pt tele-processamento *(m)*

elaborazione a domanda *(f)* It
De Abrufverarbeitung *(f)*
En demand processing
Es tratamiento inmediato *(m)*
Fr traitement immédiat *(m)*
Pt processamento de procura *(m)*

elaborazione a lotti *(f)* It
De Stapelverarbeitung *(f)*
En batch processing
Es proceso por lotes *(m)*
Fr traitement par lot *(m)*
Pt tratamento por lotes *(m)*

elaborazione automatica dei dati *(f)* It
De automatische Datenverarbeitung *(f)*
En automatic data processing
Es proceso automático de datos *(m)*
Fr traitement automatique de l'information (TAI) *(m)*
Pt tratamento automático de dados *(m)*

elaborazione concorrente *(f)* It
De verzahnt ablaufende Verarbeitung *(f)*
En concurrent processing
Es proceso concurrente *(m)*
Fr traitement en simultané *(m)*
Pt processamento concorrente *(m)*

elaborazione dei dati *(f)* It
De Datenverarbeitung *(f)*
En data processing (DP)
Es proceso de datos *(m)*
Fr traitement de l'information *(m)*
Pt tratamento de dados *(m)*

elaborazione della lista *(f)* It
De Listenverarbeitung *(f)*
En list processing
Es proceso por lista *(m)*
Fr traitement de liste *(m)*
Pt processamento de lista *(m)*

elaborazione delle informazioni *(f)* It
De Informations-verarbeitung *(f)*
En information processing
Es proceso de la información *(m)*
Fr traitement de l'information *(m)*
Pt tratamento da informação *(m)*

elaborazione delle transazioni *(f)* It
De Transaktions-verarbeitung *(f)*
En transaction processing
Es proceso de transacciones *(m)*
Fr traitement transactionnel *(m)*
Pt processamento de transacções *(m)*

elaborazione di primo piano *(f)* It
De Vordergrund-verarbeitung *(f)*
En foreground processing
Es proceso preferente *(m)*
Fr traitement de front *(m)*
Pt processamento de primeiro plano *(m)*

elaborazione di priorità *(f)* It
De Vorrangverarbeitung *(f)*
En priority processing
Es tratamiento por prioridad *(m)*
Fr traitement par priorités *(m)*
Pt processamento prioritário *(m)*

elaborazione di vettori *(f)* It
De Vektorverarbeitung *(f)*
En vector processing
Es proceso vectorial *(m)*
Fr traitement vectoriel *(m)*
Pt processamento de vectores *(m)*

elaborazione elettronica dei dati *(f)* It
De elektronische Datenverarbeitung (EDV) *(f)*
En electronic data processing (EDP)
Es proceso electrónico de datos *(m)*
Fr traitement électronique des données (TED) *(m)*
Pt tratamento electrónico de dados *(m)*

elaborazione in proprio *(f)* It
De Lokalrechnung *(f)*
En home computing
Es cálculo inicial *(m)*
Fr traitement domestique *(m)*
Pt computação doméstica *(f)*

elaborazione in serie *(f)* It
De Reihenverarbeitung *(f)*
En serial processing
Es proceso en serie *(m)*
Fr traitement série *(m)*
Pt processamento em série *(m)*

elaborazione integrata dei dati *(f)* It
De integrierte Datenverarbeitung *(f)*
En integrated data processing (IDP)
Es proceso integrado de datos *(m)*
Fr traitement intégré de l'information (TII) *(m)*
Pt tratamento integrado de dados *(m)*

elaborazione in tempo reale *(f)* It
De Uhrzeigverarbeitung *(f)*
En real-time processing
Es proceso en tiempo real *(m)*
Fr traitement en temps réel *(m)*
Pt processamento de tempo real *(m)*

elaborazione non precedenza *(f)* It
De Hintergrund-verarbeitung *(f)*
En background processing
Es proceso de programas subordinados *(m)*
Fr traitement non prioritaire *(m)*
Pt tratamento de plano de fundo *(m)*

elaborazione parallela *(f)* It
De Parallelsimultan-verarbeitung *(f)*
En parallel processing
Es proceso en paralelo *(m)*
Fr traitement en parallèle *(m)*
Pt processamento paralelo *(m)*

elaborazione ripartita *(f)* It
De verteilte Verarbeitung *(f)*
En distributed processing
Es proceso distribuido *(m)*
Fr informatique répartie *(f)*
Pt tratamento distribuido *(m)*

elaborazione sequenziale *(f)* It
De Folgeverarbeitung *(f)*
En sequential processing
Es proceso secuencial *(m)*
Fr traitement séquentiel *(m)*
Pt processamento sequencial *(m)*

elapsed time En
De verstrichene Zeit *(f)*
Es tiempo transcurrido *(m)*
Fr temps écoulé *(m)*
It tempo trascorso *(m)*
Pt tempo decorrido *(m)*

elasticidade *(f) n* Pt
De Nachgiebigkeit *(f)*
En resilience
Es resiliencia *(f)*
Fr résilience *(f)*
It resilienza *(f)*

electric (or **electrical**) *adj* En
De elektrisch
Es eléctrico
Fr électrique
It elettrico
Pt eléctrico

eléctrico *adj* Es, Pt
De elektrisch
En electric; electrical
Fr électrique
It elettrico

électrique *adj* Fr
De elektrisch
En electric; electrical
Es eléctrico
It elettrico
Pt eléctrico

electron beam recording (EBR) En
De Elektronstrahl-aufzeichnung *(f)*
Es registro por haz de electrones *(m)*
Fr enregistrement à faisceau électronique *(m)*
It registrazione a fascio di elettroni *(f)*
Pt registo de feixe de electrões *(m)*

electronic *adj* En
De elektronisch
Es electrónico
Fr électronique
It elettronico
Pt electrónico

electronic data processing (EDP) En
De elektronische Datenverarbeitung (EDV) *(f)*
Es proceso electrónico de datos *(m)*
Fr traitement électronique des données (TED) *(m)*
It elaborazione elettronica dei dati *(f)*
Pt tratamento electrónico de dados *(m)*

electrónico *adj* Es, Pt
De elektronisch
En electronic
Fr électronique
It elettronico

electronic switch En
De elektronischer Schalter *(m)*
Es conmutador electrónico *(m)*
Fr bascule électronique *(f)*
It interruttore elettronico *(m)*
Pt comutador electrónico *(m)*

électronique *adj* Fr
De elektronisch
En electronic
Es electrónico
It elettronico
Pt electrónico

electrostatic printer En
De elektrostatischer Drucker *(m)*
Es impresora electrostática *(f)*
Fr imprimante électrostatique *(f)*
It stampatrice elettrostatica *(f)*
Pt impressora electrostática *(f)*

elektrisch *adj* De
En electric; electrical
Es eléctrico
Fr électrique
It elettrico
Pt eléctrico

elektronisch *adj* De
En electronic
Es electrónico
Fr électronique
It elettronico
Pt electrónico

elektronische Datenverarbeitung (EDV) *(f)* De
En electronic data processing (EDP)
Es proceso electrónico de datos *(m)*
Fr traitement électronique des données (TED) *(m)*
It elaborazione elettronica dei dati *(f)*
Pt tratamento electrónico de dados *(m)*

elektronischer Schalter *(m)* De
En electronic switch
Es conmutador electrónico *(m)*
Fr bascule électronique *(f)*
It interruttore elettronico *(m)*
Pt comutador electrónico *(m)*

Elektronstrahl-aufzeichnung *(f) n* De
En electron beam recording (EBR)
Es registro por haz de electrones *(m)*
Fr enregistrement à faisceau électronique *(m)*
It registrazione a fascio di elettroni *(f)*
Pt registo de feixe de electrões *(m)*

elektrostatischer Drucker *(m)* De
En electrostatic printer
Es impresora electrostática *(f)*

Fr imprimante électrostatique *(f)*
It stampatrice elettrostatica *(f)*
Pt impressora electrostática *(f)*

element *n* En
De Element *(n)*
Es elemento *(m)*
Fr élément *(m)*
It elemento *(m)*
Pt elemento *(m)*

Element *(n) n* De
En element
Es elemento *(m)*
Fr élément *(m)*
It elemento *(m)*
Pt elemento *(m)*

élément *(m) n* Fr
De Element *(n)*
En element
Es elemento *(m)*
It elemento *(m)*
Pt elemento *(m)*

élément à seuil *(m)* Fr
De Schwellwertdaten-element *(n)*
En threshold element
Es elemento de umbral *(m)*
It elemento di soglia *(m)*
Pt elemento de limiar *(m)*

élément à trois entrées *(m)* Fr
De Dreieingangsdaten-element *(n)*
En three-input element
Es elemento con tres entradas *(m)*
It elemento a tre entrati *(m)*
Pt elemento de três entradas *(m)*

élément d'équivalence *(m)* Fr
De Gleichheitsfunktion *(f)*
En equivalence element
Es elemento de equivalencia *(m)*
It elemento di equivalenza *(m)*
Pt elemento de equivalência *(m)*

élément d'identification *(m)* Fr
De Einzelelement *(n)*
En identity element
Es elemento de identidad *(m)*
It elemento di identità *(m)*
Pt elemento de identidade *(m)*

elementi materiali di elaboratore *(m)* It
De Hardware *(f)*
En hardware
Es equipo físico *(m)*
Fr matériel *(m)*
Pt hardware *(m)*

élément majoritaire *(m)* Fr
De Majoritätselement *(n)*
En majority element
Es elemento mayoritario *(m)*
It elemento di maggioranza *(m)*
Pt elemento de maioria *(m)*

élément matriciel *(m)* Fr
De Matrixelement *(n)*
En matrix element
Es elemento matricial *(m)*
It elemento della matrice *(m)*
Pt elemento de matriz *(m)*

elemento *(m) n* Es, It, Pt
De Element *(n)*
En element
Fr élément *(m)*

elemento a tre entrati *(m)* It
De Dreieingangs-datenelement *(n)*
En three-input element
Es elemento con tres entradas *(m)*
Fr élément à trois entrées *(m)*
Pt elemento de três entradas *(m)*

elemento con tres entradas *(m)* Es
De Dreieingangs-datenelement *(n)*
En three-input element
Fr élément à trois entrées *(m)*
It elemento a tre entrati *(m)*
Pt elemento de três entradas *(m)*

elemento de equivalencia *(m)* Es
De Gleichheitsfunktion *(f)*
En equivalence element
Fr élément d'équivalence *(m)*
It elemento di equivalenza *(m)*
Pt elemento de equivalência *(m)*

elemento de equivalência *(m)* Pt
De Gleichheitsfunktion *(f)*
En equivalence element
Es elemento de equivalencia *(m)*
Fr élément d'équivalence *(m)*
It elemento di equivalenza *(m)*

elemento de identidad *(m)* Es
De Einzelelement *(n)*
En identity element
Fr élément d'identification *(m)*
It elemento di identità *(m)*
Pt elemento de identidade *(m)*

elemento de identidade *(m)* Pt
De Einzelelement *(n)*
En identity element
Es elemento de identidad *(m)*
Fr élément d'identification *(m)*
It elemento di identità *(m)*

elemento de ligação de dados *(m)* Pt
De Datenübermitt-lungsabschnitt *(m)*
En data link
Es enlace para transmisión de datos *(m)*
Fr liaison de transmission *(f)*
It collegamento di dati *(m)*

elemento de ligação digital *(m)* Pt
De Digitalverbindung *(f)*
En digital link
Es enlace digital *(m)*
Fr liaison numérique *(f)*
It collegamento digitale *(m)*

elemento de limiar *(m)* Pt
De Schwellwertdaten-element *(n)*
En threshold element
Es elemento de umbral *(m)*
Fr élément à seuil *(m)*
It elemento di soglia *(m)*

elemento della matrice *(m)* It
De Matrixelement *(n)*
En matrix element
Es elemento matricial *(m)*
Fr élément matriciel *(m)*
Pt elemento de matriz *(m)*

elemento de maioria *(m)* Pt
De Majoritätselement *(n)*
En majority element
Es elemento mayoritario *(m)*
Fr élément majoritaire *(m)*
It elemento di maggioranza *(m)*

elemento de matriz *(m)* Pt
De Matrixelement *(n)*
En matrix element
Es elemento matricial *(m)*
Fr élément matriciel *(m)*
It elemento della matrice *(m)*

elemento de três entradas *(m)* Pt
De Dreieingangs-datenelement *(n)*
En three-input element

Es elemento con tres entradas *(m)*
Fr élément à trois entrées *(m)*
It elemento a tre entrati *(m)*

elemento de umbral *(m)* Es
De Schwellwertdaten-element *(n)*
En threshold element
Fr élément à seuil *(m)*
It elemento di soglia *(m)*
Pt elemento de limiar *(m)*

elemento di equivalenza *(m)* It
De Gleichheitsfunktion *(f)*
En equivalence element
Es elemento de equivalencia *(m)*
Fr élément d'équivalence *(m)*
Pt elemento de equivalência *(m)*

elemento di identità *(m)* It
De Einzelelement *(n)*
En identity element
Es elemento de identidad *(m)*
Fr élément d'identification *(m)*
Pt elemento de identidade *(m)*

elemento di maggioranza *(m)* It
De Majoritätselement *(n)*
En majority element
Es elemento mayoritario *(m)*
Fr élément majoritaire *(m)*
Pt elemento de maioria *(m)*

elemento di soglia *(m)* It
De Schwellwertdaten-element *(n)*
En threshold element
Es elemento de umbral *(m)*
Fr élément à seuil *(m)*
Pt elemento de limiar *(m)*

elemento matricial *(m)* Es
De Matrixelement *(n)*
En matrix element
Fr élément matriciel *(m)*
It elemento della matrice *(m)*
Pt elemento de matriz *(m)*

elemento mayoritario *(m)* Es
De Majoritätselement *(n)*
En majority element
Fr élément majoritaire *(m)*
It elemento di maggioranza *(m)*
Pt elemento de maioria *(m)*

elenco *(m) n* It
De Inhaltsverzeichnis *(n)*
En directory
Es directorio *(m)*
Fr répertoire d'adresses *(m)*
Pt anuário *(m)*

elettrico *adj* It
De elektrisch
En electric; electrical
Es eléctrico
Fr électrique
Pt eléctrico

elettronico *adj* It
De elektronisch
En electronic
Es electrónico
Fr électronique
Pt electrónico

eliminação *(f) n* Pt
De Löschung *(f)*
En erase
Es borrado *(m)*
Fr effacement *(m)*
It cancellazione *(f)*

eliminación *(f) n* Es
De Löschung *(f)*
En deletion
Fr effacement *(m)*
It cancellazione *(f)*
Pt apagado *(m)*

élimination des zéros *(f)* Fr
De Nullunterdrückung *(f)*
En zero suppression
Es supresión de ceros *(f)*
It soppressione di zero *(f)*
Pt supressão zero *(f)*

éliminer *vb* Fr
De löschen
En delete
Es suprimir
It cancellare
Pt apagar

embobinador *(m) n* Pt
De Aufspulgerät *(n)*
En spooler
Es bobinadora *(f)*
Fr enrouleur *(m)*
It avvolgitore *(m)*

embobinagem *(f) n* Pt
De Aufspulen *(n)*
En spooling
Es bobinado *(m)*
Fr bobinage *(m)*
It bobinaggio *(m)*

embobinar *vb* Pt
De spulen
En spool
Es bobinar
Fr bobiner
It bobinare

emboîter *vb* Fr
De schachteln
En nest
Es jerarquizar
It nidificare
Pt aninhar

emendador *(m) n* Pt
De Klebegerät *(n)*
En splicer
Es empalmadora *(f)*
Fr colleuse de bandes *(f)*
It incollatrice *(f)*

émetteur-récepteur *(m) n* Fr
De Senderempfänger *(m)*
En transceiver
Es transceptor *(m)*
It ricetrasmettitore *(m)*
Pt transreceptor *(m)*

emitter-coupled logic (ECL) En
De emittergekoppelte Verknüpfung *(f)*
Es lógica de emisor acoplado *(f)*
Fr logique à couplage par émetteur *(f)*
It logica accoppiata emittitore *(f)*
Pt lógica acoplada a um emissor *(f)*

emittergekoppelte Verknüpfung *(f)* De
En emitter-coupled logic (ECL)
Es lógica de emisor acoplado *(f)*
Fr logique à couplage par émetteur *(f)*
It logica accoppiata emittitore *(f)*
Pt lógica acoplada a um emissor *(f)*

empacotar *vb* Pt
De stapeln
En pack
Es empaquetar
Fr comprimer
It impaccare

empalmadora *(f) n* Es
De Klebegerät *(n)*
En splicer
Fr colleuse de bandes *(f)*
It incollatrice *(f)*
Pt emendador *(m)*

empaquetar *vb* Es
De stapeln
En pack
Fr comprimer
It impaccare
Pt empacotar

empilhadora *(f) n* Pt
De Stapler *(m)*
En stacker
Es casillero receptor *(m)*
Fr case de réception *(f)*
It carrello elevatore *(m)*

emplacement *(m) n* Fr
De Dateilage *(f)*
En location
Es posición *(f)*
It locazione *(f)*
Pt localização *(f)*

em série Pt
De gleichzeitig
En in-line
Es lineal
Fr en ligne
It lineale

emulador *(m) n* Es, Pt
De Emulator *(m)*
En emulator
Fr émulateur *(m)*
It emulatore *(m)*

émulateur *(m) n* Fr
De Emulator *(m)*
En emulator
Es emulador *(m)*
It emulatore *(m)*
Pt emulador *(m)*

emulator *n* En
De Emulator *(m)*
Es emulador *(m)*
Fr émulateur *(m)*
It emulatore *(m)*
Pt emulador *(m)*

Emulator *(m) n* De
En emulator
Es emulador *(m)*
Fr émulateur *(m)*
It emulatore *(m)*
Pt emulador *(m)*

emulatore *(m) n* It
De Emulator *(m)*
En emulator
Es emulador *(m)*
Fr émulateur *(m)*
Pt emulador *(m)*

enable pulse En
De Aktivierpuls *(m)*
Es impulso de activación *(m)*
Fr impulsion de validation *(f)*
It impulso di abilitazione *(m)*
Pt impulso de capacitação *(m)*

enabling signal En
De Aktiviersignal *(n)*
Es señal de activación *(f)*
Fr signal de validation *(m)*
It segnale di abilitazione *(m)*
Pt sinal de capacitação *(m)*

encaminamiento de mensajes *(m)* Es
De Nachrichtenvermittlung *(f)*
En message routing
Fr acheminement des messages *(m)*
It incanalazione dei messaggi *(f)*
Pt encaminhamento de mensagens *(m)*

encaminar *vb* Es
De führen
En route
Fr acheminar
It incanalare
Pt encaminhar

encaminhamento de mensagens *(m)* Pt
De Nachrichtenvermittlung *(f)*
En message routing
Es encaminamiento de mensajes *(m)*
Fr acheminement des messages *(m)*
It incanalazione dei messaggi *(f)*

encaminhar *vb* Pt
De führen
En route
Es encaminar
Fr acheminar
It incanalare

enchimento *(m) n* Pt
De Auffüllen *(n)*
En padding
Es relleno *(m)*
Fr remplissage *(m)*
It ricaricamento *(m)*

encode *vb* En
De kodieren; verschlüsseln
Es codificar
Fr coder
It codificare
Pt codificar

encoder *n* En
De Verschlüssler *(m)*
Es codificador *(m)*
Fr codeur *(m)*
It codificatore *(m)*
Pt codificador *(m)*

encre magnétique *(f)* Fr
De Magnettinte *(f)*
En magnetic ink
Es tinta magnética *(f)*
It inchiostro magnetico *(m)*
Pt tinta magnética *(f)*

encuadre *(m) n* Es
De Rahmen *(m)*
En frame
Fr cadre *(m)*
It telaio *(m)*
Pt quadro *(m)*

Ende der Arbeit *(n)* De
En end of job (EOJ)
Es fin de trabajo *(m)*
Fr fin de travail *(f)*
It fine del lavoro *(f)*
Pt fim do trabalho *(m)*

Ende des Blockes *(n)* De
En end of block (EOB)
Es fin de bloque *(m)*
Fr fin de bloc *(f)*
It fine del blocco *(f)*
Pt fim de bloco *(m)*

endereçamento directo *(m)* Pt
De direkte Adressierung *(f)*
En direct addressing
Es direccionamiento directo *(m)*
Fr adressage direct *(m)*
It indirizzamento diretto *(m)*

endereçamento relativo *(m)* Pt
De relative Adressierung *(f)*
En relative addressing
Es direccionado relativo *(m)*
Fr adressage relatif *(m)*
It indirizzamento relativo *(m)*

endereçamento repetitivo *(m)* Pt
De wiederholte Adressierung *(f)*
En repetitive addressing
Es direccionado repetitivo *(m)*
Fr adressage sous-entendu *(m)*
It indirizzamento ripetitivo *(m)*

endereçar *vb* Pt
De adressieren
En address
Es direccionar
Fr adresser
It indirizzare

endereçável ao conteúdo Pt
De inhaltsadressierbar
En content-addressable
Es contenido direccionable
Fr contenu adressable
It contenuto indirizzabile

endereço *(m) n* Pt
De Adresse *(f)*
En address
Es dirección *(f)*
Fr adresse *(f)*
It indirizzo *(m)*

endereço da máquina *(m)* Pt
De Maschinenadresse *(f)*
En machine address
Es dirección de máquina *(f)*
Fr adresse absolue *(f)*
It indirizzo di macchina *(m)*

endereço de referência *(m)* Pt
De Bezugsadresse *(f)*
En reference address
Es dirección de referencia *(f)*
Fr adresse primitive *(f)*
It indirizzo di riferimento *(m)*

endereço de segundo nível *(m)* Pt
De Adresse der zweiten Stufe *(f)*
En second-level address
Es dirección de segundo nivel *(f)*
Fr adresse à deuxième niveau *(f)*
It indirizzo del secondo livello *(m)*

endereço imediato *(m)* Pt
De unmittelbare Adresse *(f)*
En immediate address

Es dirección inmediata *(f)*
Fr adresse immédiate *(f)*
It indirizzo immediato *(m)*

endereço indirecto *(m)* Pt
De indirekte Adresse *(f)*
En indirect address
Es dirección indirecta *(f)*
Fr adresse indirecte *(f)*
It indirizzo indiretto *(m)*

endereço real *(m)* Pt
De effektive Adresse *(f)*
En effective address
Es dirección efectiva *(f)*
Fr adresse réelle *(f)*
It indirizzo efficace *(m)*

endereço relativo *(m)* Pt
De relative Adresse *(f)*
En relative address
Es dirección relativa *(f)*
Fr adresse relative *(f)*
It indirizzo relativo *(m)*

endereço relocalizável *(m)* Pt
De verschiebliche Adresse *(f)*
En relocatable address
Es dirección reubicable *(f)*
Fr adresse translatable *(f)*
It indirizzo rilocabile *(m)*

endereço simbólico *(m)* Pt
De symbolische Adresse *(f)*
En symbolic address
Es dirección simbólica *(f)*
Fr adresse symbolique *(f)*
It indirizzo simbolico *(m)*

endereço um mais um *(m)* Pt
De Eins-plus-Eins-Adresse *(f)*
En one-plus-one address
Es dirección uno más uno *(f)*
Fr à une plus une adresse *(f)*
It indirizzo uno-più-uno *(m)*

endereço virtual *(m)* Pt
De virtuelle Adresse *(f)*
En virtual address
Es dirección virtual *(f)*
Fr adresse virtuelle *(f)*
It indirizzo virtuale *(m)*

Endezeichen *(n)* *n* De
En end mark
Es marca final *(f)*
Fr drapeau indicateur *(m)*
It marcatura di fine *(f)*
Pt marca final *(f)*

Endlosvordrucke *(pl)* *n* De
En continuous stationery
Es papel continuo *(m)*
Fr papier en continu *(m)*
It carta da tabulati a fisarmonica *(f)*
Pt continuo-estacionário *(m)*

end mark En
De Endezeichen *(n)*
Es marca final *(f)*
Fr drapeau indicateur *(m)*
It marcatura di fine *(f)*
Pt marca final *(f)*

end of block (EOB) En
De Ende des Blockes *(n)*
Es fin de bloque *(m)*
Fr fin de bloc *(f)*
It fine del blocco *(f)*
Pt fim de bloco *(m)*

end of file (EOF) En
De Dateiende *(n)*
Es fin de fichero *(m)*
Fr fin de fichier *(f)*
It fine del file *(f)*
Pt fim de arquivo *(m)*

end of job (EOJ) En
De Ende der Arbeit *(n)*
Es fin de trabajo *(m)*
Fr fin de travail *(f)*
It fine del lavoro *(f)*
Pt fim do trabalho *(m)*

end of run (EOR) En
De Ablaufende *(n)*
Es fin de pasada *(m)*
Fr fin de passage *(f)*
It fine dell'elaborazione *(f)*
Pt fim da passagem *(m)*

end of tape (EOT) En
De Bandende *(n)*
Es fin de cinta *(m)*
Fr fin de bande *(f)*
It fine del nastro *(f)*
Pt fim da fita *(m)*

Endstation *(f)* *n* De
En terminal
Es terminal *(m)*
Fr terminal *(m)*
It terminale *(m)*
Pt terminal *(m)*

Endstelle *(f)* *n* De
En termination
Es terminación *(f)*
Fr fin *(f)*
It conclusione *(f)*
Pt terminação *(f)*

energieabhängiger Speicher *(m)* De
En volatile memory
Es memoria volátil *(f)*
Fr mémoire non rémanente *(f)*
It memoria volatile *(f)*
Pt memória volátil *(f)*

engenharia de software *(f)* Pt
De Programm-ausrüstung *(f)*
En software engineering
Es ingeniería de soportes lógicos *(f)*
Fr technique du logiciel *(f)*
It ingegneria del software *(f)*

eng gekoppelt De
En tightly coupled
Es fuertemente acoplado
Fr à couplage serré
It accoppiado fortemente
Pt firmemente acoplado

engineering time En
De Zeit für technische Arbeiten *(f)*
Es tiempo de inmovilización *(m)*
Fr temps d'immobilisation *(m)*
It tempo di immobilizzazione *(m)*
Pt tempo de engenharia *(m)*

engrenar *vb* Pt
De verriegeln
En interlock
Es interbloquear
Fr verrouiller
It interbloccare

enlace *(m)* *n* Es
De Verbindung *(f)*
En linkage
Fr lien *(m)*
It interconnessione *(f)*
Pt ligação *(f)*

enlace común *(m)* Es
De Sammelverbindung *(f)*
En trunk link
Fr liaison interurbaine *(f)*
It linea principale *(f)*
Pt linha principal *(f)*

enlace digital *(m)* Es
De Digitalverbindung *(f)*
En digital link
Fr liaison numérique *(f)*
It collegamento digitale *(m)*
Pt elemento de ligação digital *(m)*

enlace para transmisión de datos *(m)* Es
De Datenübermitt-lungsabschnitt *(m)*
En data link
Fr liaison de transmission *(f)*
It collegamento di dati *(m)*
Pt elemento de ligação de dados *(m)*

en ligne Fr
De gleichzeitig
En in-line
Es lineal
It lineale
Pt em série

en línea Es
De direkt
En on-line
Fr direct
It in linea
Pt sobre a linha

enmascaramiento *(m)* *n* Es
De Maskierung *(f)*
En masking

Fr masquage *(m)*
It mascheratura *(f)*
Pt ocultação *(f)*

enmascarar *vb* Es
De maskieren
En mask
Fr masquer
It mascherare
Pt ocultar

enregistrement *(m) n* Fr
De Satz *(m)*
En record
Es registro *(m)*
It record *(m)*
Pt registo *(m)*

enregistrement à faisceau électronique *(m)* Fr
De Elektronstrahlaufzeichnung *(f)*
En electron beam recording (EBR)
Es registro por haz de electrones *(m)*
It registrazione a fascio di elettroni *(f)*
Pt registo de feixe de electrões *(m)*

enregistrement d'effacement *(m)* Fr
De Löschungssatz *(m)*
En deletion record
Es registro de eliminación *(m)*
It record di cancellazione *(m)*
Pt registo de apagamento *(m)*

enregistrement double *(m)* Fr
De Parallelaufzeichnung *(f)*
En dual recording
Es registro en paralelo *(m)*
It registrazione duplice *(f)*
Pt registo duplo *(m)*

enregistrement en chaîne *(m)* Fr
De Kettensatz *(m)*
En chained record
Es registro en cadena *(m)*
It record concatenato *(m)*
Pt registo com cadeia *(m)*

enregistrement protégé *(m)* Fr
De geschützter Satz *(m)*
En protected record
Es registro protegido *(m)*
It record protetto *(m)*
Pt registo protegido *(m)*

enregistrement sur bande Fr
De Taste auf Band
En key-to-tape
Es registro sobre cinta
It registrazione su nastro magnetico
Pt tecla-à-fita

enregistrement sur disque Fr
De Taste auf Platte
En key-to-disk
Es registro sobre disco
It registrazione su disco
Pt tecla-ao-disco

enregistrement unitaire *(m)* Fr
De Einheitssatz *(m)*
En unit record
Es registro unitario *(m)*
It record di unità *(m)*
Pt registo de unidades *(m)*

enregistrer *vb* Fr
De aufzeichnen
En record
Es registrar
It registrare
Pt registar

enregistreur automatique *(m)* Fr
De Schreibgerät *(n)*
En logger
Es registrador automático *(m)*
It registratore automatico *(m)*
Pt registador automático *(m)*

enrouleur *(m) n* Fr
De Aufspulgerät *(n)*
En spooler
Es bobinadora *(f)*
It avvolgitore *(m)*
Pt embobinador *(m)*

ensaiar *vb* Pt
De prüfen
En test
Es probar
Fr essayer
It provare

ensaio *(m) n* Pt
De Prüfung *(f)*
En test
Es prueba *(f)*
Fr essai *(m)*
It prova *(f)*

ensaio do programa *(m)* Pt
De Programmprüfung *(f)*
En program testing
Es ensayo de programa *(m)*
Fr contrôle de programme *(m)*
It collaudo del programma *(m)*

ensamblador *(m) n* Es
De Assemblierer *(m)*
En assembler
Fr assembleur *(m)*
It assemblatore *(m)*
Pt montador *(m)*

ensamblar *vb* Es
De assemblieren
En assemble
Fr assembler
It assemblare
Pt montar

ensayo a distancia *(m)* Es
De Fernprüfung *(f)*
En remote testing
Fr contrôle à distance *(m)*
It collaudo a distanza *(m)*
Pt tele-ensaio *(m)*

ensayo de aceptación *(m)* Es
De Abnahmeprüfung *(f)*
En acceptance test
Fr essai de réception *(m)*
It test di accettazione *(m)*
Pt teste de aceitação *(m)*

ensayo de aceptación por el cliente *(m)* Es
De Kundenabnahmeprüfung *(f)*
En customer-acceptance test
Fr test de réception en clientèle *(m)*
It controllo accettazione clienti *(m)*
Pt teste de aceitação de cliente *(m)*

ensayo de programa *(m)* Es
De Programmprüfung *(f)*
En program testing
Fr contrôle de programme *(m)*
It collaudo del programma *(m)*
Pt ensaio do programa *(m)*

enseignement assisté par ordinateur *(m)* Fr
De computerunterstützter Unterricht *(m)*
En computer-aided instruction
Es instrucción com la ayuda de ordenador *(f)*
It istruzione basata sull'elaboratore *(f)*
Pt instrução auxiliada por computador *(f)*

enseignement automatisé *(m)* Fr
De computerbasiertes Lernen *(n)*
En computer-based learning
Es enseñanza automatizada *(f)*
It apprendimento basato sull'elaboratore *(m)*
Pt aprendizagem baseada em computador *(f)*

ensemble *(m) n* Fr
De Menge *(f)*
En set

Es conjunto *(m)*
It insieme *(m)*
Pt conjunto *(m)*

ensemble à semiconducteurs *(m)* Fr
De Halbleiterfeld *(n)*
En semiconductor array
Es matriz de semiconductores *(f)*
It rete semiconduttori *(f)*
Pt disposição semicondutora *(f)*

ensemble de données téléphoniques *(m)* Fr
De Telefondatensatz *(m)*
En telephone data set
Es equipo de datos telefónicos *(m)*
It gruppo di dati telefonici *(m)*
Pt conjunto de dados telefónicos *(m)*

enseñanza automatizada *(f)* Es
De computerbasiertes Lernen *(n)*
En computer-based learning
Fr enseignement automatisé *(m)*
It apprendimento basato sull'elaboratore *(m)*
Pt aprendizagem baseada em computador *(f)*

en-tête *(f) n* Fr
De Kennsatz *(m)*
En header
Es cabecera *(f)*
It testata *(f)*
Pt porta-cabeças *(m)*

entrada *(f) n* Es, Pt
De Eingang *(m)*
En entry; input
Fr entrée *(f)*
It entrata *(f)*

entrada de dados *(f)* Pt
De Dateneingabe *(f)*
En data entry
Es entrada de datos *(f)*
Fr saisie de données *(f)*
It ingresso dei dati *(m)*

entrada de datos *(f)* Es
De Dateneingabe *(f)*
En data entry
Fr saisie de données *(f)*
It ingresso dei dati *(m)*
Pt entrada de dados *(f)*

entrada de trabajos a distancia *(f)* Es
De Jobfernverarbeitung *(f)*
En remote job entry
Fr télésoumission de travaux *(f)*
It entrata del lavoro a distanza *(f)*
Pt entrada de trabalho remota *(f)*

entrada de trabalho remota *(f)* Pt
De Jobfernverarbeitung *(f)*
En remote job entry
Es entrada de trabajos a distancia *(f)*
Fr télésoumission de travaux *(f)*
It entrata del lavoro a distanza *(f)*

entrada manual *(f)* Es
De Handeingabe *(f)*
En manual input
Fr introduction manuelle *(f)*
It input manuale *(m)*
Pt input manual *(m)*

entrada-sair Pt
De Eingang-Ausgang
En input-output
Es entrada-salida
Fr entrée-sortie
It entrata-uscita

entrada-salida Es
De Eingang-Ausgang
En input-output
Fr entrée-sortie
It entrata-uscita
Pt entrada-sair

entraînement d'accès double *(m)* Fr
De Doppelzugriffsantrieb *(m)*
En dual-access drive
Es unidad de doble acceso *(f)*
It unità ad accesso duplice *(f)*
Pt accionamento de acesso duplo *(m)*

entraînement du ruban *(m)* Fr
De Bandvorschub *(m)*
En tape feed
Es alimentador de cinta *(m)*
It alimentazione del nastro *(f)*
Pt alimentação de fita *(f)*

entraîner *vb* Fr
De antreiben
En drive
Es impulsar
It azionare
Pt accionar

entraîneur de papier *(m)* Fr
De Formulartraktor *(m)*
En forms tractor
Es tractor de arrastre del papel *(m)*
It trattore di moduli *(m)*
Pt tractor de formulários *(m)*

entrampar *vb* Es
De fangen
En trap
Fr piéger
It intrappolare
Pt apanhar

entrar *vb* Pt
De eingeben
En input
Es introducir
Fr entrer
It immettere

entrata *(f) n* It
De Eingang *(m)*
En entry; input
Es entrada *(f)*
Fr entrée *(f)*
Pt entrada *(f)*

entrata del lavoro a distanza *(f)* It
De Jobfernverarbeitung *(f)*
En remote job entry
Es entrada de trabajos a distancia *(f)*
Fr télésoumission de travaux *(f)*
Pt entrada de trabalho remota *(f)*

entrata-uscita It
De Eingang-Ausgang
En input-output
Es entrada-salida
Fr entrée-sortie
Pt entrada-sair

entrée *(f) n* Fr
De Eingang *(m)*
En entry; input
Es entrada *(f)*
It entrata *(f)*
Pt entrada *(f)*

entrée-sortie Fr
De Eingang-Ausgang
En input-output
Es entrada-salida
It entrata-uscita
Pt entrada-sair

entrefer *(m) n* Fr
De Magnetkopfspalt *(m)*
En head gap
Es entrehierro *(m)*
It distanza dalla testina *(f)*
Pt intervalo de cabeça *(m)*

entrehierro *(m) n* Es
De Magnetkopfspalt *(m)*
En head gap
Fr entrefer *(m)*
It distanza dalla testina *(f)*
Pt intervalo de cabeça *(m)*

entrer *vb* Fr
De eingeben
En input
Es introducir
It immettere
Pt entrar

entretien correctif *(m)* Fr
De Verbesserungs-wartung *(f)*
En corrective maintenance
Es mantenimiento correctivo *(m)*
It manutenzione correttiva *(f)*
Pt manutenção correctiva *(f)*

entretien de routine *(m)* Fr
De regelmäßige Wartung *(f)*
En routine maintenance
Es mantenimiento de rutina *(m)*
It manutenzione ordinaria *(f)*
Pt manutenção de rotina *(f)*

entretien périodique *(m)* Fr
De Terminwartung *(f)*
En scheduled maintenance
Es mantenimiento programado *(m)*
It manutenzione programmata *(f)*
Pt manutenção planificada *(f)*

entretien préventif *(m)* Fr
De vorbeugende Wartung *(f)*
En preventative maintenance
Es mantenimiento preventivo *(m)*
It manutenzione preventiva *(f)*
Pt manutenção preventiva *(f)*

entry *n* En
De Eingang *(m)*
Es entrada *(f)*
Fr entrée *(f)*
It entrata *(f)*
Pt entrada *(f)*

entry point En
De Eingangspunkt *(m)*
Es punto de entrada *(m)*
Fr point d'entrée *(m)*
It punto di entrata *(m)*
Pt ponto de entrada *(m)*

Entscheidungstabelle *(f)* *n* De
En decision table
Es tabla de decisión *(f)*
Fr table de décision *(f)*
It tavola di decisione *(f)*
Pt tabela de decisão *(f)*

entschlüsseln *vb* De
En decode
Es decodificar
Fr décoder
It decodificare
Pt descodificar

Entschlüssler *(m)* *n* De
En decoder
Es decodificador *(m)*
Fr décodeur *(m)*
It decodificatore *(m)*
Pt descodificador *(m)*

Entstellung *(f)* *n* De
En corruption
Es corrupción *(f)*
Fr corruption *(f)*
It corruzione *(f)*
Pt corrupção *(f)*

Entweder-oder-Funktion *(f)* De
En either-or operation
Es operación ambos o uno *(f)*
Fr opération soit-ou *(f)*
It operazione sia-o *(f)*
Pt operação de ou-ou *(f)*

enumerar em lista Pt
De auflisten
En list
Es listar
Fr lister
It listare

enveloped file En
De Hülldatei *(f)*
Es fichero envuelto *(m)*
Fr dossier sous enveloppe *(m)*
It file inviluppato *(m)*
Pt arquivo envolvido *(m)*

environment *n* En
De Umgebung *(f)*
Es ambiente *(m)*
Fr ambiance *(f)*
It ambiente *(m)*
Pt ambiente *(m)*

épreuve marginale *(f)* Fr
De Randwertprüfung *(f)*
En marginal test
Es prueba marginal *(f)*
It test marginale *(m)*
Pt teste marginal *(m)*

equality unit En
De Äquivalenzschaltung *(f)*
Es unidad de igualdad *(f)*
Fr unité d'égalité *(f)*
It unità di uguaglianza *(f)*
Pt unidade de igualdade *(f)*

equiparação *(f)* *n* Pt
De Übereinstimmung *(f)*
En match
Es correspondencia *(f)*
Fr assortiment *(m)*
It accoppiamento *(m)*

equipment compatibility En
De Maschinenverträglichkeit *(f)*
Es compatibilidad entre equipos *(f)*
Fr compatibilité de matériels *(f)*
It compatibilità delle apparecchiature *(f)*
Pt compatibilidade do equipamento *(f)*

equipment failure En
De Maschinenausfall *(m)*
Es fallo del equipo *(m)*
Fr panne *(f)*
It guasto delle apparecchiature *(m)*
Pt falha de equipamento *(f)*

equipo de datos telefónicos *(m)* Es
De Telefondatensatz *(m)*
En telephone data set
Fr ensemble de données téléphoniques *(m)*
It gruppo di dati telefonici *(m)*
Pt conjunto de dados telefónicos *(m)*

equipo físico *(m)* Es
De Hardware *(f)*
En hardware
Fr matériel *(m)*
It elementi materiali di elaboratore *(m)*
Pt hardware *(m)*

equipo instruccional multicapas *(m)* Es
De mehrschichtige Software *(f)*
En multilayered software
Fr software multi-couche *(m)*
It software a strato multiplo *(m)*
Pt software de camadas múltiplas *(m)*

equivalence *n* En
De Gleichheit *(f)*
Es equivalencia *(f)*
Fr équivalence *(f)*
It equivalenza *(f)*
Pt equivalência *(f)*

équivalence *(f)* *n* Fr
De Gleichheit *(f)*
En equivalence
Es equivalencia *(f)*
It equivalenza *(f)*
Pt equivalência *(f)*

equivalence element En
De Gleichheitsfunktion *(f)*
Es elemento de equivalencia *(m)*
Fr élément d'équivalence *(m)*
It elemento di equivalenza *(m)*
Pt elemento de equivalência *(m)*

equivalence operation En
De Gleichheitsbetrieb *(m)*
Es operación de equivalencia *(f)*
Fr opération d'équivalence *(f)*
It operazione di equivalenza *(f)*
Pt operação de equivalência *(f)*

equivalencia *(f)* *n* Es
De Gleichheit *(f)*
En equivalence
Fr équivalence *(f)*
It equivalenza *(f)*
Pt equivalência *(f)*

equivalência *(f)* *n* Pt
De Gleichheit *(f)*
En equivalence
Es equivalencia *(f)*
Fr équivalence *(f)*
It equivalenza *(f)*

equivalent binary digits En

De gleichwertige Binärziffern *(pl)*
Es dígitos binarios equivalentes *(m pl)*
Fr chiffres binaires équivalents *(m pl)*
It digiti binari equivalenti *(m pl)*
Pt números digitais binários equivalentes *(m pl)*

equivalenza *(f) n* It
De Gleichheit *(f)*
En equivalence
Es equivalencia *(f)*
Fr équivalence *(f)*
Pt equivalência *(f)*

erasable memory En
De löschbarer Speicher *(m)*
Es memoria borrable *(f)*
Fr mémoire effaçable *(f)*
It memoria cancellabile *(f)*
Pt memória apagável *(f)*

erasable PROM (EPROM) En
De löschbarer PROM *(m)*
Es PROM borrable *(f)*
Fr PROM effaçable *(f)*
It PROM cancellabile *(f)*
Pt PROM apagável *(f)*

erase *n* En
De Löschung *(f)*
Es borrado *(m)*
Fr effacement *(m)*
It cancellazione *(f)*
Pt eliminação *(f)*

erase *vb* En
De löschen
Es borrar
Fr effacer
It cancellare
Pt apagar

erase head En
De Löschkopf *(m)*
Es cabeza de borrado *(f)*
Fr tête d'effacement *(f)*
It testina di cancellazione *(f)*
Pt cabeça apagadora *(f)*

ergänzen *vb* De
En complement
Es complementar
Fr prendre le complément de
It complementare
Pt complementar

Ergänzung *(f) n* De
En complement
Es complemento *(m)*
Fr complément *(m)*
It complemento *(m)*
Pt complemento *(m)*

Erkennung von Magnettinten-zeichen *(f)* De
En magnetic-ink character recognition
Es reconocimiento de caracteres de tinta magnética *(m)*
Fr reconnaissance magnétique de caractères *(f)*
It riconoscimento di caratteri di inchiostro magnetico *(m)*
Pt reconhecimento de caracteres de tinta magnética *(m)*

erreur *(f) n* Fr
De Fehler *(m)*
En error
Es error *(m)*
It errore *(m)*
Pt erro *(m)*

erreur d'ambiguité *(f)* Fr
De Zweideutigkeitsfehler *(m)*
En ambiguity error
Es error de ambigüedad *(m)*
It errore di ambiguità *(m)*
Pt erro de ambiguidade *(m)*

erreur d'arrondi *(f)* Fr
De Rundungsfehler *(m)*
En rounding error
Es error de redondeo *(m)*
It errore di arrotondamento *(m)*
Pt erro de arredondamento *(m)*

erreur de parité *(f)* Fr
De Paritätsfehler *(m)*
En parity error
Es error de paridad *(m)*
It errore di parità *(m)*
Pt erro de paridade *(m)*

erreur héritée *(f)* Fr
De mitgeschleppter Fehler *(m)*
En inherited error
Es error arrastrado *(m)*
It errore ereditato *(m)*
Pt erro herdado *(m)*

erreur par troncation *(f)* Fr
De Abschneidefehler *(m)*
En truncation error
Es error de truncamiento *(m)*
It errore di troncamento *(m)*
Pt erro de truncamento *(m)*

erreur propagée *(f)* Fr
De mitlaufender Fehler *(m)*
En propagated error
Es error propagado *(m)*
It errore propagato *(m)*
Pt erro propagado *(m)*

erreur résiduelle *(f)* Fr
De Restfehler *(m)*
En residual error
Es error residual *(m)*
It errore residuo *(m)*
Pt erro residual *(m)*

erro *(m) n* Pt
De Fehler *(m)*
En error
Es error *(m)*
Fr erreur *(f)*
It errore *(m)*

erro de ambiguidade *(m)* Pt
De Zweideutigkeitsfehler *(m)*
En ambiguity error
Es error de ambigüedad *(m)*
Fr erreur d'ambiguité *(f)*
It errore di ambiguità *(m)*

erro de arredondamento *(m)* Pt
De Rundungsfehler *(m)*
En rounding error
Es error de redondeo *(m)*
Fr erreur d'arrondi *(f)*
It errore di arrotondamento *(m)*

erro de paridade *(m)* Pt
De Paritätsfehler *(m)*
En parity error
Es error de paridad *(m)*
Fr erreur de parité *(f)*
It errore di parità *(m)*

erro de truncamento *(m)* Pt
De Abschneidefehler *(m)*
En truncation error
Es error de truncamiento *(m)*
Fr erreur par troncation *(f)*
It errore di troncamento *(m)*

erro herdado *(m)* Pt
De mitgeschleppter Fehler *(m)*
En inherited error
Es error arrastrado *(m)*
Fr erreur héritée *(f)*
It errore ereditato *(m)*

erro propagado *(m)* Pt
De mitlaufender Fehler *(m)*
En propagated error
Es error propagado *(m)*
Fr erreur propagée *(f)*
It errore propagato *(m)*

error *n* En, Es *(m)*
De Fehler *(m)*
Fr erreur *(f)*
It errore *(m)*
Pt erro *(m)*

error arrastrado *(m)* Es
De mitgeschleppter Fehler *(m)*
En inherited error
Fr erreur héritée *(f)*
It errore ereditato *(m)*
Pt erro herdado *(m)*

error-correcting code En
De Fehlerkorrekturcode *(m)*

Es código de corrección de errores *(m)*
Fr code correcteur d'erreurs *(m)*
It codice di correzione errore *(m)*
Pt código de correcção de erros *(m)*

error de ambigüedad *(m)* Es
De Zweideutigkeitsfehler *(m)*
En ambiguity error
Fr erreur d'ambiguité *(f)*
It errore di ambiguità *(m)*
Pt erro de ambiguidade *(m)*

error de paridad *(m)* Es
De Paritätsfehler *(m)*
En parity error
Fr erreur de parité *(f)*
It errore di parità *(m)*
Pt erro de paridade *(m)*

error de redondeo *(m)* Es
De Rundungsfehler *(m)*
En rounding error
Fr erreur d'arrondi *(f)*
It errore di arrotondamento *(m)*
Pt erro de arredondamento *(m)*

error-detecting code En
De Fehlererkennungscode *(m)*
Es código de detección de errores *(m)*
Fr code détecteur d'erreurs *(m)*
It codice di individuazione errore *(m)*
Pt código de detecção de erros *(m)*

error de truncamiento *(m)* Es
De Abschneidefehler *(m)*
En truncation error
Fr erreur par troncation *(f)*
It errore di troncamento *(m)*
Pt erro de truncamento *(m)*

error diagnostics En
De Fehlerdiagnostik *(f)*
Es diagnosis de errores *(f)*
Fr diagnostics d'erreurs *(m)*
It diagnostica degli errori *(f)*
Pt diagnóstico de erros *(m)*

errore *(m)* *n* It
De Fehler *(m)*
En error
Es error *(m)*
Fr erreur *(f)*
Pt erro *(m)*

errore di ambiguità *(m)* It
De Zweideutigkeitsfehler *(m)*
En ambiguity error
Es error de ambigüedad *(m)*
Fr erreur d'ambiguité *(f)*
Pt erro de ambiguidade *(m)*

errore di arrotondamento *(m)* It
De Rundungsfehler *(m)*
En rounding error
Es error de redondeo *(m)*
Fr erreur d'arrondi *(f)*
Pt erro de arredondamento *(m)*

errore di parità *(m)* It
De Paritätsfehler *(m)*
En parity error
Es error de paridad *(m)*
Fr erreur de parité *(f)*
Pt erro de paridade *(m)*

errore di troncamento *(m)* It
De Abschneidefehler *(m)*
En truncation error
Es error de truncamiento *(m)*
Fr erreur par troncation *(f)*
Pt erro de truncamento *(m)*

errore ereditato *(m)* It
De mitgeschleppter Fehler *(m)*
En inherited error
Es error arrastrado *(m)*
Fr erreur héritée *(f)*
Pt erro herdado *(m)*

errore propagato *(m)* It
De mitlaufender Fehler *(m)*
En propagated error
Es error propagado *(m)*
Fr erreur propagée *(f)*
Pt erro propagado *(m)*

errore residuo *(m)* It
De Restfehler *(m)*
En residual error
Es error residual *(m)*
Fr erreur résiduelle *(f)*
Pt erro residual *(m)*

erro residual *(m)* Pt
De Restfehler *(m)*
En residual error
Es error residual *(m)*
Fr erreur résiduelle *(f)*
It errore residuo *(m)*

error message En
De Fehlernachricht *(f)*
Es mansaje de error *(m)*
Fr message d'erreur *(m)*
It messaggio errore *(m)*
Pt mensagem de erro *(f)*

error propagado *(m)* Es
De mitlaufender Fehler *(m)*
En propagated error
Fr erreur propagée *(f)*
It errore propagato *(m)*
Pt erro propagado *(m)*

error rate En
De Fehlerhäufigkeit *(f)*
Es coeficiente de errores *(m)*
Fr taux d'erreurs *(m)*
It tasso di errori *(m)*
Pt índice de erros *(m)*

error report En
De Fehlerbericht *(m)*
Es informe de errores *(m)*
Fr état sélectif *(m)*
It tabulato errori *(m)*
Pt relatório de erros *(m)*

error residual *(m)* Es
De Restfehler *(m)*
En residual error
Fr erreur résiduelle *(f)*
It errore residuo *(m)*
Pt erro residual *(m)*

error routine En
De Fehlerprogramm *(n)*
Es rutina de errores *(f)*
Fr routine de détection d'erreurs *(f)*
It routine errori *(f)*
Pt rotina de erros *(f)*

Erstbelegung *(f)* *n* De
En initialization
Es inicialización *(f)*
Fr initialisation *(f)*
It inizializzazione *(f)*
Pt inicialização *(f)*

erstgeneration *adj* De
En first-generation
Es primera-generación
Fr première-génération
It prima-generazione
Pt primeira-geração

Erstgenerationsband *(n)* *n* De
En grandfather tape
Es cinta primera generación *(f)*
Fr bande première génération *(f)*
It nastro nonno *(m)*
Pt fita avó *(f)*

erweiterter inhaltsadressierter Speicher *(m)* De
En augmented content-addressed memory (ACAM)
Es memoria asociativa ampliada *(f)*
Fr mémoire associative complétée *(f)*
It memoria a contenuto indirizzato aumentato *(f)*
Pt memória de direcção de conteúdo aumentada *(f)*

erzeugen *vb* De
En generate
Es generar
Fr générer
It generare
Pt gerar

esaminare *vb* It
De kontrollieren
En monitor
Es examinar
Fr surveiller
Pt vigiar

escala *(f) n* Es, Pt
De Skala *(f)*
En scale
Fr échelle *(f)*
It scala *(f)*

escala de tempo *(f)* Pt
De Zeitskala *(f)*
En time scale
Es escala de tiempos *(f)*
Fr échelle des temps *(f)*
It scala di tempo *(f)*

escala de tiempos *(f)* Es
De Zeitskala *(f)*
En time scale
Fr échelle des temps *(f)*
It scala di tempo *(f)*
Pt escala de tempo *(f)*

escape character En
De Datenübertragungs-umschaltung *(f)*
Es carácter de escape *(m)*
Fr caractère échappatoire *(m)*
It carattere di uscita *(m)*
Pt carácter de escape *(m)*

escrever *vb* Pt
De schreiben
En write
Es escribir
Fr écrire
It scrivere

escrever à máquina Pt
De maschinenschreiben
En type
Es escribir a máquina
Fr écrire à la machine
It scrivere a macchina

escrever em condensado Pt
De sammelnbeschreiben
En gather write
Es escribir agrupada
Fr écrire en regroupant
It scrivere di raccolta

escrever por cima Pt
De überschreiben
En overwrite
Es recubrir
Fr superposer une écriture
It inscrivere per riempimento

escribir *vb* Es
De schreiben
En write
Fr écrire
It scrivere
Pt escrever

escribir agrupada Es
De sammelnbeschreiben
En gather write
Fr écrire en regroupant
It scrivere di raccolta
Pt escrever em condensado

escribir a máquina Es
De maschinenschreiben
En type
Fr écrire à la machine
It scrivere a macchina
Pt escrever à máquina

escrita de procura *(f)* Pt
De Abrufschreiben *(n)*
En demand writing
Es escritura inmediata *(f)*
Fr écriture immédiate *(f)*
It scrittura a domanda *(f)*

escritura inmediata *(f)* Es
De Abrufschreiben *(n)*
En demand writing
Fr écriture immédiate *(f)*
It scrittura a domanda *(f)*
Pt escrita de procura *(f)*

esecuzione *(f) n* It
De Durchlauf *(m)*
En run
Es pasada *(f)*
Fr passage *(m)*
Pt passagem *(f)*

esecuzione di elaboratore *(f) n* It
De Ablauf *(m)*
En computer run
Es pasada de ordenador *(f)*
Fr phase de traitement *(f)*
Pt passagem de computador *(f)*

esecuzione di produzione *(f)* It
De Fertigungslauf *(m)*
En production run
Es pasada de producción *(f)*
Fr passage de production *(m)*
Pt passagem de produção *(f)*

esecuzione di prova *(f)* It
De Prüfablauf *(m)*
En test run
Es pasada de ensayo *(f)*
Fr passage d'essai *(m)*
Pt passagem de ensaio *(f)*

esecuzione parallela *(f)* It
De Parallellauf *(m)*
En parallel running
Es ciclo de funcionamiento en paralelo *(m)*
Fr exploitation en parallèle *(f)*
Pt passagens paralelas *(f)*

eseguire *vb* It
De aktivieren
En execute
Es ejecutar
Fr exécuter
Pt executar

espace *(m) n* Fr
De Leerstelle *(f)*
En blank
Es blanco *(m)*
It bianco *(m)*
Pt espaço *(m)*

espace interbloc *(m)* Fr
De Satzzwischenraum *(m)*
En inter-record gap
Es separación entre registros *(f)*
It distanza tra i record *(f)*
Pt intervalo entre registos *(m)*

espaço *(m) n* Pt
De Leerstelle *(f)*
En blank
Es blanco *(m)*
Fr espace *(m)*
It bianco *(m)*

espécie *(f) n* Pt
De Sortierung *(f)*
En sort
Es clasificación *(f)*
Fr tri *(m)*
It selezione *(f)*

especificação *(f) n* Pt
De Spezifikation *(f)*
En specification
Es especificación *(f)*
Fr spécification *(f)*
It specificazione *(f)*

especificação do programa *(f)* Pt
De Programmvorgabe *(f)*
En program specification
Es especificación de programa *(f)*
Fr spécification de programme *(f)*
It specificazioni del programma *(f)*

especificación *(f) n* Es
De Spezifikation *(f)*
En specification
Fr spécification *(f)*
It specificazione *(f)*
Pt especificação *(f)*

especificación de programa *(f)* Es
De Programmvorgabe *(f)*
En program specification
Fr spécification de programme *(f)*
It specificazioni del programma *(f)*
Pt especificação do programa *(f)*

esplorazione *(f) n* It
De Abtastung *(f)*
En scan
Es exploración *(f)*
Fr exploration *(f)*
Pt exploracão *(f)*

espressione *(f) n* It
De Ausdruck *(m)*
En expression
Es expresión *(f)*
Fr expression *(f)*
Pt expressão *(f)*

esquema *(m) n* Es, Pt
De Schema *(n)*
En schema
Fr schéma *(m)*
It schema *(m)*

essai *(m) n* Fr
De Prüfung *(f)*
En test
Es prueba *(f)*
It prova *(f)*
Pt ensaio *(m)*

essai de réception *(m)* Fr
De Abnahmeprüfung *(f)*
En acceptance test
Es ensayo de aceptación *(m)*
It test di accettazione *(m)*
Pt teste de aceitação *(m)*

essayer *vb* Fr
De prüfen
En test
Es probar
It provare
Pt ensaiar

estação de operação *(f)* Pt
De Arbeitsstation *(f)*
En operating station
Es estación operativa *(f)*
Fr poste d'exploitation *(m)*
It posto funzionante *(m)*

estação de subscritor *(f)* Pt
De Teilnehmerstation *(f)*
En subscriber station
Es estación de una red *(f)*
Fr poste du réseau *(m)*
It posto d'abbonato *(m)*

estação de visualização *(f)* Pt
De Anzeigestation *(f)*
En display station
Es estación de visualización *(f)*
Fr poste de visualisation *(m)*
It posto di visualizzazione *(m)*

estación de una red *(f)* Es
De Teilnehmerstation *(f)*
En subscriber station
Fr poste du réseau *(m)*
It posto d'abbonato *(m)*
Pt estação de subscritor *(f)*

estación de visualización *(f)* Es
De Anzeigestation *(f)*
En display station
Fr poste de visualisation *(m)*
It posto di visualizzazione *(m)*
Pt estação de visualização *(f)*

estación operativa *(f)* Es
De Arbeitsstation *(f)*
En operating station
Fr poste d'exploitation *(m)*
It posto funzionante *(m)*
Pt estação de operação *(f)*

estado cero *(m)* Es
De Nullzustand *(m)*
En zero state
Fr état zéro *(m)*
It stato zero *(m)*
Pt estado zero *(m)*

estado de unidade *(m)* Pt
De Einzustand *(m)*
En one state
Es estado uno *(m)*
Fr état un *(m)*
It stato uno *(m)*

estado uno *(m)* Es
De Einzustand *(m)*
En one state
Fr état un *(m)*
It stato uno *(m)*
Pt estado de unidade *(m)*

estado zero *(m)* Pt
De Nullzustand *(m)*
En zero state
Es estado cero *(m)*
Fr état zéro *(m)*
It stato zero *(m)*

estandardizar *vb* Es
De normen
En standardize
Fr standardiser
It standardizzare
Pt standardizar

estructura de redes de sistemas *(f)* Es
De Systemnetzaufbau *(m)*
En systems network architecture (SNA)
Fr architecture unifiée de réseau (AUR) *(f)*
It architettura della rete di sistemi *(f)*
Pt arquitectura de rede de sistemas *(f)*

estudio de posibilidades *(m)* Es
De Wirklichkeits-untersuchung *(f)*
En feasibility study
Fr étude de faisabilité *(f)*
It studio di fattibilità *(m)*
Pt estudo de viabilidade *(m)*

estudo de viabilidade *(m)* Pt
De Wirklichkeits-untersuchung *(f)*
En feasibility study
Es estudio de posibilidades *(m)*
Fr étude de faisabilité *(f)*
It studio di fattibilità *(m)*

état sélectif *(m)* Fr
De Fehlerbericht *(m)*
En error report
Es informe de errores *(m)*
It tabulato errori *(m)*
Pt relatório de erros *(m)*

état un *(m)* Fr
De Einzustand *(m)*
En one state
Es estado uno *(m)*
It stato uno *(m)*
Pt estado de unidade *(m)*

état zéro *(m)* Fr
De Nullzustand *(m)*
En zero state
Es estado cero *(m)*
It stato zero *(m)*
Pt estado zero *(m)*

etichetta *(f) n* It
De Schildchen *(n)*
En label
Es marbete *(m)*
Fr label *(m)*
Pt rótulo *(m)*

etichetta del file *(f)* It
De Dateikennsatz *(m)*
En file label
Es etiqueta de fichero *(f)*
Fr étiquette de fichier *(f)*
Pt rótulo de arquivo *(m)*

etichetta della testata *(f)* It
De Anfangskennsatz *(m)*
En header label
Es etiqueta de cabecera *(f)*
Fr label début *(m)*
Pt rótulo de porta-cabeças *(m)*

etichetta di fine *(f)* It
De Beisatzkennzeichen *(n)*
En trailer label
Es etiqueta de cola *(f)*
Fr label fin *(m)*
Pt rótulo de trailer *(m)*

etichetta di pista *(f)* It
De Spurkennzeichen *(n)*
En track label
Es etiqueta de pista *(f)*
Fr label piste *(m)*
Pt rótulo de pista *(m)*

Etikett *(n) n* De
En tag
Es etiqueta *(f)*
Fr étiquette *(f)*
It identificatore *(m)*
Pt etiqueta *(f)*

etiqueta *(f) n* Es, Pt
De Etikett *(n)*
En tag

Fr étiquette *(f)*
It identificatore *(m)*

etiqueta de cabecera *(f)* Es
De Anfangskennsatz *(m)*
En header label
Fr label début *(m)*
It etichetta della testata *(f)*
Pt rótulo de porta-cabeças *(m)*

etiqueta de cola *(f)* Es
De Beisatzkennzeichen *(n)*
En trailer label
Fr label fin *(m)*
It etichetta di fine *(f)*
Pt rótulo de trailer *(m)*

etiqueta de fichero *(f)* Es
De Dateikennsatz *(m)*
En file label
Fr étiquette de fichier *(f)*
It etichetta del file *(f)*
Pt rótulo de arquivo *(m)*

etiqueta de pista *(f)* Es
De Spurkennzeichen *(n)*
En track label
Fr label piste *(m)*
It etichetta di pista *(f)*
Pt rótulo de pista *(m)*

étiquette *(f)* *n* Fr
De Etikett *(n)*
En tag
Es etiqueta *(f)*
It identificatore *(m)*
Pt etiqueta *(f)*

étiquette de fichier *(f)* Fr
De Dateikennsatz *(m)*
En file label
Es etiqueta de fichero *(f)*
It etichetta del file *(f)*
Pt rótulo de arquivo *(m)*

étude de faisabilité *(f)* Fr
De Wirklichkeits-untersuchung *(f)*
En feasibility study
Es estudio de posibilidades *(m)*
It studio di fattibilità *(m)*
Pt estudo de viabilidade *(m)*

étude technique automatisée (ETA) *(f)* Fr
De automatisierte Maschinen-konstruktion *(f)*
En automated engineering design (AED)
Es diseño técnico automatizado *(m)*
It disegno di ingegneria automatizzata *(m)*
Pt desenho de engenharia automatizado *(m)*

euristica *(f)* *n* It
De Heuristik *(f)*
En heuristics
Es heurística *(f)*
Fr heuristique *(f)*
Pt heurística *(f)*

even parity En
De gerade Bitzahl *(f)*
Es paridad *(f)*
Fr parité *(f)*
It parità pari *(f)*
Pt paridade de igualdade *(f)*

examinar *vb* Es
De kontrollieren
En monitor
Fr surveiller
It esaminare
Pt vigiar

exception principle system En
De Ausnahmeprinzip-system *(n)*
Es control por excepción *(m)*
Fr gestion par exception *(f)*
It sistema a principio di eccezione *(m)*
Pt sistema de princípio de excepção *(m)*

excess fifty En
De Fünfzig-Überschuß *(m)*
Es cincuenta excedente *(f)*
Fr code plus cinquante *(m)*
It cinquanta di eccesso *(f)*
Pt cinquenta em excesso *(f)*

excess three En
De Drei-Überschuß *(m)*
Es tres excedente *(m)*
Fr code plus trois *(m)*
It tre di eccesso *(m)*
Pt três em excesso *(m)*

exchange *n* En
De Vermittlung *(f)*
Es intercambio *(m)*
Fr échange *(m)*
It scambio *(m)*
Pt intercâmbio *(m)*

exchange *vb* En
De vermitteln
Es cambiar
Fr intervenir
It scambiare
Pt intercambiar

exchangeable disk store (EDS) En
De auswechselbarer Plattenspeicher *(m)*
Es unidad de discos móviles *(f)*
Fr unité de disques à chargeur (UTC) *(f)*
It memoria a dischi inseribili *(f)*
Pt armazém de discos intercambiáveis *(m)*

exclusive-or operation En
De Antivalenzfunktion *(f)*
Es operación O exclusivo *(f)*
Fr opération OU exclusif *(f)*
It operazione o-esclusivo *(f)*
Pt operação exclusiva-ou *(f)*

executar *vb* Pt
De aktivieren
En execute
Es ejecutar
Fr exécuter
It eseguire

execute *vb* En
De aktivieren
Es ejecutar
Fr exécuter
It eseguire
Pt executar

execute phase En
De Aktivierungsphase *(f)*
Es fase de ejecución *(f)*
Fr phase opératoire *(f)*
It fase di esecuzione *(f)*
Pt fase de execução *(f)*

exécuter *vb* Fr
De aktivieren; durchlaufen
En execute; run
Es ejecutar; pasar
It eseguire; passare
Pt executar; passar

execution time En
De Aktivierungszeit *(f)*
Es tiempo de ejecución *(m)*
Fr durée d'exécution *(f)*
It tempo di esecuzione *(m)*
Pt tempo de execução *(m)*

executive program En
De Aktivierungs-programm *(n)*
Es programa ejecutivo *(m)*
Fr programme superviseur *(m)*
It programma esecutivo *(m)*
Pt programa de execução *(m)*

exit *n* En
De Ausgang *(m)*
Es salida *(f)*
Fr sortie *(f)*
It uscita *(f)*
Pt saída *(f)*

exit *vb* En
De ausgehen
Es salir
Fr sortir
It uscire
Pt sair

exploitation *(f)* *n* Fr
De Operation *(f)*
En operation
Es operación *(f)*
It operazione *(f)*
Pt operação *(f)*

exploitation en parallèle *(f)* Fr
De Parallellauf *(m)*

En parallel running
Es ciclo de funcionamiento en paralelo *(m)*
It esecuzione parallela *(f)*
Pt passagens paralelas *(f)*

exploitation NON *(f)* Fr
De NOT-Verknüpfung *(f)*
En NOT-operation
Es operación NO *(f)*
It operazione NO *(f)*
Pt operação NÃO *(f)*

exploitation NON-ET *(f)* Fr
De NAND-Verknüpfung; NICHT-UND-Verknüpfung *(f)*
En NAND-operation; NOT-AND operation
Es operación NO-Y *(f)*
It operazione NAND; operazione NO-E *(f)*
Pt operação NAND; operação NÃO-E *(f)*

exploitation NON-OU *(f)* Fr
De NOR-Verknüpfung *(f)*
En NOR-operation
Es operación NI *(f)*
It operazione NOR *(f)*
Pt operação NOR *(f)*

exploitation OU *(f)* Fr
De ODER-Verknüpfung *(f)*
En OR-operation
Es operación O *(f)*
It operazione O *(f)*
Pt operação OR *(f)*

exploracão *(f) n* Pt
De Abtastung *(f)*
En scan
Es exploración *(f)*
Fr exploration *(f)*
It esplorazione *(f)*

exploração de marca *(f)* Pt
De Kennzeichen-abtastung *(f)*
En mark scanning
Es exploración de marcas *(f)*
Fr lecture optique de marques *(f)*
It scansione di marcature *(f)*

exploración *(f) n* Es
De Abtastung *(f)*
En scan
Fr exploration *(f)*
It esplorazione *(f)*
Pt exploracão *(f)*

exploración de marcas *(f)* Es
De Kennzeichen-abtastung *(f)*
En mark scanning
Fr lecture optique de marques *(f)*
It scansione di marcature *(f)*
Pt exploração de marca *(f)*

explorador *(m) n* Es
De Abtaster *(m)*
En scanner
Fr explorateur *(m)*
It analizzatore per scansione *(m)*
Pt dispositivo de exploração *(m)*

explorador óptico *(m)* Es, Pt
De optischer Abtaster *(m)*
En optical scanner
Fr lecteur optique *(m)*
It analizzatore per scansione di caratteri ottici *(m)*

explorar *vb* Es, Pt
De abtasten
En scan
Fr explorer
It scrutare

explorateur *(m) n* Fr
De Abtaster *(m)*
En scanner
Es explorador *(m)*
It analizzatore per scansione *(m)*
Pt dispositivo de exploração *(m)*

exploration *(f) n* Fr
De Abtastung *(f)*
En scan
Es exploración *(f)*
It esplorazione *(f)*
Pt exploracão *(f)*

explorer *vb* Fr
De abtasten
En scan
Es explorar
It scrutare
Pt explorar

expresión *(f) n* Es
De Ausdruck *(m)*
En expression
Fr expression *(f)*
It espressione *(f)*
Pt expressão *(f)*

expressão *(f) n* Pt
De Ausdruck *(m)*
En expression
Es expresión *(f)*
Fr expression *(f)*
It espressione *(f)*

expression *n* En, Fr *(f)*
De Ausdruck *(m)*
Es expresión *(f)*
It espressione *(f)*
Pt expressão *(f)*

external store En
De Außenspeicher *(m)*
Es memoria externa *(f)*
Fr mémoire externe *(f)*
It memoria esterna *(f)*
Pt armazém exterior *(m)*

extraction *(f) n* Fr
De Wiederauffinden *(n)*
En retrieval
Es recuperación *(f)*
It reperimento *(m)*
Pt recuperação *(f)*

extraer *vb* Es
De ausgeben
En output
Fr sortir
It output
Pt sair

extraire de la memoire Fr
De auslesen
En read out
Es leer en salida
It leggere dalla memoria
Pt ler em saida

F

fabricación con la ayuda de ordenador *(f)* Es
De computerunter-stützte Herstellung *(f)*
En computer-aided manufacture (CAM)
Fr fabrication assistée par ordinateur (FAO) *(f)*
It produzione basata sull'elaboratore *(f)*
Pt manufactura com auxílio de computador *(f)*

fabrication assistée par ordinateur (FAO) *(f)* Fr
De computerunter-stützte Herstellung *(f)*
En computer-aided manufacture (CAM)
Es fabricación con la ayuda de ordenador *(f)*
It produzione basata sull'elaboratore *(f)*
Pt manufactura com auxílio de computador *(f)*

facsímil *(m) n* Es
De Faksimile *(n)*
En facsimile
Fr fac-similé *(m)*
It facsimile *(m)*
Pt facsímile *(m)*

facsimile *n* En; It *(m)*
De Faksimile *(n)*
Es facsímil *(m)*
Fr fac-similé *(m)*
Pt facsímile *(m)*

fac-similé *(m) n* Fr
De Faksimile *(n)*
En facsimile
Es facsímil *(m)*
It facsimile *(m)*
Pt facsímile *(m)*

facsímile *(m) n* Pt
De Faksimile *(n)*
En facsimile
Es facsímil *(m)*

Fr fac-similé *(m)*
It facsimile *(m)*

facteur de cadrage *(m)* Fr
De Skalierfaktor *(m)*
En scale factor
Es factor escalar *(m)*
It fattore di scala *(m)*
Pt factor de escala *(m)*

factor de escala *(m)* Pt
De Skalierfaktor *(m)*
En scale factor
Es factor escalar *(m)*
Fr facteur de cadrage *(m)*
It fattore di scala *(m)*

factor escalar *(m)* Es
De Skalierfaktor *(m)*
En scale factor
Fr facteur de cadrage *(m)*
It fattore di scala *(m)*
Pt factor de escala *(m)*

facultad de ser portátil *(f)* Es
De Datenaustauschbarkeit *(f)*
En portability
Fr portabilité *(f)*
It portabilità *(f)*
Pt portatilidade *(f)*

fail-safe *adj* En
De eigensicher
Es sin riesgo de fallo
Fr à sécurité intégrée
It sicuro contro guasti
Pt seguro contra falhas

failure rate En
De Ausfallhäufigkeit *(f)*
Es frecuencia de fallos *(f)*
Fr taux de défaillance *(m)*
It numero di guasti *(m)*
Pt índice de falhas *(m)*

failure recovery En
De Ausfallrückgängigkeit *(f)*
Es reparación de fallo *(f)*
Fr redressement de défaillance *(m)*
It recupero di fallimento *(m)*
Pt recuperação de falha *(f)*

faire avancer Fr
De vorschieben
En feed
Es alimentar
It alimentare
Pt alimentar

faire le double Fr
De doppeln
En duplicate
Es duplicar
It duplicare
Pt duplicar

faire un index Fr
De indizieren
En index
Es poner en un índice
It metter nell'indice
Pt pôr em índex

Faksimile *(n) n* De
En facsimile
Es facsímil *(m)*
Fr fac-similé *(m)*
It facsimile *(m)*
Pt facsímile *(m)*

falha de equipamento *(f)* Pt
De Maschinenausfall *(m)*
En equipment failure
Es fallo del equipo *(m)*
Fr panne *(f)*
It guasto delle apparecchiature *(m)*

fallo *(m) n* Es
De Defekt *(m)*
En fault
Fr faute *(f)*
It guasto *(m)*
Pt defeito *(m)*

fallo del equipo *(m)* Es
De Maschinenausfall *(m)*
En equipment failure
Fr panne *(f)*
It guasto delle apparecchiature *(m)*
Pt falha de equipamento *(f)*

falsa recuperación *(f)* Es
De unechtes Wiederauffinden *(n)*
En false retrieval
Fr référence non pertinente *(f)*
It falso reperimento *(m)*
Pt recuperação falsa *(f)*

false retrieval En
De unechtes Wiederauffinden *(n)*
Es falsa recuperación *(f)*
Fr référence non pertinente *(f)*
It falso reperimento *(m)*
Pt recuperação falsa *(f)*

falso reperimento *(m)* It
De unechtes Wiederauffinden *(n)*
En false retrieval
Es falsa recuperación *(f)*
Fr référence non pertinente *(f)*
Pt recuperação falsa *(f)*

Faltverhältnis *(n) n* De
En folding ratio
Es relación de plegado *(f)*
Fr rapport de pliage *(m)*
It rapporto pieghevole *(m)*
Pt ratio de dobragem *(f)*

fangen *vb* De
En trap
Es entrampar
Fr piéger
It intrappolare
Pt apanhar

Farbband *(n) n* De
En ink ribbon
Es cinta entintada *(f)*
Fr ruban à encre *(m)*
It nastro ad inchiostro *(m)*
Pt fita de tinta *(f)*

fare un dump It
De speicherausziehen
En dump
Es volcar
Fr vider
Pt descarregar

fase de ejecución *(f)* Es
De Aktivierungsphase *(f)*
En execute phase
Fr phase opératoire *(f)*
It fase di esecuzione *(f)*
Pt fase de execução *(f)*

fase de execução *(f)* Pt
De Aktivierungsphase *(f)*
En execute phase
Es fase de ejecución *(f)*
Fr phase opératoire *(f)*
It fase di esecuzione *(f)*

fase di esecuzione *(f)* It
De Aktivierungsphase *(f)*
En execute phase
Es fase de ejecución *(f)*
Fr phase opératoire *(f)*
Pt fase de execução *(f)*

Faseroptik *(f) n* De
Am fiber optics
En fibre optics
Es óptica de las fibras *(f)*
Fr optique à fibre *(f)*
It fibre ottiche *(f)*
Pt óptica de fibras *(f)*

Faseroptiktechnik *(f) n* De
Am optical fiber technology
En optical fibre technology
Es tecnología de las fibras ópticas *(f)*
Fr technologie des fibres optiques *(f)*
It tecnologia delle fibre ottiche *(f)*
Pt tecnologia de fibras ópticas *(f)*

father tape En
De Urband *n*
Es cinta creadora *(f)*
Fr bande créatrice *(f)*
It nastro padre *(m)*
Pt fita pai *(f)*

fatia de tempo *(f)* Pt
De Zeitscheibenverfahren *(n)*
En time slice
Es fracción de tiempo *(f)*
Fr découpage du temps *(m)*
It ripartizione di tempo *(f)*

fattore di scala *(m)* It
De Skalierfaktor *(m)*
En scale factor
Es factor escalar *(m)*
Fr facteur de cadrage *(m)*
Pt factor de escala *(m)*

fault *n* En
De Defekt *(m)*
Es fallo *(m)*
Fr faute *(f)*
It guasto *(m)*
Pt defeito *(m)*

fault-tolerant *adj* En
De defekttolerant
Es tolerante con las averías
Fr insensible aux défaillances
It tollerante di guasto
Pt tolerante relativamente a erros

faute *(f) n* Fr
De Defekt *(m)*
En fault
Es fallo *(m)*
It guasto *(m)*
Pt defeito *(m)*

fazer concordar com a escala Pt
De skalieren
En scale
Es pasar a escala
Fr cadrer
It scalare

feasibility study En
De Wirklichkeits-untersuchung *(f)*
Es estudio de posibilidades *(m)*
Fr étude de faisabilité *(f)*
It studio di fattibilità *(m)*
Pt estudo de viabilidade *(m)*

feed *n* En
De Vorschub *(m)*
Es alimentación *(f)*
Fr avance *(f)*
It alimentazione *(f)*
Pt alimentação *(f)*

feed *vb* En
De vorschieben
Es alimentar
Fr faire avancer
It alimentare
Pt alimentar

feedback *n* En
De Rückkopplung *(f)*
Es realimentación *(f)*
Fr rétroaction *(f)*
It retroazione *(f)*
Pt realimentação *(f)*

feedback control En
De rückgekoppeltes Regelungssystem *(n)*
Es control de realimentación *(m)*
Fr commande de rétroaction *(f)*
It controllo di retroazione *(m)*
Pt controle de realimentação *(m)*

feed holes En
De Taktlöcher *(n pl)*
Es perforaciones de alimentación *(f pl)*
Fr trous d'entraînement *(m pl)*
It fori di alimentazione *(m pl)*
Pt furos de alimentação *(m pl)*

Fehler *(m) n* De
En error
Es error *(m)*
Fr erreur *(f)*
It errore *(m)*
Pt erro *(m)*

Fehlerbericht *(m) n* De
En error report
Es informe de errores *(m)*
Fr état sélectif *(m)*
It tabulato errori *(m)*
Pt relatório de erros *(m)*

Fehlerdiagnostik *(f) n* De
En error diagnostics
Es diagnosis de errores *(f)*
Fr diagnostics d'erreurs *(m)*
It diagnostica degli errori *(f)*
Pt diagnóstico de erros *(m)*

Fehlererkennungscode *(m) n* De
En error-detecting code
Es código de detección de errores *(m)*
Fr code détecteur d'erreurs *(m)*
It codice di individuazione errore *(m)*
Pt código de detecção de erros *(m)*

Fehlerhäufigkeit *(f) n* De
En error rate
Es coeficiente de errores *(m)*
Fr taux d'erreurs *(m)*
It tasso di errori *(m)*
Pt índice de erros *(m)*

Fehlerkorrekturcode *(m) n* De
En error-correcting code
Es código de corrección de errores *(m)*
Fr code correcteur d'erreurs *(m)*
It codice di correzione errore *(m)*
Pt código de correcção de erros *(m)*

Fehlernachricht *(f) n* De
En error message
Es mansaje de error *(m)*
Fr message d'erreur *(m)*
It messaggio errore *(m)*
Pt mensagem de erro *(f)*

Fehlerprogramm *(n) n* De
En error routine
Es rutina de errores *(f)*
Fr routine de détection d'erreurs *(f)*
It routine errori *(f)*
Pt rotina de erros *(f)*

fehlersuchen *vb* De
En debug
Es depurar
Fr mettre au point
It mettere a punto un programma
Pt desparasitar

Fehlersuchen *(n) n* De
En trouble shooting
Es localización de errores *(f)*
Fr dépannage *(m)*
It risoluzione dei problemi organizzativi *(f)*
Pt detecção de avarias *(f)*

Fehlersuchhilfe *(f) n* De
En debugging aid
Es ayuda a la depuración *(f)*
Fr outil de mise au point *(m)*
It strumento di messa a punto (di un programma) *(m)*
Pt ajuda de desparasitação *(f)*

Feld *(n) n* De
En field
Es campo *(m)*
Fr champ *(m)*
It campo *(m)*
Pt campo *(m)*

Feldaddierer *(m) n* De
En full adder
Es adicionador completo *(m)*
Fr additionneur complet *(m)*
It addizionatore totale *(m)*
Pt somador total *(m)*

Feldeffekttransistor *(m) n* De
En field-effect transistor (FET)
Es transistor de efecto de campo *(m)*
Fr transistor à effet de champ (TEC) *(m)*
It transistore ad effetto di campo *(m)*
Pt transistor de efeito de campo *(m)*

Feldlänge *(f) n* De
En field length
Es longitud de campo *(f)*
Fr longueur de zone *(f)*
It lunghezza del campo *(f)*
Pt comprimento de campo *(m)*

Fernmeldung *(f) n* De
En telecommunication
Es telecomunicación *(f)*
Fr télécommunication *(f)*
It telecomunicazione *(f)*
Pt telecomunicação *(f)*

Fernmessung *(f) n* De
En telemetry
Es telemetría *(f)*
Fr télémesure *(f)*

It telemetria *(f)*
Pt telemetria *(f)*

Fernprüfung *(f)* *n* De
En remote testing
Es ensayo a distancia *(m)*
Fr contrôle à distance *(m)*
It collaudo a distanza *(m)*
Pt tele-ensaio *(m)*

Fernrechensystem *(n)* *n* De
En remote computing system
Es sistema de cálculo a distancia *(m)*
Fr système de traitement à distance *(m)*
It sistema di elaborazione a distanza *(m)*
Pt sistema de tele-computador *(m)*

Fernschreiber *(m)* *n* De
En teleprinter
Es teleimpresor *(m)*
Fr téléimprimeur *(m)*
It telestampatrice *(f)*
Pt tele-impressor *(m)*

Ferntext *(m)* *n* De
En teletext
Es teletexto *(m)*
Fr télétexte *(m)*
It teletesto *(m)*
Pt teletexto *(m)*

Fernverarbeitung *(f)* *n* De
En remote processing; teleprocessing
Es proceso a distancia; teleproceso *(m)*
Fr télétraitement *(m)*
It elaborazione a distanza; tele-elaborazione *(f)*
Pt tele-processamento *(m)*

ferramentas programadas automaticamente *(f pl)* Pt
De automatisch programmierte Werkzeuge *(pl)*
En automatically programmed tools (APT)
Es herramientas programadas automáticamente *(f pl)*
Fr machines-outils programmées automatiquement *(f pl)*
It strumenti programmati automaticamente *(m pl)*

ferrite core En
De Ferritkern *(m)*
Es núcleo de ferria *(m)*
Fr tore de ferrite *(f)*
It memoria di ferrite *(f)*
Pt núcleo de ferrite *(m)*

Ferritkern *(m)* *n* De
En ferrite core
Es núcleo de ferria *(m)*
Fr tore de ferrite *(f)*
It memoria di ferrite *(f)*
Pt núcleo de ferrite *(m)*

Fertigungslauf *(m)* *n* De
En production run
Es pasada de producción *(f)*
Fr passage de production *(m)*
It esecuzione di produzione *(f)*
Pt passagem de produção *(f)*

Fertigungszeit *(f)* *n* De
En productive time
Es tiempo do producción *(m)*
Fr temps productif *(m)*
It tempo produttivo *(m)*
Pt tempo produtivo *(m)*

feste Blocklänge *(f)* De
En fixed block length
Es longitud de bloque fija *(f)*
Fr bloc de longueur fixe *(m)*
It lunghezza del blocco fisso *(f)*
Pt comprimento de bloco fixo *(m)*

festes Feld *(n)* De
En fixed field
Es campo fijo *(m)*
Fr zone fixe *(f)*
It campo fisso *(m)*
Pt campo fixo *(m)*

Festparameter *(m)* *n* De
En preset parameter
Es parámetro definido previamente *(m)*
Fr paramètre pré-défini *(m)*
It parametro prestabilito *(m)*
Pt parâmetro previamente fixado *(m)*

Festplattendatei *(f)* *n* De
En fixed-disk file
Es fichero de discos fijos *(m)*
Fr fichier de disques fixes *(m)*
It file del disco fisso *(m)*
Pt arquivo de discos fixos *(m)*

Festpunktarithmetik *(f)* *n* De
En fixed-point arithmetic
Es aritmética de coma fija *(f)*
Fr arithmétique en fixe *(f)*
It aritmetica a virgola fissa *(f)*
Pt aritmética de ponto fixo *(f)*

Festschaltungsspeicher *(m)* *n* De
En solid-state memory
Es memoria de estado sólido *(f)*
Fr mémoire en état solide *(f)*
It memoria a stato solido *(f)*
Pt memória solid-state *(f)*

Festspeicher *(m)* *n* De
En read-only memory (ROM)
Es memoria fija *(f)*
Fr mémoire fixe *(f)*
It memoria soltanto di lettura *(f)*
Pt memória apenas de leitura *(f)*

fiabilidad *(f)* *n* Es
De Zuverlässigkeit *(f)*
En reliability
Fr fiabilité *(f)*
It affidabilita *(f)*
Pt confiança *(f)*

fiabilité *(f)* *n* Fr
De Zuverlässigkeit *(f)*
En reliability
Es fiabilidad *(f)*
It affidabilita *(f)*
Pt confiança *(f)*

fiber optics Am
De Faseroptik *(f)*
En fibre optics
Es óptica de las fibras *(f)*
Fr optique à fibre *(f)*
It fibre ottiche *(f)*
Pt óptica de fibras *(f)*

fibre optics En
Am fiber optics
De Faseroptik *(f)*
Es óptica de las fibras *(f)*
Fr optique à fibre *(f)*
It fibre ottiche *(f)*
Pt óptica de fibras *(f)*

fibre ottiche *(f)* It
Am fiber optics
De Faseroptik *(f)*
En fibre optics
Es óptica de las fibras *(f)*
Fr optique à fibre *(f)*
Pt óptica de fibras *(f)*

ficha *(f)* *n* Es, Pt
De Karte *(f)*
En card
Fr carte *(f)*
It scheda *(f)*

ficha de oitenta colunas *(f)* Pt
De achtzig-Spalten-Karte *(f)*
En eighty-column card
Es tarjeta de ochenta columnas *(f)*
Fr carte de quatre-vingt colonnes *(f)*
It scheda ad ottanta colonne *(f)*

ficha de silício *(f)* Pt
De Silikonchip *(m)*
En silicon chip
Es microplaqueta de silicio *(f)*

Fr puce au silicium *(f)*
It scheggia di silicone *(f)*

ficha eléctrica *(f) n* Pt
De Stecker *(m)*
En plug
Es clavija *(f)*
Fr fiche *(f)*
It spina *(f)*

ficha magnética *(f)* Es, Pt
De Magnetkarte *(f)*
En magnetic card
Fr carte magnétique *(f)*
It scheda magnetica *(f)*

ficha perforada *(f)* Es
Am punch card
De Lochkarte *(f)*
En punched card
Fr carte mécanographique *(f)*
It scheda perforata *(f)*
Pt ficha perfurada *(f)*

ficha perfurada *(f)* Pt
Am punch card
De Lochkarte *(f)*
En punched card
Es ficha perforada *(f)*
Fr carte mécanographique *(f)*
It scheda perforata *(f)*

fiche *(f) n* Fr
De Stecker *(m)*
En plug
Es clavija *(f)*
It spina *(f)*
Pt ficha eléctrica *(f)*

fiche de connexion *(f)* Fr
De Schaltschnur *(f)*
En patchcord
Es cable de conexión *(m)*
It cordone di connessione *(m)*
Pt cabo de concerto *(m)*

fichero *(m) n* Es
De Datei *(f)*
En file
Fr fichier *(m)*
It file *(m)*
Pt arquivo *(m)*

fichero archivado *(m)* Es
De archivierte Datei *(f)*
En archived file
Fr fichier archivé *(m)*
It file archiviato *(m)*
Pt dossier arquivado *(m)*

fichero de discos *(m)* Es
De Plattendatei *(f)*
En disk file
Fr fichier sur disque *(m)*
It file su disco *(m)*
Pt arquivo de discos *(m)*

fichero de discos fijos *(m)* Es
De Festplattendatei *(f)*
En fixed-disk file
Fr fichier de disques fixes *(m)*
It file del disco fisso *(m)*
Pt arquivo de discos fixos *(m)*

fichero envuelto *(m)* Es
De Hülldatei *(f)*
En enveloped file
Fr dossier sous enveloppe *(m)*
It file inviluppato *(m)*
Pt arquivo envolvido *(m)*

fichero físico *(m)* Es
De physische Datei *(f)*
En physical file
Fr fichier physique *(m)*
It file fisico *(m)*
Pt arquivo físico *(m)*

fichero maestro *(m)* Es
De Stammdatei *(f)*
En master file
Fr fichier principal *(m)*
It file principale *(m)*
Pt arquivo principal *(m)*

ficheros compartidos *(m pl)* Es
De gemeinsam benutzte Datei *(f)*
En shared files
Fr fichiers partagés *(m pl)*
It file in comune *(f pl)*
Pt arquivos compartidos *(m pl)*

fichero secuencial *(m)* Es
De Folgedatei *(f)*
En sequential file
Fr fichier séquentiel *(m)*
It file sequenziale *(m)*
Pt arquivo sequencial *(f)*

fichier *(m) n* Fr
De Datei *(f)*
En file
Es fichero *(m)*
It file *(m)*
Pt arquivo *(m)*

fichier archivé *(m)* Fr
De archivierte Datei *(f)*
En archived file
Es fichero archivado *(m)*
It file archiviato *(m)*
Pt dossier arquivado *(m)*

fichier de disques fixes *(m)* Fr
De Festplattendatei *(f)*
En fixed-disk file
Es fichero de discos fijos *(m)*
It file del disco fisso *(m)*
Pt arquivo de discos fixos *(m)*

fichier physique *(m)* Fr
De physische Datei *(f)*
En physical file
Es fichero físico *(m)*
It file fisico *(m)*
Pt arquivo físico *(m)*

fichier principal *(m)* Fr
De Stammdatei *(f)*
En master file
Es fichero maestro *(m)*
It file principale *(m)*
Pt arquivo principal *(m)*

fichier séquentiel *(m)* Fr
De Folgedatei *(f)*
En sequential file
Es fichero secuencial *(m)*
It file sequenziale *(m)*
Pt arquivo sequencial *(f)*

fichiers partagés *(m pl)* Fr
De gemeinsam benutzte Datei *(f)*
En shared files
Es ficheros compartidos *(m pl)*
It file in comune *(f pl)*
Pt arquivos compartidos *(m pl)*

fichier sur disque *(m)* Fr
De Plattendatei *(f)*
En disk file
Es fichero de discos *(m)*
It file su disco *(m)*
Pt arquivo de discos *(m)*

ficticio *adj* Es
De Schein-
En dummy
Fr fictif
It fittizio
Pt simulado

fictif *adj* Fr
De Schein-
En dummy
Es ficticio
It fittizio
Pt simulado

field *n* En
De Feld *(n)*
Es campo *(m)*
Fr champ *(m)*
It campo *(m)*
Pt campo *(m)*

field-effect transistor (FET) En
De Feldeffekttransistor *(m)*
Es transistor de efecto de campo *(m)*
Fr transistor à effet de champ (TEC) *(m)*
It transistore ad effetto di campo *(m)*
Pt transistor de efeito de campo *(m)*

field length En
De Feldlänge *(f)*
Es longitud de campo *(f)*
Fr longueur de zone *(f)*
It lunghezza del campo *(f)*
Pt comprimento de campo *(m)*

fila *(f) n* Es, It, Pt
De Zeile *(f)*
En row
Fr ligne *(f)*

fila de bits *(f)* Pt
De Binärzeichenfolge *(f)*
En bit string
Es serie de bits *(f)*
Fr chaîne de bits *(f)*
It stringa di bit *(f)*

file *n* En; It *(m)*
De Datei *(f)*
Es fichero *(m)*
Fr fichier *(m)*
Pt arquivo *(m)*

file archiviato *(m)* It
De archivierte Datei *(f)*
En archived file
Es fichero archivado *(m)*
Fr fichier archivé *(m)*
Pt dossier arquivado *(m)*

file conversion En
De Dateiumwandlung *(f)*
Es conversión de ficheros *(f)*
Fr conversion de fichiers *(f)*
It conversione del file *(f)*
Pt conversão de arquivo *(f)*

file del disco fisso *(m)* It
De Festplattendatei *(f)*
En fixed-disk file
Es fichero de discos fijos *(m)*
Fr fichier de disques fixes *(m)*
Pt arquivo de discos fixos *(m)*

file fisico *(m)* It
De physische Datei *(f)*
En physical file
Es fichero físico *(m)*
Fr fichier physique *(m)*
Pt arquivo físico *(m)*

file identification En
De Dateikennzeichnung *(f)*
Es identificación del fichero *(f)*
Fr identification de fichier *(f)*
It identificazione del file *(f)*
Pt identificação de arquivo *(f)*

file in comune *(f pl)* It
De gemeinsam benutzte Datei *(f)*
En shared files
Es ficheros compartidos *(m pl)*
Fr fichiers partagés *(m pl)*
Pt arquivos compartidos *(m pl)*

file inviluppato *(m)* It
De Hülldatei *(f)*
En enveloped file
Es fichero envuelto *(m)*
Fr dossier sous enveloppe *(m)*
Pt arquivo envolvido *(m)*

fileira *(f) n* Pt
De Folge *(f)*
En string
Es serie *(f)*
Fr chaîne *(f)*
It stringa *(f)*

file label En
De Dateikennsatz *(m)*
Es etiqueta de fichero *(f)*
Fr étiquette de fichier *(f)*
It etichetta del file *(f)*
Pt rótulo de arquivo *(m)*

file maintenance En
De Dateiwartung *(f)*
Es mantenimiento de ficheros *(m)*
Fr tenue à jour de fichier *(f)*
It manutenzione del file *(f)*
Pt manutenção de arquivo *(f)*

file principale *(m)* It
De Stammdatei *(f)*
En master file
Es fichero maestro *(m)*
Fr fichier principal *(m)*
Pt arquivo principal *(m)*

file protection En
De Dateischutz *(m)*
Es protección de fichero *(f)*
Fr protection de fichier *(f)*
It protezione del file *(f)*
Pt protecção de arquivo *(f)*

file sequenziale *(m)* It
De Folgedatei *(f)*
En sequential file
Es fichero secuencial *(m)*
Fr fichier séquentiel *(m)*
Pt arquivo sequencial *(f)*

file store *n* En
De Dateispeicher *(m)*
Es memoria fichero *(f)*
Fr mémoire fichier *(f)*
It memoria dei file *(f)*
Pt armazém de arquivo *(m)*

file su disco *(m)* It
De Plattendatei *(f)*
En disk file
Es fichero de discos *(m)*
Fr fichier sur disque *(m)*
Pt arquivo de discos *(m)*

Filmaufzeichner *(m) n* De
En film recorder
Es registrador de películas *(m)*
Fr unité d'enregistrement sur film *(f)*
It registratore di pellicole *(m)*
Pt registador de películas *(m)*

Filmleser *(m) n* De
En film reader
Es lectora de películas *(f)*
Fr lecteur de film *(m)*
It lettore di pellicole *(m)*
Pt leitor de películas *(m)*

film reader En
De Filmleser *(m)*
Es lectora de películas *(f)*
Fr lecteur de film *(m)*
It lettore di pellicole *(m)*
Pt leitor de películas *(m)*

film recorder En
De Filmaufzeichner *(m)*
Es registrador de películas *(m)*
Fr unité d'enregistrement sur film *(f)*
It registratore di pellicole *(m)*
Pt registador de películas *(m)*

filter *n* En
De Filter *(m)*
Es filtro *(m)*
Fr filtre *(m)*
It filtro *(m)*
Pt filtro *(m)*

Filter *(m) n* De
En filter
Es filtro *(m)*
Fr filtre *(m)*
It filtro *(m)*
Pt filtro *(m)*

filtre *(m) n* Fr
De Filter *(m)*
En filter
Es filtro *(m)*
It filtro *(m)*
Pt filtro *(m)*

filtro *(m) n* Es, It, Pt
De Filter *(m)*
En filter
Fr filtre *(m)*

fim da fita *(m)* Pt
De Bandende *(n)*
En end of tape (EOT)
Es fin de cinta *(m)*
Fr fin de bande *(f)*
It fine del nastro *(f)*

fim da passagem *(m)* Pt
De Ablaufende *(n)*
En end of run (EOR)
Es fin de pasada *(m)*
Fr fin de passage *(f)*
It fine dell'elaborazione *(f)*

fim de arquivo *(m)* Pt
De Dateiende *(n)*
En end of file (EOF)
Es fin de fichero *(m)*
Fr fin de fichier *(f)*
It fine del file *(f)*

fim de bloco *(m)* Pt
De Ende des Blockes *(n)*
En end of block (EOB)
Es fin de bloque *(m)*
Fr fin de bloc *(f)*
It fine del blocco *(f)*

fim do trabalho *(m)* Pt
De Ende der Arbeit *(n)*
En end of job (EOJ)
Es fin de trabajo *(m)*
Fr fin de travail *(f)*
It fine del lavoro *(f)*

fin *(f) n* Fr
De Endstelle *(f)*
En termination
Es terminación *(f)*

It conclusione *(f)*
Pt terminação *(f)*

fin de bande *(f)* Fr
De Bandende *(n)*
En end of tape (EOT)
Es fin de cinta *(m)*
It fine del nastro *(f)*
Pt fim da fita *(m)*

fin de bloc *(f)* Fr
De Ende des Blockes *(n)*
En end of block (EOB)
Es fin de bloque *(m)*
It fine del blocco *(f)*
Pt fim de bloco *(m)*

fin de bloque *(m)* Es
De Ende des Blockes *(n)*
En end of block (EOB)
Fr fin de bloc *(f)*
It fine del blocco *(f)*
Pt fim de bloco *(m)*

fin de cinta *(m)* Es
De Bandende *(n)*
En end of tape (EOT)
Fr fin de bande *(f)*
It fine del nastro *(f)*
Pt fim da fita *(m)*

fin de fichero *(m)* Es
De Dateiende *(n)*
En end of file (EOF)
Fr fin de fichier *(f)*
It fine del file *(f)*
Pt fim de arquivo *(m)*

fin de fichier *(f)* Fr
De Dateiende *(n)*
En end of file (EOF)
Es fin de fichero *(m)*
It fine del file *(f)*
Pt fim de arquivo *(m)*

fin de pasada *(m)* Es
De Ablaufende *(n)*
En end of run (EOR)
Fr fin de passage *(f)*
It fine dell'elaborazione *(f)*
Pt fim da passagem *(m)*

fin de passage *(f)* Fr
De Ablaufende *(n)*
En end of run (EOR)
Es fin de pasada *(m)*
It fine dell'elaborazione *(f)*
Pt fim da passagem *(m)*

fin de trabajo *(m)* Es
De Ende der Arbeit *(n)*
En end of job (EOJ)
Fr fin de travail *(f)*
It fine del lavoro *(f)*
Pt fim do trabalho *(m)*

fin de travail *(f)* Fr
De Ende der Arbeit *(n)*
En end of job (EOJ)
Es fin de trabajo *(m)*
It fine del lavoro *(f)*
Pt fim do trabalho *(m)*

fine del blocco *(f)* It
De Ende des Blockes *(n)*
En end of block (EOB)
Es fin de bloque *(m)*
Fr fin de bloc *(f)*
Pt fim de bloco *(m)*

fine del file *(f)* It
De Dateiende *(n)*
En end of file (EOF)
Es fin de fichero *(m)*
Fr fin de fichier *(f)*
Pt fim de arquivo *(m)*

fine del lavoro *(f)* It
De Ende der Arbeit *(n)*
En end of job (EOJ)
Es fin de trabajo *(m)*
Fr fin de travail *(f)*
Pt fim do trabalho *(m)*

fine dell'elaborazione *(f)* It
De Ablaufende *(n)*
En end of run (EOR)
Es fin de pasada *(m)*
Fr fin de passage *(f)*
Pt fim da passagem *(m)*

fine del nastro *(f)* It
De Bandende *(n)*
En end of tape (EOT)
Es fin de cinta *(m)*
Fr fin de bande *(f)*
Pt fim da fita *(m)*

firmemente acoplado Pt
De eng gekoppelt
En tightly coupled
Es fuertemente acoplado
Fr à couplage serré
It accoppiado fortemente

first-generation *adj* En
De erstgeneration
Es primera-generación
Fr première-génération
It prima-generazione
Pt primeira-geração

first in, first out (FIFO) En
De Prioritätssteuerung *(f)*
Es primero a llegar, primero que sale *(m)*
Fr premier entré, premier sorti *(m)*
It dentro il primo, fuori il primo *(m)*
Pt primeiro a entrar, primeiro a sair *(m)*

fita *(f) n* Pt
De Band *(n)*
En tape
Es cinta *(f)*
Fr bande *(f)*
It nastro *(m)*

fita avó *(f)* Pt
De Erstgenerationsband *(n)*
En grandfather tape
Es cinta primera generación *(f)*
Fr bande première génération *(f)*
It nastro nonno *(m)*

fita com controle de carro *(f)* Pt
De Wagensteuerband *(n)*
En carriage-control tape
Es cinta de control del carro *(f)*
Fr bande pilote *(f)*
It nastrino di controllo del carrello *(m)*

fita de alimentação central *(f)* Pt
Am center-feed tape
De Band mit Zentralvorschub *(n)*
En centre-feed tape
Es cinta de alimentación central *(f)*
Fr bande à entraînement central *(f)*
It nastro ad alimentazione centrale *(m)*

fita de alimentação por avanço *(f)* Pt
De Bandvorausvorschub *(m)*
En advance-feed tape
Es cinta de alimentación por arrastre *(f)*
Fr défilement-avancement bande *(m)*
It avanzare-alimentare nastro *(m)*

fita de instruções principais *(f)* Pt
De Hauptbefehlsband *(n)*
En master-instruction tape (MIT)
Es cinta programa de explotación *(f)*
Fr bande de programme d'exploitation (BPE) *(f)*
It nastro dell'istruzioni principali *(m)*

fita de papel *(f)* Pt
De Papierstreifen *(m)*
En paper tape
Es cinta de papel *(f)*
Fr bande de papier *(f)*
It nastro di carta *(m)*

fita de tinta *(f)* Pt
De Farbband *(n)*
En ink ribbon
Es cinta entintada *(f)*
Fr ruban à encre *(m)*
It nastro ad inchiostro *(m)*

fita de trabalho *(f)* Pt
De Arbeitsband *(n)*
En work tape
Es cinta de maniobra *(f)*
Fr bande de travail *(f)*
It nastro di lavoro *(m)*

fita magnética *(f)* Pt
De Magnetband *(n)*
En magnetic tape
Es cinta magnética *(f)*
Fr bande magnétique *(f)*
It nastro magnetico *(m)*

fita pai *(f)* Pt
De Urband *n*
En father tape
Es cinta creadora *(f)*
Fr bande créatrice *(f)*
It nastro padre *(m)*

fita perfurada *(f)* Pt
De Lochstreifen *(m)*
En perforated tape; punched tape
Es cinta perforada *(f)*
Fr bande perforée *(f)*
It nastro perforato *(m)*

fita principal *(f)* Pt
De Stammband *(n)*
En master tape
Es bobina emisora *(f)*
Fr bande maîtresse *(f)*
It nastro principale *(m)*

fita recortada *(f)* Pt
De geschuppter Streifen *(m)*
En chadded tape
Es cinta de perforación completa *(f)*
Fr bande à perforations complètes *(f)*
It nastro con perforazioni totali *(m)*

fita sem recorte *(f)* Pt
De Schuppenstreifen *(m)*
En chadless tape
Es cinta semiperforada *(f)*
Fr bande semi-perforée *(f)*
It nastro semiperforato *(m)*

fita virgem *(f)* Pt
De Neuband *(n)*
En virgin tape
Es cint a virgen *(f)*
Fr bande vierge *(f)*
It nastro vergine *(m)*

fittizio *adj* It
De Schein-
En dummy
Es ficticio
Fr fictif
Pt simulado

fixed block length En
De feste Blocklänge *(f)*
Es longitud de bloque fija *(f)*
Fr bloc de longueur fixe *(m)*
It lunghezza del blocco fisso *(f)*
Pt comprimento de bloco fixo *(m)*

fixed-disk file En
De Festplattendatei *(f)*
Es fichero de discos fijos *(m)*
Fr fichier de disques fixes *(m)*
It file del disco fisso *(m)*
Pt arquivo de discos fixos *(m)*

fixed field En
De festes Feld *(n)*
Es campo fijo *(m)*
Fr zone fixe *(f)*
It campo fisso *(m)*
Pt campo fixo *(m)*

fixed-point arithmetic En
De Festpunktarithmetik *(f)*
Es aritmética de coma fija *(f)*
Fr arithmétique en fixe *(f)*
It aritmetica a virgola fissa *(f)*
Pt aritmética de ponto fixo *(f)*

Fixpunkt *(m) n* De
En benchmark
Es referencia *(f)*
Fr repère *(m)*
It riferimento *(m)*
Pt referência de nível *(f)*

Flachtisch-kurvenzeichner *(m) n* De
En flat-bed plotter
Es trazador de base plana *(m)*
Fr traceur à plat *(m)*
It tracciatore in piano *(m)*
Pt plotador de leito plano *(m)*

flag *n* En
De Markierung *(f)*
Es señalizador *(m)*
Fr drapeau *(m)*
It indicatore *(m)*
Pt bandeira *(f)*

flat-bed plotter En
De Flachtisch-kurvenzeichner *(m)*
Es trazador de base plana *(m)*
Fr traceur à plat *(m)*
It tracciatore in piano *(m)*
Pt plotador de leito plano *(m)*

floating-point arithmetic En
De Flüssigpunkt-arithmetik *(f)*
Es aritmética de coma flotante *(f)*
Fr calcul en virgule flottante *(m)*
It aritmetica a virgola mobile *(f)*
Pt aritmética de ponto flutuante *(f)*

floppy disk En; It *(m)*
De Floppy Disk *(m)*
Es disco blando *(m)*
Fr disque souple *(m)*
Pt disco floppy *(m)*

Floppy Disk *(m)* De
En floppy disk
Es disco blando *(m)*
Fr disque souple *(m)*
It floppy disk *(m)*
Pt disco floppy *(m)*

Floppy-Disk-Antrieb *(m)* De
En floppy-disk drive
Es unidad de discos flexibles *(f)*
Fr unité de disque souple *(f)*
It unità floppy disk *(f)*
Pt accionamento do disco floppy *(m)*

floppy-disk drive En
De Floppy-Disk-Antrieb *(m)*
Es unidad de discos flexibles *(f)*
Fr unité de disque souple *(f)*
It unità floppy disk *(f)*
Pt accionamento do disco floppy *(m)*

flowchart *n* En
De Flußdiagramm *(n)*
Es ordinograma *(m)*
Fr organigramme *(m)*
It diagramma di flusso *(m)*
Pt gráfico de fluxo *(m)*

flowline *n* En
De Flußlinie *(f)*
Es línea de flujo *(f)*
Fr ligne de flux *(f)*
It linea di flusso *(f)*
Pt linha de fluxo *(f)*

flüchtig *adj* De
En transient
Es transitorio
Fr transitoire
It transitorio
Pt transitório

fluid logic En
De Fluidverknüpfung *(f)*
Es lógica de flúidos *(f)*
Fr logique des fluides *(f)*
It logica fluida *(f)*
Pt lógica fluida *(f)*

Fluidverknüpfung *(f) n* De
En fluid logic
Es lógica de flúidos *(f)*
Fr logique des fluides *(f)*
It logica fluida *(f)*
Pt lógica fluida *(f)*

Flußdiagramm *(n) n* De
En flowchart
Es ordinograma *(m)*
Fr organigramme *(m)*
It diagramma di flusso *(m)*
Pt gráfico de fluxo *(m)*

Flüssigpunktarithmetik *(f) n* De
En floating-point arithmetic
Es aritmética de coma flotante *(f)*
Fr calcul en virgule flottante *(m)*
It aritmetica a virgola mobile *(f)*
Pt aritmética de ponto flutuante *(f)*

Flußlinie *(f) n* De
En flowline
Es línea de flujo *(f)*
Fr ligne de flux *(f)*
It linea di flusso *(f)*
Pt linha de fluxo *(f)*

Flußwechseldichte *(f) n* De
En packing density

Es densidad de empaquetamiento *(f)*
Fr densité d'implantation *(f)*
It densita di compattezza *(f)*
Pt densidade de acumulação *(f)*

folding ratio En
De Faltverhältnis *(n)*
Es relación de plegado *(f)*
Fr rapport de pliage *(m)*
It rapporto pieghevole *(m)*
Pt ratio de dobragem *(f)*

Folge *(f) n* De
En sequence; string
Es secuencia; serie *(f)*
Fr chaîne; séquence *(f)*
It sequenza; stringa *(f)*
Pt fileira; sequência *(f)*

Folgebearbeitung *(f) n* De
En string manipulation
Es manipulación de series *(f)*
Fr manipulation de chaîne *(f)*
It manipolazione di stringa *(f)*
Pt manipulação de fileira *(f)*

Folgedatei *(f) n* De
En sequential file
Es fichero secuencial *(m)*
Fr fichier séquentiel *(m)*
It file sequenziale *(m)*
Pt arquivo sequencial *(f)*

folgen *vb* De
En sequence
Es secuenciar
Fr ordonner
It sequenziare
Pt formar sequência

Folgeprüfung *(f) n* De
En sequence check
Es verificación de secuencia *(f)*
Fr contrôle de séquence *(m)*
It controllo di sequenza *(m)*
Pt verificação de sequência *(f)*

Folgeverarbeitung *(f) n* De
En sequential processing
Es proceso secuencial *(m)*
Fr traitement séquentiel *(m)*
It elaborazione sequenziale *(f)*
Pt processamento sequencial *(m)*

Folgezugriff *(m) n* De
En sequential access
Es acceso secuencial *(m)*
Fr accès séquentiel *(m)*
It accesso sequenziale *(m)*
Pt acesso sequencial *(m)*

fonction *(f) n* Fr
De Funktion *(f)*
En function
Es función *(f)*
It funzione *(f)*
Pt função *(f)*

fonction de transfert *(f)* Fr
De Übertragungs-funktion *(f)*
En transfer function
Es función de transferencia *(f)*
It funzione di trasferimento *(f)*
Pt função de transferência *(f)*

fonctionnement à caractères Fr
De zeichenmäsig ausgerichtet
En character-orientated
Es orientado a los caracteres
It orientato a carattere
Pt orientado por caracteres

fora da linha Pt
De indirekt
En offline
Es fuera de línea
Fr hors ligne
It non collegato

forçar *vb* Pt
De zwingen
En force
Es forzar
Fr forcer
It forzare

force *vb* En
De zwingen
Es forzar
Fr forcer
It forzare
Pt forçar

forcer *vb* Fr
De zwingen
En force
Es forzar
It forzare
Pt forçar

foreground processing En
De Vordergrund-verarbeitung *(f)*
Es proceso preferente *(m)*
Fr traitement de front *(m)*
It elaborazione di primo piano *(f)*
Pt processamento de primeiro plano *(m)*

fori di alimentazione *(m pl)* It
De Taktlöcher *(n pl)*
En feed holes
Es perforaciones de alimentación *(f pl)*
Fr trous d'entraînement *(m pl)*
Pt furos de alimentação *(m pl)*

formación de colas de mensajes *(f)* Es
De Nachrichten-schlangestehen *(n)*
En message queuing
Fr mise en file d'attente de message *(f)*
It messa in coda dei messaggi *(f)*
Pt bicha de mensagens *(f)*

formar sequência Pt
De folgen
En sequence
Es secuenciar
Fr ordonner
It sequenziare

formas de partes múltiplas *(f pl)* Pt
De mehrteilige Formulare *(pl)*
En multipart forms
Es paquete de papel continuo *(m)*
Fr liasse *(f)*
It moduli a copie multiple *(m pl)*

format *n* En; Fr *(m)*
De Format *(n)*
Es formato *(m)*
It formato *(m)*
Pt formato *(m)*

Format *(n) n* De
En format
Es formato *(m)*
Fr format *(m)*
It formato *(m)*
Pt formato *(m)*

formato *(m) n* Es, It, Pt
De Format *(n)*
En format
Fr format *(m)*

formato de impresión *(m)* Es
De Druckformat *(n)*
En print format
Fr présentation de l'impression *(f)*
It formato di stampa *(m)*
Pt formato de impressão *(m)*

formato de impressão *(m)* Pt
De Druckformat *(n)*
En print format
Es formato de impresión *(m)*
Fr présentation de l'impression *(f)*
It formato di stampa *(m)*

formato de instruções *(m)* Pt
De Befehlsformat *(n)*
En instruction format
Es formato de la instrucción *(m)*

Fr structure de l'instruction *(f)*
It formato dell'istruzione *(m)*

formato de la instrucción *(m)* Es
De Befehlsformat *(n)*
En instruction format
Fr structure de l'instruction *(f)*
It formato dell'istruzione *(m)*
Pt formato de instruções *(m)*

formato dell'istruzione *(m)* It
De Befehlsformat *(n)*
En instruction format
Es formato de la instrucción *(m)*
Fr structure de l'instruction *(f)*
Pt formato de instruções *(m)*

formato di stampa *(m)* It
De Druckformat *(n)*
En print format
Es formato de impresión *(m)*
Fr présentation de l'impression *(f)*
Pt formato de impressão *(m)*

formato normalizado *(m)* Es
De Standardform *(f)*
En standard form
Fr forme normalisée *(f)*
It modulo standard *(m)*
Pt formulário standard *(m)*

formato reducido *(m)* Es
De verdichtetes Format *(n)*
En reduced format
Fr structure réduite *(f)*
It formato ridotto *(m)*
Pt formato reduzido *(m)*

formato reduzido *(m)* Pt
De verdichtetes Format *(n)*
En reduced format
Es formato reducido *(m)*
Fr structure réduite *(f)*
It formato ridotto *(m)*

formato ridotto *(m)* It
De verdichtetes Format *(n)*
En reduced format
Es formato reducido *(m)*
Fr structure réduite *(f)*
Pt formato reduzido *(m)*

forme normalisée *(f)* Fr
De Standardform *(f)*
En standard form
Es formato normalizado *(m)*
It modulo standard *(m)*
Pt formulário standard *(m)*

form feed En
De Formularvorschub *(m)*
Es alimentación del papel *(f)*
Fr alimentation en papier *(f)*
It alimentazione del modulo *(f)*
Pt alimentação de formulários *(f)*

forms *n pl* En
De Formulare *(n pl)*
Es papel *(m)*
Fr formules *(f pl)*
It moduli *(m pl)*
Pt formulários *(m pl)*

form stop En
De Formularanschlag *(m)*
Es parada del papel *(f)*
Fr arrêt de papier *(m)*
It arresto del modulo *(m)*
Pt paragem de formulários *(f)*

forms tractor En
De Formulartraktor *(m)*
Es tractor de arrastre del papel *(m)*
Fr entraîneur de papier *(m)*
It trattore di moduli *(m)*
Pt tractor de formulários *(m)*

Formularanschlag *(m) n* De
En form stop
Es parada del papel *(f)*
Fr arrêt de papier *(m)*
It arresto del modulo *(m)*
Pt paragem de formulários *(f)*

Formulare *(n pl) n* De
En forms
Es papel *(m)*
Fr formules *(f pl)*
It moduli *(m pl)*
Pt formulários *(m pl)*

formulários *(m pl) n* Pt
De Formulare *(n pl)*
En forms
Es papel *(m)*
Fr formules *(f pl)*
It moduli *(m pl)*

formulário standard *(m)* Pt
De Standardform *(f)*
En standard form
Es formato normalizado *(m)*
Fr forme normalisée *(f)*
It modulo standard *(m)*

Formulartraktor *(m) n* De
En forms tractor
Es tractor de arrastre del papel *(m)*
Fr entraîneur de papier *(m)*
It trattore di moduli *(m)*
Pt tractor de formulários *(m)*

Formularvorschub *(m) n* De
En form feed
Es alimentación del papel *(f)*
Fr alimentation en papier *(f)*
It alimentazione del modulo *(f)*
Pt alimentação de formulários *(f)*

formules *(f pl) n* Fr
De Formulare *(n pl)*
En forms
Es papel *(m)*
It moduli *(m pl)*
Pt formulários *(m pl)*

forzar *vb* Es
De zwingen
En force
Fr forcer
It forzare
Pt forçar

forzare *vb* It
De zwingen
En force
Es forzar
Fr forcer
Pt forçar

fourth-generation *adj* En
De viertgeneration
Es cuarta-generación
Fr quatrième-génération
It quarta-generazione
Pt quarta-geração

four-wire circuit En
De Vierdrahtschaltung *(f)*
Es circuito de cuatro hilos *(m)*
Fr circuit quatre fils *(m)*
It circuito a quattro fili *(m)*
Pt circuito de quatro fios *(m)*

fracción de tiempo *(f)* Es
De Zeitscheiben-verfahren *(n)*
En time slice
Fr découpage du temps *(m)*
It ripartizione di tempo *(f)*
Pt fatia de tempo *(f)*

frame *n* En
De Rahmen *(m)*
Es encuadre *(m)*
Fr cadre *(m)*
It telaio *(m)*
Pt quadro *(m)*

frecuencia de fallos *(f)* Es
De Ausfallhäufigkeit *(f)*
En failure rate
Fr taux de défaillance *(m)*
It numero di guasti *(m)*
Pt índice de falhas *(m)*

frecuencia de muestreo *(f)* Es
De Abtastfrequenz *(f)*
En sampling rate
Fr vitesse d'échantillonnage *(f)*

It volume di campionamento *(m)*
Pt índice de amostragem *(m)*

frecuencia de pulsación *(f)* Es
De Schwebungsfrequenz *(f)*
En beat frequency
Fr fréquence de battement *(f)*
It frequenza di battimento *(f)*
Pt frequência de pulso *(f)*

frecuencia de repetición de impulsos *(f)* Es
De Impulsfolgefrequenz *(f)*
En pulse repetition frequency (prf)
Fr fréquence par récurrence des impulsions *(f)*
It frequenza a ripetizione di impulsi *(f)*
Pt frequência de repetição de impulsos *(f)*

free field En
De Freifeld *(n)*
Es campo libre *(m)*
Fr champ libre *(m)*
It campo libero *(m)*
Pt campo livre *(m)*

Freifeld *(n) n* De
En free field
Es campo libre *(m)*
Fr champ libre *(m)*
It campo libero *(m)*
Pt campo livre *(m)*

fréquence de battement *(f)* Fr
De Schwebungsfrequenz *(f)*
En beat frequency
Es frecuencia de pulsación *(f)*
It frequenza di battimento *(f)*
Pt frequência de pulso *(f)*

fréquence des impulsions d'horloge *(f)* Fr
De Taktgeschwindigkeit *(f)*
En clock rate
Es velocidad de impulsos de reloj *(f)*
It frequenza degli impulsi dell'orologio *(f)*
Pt taxa de impulsos de relógio *(f)*

fréquence par récurrence des impulsions *(f)* Fr
De Impulsfolgefrequenz *(f)*
En pulse repetition frequency (prf)
Es frecuencia de repetición de impulsos *(f)*
It frequenza a ripetizione di impulsi *(f)*
Pt frequência de repetição de impulsos *(f)*

frequência de pulso *(f)* Pt
De Schwebungsfrequenz *(f)*
En beat frequency
Es frecuencia de pulsación *(f)*
Fr fréquence de battement *(f)*
It frequenza di battimento *(f)*

frequência de repetição de impulsos *(f)* Pt
De Impulsfolgefrequenz *(f)*
En pulse repetition frequency (prf)
Es frecuencia de repetición de impulsos *(f)*
Fr fréquence par récurrence des impulsions *(f)*
It frequenza a ripetizione di impulsi *(f)*

frequenza a ripetizione di impulsi *(f)* It
De Impulsfolgefrequenz *(f)*
En pulse repetition frequency (prf)
Es frecuencia de repetición de impulsos *(f)*
Fr fréquence par récurrence des impulsions *(f)*
Pt frequência de repetição de impulsos *(f)*

frequenza degli impulsi dell'orologio *(f)* It
De Taktgeschwindigkeit *(f)*
En clock rate
Es velocidad de impulsos de reloj *(f)*
Fr fréquence des impulsions d'horloge *(f)*
Pt taxa de impulsos de relógio *(f)*

frequenza di battimento *(f)* It
De Schwebungsfrequenz *(f)*
En beat frequency
Es frecuencia de pulsación *(f)*
Fr fréquence de battement *(f)*
Pt frequência de pulso *(f)*

fuera de línea Es
De indirekt
En offline
Fr hors ligne
It non collegato
Pt fora da linha

fuertemente acoplado Es
De eng gekoppelt
En tightly coupled
Fr à couplage serré
It accoppiado fortemente
Pt firmemente acoplado

fühlen *vb* De
En sense
Es detectar
Fr détecter
It rilevare
Pt pesquisar

führen *vb* De
En route
Es encaminar
Fr acheminar
It incanalare
Pt encaminhar

full adder En
De Feldaddierer *(m)*
Es adicionador completo *(m)*
Fr additionneur complet *(m)*
It addizionatore totale *(m)*
Pt somador total *(m)*

função *(f) n* Pt
De Funktion *(f)*
En function
Es función *(f)*
Fr fonction *(f)*
It funzione *(f)*

função de transferência *(f)* Pt
De Übertragungsfunktion *(f)*
En transfer function
Es función de transferencia *(f)*
Fr fonction de transfert *(f)*
It funzione di trasferimento *(f)*

función *(f) n* Es
De Funktion *(f)*
En function
Fr fonction *(f)*
It funzione *(f)*
Pt função *(f)*

función de transferencia *(f)* Es
De Übertragungsfunktion *(f)*
En transfer function
Fr fonction de transfert *(f)*
It funzione di trasferimento *(f)*
Pt função de transferência *(f)*

function *n* En
De Funktion *(f)*
Es función *(f)*
Fr fonction *(f)*
It funzione *(f)*
Pt função *(f)*

functional design En
De funktionsmäßige Konstruktion *(f)*
Es diseño funcional *(m)*
Fr conception fonctionnelle *(f)*
It disegno funzionale *(m)*
Pt desenho funcional *(m)*

function generator En
De Funktionsgeber *(m)*
Es generador de función *(m)*
Fr générateur de fonctions *(m)*
It generatore di funzioni *(m)*
Pt gerador funcional *(m)*

function key En
De Funktionsschlüssel *(m)*
Es tecla de función *(f)*
Fr touche de fonction *(f)*
It tasto di funzione *(m)*
Pt tecla de funções *(f)*

fundo para cima Pt
De kieloben
En bottom-up
Es boca-abajo
Fr ascendant
It sottosopra

Fünfzig-Überschuß *(m)* *n* De
En excess fifty
Es cincuenta excedente *(f)*
Fr code plus cinquante *(m)*
It cinquanta di eccesso *(f)*
Pt cinquenta em excesso *(f)*

Funktion *(f)* *n* De
En function
Es función *(f)*
Fr fonction *(f)*
It funzione *(f)*
Pt função *(f)*

Funktionsgeber *(m)* *n* De
En function generator
Es generador de función *(m)*
Fr générateur de fonctions *(m)*
It generatore di funzioni *(m)*
Pt gerador funcional *(m)*

funktionsmäßige Konstruktion *(f)* De
En functional design
Es diseño funcional *(m)*
Fr conception fonctionnelle *(f)*
It disegno funzionale *(m)*
Pt desenho funcional *(m)*

Funktionsschlüssel *(m)* *n* De
En function key
Es tecla de función *(f)*
Fr touche de fonction *(f)*
It tasto di funzione *(m)*
Pt tecla de funções *(f)*

funzione *(f)* *n* It
De Funktion *(f)*
En function
Es función *(f)*
Fr fonction *(f)*
Pt função *(f)*

funzione di trasferimento *(f)* It
De Übertragungs-funktion *(f)*
En transfer function
Es función de transferencia *(f)*
Fr fonction de transfert *(f)*
Pt função de transferência *(f)*

furos de alimentação *(m pl)* Pt
De Taktlöcher *(pl)*
En feed holes
Es perforaciones de alimentación *(f pl)*
Fr trous d'entraînement *(m pl)*
It fori di alimentazione *(m pl)*

furos de roda dentada *(m pl)* Pt
De Taktlöcher *(pl)*
En sprocket holes
Es perforaciones marginales *(f pl)*
Fr perforations d'entraînement *(f pl)*
It perforazioni di tabulati *(f pl)*

fusão *(f)* *n* Pt
De Fusion *(f)*
En merge
Es fusión *(f)*
Fr fusion *(f)*
It fusione *(f)*

fusion *(f)* *n* Fr
De Fusion *(f)*
En merge
Es fusión *(f)*
It fusione *(f)*
Pt fusão *(f)*

Fusion *(f)* *n* De
En merge
Es fusión *(f)*
Fr fusion *(f)*
It fusione *(f)*
Pt fusão *(f)*

fusión *(f)* *n* Es
De Fusion *(f)*
En merge
Fr fusion *(f)*
It fusione *(f)*
Pt fusão *(f)*

fusionar *vb* Es
De fusionieren
En merge
Fr fusionner
It confondere
Pt misturar

fusione *(f)* *n* It
De Fusion *(f)*
En merge
Es fusión *(f)*
Fr fusion *(f)*
Pt fusão *(f)*

fusionieren *vb* De
En merge
Es fusionar
Fr fusionner
It confondere
Pt misturar

fusionner *vb* Fr
De fusionieren
En merge
Es fusionar
It confondere
Pt misturar

G

gaiola de ficha *(f)* Pt
De Kartenkorb *(m)*
En card cage
Es caja de fichas *(f)*
Fr porte-carte *(m)*
It scatola schede *(f)*

gamma *(f)* *n* It
De Bereich *(m)*
En range
Es margen *(m)*
Fr gamme *(f)*
Pt alcance *(m)*

gamme *(f)* *n* Fr
De Bereich *(m)*
En range
Es margen *(m)*
It gamma *(f)*
Pt alcance *(m)*

Gang *(m)* *n* De
En cycle
Es ciclo *(m)*
Fr cycle *(m)*
It ciclo *(m)*
Pt ciclo *(m)*

Gangzählung *(f)* *n* De
En cycle count
Es cuenta de ciclos *(f)*
Fr comptage de cycles *(m)*
It conteggio dei cicli *(m)*
Pt contagem de ciclos *(f)*

Gänseblümchen-Typenraddrucker *(m)* De
En daisywheel printer
Es impresora de ruedas de mariposa *(f)*
Fr imprimante à marguerite *(f)*
It stampatrice daisywheel *(f)*
Pt impressora margarida *(f)*

gap *n* En
De Spalte *(f)*
Es intervalo *(m)*
Fr intervalle *(m)*

It intervallo *(m)*
Pt intervalo *(m)*

garbage *n* En
De Schund *(m)*
Es información parásita *(f)*
Fr informations parasites *(f pl)*
It rifiuti *(m pl)*
Pt refugo *(m)*

gate *n* En
De Tor *(n)*
Es puerta *(f)*
Fr porte *(f)*
It porta *(f)*
Pt porta *(f)*

gather write En
De sammelnbeschreiben
Es escribir agrupada
Fr écrire en regroupant
It scrivere di raccolta
Pt escrever em condensado

gatilho *(m) n* Pt
De Trigger *(m)*
En trigger
Es disparador *(m)*
Fr détente *(f)*
It scatto *(m)*

Gegenkompilierer *(m) n* De
En cross compiler
Es compilador cruzado *(m)*
Fr compilateur croisé *(m)*
It compilatore incrociato *(m)*
Pt compilador cruzado *(m)*

gegenprüfen *vb* De
En cross check
Es verificar por comparación
Fr contre-vérifier
It contra-verificare
Pt contra-verificar

Gegenprüfung *(f) n* De
En cross check
Es verificación cruzada *(f)*
Fr contrevérification *(f)*
It verifica generale completa *(f)*
Pt verificação cruzada *(f)*

gegliedertes Programm *(n)* De
En structured program
Es programa estructurado *(m)*
Fr programme structuré *(m)*
It programma strutturato *(m)*
Pt programa estruturado *(m)*

gekettete Liste *(f)* De
En chained list
Es lista en cadena *(f)*
Fr liste en chaîne *(f)*
It lista concatenata *(f)*
Pt lista com cadeia *(f)*

gemeinsam benutzte Datei *(f)* De
En shared files
Es ficheros compartidos *(m pl)*
Fr fichiers partagés *(m pl)*
It file in comune *(f pl)*
Pt arquivos compartidos *(m pl)*

generación del sistema *(f)* Es
De Systemgenerierung *(f)*
En system generation
Fr génération d'un système *(f)*
It generazione di sistemi *(f)*
Pt geração de sistemas *(f)*

generador *(m) n* Es
De Generator *(m)*
En generator
Fr générateur *(m)*
It generatore *(m)*
Pt gerador *(m)*

generador de función *(m)* Es
De Funktionsgeber *(m)*
En function generator
Fr générateur de fonctions *(m)*
It generatore di funzioni *(m)*
Pt gerador funcional *(m)*

generador de informes *(m)* Es
De Listengeber *(m)*
En report generator
Fr générateur d'édition *(m)*
It generatore di tabulati *(m)*
Pt gerador de relatório *(m)*

generador de números aleatorios *(m)* Es
De Zufallsnummerngeber *(m)*
En random-number generator
Fr générateur de nombres aléatoires *(m)*
It generatore di numeri casuali *(m)*
Pt gerador de números aleatórios *(m)*

generador de programas *(m)* Es
De Programmgeber *(m)*
En program generator
Fr générateur de programmes *(m)*
It generatore di programmi *(m)*
Pt gerador de programas *(m)*

generador de soportes lógicos *(m)* Es
De Programmausrüstungsgeber *(m)*
En software generator
Fr générateur de logiciel *(m)*
It generatore di software *(m)*
Pt gerador de software *(m)*

general-purpose computer En
De Allgemeinzweck-computer *(m)*
Es ordenador universal *(m)*
Fr calculateur universel *(m)*
It elaboratore a scopo generale *(m)*
Pt computador para todos os fins *(m)*

generar *vb* Es
De erzeugen
En generate
Fr générer
It generare
Pt gerar

generare *vb* It
De erzeugen
En generate
Es generar
Fr générer
Pt gerar

generate *vb* En
De erzeugen
Es generar
Fr générer
It generare
Pt gerar

générateur *(m) n* Fr
De Generator *(m)*
En generator
Es generador *(m)*
It generatore *(m)*
Pt gerador *(m)*

générateur d'édition *(m)* Fr
De Listengeber *(m)*
En report generator
Es generador de informes *(m)*
It generatore di tabulati *(m)*
Pt gerador de relatório *(m)*

générateur de fonctions *(m)* Fr
De Funktionsgeber *(m)*
En function generator
Es generador de función *(m)*
It generatore di funzioni *(m)*
Pt gerador funcional *(m)*

générateur de logiciel *(m)* Fr
De Programmausrüstungsgeber *(m)*
En software generator
Es generador de soportes lógicos *(m)*
It generatore di software *(m)*
Pt gerador de software *(m)*

générateur de nombres aléatoires *(m)* Fr
De Zufallsnummerngeber *(m)*
En random-number generator
Es generador de números aleatorios *(m)*
It generatore di numeri casuali *(m)*
Pt gerador de números aleatórios *(m)*

générateur de programmes *(m)* Fr
De Programmgeber *(m)*
En program generator
Es generador de programas *(m)*
It generatore di programmi *(m)*
Pt gerador de programas *(m)*

génération d'un système *(f)* Fr
De Systemgenerierung *(f)*
En system generation
Es generación del sistema *(f)*
It generazione di sistemi *(f)*
Pt geração de sistemas *(f)*

generator *n* En
De Generator *(m)*
Es generador *(m)*
Fr générateur *(m)*
It generatore *(m)*
Pt gerador *(m)*

Generator *(m) n* De
En generator
Es generador *(m)*
Fr générateur *(m)*
It generatore *(m)*
Pt gerador *(m)*

generatore *(m) n* It
De Generator *(m)*
En generator
Es generador *(m)*
Fr générateur *(m)*
Pt gerador *(m)*

generatore di funzioni *(m)* It
De Funktionsgeber *(m)*
En function generator
Es generador de función *(m)*
Fr générateur de fonctions *(m)*
Pt gerador funcional *(m)*

generatore di numeri casuali *(m)* It
De Zufallsnummerngeber *(m)*
En random-number generator
Es generador de números aleatorios *(m)*
Fr générateur de nombres aléatoires *(m)*
Pt gerador de números aleatórios *(m)*

generatore di programmi *(m)* It
De Programmgeber *(m)*
En program generator
Es generador de programas *(m)*
Fr générateur de programmes *(m)*
Pt gerador de programas *(m)*

generatore di software *(m)* It
De Programmausrüstungsgeber *(m)*
En software generator
Es generador de soportes lógicos *(m)*
Fr générateur de logiciel *(m)*
Pt gerador de software *(m)*

generatore di tabulati *(m)* It
De Listengeber *(m)*
En report generator
Es generador de informes *(m)*
Fr générateur d'édition *(m)*
Pt gerador de relatório *(m)*

generazione di sistemi *(f)* It
De Systemgenerierung *(f)*
En system generation
Es generación del sistema *(f)*
Fr génération d'un système *(f)*
Pt geração de sistemas *(f)*

générer *vb* Fr
De erzeugen
En generate
Es generar
It generare
Pt gerar

geração de sistemas *(f)* Pt
De Systemgenerierung *(f)*
En system generation
Es generación del sistema *(f)*
Fr génération d'un système *(f)*
It generazione di sistemi *(f)*

gerade Bitzahl *(f)* De
En even parity
Es paridad *(f)*
Fr parité *(f)*
It parità pari *(f)*
Pt paridade de igualdade *(f)*

gerade-ungerade Paritätsprüfung *(f)* De
En odd-even check
Es control de paridad par-impar *(m)*
Fr contrôle de parité pair-impair *(m)*
It controllo pari-dispari *(m)*
Pt verificação par-impar *(f)*

gerador *(m) n* Pt
De Generator *(m)*
En generator
Es generador *(m)*
Fr générateur *(m)*
It generatore *(m)*

gerador de números aleatórios *(m)* Pt
De Zufallsnummerngeber *(m)*
En random-number generator
Es generador de números aleatorios *(m)*
Fr générateur de nombres aléatoires *(m)*
It generatore di numeri casuali *(m)*

gerador de programas *(m)* Pt
De Programmgeber *(m)*
En program generator
Es generador de programas *(m)*
Fr générateur de programmes *(m)*
It generatore di programmi *(m)*

gerador de relatório *(m)* Pt
De Listengeber *(m)*
En report generator
Es generador de informes *(m)*
Fr générateur d'édition *(m)*
It generatore di tabulati *(m)*

gerador de software *(m)* Pt
De Programmausrüstungsgeber *(m)*
En software generator
Es generador de soportes lógicos *(m)*
Fr générateur de logiciel *(m)*
It generatore di software *(m)*

gerador funcional *(m)* Pt
De Funktionsgeber *(m)*
En function generator
Es generador de función *(m)*
Fr générateur de fonctions *(m)*
It generatore di funzioni *(m)*

gerar *vb* Pt
De erzeugen
En generate
Es generar
Fr générer
It generare

geschaltetes Nachrichtennetz *(n)* De
En switched-message network

Es red de conmutación de mensajes *(f)*
Fr réseau de messages commutés *(m)*
It rete di messaggi commutati *(f)*
Pt rede de mensagens comutadas *(f)*

geschlossene Schleife *(f)* De
En closed loop
Es circuito cerrado *(m)*
Fr boucle fermée *(f)*
It ciclo chiuso *(m)*
Pt circuito fechado *(m)*

geschuppter Streifen *(m)* De
En chadded tape
Es cinta de perforación completa *(f)*
Fr bande à perforations complètes *(f)*
It nastro con perforazioni totali *(m)*
Pt fita recortada *(f)*

geschützter Ort *(m)* De
En protected location
Es posición protegida *(f)*
Fr position protégée *(f)*
It locazione protetta *(f)*
Pt localização protegida *(f)*

geschützter Satz *(m)* De
En protected record
Es registro protegido *(m)*
Fr enregistrement protégé *(m)*
It record protetto *(m)*
Pt registo protegido *(m)*

gespeichertes Programm *(n)* De
En stored program
Es programa almacenado *(m)*
Fr programme enregistré *(m)*
It programma memorizzato *(m)*
Pt programa armazenado *(m)*

gestion par exception *(f)* Fr
De Ausnahmeprinzip-system *(n)*
En exception principle system
Es control por excepción *(m)*
It sistema a principio di eccezione *(m)*
Pt sistema de princípio de excepção *(m)*

giro della macchina *(m)* It
De Maschinenlauf *(m)*
En machine run
Es pasada de máquina *(f)*
Fr passage en machine *(m)*
Pt passagem da máquina *(f)*

giustificare *vb* It
De bündig machen
En justify
Es justificar
Fr justifier
Pt justificar

giustificato a destra It
De rechtsbündig
En right-justified
Es justificado a la derecha
Fr cadré à droite
Pt justificado à direita

giustificato a sinistra It
De linksbündig
En left-justified
Es justificado a la izquierda
Fr cadré à gauche
Pt justificado à esquerda

Gleichheit *(f) n* De
En equivalence
Es equivalencia *(f)*
Fr équivalence *(f)*
It equivalenza *(f)*
Pt equivalência *(f)*

Gleichheitsbetrieb *(m) n* De
En equivalence operation
Es operación de equivalencia *(f)*
Fr opération d'équivalence *(f)*
It operazione di equivalenza *(f)*
Pt operação de equivalência *(f)*

Gleichheitsfunktion *(f) n* De
En equivalence element
Es elemento de equivalencia *(m)*
Fr élément d'équivalence *(m)*
It elemento di equivalenza *(m)*
Pt elemento de equivalência *(m)*

gleichwertige Binärziffern *(pl)* De
En equivalent binary digits
Es dígitos binarios equivalentes *(m pl)*
Fr chiffres binaires équivalents *(m pl)*
It digiti binari equivalenti *(m pl)*
Pt números digitais binários equivalentes *(m pl)*

gleichzeitig *adj* De
En in-line
Es lineal
Fr en ligne
It lineale
Pt em série

gleichzeitiger Zugriff *(m)* De
En simultaneous access
Es acceso simultáneo *(m)*
Fr accès simultané *(m)*
It accesso simultaneo *(m)*
Pt acesso simultâneo *(m)*

Gliederdrucker *(m) n* De
En train printer
Es impresora de cadena *(f)*
Fr imprimante à train de caractères *(f)*
It stampatrice a treno di caratteri *(f)*
Pt impressora de trem *(f)*

go down En
De abgehen
Es tener una avería
Fr tomber en panne
It avere una panna
Pt avariar

golfball printer En
De Kugelkopfdrucker *(m)*
Es impresora de esfera *(f)*
Fr imprimante à sphère *(f)*
It stampatrice a pallina *(f)*
Pt impressora de bola de golf *(f)*

grafica *(f) n* It
De Zeichen *(n)*
En graphics
Es gráfica *(f)*
Fr graphisme *(m)*
Pt gráfica *(f)*

gráfica *(f) n* Es, Pt
De Zeichen *(n)*
En graphics
Fr graphisme *(m)*
It grafica *(f)*

gráfico de fluxo *(m)* Pt
De Flußdiagramm *(n)*
En flowchart
Es ordinograma *(m)*
Fr organigramme *(m)*
It diagramma di flusso *(m)*

grandfather tape En
De Erstgenerationsband *(n)*
Es cinta primera generación *(f)*
Fr bande première génération *(f)*
It nastro nonno *(m)*
Pt fita avó *(f)*

graphic panel En
De Symboltafel *(f)*
Es panel gráfico *(m)*
Fr tableau graphique *(m)*
It pannello grafico *(m)*
Pt painel de gráficos *(m)*

graphics *n* En
De Zeichen *(n)*
Es gráfica *(f)*
Fr graphisme *(m)*
It grafica *(f)*
Pt gráfica *(f)*

graphics display En
De Zeichenanzeige *(f)*
Es representación gráfica *(f)*
Fr visualisation graphique *(f)*
It visualizzatore grafico *(m)*
Pt representação gráfica *(f)*

graphics printer En
De Zeichendrucker *(m)*
Es impresora gráfica *(f)*
Fr imprimante graphique *(f)*
It stampatrice grafica *(f)*
Pt impressora gráfica *(f)*

graphics terminal En
De Zeichenstation *(f)*
Es terminal gráfico *(m)*
Fr terminal graphique *(m)*
It terminale grafico *(m)*
Pt terminal gráfico *(m)*

graphisme *(m) n* Fr
De Zeichen *(n)*
En graphics
Es gráfica *(f)*
It grafica *(f)*
Pt gráfica *(f)*

graph plotter En
De Kurvenzeichner *(m)*
Es trazador de curvas *(m)*
Fr traceur de courbes *(m)*
It tracciatore di grafici *(m)*
Pt plotador de gráficos *(m)*

Gray code En
De Gray-Code *(n)*
Es código Gray *(m)*
Fr code Gray *(m)*
It codice Gray *(m)*
Pt código Gray *(m)*

Gray-Code *(n) n* De
En Gray code
Es código Gray *(m)*
Fr code Gray *(m)*
It codice Gray *(m)*
Pt código Gray *(m)*

Grenzwertvergleicher *(m) n* De
En comparator
Es comparador *(m)*
Fr comparateur *(m)*
It comparatore *(m)*
Pt comparador *(m)*

Groβintegration *(f) n* De
En large-scale integration
Es integración en gran escala *(f)*
Fr intégration à grande échelle *(f)*
It integrazione su grande scala *(f)*
Pt integração à grande escala *(f)*

Groβsignalsprache *(f) n* De
En high-level language
Es lenguaje de alto nivel *(m)*
Fr langage évolué *(m)*
It linguaggio di alto livello *(m)*
Pt linguagem de alto nível *(f)*

Groβspeicher *(m) n* De
En bulk store
Es memoria de gran capacidad *(f)*
Fr mémoire de masse *(f)*
It memoria di massa *(f)*
Pt memória global *(f)*

group *n* En
De Gruppe *(f)*
Es grupo *(m)*
Fr groupe *(m)*
It gruppo *(m)*
Pt grupo *(m)*

groupage enregistrement *(m)* Fr
De Satzblockierung *(f)*
En record blocking
Es bloqueo de registro *(m)*
It bloccaggio di record *(m)*
Pt bloqueio de registo *(m)*

groupe *(m) n* Fr
De Gruppe *(f)*
En group
Es grupo *(m)*
It gruppo *(m)*
Pt grupo *(m)*

groupement d'utilisateurs *(m)* Fr
De Benutzergruppe *(f)*
En user group
Es grupo de usuarios *(m)*
It gruppo di utenti *(m)*
Pt group utente *(m)*

grouper *vb* Fr
De zusammenfügen
En join
Es unir
It unire
Pt unir

group mark En
De Trennmarke *(f)*
Es marca de grupo *(f)*
Fr drapeau groupe *(m)*
It segno di gruppo *(m)*
Pt marca de grupo *(f)*

group utente *(m)* Pt
De Benutzergruppe *(f)*
En user group
Es grupo de usuarios *(m)*
Fr groupement d'utilisateurs *(m)*
It gruppo di utenti *(m)*

grupo *(m) n* Es, Pt
De Gruppe *(f)*
En group
Fr groupe *(m)*
It gruppo *(m)*

grupo de usuarios *(m)* Es
De Benutzergruppe *(f)*
En user group
Fr groupement d'utilisateurs *(m)*
It gruppo di utenti *(m)*
Pt group utente *(m)*

Gruppe *(f) n* De
En group
Es grupo *(m)*
Fr groupe *(m)*
It gruppo *(m)*
Pt grupo *(m)*

gruppo *(m) n* It
De Gruppe *(f)*
En group
Es grupo *(m)*
Fr groupe *(m)*
Pt grupo *(m)*

gruppo di caratteri *(m)* It
De Zeichensatz *(m)*
En character set
Es juego de caracteres *(m)*
Fr jeu de caractères *(m)*
Pt jogo de caracteres *(m)*

gruppo di dati telefonici *(m)* It
De Telefondatensatz *(m)*
En telephone data set
Es equipo de datos telefónicos *(m)*
Fr ensemble de données téléphoniques *(m)*
Pt conjunto de dados telefónicos *(m)*

gruppo di istruzioni *(m)* It
De Befehlsvorrat *(m)*
En instruction set
Es juego de instrucciones *(m)*
Fr jeu d'instructions *(m)*
Pt conjunto de instruções *(m)*

gruppo di utenti *(m)* It
De Benutzergruppe *(f)*
En user group
Es grupo de usuarios *(m)*
Fr groupement d'utilisateurs *(m)*
Pt group utente *(m)*

guard band En
De Schutzband *(n)*
Es banda de guardia *(f)*
Fr bande protection *(f)*
It banda di guardia *(f)*
Pt banda de protecção *(f)*

guasto *(m) n* It
De Defekt *(m)*
En fault
Es fallo *(m)*
Fr faute *(f)*
Pt defeito *(m)*

guasto delle apparecchiature *(m)* It

De Maschinenausfall *(m)*
En equipment failure
Es fallo del equipo *(m)*
Fr panne *(f)*
Pt falha de equipamento *(f)*

guida del nastro *(f)* It
De Bandantrieb *(m)*
En tape drive
Es impulsor de cinta *(m)*
Fr dérouleur de bande *(m)*
Pt accionamento da fita *(m)*

Gültigkeitsprüfung *(f) n* De
En validity check
Es verificación de validez *(f)*
Fr contrôle de vraisemblance *(m)*
It controllo di validità *(m)*
Pt verificação de validez *(f)*

H

Haftstelle *(f) n* De
En trap
Es trampa *(f)*
Fr piège *(m)*
It trappola *(f)*
Pt armadilha *(f)*

Halbaddierglied *(n) n* De
En half adder
Es semi-sumador *(m)*
Fr demi-additionneur *(m)*
It metà addizionatore *(m)*
Pt semi-somador *(m)*

halbautomatisch *adj* De
En semi-automatic
Es semiautomático
Fr semiautomatique
It semiautomatico
Pt semiautomático

Halbduplex *(m) n* De
En half duplex
Es semiduplex *(m)*
Fr semi-duplex *(m)*
It metà duplex *(m)*
Pt semi-duplex *(m)*

Halbleiter *(m) n* De
En semiconductor
Es semiconductor *(m)*
Fr semiconducteur *(m)*
It semiconduttore *(m)*
Pt semicondutor *(m)*

Halbleiterfeld *(n) n* De
En semiconductor array
Es matriz de semiconductores *(f)*
Fr ensemble à semiconducteurs *(m)*
It rete semiconduttori *(f)*
Pt disposição semicondutora *(f)*

Halbleiterspeicher *(m) n* De
En semiconductor memory
Es memoria de semiconductores *(f)*
Fr mémoire à semiconducteurs *(f)*
It memoria a semiconduttori *(f)*
Pt memória semi-condutora *(f)*

Halbsubtrahierer *(m) n* De
En half subtractor
Es semi-sustractor *(m)*
Fr semi-soustracteur *(m)*
It metà sottrattore *(m)*
Pt semi-subtractor *(m)*

Halbwort *(n) n* De
En half word
Es media palabra *(f)*
Fr demi-mot *(m)*
It metà voce *(f)*
Pt meia-palavra *(f)*

half adder En
De Halbaddierglied *(n)*
Es semi-sumador *(m)*
Fr demi-additionneur *(m)*
It metà addizionatore *(m)*
Pt semi-somador *(m)*

half duplex En
De Halbduplex *(m)*
Es semiduplex *(m)*
Fr semi-duplex *(m)*
It metà duplex *(m)*
Pt semi-duplex *(m)*

half subtractor En
De Halbsubtrahierer *(m)*
Es semi-sustractor *(m)*
Fr semi-soustracteur *(m)*
It metà sottrattore *(m)*
Pt semi-subtractor *(m)*

half word En
De Halbwort *(n)*
Es media palabra *(f)*
Fr demi-mot *(m)*
It metà voce *(f)*
Pt meia-palavra *(f)*

halt *n* En
De Stopp *(m)*
Es parada *(f)*
Fr arrêt *(m)*
It arresto *(m)*
Pt paragem *(f)*

Handeingabe *(f) n* De
En manual input
Es entrada manual *(f)*
Fr introduction manuelle *(f)*
It input manuale *(m)*
Pt input manual *(m)*

Handsteuerung *(f) n* De
En manual control
Es control manual *(m)*
Fr commande manuelle *(f)*
It controllo manuale *(m)*
Pt controle manual *(m)*

hard copy En
De dauerhafter Text *(m)*
Es salida impresa *(f)*
Fr document en clair *(m)*
It copia stampata *(f)*
Pt cópia dura *(f)*

hard disk En
De Hartplatte *(f)*
Es disco duro *(m)*
Fr disque dur *(m)*
It discho duro *(m)*
Pt disco duro *(m)*

hardware *n* En; Pt *(m)*
De Hardware *(f)*
Es equipo físico *(m)*
Fr matériel *(m)*
It elementi materiali di elaboratore *(m)*

Hardware *(f) n* De
En hardware
Es equipo físico *(m)*
Fr matériel *(m)*
It elementi materiali di elaboratore *(m)*
Pt hardware *(m)*

Hartplatte *(f) n* De
En hard disk
Es disco duro *(m)*
Fr disque dur *(m)*
It discho duro *(m)*
Pt disco duro *(m)*

Hauptbefehlsband *(n) n* De
En master-instruction tape (MIT)
Es cinta programa de explotación *(f)*
Fr bande de programme d'exploitation (BPE) *(f)*
It nastro dell'istruzioni principali *(m)*
Pt fita de instruções principais *(f)*

Hauptrechner *(m) n* De
En mainframe computer
Es computador principal *(m)*
Fr ordinateur principal *(m)*
It calcolatore principale *(m)*
Pt computador principal *(m)*

Hauptsatz *(m) n* De
En master record
Es registro maestro *(m)*
Fr article du fichier permanent *(m)*
It record principale *(m)*
Pt registo principal *(m)*

Hauptspeicher *(m) n* De
En main memory
Es memoria principal *(f)*
Fr mémoire centrale *(f)*
It memoria principale *(f)*
Pt memória principal *(f)*

Hauptspeicherung *(f) n* De
En main storage
Es almacenamiento principal *(m)*
Fr stockage central *(m)*
It immagazzinamento principale *(m)*
Pt armazenagem principal *(f)*

Hauptverbindung *(f) n* De
En bus
Es conductor común *(m)*
Fr bus *(m)*
It barra *(f)*
Pt condutor *(m)*

head *n* En
De Magnetkopf *(m)*
Es cabeza *(f)*
Fr tête *(f)*
It testina *(f)*
Pt cabeça *(f)*

header *n* En
De Kennsatz *(m)*
Es cabecera *(f)*
Fr en-tête *(f)*
It testata *(f)*
Pt porta-cabeças *(m)*

header label En
De Anfangskennsatz *(m)*
Es etiqueta de cabecera *(f)*
Fr label début *(m)*
It etichetta della testata *(f)*
Pt rótulo de porta-cabeças *(m)*

head gap En
De Magnetkopfspalt *(m)*
Es entrehierro *(m)*
Fr entrefer *(m)*
It distanza dalla testina *(f)*
Pt intervalo de cabeça *(m)*

Herkunftsort *(m) n* De
En origin
Es origen *(m)*
Fr origine *(f)*
It origine *(f)*
Pt origem *(f)*

herramientas programadas automáticamente *(f pl)* Es
De automatisch programmierte Werkzeuge *(pl)*
En automatically programmed tools (APT)
Fr machines-outils programmées automatiquement *(f pl)*
It strumenti programmati automaticamente *(m pl)*
Pt ferramentas programadas automaticamente *(f pl)*

heurística *(f) n* Es, Pt
De Heuristik *(f)*
En heuristics
Fr heuristique *(f)*
It euristica *(f)*

heuristic program En
De heuristisches Programm *(n)*
Es programa heurístico *(m)*
Fr programme heuristique *(m)*
It programma euristico *(m)*
Pt programa heurístico *(m)*

heuristics *n* En
De Heuristik *(f)*
Es heurística *(f)*
Fr heuristique *(f)*
It euristica *(f)*
Pt heurística *(f)*

Heuristik *(f) n* De
En heuristics
Es heurística *(f)*
Fr heuristique *(f)*
It euristica *(f)*
Pt heurística *(f)*

heuristique *(f) n* Fr
De Heuristik *(f)*
En heuristics
Es heurística *(f)*
It euristica *(f)*
Pt heurística *(f)*

heuristisches Programm *(n)* De
En heuristic program
Es programa heurístico *(m)*
Fr programme heuristique *(m)*
It programma euristico *(m)*
Pt programa heurístico *(m)*

hexadecimal notation En
De hexadezimale Darstellung *(f)*
Es notación hexadecimal *(f)*
Fr notation hexadécimale *(f)*
It notazione esadecimale *(f)*
Pt notação hexadecimal *(f)*

hexadezimale Darstellung *(f)* De
En hexadecimal notation
Es notación hexadecimal *(f)*
Fr notation hexadécimale *(f)*
It notazione esadecimale *(f)*
Pt notação hexadecimal *(f)*

hidden-line algorithm En
De Versteckzeilen-algorithmus *(m)*
Es algoritmo de línea oculta *(m)*
Fr algorithme ligne cachée *(m)*
It algoritmo a linea nascosta *(m)*
Pt algoritmo de linha oculta *(m)*

high-level language En
De Groβsignalsprache *(f)*
Es lenguaje de alto nivel *(m)*
Fr langage évolué *(m)*
It linguaggio di alto livello *(m)*
Pt linguagem de alto nível *(f)*

high-level recovery En
De Wiederherstellung der höheren Übermittlungsstufe *(f)*
Es recuperación de alto nivel *(f)*
Fr redressement évolué *(m)*
It ricupero di alto livello *(m)*
Pt recuperação de alto nível *(f)*

high order En
De hoher Grad *(m)*
Es orden superior *(m)*
Fr ordre haut *(m)*
It ordine elevato *(m)*
Pt ordem elevada *(f)*

Hilfsprogramm *(n) n* De
En utility program
Es programa de utilidad *(m)*
Fr programme utilitaire *(m)*
It programma di utilità *(m)*
Pt programa de utilidade *(m)*

Hilfsspeicher *(m) n* De
En backing store
Es memoria auxiliar *(f)*
Fr mémoire auxiliaire *(f)*
It memoria ausiliaria *(f)*
Pt armazém de apoio *(m)*

Hintergrundprogramm *(n) n* De
En background program
Es programa subordinado *(m)*
Fr programme non prioritaire *(m)*
It programma non precedenza *(m)*
Pt programa de plano de fundo *(m)*

Hintergrund-verarbeitung *(f) n* De
En background processing
Es proceso de programas subordinados *(m)*
Fr traitement non prioritaire *(m)*

It elaborazione non precedenza *(f)*
Pt tratamento de plano de fundo *(m)*

hoher Grad *(m)* De
En high order
Es orden superior *(m)*
Fr ordre haut *(m)*
It ordine elevato *(m)*
Pt ordem elevada *(f)*

hold *vb* En
De anhalten
Es mantener
Fr tenir
It mantenere
Pt manter

Hollerith code En
De Hollerith-Code *(m)*
Es código Hollerith *(m)*
Fr code Hollerith *(m)*
It codice di Hollerith *(m)*
Pt código Hollerith *(m)*

Hollerith-Code *(m) n* De
En Hollerith code
Es código Hollerith *(m)*
Fr code Hollerith *(m)*
It codice di Hollerith *(m)*
Pt código Hollerith *(m)*

holographic memory En
De holographischer Speicher *(m)*
Es memoria holográfica *(f)*
Fr mémoire holographique *(f)*
It memoria olografica *(f)*
Pt memória holográfica *(f)*

holographischer Speicher *(m)* De
En holographic memory
Es memoria holográfica *(f)*
Fr mémoire holographique *(f)*
It memoria olografica *(f)*
Pt memória holográfica *(f)*

home computing En
De Lokalrechnung *(f)*
Es cálculo inicial *(m)*
Fr traitement domestique *(m)*
It elaborazione in proprio *(f)*
Pt computação doméstica *(f)*

homeostase *(f) n* Pt
De Homöostase *(f)*
En homeostasis
Es homeostasis *(f)*
Fr homéostasie *(f)*
It omeostasi *(f)*

homéostasie *(f) n* Fr
De Homöostase *(f)*
En homeostasis
Es homeostasis *(f)*
It omeostasi *(f)*
Pt homeostase *(f)*

homeostasis *n* En; Es *(f)*
De Homöostase *(f)*
Fr homéostasie *(f)*
It omeostasi *(f)*
Pt homeostase *(f)*

Homöostase *(f) n* De
En homeostasis
Es homeostasis *(f)*
Fr homéostasie *(f)*
It omeostasi *(f)*
Pt homeostase *(f)*

hopper *n* En
De Magazin *(n)*
Es depósito de alimentación *(m)*
Fr magasin d'alimentation *(m)*
It serbatoio di alimentazione (schede) *(m)*
Pt tremonha *(f)*

horizontal feed En
De Horizontalvorschub *(m)*
Es alimentación horizontal *(f)*
Fr avance horizontale *(f)*
It alimentazione orizzontale *(f)*
Pt alimentação horizontal *(f)*

Horizontalvorschub *(m) n* De
En horizontal feed
Es alimentación horizontal *(f)*
Fr avance horizontale *(f)*
It alimentazione orizzontale *(f)*
Pt alimentação horizontal *(f)*

horloge *(f) n* Fr
De Taktgeber *(m)*
En clock
Es reloj *(m)*
It orologio *(m)*
Pt relógio *(m)*

horloge numérique *(f)* Fr
De Digitalzeitgeber *(m)*
En digital clock
Es reloj digital *(m)*
It orologio digitale *(m)*
Pt relógio digital *(m)*

horloge pilote *(f)* Fr
De Stammzeitgeber *(m)*
En master clock
Es reloj maestro *(m)*
It orologio principale *(m)*
Pt relógio principal *(m)*

horloge temps réel *(f)* Fr
De Uhrzeitgeber *(m)*
En real-time clock
Es reloj binario *(m)*
It orologio di tempo reale *(m)*
Pt relógio de tempo real *(m)*

hors ligne Fr
De indirekt
En offline
Es fuera de línea
It non collegato
Pt fora da linha

host computer En
De Wirtsrechner *(m)*
Es ordenador anfitrión *(m)*
Fr ordinateur central *(m)*
It elaboratore per conto terzi *(m)*
Pt computador hospedeiro *(m)*

hub *n* En
De Nabe *(f)*
Es boca *(f)*
Fr moyeu porte-bobine *(m)*
It mozzo *(m)*
Pt cubo *(m)*

Hülldatei *(f) n* De
En enveloped file
Es fichero envuelto *(m)*
Fr dossier sous enveloppe *(m)*
It file inviluppato *(m)*
Pt arquivo envolvido *(m)*

hybrid computer En
De Hybridrechner *(m)*
Es ordenador híbrido *(m)*
Fr calculateur hybride *(m)*
It elaboratore ibrido *(m)*
Pt computador híbrido *(m)*

Hybridrechner *(m) n* De
En hybrid computer
Es ordenador híbrido *(m)*
Fr calculateur hybride *(m)*
It elaboratore ibrido *(m)*
Pt computador híbrido *(m)*

I

identificação de arquivo *(f)* Pt
De Dateikennzeichnung *(f)*
En file identification
Es identificación del fichero *(f)*
Fr identification de fichier *(f)*
It identificazione del file *(f)*

identificación del fichero *(f)* Es
De Dateikennzeichnung *(f)*

En file identification
Fr identification de fichier *(f)*
It identificazione del file *(f)*
Pt identificação de arquivo *(f)*

identificador *(m) n* Es, Pt
De Bezeichner *(m)*
En identifier
Fr identificateur *(m)*
It identificatore *(m)*

identificateur *(m) n* Fr
De Bezeichner *(m)*
En identifier
Es identificador *(m)*
It identificatore *(m)*
Pt identificador *(m)*

identification de fichier *(f)* Fr
De Dateikennzeichnung *(f)*
En file identification
Es identificación del fichero *(f)*
It identificazione del file *(f)*
Pt identificação de arquivo *(f)*

identificativo *(m) n* It
De Kennzeichner *(m)*
En marker
Es marcador *(m)*
Fr repère *(m)*
Pt marcador *(m)*

identificatore *(m) n* It
De Bezeichner; Etikett *(m n)*
En identifier; tag
Es etiqueta; identificador *(f m)*
Fr étiquette; identificateur *(f m)*
Pt etiqueta; identificador *(f m)*

identificazione del file *(f)* It
De Dateikennzeichnung *(f)*
En file identification
Es identificación del fichero *(f)*
Fr identification de fichier *(f)*
Pt identificação de arquivo *(f)*

identifier *n* En
De Bezeichner *(m)*
Es identificador *(m)*
Fr identificateur *(m)*
It identificatore *(m)*
Pt identificador *(m)*

identity element En
De Eizelelement *(n)*
Es elemento de identidad *(m)*
Fr élément d'identification *(m)*
It elemento di identità *(m)*
Pt elemento de identidade *(m)*

identity unit En
De Einzeleinheit *(f)*
Es unidad de identidad *(f)*
Fr unité d'identification *(f)*
It unità di identità *(f)*
Pt unidade de identidade *(f)*

idle time En
De Leerlaufzeit *(f)*
Es tiempo pasivo *(m)*
Fr temps en chômage *(m)*
It tempo passivo *(m)*
Pt tempo de functionamento em vazio *(m)*

if-then operation En
De Implikationsfunktion *(f)*
Es operación condicional *(f)*
Fr opération conditionnelle *(f)*
It operazione se-allora *(f)*
Pt operação se-então *(f)*

ignore character En
De Übergehenzeichen *(n)*
Es carácter de supresión *(m)*
Fr caractère d'omission *(m)*
It carattere di ignorare *(m)*
Pt carácter ignore *(m)*

illegal character En
De unzulässiges Zeichen *(n)*
Es carácter no válido *(m)*
Fr caractère interdit *(m)*
It carattere illegale *(m)*
Pt carácter ilegal *(m)*

image *n* En, Fr *(f)*
De Wiedergabe *(f)*
Es imagen *(f)*
It immagine *(f)*
Pt imagem *(f)*

imagem *(f) n* Pt
De Wiedergabe *(f)*
En image
Es imagen *(f)*
Fr image *(f)*
It immagine *(f)*

imagen *(f) n* Es
De Wiedergabe *(f)*
En image
Fr image *(f)*
It immagine *(f)*
Pt imagem *(f)*

immagazzinamento *(m) n* It
De Speicherung *(f)*
En storage
Es almacenamiento *(m)*
Fr stockage *(m)*
Pt armazenamento *(m)*

immagazzinamento principale *(m)* It
De Hauptspeicherung *(f)*
En main storage
Es almacenamiento principal *(m)*
Fr stockage central *(m)*
Pt armazenagem principal *(f)*

immagine *(f) n* It
De Wiedergabe *(f)*
En image
Es imagen *(f)*
Fr image *(f)*
Pt imagem *(f)*

immediate access En
De unmittelbarer Zugriff *(m)*
Es acceso inmediato *(m)*
Fr accès immédiat *(m)*
It accesso immediato *(m)*
Pt acesso imediato *(m)*

immediate address En
De unmittelbare Adresse *(f)*
Es dirección inmediata *(f)*
Fr adresse immédiate *(f)*
It indirizzo immediato *(m)*
Pt endereço imediato *(m)*

immettere *vb* It
De eingeben
En input
Es introducir
Fr entrer
Pt entrar

impaccare *vb* It
De stapeln
En pack
Es empaquetar
Fr comprimer
Pt empacotar

impact printer En
De mechanischer Drucker *(m)*
Es impresora a percusión *(f)*
Fr imprimante à percussion *(f)*
It stampatrice ad impatto *(f)*
Pt impressora de impacto *(f)*

imparidad *(f) n* Es
De ungerade Parität *(f)*
En odd parity
Fr imparité *(f)*
It parità dispari *(f)*
Pt paridade impar *(f)*

imparité *(f) n* Fr
De ungerade Parität *(f)*
En odd parity
Es imparidad *(f)*
It parità dispari *(f)*
Pt paridade impar *(f)*

implementação *(f) n* Pt
De Durchführung *(f)*
En implementation
Es realización *(f)*
Fr mise en application *(f)*
It implementazione *(f)*

implementation *n* En
De Durchführung *(f)*
Es realización *(f)*
Fr mise en application *(f)*
It implementazione *(f)*
Pt implementação *(f)*

implementazione *(f) n* It
De Durchführung *(f)*
En implementation
Es realización *(f)*
Fr mise en application *(f)*
Pt implementação *(f)*

implicação condicional *(f)* Pt
De bedingte Funktion *(f)*
En conditional implication
Es implicación condicional *(f)*
Fr implication conditionnelle *(f)*
It implicazione condizionale *(f)*

implicación condicional *(f)* Es
De bedingte Funktion *(f)*
En conditional implication
Fr implication conditionnelle *(f)*
It implicazione condizionale *(f)*
Pt implicação condicional *(f)*

implication conditionnelle *(f)* Fr
De bedingte Funktion *(f)*
En conditional implication
Es implicación condicional *(f)*
It implicazione condizionale *(f)*
Pt implicação condicional *(f)*

implicazione condizionale *(f)* It
De bedingte Funktion *(f)*
En conditional implication
Es implicación condicional *(f)*
Fr implication conditionnelle *(f)*
Pt implicação condicional *(f)*

Implikationsfunktion *(f) n* De
En if-then operation
Es operación condicional *(f)*
Fr opération conditionnelle *(f)*
It operazione se-allora *(f)*
Pt operação se-então *(f)*

impresora *(f) n* Es
De Drucker *(m)*
En printer
Fr imprimante *(f)*
It stampatrice *(f)*
Pt impressora *(f)*

impresora a percusión *(f)* Es
De mechanischer Drucker *(m)*
En impact printer
Fr imprimante à percussion *(f)*
It stampatrice ad impatto *(f)*
Pt impressora de impacto *(f)*

impresora a tambor *(f)* Es
De Trommeldrucker *(m)*
En drum printer
Fr imprimante à tambour *(f)*
It stampatrice a tamburo *(f)*
Pt impressora de tambor *(f)*

impresora de cadena *(f)* Es
De Kettendrucker *(m)*
En chain printer
Fr imprimante à chaîne *(f)*
It stampatrice a catena *(f)*
Pt impressora de cadeia *(f)*

impresora de cadena *(f)* Es
De Gliederdrucker *(m)*
En train printer
Fr imprimante à train de caractères *(f)*
It stampatrice a treno di caratteri *(f)*
Pt impressora de trem *(f)*

impresora de esfera *(f)* Es
De Kugelkopfdrucker *(m)*
En golfball printer
Fr imprimante à sphère *(f)*
It stampatrice a pallina *(f)*
Pt impressora de bola de golf *(f)*

impresora de laser *(f)* Es
De Laserdrucker *(m)*
En laser printer
Fr imprimante à laser *(f)*
It stampatrice a laser *(f)*
Pt impressora laser *(f)*

impresora de líneas *(f)* Es
De Zeilendrucker *(m)*
En line printer
Fr imprimante ligne par ligne *(f)*
It stampatrice a linea *(f)*
Pt impressora de linha *(f)*

impresora de matriz *(f)* Es
De Matrizendrucker *(m)*
En matrix printer
Fr imprimante matricielle *(f)*
It stampatrice a matrice *(f)*
Pt impressora de matriz *(f)*

impresora de rodillo *(f)* Es
De Trommeldrucker *(m)*
En barrel printer
Fr imprimante à tambour *(f)*
It stampatrice a tamburo *(f)*
Pt impressora de tambor *(f)*

impresora de ruedas *(f)* Es
De Typenraddrucker *(m)*
En wheel printer
Fr imprimante à roues *(f)*
It stampatrice di ruota *(f)*
Pt impressora de roda *(f)*

impresora de ruedas de mariposa *(f)* Es
De Gänseblümchen-Typenraddrucker *(m)*
En daisywheel printer
Fr imprimante à marguerite *(f)*
It stampatrice daisywheel *(f)*
Pt impressora margarida *(f)*

impresora electrostática *(f)* Es
De elektrostatischer Drucker *(m)*
En electrostatic printer
Fr imprimante électrostatique *(f)*
It stampatrice elettrostatica *(f)*
Pt impressora electrostática *(f)*

impresora en serie *(f)* Es
De Reihendrucker *(m)*
En serial printer
Fr imprimante série *(f)*
It stampatrice in serie *(f)*
Pt impressora em série *(f)*

impresora gráfica *(f)* Es
De Zeichendrucker *(m)*
En graphics printer
Fr imprimante graphique *(f)*
It stampatrice grafica *(f)*
Pt impressora gráfica *(f)*

impresora por páginas *(f)* Es
De Seitendrucker *(m)*
En page printer
Fr imprimante page par page *(f)*
It stampatrice di pagina *(f)*
Pt impressora de página *(f)*

impresora por puntos *(f)* Es
De Punktdrucker *(m)*
En dot printer

Fr imprimante par points *(f)*
It stampatrice a punti *(f)*
Pt impressora de pontos *(f)*

impresora sin percusión *(f)* Es
De nicht mechanischer Drucker *(m)*
En nonimpact printer
Fr imprimante non à percussion *(f)*
It stampatrice non ad impatto *(f)*
Pt impressora sem impacto *(f)*

impresora xerográfica *(f)* Es
De xerographischer Drucker *(m)*
En xerographic printer
Fr imprimante xérographique *(f)*
It stampatrice xerografica *(f)*
Pt impressora xerográfica *(f)*

impressão *(f) n* Pt
De Ausdruck *(m)*
En printout
Es vaciado a la impresora *(m)*
Fr sortie sur imprimante *(f)*
It stampato *(m)*

impression sur microfilm *(f)* Fr
De Computerausgang auf Mikrofilm *(m)*
En computer output on microfilm (COM)
Es salida de ordenador en microfilm *(f)*
It output del elaboratore su microfilm *(m)*
Pt output de computador em microfilme *(m)*

impressora *(f) n* Pt
De Drucker *(m)*
En printer
Es impresora *(f)*
Fr imprimante *(f)*
It stampatrice *(f)*

impressora de bola de golf *(f)* Pt
De Kugelkopfdrucker *(m)*
En golfball printer
Es impresora de esfera *(f)*
Fr imprimante à sphère *(f)*
It stampatrice a pallina *(f)*

impressora de cadeia *(f)* Pt
De Kettendrucker *(m)*
En chain printer
Es impresora de cadena *(f)*
Fr imprimante à chaîne *(f)*
It stampatrice a catena *(f)*

impressora de impacto *(f)* Pt
De mechanischer Drucker *(m)*
En impact printer
Es impresora a percusión *(f)*
Fr imprimante à percussion *(f)*
It stampatrice ad impatto *(f)*

impressora de linha *(f)* Pt
De Zeilendrucker *(m)*
En line printer
Es impresora de líneas *(f)*
Fr imprimante ligne par ligne *(f)*
It stampatrice a linea *(f)*

impressora de matriz *(f)* Pt
De Matrizendrucker *(m)*
En matrix printer
Es impresora de matriz *(f)*
Fr imprimante matricielle *(f)*
It stampatrice a matrice *(f)*

impressora de página *(f)* Pt
De Seitendrucker *(m)*
En page printer
Es impresora por páginas *(f)*
Fr imprimante page par page *(f)*
It stampatrice di pagina *(f)*

impressora de pontos *(f)* Pt
De Punktdrucker *(m)*
En dot printer
Es impresora por puntos *(f)*
Fr imprimante par points *(f)*
It stampatrice a punti *(f)*

impressora de roda *(f)* Pt
De Typenraddrucker *(m)*
En wheel printer
Es impresora de ruedas *(f)*
Fr imprimante à roues *(f)*
It stampatrice di ruota *(f)*

impressora de tambor *(f)* Pt
De Trommeldrucker *(m)*
En barrel printer; drun printer
Es impresora a tambor; impresora de rodillo *(f)*
Fr imprimante à tambour *(f)*
It stampatrice a tamburo *(f)*

impressora de trem *(f)* Pt
De Gliederdrucker *(m)*
En train printer
Es impresora de cadena *(f)*
Fr imprimante à train de caractères *(f)*
It stampatrice a treno di caratteri *(f)*

impressora electrostática *(f)* Pt
De elektrostatischer Drucker *(m)*
En electrostatic printer
Es impresora electrostática *(f)*
Fr imprimante électrostatique *(f)*
It stampatrice elettrostatica *(f)*

impressora em série *(f)* Pt
De Reihendrucker *(m)*
En serial printer
Es impresora en serie *(f)*
Fr imprimante série *(f)*
It stampatrice in serie *(f)*

impressora gráfica *(f)* Pt
De Zeichendrucker *(m)*
En graphics printer
Es impresora gráfica *(f)*
Fr imprimante graphique *(f)*
It stampatrice grafica *(f)*

impressora laser *(f)* Pt
De Laserdrucker *(m)*
En laser printer
Es impresora de laser *(f)*
Fr imprimante à laser *(f)*
It stampatrice a laser *(f)*

impressora margarida *(f)* Pt
De Gänseblümchen-Typenraddrucker *(m)*
En daisywheel printer
Es impresora de ruedas de mariposa *(f)*
Fr imprimante à marguerite *(f)*
It stampatrice daisywheel *(f)*

impressora sem impacto *(f)* Pt
De nicht mechanischer Drucker *(m)*
En nonimpact printer
Es impresora sin percusión *(f)*
Fr imprimante non à percussion *(f)*
It stampatrice non ad impatto *(f)*

impressora xerográfica *(f)* Pt
De xerographischer Drucker *(m)*
En xerographic printer
Es impresora xerográfica *(f)*
Fr imprimante xérographique *(f)*
It stampatrice xerografica *(f)*

imprimante *(f) n* Fr
De Drucker *(m)*
En printer
Es impresora *(f)*
It stampatrice *(f)*
Pt impressora *(f)*

imprimante à chaîne *(f)* Fr
De Kettendrucker *(m)*
En chain printer
Es impresora de cadena *(f)*
It stampatrice a catena *(f)*
Pt impressora de cadeia *(f)*

imprimante à laser *(f)* Fr
De Laserdrucker *(m)*
En laser printer
Es impresora de laser *(f)*
It stampatrice a laser *(f)*
Pt impressora laser *(f)*

imprimante à marguerite *(f)* Fr
De Gänseblümchen-Typenraddrucker *(m)*
En daisywheel printer
Es impresora de ruedas de mariposa *(f)*
It stampatrice daisywheel *(f)*
Pt impressora margarida *(f)*

imprimante à percussion *(f)* Fr
De mechanischer Drucker *(m)*
En impact printer
Es impresora a percusión *(f)*
It stampatrice ad impatto *(f)*
Pt impressora de impacto *(f)*

imprimante à roues *(f)* Fr
De Typenraddrucker *(m)*
En wheel printer
Es impresora de ruedas *(f)*
It stampatrice di ruota *(f)*
Pt impressora de roda *(f)*

imprimante à sphère *(f)* Fr
De Kugelkopfdrucker *(m)*
En golfball printer
Es impresora de esfera *(f)*
It stampatrice a pallina *(f)*
Pt impressora de bola de golf *(f)*

imprimante à tambour *(f)* Fr
De Trommeldrucker *(m)*
En barrel printer; drun printer
Es impresora a tambor; impresora de rodillo *(f)*
It stampatrice a tamburo *(f)*
Pt impressora de tambor *(f)*

imprimante à train de caractères *(f)* Fr
De Gliederdrucker *(m)*
En train printer
Es impresora de cadena *(f)*
It stampatrice a treno di caratteri *(f)*
Pt impressora de trem *(f)*

imprimante électrostatique *(f)* Fr
De elektrostatischer Drucker *(m)*
En electrostatic printer
Es impresora electrostática *(f)*
It stampatrice elettrostatica *(f)*
Pt impressora electrostática *(f)*

imprimante graphique *(f)* Fr
De Zeichendrucker *(m)*
En graphics printer
Es impresora gráfica *(f)*
It stampatrice grafica *(f)*
Pt impressora gráfica *(f)*

imprimante ligne par ligne *(f)* Fr
De Zeilendrucker *(m)*
En line printer
Es impresora de líneas *(f)*
It stampatrice a linea *(f)*
Pt impressora de linha *(f)*

imprimante matricielle *(f)* Fr
De Matrizendrucker *(m)*
En matrix printer
Es impresora de matriz *(f)*
It stampatrice a matrice *(f)*
Pt impressora de matriz *(f)*

imprimante non à percussion *(f)* Fr
De nicht mechanischer Drucker *(m)*
En nonimpact printer
Es impresora sin percusión *(f)*
It stampatrice non ad impatto *(f)*
Pt impressora sem impacto *(f)*

imprimante page par page *(f)* Fr
De Seitendrucker *(m)*
En page printer
Es impresora por páginas *(f)*
It stampatrice di pagina *(f)*
Pt impressora de página *(f)*

imprimante par points *(f)* Fr
De Punktdrucker *(m)*
En dot printer
Es impresora por puntos *(f)*
It stampatrice a punti *(f)*
Pt impressora de pontos *(f)*

imprimante série *(f)* Fr
De Reihendrucker *(m)*
En serial printer
Es impresora en serie *(f)*
It stampatrice in serie *(f)*
Pt impressora em série *(f)*

imprimante xérographique *(f)* Fr
De xerographischer Drucker *(m)*
En xerographic printer
Es impresora xerográfica *(f)*
It stampatrice xerografica *(f)*
Pt impressora xerográfica *(f)*

Impuls *(m) n* De
En pulse
Es impulso *(m)*
Fr impulsion *(f)*
It impulso *(m)*
Pt impulso *(m)*

impulsar *vb* Es
De antreiben
En drive
Fr entraîner
It azionare
Pt accionar

Impulsfolge *(f) n* De
En pulse train
Es tren de impulsos *(m)*
Fr train d'impulsions *(m)*
It treno d'impulsi *(m)*
Pt trem de impulsos *(m)*

Impulsfolgefrequenz *(f) n* De
En pulse repetition frequency (prf)
Es frecuencia de repetición de impulsos *(f)*
Fr fréquence par récurrence des impulsions *(f)*
It frequenza a ripetizione di impulsi *(f)*
Pt frequência de repetição de impulsos *(f)*

impulsi dell'orologio *(m pl)* It
De Taktimpulse *(pl)*
En clock pulses
Es impulsos de reloj *(m pl)*
Fr impulsions d'horloge *(f pl)*
Pt impulsos de relógio *(m pl)*

impulsion *(f) n* Fr
De Impuls *(m)*
En pulse
Es impulso *(m)*

It impulso *(m)*
Pt impulso *(m)*

impulsion de synchronisation *(f)* Fr
De Taktpulse *(pl)*
En sprocket pulse
Es impulso de sincronización *(m)*
It impulso del rocchetto *(m)*
Pt impulso de roda dentada *(m)*

impulsion de validation *(f)* Fr
De Aktivierpuls *(m)*
En enable pulse
Es impulso de activación *(m)*
It impulso di abilitazione *(m)*
Pt impulso de capacitação *(m)*

impulsion d'interdiction *(f)* Fr
De Sperrimpuls *(m)*
En inhibit pulse
Es impulso de bloqueo *(m)*
It impulso inibitore *(m)*
Pt impulso de inibição *(m)*

impulsion RAZ *(f)* Fr
De Rückstellenpuls *(m)*
En reset pulse
Es impulso de reposición *(m)*
It impulso di riazzeramento *(m)*
Pt impulso de reacerto *(m)*

impulsions d'horloge *(f pl)* Fr
De Taktimpulse *(pl)*
En clock pulses
Es impulsos de reloj *(m pl)*
It impulsi dell'orologio *(m pl)*
Pt impulsos de relógio *(m pl)*

impulso *(m)* *n* Es, It, Pt
De Impuls *(m)*
En pulse
Fr impulsion *(f)*

impulso de activación *(m)* Es
De Aktivierpuls *(m)*
En enable pulse
Fr impulsion de validation *(f)*
It impulso di abilitazione *(m)*
Pt impulso de capacitação *(m)*

impulso de bloqueo *(m)* Es
De Sperrimpuls *(m)*
En inhibit pulse
Fr impulsion d'interdiction *(f)*
It impulso inibitore *(m)*
Pt impulso de inibição *(m)*

impulso de capacitação *(m)* Pt
De Aktivierpuls *(m)*
En enable pulse
Es impulso de activación *(m)*
Fr impulsion de validation *(f)*
It impulso di abilitazione *(m)*

impulso de inibição *(m)* Pt
De Sperrimpuls *(m)*
En inhibit pulse
Es impulso de bloqueo *(m)*
Fr impulsion d'interdiction *(f)*
It impulso inibitore *(m)*

impulso del rocchetto *(m)* It
De Taktpulse *(pl)*
En sprocket pulse
Es impulso de sincronización *(m)*
Fr impulsion de synchronisation *(f)*
Pt impulso de roda dentada *(m)*

impulso de reacerto *(m)* Pt
De Rückstellenpuls *(m)*
En reset pulse
Es impulso de reposición *(m)*
Fr impulsion RAZ *(f)*
It impulso di riazzeramento *(m)*

impulso de reposición *(m)* Es
De Rückstellenpuls *(m)*
En reset pulse
Fr impulsion RAZ *(f)*
It impulso di riazzeramento *(m)*
Pt impulso de reacerto *(m)*

impulso de roda dentada *(m)* Pt
De Taktpulse *(pl)*
En sprocket pulse
Es impulso de sincronización *(m)*
Fr impulsion de synchronisation *(f)*
It impulso del rocchetto *(m)*

impulso de sincronización *(m)* Es
De Taktpulse *(pl)*
En sprocket pulse
Fr impulsion de synchronisation *(f)*
It impulso del rocchetto *(m)*
Pt impulso de roda dentada *(m)*

impulso di abilitazione *(m)* It
De Aktivierpuls *(m)*
En enable pulse
Es impulso de activación *(m)*
Fr impulsion de validation *(f)*
Pt impulso de capacitação *(m)*

impulso di riazzeramento *(m)* It
De Rückstellenpuls *(m)*
En reset pulse
Es impulso de reposición *(m)*
Fr impulsion RAZ *(f)*
Pt impulso de reacerto *(m)*

impulso inibitore *(m)* It
De Sperrimpuls *(m)*
En inhibit pulse
Es impulso de bloqueo *(m)*
Fr impulsion d'interdiction *(f)*
Pt impulso de inibição *(m)*

impulsor de cinta *(m)* Es
De Bandantrieb *(m)*
En tape drive
Fr dérouleur de bande *(m)*
It guida del nastro *(f)*
Pt accionamento da fita *(m)*

impulsore *(m)* *n* It
De Reißer *(m)*
En burster
Es separadora de hojas *(f)*
Fr rupteuse *(f)*
Pt separador de folha *(m)*

impulsos de relógio *(m pl)* Pt
De Taktimpulse *(pl)*
En clock pulses
Es impulsos de reloj *(m pl)*
Fr impulsions d'horloge *(f pl)*
It impulsi dell'orologio *(m pl)*

impulsos de reloj *(m pl)* Es
De Taktimpulse *(pl)*
En clock pulses
Fr impulsions d'horloge *(f pl)*
It impulsi dell'orologio *(m pl)*
Pt impulsos de relógio *(m pl)*

inactive *adj* En
De unbewegt
Es inactivo
Fr non mouvementé
It inattivo
Pt inactivo

inactivo *adj* Es, Pt
De unbewegt
En inactive
Fr non mouvementé
It inattivo

inattivo *adj* It
De unbewegt
En inactive
Es inactivo

Fr non mouvementé
Pt inactivo

in Ausgangsstellung bringen De
En restore
Es restaurar
Fr rétablir
It ripristinare
Pt rearmazenar

incanalare *vb* It
De führen
En route
Es encaminar
Fr acheminar
Pt encaminhar

incanalazione dei messaggi *(f)* It
De Nachrichtenvermittlung *(f)*
En message routing
Es encaminamiento de mensajes *(m)*
Fr acheminement des messages *(m)*
Pt encaminhamento de mensagens *(m)*

inceppamento *(m) n* It
De Verklemmung *(f)*
En jam
Es atascamiento *(m)*
Fr bourrage *(m)*
Pt congestionamento *(m)*

inchiostro magnetico *(m)* It
De Magnettinte *(f)*
En magnetic ink
Es tinta magnética *(f)*
Fr encre magnétique *(f)*
Pt tinta magnética *(f)*

incidentals time En
De Nebenzeiten *(pl)*
Es tiempo de actividades anexas *(m)*
Fr temps d'activités annexes *(m)*
It tempo di attività eventuale *(m)*
Pt tempo de incidentes *(m)*

inclusive-or operation En
De ODER-Verknüpfung *(f)*
Es operación O inclusivo *(m)*
Fr opération OU inclusif *(f)*
It operazione inclusivo-o *(f)*
Pt operação inclusivé-ou *(f)*

incollatrice *(f) n* It
De Klebegerät *(n)*
En splicer
Es empalmadora *(f)*
Fr colleuse de bandes *(f)*
Pt emendador *(m)*

incremental plotter En
De schrittweiser Kurvenzeichner *(m)*
Es trazador incremental *(m)*
Fr traceur incrémentiel *(m)*
It tracciatore incrementale *(m)*
Pt plotador incremental *(m)*

incremental representation En
De schrittweise Darstellung *(f)*
Es representación incremental *(f)*
Fr représentation incrémentielle *(f)*
It rappresentazione incrementale *(f)*
Pt representação incremental *(f)*

indépendance de gamme *(f)* Fr
De Bereichsunabhängigkeit *(f)*
En range independence
Es independencia del margen *(f)*
It indipendenza di gamma *(f)*
Pt independência do alcance *(f)*

independencia del margen *(f)* Es
De Bereichsunabhängigkeit *(f)*
En range independence
Fr indépendance de gamme *(f)*
It indipendenza di gamma *(f)*
Pt independência do alcance *(f)*

independência do alcance *(f)* Pt
De Bereichsunabhängigkeit *(f)*
En range independence
Es independencia del margen *(f)*
Fr indépendance de gamme *(f)*
It indipendenza di gamma *(f)*

indépendent de la machine Fr
De maschinenunabhängig
En machine-independent
Es independiente de la máquina
It indipendente dalla macchina
Pt independente da máquina

independente da máquina Pt
De maschinenunabhängig
En machine-independent
Es independiente de la máquina
Fr indépendent de la machine
It indipendente dalla macchina

independiente de la máquina Es
De maschinenunabhängig
En machine-independent
Fr indépendent de la machine
It indipendente dalla macchina
Pt independente da máquina

index *n* En, Fr, Pt *(m)*
De Sachwörterverzeichnis *(n)*
Es índice *(m)*
It indice *(m)*

index *vb* En
De indizieren
Es poner en un índice
Fr faire un index
It metter nell'indice
Pt pôr em índex

indicação *(f) n* Pt
De Vorzeichen *(n)*
En sign
Es signo *(m)*
Fr signe *(m)*
It segno *(m)*

indicación *(f) n* Es
De Kennzeichnung *(f)*
En designation
Fr indication *(f)*
It designazione *(f)*
Pt designação *(f)*

indicador *(m) n* Es
De Zeiger *(m)*
En pointer
Fr indicateur *(m)*
It lancetta *(f)*
Pt ponteiro *(m)*

indicador de prioridad *(m)* Es
De Vorranganzeiger *(m)*
En priority indicator
Fr indicateur prioritaire *(m)*
It indicatore di priorità *(m)*
Pt indicador de prioridade *(m)*

indicador de prioridade *(m)* Pt
De Vorranganzeiger *(m)*
En priority indicator
Es indicador de prioridad *(m)*
Fr indicateur prioritaire *(m)*
It indicatore di priorità *(m)*

indicador de verificação *(m)* Pt
De Prüfanzeiger *(m)*
En check indicator

Es indicador de verificación *(m)*
Fr indicateur de contrôle *(m)*
It indicatore di controllo *(m)*

indicador de verificação de sinal *(m)* Pt
De Vorzeichen-prüfanzeiger *(m)*
En sign-check indicator
Es indicador de verificación de signo *(m)*
Fr indicateur de contrôle de signes *(m)*
It indicatore del controllo di segno *(m)*

indicador de verificación *(m)* Es
De Prüfanzeiger *(m)*
En check indicator
Fr indicateur de contrôle *(m)*
It indicatore di controllo *(m)*
Pt indicador de verificação *(m)*

indicador de verificación de signo *(m)* Es
De Vorzeichen-prüfanzeiger *(m)*
En sign-check indicator
Fr indicateur de contrôle de signes *(m)*
It indicatore del controllo di segno *(m)*
Pt indicador de verificação de sinal *(m)*

indicateur *(m)* *n* Fr
De Zeiger *(m)*
En pointer
Es indicador *(m)*
It lancetta *(f)*
Pt ponteiro *(m)*

indicateur de contrôle *(m)* Fr
De Prüfanzeiger *(m)*
En check indicator
Es indicador de verificación *(m)*
It indicatore di controllo *(m)*
Pt indicador de verificação *(m)*

indicateur de contrôle de signes *(m)* Fr
De Vorzeichen-prüfanzeiger *(m)*
En sign-check indicator
Es indicador de verificación de signo *(m)*
It indicatore del controllo di segno *(m)*
Pt indicador de verificação de sinal *(m)*

indicateur prioritaire *(m)* Fr
De Vorranganzeiger *(m)*
En priority indicator
Es indicador de prioridad *(m)*
It indicatore di priorità *(m)*
Pt indicador de prioridade *(m)*

indication *(f)* *n* Fr
De Kennzeichnung *(f)*
En designation
Es indicación *(f)*
It designazione *(f)*
Pt designação *(f)*

indicatore *(m)* *n* It
De Markierung *(f)*
En flag
Es señalizador *(m)*
Fr drapeau *(m)*
Pt bandeira *(f)*

indicatore del controllo di segno *(m)* It
De Vorzeichen-prüfanzeiger *(m)*
En sign-check indicator
Es indicador de verificación de signo *(m)*
Fr indicateur de contrôle de signes *(m)*
Pt indicador de verificação de sinal *(m)*

indicatore di controllo *(m)* It
De Prüfanzeiger *(m)*
En check indicator
Es indicador de verificación *(m)*
Fr indicateur de contrôle *(m)*
Pt indicador de verificação *(m)*

indicatore di priorità *(m)* It
De Vorranganzeiger *(m)*
En priority indicator
Es indicador de prioridad *(m)*
Fr indicateur prioritaire *(m)*
Pt indicador de prioridade *(m)*

indice *(m)* *n* It
De Sachwörter-verzeichnis *(n)*
En index
Es índice *(m)*
Fr index *(m)*
Pt índex *(m)*

índice *(m)* *n* Es
De Sachwörter-verzeichnis *(n)*
En index
Fr index *(m)*
It indice *(m)*
Pt índex *(m)*

índice de amostragem *(m)* Pt
De Abtastfrequenz *(f)*
En sampling rate
Es frecuencia de muestreo *(f)*
Fr vitesse d'échantillonnage *(f)*
It volume di campionamento *(m)*

índice de erros *(m)* Pt
De Fehlerhäufigkeit *(f)*
En error rate
Es coeficiente de errores *(m)*
Fr taux d'erreurs *(m)*
It tasso di errori *(m)*

índice de falhas *(m)* Pt
De Ausfallhäufigkeit *(f)*
En failure rate
Es frecuencia de fallos *(f)*
Fr taux de défaillance *(m)*
It numero di guasti *(m)*

índice de perfuração *(m)* Pt
De Lochungs-geschwindigkeit *(f)*
En perforation rate; punching rate
Es velocidad de perforación *(f)*
Fr vitesse de perforation *(f)*
It volume di perforazione *(m)*

índice de sinalização *(m)* Pt
De Signalisier-geschwindigkeit *(f)*
En signalling rate
Es velocidad de transmisión de señal *(f)*
Fr vitesse de signalisation *(f)*
It velocità dai segnali *(f)*

indice de transferencia *(m)* Es
De Übertragungs-frequenz *(f)*
En transfer rate
Fr vitesse de transfert *(f)*
It volume di trasferimento *(m)*
Pt índice de transferência *(m)*

índice de transferência *(m)* Pt
De Übertragungs-frequenz *(f)*
En transfer rate
Es indice de transferencia *(m)*
Fr vitesse de transfert *(f)*
It volume di trasferimento *(m)*

indipendente dalla macchina It
De maschinen-unabhängig
En machine-independent
Es independiente de la máquina
Fr indépendent de la machine

Pt independente da máquina

indipendenza di gamma *(f)* It
De Bereichs-unabhängigkeit *(f)*
En range independence
Es independencia del margen *(f)*
Fr indépendance de gamme *(f)*
Pt independência do alcance *(f)*

indirect address En
De indirekte Adresse *(f)*
Es dirección indirecta *(f)*
Fr adresse indirecte *(f)*
It indirizzo indiretto *(m)*
Pt endereço indirecto *(m)*

indirekt *adj* De
En offline
Es fuera de línea
Fr hors ligne
It non collegato
Pt fora da linha

indirekte Adresse *(f)* De
En indirect address
Es dirección indirecta *(f)*
Fr adresse indirecte *(f)*
It indirizzo indiretto *(m)*
Pt endereço indirecto *(m)*

indirizzamento diretto *(m)* It
De direkte Adressierung *(f)*
En direct addressing
Es direccionamiento directo *(m)*
Fr adressage direct *(m)*
Pt enderaçamento directo *(m)*

indirizzamento relativo *(m)* It
De relative Adressierung *(f)*
En relative addressing
Es direccionado relativo *(m)*
Fr adressage relatif *(m)*
Pt endereçamento relativo *(m)*

indirizzamento ripetitivo *(m)* It
De wiederholte Adressierung *(f)*
En repetitive addressing
Es direccionado repetitivo *(m)*
Fr adressage sous-entendu *(m)*
Pt endereçamento repetitivo *(m)*

indirizzare *vb* It
De adressieren
En address
Es direccionar
Fr adresser
Pt endereçar

indirizzo *(m) n* It
De Adresse *(f)*
En address
Es dirección *(f)*
Fr adresse *(f)*
Pt endereço *(m)*

indirizzo assoluto *(m)* It
De absolute Adresse *(f)*
En absolute address
Es dirección absoluta *(f)*
Fr adresse absolue *(f)*
Pt direcção absoluta *(f)*

indirizzo base *(m)* It
De Basisadresse *(f)*
En base address
Es dirección de base *(f)*
Fr adresse de base *(f)*
Pt direcção de base *(f)*

indirizzo del secondo livello *(m)* It
De Adresse der zweiten Stufe *(f)*
En second-level address
Es dirección de segundo nivel *(f)*
Fr adresse à deuxième niveau *(f)*
Pt endereço de segundo nivel *(m)*

indirizzo di macchina *(m)* It
De Maschinenadresse *(f)*
En machine address
Es dirección de máquina *(f)*
Fr adresse absolue *(f)*
Pt endereço da máquina *(m)*

indirizzo di riferimento *(m)* It
De Bezugsadresse *(f)*
En reference address
Es dirección de referencia *(f)*
Fr adresse primitive *(f)*
Pt endereço de referência *(m)*

indirizzo effettivo *(m)* It
De echte Adresse *(f)*
En actual address
Es dirección real *(f)*
Fr adresse réelle *(f)*
Pt direcção real *(f)*

indirizzo efficace *(m)* It
De effektive Adresse *(f)*
En effective address
Es dirección efectiva *(f)*
Fr adresse réelle *(f)*
Pt endereço real *(m)*

indirizzo immediato *(m)* It
De unmittelbare Adresse *(f)*
En immediate address
Es dirección inmediata *(f)*
Fr adresse immédiate *(f)*
Pt endereço imediato *(m)*

indirizzo indiretto *(m)* It
De indirekte Adresse *(f)*
En indirect address
Es dirección indirecta *(f)*
Fr adresse indirecte *(f)*
Pt endereço indirecto *(m)*

indirizzo parziale *(m)* It
De Adressenteil *(n)*
En address part
Es parte de la dirección *(f)*
Fr partie d'adresse *(f)*
Pt parte de endereço *(f)*

indirizzo relativo *(m)* It
De relative Adresse *(f)*
En relative address
Es dirección relativa *(f)*
Fr adresse relative *(f)*
Pt endereço relativo *(m)*

indirizzo rilocabile *(m)* It
De verschiebliche Adresse *(f)*
En relocatable address
Es dirección reubicable *(f)*
Fr adresse translatable *(f)*
Pt endereço relocalizável *(m)*

indirizzo simbolico *(m)* It
De symbolische Adresse *(f)*
En symbolic address
Es dirección simbólica *(f)*
Fr adresse symbolique *(f)*
Pt endereço simbólico *(m)*

indirizzo uno-più-uno *(m)* It
De Eins-plus-Eins-Adresse *(f)*
En one-plus-one address
Es dirección uno más uno *(f)*
Fr à une plus une adresse *(f)*
Pt endereço um mais um *(m)*

indirizzo virtuale *(m)* It
De virtuelle Adresse *(f)*
En virtual address
Es dirección virtual *(f)*
Fr adresse virtuelle *(f)*
Pt endereço virtual *(m)*

indizieren *vb* De
En index
Es poner en un índice
Fr faire un index
It metter nell'indice
Pt pôr em índex

ineffective time En
De unwirksame Zeit *(f)*
Es tiempo ineficaz *(m)*
Fr temps ineffectif *(m)*
It tempo inefficace *(m)*
Pt tempo irreal *(m)*

informação *(f) n* Pt
De Information *(f)*
En information
Es información *(f)*
Fr informations *(f pl)*
It informazioni *(f pl)*

información *(f) n* Es
De Information *(f)*
En information
Fr informations *(f pl)*
It informazioni *(f pl)*
Pt informação *(f)*

información parásita *(f)* Es
De Schund *(m)*
En garbage
Fr informations parasites *(f pl)*
It rifiuti *(m pl)*
Pt refugo *(m)*

information *n* En
De Information *(f)*
Es información *(f)*
Fr informations *(f pl)*
It informazioni *(f pl)*
Pt informação *(f)*

Information *(f) n* De
En information
Es información *(f)*
Fr informations *(f pl)*
It informazioni *(f pl)*
Pt informação *(f)*

information processing En
De Informations-verarbeitung *(f)*
Es proceso de la información *(m)*
Fr traitement de l'information *(m)*
It elaborazione delle informazioni *(f)*
Pt tratamento da informação *(m)*

information retrieval En
De Wiederauffinden von Informationen *(n)*
Es recuperación de la información *(f)*
Fr recherche documentaire *(f)*
It reperimento delle informazioni *(m)*
Pt recuperação da informação *(f)*

informations *(f pl) n* Fr
De Information *(f)*
En information
Es información *(f)*
It informazioni *(f pl)*
Pt informação *(f)*

informations parasites *(f pl)* Fr
De Schund *(m)*
En garbage
Es información parásita *(f)*
It rifiuti *(m pl)*
Pt refugo *(m)*

Informations-system *(n) n* De
En information system
Es sistema de información *(m)*
Fr système informatique *(m)*
It sistema di informazioni *(m)*
Pt sistema de informação *(m)*

Informations-theorie *(f) n* De
En information theory
Es teoría de la información *(f)*
Fr théorie de l'information *(f)*
It teoria delle informazioni *(f)*
Pt teoria de informação *(f)*

Informations-verarbeitung *(f) n* De
En information processing
Es proceso de la información *(m)*
Fr traitement de l'information *(m)*
It elaborazione delle informazioni *(f)*
Pt tratamento da informação *(m)*

information system En
De Informationssystem *(n)*
Es sistema de información *(m)*
Fr système informatique *(m)*
It sistema di informazioni *(m)*
Pt sistema de informação *(m)*

information theory En
De Informationstheorie *(f)*
Es teoría de la información *(f)*
Fr théorie de l'information *(f)*
It teoria delle informazioni *(f)*
Pt teoria de informação *(f)*

informatique répartie *(f)* Fr
De verteilte Verarbeitung *(f)*
En distributed processing
Es proceso distribuido *(m)*
It elaborazione ripartita *(f)*
Pt tratamento distribuido *(m)*

informazioni *(f pl) n* It
De Information *(f)*
En information
Es información *(f)*
Fr informations *(f pl)*
Pt informação *(f)*

informe de errores *(m)* Es
De Fehlerbericht *(m)*
En error report
Fr état sélectif *(m)*
It tabulato errori *(m)*
Pt relatório de erros *(m)*

ingegneria del software *(f)* It
De Programmaus-rüstung *(f)*
En software engineering
Es ingeniería de soportes lógicos *(f)*
Fr technique du logiciel *(f)*
Pt engenharia de software *(f)*

ingeniería de soportes lógicos *(f)* Es
De Programmaus-rüstung *(f)*
En software engineering
Fr technique du logiciel *(f)*
It ingegneria del software *(f)*
Pt engenharia de software *(f)*

ingresso dei dati *(m)* It
De Dateneingabe *(f)*
En data entry
Es entrada de datos *(f)*
Fr saisie de données *(f)*
Pt entrada de dados *(f)*

Inhalt *(m) n* De
En content
Es contenido *(m)*
Fr contenu *(m)*
It contenuto *(m)*
Pt conteúdo *(m)*

inhaltsadressierbar De
En content-addressable
Es contenido direccionable
Fr contenu adressable
It contenuto indirizzabile
Pt endereçável ao conteúdo

Inhaltsverzeichnis *(n) n* De
En directory
Es directorio *(m)*
Fr répertoire d'adresses *(m)*
It elenco *(m)*
Pt anuário *(m)*

inherited error En
De mitgeschleppter Fehler *(m)*
Es error arrastrado *(m)*
Fr erreur héritée *(f)*
It errore ereditato *(m)*
Pt erro herdado *(m)*

inhiber *vb* Fr
De sperren
En inhibit
Es inhibir
It inibire
Pt inibir

inhibir *vb* Es
De sperren
En inhibit
Fr inhiber
It inibire
Pt inibir

inhibit *vb* En
De sperren
Es inhibir
Fr inhiber
It inibire
Pt inibir

inhibiting signal En
De Sperrsignal *(n)*
Es señal inhibidora *(f)*
Fr signal d'interdiction *(m)*
It segnale inibitore *(m)*
Pt sinal de inibição *(m)*

inhibit pulse En
De Sperrimpuls *(m)*
Es impulso de bloqueo *(m)*
Fr impulsion d'interdiction *(f)*
It impulso inibitore *(m)*
Pt impulso de inibição *(m)*

inibir *vb* Pt
De sperren
En inhibit
Es inhibir
Fr inhiber
It inibire

inibire *vb* It
De sperren
En inhibit
Es inhibir
Fr inhiber
Pt inibir

inicialização *(f) n* Pt
De Erstbelegung *(f)*
En initialization
Es inicialización *(f)*
Fr initialisation *(f)*
It inizializzazione *(f)*

inicialización *(f) n* Es
De Erstbelegung *(f)*
En initialization
Fr initialisation *(f)*
It inizializzazione *(f)*
Pt inicialização *(f)*

inicializar *vb* Es, Pt
De initialisieren
En initialize
Fr initialiser
It inizializzare

initialisation *(f) n* Fr
De Erstbelegung *(f)*
En initialization
Es inicialización *(f)*
It inizializzazione *(f)*
Pt inicialização *(f)*

initialiser *vb* Fr
De initialisieren
En initialize
Es inicializar
It inizializzare
Pt inicializar

initialisieren *vb* De
En initialize
Es inicializar
Fr initialiser
It inizializzare
Pt inicializar

initialization *n* En
De Erstbelegung *(f)*
Es inicialización *(f)*
Fr initialisation *(f)*
It inizializzazione *(f)*
Pt inicialização *(f)*

initialize *vb* En
De initialisieren
Es inicializar
Fr initialiser
It inizializzare
Pt inicializar

inizializzare *vb* It
De initialisieren
En initialize
Es inicializar
Fr initialiser
Pt inicializar

inizializzazione *(f) n* It
De Erstbelegung *(f)*
En initialization
Es inicialización *(f)*
Fr initialisation *(f)*
Pt inicialização *(f)*

Inklusiv-ODER-Verknüpfung *(f)* De
En disjunction; inclusive-or operation
Es operación O inclusivo *(f)*
Fr opération OU inclusif *(f)*
It operazione inclusivo-o *(f)*
Pt operação inclusivé-ou *(f)*

ink ribbon En
De Farbband *(n)*
Es cinta entintada *(f)*
Fr ruban à encre *(m)*
It nastro ad inchiostro *(m)*
Pt fita de tinta *(f)*

in-line *adj* En
De gleichzeitig
Es lineal
Fr en ligne
It lineale
Pt em série

in linea It
De direkt
En on-line
Es en línea
Fr direct
Pt sobre a linha

Innenspeicher *(m) n* De
En internal store
Es memoria interna *(f)*
Fr mémoire interne *(f)*
It memoria interna *(f)*
Pt armazém interno *(m)*

innescare *vb* It
De triggern
En trigger
Es disparar
Fr declencher
Pt disparar

input *n* En
De Eingang *(m)*
Es entrada *(f)*
Fr entrée *(f)*
It entrata *(f)*
Pt entrada *(f)*

input *vb* En
De eingeben
Es introducir
Fr entrer
It immettere
Pt entrar

input buffer En
De Eingangspuffer *(m)*
Es memoria intermedia de entrada *(f)*
Fr tampon d'entrée *(m)*
It memoria di transito dell'entrata *(f)*
Pt separador de entrada *(m)*

input device En
De Eingangs-vorrichtung *(f)*
Es dispositivo de entrada *(m)*
Fr périphérique d'entrée *(m)*
It organo di entrata *(m)*
Pt dispositivo de entrada *(m)*

input manual *(m)* Pt
De Handeingabe *(f)*
En manual input
Es entrada manual *(f)*
Fr introduction manuelle *(f)*
It input manuale *(m)*

input manuale *(m)* It
De Handeingabe *(f)*
En manual input
Es entrada manual *(f)*
Fr introduction manuelle *(f)*
Pt input manual *(m)*

input-output En
De Eingang-Ausgang
Es entrada-salida
Fr entrée-sortie
It entrata-uscita
Pt entrada-sair

input-output buffer En
De Eingangs-Ausgangspuffer *(m)*
Es memoria intermedia de entrada-salida *(f)*
Fr tampon entrée-sortie *(m)*
It memoria di transito entrata-uscita *(f)*
Pt separador de entrada-sair *(m)*

input-output device En
De Eingangs-Ausgangs-vorrichtung *(f)*
Es dispositivo de entrada-salida *(m)*
Fr périphérique entrée-sortie *(m)*
It organo di entrata-uscita *(m)*
Pt dispositivo de entrada-sair *(m)*

input-output port En
De Eingangs-Ausgangsanschluß *(m)*
Es puerta de entrada-salida *(f)*

Fr point d'accès entrée-sortie *(m)*
It porto entrata-uscita *(m)*
Pt abertura de entrada-sair *(f)*

inquiry terminal En
De Abfragestation *(f)*
Es terminal de interrogación *(m)*
Fr poste d'interrogation *(m)*
It terminale per informazioni *(m)*
Pt terminal de indagação *(m)*

inscrever *vb* Pt
De beschriften
En inscribe
Es marcar
Fr marquer
It inscrivere

inscribe *vb* En
De beschriften
Es marcar
Fr marquer
It inscrivere
Pt inscrever

inscrivere *vb* It
De beschriften
En inscribe
Es marcar
Fr marquer
Pt inscrever

inscrivere per riempimento It
De überschreiben
En overwrite
Es recubrir
Fr superposer une écriture
Pt escrever por cima

insensible aux défaillances Fr
De defekttolerant
En fault-tolerant
Es tolerante con las averias
It toante di quasto
Pt tolerante relativamente a erros

inserire *vb* It
De kollationieren
En collate
Es intercalar
Fr interclasser
Pt conferir

inseritrice *(f) n* It
De Kollationierer *(m)*
En collator
Es intercaladora *(f)*
Fr interclasseuse *(f)*
Pt conferidor *(m)*

insieme *(m) n* It
De Menge *(f)*
En set
Es conjunto *(m)*
Fr ensemble *(m)*
Pt conjunto *(m)*

instalar *vb* Pt
De einrichten
En set up
Es montar
Fr mettre en place
It mettere a punto

instrução *(f) n* Pt
De Anweisung; Befehl *(f m)*
En instruction
Es instrucción *(f)*
Fr instruction *(f)*
It istruzione *(f)*

instrução aritmética *(f)* Pt
De arithmetische Anweisung *(f)*
En arithmetic instruction
Es instrucción aritmética *(f)*
Fr instruction arithmétique *(f)*
It istruzione aritmetica *(f)*

instrução auxiliada por computador *(f)* Pt
De computer-unterstützter Unterricht *(m)*
En computer-aided instruction
Es instrucción com la ayuda de ordenador *(f)*
Fr enseignement assisté par ordinateur *(m)*
It istruzione basata sull'elaboratore *(f)*

instrução de dois endereços *(f)* Pt
De Zweiadressen-anweisung *(f)*
En two-address instruction
Es instrucción con dos direcciones *(f)*
Fr instruction à deux adresses *(f)*
It istruzione a due indirizzi *(f)*

instrução de endereço múltiplo *(f)* Pt
De Mehrfachadress-befehl *(m)*
En multiple-address instruction
Es instrucción de direcciones múltiples *(f)*
Fr instruction multi-adresse *(f)*
It istruzione ad indirizzo multiplo *(f)*

instrução de endereço único *(f)* Pt
De Einzeladress-anweisung *(f)*
En single-address instruction
Es instrucción de una sola dirección *(f)*
Fr instruction à une adresse *(f)*
It istruzione ad indirizzo singolo *(f)*

instrução de endereço zero *(f)* Pt
De Nulladress-enanweisung *(f)*
En zero-address instruction
Es instrucción de dirección cero *(f)*
Fr instruction sans adresse *(f)*
It istruzione ad indirizzo zero *(f)*

instrução de não-endereço *(f)* Pt
De Kein-Adressenbefehl *(m)*
En no-address instruction
Es instrucción sin dirección *(f)*
Fr instruction sans adresse *(f)*
It istruzione a non indirizzo *(f)*

instrução de ramificação condicional *(f)* Pt
De bedingter Verzweigungsbefehl *(m)*
En conditional branch instruction
Es instrucción de bifurcación condicional *(f)*
Fr instruction de branchement conditionnelle *(f)*
It istruzione di diramazione condizionale *(f)*

instrução de ramo incondicional *(f)* Pt
De unbedingte Verzweigungs-anweisung *(f)*
En unconditional branch instruction
Es instrucción de bifurcación incondicional *(f)*
Fr instruction de branchement inconditionnel *(f)*
It istruzione di diramazione non condizionale *(f)*

instrução de regresso *(f)* Pt
De Rücklaufanweisung *(f)*
En return instruction
Es instrucción de retorno *(f)*
Fr instruction de retour *(f)*
It istruzione di ritorno *(f)*

instrução de repetição *(f)* Pt
De Wiederholungsbefehl *(m)*
En repetition instruction
Es instrucción de repetición *(f)*
Fr répertoire d'instructions *(m)*
It istruzione di ripetizione *(f)*

instrução de transferência *(f)* Pt
De Übertragungsanweisung *(f)*
En transfer instruction
Es instrucción de transferencia *(f)*
Fr instruction de branchement *(f)*
It istruzione di trasferimento *(f)*

instrução de três endereços *(f)* Pt
De Dreiadressenanweisung *(f)*
En three-address instruction
Es instrucción con tres direcciones *(f)*
Fr instruction à trois adresses *(f)*
It istruzione a tre indirizzi *(f)*

instrução simulada *(f)* Pt
De Blindbefehl *(m)*
En dummy instruction
Es instrucción ficticia *(f)*
Fr instruction fictive *(f)*
It istruzione fittizia *(f)*

instrucción *(f)* *n* Es
De Anweisung; Befehl *(f m)*
En instruction
Fr instruction *(f)*
It istruzione *(f)*
Pt instrução *(f)*

instrucción aritmética *(f)* Es
De arithmetische Anweisung *(f)*
En arithmetic instruction
Fr instruction arithmétique *(f)*
It istruzione aritmetica *(f)*
Pt instrução aritmética *(f)*

instrucción com la ayuda de ordenador *(f)* Es
De computerunterstützter Unterricht *(m)*
En computer-aided instruction
Fr enseignement assisté par ordinateur *(m)*
It istruzione basata sull'elaboratore *(f)*
Pt instrução auxiliada por computador *(f)*

instrucción con dos direcciones *(f)* Es
De Zweiadressenanweisung *(f)*
En two-address instruction
Fr instruction à deux adresses *(f)*
It istruzione a due indirizzi *(f)*
Pt instrução de dois endereços *(f)*

instrucción con tres direcciones *(f)* Es
De Dreiadressenanweisung *(f)*
En three-address instruction
Fr instruction à trois adresses *(f)*
It istruzione a tre indirizzi *(f)*
Pt instrução de três endereços *(f)*

instrucción de bifurcación *(f)* Es
De Verzweigungsbefehl *(m)*
En branch instruction
Fr instruction de branchement *(f)*
It istruzione di diramazione *(f)*
Pt instruções para ligar *(f)*

instrucción de bifurcación condicional *(f)* Es
De bedingter Verzweigungsbefehl *(m)*
En conditional branch instruction
Fr instruction de branchement conditionnelle *(f)*
It istruzione di diramazione condizionale *(f)*
Pt instrução de ramificação condicional *(f)*

instrucción de bifurcación incondicional *(f)* Es
De unbedingte Verzweigungsanweisung *(f)*
En unconditional branch instruction
Fr instruction de branchement inconditionnel *(f)*
It istruzione di diramazione non condizionale *(f)*
Pt instrução de ramo incondicional *(f)*

instrucción de dirección cero *(f)* Es
De Nulladressenanweisung *(f)*
En zero-address instruction
Fr instruction sans adresse *(f)*
It istruzione ad indirizzo zero *(f)*
Pt instrução de endereço zero *(f)*

instrucción de direcciones múltiples *(f)* Es
De Mehrfachadressbefehl *(m)*
En multiple-address instruction
Fr instruction multi-adresse *(f)*
It istruzione ad indirizzo multiplo *(f)*
Pt instrução de endereço múltiplo *(f)*

instrucción de punto de interrupción *(f)* Es
De Ausgleichspunktbefehl *(m)*
En breakpoint instruction
Fr instruction de point de rupture *(f)*
It istruzione del punto di arresto *(f)*
Pt instruções de ponto de rotura *(f)*

instrucción de repetición *(f)* Es
De Wiederholungsbefehl *(m)*
En repetition instruction
Fr répertoire d'instructions *(m)*
It istruzione di ripetizione *(f)*
Pt instrução de repetição *(f)*

instrucción de retorno *(f)* Es
De Rücklaufanweisung *(f)*
En return instruction
Fr instruction de retour *(f)*
It istruzione di ritorno *(f)*
Pt instrução de regresso *(f)*

instrucción de transferencia *(f)* Es
De Übertragungsanweisung *(f)*
En transfer instruction
Fr instruction de branchement *(f)*
It istruzione di trasferimento *(f)*
Pt instrução de transferência *(f)*

instrucción de una sola dirección *(f)* Es
De Einzeladressanweisung *(f)*
En single-address instruction
Fr instruction à une adresse *(f)*
It istruzione ad indirizzo singolo *(f)*
Pt instrução de endereço único *(f)*

instrucción ficticia *(f)* Es
De Blindbefehl *(m)*
En dummy instruction
Fr instruction fictive *(f)*
It istruzione fittizia *(f)*
Pt instrução simulada *(f)*

instrucción mnemotécnica *(f)* Es
De Befehlsmnemonik *(f)*
En instruction mnemonic
Fr mnémonique d'instruction *(f)*
It mnemonica dell'istruzione *(f)*

Pt mnemónica de instruções *(f)*

instrucción sin dirección *(f)* Es
De Kein-Adressenbefehl *(m)*
En no-address instruction
Fr instruction sans adresse *(f)*
It istruzione a non indirizzo *(f)*
Pt instrução de não-endereço *(f)*

instruções de ponto de rotura *(f)* Pt
De Ausgleichspunkt-befehl *(m)*
En breakpoint instruction
Es instrucción de punto de interrupción *(f)*
Fr instruction de point de rupture *(f)*
It istruzione del punto di arresto *(f)*

instruções para ligar *(f)* Pt
De Verzweigungsbefehl *(m)*
En branch instruction
Es instrucción de bifurcación *(f)*
Fr instruction de branchement *(f)*
It istruzione di diramazione *(f)*

instruction *n* En, Fr *(f)*
De Anweisung; Befehl *(f m)*
Es instrucción *(f)*
It istruzione *(f)*
Pt instrução *(f)*

instruction-address register En
De Befehlsadressen-register *(n)*
Es registro de instruccióndirección *(m)*
Fr registre d'adresse de l'instruction *(m)*
It registro dell'indirizzo dell'istruzione *(m)*
Pt registo de endereço de instrução *(m)*

instruction à deux adresses *(f)* Fr
De Zweiadressen-anweisung *(f)*
En two-address instruction
Es instrucción con dos direcciones *(f)*
It istruzione a due indirizzi *(f)*
Pt instrução de dois endereços *(f)*

instruction arithmétique *(f)* Fr
De arithmetische Anweisung *(f)*
En arithmetic(al) instruction
Es instrucción aritmética *(f)*
It istruzione aritmetica *(f)*
Pt instrução aritmética *(f)*

instruction à trois adresses *(f)* Fr
De Dreiadressen-anweisung *(f)*
En three-address instruction
Es instrucción con tres direcciones *(f)*
It istruzione a tre indirizzi *(f)*
Pt instrução de três endereços *(f)*

instruction à une adresse *(f)* Fr
De Einzeladress-anweisung *(f)*
En single-address instruction
Es instrucción de una sola dirección *(f)*
It istruzione ad indirizzo singolo *(f)*
Pt instrução de endereço único *(f)*

instruction code En
De Befehlscode *(m)*
Es código de instrucción *(m)*
Fr code d'instruction *(m)*
It codice dell'istruzione *(m)*
Pt código de instruções *(m)*

instruction de branchement *(f)* Fr
De Verzweigungsbefehl *(m)*
En branch instruction
Es instrucción de bifurcación *(f)*
It istruzione di diramazione *(f)*
Pt instruções para ligar *(f)*

instruction de branchement *(f)* Fr
De Übertragungs-anweisung *(f)*
En transfer instruction
Es instrucción de transferencia *(f)*
It istruzione di trasferimento *(f)*
Pt instrução de transferência *(f)*

instruction de branchement conditionnelle *(f)* Fr
De bedingter Verzweigungsbefehl *(m)*
En conditional branch instruction
Es instrucción de bifurcación condicional *(f)*
It istruzione di diramazione condizionale *(f)*
Pt instrução de ramificação condicional *(f)*

instruction de branchement inconditionnel *(f)* Fr
De unbedingte Verzweigungs-anweisung *(f)*
En unconditional branch instruction
Es instrucción de bifurcación incondicional *(f)*
It istruzione di diramazione non condizionale *(f)*
Pt instrução de ramo incondicional *(f)*

instruction déclarative *(f)* Fr
De Prozeduranweisung *(f)*
En declarative statement
Es sentencia de declaración *(f)*
It statement di dichiarazione *(m)*
Pt afirmação declarativa *(f)*

instruction de point de rupture *(f)* Fr
De Ausgleichspunkt-befehl *(m)*
En breakpoint instruction
Es instrucción de punto de interrupción *(f)*
It istruzione del punto di arresto *(f)*
Pt instruções de ponto de rotura *(f)*

instruction de retour *(f)* Fr
De Rücklaufanweisung *(f)*
En return instruction
Es instrucción de retorno *(f)*
It istruzione di ritorno *(f)*
Pt instrução de regresso *(f)*

instruction fictive *(f)* Fr
De Blindbefehl *(m)*
En dummy instruction
Es instrucción ficticia *(f)*
It istruzione fittizia *(f)*
Pt instrução simulada *(f)*

instruction format En
De Befehlsformat *(n)*
Es formato de la instrucción *(m)*
Fr structure de l'instruction *(f)*
It formato dell'istruzione *(m)*
Pt formato de instruções *(m)*

instruction mnemonic En
De Befehlsmnemonik *(f)*
Es instrucción mnemotécnica *(f)*
Fr mnémonique d'instruction *(f)*
It mnemonica dell'istruzione *(f)*
Pt mnemónica de instruções *(f)*

instruction multi-adresse *(f)* Fr
De Mehrfachadressbefehl *(m)*
En multiple-address instruction
Es instrucción de direcciones múltiples *(f)*
It istruzione ad indirizzo multiplo *(f)*
Pt instrução de endereço múltiplo *(f)*

instructions *(f pl) n* Fr
De Anweisung *(f)*
En statement
Es sentencia *(f)*
It statement *(m)*
Pt afirmação *(f)*

instruction sans adresse *(f)* Fr
De Kein-Adressenbefehl; Nulladressenanweisung *(m f)*
En no-address instruction; zero-address instruction
Es instrucción de dirección cero; instrucción sin dirección *(f)*
It istruzione ad indirizzo zero; istruzione a non indirizzo *(f)*
Pt instrução de endereço zero; instrução de não-endereço *(f)*

instruction set En
De Befehlsvorrat *(m)*
Es juego de instrucciones *(m)*
Fr jeu d'instructions *(m)*
It gruppo di istruzioni *(m)*
Pt conjunto de instruções *(m)*

instruction time En
De Befehlszeit *(f)*
Es tiempo de una instrucción *(m)*
Fr temps d'exécution d'une instruction *(m)*
It tempo per l'istruzione *(m)*
Pt tempo de instruções *(m)*

insuccesso *(m) n* It
De Blockabbruch *(m)*
En abort
Es suspensión *(f)*
Fr suspension d'exécution *(f)*
Pt aborto *(m)*

integração à grande escala *(f)* Pt
De Groβintegration *(f)*
En large-scale integration
Es integración en gran escala *(f)*
Fr intégration à grande échelle *(f)*
It integrazione su grande scala *(f)*

integración en gran escala *(f)* Es
De Grointegration *(f)*
En large-scale integration
Fr intégration à grande échelle *(f)*
It integrazione su grande scala *(f)*
Pt integração à grande escala *(f)*

integrador *(m) n* Es, Pt
De Integrator *(m)*
En integrator
Fr intégrateur *(m)*
It integratore *(m)*

integral memory En
De Integralspeicher *(m)*
Es memoria integral *(f)*
Fr mémoire intégrée *(f)*
It memoria integrale *(f)*
Pt memória integral *(f)*

Integralspeicher *(m) n* De
En integral memory
Es memoria integral *(f)*
Fr mémoire intégrée *(f)*
It memoria integrale *(f)*
Pt memória integral *(f)*

integrated circuit En
De integrierte Schaltung *(f)*
Es circuito integrado *(m)*
Fr circuit intégré *(m)*
It circuito integrato *(m)*
Pt circuito integrado *(m)*

integrated data processing (IDP) En
De integrierte Datenverarbeitung *(f)*
Es proceso integrado de datos *(m)*
Fr traitement intégré de l'information (TII) *(m)*
It elaborazione integrata dei dati *(f)*
Pt tratamento integrado de dados *(m)*

integrated injection logic En
De integrierte Injektionsverknüpfung *(f)*
Es lógica de inyección integrada *(f)*
Fr logique d'injection intégrée *(f)*
It logica di iniezione integrata *(f)*
Pt lógica de injecção integrada *(f)*

intégrateur *(m) n* Fr
De Integrator *(m)*
En integrator
Es integrador *(m)*
It integratore *(m)*
Pt integrador *(m)*

intégration à grande échelle *(f)* Fr
De Grosintegration *(f)*
En large-scale integration
Es integración en gran escala *(f)*
It integrazione su grande scala *(f)*
Pt integração à grande escala *(f)*

integrator *n* En
De Integrator *(m)*
Es integrador *(m)*
Fr intégrateur *(m)*
It integratore *(m)*
Pt integrador *(m)*

Integrator *(m) n* De
En integrator
Es integrador *(m)*
Fr intégrateur *(m)*
It integratore *(m)*
Pt integrador *(m)*

integratore *(m) n* It
De Integrator *(m)*
En integrator
Es integrador *(m)*
Fr intégrateur *(m)*
Pt integrador *(m)*

integrazione su grande scala *(f)* It
De Groβintegration *(f)*
En large-scale integration
Es integración en gran escala *(f)*
Fr intégration à grande échelle *(f)*
Pt integração à grande escala *(f)*

integridad *(f) n* Es
De Sicherheit *(f)*
En integrity
Fr intégrité *(f)*
It integrità *(f)*
Pt integridade *(f)*

integridade *(f) n* Pt
De Sicherheit *(f)*
En integrity
Es integridad *(f)*
Fr intégrité *(f)*
It integrità *(f)*

integrierte Datenverarbeitung *(f)* De
En integrated data processing (IDP)
Es proceso integrado de datos *(m)*
Fr traitement intégré de l'information (TII) *(m)*
It elaborazione integrata dei dati *(f)*
Pt tratamento integrado de dados *(m)*

integrierte Injektionsverknüpfung *(f)* De
En integrated injection logic
Es lógica de inyección integrada *(f)*
Fr logique d'injection intégrée *(f)*
It logica di iniezione integrata *(f)*
Pt lógica de injecção integrada *(f)*

integrierte Schaltung *(f)* De
En integrated circuit
Es circuito integrado *(m)*
Fr circuit intégré *(m)*

It circuito integrato *(m)*
Pt circuito integrado *(m)*

integrità *(f) n* It
De Sicherheit *(f)*
En integrity
Es integridad *(f)*
Fr intégrité *(f)*
Pt integridade *(f)*

intégrité *(f) n* Fr
De Sicherheit *(f)*
En integrity
Es integridad *(f)*
It integrità *(f)*
Pt integridade *(f)*

integrity *n* En
De Sicherheit *(f)*
Es integridad *(f)*
Fr intégrité *(f)*
It integrità *(f)*
Pt integridade *(f)*

inteligencia artificial *(f)* Es
De künstliche Intelligenz *(f)*
En artificial intelligence (AI)
Fr intelligence artificielle (IA) *(f)*
It intelligenza artificiale *(f)*
Pt inteligência artificial *(f)*

inteligência artificial *(f)* Pt
De künstliche Intelligenz *(f)*
En artificial intelligence (AI)
Es inteligencia artificial *(f)*
Fr intelligence artificielle (IA) *(f)*
It intelligenza artificiale *(f)*

inteligência da máquina *(f)* Pt
De Maschinen-programmierung *(f)*
En machine intelligence
Es inteligencia de máquina *(f)*
Fr intelligence-machine *(f)*
It intelligenza della macchina *(f)*

inteligencia de máquina *(f)* Es
De Maschinen-programmierung *(f)*
En machine intelligence
Fr intelligence-machine *(f)*
It intelligenza della macchina *(f)*
Pt inteligência da máquina *(f)*

intelligence artificielle (IA) *(f)* Fr
De künstliche Intelligenz *(f)*
En artificial intelligence (AI)
Es inteligencia artificial *(f)*
It intelligenza artificiale *(f)*
Pt inteligência artificial *(f)*

intelligence-machine *(f)* Fr
De Maschinen-programmierung *(f)*
En machine intelligence
Es inteligencia de máquina *(f)*
It intelligenza della macchina *(f)*
Pt inteligência da máquina *(f)*

intelligent terminal En
De programmierbare Station *(f)*
Es terminal inteligente *(m)*
Fr terminal intelligent *(m)*
It terminale intelligente *(m)*
Pt terminal inteligente *(m)*

intelligenza artificiale *(f)* It
De künstliche Intelligenz *(f)*
En artificial intelligence (AI)
Es inteligencia artificial *(f)*
Fr intelligence artificielle (IA) *(f)*
Pt inteligência artificial *(f)*

intelligenza della macchina *(f)* It
De Maschinen-programmierung *(f)*
En machine intelligence
Es inteligencia de máquina *(f)*
Fr intelligence-machine *(f)*
Pt inteligência da máquina *(f)*

interacção homem-máquina *(f)* Pt
De Personal-Maschinen Wechselwirkung *(f)*
En man-machine interaction
Es interacción hombre-máquina *(f)*
Fr interaction homme-machine *(f)*
It interazione uomo-macchina *(f)*

interacción hombre-máquina *(f)* Es
De Personal-Maschinen Wechselwirkung *(f)*
En man-machine interaction
Fr interaction homme-machine *(f)*
It interazione uomo-macchina *(f)*
Pt interacção homem-máquina *(f)*

interactif *adj* Fr
De interaktiv
En interactive
Es interactivo
It interattivo
Pt interactivo

interaction homme-machine *(f)* Fr
De Personal-Maschinen Wechselwirkung *(f)*
En man-machine interaction
Es interacción hombre-máquina *(f)*
It interazione uomo-macchina *(f)*
Pt interacção homem-máquina *(f)*

interactive *adj* En
De interaktiv
Es interactivo
Fr interactif
It interattivo
Pt interactivo

interactive computing En
De Dialogbetrieb *(m)*
Es cálculo interactivo *(m)*
Fr traitement interactif *(m)*
It calcoli interattivi *(m)*
Pt computação interactiva *(f)*

interactive display En
De Dialoganzeige *(f)*
Es representación interactiva *(f)*
Fr visualisation interactive *(f)*
It visualizzatore interattivo *(m)*
Pt visualização interactiva *(f)*

interactive mode En
De interaktive Betriebsart *(f)*
Es modo interactivo *(m)*
Fr mode interactif *(m)*
It modalità interattiva *(f)*
Pt modo interactivo *(m)*

interactive terminal En
De Dialogdatenstation *(f)*
Es terminal interactivo *(m)*
Fr terminal interactif *(m)*
It terminale interattivo *(m)*
Pt terminal interactivo *(m)*

interactivo *adj* Es, Pt
De interaktiv
En interactive
Fr interactif
It interattivo

interaktiv *adj* De
En interactive
Es interactivo
Fr interactif
It interattivo
Pt interactivo

interaktive Betriebsart *(f)* De
- En interactive mode
- Es modo interactivo *(m)*
- Fr mode interactif *(m)*
- It modalità interattiva *(f)*
- Pt modo interactivo *(m)*

interattivo *adj* It
- De interaktiv
- En interactive
- Es interactivo
- Fr interactif
- Pt interactivo

interazione uomo-macchina *(f)* It
- De Personal-Maschinen Wechselwirkung *(f)*
- En man-machine interaction
- Es interacción hombre-máquina *(f)*
- Fr interaction homme-machine *(f)*
- Pt interacção homem-máquina *(f)*

interbloccare *vb* It
- De verriegeln
- En interlock
- Es interbloquear
- Fr verrouiller
- Pt engrenar

interbloquear *vb* Es
- De verriegeln
- En interlock
- Fr verrouiller
- It interbloccare
- Pt engrenar

intercaladora *(f) n* Es
- De Kollationierer
- En collator
- Fr interclasseuse *(f)*
- It inseritrice *(f)*
- Pt conferidor *(m)*

intercalar *vb* Es
- De kollationieren
- En collate
- Fr interclasser
- It inserire
- Pt conferir

intercambiar *vb* Pt
- De vermitteln
- En exchange
- Es cambiar
- Fr intervenir
- It scambiare

intercambio *(m) n* Es
- De Vermittlung *(f)*
- En exchange
- Fr échange *(m)*
- It scambio *(m)*
- Pt intercâmbio *(m)*

intercâmbio *(m) n* Pt
- De Vermittlung *(f)*
- En exchange
- Es intercambio *(m)*
- Fr échange *(m)*
- It scambio *(m)*

interclasser *vb* Fr
- De kollationieren
- En collate
- Es intercalar
- It inserire
- Pt conferir

interclasseuse *(f) n* Fr
- De Kollationierer
- En collator
- Es intercaladora *(f)*
- It inseritrice *(f)*
- Pt conferidor *(m)*

interconnessione *(f) n* It
- De Verbindung *(f)*
- En linkage
- Es enlace *(m)*
- Fr lien *(m)*
- Pt ligação *(f)*

interfaccia *(f) n* It
- De Schnittstelle *(f)*
- En interface
- Es acoplamiento mutuo *(m)*
- Fr interface *(f)*
- Pt interface *(f)*

interfaccia del ciclo corrente *(f)* It
- De Stromschleifen-Schnittstelle *(f)*
- En current-loop interface
- Es acoplamiento mutuo por bucle de corriente *(m)*
- Fr interface boucle courant *(f)*
- Pt interface de circuito de corrente *(f)*

interfaccia di trasmissione *(f)* It
- De Übertragungs-schnittstelle *(f)*
- En transmission interface
- Es interfase de transmisión *(f)*
- Fr interface de transmission *(f)*
- Pt interface de transmissão *(f)*

interfaccia parallela *(f)* It
- De Parallelschnittstelle *(f)*
- En parallel interface
- Es interfase en paralelo *(f)*
- Fr interface en parallèle *(f)*
- Pt interface paralela *(f)*

interfaccia standard *(f)* It
- De Standardschnittstelle *(f)*
- En standard interface
- Es interfase normalizada *(f)*
- Fr interface normalisée *(f)*
- Pt interface standard *(f)*

interfaccia uomo-macchina *(f)* It
- De Personal-Maschinen Schnittstelle *(f)*
- En man-machine interface
- Es acoplamiento hombre-máquina *(m)*
- Fr interface homme-machine *(f)*
- Pt interface homem-máquina *(f)*

interface *n* En, Fr, Pt *(f)*
- De Schnittstelle *(f)*
- Es acoplamiento mutuo *(m)*
- It interfaccia *(f)*

interface boucle courant *(f)* Fr
- De Stromschleifen-Schnittztelle *(f)*
- En current-loop interface
- Es acoplamiento mutuo por bucle de corriente *(m)*
- It interfaccia del ciclo corrente *(f)*
- Pt interface de circuito de corrente *(f)*

interface de circuito de corrente *(f)* Pt
- De Stromschleifen-Schnittstelle *(f)*
- En current-loop interface
- Es acoplamiento mutuo por bucle de corriente *(m)*
- Fr interface boucle courant *(f)*
- It interfaccia del ciclo corrente *(f)*

interface de transmissão *(f)* Pt
- De Übertragungs-schnittstelle *(f)*
- En transmission interface
- Es interfase de transmisión *(f)*
- Fr interface de transmission *(f)*
- It interfaccia di trasmissione *(f)*

interface de transmission *(f)* Fr
- De Übertragungs-schnittstelle *(f)*
- En transmission interface
- Es interfase de transmisión *(f)*
- It interfaccia di trasmissione *(f)*
- Pt interface de transmissão *(f)*

interface en parallèle *(f)* Fr
- De Parallelschnittstelle *(f)*
- En parallel interface
- Es interfase en paralelo *(f)*
- It interfaccia parallela *(f)*
- Pt interface paralela *(f)*

interface homem-máquina *(f)* Pt
- De Personal-Maschinen Schnittstelle *(f)*
- En man-machine interface

Es acoplamiento hombre-máquina *(m)*
Fr interface homme-machine *(f)*
It interfaccia uomo-macchina *(f)*

interface homme-machine *(f)* Fr
De Personal-Maschinen Schnittstelle *(f)*
En man-machine interface
Es acoplamiento hombre-máquina *(m)*
It interfaccia uomo-macchina *(f)*
Pt interface homem-máquina *(f)*

interface normalisée *(f)* Fr
De Standardschnittstelle *(f)*
En standard interface
Es interfase normalizada *(f)*
It interfaccia standard *(f)*
Pt interface standard *(f)*

interface paralela *(f)* Pt
De Parallelschnittstelle *(f)*
En parallel interface
Es interfase en paralelo *(f)*
Fr interface en parallèle *(f)*
It interfaccia parallela *(f)*

interface standard *(f)* Pt
De Standardschnittstelle *(f)*
En standard interface
Es interfase normalizada *(f)*
Fr interface normalisée *(f)*
It interfaccia standard *(f)*

interfase de transmisión *(f)* Es
De Übertragungs-schnittstelle *(f)*
En transmission interface
Fr interface de transmission *(f)*
It interfaccia di trasmissione *(f)*
Pt interface de transmissão *(f)*

interfase en paralelo *(f)* Es
De Parallelschnittstelle *(f)*
En parallel interface
Fr interface en parallèle *(f)*
It interfaccia parallela *(f)*
Pt interface paralela *(f)*

interfase normalizada *(f)* Es
De Standardschnittstelle *(f)*
En standard interface
Fr interface normalisée *(f)*
It interfaccia standard *(f)*
Pt interface standard *(f)*

interfogliare *(m) n* It
De Verzahnung *(f)*
En interleaving
Es interfolición *(f)*
Fr interfoliage *(m)*
Pt interfolição *(f)*

interfoliage *(m) n* Fr
De Verzahnung *(f)*
En interleaving
Es interfolición *(f)*
It interfogliare *(m)*
Pt interfolição *(f)*

interfolição *(f) n* Pt
De Verzahnung *(f)*
En interleaving
Es interfolición *(f)*
Fr interfoliage *(m)*
It interfogliare *(m)*

interfolición *(f) n* Es
De Verzahnung *(f)*
En interleaving
Fr interfoliage *(m)*
It interfogliare *(m)*
Pt interfolição *(f)*

interleaving *n* En
De Verzahnung *(f)*
Es interfolición *(f)*
Fr interfoliage *(m)*
It interfogliare *(m)*
Pt interfolição *(f)*

interlock *vb* En
De verriegeln
Es interbloquear
Fr verrouiller
It interbloccare
Pt engrenar

intermediate storage En
De Zwischen-speicherung *(f)*
Es memoria intermedia *(f)*
Fr mémoire intermédiaire *(f)*
It memoria intermedia *(f)*
Pt armazenagem intermediária *(m)*

internal store En
De Innenspeicher *(m)*
Es memoria interna *(f)*
Fr mémoire interne *(f)*
It memoria interna *(f)*
Pt armazém interno *(m)*

interpolador *(m) n* Es, Pt
De Interpolator *(m)*
En interpolator
Fr interpolateur *(m)*
It interpolatore *(m)*

interpolateur *(m) n* Fr
De Interpolator *(m)*
En interpolator
Es interpolador *(m)*
It interpolatore *(m)*
Pt interpolador *(m)*

interpolator *n* En
De Interpolator *(m)*
Es interpolador *(m)*
Fr interpolateur *(m)*
It interpolatore *(m)*
Pt interpolador *(m)*

Interpolator *(m) n* De
En interpolator
Es interpolador *(m)*
Fr interpolateur *(m)*
It interpolatore *(m)*
Pt interpolador *(m)*

interpolatore *(m) n* It
De Interpolator *(m)*
En interpolator
Es interpolador *(m)*
Fr interpolateur *(m)*
Pt interpolador *(m)*

interpret *vb* En
De lochschrift-übersetzen
Es interpretar
Fr interpréter
It interpretare
Pt interpretar

interpretadora *(f) n* Es
De Lochschrift-übersetzer *(m)*
En interpreter
Fr traductrice *(f)*
It interprete *(m)*
Pt intérprete *(m)*

interpretar *vb* Es, Pt
De lochschrift-übersetzen
En interpret
Fr interpréter
It interpretare

interpretare *vb* It
De lochschrift-übersetzen
En interpret
Es interpretar
Fr interpréter
Pt interpretar

interprete *(m) n* It
De Lochschrift-übersetzer *(m)*
En interpreter
Es interpretadora *(f)*
Fr traductrice *(f)*
Pt intérprete *(m)*

intérprete *(m) n* Pt
De Lochschrift-übersetzer *(m)*
En interpreter
Es interpretadora *(f)*
Fr traductrice *(f)*
It interprete *(m)*

internpreter *n* En
De Lochschrift-übersetzer *(m)*
Es interpretadora *(f)*
Fr traductrice *(f)*
It interprete *(m)*
Pt intérprete *(m)*

interpréter *vb* Fr
De lochschrift-übersetzen
En interpret
Es interpretar

It interpretare
Pt interpretar

inter-record gap En
De Satzzwischenraum *(m)*
Es separación entre registros *(f)*
Fr espace interbloc *(m)*
It distanza tra i record *(f)*
Pt intervalo entre registos *(m)*

interromper *vb* Pt
De unterbrechen
En interrupt
Es interrumpir
Fr interrompre
It interrompere

interrompere *vb* It
De unterbrechen
En interrupt
Es interrumpir
Fr interrompre
Pt interromper

interrompre *vb* Fr
De unterbrechen
En interrupt
Es interrumpir
It interrompere
Pt interromper

interrumpir *vb* Es
De unterbrechen
En interrupt
Fr interrompre
It interrompere
Pt interromper

interrupção *(f) n* Pt
De Unterbrechung *(f)*
En interrupt
Es interrupción *(f)*
Fr interruption *(f)*
It interruzione *(f)*

interrupção automática *(f)* Pt
De automatische Unterbrechung *(f)*
En automatic interrupt
Es interrupción automática *(f)*
Fr interruption automatique *(f)*
It interruzione automatica *(f)*

interrupción *(f) n* Es
De Unterbrechung *(f)*
En interrupt
Fr interruption *(f)*
It interruzione *(f)*
Pt interrupção *(f)*

interrupción automática *(f)* Es
De automatische Unterbrechung *(f)*
En automatic interrupt
Fr interruption automatique *(f)*
It interruzione automatica *(f)*
Pt interrupção automática *(f)*

interrupt *n* En
De Unterbrechung *(f)*
Es interrupción *(f)*
Fr interruption *(f)*
It interruzione *(f)*
Pt interrupção *(f)*

interrupt *vb* En
De unterbrechen
Es interrumpir
Fr interrompre
It interrompere
Pt interromper

interrupteur *(m) n* Fr
De Schalter *(m)*
En switch
Es conmutador *(m)*
It interruttore *(m)*
Pt comutador *(m)*

interruption *(f) n* Fr
De Unterbrechung *(f)*
En interrupt
Es interrupción *(f)*
It interruzione *(f)*
Pt interrupção *(f)*

interruption automatique *(f)* Fr
De automatische Unterbrechung *(f)*
En automatic interrupt
Es interrupción automática *(f)*
It interruzione automatica *(f)*
Pt interrupção automática *(f)*

interruption prioritaire *(f)* Fr
De Unterbrechungs-priorität *(f)*
En interrupt priority
Es prioridad de interrupción *(f)*
It priorità di interruzione *(f)*
Pt prioridade de interrupção *(f)*

interrupt priority En
De Unterbrechungs-priorität *(f)*
Es prioridad de interrupción *(f)*
Fr interruption prioritaire *(f)*
It priorità di interruzione *(f)*
Pt prioridade de interrupção *(f)*

interruttore *(m) n* It
De Schalter *(m)*
En switch
Es conmutador *(m)*
Fr interrupteur *(m)*
Pt comutador *(m)*

interruttore elettronico *(m)* It
De elektronischer Schalter *(m)*
En electronic switch
Es conmutador electrónico *(m)*
Fr bascule électronique *(f)*
Pt comutador electrónico *(m)*

interruzione *(f) n* It
De Unterbrechung *(f)*
En interrupt
Es interrupción *(f)*
Fr interruption *(f)*
Pt interrupção *(f)*

interruzione automatica *(f)* It
De automatische Unterbrechung *(f)*
En automatic interrupt
Es interrupción automática *(f)*
Fr interruption automatique *(f)*
Pt interrupção automática *(f)*

intersystem communications *n pl* En
De Zwischensystem-Verbindungswege *(pl)*
Es comunicaciones entre sistemas *(f pl)*
Fr transmission inter-système *(f)*
It comunicazioni tra sistemi *(f pl)*
Pt comunicações entre sistemas *(f pl)*

intervalle *(m) n* Fr
De Spalte *(f)*
En gap
Es intervalo *(m)*
It intervallo *(m)*
Pt intervalo *(m)*

intervallo *(m) n* It
De Spalte *(f)*
En gap
Es intervalo *(m)*
Fr intervalle *(m)*
Pt intervalo *(m)*

intervalo *(m) n* Es, Pt
De Spalte *(f)*
En gap
Fr intervalle *(m)*
It intervallo *(m)*

intervalo de cabeça *(m)* Pt
De Magnetkopfspalt *(m)*
En head gap
Es entrehierro *(m)*
Fr entrefer *(m)*
It distanza dalla testina *(f)*

intervalo entre registos *(m)* Pt
De Satzzwischenraum *(m)*
En inter-record gap
Es separación entre registros *(f)*
Fr espace interbloc *(m)*
It distanza tra i record *(f)*

intervenir *vb* Fr
De vermitteln
En exchange
Es cambiar
It scambiare
Pt intercambiar

intrappolare *vb* It
De fangen
En trap
Es entrampar
Fr piéger
Pt apanhar

introducir *vb* Es
De eingeben
En input
Fr entrer
It immettere
Pt entrar

introducir desde teclado Es
De eintasten
En keyboard
Fr introduire par clavier
It introdurre (dati) mediante la tastiera
Pt introduzir desde teclado

introduction manuelle *(f)* Fr
De Handeingabe *(f)*
En manual input
Es entrada manual *(f)*
It input manuale *(m)*
Pt input manual *(m)*

introduire par clavier Fr
De eintasten
En keyboard
Es introducir desde teclado
It introdurre (dati) mediante la tastiera
Pt introduzir desde teclado

introdurre (dati) mediante la tastiera It
De eintasten
En keyboard
Es introducir desde teclado
Fr introduire par clavier
Pt introduzir desde teclado

introduzir desde teclado Pt
De eintasten
En keyboard
Es introducir desde teclado
Fr introduire par clavier
It introdurre (dati) mediante la tastiera

inversão *(f) n* Pt
De Inversion *(f)*
En inversion
Es inversión *(f)*
Fr inversion *(f)*
It inversione *(f)*

inversão de matriz *(f)* Pt
De Matrizeninversion *(f)*
En matrix inversion
Es inversión de matriz *(f)*
Fr inversion matricielle *(f)*
It inversione di matrice *(f)*

inverser *vb* Fr
De invertieren
En invert
Es invertir
It invertire
Pt inverter

inverseur *(m) n* Fr
De Binärinverter *(m)*
En inverter
Es inversor *(m)*
It invertitore *(m)*
Pt inversor *(m)*

inversion *n* En, Fr *(f)*
De Inversion *(f)*
Es inversión *(f)*
It inversione *(f)*
Pt inversão *(f)*

Inversion *(f) n* De
En inversion
Es inversión *(f)*
Fr inversion *(f)*
It inversione *(f)*
Pt inversão *(f)*

inversión *(f) n* Es
De Inversion *(f)*
En inversion
Fr inversion *(f)*
It inversione *(f)*
Pt inversão *(f)*

inversión de matriz *(f)* Es
De Matrizeninversion *(f)*
En matrix inversion
Fr inversion matricielle *(f)*
It inversione di matrice *(f)*
Pt inversão de matriz *(f)*

inversione *(f) n* It
De Inversion *(f)*
En inversion
Es inversión *(f)*
Fr inversion *(f)*
Pt inversão *(f)*

inversione di matrice *(f)* It
De Matrizeninversion *(f)*
En matrix inversion
Es inversión de matriz *(f)*
Fr inversion matricielle *(f)*
Pt inversão de matriz *(f)*

inversion matricielle *(f)* Fr
De Matrizeninversion *(f)*
En matrix inversion
Es inversión de matriz *(f)*
It inversione di matrice *(f)*
Pt inversão de matriz *(f)*

inversor *(m) n* Es, Pt
De Binärinverter *(m)*
En inverter
Fr inverseur *(m)*
It invertitore *(m)*

invert *vb* En
De invertieren
Es invertir
Fr inverser
It invertire
Pt inverter

inverter *n* En
De Binärinverter *(m)*
Es inversor *(m)*
Fr inverseur *(m)*
It invertitore *(m)*
Pt inversor *(m)*

inverter *vb* Pt
De invertieren
En invert
Es invertir
Fr inverser
It invertire

invertieren *vb* De
En invert
Es invertir
Fr inverser
It invertire
Pt inverter

invertir *vb* Es
De invertieren
En invert
Fr inverser
It invertire
Pt inverter

invertire *vb* It
De invertieren
En invert
Es invertir
Fr inverser
Pt inverter

invertitore *(m) n* It
De Binärinverter *(m)*
En inverter
Es inversor *(m)*
Fr inverseur *(m)*
Pt inversor *(m)*

investigação operacional *(f)* Pt
De Unternehmungsforschung *(f)*
En operational research (OR)
Es investigación operativa *(f)*
Fr recherche opérationnelle *(f)*
It ricerca operativa *(f)*

investigación operativa *(f)* Es
De Unternehmungsforschung *(f)*
En operational research (OR)
Fr recherche opérationnelle *(f)*
It ricerca operativa *(f)*
Pt investigação operacional *(f)*

investigar *vb* Es
De suchen
En search
Fr chercher
It ricercare
Pt procurar

istruzione *(f) n* It
De Anweisung; Befehl *(f m)*
En instruction
Es instrucción *(f)*
Fr instruction *(f)*
Pt instrução *(f)*

istruzione ad indirizzo multiplo *(f)* It
De Mehrfachadress-befehl *(m)*
En multiple-address instruction
Es instrucción de direcciones múltiples *(f)*
Fr instruction multi-adresse *(f)*
Pt instrução de endereço múltiplo *(f)*

istruzione ad indirizzo singolo *(f)* It
De Einzeladress-anweisung *(f)*
En single-address instruction
Es instrucción de una sola dirección *(f)*
Fr instruction à une adresse *(f)*
Pt instrução de endereço único *(f)*

istruzione ad indirizzo zero *(f)* It
De Nulladressen-anweisung *(f)*
En zero-address instruction
Es instrucción de dirección cero *(f)*
Fr instruction sans adresse *(f)*
Pt instrução de endereço zero *(f)*

istruzione a due indirizzi *(f)* It
De Zweiadressen-anweisung *(f)*
En two-address instruction
Es instrucción con dos direcciones *(f)*
Fr instruction à deux adresses *(f)*
Pt instrução de dois endereços *(f)*

istruzione a non indirizzo *(f)* It
De Kein-Adressenbefehl *(m)*
En no-address instruction
Es instrucción sin dirección *(f)*
Fr instruction sans adresse *(f)*
Pt instrução de não-endereço *(f)*

istruzione aritmetica *(f)* It
De arithmetische Anweisung *(f)*
En arithmetic instruction
Es instrucción aritmética *(f)*
Fr instruction arithmétique *(f)*
Pt instrução aritmética *(f)*

istruzione a tre indirizzi *(f)* It
De Dreiadressen-anweisung *(f)*
En three-address instruction
Es instrucción con tres direcciones *(f)*
Fr instruction à trois adresses *(f)*
Pt instrução de três endereços *(f)*

istruzione basata sull'elaboratore *(f)* It
De computerunter-stützter Unterricht *(m)*
En computer-aided instruction
Es instrucción com la ayuda de ordenador *(f)*
Fr enseignement assisté par ordinateur *(m)*
Pt instrução auxiliada por computador *(f)*

istruzione del punto di arresto *(f)* It
De Ausgleichspunkt-befehl *(m)*
En breakpoint instruction
Es instrucción de punto de interrupción *(f)*
Fr instruction de point de rupture *(f)*
Pt instruções de ponto de rotura *(f)*

istruzione di diramazione *(f)* It
De Verzweigungsbefehl *(m)*
En branch instruction
Es instrucción de bifurcación *(f)*
Fr instruction de branchement *(f)*
Pt instruções para ligar *(f)*

istruzione di diramazione condizionale *(f)* It
De bedingter Verzweigungsbefehl *(m)*
En conditional branch instruction
Es instrucción de bifurcación condicional *(f)*
Fr instruction de branchement conditionnelle *(f)*
Pt instrução de ramificação condicional *(f)*

istruzione di diramazione non condizionale *(f)* It
De unbedingte Verzweigungs-anweisung *(f)*
En unconditional branch instruction
Es instrucción de bifurcación incondicional *(f)*
Fr instruction de branchement inconditionnel *(f)*
Pt instrução de ramo incondicional *(f)*

istruzione di ripetizione *(f)* It
De Wiederholungsbefehl *(m)*
En repetition instruction
Es instrucción de repetición *(f)*
Fr répertoire d'instructions *(m)*
Pt instrução de repetição *(f)*

istruzione di ritorno *(f)* It
De Rücklaufanweisung *(f)*
En return instruction
Es instrucción de retorno *(f)*
Fr instruction de retour *(f)*
Pt instrução de regresso *(f)*

istruzione di trasferimento *(f)* It
De Übertragungs-anweisung *(f)*
En transfer instruction
Es instrucción de transferencia *(f)*
Fr instruction de branchement *(f)*
Pt instrução de transferência *(f)*

istruzione fittizia *(f)* It
De Blindbefehl *(m)*
En dummy instruction
Es instrucción ficticia *(f)*
Fr instruction fictive *(f)*
Pt instrução simulada *(f)*

istruzioni di avviamento *(f)* It
De Startroutine *(f)*
En bootstrap
Es autocargador *(m)*
Fr amorce *(f)*
Pt bootstrap *(m)*

item de dados *(m)* Pt
De Datenfeld *(n)*
En data item
Es unidad de información *(f)*
Fr donnée élémentaire *(f)*
It voce di dato *(f)*

item design En
De Datenfeld-konstruktion *(f)*
Es diseño de elementos *(m)*
Fr définition du découpage des articles *(f)*
It disegno dell voci *(m)*
Pt desenho de item *(m)*

iteração *(f)* *n* Pt
De Wiederholung *(f)*
En iteration
Es iteración *(f)*
Fr itération *(f)*
It iterazione *(f)*

iteración *(f)* *n* Es
De Wiederholung *(f)*
En iteration
Fr itération *(f)*

It iterazione *(f)*
Pt iteração *(f)*

itératif *adj* Fr
De wiederholend
En iterative
Es iterativo
It iterativo
Pt iterativo

iteration *n* En
De Wiederholung *(f)*
Es iteración *(f)*
Fr itération *(f)*
It iterazione *(f)*
Pt iteração *(f)*

itération *(f) n* Fr
De Wiederholung *(f)*
En iteration
Es iteración *(f)*
It iterazione *(f)*
Pt iteração *(f)*

iterative *adj* En
De wiederholend
Es iterativo
Fr itératif
It iterativo
Pt iterativo

iterativo *adj* Es, It, Pt
De wiederholend
En iterative
Fr itératif

iterazione *(f) n* It
De Wiederholung *(f)*
En iteration
Es iteración *(f)*
Fr itération *(f)*
Pt iteração *(f)*

itinéraire *(m) n* Fr
De Leitweg *(m)*
En route
Es ruta *(f)*
It pista *(f)*
Pt caminho *(m)*

J

jam *n* En
De Verklemmung *(f)*
Es atascamiento *(m)*
Fr bourrage *(m)*
It inceppamento *(m)*
Pt congestionamento *(m)*

jerarquizar *vb* Es
De schachteln
En nest
Fr emboîter
It nidificare
Pt aninhar

jeu de caractères *(m)* Fr
De Zeichensatz *(m)*
En character set
Es juego de caracteres *(m)*
It gruppo di caratteri *(m)*
Pt jogo de caracteres *(m)*

jeu d'instructions *(m)* Fr
De Befehlsvorrat *(m)*
En instruction set
Es juego de instrucciones *(m)*
It gruppo di istruzioni *(m)*
Pt conjunto de instruções *(m)*

job *n* En
De Job *(m)*
Es trabajo *(m)*
Fr travail *(m)*
It lavoro *(m)*
Pt trabalho *(m)*

Job *(m) n* De
En job
Es trabajo *(m)*
Fr travail *(m)*
It lavoro *(m)*
Pt trabalho *(m)*

job control language (JCL) En
De Jobkontrollsprache *(f)*
Es lenguaje de control de trabajos *(m)*
Fr langage de contrôle de travaux (LCT) *(m)*
It linguaggio di controllo del lavoro *(m)*
Pt linguagem de controle de trabalho *(f)*

job control system En
De Jobkontrollsystem *(n)*
Es sistema de control de trabajos *(m)*
Fr système de contrôle des travaux *(m)*
It sistema di controllo olei lavori *(m)*
Pt sistema de controle de trabalho *(m)*

Jobfernverarbeitung *(f) n* De
En remote job entry
Es entrada de trabajos a distancia *(f)*
Fr télésoumission de travaux *(f)*
It entrata del lavoro a distanza *(f)*
Pt entrada de trabalho remota *(f)*

Jobkontrollsprache *(f) n* De
En job control language (JCL)
Es lenguaje de control de trabajos *(m)*
Fr langage de contrôle de travaux (LCT) *(m)*
It linguaggio di controllo del lavoro *(m)*
Pt linguagem de controle de trabalho *(f)*

Jobkontrollsystem *(n) n* De
En job control system
Es sistema de control de trabajos *(m)*
Fr système de contrôle des travaux *(m)*
It sistema di controllo olei lavori *(m)*
Pt sistema de controle de trabalho *(m)*

job scheduler En
De Jobscheduler *(m)*
Es planificador de trabajos *(m)*
Fr programmateur des travaux *(m)*
It pianificatore dei lavoratori *(m)*
Pt planificador de trabalhos *(m)*

Jobscheduler *(m) n* De
En job scheduler
Es planificador de trabajos *(m)*
Fr programmateur des travaux *(m)*
It pianificatore dei lavoratori *(m)*
Pt planificador de trabalhos *(m)*

jogo de caracteres *(m)* Pt
De Zeichensatz *(m)*
En character set
Es juego de caracteres *(m)*
Fr jeu de caractères *(m)*
It gruppo di caratteri *(m)*

join *vb* En
De zusammenfügen
Es unir
Fr grouper
It unire
Pt unir

Journal *(n) n* De
En log
Es registro *(m)*
Fr consignation *(f)*
It registro *(m)*
Pt diário *(m)*

juego de caracteres *(m)* Es
De Zeichensatz *(m)*
En character set
Fr jeu de caractères *(m)*
It gruppo di caratteri *(m)*
Pt jogo de caracteres *(m)*

juego de instrucciones *(m)* Es
De Befehlsvorrat *(m)*
En instruction set
Fr jeu d'instructions *(m)*
It gruppo di istruzioni *(m)*

Pt conjunto de instruções *(m)*

jump *n* En
De Sprung *(m)*
Es salto *(m)*
Fr saut *(m)*
It salto *(m)*
Pt salto *(m)*

jump *vb* En
De überspringen
Es saltar
Fr sauter
It saltare
Pt saltar

justificado à direita Pt
De rechtsbündig
En right-justified
Es justificado a la derecha
Fr cadré à droite
It giustificato a destra

justificado à esquerda Pt
De linksbündig
En left-justified
Es justificado a la izquierda
Fr cadré à gauche
It giustificato a sinistra

justificado a la derecha Es
De rechtsbündig
En right-justified
Fr cadré à droite
It giustificato a destra
Pt justificado à direita

justificado a la izquierda Es
De linksbündig
En left-justified
Fr cadré à gauche
It giustificato a sinistra
Pt justificado à esquerda

justificar *vb* Es, Pt
De bündig machen
En justify
Fr justifier
It giustificare

justifier *vb* Fr
De bündig machen
En justify
Es justificar
It giustificare
Pt justificar

justify *vb* En
De bündig machen
Es justificar
Fr justifier
It giustificare
Pt justificar

K

Kanal *(m) n* De
En channel
Es canal *(m)*
Fr canal *(m)*
It canale *(m)*
Pt canal *(m)*

Kapazität *(f) n* De
En capacity
Es capacidad *(f)*
Fr capacité *(f)*
It capacità *(f)*
Pt capacidade *(f)*

Karte *(f) n* De
En card
Es ficha *(f)*
Fr carte *(f)*
It scheda *(f)*
Pt ficha *(f)*

Kartenkorb *(m) n* De
En card cage
Es caja de fichas *(f)*
Fr porte-carte *(m)*
It scatola schede *(f)*
Pt gaiola de ficha *(f)*

Kartenleser *(m) n* De
En card reader
Es lectora de fichas *(f)*
Fr lecteur de cartes *(m)*
It lettore di schede *(m)*
Pt leitor de fichas *(m)*

Kartenlocher *(m) n* De
En card punch
Es perforadora de fichas *(f)*
Fr perforatrice de cartes *(f)*
It perforatrice di schede *(f)*
Pt perfuradora de ficha *(f)*

Kartenprüfung *(f) n* De
En card verifying
Es verificación de fichas *(f)*
Fr vérification de cartes *(f)*
It verifica delle schede *(f)*
Pt verificação de fichas *(f)*

Kartensatz *(m) n* De
Am deck (of cards)
En pack (of cards)
Es baraja *(f)*
Fr paquet de cartes *(m)*
It mazzo *(m)*
Pt baralho (de cartas) *(m)*

Kaskadenprogramme *(pl) n* De
En cascaded programs
Es programas en cascada *(m pl)*
Fr programmes en cascade *(m pl)*
It programmi in cascata *(m pl)*
Pt programas em cascada *(m pl)*

Kassette *(f) n* De
En cassette
Es cassette *(f)*
Fr cassette *(f)*
It cassetta *(f)*
Pt cassette *(f)*

Kathodenstrahlröhre *(f) n* De
En cathode-ray tube (CRT)
Es tubo de rayos catódicos (TRC) *(m)*
Fr tube à rayons cathodiques *(m)*
It tubo a raggi catodici *(m)*
Pt válvula catódica *(f)*

Kein-Adressenbefehl *(m)* De
En no-address instruction
Es instrucción sin dirección *(f)*
Fr instruction sans adresse *(f)*
It istruzione a non indirizzo *(f)*
Pt instrução de não-endereço *(f)*

Kennsatz *(m) n* De
En header
Es cabecera *(f)*
Fr en-tête *(f)*
It testata *(f)*
Pt porta-cabeças *(m)*

Kennwort *(n) n* De
En password
Es contraseña *(f)*
Fr mot de passe *(m)*
It parola d'ordine *(f)*
Pt contra-senha *(f)*

Kennzeichen *(n) n* De
En mark
Es marca *(f)*
Fr marque *(f)*
It marca *(f)*
Pt marca *(f)*

Kennzeichenabtastung *(f) n* De
En mark scanning
Es exploración de marcas *(f)*
Fr lecture optique de marques *(f)*
It scansione di marcature *(f)*
Pt exploração de marca *(f)*

Kennzeichenfühlung *(f) n* De
En mark sensing
Es lectura de marcas *(f)*
Fr lecture de marques *(f)*
It lettura di marcature *(f)*
Pt determinacáo da marco *(f)*

Kennzeichner *(m) n* De
En marker
Es marcador *(m)*
Fr repère *(m)*
It identificativo *(m)*
Pt marcador *(m)*

Kennzeichnung *(f) n* De
En designation
Es indicación *(f)*
Fr indication *(f)*
It designazione *(f)*
Pt designação *(f)*

Kern *(m) n* De
En core
Es núcleo *(m)*
Fr mémoire centrale *(f)*
It memoria centrale *(f)*
Pt núcleo *(m)*

Kernspeicher *(m) n* De
En core memory; store
Es memoria de núcleos *(f)*
Fr mémoire à tores *(f)*
It memoria a nuclei *(f)*
Pt memória de núcleo *(f)*

Kette *(f) n* De
En chain
Es cadena *(f)*
Fr chaîne *(f)*
It catena *(f)*
Pt cadeia *(f)*

Kettencode *(m) n* De
En chain code
Es código en cadena *(m)*
Fr code à enchaînement *(m)*
It codice di catena *(m)*
Pt código de cadeia *(m)*

Kettendrucker *(m) n* De
En chain printer
Es impresora de cadena *(f)*
F imprimante à chaîne *(f)*
It stampatrice a catena *(f)*
Pt impressora de cadeia *(f)*

Kettensatz *(m) n* De
En chained record
Es registro en cadena *(m)*
Fr enregistrement en chaîne *(m)*
It record concatenato *(m)*
Pt registo com cadeia *(m)*

Kettensuche *(f) n* De
En chaining search
Es búsqueda de la cadena *(f)*
Fr recherche par chaînage *(f)*
It ricerca concatenata *(f)*
Pt busca de cadeia *(f)*

key *n* En
De Schlüssel *(m)*
Es tecla *(f)*
Fr touche *(f)*
It tasto *(m)*
Pt tecla *(f)*

keyboard *n* En
De Tastatur *(m)*
Es teclado *(m)*
Fr clavier *(m)*
It tastiera *(f)*
Pt teclado *(m)*

keyboard *vb* En
De eintasten
Es introducir desde teclado
Fr introduire par clavier
It introdurre (dati) mediante la tastiera
Pt introduzir desde teclado

key punch En
De Locher mit Tastatur *(m)*
Es perforadora de tecla *(f)*
Fr perforatrice à clavier *(f)*
It perforatrice a tastiera *(f)*
Pt perfuradora de tecla *(f)*

key-to-disk En
De Taste auf Platte
Es registro sobre disco
Fr enregistrement sur disque
It registrazione su disco
Pt tecla-ao-disco

key-to-tape En
De Taste auf Band
Es registro sobre cinta
Fr enregistrement sur bande
It registrazione su nastro magnetico
Pt tecla-à-fita

keyword *n* En
De Schlüsselwort *(n)*
Es palabra clave *(f)*
Fr mot-clé *(m)*
It parola chiave *(f)*
Pt palavra chave *(f)*

kieloben *adj* De
En bottom-up
Es boca-abajo
Fr ascendant
It sottosopra
Pt fundo para cima

kilobit *n* En; Es, Fr, Pt *(m)*
De Kilobit *(m)*
It chilobit *(m)*

Kilobit *(m) n* De
En kilobit
Es kilobit *(m)*
Fr kilobit *(m)*
It chilobit *(m)*
Pt kilobit *(m)*

kilobyte *n* En, Pt *(m)*
De Kilobyte *(m)*
Es kilo-octeto *(m)*
Fr kilomultiplet *(m)*
It chilobyte *(m)*

Kilobyte *(m) n* De
En kilobyte
Es kilo-octeto *(m)*
Fr kilomultiplet *(m)*
It chilobyte *(m)*
Pt kilobyte *(m)*

kilo core seconds (KCS) En
De Kilokern Sekunden *(pl)*
Es kilonúcleo segundos *(m pl)*
Fr kilo tores secondes (KTS) *(f pl)*
It chilo secondi di memoria *(m pl)*
Pt kilo core segundos *(m pl)*

kilo core segundos *(m pl)* Pt
De Kilokern Sekunden *(pl)*
En kilo core seconds (KCS)
Es kilonúcleo segundos *(m pl)*
Fr kilo tores secondes (KTS) *(f pl)*
It chilo secondi di memoria *(m pl)*

Kilokern Sekunden *(pl)* De
En kilo core seconds (KCS)
Es kilonúcleo segundos *(m pl)*
Fr kilo tores secondes (KTS) *(f pl)*
It chilo secondi di memoria *(m pl)*
Pt kilo core segundos *(m pl)*

kilomultiplet *(m) n* Fr
De Kilobyte *(m)*
En kilobyte
Es kilo-octeto *(m)*
It chilobyte *(m)*
Pt kilobyte *(m)*

kilonúcleo segundos *(m pl)* Es
De Kilokern Sekunden *(pl)*
En kilo core seconds (KCS)
Fr kilo tores secondes (KTS) *(f pl)*
It chilo secondi di memoria *(m pl)*
Pt kilo core segundos *(m pl)*

kilo-octeto *(m) n* Es
De Kilobyte *(m)*
En kilobyte
Fr kilomultiplet *(m)*
It chilobyte *(m)*
Pt kilobyte *(m)*

kilo tores secondes (KTS) *(f pl)* Fr
De Kilokern Sekunden *(pl)*
En kilo core seconds (KCS)
Es kilonúcleo segundos *(m pl)*
It chilo secondi di memoria *(m pl)*
Pt kilo core segundos *(m pl)*

Klebegerät *(n) n* De
En splicer
Es empalmadora *(f)*
Fr colleuse de bandes *(f)*

It incollatrice *(f)*
Pt emendador *(m)*

Kleinsignalsprache *(f) n* De
En low-level language
Es lenguaje de bajo nivel *(m)*
Fr langage bas de gamme *(m)*
It linguaggio di basso livello *(m)*
Pt linguagem de baixo nível *(f)*

Knotenpunkt *(m) n* De
En node
Es nodo *(m)*
Fr noeud *(m)*
It nodo *(m)*
Pt nó *(m)*

kodieren *vb* De
En code; encode
Es codificar
Fr coder
It codificare
Pt codificar

Kodierung *(f) n* De
En coding
Es codificación *(f)*
Fr codage *(m)*
It codificazione *(f)*
Pt codificação *(f)*

Kodierungsprüfung *(f) n* De
En coding check
Es verificación de la codificación *(f)*
Fr contrôle de codage *(m)*
It controllo di codificazione *(m)*
Pt verificação de codificação *(f)*

kollationieren *vb* De
En collate
Es intercalar
Fr interclasser
It inserire
Pt conferir

Kollationierer *(m)*
En collator
Es intercaladora *(f)*
Fr interclasseuse *(f)*
It inseritrice *(f)*
Pt conferidor *(m)*

Kommentar *(m) n* De
En comment
Es comentario *(m)*
Fr commentaire *(m)*
It commento *(m)*
Pt comentário *(m)*

Kommunikation *(f) n* De
En communication
Es comunicación *(f)*
Fr communication *(f)*
It comunicazione *(f)*
Pt comunicação *(f)*

Kommunikationskanal *(m) n* De
En communication channel
Es canal de comunicación *(m)*
Fr voie de communication *(f)*
It canale di comunicazione *(m)*
Pt canal de comunicação *(m)*

Kommunikationsnetz *(n) n* De
En communication network
Es red de comunicaciones *(f)*
Fr réseau de communication *(m)*
It rete di comunicazione *(f)*
Pt rede de comunicação *(f)*

Kommunikationssystem *(n) n* De
En communication system
Es sistema de comunicaciones *(m)*
Fr système de communication *(m)*
It sistema di comunicazione *(m)*
Pt sistema de comunicaćão *(m)*

kompilieren *vb* De
En compile
Es compilar
Fr compiler
It compilare
Pt compilar

Kompilierer *(m) n* De
En compiler
Es compilador *(m)*
Fr compilateur *(m)*
It compilatore *(m)*
Pt compilador *(m)*

Kompilierung *(f) n* De
En compilation
Es compilación *(f)*
Fr compilation *(f)*
It compilazione *(f)*
Pt compilação *(f)*

komplementäre Funktion *(f)* De
En complementary operation
Es operación complementaria *(f)*
Fr opération complémentaire *(f)*
It operazione complementare *(f)*
Pt operação complementar *(f)*

komplementäres MOS *(n)* De
En complementary MOS
Es MOS suplementario *(m)*
Fr MOS complémentaire *(m)*
It MOS complementare *(m)*
Pt MOS complementar *(m)*

Konfiguration *(f) n* De
En configuration
Es configuración *(f)*
Fr configuration *(f)*
It configurazione *(f)*
Pt configuração *(f)*

Konjunktion *(f) n* De
En conjunction
Es conjunción *(f)*
Fr conjonction *(f)*
It congiunzione *(f)*
Pt conjunção *(f)*

Konsolenschreibmaschine *(f) n* De
En console typewriter
Es máquina de escribir de consola *(f)*
Fr machine à écrire de pupitre *(f)*
It macchina da scrivere a console *(f)*
Pt máquina de escrever de consola *(f)*

Konstantbereich *(m) n* De
En constant area
Es área constante *(f)*
Fr aire constante *(f)*
It area costante *(f)*
Pt área constante *(f)*

Konstante *(pl) n* De
En constants
Es constantes *(f pl)*
Fr constantes *(f pl)*
It costanti *(m pl)*
Pt constantes *(f pl)*

Kontrolle der Konsistenz *(f)* De
En consistency check
Es control de uniformidad *(m)*
Fr contrôle de cohérence *(m)*
It controllo di consistenza *(m)*
Pt verificação de congruência *(f)*

kontrollieren *vb* De
En monitor
Es examinar
Fr surveiller
It esaminare
Pt vigiar

Kontrollpunkt *(m) n* De
En checkpoint
Es punto de control *(m)*
Fr point de contrôle *(m)*
It punto di controllo *(m)*
Pt ponto de verificação *(m)*

Kontrollsumme *(f) n* De
En control total; proof total
Es total de control *(m)*
Fr total de contrôle *(m)*
It totale di controllo *(m)*
Pt total de controlo *(m)*

Kontroll-Summenfeld *(n)* De
En accumulator
Es acumulador *(m)*
Fr accumulateur *(m)*
It accumulatore *(m)*
Pt acumulador *(m)*

Kontrollzeit *(f) n* De
En proving time
Es tiempo de ensayo *(m)*
Fr durée d´essai de fonctionnement *(f)*
It tempo di prova *(m)*
Pt tempo de prova *(m)*

kopieren *vb* De
En copy
Es copiar
Fr copier
It copiare
Pt copiar

Kopierer *(m) n* De
En reproducer
Es reproductor *(m)*
Fr reproductrice *(f)*
It riproduttore *(m)*
Pt reprodutor *(m)*

Korrektur *(f) n* De
En patch
Es parche *(m)*
Fr correction *(f)*
It connessione *(f)*
Pt remendo *(m)*

korrigieren (ein Programm) De
En patch
Es parchear un programa
Fr corriger un programme
It correggere un programma
Pt remendar uma programa

kryogenischer Speicher *(m)* De
En cryogenic memory
Es memoria criogénica *(f)*
Fr mémoire cryogénique *(f)*
It memoria criogenica *(f)*
Pt memória criogénica *(f)*

Kugel *(f) n* De
En bead
Es perla *(f)*
Fr perle *(f)*
It perla *(f)*
Pt boleado *(m)*

Kugelkopfdrucker *(m) n* De
En golfball printer
Es impresora de esfera *(f)*
Fr imprimante à sphère *(f)*
It stampatrice a pallina *(f)*
Pt impressora de bola de golf *(f)*

Kundenabnahmeprüfung *(f) n* De
En customer-acceptance test
Es ensayo de aceptación por el cliente *(m)*
Fr test de réception en clientèle *(m)*
It controllo accettazione clienti *(m)*
Pt teste de aceitação de cliente *(m)*

künstliche Intelligenz *(f)* De
En artificial intelligence (AI)
Es inteligencia artificial *(f)*
Fr intelligence artificielle (IA) *(f)*
It intelligenza artificiale *(f)*
Pt inteligência artificial *(f)*

künstliche Sprache *(f)* De
En synthetic language
Es lenguaje sintético *(m)*
Fr langage synthétique *(m)*
It linguaggio sintetico *(m)*
Pt linguagem sintética *(f)*

Kurvenzeichner *(m) n* De
En graph plotter
Es trazador de curvas *(m)*
Fr traceur de courbes *(m)*
It tracciatore di grafici *(m)*
Pt plotador de gráficos *(m)*

Kybernetik *(f) n* De
En cybernetics
Es cibernética *(f)*
Fr cybernétique *(f)*
It cibernetica *(f)*
Pt cibernética *(f)*

L

label *n* En; Fr *(m)*
De Schildchen *(n)*
Es marbete *(m)*
It etichetta *(f)*
Pt rótulo *(m)*

label début *(m)* Fr
De Anfangskennsatz *(m)*
En header label
Es etiqueta de cabecera *(f)*
It etichetta della testata *(f)*
Pt rótulo de porta-cabeças *(m)*

label fin *(m)* Fr
De Beisatzkennzeichen *(n)*
En trailer label
Es etiqueta de cola *(f)*
It etichetta di fine *(f)*
Pt rótulo de trailer *(m)*

label piste *(m)* Fr
De Spurkennzeichen *(n)*
En track label
Es etiqueta de pista *(f)*
It etichetta di pista *(f)*
Pt rótulo de pista *(m)*

lâchement couplé Fr
De lose gekoppelt
En loosely coupled
Es débilmente acoplado
It accoppiado lentamente
Pt acoplado de forma solta

Ladeadresse *(f) n* De
En load point
Es punto de carga *(m)*
Fr point de chargement *(m)*
It punto di caricamento *(m)*
Pt ponto de carga *(m)*

laden *vb* De
En load
Es cargar
Fr charger
It caricare
Pt carregar

Ladeprogramm *(n) n* De
En loading routine
Es rutina de carga *(f)*
Fr programme de chargement *(m)*
It routine di caricamento *(f)*
Pt rotina de carga *(f)*

Lader *(m) n* De
En loader
Es cargador *(m)*
Fr chargeur *(m)*
It caricatore *(m)*
Pt carregador *(m)*

ladungsgekoppelte Vorrichtung *(f)* De
En charge-coupled device (CCD)
Es dispositivo acoplado por carga *(m)*
Fr dispositif à couplage de charge (DCC) *(m)*
It dispositivo accoppiato a carica *(m)*
Pt dispositivo de acoplamento por carga *(m)*

Ladungsträger *(m) n* De
En carrier
Es portador *(m)*
Fr courant porteur *(m)*
It supporto *(m)*
Pt portador *(m)*

lancetta *(f) n* It
De Zeiger *(m)*
En pointer
Es indicador *(m)*
Fr indicateur *(m)*
Pt ponteiro *(m)*

langage *(m) n* Fr
De Sprache *(f)*
En language

Es lenguaje *(m)*
It linguaggio *(m)*
Pt linguagem *(f)*

langage bas de gamme *(m)* Fr
De Kleinsignalsprache *(f)*
En low-level language
Es lenguaje de bajo nivel *(m)*
It linguaggio di basso livello *(m)*
Pt linguagem de baixo nível *(f)*

langage d'assemblage *(m)* Fr
De Assembliersprache *(f)*
En assembly language
Es lenguaje ensamblador *(m)*
It linguaggio assemblatore *(m)*
Pt linguagem de montagem *(f)*

langage de commande *(m)* Fr
De Befehlssprache *(f)*
En command language
Es lenguaje de orden *(m)*
It linguaggio del comando *(m)*
Pt linguagem de ordem *(f)*

langage de contrôle *(m)* Fr
De Steuersprache *(f)*
En control language
Es lenguaje de control *(m)*
It linguaggio di controllo *(m)*
Pt linguagem de controlo *(f)*

langage de contrôle de travaux (LCT) *(m)* Fr
De Jobkontrollsprache *(f)*
En job control language (JCL)
Es lenguaje de control de trabajos *(m)*
It linguaggio di controllo del lavoro *(m)*
Pt linguagem de controle de trabalho *(f)*

langage de description des données *(m)* Fr
De Datenbeschreibungssprache *(f)*
En data description language (DDL)
Es lenguaje de descripción de datos *(m)*
It linguaggio di descrizione dei dati *(m)*
Pt linguagem de descrição de dados *(f)*

langage de programmation *(m)* Fr
De Programmiersprache *(f)*
En programming language
Es lenguaje de programación *(m)*
It linguaggio di programmazione *(m)*
Pt linguagem de programação *(f)*

langage évolué *(m)* Fr
De Groβsignalsprache *(f)*
En high-level language
Es lenguaje de alto nivel *(m)*
It linguaggio di alto livello *(m)*
Pt linguagem de alto nível *(f)*

langage généré *(m)* Fr
De Zielsprache *(f)*
En target language
Es lenguaje resultante *(m)*
It linguaggio risultante *(m)*
Pt linguagem de objectivo *(f)*

langage machine *(m)* Fr
De Maschinensprache *(f)*
En machine language
Es lenguaje de máquina *(m)*
It linguaggio macchina *(m)*
Pt linguagem da máquina *(f)*

langage objet *(m)* Fr
De Objektsprache *(f)*
En object language
Es lenguaje objeto *(m)*
It linguaggio oggetto *(m)*
Pt linguagem de objecto *(f)*

langage orienté à la procédure *(m)* Fr
De verfahrenbasierte Sprache *(f)*
En procedure-orientated language
Es lenguaje orientado a los procedimientos *(m)*
It linguaggio orientato alla procedura *(m)*
Pt linguagem orientada pelo procedimento *(f)*

langage orienté aux problèmes *(m)* Fr
De problembasierte Sprache *(f)*
En problem-orientated language
Es lenguaje orientado a los problemas *(m)*
It linguaggio orientato alle probleme *(m)*
Pt linguagem orientada peros problemas *(f)*

langage source *(m)* Fr
De Quellsprache *(f)*
En source language
Es lenguaje fuente *(m)*
It linguaggio origine *(m)*
Pt linguagem de origem *(f)*

langage symbolique *(m)* Fr
De symbolische Sprache *(f)*
En symbolic language
Es lenguaje simbólico *(m)*
It linguaggio simbolico *(m)*
Pt linguagem simbólica *(f)*

langage synthétique *(m)* Fr
De künstliche Sprache *(f)*
En synthetic language
Es lenguaje sintético *(m)*
It linguaggio sintetico *(m)*
Pt linguagem sintética *(f)*

langage tabulaire *(m)* Fr
De tabellarische Sprache *(f)*
En tabular language
Es lenguaje tabular *(m)*
It linguaggio tabulare *(m)*
Pt linguagem tabelar *(f)*

language *n* En
De Sprache *(f)*
Es lenguaje *(m)*
Fr langage *(m)*
It linguaggio *(m)*
Pt linguagem *(f)*

lápiz fotosensible *(f)* Es
De Lichtschreiber *(m)*
En light pen
Fr photo-style *(f)*
It penna luminosa *(f)*
Pt caneta de luz *(f)*

large-scale integration En
De Groβintegration *(f)*
Es integración en gran escala *(f)*
Fr intégration à grande échelle *(f)*
It integrazione su grande scala *(f)*
Pt integração à grande escala *(f)*

largeur de bande *(f)* Fr
De Bandbreite *(f)*
En bandwidth
Es anchura de banda *(f)*
It larghezza di banda *(f)*
Pt largura de banda *(f)*

larghezza di banda *(f)* It
De Bandbreite *(f)*
En bandwidth
Es anchura de banda *(f)*
Fr largeur de bande *(f)*
Pt largura de banda *(f)*

largura de banda *(f)* Pt
De Bandbreite *(f)*
En bandwidth
Es anchura de banda *(f)*
Fr largeur de bande *(f)*
It larghezza di banda *(f)*

lasca *(f) n* Pt
De Chip *(m)*
En chip
Es microplaqueta *(f)*
Fr puce *(f)*
It chip *(m)*

Laserdrucker *(m) n* De
En laser printer
Es impresora de laser *(f)*
Fr imprimante à laser *(f)*
It stampatrice a laser *(f)*
Pt impressora laser *(f)*

laser printer En
De Laserdrucker *(m)*
Es impresora de laser *(f)*
Fr imprimante à laser *(f)*
It stampatrice a laser *(f)*
Pt impressora laser *(f)*

latence *(f) n* Fr
De Zugriffsverzögerung *(f)*
En latency
Es latencia *(f)*
It latenza *(f)*
Pt latência *(f)*

latencia *(f) n* Es
De Zugriffsverzögerung *(f)*
En latency
Fr latence *(f)*
It latenza *(f)*
Pt latência *(f)*

latência *(f) n* Pt
De Zugriffsverzögerung *(f)*
En latency
Es latencia *(f)*
Fr latence *(f)*
It latenza *(f)*

latency *n* En
De Zugriffsverzögerung *(f)*
Es latencia *(f)*
Fr latence *(f)*
It latenza *(f)*
Pt latência *(f)*

latenza *(f) n* It
De Zugriffsverzögerung *(f)*
En latency
Es latencia *(f)*
Fr latence *(f)*
Pt latência *(f)*

lavoro *(m) n* It
De Job *(m)*
En job
Es trabajo *(m)*
Fr travail *(m)*
Pt trabalho *(m)*

lavoro a lotti *(m)* It
De Stapelarbeit *(f)*
En batch job
Es trabajo por lotes *(m)*
Fr travail en traitement par lots *(m)*
Pt trabalho por lotes *(m)*

lavoro di multi-programmazione *(m)* It
De Zeitteilung *(f)*
En time sharing
Es tiempo compartido *(m)*
Fr utilisation en temps partagé *(f)*
Pt compartido tempo *(m)*

lecteur *(m) n* Fr
De Leser *(m)*
En reader
Es lectora *(f)*
It lettore *(m)*
Pt leitor *(m)*

lecteur de bande *(m)* Fr
De Bandleser *(m)*
En tape reader
Es lectora de cinta *(f)*
It lettore di nastri *(m)*
Pt leitor de fita *(m)*

lecteur de bande perforée *(m)* Fr
De Lochstreifenleser *(m)*
En paper-tape reader
Es lectora de cinta de papel *(f)*
It lettore di nastri di carta *(m)*
Pt leitor de fita de papel *(m)*

lecteur de caractères *(m)* Fr
De Zeichenleser *(m)*
En character reader
Es lectora de caracteres *(f)*
It lettore di caratteri *(m)*
Pt leitor de caracteres *(m)*

lecteur de cartes *(m)* Fr
De Kartenleser *(m)*
En card reader
Es lectora de fichas *(f)*
It lettore di schede *(m)*
Pt leitor de fichas *(m)*

lecteur de film *(m)* Fr
De Filmleser *(m)*
En film reader
Es lectora de películas *(f)*
It lettore di pellicole *(m)*
Pt leitor de películas *(m)*

lecteur optique *(m)* Fr
De optischer Abtaster *(m)*
En optical scanner
Es explorador óptico *(m)*
It analizzatore per scansione di caratteri ottici *(m)*
Pt explorador óptico *(m)*

lecteur optique des caractères *(m)* Fr
De optischer Zeichenleser *(m)*
En optical character reader
Es lectora óptica de caracteres *(f)*
It lettore di caratteri ottici *(m)*
Pt leitor de caracteres ópticos *(m)*

lectora *(f) n* Es
De Leser *(m)*
En reader
Fr lecteur *(m)*
It lettore *(m)*
Pt leitor *(m)*

lectora de caracteres *(f)* Es
De Zeichenleser *(m)*
En character reader
Fr lecteur de caractères *(m)*
It lettore di caratteri *(m)*
Pt leitor de caracteres *(m)*

lectora de cinta *(f)* Es
De Bandleser *(m)*
En tape reader
Fr lecteur de bande *(m)*
It lettore di nastri *(m)*
Pt leitor de fita *(m)*

lectora de cinta de papel *(f)* Es
De Lochstreifenleser *(m)*
En paper-tape reader
Fr lecteur de bande perforée *(m)*
It lettore di nastri di carta *(m)*
Pt leitor de fita de papel *(m)*

lectora de fichas *(f)* Es
De Kartenleser *(m)*
En card reader
Fr lecteur de cartes *(m)*
It lettore di schede *(m)*
Pt leitor de fichas *(m)*

lectora de películas *(f)* Es
De Filmleser *(m)*
En film reader
Fr lecteur de film *(m)*
It lettore di pellicole *(m)*
Pt leitor de películas *(m)*

lectora óptica de caracteres *(f)* Es
De optischer Zeichenleser *(m)*
En optical character reader
Fr lecteur optique des caractères *(m)*
It lettore di caratteri ottici *(m)*
Pt leitor de caracteres ópticos *(m)*

lectura *(f) n* Es
De Lesung *(f)*
En read
Fr lecture *(f)*
It lettura *(f)*
Pt leitura *(f)*

lectura de marcas *(f)* Es
De Kennzeichenfühlung *(f)*
En mark sensing
Fr lecture de marques *(f)*
It lettura di marcature *(f)*
Pt determinação da marca *(f)*

lectura de salida *(f)* Es
De Ausleser *(m)*
En read-out
Fr sortie de lecture *(f)*

It lettura dalla memoria (f)
Pt leitura de saida (f)

lectura destructiva (f) Es
De Löschen der Auslesung (n)
En destructive read-out
Fr lecture destructive (f)
It lettura distruttiva (f)
Pt leitura destrutiva (f)

lectura inmediata (f) Es
De Abruflesen (n)
En demand reading
Fr lecture immédiate (f)
It lettura a domanda (f)
Pt leitura de procura (f)

lectura no destructiva (f) Es
De zerstörungsfreie Auslesung (f)
En nondestructive read
Fr lecture non destructive (f)
It lettura non distruttiva (f)
Pt leitura não destrutiva (f)

lectura regenerativa (f) Es
De regenerative Auslesung (f)
En regenerative read
Fr lecture régénératrice (f)
It lettura rigenerativa (f)
Pt leitura regenerativa (f)

lecture (f) n Fr
De Lesung (f)
En read
Es lectura (f)
It lettura (f)
Pt leitura (f)

lecture de marques (f) Fr
De Kennzeichenfühlung (f)
En mark sensing
Es lectura de marcas (f)
It lettura di marcature (f)
Pt determinação da marca (f)

lecture destructive (f) Fr
De Löschen der Auslesung (n)
En destructive read-out
Es lectura destructiva (f)
It lettura distruttiva (f)
Pt leitura destrutiva (f)

lecture immédiate (f) Fr
De Abruflesen (n)
En demand reading
Es lectura inmediata (f)
It lettura a domanda (f)
Pt leitura de procura (f)

lecture non destructive (f) Fr
De zerstörungsfreie Auslesung (f)
En nondestructive read
Es lectura no destructiva (f)
It lettura non distruttiva (f)
Pt leitura não destrutiva (f)

lecture optique de marques (f) Fr
De Kennzeichen-abtastung (f)
En mark scanning
Es exploración de marcas (f)
It scansione di marcature (f)
Pt exploração de marca (f)

lecture régénératrice (f) Fr
De regenerative Auslesung (f)
En regenerative read
Es lectura regenerativa (f)
It lettura rigenerativa (f)
Pt leitura regenerativa (f)

leer vb Es
De lesen
En read
Fr lire
It leggere
Pt ler

leer en salida Es
De auslesen
En read out
Fr extraire de la memoire
It leggere dalla memoria
Pt ler em saida

Leerlaufzeit (f) n De
En idle time
Es tiempo pasivo (m)
Fr temps en chômage (m)
It tempo passivo (m)
Pt tempo de functionamento em vazio (m)

Leerstelle (f) n De
En blank
Es blanco (m)
Fr espace (m)
It bianco (m)
Pt espaço (m)

Leerstellenzeichen (n) n De
En space character
Es carácter blanco (m)
Fr caractère blanc (m)
It carattere di spazio (m)
Pt carácter de espaço (m)

left-justified adj En
De linksbündig
Es justificado a la izquierda
Fr cadré à gauche
It giustificato a sinistra
Pt justificado à esquerda

left shift En
De Linksverschiebung (f)
Es desplazamiento a la izguierda (m)
Fr décalage à gauche (m)
It spostamento a sinistra (m)
Pt mudança à esquerda (f)

leggere vb It
De lesen
En read
Es leer
Fr lire
Pt ler

leggere dalla memoria It
De auslesen
En read out
Es leer en salida
Fr extraire de la memoire
Pt ler em saida

leggibile dalla macchina It
De maschinenlesbar
En machine-readable
Es legible por la máquina
Fr compréhensible par une machine
Pt legível pela máquina

legible por la máquina Es
De maschinenlesbar
En machine-readable
Fr compréhensible par une machine
It leggibile dalla macchina
Pt legível pela máquina

legível pela máquina Pt
De maschinenlesbar
En machine-readable
Es legible por la máquina
Fr compréhensible par une machine
It leggibile dalla macchina

leitor (m) n Pt
De Leser (m)
En reader
Es lectora (f)
Fr lecteur (m)
It lettore (m)

leitor de caracteres (m) Pt
De Zeichenleser (m)
En character reader
Es lectora de caracteres (f)
Fr lecteur de caractères (m)
It lettore di caratteri (m)

leitor de caracteres ópticos (m) Pt
De optischer Zeichenleser (m)
En optical character reader
Es lectora óptica de caracteres (f)
Fr lecteur optique des caractères (m)

It lettore di caratteri ottici *(m)*

leitor de fichas *(m)* Pt
De Kartenleser *(m)*
En card reader
Es lectora de fichas *(f)*
Fr lecteur de cartes *(m)*
It lettore di schede *(m)*

leitor de fita *(m)* Pt
De Bandleser *(m)*
En tape reader
Es lectora de cinta *(f)*
Fr lecteur de bande *(m)*
It lettore di nastri *(m)*

leitor de fita de papel *(m)* Pt
De Lochstreifenleser *(m)*
En paper-tape reader
Es lectora de cinta de papel *(f)*
Fr lecteur de bande perforée *(m)*
It lettore di nastri di carta *(m)*

leitor de películas *(m)* Pt
De Filmleser *(m)*
En film reader
Es lectora de películas *(f)*
Fr lecteur de film *(m)*
It lettore di pellicole *(m)*

Leitungsschalten *(n)* *n* De
En line switching
Es conmutación de líneas *(f)*
Fr commutation de lignes *(f)*
It commutazione di linea *(f)*
Pt comutação de linha *(f)*

leitura *(f)* *n* Pt
De Lesung *(f)*
En read
Es lectura *(f)*
Fr lecture *(f)*
It lettura *(f)*

leitura de procura *(f)* Pt
De Abruflesen *(n)*
En demand reading
Es lectura inmediata *(f)*
Fr lecture immédiate *(f)*
It lettura a domanda *(f)*

leitura de saida *(f)* Pt
De Ausleser *(m)*
En read-out
Es lectura de salida *(f)*
Fr sortie de lecture *(f)*
It lettura dalla memoria *(f)*

leitura destrutiva *(f)* Pt
De Löschen der Auslesung *(m)*
En destructive read-out
Es lectura destructiva *(f)*
Fr lecture destructive *(f)*
It lettura distruttiva *(f)*

leitura não destrutiva *(f)* Pt
De zerstörungsfreie Auslesung *(f)*
En nondestructive read
Es lectura no destructiva *(f)*
Fr lecture non destructive *(f)*
It lettura non distruttiva *(f)*

leitura regenerativa *(f)* Pt
De regenerative Auslesung *(f)*
En regenerative read
Es lectura regenerativa *(f)*
Fr lecture régénératrice *(f)*
It lettura rigenerativa *(f)*

Leitweg *(m)* *n* De
En route
Es ruta *(f)*
Fr itinéraire *(m)*
It pista *(f)*
Pt caminho *(m)*

Leitwerk *(n)* *n* De
En control unit
Es unidad de control *(f)*
Fr unité de contrôle *(f)*
It unità di controllo *(f)*
Pt unidade de controlo *(f)*

lenguaje *(m)* *n* Es
De Sprache *(f)*
En language
Fr langage *(m)*
It linguaggio *(m)*
Pt linguagem *(f)*

lenguaje de alto nivel *(m)* Es
De Groβsignalsprache *(f)*
En high-level language
Fr langage évolué *(m)*
It linguaggio di alto livello *(m)*
Pt linguagem de alto nível *(f)*

lenguaje de bajo nivel *(m)* Es
De Kleinsignalsprache *(f)*
En low-level language
Fr langage bas de gamme *(m)*
It linguaggio di basso livello *(m)*
Pt linguagem de baixo nível *(f)*

lenguaje de control *(m)* Es
De Steuersprache *(f)*
En control language
Fr langage de contrôle *(m)*
It linguaggio di controllo *(m)*
Pt linguagem de controlo *(f)*

lenguaje de control de trabajos *(m)* Es
De Jobkontrollsprache *(f)*
En job control language (JCL)
Fr langage de contrôle de travaux (LCT) *(m)*
It linguaggio di controllo del lavoro *(m)*
Pt linguagem de controle de trabalho *(f)*

lenguaje de descripción de datos *(m)* Es
De Datenbeschreibungssprache *(f)*
En data description language (DDL)
Fr langage de description des données *(m)*
It linguaggio di descrizione dei dati *(m)*
Pt linguagem de descrição de dados *(f)*

lenguaje de máquina *(m)* Es
De Maschinensprache *(f)*
En machine language
Fr langage machine *(m)*
It linguaggio macchina *(m)*
Pt linguagem da máquina *(f)*

lenguaje de orden *(m)* Es
De Befehlssprache *(f)*
En command language
Fr langage de commande *(m)*
It linguaggio del comando *(m)*
Pt linguagem de ordem *(f)*

lenguaje de programación *(m)* Es
De Programmiersprache *(f)*
En programming language
Fr langage de programmation *(m)*
It linguaggio di programmazione *(m)*
Pt linguagem de programação *(f)*

lenguaje ensamblador *(m)* Es
De Assembliersprache *(f)*
En assembly language
Fr langage d'assemblage *(m)*
It linguaggio assemblatore *(m)*
Pt linguagem de montagem *(f)*

lenguaje fuente *(m)* Es
De Quellsprache *(f)*
En source language
Fr langage source *(m)*
It linguaggio origine *(m)*
Pt linguagem de origem *(f)*

lenguaje objeto *(m)* Es
De Objektsprache *(f)*
En object language
Fr langage objet *(m)*
It linguaggio oggetto *(m)*

Pt linguagem de objecto *(f)*

lenguaje orientado a los problemas *(m)* Es
De problembasierte Sprache *(f)*
En problem-orientated language
Fr langage orienté aux problèmes *(m)*
It linguaggio orientato alle probleme *(m)*
Pt linguagem orientada peros problemas *(f)*

lenguaje orientado a los procedimientos *(m)* Es
De verfahrenbasierte Sprache *(f)*
En procedure-orientated language
Fr langage orienté à la procédure *(m)*
It linguaggio orientato alla procedura *(m)*
Pt linguagem orientada pelo procedimento *(f)*

lenguaje resultante *(m)* Es
De Zielsprache *(f)*
En target language
Fr langage généré *(m)*
It linguaggio risultante *(m)*
Pt linguagem de objectivo *(f)*

lenguaje simbólico *(m)* Es
De symbolische Sprache *(f)*
En symbolic language
Fr langage symbolique *(m)*
It linguaggio simbolico *(m)*
Pt linguagem simbólica *(f)*

lenguaje sintético *(m)* Es
De künstliche Sprache *(f)*
En synthetic language
Fr langage synthétique *(m)*
It linguaggio sintetico *(m)*
Pt linguagem sintética *(f)*

lenguaje tabular *(m)* Es
De tabellarische Sprache *(f)*
En tabular language
Fr langage tabulaire *(m)*
It linguaggio tabulare *(m)*
Pt linguagem tabelar *(f)*

ler *vb* Pt
De lesen
En read
Es leer
Fr lire
It leggere

ler em saida Pt
De auslesen
En read out
Es leer en salida
Fr extraire de la memoire
It leggere dalla memoria

Lesekopf *(m) n* De
En read head
Es cabeza de lectura *(f)*
Fr tête de lecture *(f)*
It testina di lettura *(f)*
Pt cabeça leitora *(f)*

lesen *vb* De
En read
Es leer
Fr lire
It leggere
Pt ler

Lesen-Schreiben-Kanal *(m)* De
En read-write channel
Es canal de lectura-escritura *(m)*
Fr voie lecture-écriture *(f)*
It canale di lettura-scrittura *(m)*
Pt canal de leitura-escrita *(m)*

Leser *(m) n* De
En reader
Es lectora *(f)*
Fr lecteur *(m)*
It lettore *(m)*
Pt leitor *(m)*

Les-Schreibkopf *(m) n* De
En read-write head
Es cabeza de lectura-escritura *(f)*
Fr tête lecture-écriture *(f)*
It testina di lettura-scrittura *(f)*
Pt cabeça de leitura-escrita *(f)*

Lesung *(f) n* De
En read
Es lectura *(f)*
Fr lecture *(f)*
It lettura *(f)*
Pt leitura *(f)*

lettore *(m) n* It
De Leser *(m)*
En reader
Es lectora *(f)*
Fr lecteur *(m)*
Pt leitor *(m)*

lettore di caratteri *(m)* It
De Zeichenleser *(m)*
En character reader
Es lectora de caracteres *(f)*
Fr lecteur de caractères *(m)*
Pt leitor de caracteres *(m)*

lettore di caratteri ottici *(m)* It
De optischer Zeichenleser *(m)*
En optical character reader
Es lectora óptica de caracteres *(f)*
Fr lecteur optique des caractères *(m)*
Pt leitor de caracteres ópticos *(m)*

lettore di nastri *(m)* It
De Bandleser *(m)*
En tape reader
Es lectora de cinta *(f)*
Fr lecteur de bande *(m)*
Pt leitor de fita *(m)*

lettore di nastri di carta *(m)* It
De Lochstreifenleser *(m)*
En paper-tape reader
Es lectora de cinta de papel *(f)*
Fr lecteur de bande perforée *(m)*
Pt leitor de fita de papel *(m)*

lettore di pellicole *(m)* It
De Filmleser *(m)*
En film reader
Es lectora de películas *(f)*
Fr lecteur de film *(m)*
Pt leitor de películas *(m)*

lettore di schede *(m)* It
De Kartenleser *(m)*
En card reader
Es lectora de fichas *(f)*
Fr lecteur de cartes *(m)*
Pt leitor de fichas *(m)*

lettura *(f) n* It
De Lesung *(f)*
En read
Es lectura *(f)*
Fr lecture *(f)*
Pt leitura *(f)*

lettura a domanda *(f)* It
De Abruflesen *(n)*
En demand reading
Es lectura inmediata *(f)*
Fr lecture immédiate *(f)*
Pt leitura de procura *(f)*

lettura dalla memoria *(f)* It
De Ausleser *(m)*
En read-out
Es lectura de salida *(f)*
Fr sortie de lecture *(f)*
Pt leitura de saida *(f)*

lettura di marcature *(f)* It
De Kennzeichenfühlung *(f)*
En mark sensing
Es lectura de marcas *(f)*
Fr lecture de marques *(f)*
Pt determinação da marca *(f)*

lettura distruttiva *(f)* It
De Löschen der Auslesung *(n)*
En destructive read-out
Es lectura destructiva *(f)*
Fr lecture destructive *(f)*
Pt leitura destrutiva *(f)*

lettura non distruttiva *(f)* It
De zerstörungsfreie Auslesung *(f)*
En nondestructive read
Es lectura no destructiva *(f)*
Fr lecture non destructive *(f)*
Pt leitura não destrutiva *(f)*

lettura rigenerativa *(f)* It
De regenerative Auslesung *(f)*
En regenerative read
Es lectura regenerativa *(f)*
Fr lecture régénératrice *(f)*
Pt leitura regenerativa *(f)*

Leuchtdiode *(f) n* De
En light-emitting diode (LED)
Es diodo luminoso *(m)*
Fr diode électro-luminescente *(f)*
It diodo emittente luce *(m)*
Pt díodo emissor de luz *(m)*

liaison de transmission *(f)* Fr
De Datenübermittlungsabschnitt *(m)*
En data link
Es enlace para transmisión de datos *(m)*
It collegamento di dati *(m)*
Pt elemento de ligação de dados *(m)*

liaison interurbaine *(f)* Fr
De Sammelverbindung *(f)*
En trunk link
Es enlace común *(m)*
It linea principale *(f)*
Pt linha principal *(f)*

liaison numérique *(f)* Fr
De Digitalverbindung *(f)*
En digital link
Es enlace digital *(m)*
It collegamento digitale *(m)*
Pt elemento de ligação digital *(m)*

liasse *(f) n* Fr
De mehrteilige Formulare *(pl)*
En multipart forms
Es paquete de papel continuo *(m)*
It moduli a copie multiple *(m pl)*
Pt formas de partes múltiplas *(f pl)*

liberar *vb* Es
De auslösen
En release
Fr libérer
It rilasciare
Pt libertar

libérer *vb* Fr
De auslösen
En release
Es liberar
It rilasciare
Pt libertar

libertar *vb* Pt
De auslösen
En release
Es liberar
Fr libérer
It rilasciare

library *n* En
De Bibliothek *(f)*
Es biblioteca *(f)*
Fr bibliothèque *(f)*
It libreria *(f)*
Pt biblioteca *(f)*

libreria *(f) n* It
De Bibliothek *(f)*
En library
Es biblioteca *(f)*
Fr bibliothèque *(f)*
Pt biblioteca *(f)*

libreria dei nastri *(f)* It
De Bandbibliothek *(f)*
En tape library
Es biblioteca de cintas *(f)*
Fr bandothèque *(f)*
Pt biblioteca de fitas *(f)*

libreria dei programmi *(f)* It
De Programmbibliothek *(f)*
En program library
Es biblioteca de programas *(f)*
Fr bibliothèque de programmes *(f)*
Pt biblioteca de programas *(f)*

libreria dei programmi applicativi *(f)* It
De Bibliothek der Anwendungsprogramme *(f)*
En application programs library (APL)
Es biblioteca de programas de aplicación *(f)*
Fr bibliothèque des programmes d'application *(f)*
Pt biblioteca de programas de aplicação *(f)*

Lichtschreiber *(m) n* De
En light pen
Es lápiz fotosensible *(f)*
Fr photo-style *(f)*
It penna luminosa *(f)*
Pt caneta de luz *(f)*

lien *(m) n* Fr
De Verbindung *(f)*
En linkage
Es enlace *(m)*
It interconnessione *(f)*
Pt ligação *(f)*

ligação *(f) n* Pt
De Verbindung *(f)*
En linkage
Es enlace *(m)*
Fr lien *(m)*
It interconnessione *(f)*

ligar *vb* Pt
De abzweigen
En branch
Es bifurcar
Fr brancher
It diramarsi

light-emitting diode (LED) En
De Leuchtdiode *(f)*
Es diodo luminoso *(m)*
Fr diode électro-luminescente *(f)*
It diodo emittente luce *(m)*
Pt díodo emissor de luz *(m)*

light pen En
De Lichtschreiber *(m)*
Es lápiz fotosensible *(f)*
Fr photo-style *(f)*
It penna luminosa *(f)*
Pt caneta de luz *(f)*

ligne *(f) n* Fr
De Zeile *(f)*
En row
Es fila *(f)*
It fila *(f)*
Pt fila *(f)*

ligne à retard *(f)* Fr
De Verzögerungsleitung *(f)*
En delay line
Es línea de retardo *(f)*
It linea di ritardo *(f)*
Pt linha de atraso *(f)*

ligne de flux *(f)* Fr
De Fluβlinie *(f)*
En flowline
Es línea de flujo *(f)*
It linea di flusso *(f)*
Pt linha de fluxo *(f)*

lignes par minute *(f pl)* Fr
De Zeilen pro Minute *(pl)*
En lines per minute (lpm)
Es líneas por minuto *(f pl)*
It linee al minuto *(f pl)*
Pt linhas por minuto *(f pl)*

limitado ao processor Pt
De verarbeiter-beschränkt
En processor-limited
Es limitado por la procesador
Fr limité par la vitesse de traitement
It limitato per velocitá di elaborazione

limitado por la procesador Es
De verarbeiter-beschränkt
En processor-limited

Fr limité par la vitesse de traitement
It limitato per velocitá di elaborazione
Pt limitado ao processor

limitado por los periféricos Es
De peripherebegrenzt
En peripheral-limited
Fr limité par les périphériques
It limitato per periferichi
Pt perifericamente limitado

limitato per periferichi It
De peripherebegrenzt
En peripheral-limited
Es limitado por los periféricos
Fr limité par les périphériques
Pt perifericamente limitado

limitato per velocitá di elaborazione It
De verarbeiter-beschränkt
En processor-limited
Es limitado por la procesador
Fr limité par la vitesse de traitement
Pt limitado ao processor

limitazione poligonale *(f)* It
De Vieleckbegrenzung *(f)*
En polygon clipping
Es recorte poligonal *(m)*
Fr écrêtage polygone *(m)*
Pt recorte poligonal *(m)*

limité par la vitesse de traitement Fr
De verarbeiter-beschränkt
En processor-limited
Es limitado por la procesador
It limitato per velocitá di elaborazione
Pt limitado ao processor

limité par les périphériques Fr
De peripherebegrenzt
En peripheral-limited
Es limitado por los periféricos
It limitato per periferichi
Pt perifericamente limitado

limpar *vb* Pt
De löschen
En clear
Es despejar
Fr remettre à zéro
It rimettere a zero

limpieza de los datos *(f)* Es
De Datenlöschung *(f)*
En data cleaning
Fr nettoyage de données *(f)*
It pulizia dei dati *(f)*
Pt apagamento de dados *(m)*

línea de flujo *(f)* Es
De Flußlinie *(f)*
En flowline
Fr ligne de flux *(f)*
It linea di flusso *(f)*
Pt linha de fluxo *(f)*

línea de retardo *(f)* Es
De Verzögerungsleitung *(f)*
En delay line
Fr ligne à retard *(f)*
It linea di ritardo *(f)*
Pt linha de atraso *(f)*

linea di flusso *(f)* It
De Flußlinie *(f)*
En flowline
Es línea de flujo *(f)*
Fr ligne de flux *(f)*
Pt linha de fluxo *(f)*

linea di ritardo *(f)* It
De Verzögerungsleitung *(f)*
En delay line
Es línea de retardo *(f)*
Fr ligne à retard *(f)*
Pt linha de atraso *(f)*

lineal *adj* Es
De gleichzeitig
En in-line
Fr en ligne
It lineale
Pt em série

lineale *adj* It
De gleichzeitig
En in-line
Es lineal
Fr en ligne
Pt em série

linea principale *(f)* It
De Sammelverbindung *(f)*
En trunk link
Es enlace común *(m)*
Fr liaison interurbaine *(f)*
Pt linha principal *(f)*

lineare Programmierung *(f)* De
En linear programming (LP)
Es programaciòn lineal *(f)*
Fr programmation linéaire (PL) *(f)*
It programmazione lineare *(f)*
Pt programação linear *(f)*

linear programming (LP) En
De lineare Programmierung *(f)*
Es programación lineal *(f)*
Fr programmation linéaire (PL) *(f)*
It programmazione lineare *(f)*
Pt programação linear *(f)*

líneas por minuto *(f pl)* Es
De Zeilen pro Minute *(pl)*
En lines per minute (lpm)
Fr lignes par minute *(f pl)*
It linee al minuto *(f pl)*
Pt linhas por minuto *(f pl)*

linee al minuto *(f pl)* It
De Zeilen pro Minute *(pl)*
En lines per minute (lpm)
Es líneas por minuto *(f pl)*
Fr lignes par minute *(f pl)*
Pt linhas por minuto *(f pl)*

line printer En
De Zeilendrucker *(m)*
Es impresora de líneas *(f)*
Fr imprimante ligne par ligne *(f)*
It stampatrice a linea *(f)*
Pt impressora de linha *(f)*

lines per minute (lpm) En
De Zeilen pro Minute *(pl)*
Es líneas por minuto *(f pl)*
Fr lignes par minute *(f pl)*
It linee al minuto *(f pl)*
Pt linhas por minuto *(f pl)*

line switching En
De Leitungsschalten *(n)*
Es conmutación de líneas *(f)*
Fr commutation de lignes *(f)*
It commutazione di linea *(f)*
Pt comutação de linha *(f)*

linguagem *(f) n* Pt
De Sprache *(f)*
En language
Es lenguaje *(m)*
Fr langage *(m)*
It linguaggio *(m)*

linguagem da máquina *(f)* Pt
De Maschinensprache *(f)*
En machine language
Es lenguaje de máquina *(m)*
Fr langage machine *(m)*
It linguaggio macchina *(m)*

linguagem de alto nível *(f)* Pt
De Groβsignalsprache *(f)*
En high-level language
Es lenguaje de alto nivel *(m)*
Fr langage évolué *(m)*
It linguaggio di alto livello *(m)*

linguagem de baixo nível *(f)* Pt
De Kleinsignalsprache *(f)*
En low-level language
Es lenguaje de bajo nivel *(m)*
Fr langage bas de gamme *(m)*
It linguaggio di basso livello *(m)*

linguagem de controle de trabalho *(f)* Pt
De Jobkontrollsprache *(f)*
En job control language (JCL)
Es lenguaje de control de trabajos *(m)*
Fr langage de contrôle de travaux (LCT) *(m)*
It linguaggio di controllo del lavoro *(m)*

linguagem de controlo *(f)* Pt
De Steuersprache *(f)*
En control language
Es lenguaje de control *(m)*
Fr langage de contrôle *(m)*
It linguaggio di controllo *(m)*

linguagem de descrição de dados *(f)* Pt
De Datenbeschreibungssprache *(f)*
En data description language (DDL)
Es lenguaje de descripción de datos *(m)*
Fr langage de description des données *(m)*
It linguaggio di descrizione dei dati *(m)*

linguagem de montagem *(f)* Pt
De Assembliersprache *(f)*
En assembly language
Es lenguaje ensamblador *(m)*
Fr langage d'assemblage *(m)*
It linguaggio assemblatore *(m)*

linguagem de objectivo *(f)* Pt
De Zielsprache *(f)*
En target language
Es lenguaje resultante *(m)*
Fr langage généré *(m)*
It linguaggio risultante *(m)*

linguagem de objecto *(f)* Pt
De Objektsprache *(f)*
En object language
Es lenguaje objeto *(m)*
Fr langage objet *(m)*
It linguaggio oggetto *(m)*

linguagem de ordem *(f)* Pt
De Befehlssprache *(f)*
En command language
Es lenguaje de orden *(m)*
Fr langage de commande *(m)*
It linguaggio del comando *(m)*

linguagem de origem *(f)* Pt
De Quellsprache *(f)*
En source language
Es lenguaje fuente *(m)*
Fr langage source *(m)*
It linguaggio origine *(m)*

linguagem de programação *(f)* Pt
De Programmiersprache *(f)*
En programming language
Es lenguaje de programación *(m)*
Fr langage de programmation *(m)*
It linguaggio di programmazione *(m)*

linguagem orientada pelo procedimento *(f)* Pt
De verfahrenbasierte Sprache *(f)*
En procedure-orientated language
Es lenguaje orientado a los procedimientos *(m)*
Fr langage orienté à la procédure *(m)*
It linguaggio orientato alla procedura *(m)*

linguagem orientada peros problemas *(f)* Pt
De problembasierte Sprache *(f)*
En problem-orientated language
Es lenguaje orientado a los problemas *(m)*
Fr langage orienté aux problèmes *(m)*
It linguaggio orientato alle probleme *(m)*

linguagem simbólica *(f)* Pt
De symbolische Sprache *(f)*
En symbolic language
Es lenguaje simbólico *(m)*
Fr langage symbolique *(m)*
It linguaggio simbolico *(m)*

linguagem sintética *(f)* Pt
De künstliche Sprache *(f)*
En synthetic language
Es lenguaje sintético *(m)*
Fr langage synthétique *(m)*
It linguaggio sintetico *(m)*

linguagem tabelar *(f)* Pt
De tabellarische Sprache *(f)*
En tabular language
Es lenguaje tabular *(m)*
Fr langage tabulaire *(m)*
It linguaggio tabulare *(m)*

linguaggio *(m) n* It
De Sprache *(f)*
En language
Es lenguaje *(m)*
Fr langage *(m)*
Pt linguagem *(f)*

linguaggio assemblatore *(m)* It
De Assembliersprache *(f)*
En assembly language
Es lenguaje ensamblador *(m)*
Fr langage d'assemblage *(m)*
Pt linguagem de montagem *(f)*

linguaggio del comando *(m)* It
De Befehlssprache *(f)*
En command language
Es lenguaje de orden *(m)*
Fr langage de commande *(m)*
Pt linguagem de ordem *(f)*

linguaggio di alto livello *(m)* It
De Großsignalsprache *(f)*
En high-level language
Es lenguaje de alto nivel *(m)*
Fr langage évolué *(m)*
Pt linguagem de alto nível *(f)*

linguaggio di basso livello *(m)* It
De Kleinsignalsprache *(f)*
En low-level language
Es lenguaje de bajo nivel *(m)*
Fr langage bas de gamme *(m)*
Pt linguagem de baixo nível *(f)*

linguaggio di controllo *(m)* It
De Steuersprache *(f)*
En control language
Es lenguaje de control *(m)*
Fr langage de contrôle *(m)*
Pt linguagem de controlo *(f)*

linguaggio di controllo del lavoro *(m)* It
De Jobkontrollsprache *(f)*
En job control language (JCL)
Es lenguaje de control de trabajos *(m)*
Fr langage de contrôle de travaux (LCT) *(m)*
Pt linguagem de

controle de trabalho *(f)*

linguaggio di descrizione dei dati *(m)* It
De Datenbeschreibungssprache *(f)*
En data description language (DDL)
Es lenguaje de descripción de datos *(m)*
Fr langage de description des données *(m)*
Pt linguagem de descrição de dados *(f)*

linguaggio di programmazione *(m)* It
De Programmiersprache *(f)*
En programming language
Es lenguaje de programación *(m)*
Fr langage de programmation *(m)*
Pt linguagem de programação *(f)*

linguaggio macchina *(m)* It
De Maschinensprache *(f)*
En machine language
Es lenguaje de máquina *(m)*
Fr langage machine *(m)*
Pt linguagem da máquina *(f)*

linguaggio oggetto *(m)* It
De Objektsprache *(f)*
En object language
Es lenguaje objeto *(m)*
Fr langage objet *(m)*
Pt linguagem de objecto *(f)*

linguaggio orientato alla procedura *(m)* It
De verfahrenbasierte Sprache *(f)*
En procedure-orientated language
Es lenguaje orientado a los procedimientos *(m)*
Fr langage orienté à la procédure *(m)*
Pt linguagem orientada pelo procedimento *(f)*

linguaggio orientato alle probleme *(m)* It
De problembasierte Sprache *(f)*
En problem-orientated language
Es lenguaje orientado a los problemas *(m)*
Fr langage orienté aux problèmes *(m)*
Pt linguagem orientada peros problemas *(f)*

linguaggio origine *(m)* It
De Quellsprache *(f)*
En source language
Es lenguaje fuente *(m)*
Fr langage source *(m)*
Pt linguagem de origem *(f)*

linguaggio risultante *(m)* It
De Zielsprache *(f)*
En target language
Es lenguaje resultante *(m)*
Fr langage généré *(m)*
Pt linguagem de objectivo *(f)*

linguaggio simbolico *(m)* It
De symbolische Sprache *(f)*
En symbolic language
Es lenguaje simbólico *(m)*
Fr langage symbolique *(m)*
Pt linguagem simbólica *(f)*

linguaggio sintetico *(m)* It
De künstliche Sprache *(f)*
En synthetic language
Es lenguaje sintético *(m)*
Fr langage synthétique *(m)*
Pt linguagem sintética *(f)*

linguaggio tabulare *(m)* It
De tabellarische Sprache *(f)*
En tabular language
Es lenguaje tabular *(m)*
Fr langage tabulaire *(m)*
Pt linguagem tabelar *(f)*

linha de atraso *(f)* Pt
De Verzögerungsleitung *(f)*
En delay line
Es línea de retardo *(f)*
Fr ligne à retard *(f)*
It linea di ritardo *(f)*

linha de fluxo *(f)* Pt
De Fluβlinie *(f)*
En flowline
Es línea de flujo *(f)*
Fr ligne de flux *(f)*
It linea di flusso *(f)*

linha principal *(f)* Pt
De Sammelverbindung *(f)*
En trunk link
Es enlace común *(m)*
Fr liaison interurbaine *(f)*
It linea principale *(f)*

linhas por minuto *(f pl)* Pt
De Zeilen pro Minute *(pl)*
En lines per minute (lpm)
Es líneas por minuto *(f pl)*
Fr lignes par minute *(f pl)*
It linee al minuto *(f pl)*

linkage *n* En
De Verbindung *(f)*
Es enlace *(m)*
Fr lien *(m)*
It interconnessione *(f)*
Pt ligação *(f)*

linksbündig *adj* De
En left-justified
Es justificado a la izquierda
Fr cadré à gauche
It giustificato a sinistra
Pt justificado à esquerda

Linksverschiebung *(f) n* De
En left shift
Es desplazamiento a la izquierda *(m)*
Fr décalage à gauche *(m)*
It spostamento a sinistra *(m)*
Pt mudança à esquerda *(f)*

lire *vb* Fr
De lesen
En read
Es leer
It leggere
Pt ler

list *n* En
De Liste *(f)*
Es lista *(f)*
Fr liste *(f)*
It lista *(f)*
Pt lista *(f)*

list *vb* En
De auflisten
Es listar
Fr lister
It listare
Pt enumerar em lista

lista *(f) n* Es, It, Pt
De Liste *(f)*
En list
Fr liste *(f)*

lista com cadeia *(f)* Pt
De gekettete Liste *(f)*
En chained list
Es lista en cadena *(f)*
Fr liste en chaîne *(f)*
It lista concatenata *(f)*

lista concatenata *(f)* It
De gekettete Liste *(f)*
En chained list
Es lista en cadena *(f)*
Fr liste en chaîne *(f)*
Pt lista com cadeia *(f)*

lista de referencias *(f)* Es
De Bezugsliste *(f)*
En reference listing
Fr listage primitif *(m)*
It listato di riferimento *(m)*
Pt listagem de referência *(f)*

lista di verifica *(f)* It
De Prüfliste *(f)*
En audit trail
Es pista de auditoría *(f)*
Fr vérification à rebours *(f)*
Pt trilho de verificação *(m)*

lista en cadena *(f)* Es
De gekettete Liste *(f)*
En chained list
Fr liste en chaîne *(f)*
It lista concatenata *(f)*
Pt lista com cadeia *(f)*

listagem de referência *(f)* Pt
De Bezugsliste *(f)*
En reference listing
Es lista de referencias *(f)*
Fr listage primitif *(m)*
It listato di riferimento *(m)*

listage primitif *(m)* Fr
De Bezugsliste *(f)*
En reference listing
Es lista de referencias *(f)*
It listato di riferimento *(m)*
Pt listagem de referência *(f)*

listar *vb* Es
De auflisten
En list
Fr lister
It listare
Pt enumerar em lista

listare *vb* It
De auflisten
En list
Es listar
Fr lister
Pt enumerar em lista

listato di riferimento *(m)* It
De Bezugsliste *(f)*
En reference listing
Es lista de referencias *(f)*
Fr listage primitif *(m)*
Pt listagem de referência *(f)*

liste *(f)* *n* Fr
De Liste *(f)*
En list
Es lista *(f)*
It lista *(f)*
Pt lista *(f)*

Liste *(f)* *n* De
En list
Es lista *(f)*
Fr liste *(f)*
It lista *(f)*
Pt lista *(f)*

liste en chaîne *(f)* Fr
De gekettete Liste *(f)*
En chained list
Es lista en cadena *(f)*
It lista concatenata *(f)*
Pt lista com cadeia *(f)*

Listengeber *(m)* *n* De
En report generator
Es generador de informes *(m)*
Fr générateur d'édition *(m)*
It generatore di tabulati *(m)*
Pt gerador de relatório *(m)*

Listenprogramm *(n)* *n* De
En report program
Es programa de informes *(m)*
Fr programme des informations *(m)*
It programma di tabulati *(m)*
Pt programa de relatórios *(m)*

Listenverarbeitung *(f)* *n* De
En list processing
Es proceso por lista *(m)*
Fr traitement de liste *(m)*
It elaborazione della lista *(f)*
Pt processamento de lista *(m)*

lister *vb* Fr
De auflisten
En list
Es listar
It listare
Pt enumerar em lista

list processing En
De Listenbverarbeitung *(f)*
Es proceso por lista *(m)*
Fr traitement de liste *(m)*
It elaborazione della lista *(f)*
Pt processamento de lista *(m)*

livello di accesso *(m)* It
De Zugriffsstufe *(f)*
En access level
Es nivel de acceso *(m)*
Fr niveau d'accès *(m)*
Pt nível de acesso *(m)*

llamada *(f)* *n* Es
De Aufruf *(m)*
En call
Fr appel *(m)*
It chiamata *(f)*
Pt chamada *(f)*

llamar *vb* Es
De aufrufen
En call
Fr appeler
It chiamare
Pt chamar

load *vb* En
De laden
Es cargar
Fr charger
It caricare
Pt carregar

load and go En
De umwandeln und ausführen
Es cargar y ejecutar
Fr charger et exécuter
It caricare e eseguire
Pt carregar e seguir

loader *n* En
De Lader *(m)*
Es cargador *(m)*
Fr chargeur *(m)*
It caricatore *(m)*
Pt carregador *(m)*

loading routine En
De Ladeprogramm *(n)*
Es rutina de carga *(f)*
Fr programme de chargement *(m)*
It routine di caricamento *(f)*
Pt rotina de carga *(f)*

load point En
De Ladeadresse *(f)*
Es punto de carga *(m)*
Fr point de chargement *(m)*
It punto di caricamento *(m)*
Pt ponto de carga *(m)*

localização *(f)* *n* Pt
De Dateilage *(f)*
En location
Es posición *(f)*
Fr emplacement *(m)*
It locazione *(f)*

localização de bit *(f)* Pt
De Binärzeichenortung *(f)*
En bit location
Es posición de bit *(f)*
Fr position de bits *(f)*
It locazione del bit *(f)*

localização protegida *(f)* Pt
De geschützter Ort *(m)*
En protected location
Es posición protegida *(f)*
Fr position protégée *(f)*
It locazione protetta *(f)*

localización de errores *(f)* Es
De Fehlersuchen *(n)*
En trouble shooting
Fr dépannage *(m)*
It risoluzione dei problemi organizzativi *(f)*
Pt detecção de avarias *(f)*

location *n* En
De Dateilage *(f)*
Es posición *(f)*
Fr emplacement *(m)*
It locazione *(f)*
Pt localização *(f)*

location counter En
De Dateilagezähler *(m)*
Es contador de posiciones *(m)*
Fr compteur d'emplacement *(m)*
It contatore di locazioni *(m)*
Pt contador de localização *(m)*

locazione *(f) n* It
De Dateilage *(f)*
En location
Es posición *(f)*
Fr emplacement *(m)*
Pt localização *(f)*

locazione del bit *(f)* It
De Binärzeichenortung *(f)*
En bit location
Es posición de bit *(f)*
Fr position de bits *(f)*
Pt localização de bit *(f)*

locazione protetta *(f)* It
De geschützter Ort *(m)*
En protected location
Es posición protegida *(f)*
Fr position protégée *(f)*
Pt localização protegida *(f)*

Lochbandlocher *(m) n* De
En perforator
Es perforador *(m)*
Fr perforatrice *(f)*
It perforatrice *(f)*
Pt perfuradora *(f)*

lochen *vb* De
En punch
Es perforar
Fr perforer
It perforare
Pt perfurar

Locher *(m) n* De
En punch
Es perforadora *(f)*
Fr perforatrice *(f)*
It perforatrice *(f)*
Pt perfuradora *(f)*

Locher mit Tastatur *(m)* De
En key punch
Es perforadora de tecla *(f)*
Fr perforatrice à clavier *(f)*
It perforatrice a tastiera *(f)*
Pt perfuradora de tecla *(f)*

Lochkarte *(f) n* De
Am punch card
En punched card
Es ficha perforada *(f)*
Fr carte mécanographique *(f)*
It scheda perforata *(f)*
Pt ficha perfurada *(f)*

Lochkartenspalte *(f) n* De
En card column
Es columna de ficha *(f)*
Fr colonne de carte *(f)*
It colonna della scheda *(f)*
Pt coluna de ficha *(f)*

lochschrift- übersetzen De
En interpret
Es interpretar
Fr interpréter
It interpretare
Pt interpretar

Lochschrift- übersetzer *(m) n* De
En interpreter
Es interpretadora *(f)*
Fr traductrice *(f)*
It interprete *(m)*
Pt intérprete *(m)*

Lochstellung *(f) n* De
En punching position
Es posición de perforación *(f)*
Fr position de perforation *(f)*
It posizione di perforazione *(f)*
Pt posição de perfuração *(f)*

Lochstreifen *(m) n* De
En perforated tape
Es cinta perforada *(f)*
Fr bande perforée *(f)*
It nastro perforato *(m)*
Pt fita perfurada *(f)*

Lochstreifenleser *(m) n* De
En paper-tape reader
Es lectora de cinta de papel *(f)*
Fr lecteur de bande perforée *(m)*
It lettore di nastri di carta *(m)*
Pt leitor de fita de papel *(m)*

Lochstreifenlocher *(m) n* De
En paper-tape punch
Es perforador de cinta *(m)*
Fr perforatrice à papier *(f)*
It perforatrice di nastri di carta *(f)*
Pt perfuradora de fita de papel *(f)*

Lochungs- geschwindigkeit *(f) n* De
En perforation rate
Es velocidade de perforación *(f)*
Fr vitesse de perforation *(f)*
It volume di perforazione *(m)*
Pt índice de perfuração *(m)*

Lochungsprüfer *(m) n* De
En punch verifier
Es verificador de perforación *(m)*
Fr vérificatrice de perforations *(f)*
It verificatrice della perforazione *(f)*
Pt verificador de perfuração *(m)*

lock out En
De sperren
Es bloquear
Fr bloquer
It chiudere fuori
Pt bloquear

log *n* En
De Journal *(n)*
Es registro *(m)*
Fr consignation *(f)*
It registro *(m)*
Pt diário *(m)*

log *vb* En
De senden
Es registrar
Fr consigner
It registrare
Pt registar em diário

logger *n* En
De Schreibgerät *(n)*
Es registrador automático *(m)*
Fr enregistreur automatique *(m)*
It registratore automatico *(m)*
Pt registador automático *(m)*

logic *n* En
De Verknüpfung *(f)*
Es lógica *(f)*
Fr logique *(f)*
It logica *(f)*
Pt lógica *(f)*

logica *(f) n* It
De Verknüpfung *(f)*
En logic
Es lógica *(f)*
Fr logique *(f)*
Pt lógica *(f)*

lógica *(f) n* Es, Pt
De Verknüpfung *(f)*
En logic
Fr logique *(f)*
It logica *(f)*

logica accoppiata emittitore *(f)* It
De emittergekoppelte Verknüpfung *(f)*
En emitter-coupled logic (ECL)
Es lógica de emisor acoplado *(f)*
Fr logique à couplage par émetteur *(f)*
Pt lógica acoplada a um emissor *(f)*

lógica acoplada a um emissor *(f)* Pt
De emittergekoppelte Verknüpfung *(f)*
En emitter-coupled logic (ECL)
Es lógica de emisor acoplado *(f)*
Fr logique à couplage par émetteur *(f)*
It logica accoppiata emittitore *(f)*

lógica de emisor acoplado *(f)* Es
De emittergekoppelte Verknüpfung *(f)*
En emitter-coupled logic (ECL)
Fr logique à couplage par émetteur *(f)*

It logica accoppiata emittitore *(f)*
Pt lógica acoplada a um emissor *(f)*

lógica de flúidos *(f)* Es
De Fluidverknüpfung *(f)*
En fluid logic
Fr logique des fluides *(f)*
It logica fluida *(f)*
Pt lógica fluida *(f)*

lógica de injecção integrada *(f)* Pt
De integrierte Injektions-verknüpfung *(f)*
En integrated injection logic
Es lógica de inyección integrada *(f)*
Fr logique d'injection intégrée *(f)*
It logica di iniezione integrata *(f)*

lógica de inyección integrada *(f)* Es
De integrierte Injektions-verknüpfung *(f)*
En integrated injection logic
Fr logique d'injection intégrée *(f)*
It logica di iniezione integrata *(f)*
Pt lógica de injecção integrada *(f)*

lógica de resistencia-transistor *(f)* Es
De Widerstand-Transistor-verknüpfung *(f)*
En resistor-transistor logic (RTL)
Fr logique résistance-transistor *(f)*
It logica resistore-transistore *(f)*
Pt lógica de resistor-transistor *(f)*

lógica de resistor-transistor *(f)* Pt
De Widerstand-Transistor-verknüpfung *(f)*
En resistor-transistor logic (RTL)
Es lógica de resistencia-transistor *(f)*
Fr logique résistance-transistor *(f)*
It logica resistore-transistore *(f)*

lógica de transistor de díodo *(f)* Pt
De Diodentransistor-verknüpfung *(f)*
En diode-transistor ligic (DTL)
Es lógica diodo-transistor *(f)*
Fr logique à diodes et transistors *(f)*
It logica diodo-transistore *(f)*

lógica de transistor-transistor *(f)* Es
De Transistor-Transistor-Verknüpfung *(f)*
En transistor-transistor logic (TTL)
Fr logique transistor-transistor *(f)*
It logica transistore-transistore *(f)*
Pt lógica transistor-transistor *(f)*

logica di iniezione integrata *(f)* It
De integrierte Injektions-verknüpfung *(f)*
En integrated injection logic
Es lógica de inyección integrada *(f)*
Fr logique d'injection intégrée *(f)*
Pt lógica de injecção integrada *(f)*

lógica diodo-transistor *(f)* Es
De Diodentransistor-verknüpfung *(f)*
En diode-transistor logic (DTL)
Fr logique à diodes et transistors *(f)*
It logica diodo-transistore *(f)*
Pt lógica de transistor de díodo *(f)*

logica diodo-transistore *(f)* It
De Diodentransistor-verknüpfung *(f)*
En diode-transistor logic (DTL)
Es lógica diodo-transistor *(f)*
Fr logique à diodes et transistors *(f)*
Pt lógica de transistor de díodo *(f)*

logica fluida *(f)* It
De Fluidverknüpfung *(f)*
En fluid logic
Es lógica de flúidos *(f)*
Fr logique des fluides *(f)*
Pt lógica fluida *(f)*

lógica fluida *(f)* Pt
De Fluidverknüpfung *(f)*
En fluid logic
Es lógica de flúidos *(f)*
Fr logique des fluides *(f)*
It logica fluida *(f)*

logica resistore-transistore *(f)* It
De Widerstand-Transistor-verknüpfung *(f)*
En resistor-transistor logic (RTL)
Es lógica de resistencia-transistor *(f)*
Fr logique résistance-transistor *(f)*
Pt lógica de resistor-transistor *(f)*

logica simbolica *(f)* It
De symbolische Verknüpfung *(f)*
En symbolic logic
Es lógica simbólica *(f)*
Fr logique symbolique *(f)*
Pt lógica simbólica *(f)*

lógica simbólica *(f)* Es, Pt
De symbolische Verknüpfung *(f)*
En symbolic logic
Fr logique symbolique *(f)*
It logica simbolica *(f)*

logica transistore-transistore *(f)* It
De Transistor-Transistor-Verknüpfung *(f)*
En transistor-transistor logic (TTL)
Es lógica de transistor-transistor *(f)*
Fr logique transistor-transistor *(f)*
Pt lógica transistor-transistor *(f)*

lógica transistor-transistor *(f)* Pt
De Transistor-Transistor-Verknüpfung *(f)*
En transistor-transistor logic (TTL)
Es lógica de transistor-transistor *(f)*
Fr logique transistor-transistor *(f)*
It logica transistore-transistore *(f)*

logic circuit En
De Verknüpfungs-schaltung *(f)*
Es circuito lógico *(m)*
Fr circuit logique *(m)*
It circuito logico *(m)*
Pt circuito lógico *(m)*

logic diagram En
De Verknüpfungs-diagramm *(n)*
Es diagrama lógico *(m)*
Fr schéma logique *(m)*
It diagramma logico *(m)*
Pt diagrama lógico *(m)*

logic gate En
De Verknüpfungstor *(n)*
Es puerta lógica *(f)*

Fr porte logique *(f)*
It porta logica *(f)*
Pt porta lógica *(f)*

logiciel *(m) n* Fr
De Software *(f)*
En software
Es soporte lógico *(m)*
It software *(m)*
Pt software *(m)*

logic(al) operation En
De logische Funktion *(f)*
Es operación lógica *(f)*
Fr opération logique *(f)*
It operazione logica *(f)*
Pt operação lógica *(f)*

logic(al) operator En
De Boolescher Operator *(m)*
Es operador lógico *(m)*
Fr opérateur logique *(m)*
It operatore logico *(m)*
Pt operador lógico *(m)*

logic(al) shift En
De logische Verschiebung *(f)*
Es desplazamiento lógico *(m)*
Fr décalage logique *(m)*
It spostamento logico *(m)*
Pt mudança lógica *(f)*

logic(al) unit (LU) En
De logische Einheit *(f)*
Es unidad lógica *(f)*
Fr unité logique *(f)*
It unità logica *(f)*
Pt unidade lógica *(f)*

logic symbol En
De logisches Symbol *(n)*
Es símbolo lógico *(m)*
Fr symbole logique *(m)*
It simbolo logico *(m)*
Pt símbolo lógico *(m)*

logique *(f) n* Fr
De Verknüpfung *(f)*
En logic
Es lógica *(f)*
It logica *(f)*
Pt lógica *(f)*

logique à couplage par émetteur *(f)* Fr
De emittergekoppelte Verknüpfung *(f)*
En emitter-coupled logic (ECL)
Es lógica de emisor acoplado *(f)*
It logica accoppiata emittitore *(f)*
Pt lógica acoplada a um emissor *(f)*

logique à diodes et transistors *(f)* Fr
De Diodentransistor-verknüpfung *(f)*
En diode-transistor logic (DTL)
Es lógica diodo-transistor *(f)*
It logica diodo-transistore *(f)*
Pt lógica de transistor de díodo *(f)*

logique des fluides *(f)* Fr
De Fluidverknüpfung *(f)*
En fluid logic
Es lógica de flúidos *(f)*
It logica fluida *(f)*
Pt lógica fluida *(f)*

logique d'injection intégrée *(f)* Fr
De integrierte Injektions-verknüpfung *(f)*
En integrated injection logic
Es lógica de inyección integrada *(f)*
It logica di iniezione integrata *(f)*
Pt lógica de injecção integrada *(f)*

logique résistance-transistor *(f)* Fr
De Widerstand-Transistor-verknüpfung *(f)*
En resistor-transistor logic (RTL)
Es lógica de resistencia-transistor *(f)*
It logica resistore-transistore *(f)*
Pt lógica de resistor-transistor *(f)*

logique symbolique *(f)* Fr
De symbolische Verknüpfung *(f)*
En symbolic logic
Es lógica simbólica *(f)*
It logica simbolica *(f)*
Pt lógica simbólica *(f)*

logique transistor-transistor *(f)* Fr
De Transistor-Transistor-Verknüpfung *(f)*
En transistor-transistor logic (TTL)
Es lógica de transistor-transistor *(f)*
It logica transistore-transistore *(f)*
Pt lógica transistor-transistor *(f)*

logische Einheit *(f)* De
En logic(al) unit (LU)
Es unidad lógica *(f)*
Fr unité logique *(f)*
It unità logica *(f)*
Pt unidade lógica *(f)*

logische Funktion *(f)* De
En logic(al) operation
Es operación lógica *(f)*
Fr opération logique *(f)*
It operazione logica *(f)*
Pt operação lógica *(f)*

logisches Symbol *(n)* De
En logic symbol
Es símbolo lógico *(m)*
Fr symbole logique *(m)*
It simbolo logico *(m)*
Pt símbolo lógico *(m)*

logische Verschiebung *(f)* De
En logic(al) shift
Es desplazamiento lógico *(m)*
Fr décalage logique *(m)*
It spostamento logico *(m)*
Pt mudança lógica *(f)*

Lokalrechnung *(f) n* De
En home computing
Es cálculo inicial *(m)*
Fr traitement domestique *(m)*
It elaborazione in proprio *(f)*
Pt computação doméstica *(f)*

longitud de bloque *(f)* Es
De Blocklänge *(f)*
En block length
Fr longueur de bloc *(f)*
It lunghezza del blocco *(m)*
Pt comprimento de bloco *(m)*

longitud de bloque fija *(f)* Es
De feste Blocklänge *(f)*
En fixed block length
Fr bloc de longueur fixe *(m)*
It lunghezza del blocco fisso *(f)*
Pt comprimento de bloco fixo *(m)*

longitud de campo *(f)* Es
De Feldlänge *(f)*
En field length
Fr longueur de zone *(f)*
It lunghezza del campo *(f)*
Pt comprimento de campo *(m)*

longitud de palabra *(f)* Es
De Wortlänge *(f)*
En word length
Fr longueur de mot *(f)*
It lunghezza della voce *(f)*
Pt comprimento de palavra *(m)*

longitud de registro *(f)* Es
De Satzlänge *(f)*
En record length
Fr longueur d'enregistrement *(f)*
It lunghezza del record *(f)*
Pt comprimento de registo *(m)*

longueur de bloc *(f)* Fr
De Blocklänge *(f)*
En block length
Es longitud de bloque *(f)*
It lunghezza del blocco *(m)*
Pt comprimento de bloco *(m)*

longueur de mot *(f)* Fr
De Wortlänge *(f)*
En word length
Es longitud de palabra *(f)*
It lunghezza della voce *(f)*
Pt comprimento de palavra *(m)*

longueur d'enregistrement *(f)* Fr
De Satzlänge *(f)*
En record length
Es longitud de registro *(f)*
It lunghezza del record *(f)*
Pt comprimento de registo *(m)*

longueur de zone *(f)* Fr
De Feldlänge *(f)*
En field length
Es longitud de campo *(f)*
It lunghezza del campo *(f)*
Pt comprimento de campo *(m)*

longueur double *(f)* Fr
De Doppellänge *(f)*
En double-length
Es doble longitud *(f)*
It lunghezza doppia *(f)*
Pt comprimento duplo *(m)*

look up En
De aufsuchen
Es consultar
Fr consulter
It consultare
Pt consultar

look-up table En
De Nachschlagetabelle *(f)*
Es tabla de consulta *(f)*
Fr table à consulter *(f)*
It tavola di consultazione *(f)*
Pt tabela de consulta *(f)*

loop *n* En
De Schleife *(f)*
Es bucle *(m)*
Fr boucle *(f)*
It ciclo *(m)*
Pt circuito *(m)*

loosely coupled En
De lose gekoppelt
Es débilmente acoplado
Fr lâchement couplé
It accoppiado lentamente
Pt acoplado de forma solta

löschbarer PROM *(m)* De
En erasable PROM (EPROM)
Es PROM borrable *(f)*
Fr PROM effaçable *(f)*
It PROM cancellabile *(f)*
Pt PROM apagável *(f)*

löschbarer Speicher *(m)* De
En erasable memory
Es memoria borrable *(f)*
Fr mémoire effaçable *(f)*
It memoria cancellabile *(f)*
Pt memória apagável *(f)*

löschen *vb* De
En clear; delete; erase
Es borrar; despejar; suprimir
Fr effacer; éliminer, remettre à zéro
It cancellare; rimettere a zero
Pt apagar; limpar

Löschen der Addition *(n)* De
En destructive addition
Es suma destructiva *(f)*
Fr addition destructive *(f)*
It addizione distruttiva *(f)*
Pt adição destrutiva *(f)*

Löschen der Auslesung *(n)* De
En destructive read-out
Es lectura destructiva *(f)*
Fr lecture destructive *(f)*
It lettura distruttiva *(f)*
Pt leitura destrutiva *(f)*

Löschkopf *(m)* *n* De
En erase head
Es cabeza de borrado *(f)*
Fr tête d'effacement *(f)*
It testina di cancellazione *(f)*
Pt cabeça apagadora *(f)*

Löschung *(f)* *n* De
En deletion; erase
Es borrado; eliminación *(m f)*
Fr effacement *(m)*
It cancellazione *(f)*
Pt apagado; eliminação *(m f)*

Löschungssatz *(m)* *n* De
En deletion record
Es registro de eliminación *(m)*
Fr enregistrement d'effacement *(m)*
It record di cancellazione *(m)*
Pt registo de apagamento *(m)*

lose gekoppelt De
En loosely coupled
Es débilmente acoplado
Fr lâchement couplé
It accoppiado lentamente
Pt acoplado de forma solta

loss *n* En
De Verlust *(m)*
Es pérdida *(f)*
Fr perte *(f)*
It perdita *(f)*
Pt perda *(f)*

low-level language En
De Kleinsignalsprache *(f)*
Es lenguaje de bajo nivel *(m)*
Fr langage bas de gamme *(m)*
It linguaggio di basso livello *(m)*
Pt linguagem de baixo nível *(f)*

low order En
De niedriger Grad *(m)*
Es orden inferior *(m)*
Fr ordre bas *(m)*
It ordine basso *(m)*
Pt ordem de baixo nível *(f)*

lunghezza del blocco *(m)* It
De Blocklänge *(f)*
En block length
Es longitud de bloque *(f)*
Fr longueur de bloc *(f)*
Pt comprimento de bloco *(m)*

lunghezza del blocco fisso *(f)* It
De feste Blocklänge *(f)*
En fixed block length
Es longitud de bloque fija *(f)*
Fr bloc de longueur fixe *(m)*
Pt comprimento de bloco fixo *(m)*

lunghezza del campo *(f)* It
De Feldlänge *(f)*
En field length
Es longitud de campo *(f)*
Fr longueur de zone *(f)*
Pt comprimento de campo *(m)*

lunghezza della voce *(f)* It
De Wortlänge *(f)*
En word length
Es longitud de palabra *(f)*
Fr longueur de mot *(f)*
Pt comprimento de palavra *(m)*

lunghezza del record *(f)* It
De Satzlänge *(f)*
En record length
Es longitud de registro *(f)*
Fr longueur d'enregistrement *(f)*
Pt comprimento de registo *(m)*

lunghezza doppia *(f)* It
De Doppellänge *(f)*
En double-length
Es doble longitud *(f)*

Fr longueur double *(f)*
Pt comprimento duplo *(m)*

M

macchina da scrivere *(f)* It
De Screibmaschine *(f)*
En typewriter
Es máquina de escribir *(f)*
Fr machine à écrire *(f)*
Pt máquina de escrever *(f)*

macchina da scrivere a console *(f)* It
De Konsolenschreib-maschine *(f)*
En console typewriter
Es máquina de escribir de consola *(f)*
Fr machine à écrire de pupitre *(f)*
Pt máquina de escrever de consola *(f)*

macchina di Turing universale *(f)* It
De Turings-Universalmaschine *(f)*
En universal Turing machine
Es máquina de Turing universal *(f)*
Fr machine de Turing universelle *(f)*
Pt máquina Turing universal *(f)*

macchina virtuale *(f)* It
De virtuelle Maschine *(f)*
En virtual machine
Es máquina virtual *(f)*
Fr machine virtuelle *(f)*
Pt máquina virtual *(f)*

machine address En
De Maschinenadresse *(f)*
Es dirección de máquina *(f)*
Fr adresse absolue *(f)*
It indirizzo di macchina *(m)*
Pt endereço da máquina *(m)*

machine à écrire *(f)* Fr
De Schreibmaschine *(f)*
En typewriter
Es máquina de escribir *(f)*
It macchina da scrivere *(f)*
Pt máquina de escrever *(f)*

machine à écrire de pupitre *(f)* Fr
De Konsolenschreib-maschine *(f)*
En console typewriter
Es máquina de escribir de consola *(f)*
It macchina da scrivere a console *(f)*
Pt máquina de escrever de consola *(f)*

machine code En
De Maschinencode *(m)*
Es código de máquina *(m)*
Fr code machine *(m)*
It codice macchina *(m)*
Pt código da máquina *(m)*

machine de Turing universelle *(f)* Fr
De Turings-Universalmaschine *(f)*
En universal Turing machine
Es máquina de Turing universal *(f)*
It macchina di Turing universale *(f)*
Pt máquina Turing universal *(f)*

machine-independent *adj* En
De maschinen-unabhängig
Es independiente de la máquina
Fr indépendent de la machine
It indipendente dalla macchina
Pt independente da máquina

machine intelligence En
De Maschinen-programmierung *(f)*
Es inteligencia de máquina *(f)*
Fr intelligence-machine *(f)*
It intelligenza della macchina *(f)*
Pt inteligência da máquina *(f)*

machine language En
De Maschinensprache *(f)*
Es lenguaje de máquina *(m)*
Fr langage machine *(m)*
It linguaggio macchina *(m)*
Pt linguagem da máquina *(f)*

machine-readable *adj* En
De maschinenlesbar
Es legible por la máquina
Fr compréhensible par une machine
It leggibile dalla macchina
Pt legível pela máquina

machine room En
De Maschinenraum *(m)*
Es sala de máquinas *(f)*
Fr salle des machines *(f)*
It sala macchine *(f)*
Pt sala de máquinas *(f)*

machine run En
De Maschinenlauf *(m)*
Es pasada de máquina *(f)*
Fr passage en machine *(m)*
It giro della macchina *(m)*
Pt passagem da máquina *(f)*

machines-outils programmées automatiquement *(f pl)* Fr
De automatisch programmierte Werkzeuge *(pl)*
En automatically programmed tools (APT)
Es herramientas programadas automáticamente *(f pl)*
It strumenti programmati automaticamente *(m pl)*
Pt ferramentas programadas automaticamente *(f pl)*

machine virtuelle *(f)* Fr
De virtuelle Maschine *(f)*
En virtual machine
Es máquina virtual *(f)*
It macchina virtuale *(f)*
Pt máquina virtual *(f)*

machine word En
De Maschinenwort *(n)*
Es palabra de máquina *(f)*
Fr mot machine *(m)*
It voce macchina *(f)*
Pt palavra da máquina *(f)*

macro *adj* En, Es, Fr, It, Pt
De Makro

macro-instrução *(f) n* Pt
De Makrobefehl *(m)*
En macro instruction
Es macroinstrucción *(f)*
Fr macro-instruction *(f)*
It macroistruzione *(f)*

macroinstrucción *(f) n* Es
De Makrobefehl *(m)*
En macro instruction
Fr macro-instruction *(f)*
It macroistruzione *(f)*
Pt macro-instrução *(f)*

macro instruction En
De Makrobefehl *(m)*
Es macroinstrucción *(f)*
Fr macro-instruction *(f)*
It macroistruzione *(f)*
Pt macro-instrução *(f)*

macro-instruction *(f) n* Fr
De Makrobefehl *(m)*
En macro instruction
Es macroinstrucción *(f)*

It macroistruzione *(f)*
Pt macro-instrução *(f)*

macroistruzione *(f)* *n* It
De Makrobefehl *(m)*
En macro instruction
Es macroinstrucción *(f)*
Fr macro-instruction *(f)*
Pt macro-instrução *(f)*

macroprogramação *(f)* *n* Pt
De Makro-programmierung *(f)*
En macroprogramming
Es macroprogramación *(f)*
Fr macro-programmation *(f)*
It macro-programmazione *(f)*

macroprogramación *(f)* *n* Es
De Makro-programmierung *(f)*
En macroprogramming
Fr macro-programmation *(f)*
It macro-programmazione *(f)*
Pt macroprogramação *(f)*

macro-programmation *(f)* *n* Fr
De Makro-programmierung *(f)*
En macroprogramming
Es macroprogramación *(f)*
It macro-programmazione *(f)*
Pt macroprogramação *(f)*

macroprogrammazione *(f)* *n* It
De Makro-programmierung *(f)*
En macroprogramming
Es macroprogramación *(f)*
Fr macro-programmation *(f)*
Pt macroprogramação *(f)*

macroprogramming *n* En
De Makro-programmierung *(f)*
Es macroprogramación *(f)*
Fr macro-programmation *(f)*
It macro-programmazione *(f)*
Pt macroprogramação *(f)*

magasin *(m)* *n* Fr
De Magazin *(n)*
En magazine
Es almacén *(m)*
It caricatore *(m)*
Pt armazém *(m)*

magasin d'alimentation *(m)* Fr
De Magazin *(n)*
En hopper
Es depósito de alimentación *(m)*
It serbatoio di alimentazione (schede) *(m)*
Pt tremonha *(f)*

Magazin *(n)* *n* De
En hopper; magazine
Es almavén; depósito de alimentación *(m)*
Fr magasin; magasin d'alimentation *(m)*
It caricatore; serbatoio di alimentazione (schede) *(m)*
Pt armazém; tremonha *(m f)*

magazine *n* En
De Magazin *(n)*
Es almacén *(m)*
Fr magasin *(m)*
It caricatore *(m)*
Pt armazém *(m)*

Magnetband *(n)* *n* De
En magnetic tape
Es cinta magnética *(f)*
Fr bande magnétique *(f)*
It nastro magnetico *(m)*
Pt fita magnética *(f)*

Magnetelement *(n)* *n* De
En magnetic cell
Es celda magnética *(f)*
Fr cellule magnétique *(f)*
It cellula magnetica *(f)*
Pt célula magnética *(f)*

magnetic card En
De Magnetkarte *(f)*
Es ficha magnética *(f)*
Fr carte magnétique *(f)*
It scheda magnetica *(f)*
Pt ficha magnética *(f)*

magnetic cell En
De Magnetelement *(n)*
Es celda magnética *(f)*
Fr cellule magnétique *(f)*
It cellula magnetica *(f)*
Pt célula magnética *(f)*

magnetic core En
De Magnetkern *(m)*
Es núcleo magnético *(m)*
Fr tore magnétique *(m)*
It nucleo magnetico *(m)*
Pt núcleo magnético *(m)*

magnetic disk En
De Magnetplatte *(f)*
Es disco magnético *(m)*
Fr disque magnétique *(m)*
It disco magnetico *(m)*
Pt disco magnético *(m)*

magnetic drum En
De Magnettrommel *(f)*
Es tambor magnético *(m)*
Fr tambour magnétique *(m)*
It tamburo magnetico *(m)*
Pt tambor magnético *(m)*

magnetic ink En
De Magnettinte *(f)*
Es tinta magnética *(f)*
Fr encre magnétique *(f)*
It inchiostro magnetico *(m)*
Pt tinta magnética *(f)*

magnetic-ink character recognition En
De Erkennung von Magnettintenzeichen *(f)*
Es reconocimiento de caracteres de tinta magnética *(m)*
Fr reconnaissance magnétique de caractères *(f)*
It riconoscimento di caratteri di inchiostro magnetico *(m)*
Pt reconhecimento de caracteres de tinta magnética *(m)*

magnetic media En
De magnetisches Aufzeichnungsmittel *(n)*
Es medios magnéticos *(m pl)*
Fr milieux magnétiques *(m pl)*
It mezzi magnetici *(m pl)*
Pt meios magnéticos *(m pl)*

magnetic memory En
De Magnetspeicher *(m)*
Es memoria magnética *(f)*
Fr mémoire magnétique *(f)*
It memoria magnetica *(f)*
Pt memória magnética *(f)*

magnetic tape En
De Magnetband *(n)*
Es cinta magnética *(f)*
Fr bande magnétique *(f)*
It nastro magnetico *(m)*
Pt fita magnética *(f)*

magnetisches Aufzeichnungsmittel *(n)* De
En magnetic media
Es medios magnéticos *(m pl)*
Fr milieux magnétiques *(m pl)*
It mezzi magnetici *(m pl)*
Pt meios magnéticos *(m pl)*

Magnetkarte *(f)* *n* De
En magnetic card
Es ficha magnética *(f)*
Fr carte magnétique *(f)*
It scheda magnetica *(f)*
Pt ficha magnética *(f)*

Magnetkern *(m)* *n* De
En magnetic core

Es núcleo magnético *(m)*
Fr tore magnétique *(m)*
It nucleo magnetico *(m)*
Pt núcleo magnético *(m)*

Magnetkopf *(m) n* De
En head
Es cabeza *(f)*
Fr tête *(f)*
It testina *(f)*
Pt cabeça *(f)*

Magnetkopfspalt *(m) n* De
En head gap
Es entrehierro *(m)*
Fr entrefer *(m)*
It distanza dalla testina *(f)*
Pt intervalo de cabeça *(m)*

magnetoestricción *(f) n* Es
De Magnetostriktion *(f)*
En magnetostriction
Fr magnétostriction *(f)*
It magneto-strizione *(f)*
Pt magnetostrição *(f)*

magnetostrição *(f) n* Pt
De Magnetostriktion *(f)*
En magnetostriction
Es magnetoestricción *(f)*
Fr magnétostriction *(f)*
It magneto-strizione *(f)*

magnetostriction *n* En
De Magnetostriktion *(f)*
Es magnetoestricción *(f)*
Fr magnétostriction *(f)*
It magneto-strizione *(f)*
Pt magnetostrição *(f)*

magnétostriction *(f) n* Fr
De Magnetostriktion *(f)*
En magnetostriction
Es magnetoestricción *(f)*
It magneto-strizione *(f)*
Pt magnetostrição *(f)*

Magnetostriktion *(f) n* De
En magnetostriction
Es magnetoestricción *(f)*
Fr magnétostriction *(f)*
It magneto-strizione *(f)*
Pt magnetostrição *(f)*

magneto-strizione *(f) n* It
De Magnetostriktion *(f)*
En magnetostriction
Es magnetoestricción *(f)*
Fr magnétostriction *(f)*
Pt magnetostrição *(f)*

Magnetplatte *(f) n* De
En magnetic disk
Es disco magnético *(m)*
Fr disque magnétique *(m)*
It disco magnetico *(m)*
Pt disco magnético *(m)*

Magnetplatten-installation *(f) n* De
En disk pack
Es pila de discos *(f)*
Fr dispac *(m)*
It pacco di dischi *(m)*
Pt pacote de discos *(m)*

Magnetspeicher *(m) n* De
En magnetic memory
Es memoria magnética *(f)*
Fr mémoire magnétique *(f)*
It memoria magnetica *(f)*
Pt memória magnética *(f)*

Magnettinte *(f) n* De
En magnetic ink
Es tinta magnética *(f)*
Fr encre magnétique *(f)*
It inchiostro magnetico *(m)*
Pt tinta magnética *(f)*

Magnettrommel *(f) n* De
En magnetic drum
Es tambor magnético *(m)*
Fr tambour magnétique *(m)*
It tamburo magnetico *(m)*
Pt tambor magnético *(m)*

mainframe computer *n* En
De Hauptrechner *(m)*
Es computador principal *(m)*
Fr ordinateur principal *(m)*
It calcolatore principale *(m)*
Pt computador principal *(m)*

main memory En
De Hauptspeicher *(m)*
Es memoria principal *(f)*
Fr mémoire centrale *(f)*
It memoria principale *(f)*
Pt memória principal *(f)*

main storage En
De Hauptspeicherung *(f)*
Es almacenamiento principal *(m)*
Fr stockage central *(m)*
It immagazzinamento principale *(m)*
Pt armazenagem principal *(f)*

maintenance *n* En; Fr *(f)*
De Wartung *(f)*
Es mantenimiento *(m)*
It manutenzione *(f)*
Pt manutenção *(f)*

maintenance supplémentaire *(f)* Fr
De Zusatzwartung *(f)*
En supplementary maintenance
Es mantenimiento suplementario *(m)*
It manutenzione supplementare *(f)*
Pt manutenção suplementária *(f)*

Majoritätselement *(n) n* De
En majority element
Es elemento mayoritario *(m)*
Fr élément majoritaire *(m)*
It elemento di maggioranza *(m)*
Pt elemento de maioria *(m)*

majority element En
De Majoritätselement *(n)*
Es elemento mayoritario *(m)*
Fr élément majoritaire *(m)*
It elemento di maggioranza *(m)*
Pt elemento de maioria *(m)*

Makro *adj* De
En macro
Es macro
Fr macro
It macro
Pt macro

Makrobefehl *(m) n* De
En macro instruction
Es macroinstrucción *(f)*
Fr macro-instruction *(f)*
It macroistruzione *(f)*
Pt macro-instrução *(f)*

Makroprogrammierung *(f) n* De
En macroprogramming
Es macroprogramación *(f)*
Fr macro-programmation *(f)*
It macro-programmazione *(f)*
Pt macroprogramação *(f)*

malograrse *vb* Es
De abbrechen
En abort
Fr suspendre
It abortire
Pt abortar

manipolare *vb* It
De edieren
En edit
Es editar
Fr mettre en forme
Pt editar

manipolazione di stringa *(f)* It
De Folgebearbeitung *(f)*
En string manipulation
Es manipulación de series *(f)*
Fr manipulation de chaîne *(f)*
Pt manipulação de fileira *(f)*

manipulação de fileira *(f)* Pt
De Folgebearbeitung *(f)*
En string manipulation
Es manipulación de series *(f)*

Fr manipulation de chaîne *(f)*
It manipolazione di stringa *(f)*

manipulación de series *(f)* Es
De Folgebearbeitung *(f)*
En string manipulation
Fr manipulation de chaîne *(f)*
It manipolazione di stringa *(f)*
Pt manipulação de fileira *(f)*

manipulated variable En
De Stellgröβe *(f)*
Es variable manipulada *(f)*
Fr variable manipulée *(f)*
It variabile manipolata *(f)*
Pt variável manipulada *(f)*

manipulation de chaîne *(f)* Fr
De Folgebearbeitung *(f)*
En string manipulation
Es manipulación de series *(f)*
It manipolazione di stringa *(f)*
Pt manipulação de fileira *(f)*

man-machine interaction En
De Personal-Maschinen Wechselwirkung *(f)*
Es interacción hombre-máquina *(f)*
Fr interaction homme-machine *(f)*
It interazione uomo-macchina *(f)*
Pt interacção homem-máquina *(f)*

man-machine interface En
De Personal-Maschinen Schnittstelle *(f)*
Es acoplamiento hombre-máquina *(m)*
Fr interface homme-machine *(f)*
It interfaccia uomo-macchina *(f)*
Pt interface homem-máquina *(f)*

mansaje de error *(m)* Es
De Fehlernachricht *(f)*
En error message
Fr message d'erreur *(m)*
It messaggio errore *(m)*
Pt mensagem de erro *(f)*

mantener *vb* Es
De anhalten
En hold
Fr tenir
It mantenere
Pt manter

mantenere *vb* It
De anhalten
En hold
Es mantener
Fr tenir
Pt manter

mantenimiento *(m) n* Es
De Wartung *(f)*
En maintenance
Fr maintenance *(f)*
It manutenzione *(f)*
Pt manutenção *(f)*

mantenimiento correctivo *(m)* Es
De Verbesserungs-wartung *(f)*
En corrective maintenance
Fr entretien correctif *(m)*
It manutenzione correttiva *(f)*
Pt manutenção correctiva *(f)*

mantenimiento de ficheros *(m)* Es
De Dateiwartung *(f)*
En file maintenance
Fr tenue à jour de fichier *(f)*
It manutenzione del file *(f)*
Pt manutenção de arquivo *(f)*

mantenimiento de rutins *(m)* Es
De regelmäsige Wartung *(f)*
En routine maintenance
Fr entretien de routine *(m)*
It manutenzione ordinaria *(f)*
Pt manutenção de rotina *(f)*

mantenimiento preventivo *(m)* Es
De vorbeugende Wartung *(f)*
En preventative maintenance
Fr entretien préventif *(m)*
It manutenzione preventiva *(f)*
Pt manutenção preventiva *(f)*

mantenimiento programado *(m)* Es
De Terminwartung *(f)*
En scheduled maintenance
Fr entretien périodique *(m)*
It manutenzione programmata *(f)*
Pt manutenção planificada *(f)*

mantenimiento suplementario *(m)* Es
De Zusatzwartung *(f)*
En supplementary maintenance
Fr maintenance supplémentaire *(f)*
It manutenzione supplementare *(f)*
Pt manutenção suplementária *(f)*

manter *vb* Pt
De anhalten
En hold
Es mantener
Fr tenir
It mantenere

manual control En
De Handsteuerung *(f)*
Es control manual *(m)*
Fr commande manuelle *(f)*
It controllo manuale *(m)*
Pt controle manual *(m)*

manual input En
De Handeingabe *(f)*
Es entrada manual *(f)*
Fr introduction manuelle *(f)*
It input manuale *(m)*
Pt input manual *(m)*

manufactura com auxílio de computador *(f)* Pt
De computerunter-stützte Herstellung *(f)*
En computer-aided manufacture (CAM)
Es fabricación con la ayuda de ordenador *(f)*
Fr fabrication assistée par ordinateur (FAO) *(f)*
It produzione basata sull'elaboratore *(f)*

manutenção *(f) n* Pt
De Wartung *(f)*
En maintenance
Es mantenimiento *(m)*
Fr maintenance *(f)*
It manutenzione *(f)*

manutenção correctiva *(f)* Pt
De Verbesserungs-wartung *(f)*
En corrective maintenance
Es mantenimiento correctivo *(m)*
Fr entretien correctif *(m)*
It manutenzione correttiva *(f)*

manutenção de arquivo *(f)* Pt
De Dateiwartung *(f)*
En file maintenance
Es mantenimiento de ficheros *(m)*
Fr tenue à jour de fichier *(f)*
It manutenzione del file *(f)*

manutenção de rotina *(f)* Pt
De regelmäβige Wartung *(f)*
En routine maintenance
Es mantenimiento de rutina *(m)*
Fr entretien de routine *(m)*
It manutenzione ordinaria *(f)*

manutenção planificada *(f)* Pt
De Terminwartung *(f)*
En scheduled maintenance
Es mantenimiento programado *(m)*
Fr entretien périodique *(m)*
It manutenzione programmata *(f)*

manutenção preventiva *(f)* Pt
De vorbeugende Wartung *(f)*
En preventative maintenance
Es mantenimiento preventivo *(m)*
Fr entretien préventif *(m)*
It manutenzione preventiva *(f)*

manutenção suplementária *(f)* Pt
De Zusatzwartung *(f)*
En supplementary maintenance
Es mantenimiento suplementario *(m)*
Fr maintenance supplémentaire *(f)*
It manutenzione supplementare *(f)*

manutenzione *(f) n* It
De Wartung *(f)*
En maintenance
Es mantenimiento *(m)*
Fr maintenance *(f)*
Pt manutenção *(f)*

manutenzione correttiva *(f)* It
De Verbesserungswartung *(f)*
En corrective maintenance
Es mantenimiento correctivo *(m)*
Fr entretien correctif *(m)*
Pt manutenção correctiva *(f)*

manutenzione del file *(f)* It
De Dateiwartung *(f)*
En file maintenance
Es mantenimiento de ficheros *(m)*
Fr tenue à jour de fichier *(f)*
Pt manutenção de arquivo *(f)*

manutenzione ordinaria *(f)* It
De regelmäßige Wartung *(f)*
En routine maintenance
Es mantenimiento de rutina *(m)*
Fr entretien de routine *(m)*
Pt manutenção de rotina *(f)*

manutenzione preventiva *(f)* It
De vorbeugende Wartung *(f)*
En preventative maintenance
Es mantenimiento preventivo *(m)*
Fr entretien préventif *(m)*
Pt manutenção preventiva *(f)*

manutenzione programmata *(f)* It
De Terminwartung *(f)*
En scheduled maintenance
Es mantenimiento programado *(m)*
Fr entretien périodique *(m)*
Pt manutenção planificada *(f)*

manutenzione supplementare *(f)* It
De Zusatzwartung *(f)*
En supplementary maintenance
Es mantenimiento suplementario *(m)*
Fr maintenance supplémentaire *(f)*
Pt manutenção suplementária *(f)*

map *n* En
De Bildschirmformat *(n)*
Es mapa *(m)*
Fr carte *(f)*
It mappa *(f)*
Pt mapa *(m)*

mapa *(m) n* Es, Pt
De Bildschirmformat *(n)*
En map
Fr carte *(f)*
It mappa *(f)*

mappa *(f) n* It
De Bildschirmformat *(n)*
En map
Es mapa *(m)*
Fr carte *(f)*
Pt mapa *(m)*

máquina de escrever *(f)* Pt
De Schreibmaschine *(f)*
En typewriter
Es máquina de escribir *(f)*
Fr machine à écrire *(f)*
It macchina da scrivere *(f)*

máquina de escrever de consola *(f)* Pt
De Konsolenschreibmaschine *(f)*
En console typewriter
Es máquina de escribir de consola *(f)*
Fr machine à écrire de pupitre *(f)*
It macchina da scrivere a console *(f)*

máquina de escribir *(f)* Es
De Schreibmaschine *(f)*
En typewriter
Fr machine à écrire *(f)*
It macchina da scrivere *(f)*
Pt máquina de escrever *(f)*

máquina de escribit de consola *(f)* Es
De Konsolenschreibmaschine *(f)*
En console typewriter
Fr machine à écrire de pupitre *(f)*
It macchina da scrivere a console *(f)*
Pt máquina de escrever de consola *(f)*

máquina de Turing universal *(f)* Es
De Turings-Universalmaschine *(f)*
En universal Turing machine
Fr machine de Turing universelle *(f)*
It macchina di Turing universale *(f)*
Pt máquina Turing universal *(f)*

máquina Turing universal *(f)* Pt
De Turings-Universalmaschine *(f)*
En universal Turing machine
Es máquina de Turing universal *(f)*
Fr machine de Turing universelle *(f)*
It macchina di Turing universale *(f)*

máquina virtual *(f)* Es, Pt
De virtuelle Maschine *(f)*
En virtual machine

marbete *(m) n* Es
De Schildchen *(n)*
Es label
Fr tabel *(m)*
It etichetta *(f)*
Pt rótulo *(m)*

marca *(f) n* Es, It, Pt
De Kennzeichen *(n)*
En mark
Fr marque *(f)*

marca de cinta *(f)* Es
De Bandkennzeichen *(n)*
En tape mark
Fr marque de bande *(f)*
It segno del nastro *(m)*
Pt marca de fita *(f)*

marca de fita *(f)* Pt
De Bandkennzeichen *(n)*
En tape mark
Es marca de cinta *(f)*
Fr marque de bande *(f)*
It segno del nastro *(m)*

marca de grupo *(f)* Es, Pt
De Trennmarke *(f)*
En group mark
Fr drapeau groupe *(m)*
It segno di gruppo *(m)*

marca de segmento *(f)* Es, Pt
De Segmentmarke *(f)*
En segment mark
Fr marque de segment *(f)*
It marca di segmento *(f)*

marca di segmento *(f)* It
De Segmentmarke *(f)*
En segment mark
Es marca de segmento *(f)*
Fr marque de segment *(f)*
Pt marca de segmento *(f)*

marcador *(m) n* Es, Pt
De Kennzeichner *(m)*
En marker
Fr repère *(m)*
It identificativo *(m)*

marca final *(f)* Es, Pt
De Endezeichen *(n)*
En end mark
Fr drapeau indicateur *(m)*
It marcatura di fine *(f)*

marcar *vb* Es
De beschriften
En inscribe
Fr marquer
It inscrivere
Pt inscrever

marcatura di fine *(f)* It
De Endezeichen *(n)*
En end mark
Es marca final *(f)*
Fr drapeau indicateur *(m)*
Pt marca final *(f)*

margen *(m) n* Es
De Bereich *(m)*
En range
Fr gamme *(f)*
It gamma *(f)*
Pt alcance *(m)*

marginal test En
De Randwertprüfung *(f)*
Es prueba marginal *(f)*
Fr épreuve marginale *(f)*
It test marginale *(m)*
Pt teste marginal *(m)*

mark *n* En
De Kennzeichen *(n)*
Es marca *(f)*
Fr marque *(f)*
It marca *(f)*
Pt marca *(f)*

marker *n* En
De Kennzeichner *(m)*
Es marcador *(m)*
Fr repère *(m)*
It identificativo *(m)*
Pt marcador *(m)*

Markierung *(f) n* De
En flag
Es señalizador *(m)*
Fr drapeau *(m)*
It indicatore *(m)*
Pt bandeira *(f)*

mark scanning En
De Kennzeichen-abtastung *(f)*
Es exploración de marcas *(f)*
Fr lecture optique de marques *(f)*
It scansione di marcature *(f)*
Pt exploração de marca *(f)*

mark sensing En
De Kennzeichenfühlung *(f)*
Es lectura de marcas *(f)*
Fr lecture de marques *(f)*
It lettura di marcature *(f)*
Pt determinação da marca *(f)*

marque *(f) n* Fr
De Kennzeichen *(n)*
En mark
Es marca *(f)*
It marca *(f)*
Pt marca *(f)*

marque de bande *(f)* Fr
De Bandkennzeichen *(n)*
En tape mark
Es marca de cinta *(f)*
It segno del nastro *(m)*
Pt marca de fita *(f)*

marque de segment *(f)* Fr
De Segmentmarke *(f)*
En segment mark
Es marca de segmento *(f)*
It marca di segmento *(f)*
Pt marca de segmento *(f)*

marquer *vb* Fr
De beschriften
En inscribe
Es marcar
It inscrivere
Pt inscrever

máscara *(f) n* Es, Pt
De Maske *(f)*
En mask
Fr masque *(m)*
It maschera *(f)*

mascarar *vb* Pt
De schirmen
En screen
Es cribar
Fr sélectionner
It schermare

maschera *(f) n* It
De Maske *(f)*
En mask
Es máscara *(f)*
Fr masque *(m)*
Pt máscara *(f)*

mascherare *vb* It
De maskieren
En mask
Es enmascarar
Fr masquer
Pt ocultar

mascheratura *(f) n* It
De Maskierung *(f)*
En masking
Es enmascaramiento *(m)*
Fr masquage *(m)*
Pt ocultação *(f)*

Maschinenadresse *(f) n* De
En machine address
Es dirección de máquina *(f)*
Fr adresse absolue *(f)*
It indirizzo di macchina *(m)*
Pt endereço da máquina *(m)*

Maschinenausfall *(m) n* De
En equipment failure
Es fallo del equipo *(m)*
Fr panne *(f)*
It guasto delle apparecchiature *(m)*
Pt falha de equipamento *(f)*

Maschinencode *(m) n* De
En machine code
Es código de máquina *(m)*
Fr code machine *(m)*
It codice macchina *(m)*
Pt código da máquina *(m)*

Maschinenlauf *(m) n* De
En machine run
Es pasada de máquina
Fr passage en machine *(m)*
It giro della macchina *(m)*
Pt passagem da máquina *(f)*

maschinenlesbar *adj* De
En machine-readable
Es legible por la máquina
Fr compréhensible par une machine
It leggibile dalla macchina
Pt legível pela máquina

Maschinen-programmierung *(f) n* De
En machine intelligence
Es inteligencia de máquina *(f)*
Fr intelligence-machine *(f)*
It intelligenza della macchina *(f)*
Pt inteligência da máquina *(f)*

Maschinenraum *(m) n* De
En machine room
Es sala de máquinas *(f)*
Fr salle des machines *(f)*
It sala macchine *(f)*
Pt sala de máquinas *(f)*

maschinenschreiben *vb* De
En type
Es escribir a máquina
Fr écrire à la machine
It scrivere a macchina
Pt escrever à máquina

Maschinensprache *(f) n* De
En machine language
Es lenguaje de máquina *(m)*
Fr langage machine *(m)*
It linguaggio macchina *(m)*
Pt linguagem da máquina *(f)*

maschinenunabhängig *adj* De
En machine-independent
Es independiente de la máquina
Fr indépendent de la machine
It indipendente dalla macchina
Pt independente da máquina

Maschinenverträglichkeit *(f) n* De
En equipment compatibility
Es compatibilidad entre equipos *(f)*
Fr compatibilité de matériels *(f)*
It compatibilità delle apparecchiature *(f)*
Pt compatibilidade do equipamento *(f)*

Maschinenwort *(n) n* De
En machine word
Es palabra de máquina *(f)*
Fr mot machine *(m)*
It voce macchina *(f)*
Pt palavra da máquina *(f)*

mask *n* En
De Maske *(f)*
Es máscara *(f)*
Fr masque *(m)*
It maschera *(f)*
Pt máscara *(f)*

mask *vb* En
De maskieren
Es enmascarar
Fr masquer
It mascherare
Pt ocultar

Maske *(f) n* De
En mask
Es máscara *(f)*
Fr masque *(m)*
It maschera *(f)*
Pt máscara *(f)*

maskieren *vb* De
En mask
Es enmascarar
Fr masquer
It mascherare
Pt ocultar

Maskierung *(f) n* De
En masking
Es enmascaramiento *(m)*
Fr masquage *(m)*
It mascheratura *(f)*
Pt ocultação *(f)*

masking *n* En
De Maskierung *(f)*
Es enmascaramiento *(m)*
Fr masquage *(m)*
It mascheratura *(f)*
Pt ocultação *(f)*

masquage *(m) n* Fr
De Maskierung *(f)*
En masking
Es enmascaramiento *(m)*
It mascheratura *(f)*
Pt ocultação *(f)*

masque *(m) n* Fr
De Maske *(f)*
En mask
Es máscara *(f)*
It maschera *(f)*
Pt máscara *(f)*

masquer *vb* Fr
De maskieren
En mask
Es enmascarar
It mascherare
Pt ocultar

Massenspeicher *(m) n* De
En mass store
Es memoria de gran capacidad *(f)*
Fr mémoire de grande capacité *(f)*
It memoria di massa *(f)*
Pt armazém de massa *(m)*

mass store En
De Massenspeicher *(m)*
Es memoria de gran capacidad *(f)*
Fr mémoire de grande capacité *(f)*
It memoria di massa *(f)*
Pt armazém de massa *(m)*

master clock En
De Stammzeitgeber *(m)*
Es reloj maestro *(m)*
Fr horloge pilote *(f)*
It orologio principale *(m)*
Pt relógio principal *(m)*

master file En
De Stammdatei *(f)*
Es fichero maestro *(m)*
Fr fichier principal *(m)*
It file principale *(m)*
Pt arquivo principal *(m)*

master-instruction tape (MIT) En
De Hauptbefehlsband *(n)*
Es cinta programa de explotación *(f)*
Fr bande de programme d'exploitation (BPE) *(f)*
It nastro dell'istruzioni principali *(m)*
Pt fita de instruções principais *(f)*

master record En
De Hauptsatz *(m)*
Es registro maestro *(m)*
Fr article du fichier permanent *(m)*
It record principale *(m)*
Pt registo principal *(m)*

Master-Slave-Anordnung *(f)* De
En master-slave system
Es sistema combinado maestro-satélite *(m)*
Fr système pilote-asservi *(m)*
It sistema maestro-schiavo *(m)*
Pt sistema mestre-escravo *(m)*

master-slave system En
De Master-Slave-Anordnung *(f)*
Es sistema combinado maestro-satélite *(m)*
Fr système pilote-asservi *(m)*
It sistema maestro-schiavo *(m)*
Pt sistema mestre-escravo *(m)*

master tape En
De Stammband *(n)*
Es bobina emisora *(f)*
Fr bande maîtresse *(f)*
It nastro principale *(m)*
Pt fita principal *(f)*

match *n* En
De Übereinstimmung *(f)*
Es correspondencia *(f)*
Fr assortiment *(m)*
It accoppiamento *(m)*
Pt equiparaćão *(f)*

matériel *(m) n* Fr
De Hardware *(f)*
En hardware
Es equipo físico *(m)*
It elementi materiali di elaboratore *(m)*
Pt hardware *(m)*

mathematical programming En
De mathematische Programmierung *(f)*
Es programación matemática *(f)*
Fr programmation mathématique *(f)*
It programmazione matematica *(f)*
Pt programação matemática *(f)*

mathematische Programmierung *(f)* De
En mathematical programming
Es programación matemática *(f)*

Fr programmation mathématique *(f)*
It programmazione matematica *(f)*
Pt programação matemática *(f)*

matrice *(f) n* Fr, It
De Matrix *(f)*
En matrix
Es matriz *(f)*
Pt matriz *(f)*

matrice di punti *(f)* It
De Punktmatrix *(f)*
En dot matrix
Es matriz de puntos *(f)*
Fr matrice par points *(f)*
Pt matriz de pontos *(f)*

matrice par points *(f)* Fr
De Punktmatrix *(f)*
En dot matrix
Es matriz de puntos *(f)*
It matrice di punti *(f)*
Pt matriz de pontos *(f)*

matrix *n* En
De Matrix *(f)*
Es matriz *(f)*
Fr matrice *(f)*
It matrice *(f)*
Pt matriz *(f)*

Matrix *(f) n* De
En matrix
Es matriz *(f)*
Fr matrice *(f)*
It matrice *(f)*
Pt matriz *(f)*

matrix arithmetic En
De Matrixarithmetik *(f)*
Es aritmética matricial *(f)*
Fr arithmétique matricielle *(f)*
It aritmetica delle matrici *(f)*
Pt aritmética de matriz *(f)*

Matrixarithmetik *(f) n* De
En matrix arithmetic
Es aritmética matricial *(f)*
Fr arithmétique matricielle *(f)*
It aritmetica delle matrici *(f)*
Pt aritmética de matriz *(f)*

matrix element En
De Matrixelement *(n)*
Es elemento matricial *(m)*
Fr élément matriciel *(m)*
It elemento della matrice *(m)*
Pt elemento de matriz *(m)*

Matrixelement *(n) n* De
En matrix element
Es elemento matricial *(m)*
Fr élément matriciel *(m)*
It elemento della matrice *(m)*
Pt elemento de matriz *(m)*

matrix inversion En
De Matrizeninversion *(f)*
Es inversión de matriz *(f)*
Fr inversion matricielle *(f)*
It inversione di matrice *(f)*
Pt inversão de matriz *(f)*

matrix printer En
De Matrizendrucker *(m)*
Es impresora de matriz *(f)*
Fr imprimante matricielle *(f)*
It stampatrice a matrice *(f)*
Pt impressora de matriz *(f)*

matrix store En
De Matrizenspeicher *(m)*
Es memoria matricial *(f)*
Fr mémoire matricielle *(f)*
It memoria a matrice *(f)*
Pt armazém de matriz *(m)*

matriz *(f) n* Es
De Matrix *(f)*
En matrix
Fr matrice *(f)*
It matrice *(f)*
Pt matriz *(f)*

matriz *(f) n* Pt
De Matrix *(f)*
En matrix
Es matriz *(f)*
Fr matrice *(f)*
It matrice *(f)*

matriz de pontos *(f)* Pt
De Punktmatrix *(f)*
En dot matrix
Es matriz de puntos *(f)*
Fr matrice par points *(f)*
It matrice di punti *(f)*

matriz de puntos *(f)* Es
De Punktmatrix *(f)*
En dot matrix
Fr matrice par points *(f)*
It matrice di punti *(f)*
Pt matriz de pontos *(f)*

matriz de semiconductores *(f)* Es
De Halbleiterfeld *(n)*
En semiconductor array
Fr ensemble à semiconducteurs *(m)*
It rete semiconduttori *(f)*
Pt disposição semicondutora *(f)*

Matrizendrucker *(m) n* De
En matrix printer
Es impresora de matriz *(f)*
Fr imprimante matricielle *(f)*
It stampatrice a matrice *(f)*
Pt impressora de matriz *(f)*

Matrizeninversion *(f) n* De
En matrix inversion
Es inversión de matriz *(f)*
Fr inversion matricielle *(f)*
It inversione di matrice *(f)*
Pt inversão de matriz *(f)*

Matrizenspeicher *(m) n* De
En matrix store
Es memoria matricial *(f)*
Fr mémoire matricielle *(f)*
It memoria a matrice *(f)*
Pt armazém de matriz *(m)*

mazzo *(m) n* It
Am deck (of cards)
De Kartensatz *(m)*
En pack (of cards9
Es baraja *(f)*
Fr paquet de cartes *(m)*
Pt baralho (de cartas) *(m)*

mean repair time En
De effektive Reparaturzeit *(f)*
Es tiempo medio para reparación *(m)*
Fr temps moyen de réparation *(m)*
It tempo di riparazione medio *(m)*
Pt tempo médio de reparação *(m)*

mean time between failures En
De Effektivzeit zwischen Ausfällen *(f)*
Es tiempo medio entre fallos *(m)*
Fr moyenne des temps de bon fonctionnement *(f)*
It tempo medio tra i guasti *(m)*
Pt tempo médio entre falhas *(m)*

mechanischer Drucker *(m)* De
En impact printer
Es impresora a percusión *(f)*
Fr imprimante à percussion *(f)*
It stampatrice ad impatto *(f)*
Pt impressora de impacto *(f)*

media palabra *(f)* Es
De Halbwort *(n)*
En half word
Fr demi-mot *(m)*
It metà voce *(f)*
Pt meia-palavra *(f)*

medio *(m) n* Es
De Mittel *(n)*
En medium
Fr milieu *(m)*

It mezzo *(m)*
Pt meio *(m)*

medios magnéticos *(m pl)* Es
De magnetisches Aufzeichnungsmittel *(n)*
En magnetic media
Fr milieux magnétiques *(m pl)*
It mezzi magnetici *(m pl)*
Pt meios magnéticos *(m pl)*

medium *n* En
De Mittel *(n)*
Es medio *(m)*
Fr milieu *(m)*
It mezzo *(m)*
Pt meio *(m)*

megabit *n* En, Es, It, Pt *(m)*
De Megabit *(m)*
Fr million de bits *(m)*

Megabit *(m) n* De
En megabit
Es megabit *(m)*
Fr million de bits *(m)*
It megabit *(m)*
Pt megabit *(m)*

megabyte *n* En, Es, It, Pt *(m)*
De Megabyte *(m)*
Fr million d'octets *(m)*

Megabyte *(m) n* De
En megabyte
Es megabyte *(m)*
Fr million d'octets *(m)*
It megabyte *(m)*
Pt megabyte *(m)*

megaocteto *(m) n* Es
De Megabyte *(m)*
En megabyte
Fr million d'octets *(m)*
It megabyte *(m)*
Pt megabyte *(m)*

Mehrfachadressbefehl *(m) n* De
En multiple-address instruction
Es instrucción de direcciones múltiples *(f)*
Fr instruction multi-adresse *(f)*
It istruzione ad indirizzo multiplo *(f)*
Pt instrução de endereço múltiplo *(f)*

Mehrfachbenutzersystem *(n) n* De
En multiuser system
Es sistema para usuarios múltiples *(m)*
Fr système à utilisateurs multiples *(m)*
It sistema per utenti multipli *(m)*
Pt sistema de utentes múltiplos *(m)*

Mehrfachzugriff *adj* De
En multi-access
Es acceso-múltiple
Fr accès-multiples
It accesso-multiplo
Pt multi-acesso

Mehrfachzugriffsrechnen *(n) n* De
En multi-access computing (MAC)
Es cálculo de acceso múltiple *(m)*
Fr traitement à accès multiple (TAM) *(m)*
It calcolo ad accesso multiplo *(m)*
Pt computação de multi-acesso *(f)*

Mehrprozessorsystem *(n) n* De
En multiprocessor
Es procesador múltiple *(m)*
Fr multicalculateur *(m)*
It elaboratore multiplo *(m)*
Pt multiprocessador *(m)*

Mehrpunktnetz *(n) n* De
En multipoint network
Es red de puntos múltiples *(f)*
Fr réseau multi-point *(m)*
It rete a punti multipli *(f)*
Pt rede de pontos múltiplos *(f)*

mehrschichtige Software *(f)* De
En multilayered software
Es equipo instruccional multicapas *(m)*
Fr software multi-couche *(m)*
It software a strato multiplo *(m)*
Pt software de camadas múltiplas *(m)*

mehrteilige Formulare *(pl)* De
En multipart forms
Es paquete de papel continuo *(m)*
Fr liasse *(f)*
It moduli a copie multiple *(m pl)*
Pt formas de partes múltiplas *(f pl)*

meia-palavra *(f) n* Pt
De Halbwort *(n)*
En half word
Es media palabra *(f)*
Fr demi-mot *(m)*
It metà voce *(f)*

meio *(m) n* Pt
De Mittel *(n)*
En medium
Es medio *(m)*
Fr milieu *(m)*
It mezzo *(m)*

meios magnéticos *(m pl)* Pt
De magnetisches Aufzeichnungsmittel *(n)*
En magnetic media
Es medios magnéticos *(m pl)*
Fr milieux magnétiques *(m pl)*
It mezzi magnetici *(m pl)*

mémoire *(f) n* Fr
De Speicher *(m)*
En memory; store
Es memoria *(f)*
It memoria *(f)*
Pt armazém; memória *(m f)*

mémoire à accès sélectif *(f)* Fr
De Direktzugriffsspeicher *(m)*
En random-access memory (RAM)
Es memoria de acceso al azar *(f)*
It memoria ad accesso casuale *(f)*
Pt memória de acesso aleatório *(f)*

mémoire à bulles *(f)* Fr
De Perlspeicher *(m)*
En bubble memory
Es memoria de burbuja *(f)*
It memoria a bolle *(f)*
Pt memória de bolha *(f)*

mémoire à couche mince *(f)* Fr
De Dünnfilmspeicher *(m)*
En thin-film memory
Es memoria de película delgada *(f)*
It memoria a pellicola sottile *(f)*
Pt memória de película fina *(f)*

mémoire à faisceau *(f)* Fr
De Strahlenspeicher *(m)*
En beam store
Es memoria a rayos *(f)*
It memoria a fascio *(f)*
Pt armazém de raio *(m)*

mémoire à régénération *(f)* Fr
De regenerativer Speicher *(m)*
En regenerative store
Es memoria regenerativa *(f)*
It memoria rigenerativa *(f)*
Pt armazém regenerativo *(m)*

mémoire à semiconducteurs *(f)* Fr
De Halbleiterspeicher *(m)*
En semiconductor memory
Es memoria de semiconductores *(f)*

It memoria a semiconduttori *(f)*
Pt memória semi-condutora *(f)*

mémoire asservie *(f)* Fr
De Nebenspeicher *(m)*
En slave store
Es memoria sin parte residente *(f)*
It memoria satellite *(f)*
Pt armazém escravo *(m)*

mémoire associative *(f)* Fr
De Assoziativspeicher *(m)*
En associative memory
Es memoria asociativa *(f)*
It memoria associativa *(f)*
Pt memória associativa *(f)*

mémoire associative complétée *(f)* Fr
De erweiterter inhaltsadressierter Speicher *(m)*
En augmented content-addressed memory (ACAM)
Es memoria asociativa ampliada *(f)*
It memoria a contenuto indirizzato aumentato *(f)*
Pt memória de direcção de conteúdo aumentada *(f)*

mémoire à tores *(f)* Fr
De Kernspeicher *(m)*
En core memory (or store)
Es memoria de núcleos *(f)*
It memoria a nuclei *(f)*
Pt memória de núcleo *(f)*

mémoire à un niveau *(f)* Fr
De Einstufenspeicher *(m)*
En one-level store
Es memoria de un solo nivel *(f)*
It memoria ad un livello *(f)*
Pt armazém de um só nível *(m)*

mémoire auxiliaire *(f)* Fr
De Hilfsspeicher *(m)*
En backing store
Es memoria auxiliar *(f)*
It memoria ausiliaria *(f)*
Pt armazém de apoio *(m)*

mémoire centrale *(f)* Fr
De Hauptspeicher; Kern; Primärspeicher *(m)*
En core; main memory; primary store
Es memoria principal; núcleo *(f m)*
It memoria centrale; memoria principale *(f)*
Pt armazém primária; memória principal; núcleo *(m f m)*

mémoire cryogénique *(f)* Fr
De kryogenischer Speicher *(m)*
En cryogenic memory
Es memoria criogénica *(f)*
It memoria criogenica *(f)*
Pt memória criogénica *(f)*

mémoire de grande capacité *(f)* Fr
De Massenspeicher *(m)*
En mass store
Es memoria de gran capacidad *(f)*
It memoria di massa *(f)*
Pt armazém de massa *(m)*

mémoire de masse *(f)* Fr
De Groβspeicher *(m)*
En bulk store
Es memoria de gran capacidad *(f)*
It memoria di massa *(f)*
Pt memória global *(f)*

mémoire de travail *(f)* Fr
De Arbeitspuffer *(m)*
En scratch pad
Es bloc de notas *(m)*
It bloc-notes *(m)*
Pt almofada de raspar *(f)*

mémoire dynamique *(f)* Fr
De dynamischer Speicher *(m)*
En dynamic memory
Es memoria dinámica *(f)*
It memoria dinamica *(f)*
Pt memória dinâmico *(f)*

mémoire effaçable *(f)* Fr
De löschbarer Speicher *(m)*
En erasable memory
Es memoria borrable *(f)*
It memoria cancellabile *(f)*
Pt memória apagável *(f)*

mémoire en état solide *(f)* Fr
De Festschaltungs-speicher *(m)*
En solid-state memory
Es memoria de estado sólido *(f)*
It memoria a stato solido *(f)*
Pt memória solid-state *(f)*

mémoire externe *(f)* Fr
De Auβpeicher *(m)*
En external store
Es memoria externa *(f)*
It memoria esterna *(f)*
Pt armazém exterior *(m)*

mémoire fichier *(f)* Fr
De Dateispeicher *(m)*
En file store
Es memoria fichero *(f)*
It memoria dei file *(f)*
Pt armazém de arquivo *(m)*

mémoire fixe *(f)* Fr
De Festspeicher *(m)*
En read-only memory (ROM)
Es memoria fija *(f)*
It memoria soltanto di lettura *(f)*
Pt memória apenas de leitura *(f)*

mémoire holographique *(f)* Fr
De holographischer Speicher *(m)*
En holographic memory
Es memoria holográfica *(f)*
It memoria olografica *(f)*
Pt memória holográfica *(f)*

mémoire intégrée *(f)* Fr
De Integralspeicher *(m)*
En integral memory
Es memoria integral *(f)*
It memoria integrale *(f)*
Pt memória integral *(f)*

mémoire intermédiaire *(f)* Fr
De Zwischen-speicherung *(f)*
En intermediate storage
Es memoria intermedia *(f)*
It memoria intermedia *(f)*
Pt armazenagem intermediária *(m)*

mémoire intermédiaire *(f)* Fr
De vorübergehende Speicherung *(f)*
En temporary storage
Es memoria temporal *(f)*
It memoria temporanea *(f)*
Pt armazenamento temporário *(m)*

mémoire interne *(f)* Fr
De Innenspeicher *(m)*
En internal store
Es memoria interna *(f)*
It memoria interna *(f)*
Pt armazém interno *(m)*

mémoire magnétique *(f)* Fr
De Magnetspeicher *(m)*
En magnetic memory
Es memoria magnética *(f)*
It memoria magnetica *(f)*
Pt memória magnética *(f)*

mémoire matricielle *(f)* Fr
De Matrizenspeicher *(m)*
En matrix store
Es memoria matricial *(f)*
It memoria a matrice *(f)*
Pt armazém de matriz *(m)*

mémoire morte programmable *(f)* Fr
De programmierbarer Festspeicher *(m)*
En programmable read-only memory (PROM)
Es memoria fija programable *(f)*
It memoria soltanto di lettura programmabile *(f)*
Pt memória apenas de leitura programável *(f)*

mémoire non effaçable *(f)* Fr
De nicht löschbarer Speicher *(m)*
En nonerasable store
Es memoria imborrable *(f)*
It memoria non cancellabile *(f)*
Pt armazém não apagável *(m)*

mémoire non rémanente *(f)* Fr
De energieabhängiger Speicher *(m)*
En volatile memory
Es memoria volátil *(f)*
It memoria volatile *(f)*
Pt memória volátil *(f)*

mémoire organisée en pages *(f)* Fr
De paginierter Speicher *(m)*
En paged memory
Es memoria organizada en páginas *(f)*
It memoria per pagine *(f)*
Pt memória com páginas *(f)*

mémoire permanente *(f)* Fr
De Dauerspeicher *(m)*
En permanent memory
Es memoria permanente *(f)*
It memoria permanente *(f)*
Pt memória permanente *(f)*

mémoire réelle *(f)* Fr
De Realspeicher *(m)*
En real store
Es memoria real *(f)*
It memoria reale *(f)*
Pt armazém real *(m)*

mémoire rémanente *(f)* Fr
De nicht veränderlicher Speicher *(m)*
En nonvolatile memory
Es memoria estable *(f)*
It memoria non volatile *(f)*
Pt memória não volátil *(f)*

mémoire statique *(f)* Fr
De statischer Speicher *(m)*
En static store
Es memoria estática *(f)*
It memoria statica *(f)*
Pt armazém estático *(m)*

mémoire tampon *(f)* Fr
De Pufferspeicher *(m)*
En buffer store
Es registro intermedio *(m)*
It memoria di transito *(f)*
Pt memória buffer *(f)*

mémoire virtuelle *(f)* Fr
De virtueller Speicher *(m)*
En virtual store (VS)
Es memoria virtual *(f)*
It memoria virtuale *(f)*
Pt memória virtual *(f)*

memoria *(f)* *n* Es, It
De Speicher *(m)*
En memory
Fr mémoire *(f)*
Pt memória *(f)*

memoria *(f)* *n* Es, It
De Speicher *(m)*
En store
Fr mémoire *(f)*
Pt armazém *(m)*

memória *(f)* *n* Pt
De Speicher *(m)*
En memory
Es memoria *(f)*
Fr mémoire *(f)*
It memoria *(f)*

memoria a bolle *(f)* It
De Perlspeicher *(m)*
En bubble memory
Es memoria de burbuja *(f)*
Fr mémoire à bulles *(f)*
Pt memória de bolha *(f)*

memoria a contenuto indirizzato aumentato *(f)* It
De erweiterter inhaltsadressierter Speicher *(m)*
En augmented content-addressed memory (ACAM)
Es memoria asociativa ampliada *(f)*
Fr mémoire associative complétée *(f)*
Pt memória de direcção de conteúdo aumentada *(f)*

memoria ad accesso casuale *(f)* It
De Direktzugriffsspeicher *(m)*
En random-access memory (RAM)
Es memoria de acceso al azar *(f)*
Fr mémoire à accès sélectif *(f)*
Pt memória de acesso aleatório *(f)*

memoria a dischi inseribili *(f)* It
De auswechselbarer Plattenspeicher *(m)*
En exchangeable disk store (EDS)
Es unidad de discos móviles *(f)*
Fr unité de disques à chargeur (UTC) *(f)*
Pt armazém de discos intercambiáveis *(m)*

memoria ad un livello *(f)* It
De Einstufenspeicher *(m)*
En one-level store
Es memoria de un solo nivel *(f)*
Fr mémoire à un niveau *(f)*
Pt armazém de um só nível *(m)*

memoria a fascio *(f)* It
De Strahlenspeicher *(m)*
En beam store
Es memoria a rayos *(f)*
Fr mémoire à faisceau *(f)*
Pt armazém de raio *(m)*

memoria a matrice *(f)* It
De Matrizenspeicher *(m)*
En matrix store
Es memoria matricial *(f)*
Fr mémoire matricielle *(f)*
Pt armazém de matriz *(m)*

memoria a nuclei *(f)* It
De Kernspeicher *(m)*
En core memory (or store)
Es memoria de núcleos *(f)*
Fr mémoire à tores *(f)*
Pt memória de núcleo *(f)*

memória apagável *(f)* Pt
De löschbarer Speicher *(m)*
En erasable memory
Es memoria borrable *(f)*
Fr mémoire effaçable *(f)*
It memoria cancellabile *(f)*

memoria a pellicola sottile *(f)* It
De Dünnfilmspeicher *(m)*
En thin-film memory
Es memoria de película delgada *(f)*
Fr mémoire à couche mince *(f)*
Pt memória de película fina *(f)*

memória apenas de leitura *(f)* Pt
De Festspeicher *(m)*
En read-only memory (ROM)
Es memoria fija *(f)*
Fr mémoire fixe *(f)*
It memoria soltanto di lettura *(f)*

memória apenas de leitura programável *(f)* Pt
De programmierbarer Festspeicher *(m)*

En programmable read-only memory (PROM)
Es memoria fija programable *(f)*
Fr mémoire morte programmable *(f)*
It memoria soltanto di lettura programmabile *(f)*

memoria a rayos *(f)* Es
De Strahlenspeicher *(m)*
En beam store
Fr mémoire à faisceau *(f)*
It memoria a fascio *(f)*
Pt armazém de raio *(m)*

memoria a semiconduttori *(f)* It
De Halbleiterspeicher *(m)*
En semiconductor memory
Es memoria de semiconductores *(f)*
Fr mémoire à semiconducteurs *(f)*
Pt memória semi-condutora *(f)*

memoria asociativa *(f)* Es
De Assoziativspeicher *(m)*
En associative memory
Fr mémoire associative *(f)*
It memoria associativa *(f)*
Pt memória associativa *(f)*

memoria asociativa ampliada *(f)* Es
De erweiterter inhaltsadressierter Speicher *(m)*
En augmented content-addressed memory (ACAM)
Fr mémoire associative complétée *(f)*
It memoria a contenuto indirizzato aumentato *(f)*
Pt memória de direcção de conteúdo aumentada *(f)*

memoria associativa *(f)* It
De Assoziativspeicher *(m)*
En associative memory
Es memoria asociativa *(f)*
Fr mémoire associative *(f)*
Pt memória associativa *(f)*

memória associativa *(f)* Pt
De Assoziativspeicher *(m)*
En associative memory
Es memoria asociativa *(f)*
Fr mémoire associative *(f)*
It memoria associativa *(f)*

memoria a stato solido *(f)* It
De Festschaltungs-speicher *(m)*
En solid-state memory
Es memoria de estado sólido *(f)*
Fr mémoire en état solide *(f)*
Pt memória solid-state *(f)*

memoria ausiliaria *(f)* It
De Hilfsspeicher *(m)*
En backing store
Es memoria auxiliar *(f)*
Fr mémoire auxiliaire *(f)*
Pt armazém de apoio *(m)*

memoria auxiliar *(f)* Es
De Hilfsspeicher *(m)*
En backing store
Fr mémoire auxiliaire *(f)*
It memoria ausiliaria *(f)*
Pt armazém de apoio *(m)*

memoria bidimensional *(f)* Es
De zweidimensionale Speicherung *(f)*
En two-dimensional storage
Fr stockage à double entrée *(m)*
It memoria bidimensionale *(f)*
Pt armazenamento bidimensional *(m)*

memoria bidimensionale *(f)* It
De zweidimensionale Speicherung *(f)*
En two-dimensional storage
Es memoria bidimensional *(f)*
Fr stockage à double entrée *(m)*
Pt armazenamento bidimensional *(m)*

memoria borrable *(f)* Es
De löschbarer Speicher *(m)*
En erasable memory
Fr mémoire effaçable *(f)*
It memoria cancellabile *(f)*
Pt memória apagável *(f)*

memória buffer *(f)* Pt
De Pufferspeicher *(m)*
En buffer store
Es registro intermedio *(m)*
Fr mémoire tampon *(f)*
It memoria di transito *(f)*

memoria cancellabile *(f)* It
De löschbarer Speicher *(m)*
En erasable memory
Es memoria borrable *(f)*
Fr mémoire effaçable *(f)*
Pt memória apagável *(f)*

memoria centrale *(f)* It
De Kern; Primärspeicher *(m)*
En core; primary store
Es memoria principal; núcleo *(f m)*
Fr mémoire centrale *(f)*
Pt núcleo *(m)*

memória com páginas *(f)* Pt
De paginierter Speicher *(m)*
En paged memory
Es memoria organizada en páginas *(f)*
Fr mémoire organisée en pages *(f)*
It memoria per pagine *(f)*

memoria criogenica *(f)* It
De kryogenischer Speicher *(m)*
En cryogenic memory
Es memoria criogénica *(f)*
Fr mémoire cryogénique *(f)*
Pt memória criogénica *(f)*

memoria criogénica *(f)* Es
De kryogenischer Speicher *(m)*
En cryogenic memory
Fr mémoire cryogénique *(f)*
It memoria criogenica *(f)*
Pt memória criogénica *(f)*

memória criogénica *(f)* Pt
De kryogenischer Speicher *(m)*
En cryogenic memory
Es memoria criogénica *(f)*
Fr mémoire cryogénique *(f)*
It memoria criogenica *(f)*

memoria de acceso al azar *(f)* Es
De Direktzugriffsspeicher *(m)*
En random-access memory (RAM)
Fr mémoire à accès sélectif *(f)*
It memoria ad accesso casuale *(f)*
Pt memória de acesso aleatório *(f)*

memória de acesso aleatório *(f)* Pt
De Direktzugriffsspeicher *(m)*
En random-access memory (RAM)
Es memoria de acceso al azar *(f)*
Fr mémoire à accès sélectif *(f)*

It memoria ad accesso casuale *(f)*

memória de bolha *(f)* Pt
De Perlspeicher *(m)*
En bubble memory
Es memoria de burbuja *(f)*
Fr mémoire à bulles *(f)*
It memoria a bolle *(f)*

memoria de burbuja *(f)* Es
De Perlspeicher *(m)*
En bubble memory
Fr mémoire à bulles *(f)*
It memoria a bolle *(f)*
Pt memória de bolha *(f)*

memória de direcção de conteúdo aumentada *(f)* Pt
De erweiterter inhaltsadressierter Speicher *(m)*
En augmented content-addressed memory (ACAM)
Es memoria asociativa ampliada *(f)*
Fr mémoire associative complétée *(f)*
It memoria a contenuto indirizzato aumentato *(f)*

memoria de estado sólido *(f)* Es
De Festschaltungs-speicher *(m)*
En solid-state memory
Fr mémoire en état solide *(f)*
It memoria a stato solido *(f)*
Pt memória solid-state *(f)*

memoria de gran capacidad *(f)* Es
De Groβspeicher; Massenspeicher *(m)*
En bulk store; mass store
Fr mémoire de grande capacité; mémoire de masse *(f)*
It memoria di massa *(f)*
Pt armazém de massa; memória global *(m f)*

memoria dei file *(f)* It
De Dateispeicher *(m)*
En file store
Es memoria fichero *(f)*
Fr mémoire fichier *(f)*
Pt armazém de arquivo *(m)*

memória de núcleo *(f)* Pt
De Kernspeicher *(m)*
En core memory (or store)
Es memoria de núcleos *(f)*
Fr mémoire à tores *(f)*
It memoria a nuclei *(f)*

memoria de núcleos *(f)* Es
De Kernspeicher *(m)*
En core memory (or store)
Fr mémoire à tores *(f)*
It memoria a nuclei *(f)*
Pt memória de núcleo *(f)*

memoria de película delgada *(f)* Es
De Dünnfilmspeicher *(m)*
En thin-film memory
Fr mémoire à couche mince *(f)*
It memoria a pellicola sottile *(f)*
Pt memória de película fina *(f)*

memória de película fina *(f)* Pt
De Dünnfilmspeicher *(m)*
En thin-film memory
Es memoria de película delgada *(f)*
Fr mémoire à couche mince *(f)*
It memoria a pellicola sottile *(f)*

memoria de semiconductores *(f)* Es
De Halbleiterspeicher *(m)*
En semiconductor memory
Fr mémoire à semiconducteurs *(f)*
It memoria a semiconduttori *(f)*
Pt memória semi-condutora *(f)*

memoria de un solo nivel *(f)* Es
De Einstufenspeicher *(m)*
En one-level store
Fr mémoire à un niveau *(f)*
It memoria ad un livello *(f)*
Pt armazém de um só nível *(m)*

memoria di ferrite *(f)* It
De Ferritkern *(m)*
En ferrite core
Es núcleo de ferria *(m)*
Fr tore de ferrite *(f)*
Pt núcleo de ferrite *(m)*

memoria di massa *(f)* It
De Groβspeicher; Massenspeicher *(m)*
En bulk store; mass store
Es memoria de gran capacidad *(f)*
Fr mémoire de grande capacité; mémoire de masse *(f)*
Pt armazém de massa; memória global *(m f)*

memoria dinamica *(f)* It
De dynamischer Speicher *(m)*
En dynamic memory
Es memoria dinámica *(f)*
Fr mémoire dynamique *(f)*
Pt memória dinâmico *(f)*

memoria dinámica *(f)* Es
De dynamischer Speicher *(m)*
En dynamic memory
Fr mémoire dynamique *(f)*
It memoria dinamica *(f)*
Pt memória dinâmico *(f)*

memória dinâmico *(f)* Pt
De dynamischer Speicher *(m)*
En dynamic memory
Es memoria dinámica *(f)*
Fr mémoire dynamique *(f)*
It memoria dinamica *(f)*

memoria di transito *(f)* It
De Pufferspeicher *(m)*
En buffer store
Es registro intermedio *(m)*
Fr mémoire tampon *(f)*
Pt memória buffer *(f)*

memoria di transito dell'entrata *(f)* It
De Eingangspuffer *(m)*
En input buffer
Es memoria intermedia de entrada *(f)*
Fr tampon d'entrée *(m)*
Pt separador de entrada *(m)*

memoria di transito entrata-uscita *(f)* It
De Eingangs-Ausgangspuffer *(m)*
En input-output buffer
Es memoria intermedia de entrada-salida *(f)*
Fr tampon entrée-sortie *(m)*
Pt separador de entrada-sair *(m)*

memoria estable *(f)* Es
De nicht veränderlicher Speicher *(m)*
En nonvolatile memory
Fr mémoire rémanente *(f)*
It memoria non volatile *(f)*
Pt memória não volátil *(f)*

memoria estática *(f)* Es
De statischer Speicher *(m)*
En static store
Fr mémoire statique *(f)*
It memoria statica *(f)*
Pt armazém estático *(m)*

memoria esterna *(f)* It
De Auβens Speicher *(m)*
En external store
Es memoria externa *(f)*
Fr mémoire externe *(f)*
Pt armazém exterior *(m)*

memoria externa *(f)* Es
De Auβens Speicher *(m)*
En external store
Fr mémoire externe *(f)*
It memoria esterna *(f)*
Pt armazém exterior *(m)*

memoria fichero *(f)* Es
De Dateispeicher *(m)*
En file store
Fr mémoire fichier *(f)*
It memoria dei file *(f)*
Pt armazém de arquivo *(m)*

memoria fija *(f)* Es
De Festspeicher *(m)*
En read-only memory (ROM)
Fr mémoire fixe *(f)*
It memoria soltanto di lettura *(f)*
Pt memória apenas de leitura *(f)*

memoria fija programable *(f)* Es
De programmierbarer Festspeicher *(m)*
En programmable read-only memory (PROM)
Fr mémoire morte programmable *(f)*
It memoria soltanto di lettura programmabile *(f)*
Pt memória apenas de leitura programável *(f)*

memória global *(f)* Pt
De Groβspeicher *(m)*
En bulk store
Es memoria de gran capacidad *(f)*
Fr mémoire de masse *(f)*
It memoria di massa *(f)*

memoria holográfica *(f)* Es
De holographischer Speicher *(m)*
En holographic memory
Fr mémoire holographique *(f)*
It memoria olografica *(f)*
Pt memória holográfica *(f)*

memória holográfica *(f)* Pt
De holographischer Speicher *(m)*
En holographic memory
Es memoria holográfica *(f)*
Fr mémoire holographique *(f)*
It memoria olografica *(f)*

memoria imborrable *(f)* Es
De nicht löschbarer Speicher *(m)*
En nonerasable store
Fr mémoire non effaçable *(f)*
It memoria non cancellabile *(f)*
Pt armazém não apagável *(m)*

memoria integral *(f)* Es
De Integralspeicher *(m)*
En integral memory
Fr mémoire intégrée *(f)*
It memoria integrale *(f)*
Pt memória integral *(f)*

memória integral *(f)* Pt
De Integralspeicher *(m)*
En integral memory
Es memoria integral *(f)*
Fr mémoire intégrée *(f)*
It memoria integrale *(f)*

memoria integrale *(f)* It
De Integralspeicher *(m)*
En integral memory
Es memoria integral *(f)*
Fr mémoire intégrée *(f)*
Pt memória integral *(f)*

memoria intermedia *(f)* Es, It
De Zwischenspeicherung *(f)*
En intermediate storage
Fr mémoire intermédiaire *(f)*
Pt armazenagem intermediária *(m)*

memoria intermedia de entrada *(f)* Es
De Eingangspuffer *(m)*
En input buffer
Fr tampon d'entrée *(m)*
It memoria di transito dell'entrata *(f)*
Pt separador de entrada *(m)*

memoria intermedia de entrada-salida *(f)* Es
De Eingangs-Ausgangspuffer *(m)*
En input-output buffer
Fr tampon entrée-sortie *(m)*
It memoria di transito entrata-uscita *(f)*
Pt separador de entrada-sair *(m)*

memoria interna *(f)* Es, It
De Innenspeicher *(m)*
En internal store
Fr mémoire interne *(f)*
Pt armazém interno *(m)*

memoria magnetica *(f)* It
De Magnetspeicher *(m)*
En magnetic memory
Es memoria magnética *(f)*
Fr mémoire magnétique *(f)*
Pt memória magnética *(f)*

memoria magnética *(f)* Es
De Magnetspeicher *(m)*
En magnetic memory
Fr mémoire magnétique *(f)*
It memoria magnetica *(f)*
Pt memória magnética *(f)*

memória magnética *(f)* Pt
De Magnetspeicher *(m)*
En magnetic memory
Es memoria magnética *(f)*
Fr mémoire magnétique *(f)*
It memoria magnetica *(f)*

memoria matricial *(f)* Es
De Matrizenspeicher *(m)*
En matrix store
Fr mémoire matricielle *(f)*
It memoria a matrice *(f)*
Pt armazém de matriz *(m)*

memória não volátil *(f)* Pt
De nicht veränderlicher Speicher *(m)*
En nonvolatile memory
Es memoria estable *(f)*
Fr mémoire rémanente *(f)*
It memoria non volatile *(f)*

memoria non cancellabile *(f)* It
De nicht löschbarer Speicher *(m)*
En nonerasable store
Es memoria imborrable *(f)*
Fr mémoire non effaçable *(f)*
Pt armazém não apagável *(m)*

memoria non volatile *(f)* It
De nicht veränderlicher Speicher *(m)*
En nonvolatile memory
Es memoria estable *(f)*
Fr mémoire rémanente *(f)*
Pt memória não volátil *(f)*

memoria olografica *(f)* It
De holographischer Speicher *(m)*
En holographic memory
Es memoria holográfica *(f)*
Fr mémoire holographique *(f)*
Pt memória holográfica *(f)*

memoria organizada en páginas *(f)* Es
De paginierter Speicher *(m)*
En paged memory
Fr mémoire organisée en pages *(f)*
It memoria per pagine *(f)*
Pt memória com páginas *(f)*

memoria permanente *(f)* Es, It
De Dauerspeicher *(m)*
En permanent memory
Fr mémoire permanente *(f)*
Pt memória permanente *(f)*

memória permanente *(f)* Pt
De Dauerspeicher *(m)*
En permanent memory
Es memoria permanente *(f)*
Fr mémoire permanente *(f)*
It memoria permanente *(f)*

memoria per pagine *(f)* It
De paginierter Speicher *(m)*
En paged memory
Es memoria organizada en páginas *(f)*
Fr mémoire organisée en pages *(f)*
Pt memória com páginas *(f)*

memoria principal *(f)* Es
De Hauptspeicher; Primärspeicher *(m)*
En main memory; primary store
Fr mémoire centrale *(f)*
It memoria centrale; memoria principale *(f)*
Pt armázem primaria; memória principal *(f)*

memória principal *(f)* Pt
De Hauptspeicher *(m)*
En main memory
Es memoria principal *(f)*
Fr mémoire centrale *(f)*
It memoria principale *(f)*

memoria principale *(f)* It
De Hauptspeicher *(m)*
En main memory
Es memoria principal *(f)*
Fr mémoire centrale *(f)*
Pt memória principal *(f)*

memoria real *(f)* Es
De Realspeicher *(m)*
En real store
Fr mémoire réelle *(f)*
It memoria reale *(f)*
Pt armazém real *(m)*

memoria reale *(f)* It
De Realspeicher *(m)*
En real store
Es memoria real *(f)*
Fr mémoire réelle *(f)*
Pt armazém real *(m)*

memoria regenerativa *(f)* Es
De regenerativer Speicher *(m)*
En regenerative store
Fr mémoire à régénération *(f)*
It memoria rigenerativa *(f)*
Pt armazém regenerativo *(m)*

memoria rigenerativa *(f)* It
De regenerativer Speicher *(m)*
En regenerative store
Es memoria regenerativa *(f)*
Fr mémoire à régénération *(f)*

memoria satellite *(f)* It
De Nebenspeicher *(m)*
En slave store
Es memoria sin parte residente *(f)*
Fr mémoire asservie *(f)*
Pt armazém escravo *(m)*

memória semi-condutora *(f)* Pt
De Halbleiterspeicher *(m)*
En semiconductor memory
Es memoria de semiconductores *(f)*
Fr mémoire à semiconducteurs *(f)*
It memoria a semiconduttori *(f)*

memoria sin parte residente *(f)* Es
De Nebenspeicher *(m)*
En slave store
Fr mémoire asservie *(f)*
It memoria satellite *(f)*
Pt armazém escravo *(m)*

memória solid-state *(f)* Pt
De Festschaltungs-speicher *(m)*
En solid-state memory
Es memoria de estado sólido *(f)*
Fr mémoire en état solide *(f)*
It memoria a stato solido *(f)*

memoria soltanto di lettura *(f)* It
De Festspeicher *(m)*
En read-only memory (ROM)
Es memoria fija *(f)*
Fr mémoire fixe *(f)*
Pt memória apenas de leitura *(f)*

memoria soltanto di lettura programmabile *(f)* It
De programmierbarer Festspeicher *(m)*
En programmable read-only memory (PROM)
Es memoria fija programable *(f)*
Fr mémoire morte programmable *(f)*
Pt memória apenas de leitura programável *(f)*

memoria statica *(f)* It
De statischer Speicher *(m)*
En static store
Es memoria estática *(f)*
Fr mémoire statique *(f)*
Pt armazém estático *(m)*

memoria temporal *(f)* Es
De vorübergehende Speicherung *(f)*
En temporary storage
Fr mémoire intermédiaire *(f)*
It memoria temporanea *(f)*
Pt armazenamento temporário *(m)*

memoria temporanea *(f)* It
De vorübergehende Speicherung *(f)*
En temporary storage
Es memoria temporal *(f)*
Fr mémoire intermédiaire *(f)*
Pt armazenamento temporário *(m)*

memoria virtual *(f)* Es
De virtueller Speicher *(m)*
En virtual store (VS)
Fr mémoire virtuelle *(f)*
It memoria virtuale *(f)*
Pt memória virtual *(f)*

memória virtual *(f)* Pt
De virtueller Speicher *(m)*
En virtual store (VS)
Es memoria virtual *(f)*
Fr mémoire virtuelle *(f)*
It memoria virtuale *(f)*

memoria virtuale *(f)* It
De virtueller Speicher *(m)*
En virtual store (VS)
Es memoria virtual *(f)*
Fr mémoire virtuelle *(f)*
Pt memória virtual *(f)*

memoria volátil *(f)* Es
De energieabhängiger Speicher *(m)*
En volatile memory
Fr mémoire non rémanente *(f)*
It memoria volatile *(f)*
Pt memória volátil *(f)*

memória volátil *(f)* Pt
De energieabhängiger Speicher *(m)*
En volatile memory
Es memoria volátil *(f)*
Fr mémoire non rémanente *(f)*
It memoria volatile *(f)*

memoria volatile *(f)* It
De energieabhängiger Speicher *(m)*
En volatile memory
Es memoria volátil *(f)*
Fr mémoire non rémanente *(f)*
Pt memória volátil *(f)*

mémoriser *vb* Fr
De speichern
En store
Es almacenar
It memorizzare
Pt armazenar

memorizzare *vb* It
De speichern
En store

Es almacenar
Fr mémoriser
Pt armazenar

memory *n* En
De Speicher *(m)*
Es memoria *(f)*
Fr mémoire *(f)*
It memoria *(f)*
Pt memória *(f)*

memory dump En
De Speicherauszug *(m)*
Es vuelco de la memoria *(m)*
Fr vidage de la mémoire *(m)*
It dump della memoria *(m)*
Pt descarregador de memória *(m)*

memory protection En
De Speicherschutz *(m)*
Es protección de la memoria *(f)*
Fr protection de la mémoire *(f)*
It protezione della memoria *(f)*
Pt protecção de memória *(f)*

Menge *(f) n* De
En set
Es conjunto *(m)*
Fr ensemble *(m)*
It insieme *(m)*
Pt conjunto *(m)*

mensagem de erro *(f)* Pt
De Fehlernachricht *(f)*
En error message
Es mansaje de error *(m)*
Fr message d'erreur *(m)*
It messaggio errore *(m)*

merge *n* En
De Fusion *(f)*
Es fusión *(f)*
Fr fusion *(f)*
It fusione *(f)*
Pt fusão *(f)*

merge *vb* En
De fusionieren
Es fusionar
Fr fusionner
It confondere
Pt misturar

mesa de ensaio *(f)* Pt
De Prüfstand *(m)*
En test bed
Es bancada de prueba *(f)*
Fr piste d'entraînement de test *(f)*
It banco di prova *(m)*

message d'erreur *(m)* Fr
De Fehlernachricht *(f)*
En error message
Es mansaje de error *(m)*
It messaggio errore *(m)*
Pt mensagem de erro *(f)*

message queuing En
De Nachrichten-schlangestehen *(n)*
Es formación de colas de mensajes *(f)*
Fr mise en file d'attente de message *(f)*
It messa in coda dei messaggi *(f)*
Pt bicha de mensagens *(f)*

message routing En
De Nachrichten-vermittlung *(f)*
Es encaminamiento de mensajes *(m)*
Fr acheminement des messages *(m)*
It incanalazione dei messaggi *(f)*
Pt encaminhamento de mensagens *(m)*

message switching En
De Nachrichten-verteilung *(f)*
Es conmutación de mensajes *(f)*
Fr commutation de messages *(f)*
It commutazione di messaggi *(f)*
Pt comutação de mensagem *(f)*

messaggio errore *(m)* It
De Fehlernachricht *(f)*
En error message
Es mansaje de error *(m)*
Fr message d'erreur *(m)*
Pt mensagem de erro *(f)*

messa in coda dei messaggi *(f)* It
De Nachrichten-schlangestehen *(n)*
En message queuing
Es formación de colas de mensajes *(f)*
Fr mise en file d'attente de message *(f)*
Pt bicha de mensagens *(f)*

metà addizionatore *(m)* It
De Halbaddierglied *(n)*
En half adder
Es semi-sumador *(m)*
Fr demi-additionneur *(m)*
Pt semi-somador *(m)*

metà duplex *(m)* It
De Halbduplex *(m)*
En half duplex
Es semiduplex *(m)*
Fr semi-duplex *(m)*
Pt semi-duplex *(m)*

Metalloxydhalbleiter *(m) n* De
En metal-oxide semiconductor (MOS)
Es semiconductor de óxido metálico *(m)*
Fr semiconducteur à oxyde métallique *(m)*
It semiconduttore ad ossidi metallici *(m)*
Pt semi-condutor de óxido de metal *(m)*

Metalloxyd- halbleiter-Feldeffekt-transistor *(m) n* De
En MOS field-effect transistor (MOSFET)
Es transistor MOS de efecto de campo *(m)*
Fr transistor à effet de champ à oxydes métalliques *(m)*
It transistore ad effetto di campo MOS *(m)*
Pt transistor de efeito de campo MOS *(m)*

metal-oxide semiconductor (MOS) En
De Metalloxydhalbleiter *(m)*
Es semiconductor de óxido metálico *(m)*
Fr semiconducteur à oxyde métallique *(m)*
It semiconduttore ad ossidi metallici *(m)*
Pt semi-condutor de óxido de metal *(m)*

metà sottrattore *(m)* It
De Halbsubtrahierer *(m)*
En half subtractor
Es semi-sustractor *(m)*
Fr semi-soustracteur *(m)*
Pt semi-subtractor *(m)*

metà voce *(f)* It
De Halbwort *(n)*
En half word
Es media palabra *(f)*
Fr demi-mot *(m)*
Pt meia-palavra *(f)*

méthode de Monte-Carlo *(f)* Fr
De Monte-Carlo-Methode *(f)*
En Monte Carlo method
Es método Montecarlo *(m)*
It metodo di Montecarlo *(m)*
Pt método de Monte-Carlo *(m)*

método de Monte-Carlo *(m)* Pt
De Monte-Carlo-Methode *(f)*
En Monte Carlo method
Es método Montecarlo *(m)*
Fr méthode de Monte-Carlo *(f)*
It metodo di Montecarlo *(m)*

método de planificación y control de proyectos *(m)* Es
De Projektaus-wertungsund Übersichttechnik *(f)*
En project evaluation and review technique (PERT)
Fr système d'ordonnancement des opérations et du personnel *(m)*
It technica di revisione e valutazione de progetto *(f)*

Pt técnica de avaliação e revisão de projectos *(f)*

metodo di Montecarlo *(m)* It
De Monte-Carlo-Methode *(f)*
En Monte Carlo method
Es método Montecarlo *(m)*
Fr méthode de Monte-Carlo *(f)*
Pt método de Monte-Carlo *(m)*

método Montecarlo *(m)* Es
De Monte-Carlo-Methode *(f)*
En Monte Carlo method
Fr méthode de Monte-Carlo *(f)*
It metodo di Montecarlo *(m)*
Pt método de Monte-Carlo *(m)*

mettere a punto It
De einrichten
En set up
Es montar
Fr mettre en place
Pt instalar

mettere a punto un programma It
De fehlersuchen
En debug
Es depurar
Fr mettre au point
Pt desparasitar

metter nell'indice It
De indizieren
En index
Es poner en un índice
Fr faire un index
Pt pôr em índex

mettre à jour Fr
De auf den neuesten Stand bringen
En update
Es actualizar
It aggiornare
Pt actualizar

mettre au point Fr
De fehlersuchen
En debug
Es depurar
It mettere a punto un programma
Pt desparasitar

mettre à zéro Fr
De rückstellen
En reset
Es reajustar
It riazzerare
Pt tornar a acertar

mettre en forme Fr
De edieren
En edit
Es editar
It manipolare
Pt editar

mettre en place Fr
De einrichten
En set up
Es montar
It mettere a punto
Pt instalar

mezzi magnetici *(m pl)* It
De magnetisches Aufzeichnungsmittel *(n)*
En magnetic media
Es medios magnéticos *(m pl)*
Fr milieux magnétiques *(m pl)*
Pt meios magnéticos *(m pl)*

mezzo *(m) n* It
De Mittel *(n)*
En medium
Es medio *(m)*
Fr milieu *(m)*
Pt meio *(m)*

micro *adj* En, Es, Fr, It, Pt
De Mikro

microchip *n* En, It, Pt *(m)*
De Mikrochip *(m)*
Es microplaqueta *(f)*
Fr micro-puce *(f)*

microcomputador *(m) n* Pt
De Mikrocomputer *(m)*
En microcomputer
Es microordenador *(m)*
Fr micro-ordinateur *(m)*
It microelaboratore *(m)*

microcomputer *n* En
De Mikrocomputer *(m)*
Es microordenador *(m)*
Fr micro-ordinateur *(m)*
It microelaboratore *(m)*
Pt microcomputador *(m)*

microelaboratore *(m) n* It
De Mikrocomputer; Mikroprozessor *(m)*
En microcomputer; microprocessor
Es microordenador; microprocesador *(m)*
Fr micro-ordinateur; microprocesseur *(m)*
Pt microcomputador; microprocessador *(m)*

microelectrónica *(f) n* Es, Pt
De Mikroelektronik *(f)*
En microelectronics
Fr micro-électronique *(f)*
It microelettronica *(f)*

microelectronics *n* En
De Mikroelektronik *(f)*
Es microelectrónica *(f)*
Fr micro-électronique *(f)*
It microelettronica *(f)*
Pt microelectrónica *(f)*

micro-électronique *(f) n* Fr
De Mikroelektronik *(f)*
En microelectronics
Es microelectrónica *(f)*
It microelettronica *(f)*
Pt microelectrónica *(f)*

microelettronica *(f) n* It
De Mikroelektronik *(f)*
En microelectronics
Es microelectrónica *(f)*
Fr micro-électronique *(f)*
Pt microelectrónica *(f)*

microficha *(f) n* Es, Pt
De Mikrofiche *(f)*
En microfiche
Fr micro-fiche *(f)*
It scheda microfilm *(f)*

microfiche *n* En
De Mikrofiche *(f)*
Es microficha *(f)*
Fr micro-fiche *(f)*
It scheda microfilm *(f)*
Pt microficha *(f)*

micro-fiche *(f) n* Fr
De Mikrofiche *(f)*
En microfiche
Es microficha *(f)*
It scheda microfilm *(f)*
Pt microficha *(f)*

microfilm *n* En, Es, It *(m)*
De Mikrofilm *(m)*
Fr micro-film *(m)*
Pt microfilme *(m)*

micro-film *(m) n* Fr
De Mikrofilm *(m)*
En microfilm
Es microfilm *(m)*
It microfilm *(m)*
Pt microfilme *(m)*

microfilme *(m) n* Pt
De Mikrofilm *(m)*
En microfilm
Es microfilm *(m)*
Fr micro-film *(m)*
It microfilm *(m)*

microinstrução *(f) n* Pt
De Mikrobefehl *(m)*
En microinstruction
Es microinstrucción *(f)*
Fr micro-instructions *(f pl)*
It microistruzione *(f)*

microinstrucción *(f) n* Es
De Mikrobefehl *(m)*
En microinstruction
Fr micro-instructions *(f pl)*
It microistruzione *(f)*
Pt microinstrução *(f)*

microinstruction *n* En
De Mikrobefehl *(m)*
Es microinstrucción *(f)*
Fr micro-instructions *(f pl)*
It microistruzione *(f)*
Pt microinstrução *(f)*

micro-instructions *(f pl) n* Fr
De Mikrobefehl *(m)*
En microinstruction
Es microinstrucción *(f)*
It microistruzione *(f)*
Pt microinstrução *(f)*

microistruzione *(f)* *n* It
De Mikrobefehl *(m)*
En microinstruction
Es microinstrucción *(f)*
Fr micro-instructions *(f pl)*
Pt microinstrução *(f)*

microordenador *(m)* *n* Es
De Mikrocomputer *(m)*
En microcomputer
Fr micro-ordinateur *(m)*
It microelaboratore *(m)*
Pt microcomputador *(m)*

micro-ordinateur *(m)* *n* Fr
De Mikrocomputer *(m)*
En microcomputer
Es microordenador *(m)*
It microelaboratore *(m)*
Pt microcomputador *(m)*

microplaqueta *(f)* *n* Es
De Mikrochip *(m)*
En microchip
Fr micro-puce *(f)*
It microchip *(m)*
Pt microchip *(m)*

microplaqueta de silicio *(f)* Es
De Silikonchip *(m)*
En silicon chip
Fr puce au silicium *(f)*
It scheggia di silicone *(f)*
Pt ficha de silício *(f)*

microprocesador *(m)* *n* Es
De Mikroprozessor *(m)*
En microprocessor
Fr microprocesseur *(m)*
It microelaboratore *(m)*
Pt microprocessador *(m)*

microprocessador *(m)* *n* Pt
De Mikroprozessor *(m)*
En microprocessor
Es microprocesador *(m)*
Fr microprocesseur *(m)*
It microelaboratore *(m)*

microprocesseur *(m)* *n* Fr
De Mikroprozessor *(m)*
En microprocessor
Es microprocesador *(m)*
It microelaboratore *(m)*
Pt microprocessador *(m)*

microprocessor *n* En
De Mikroprozessor *(m)*
Es microprocesador *(m)*
Fr microprocesseur *(m)*
It microelaboratore *(m)*
Pt microprocessador *(m)*

microprogram *n* En
De Mikroprogramm *(n)*
Es microprograma *(m)*
Fr microprogramme *(m)*
It microprogramma *(m)*
Pt microprograma *(m)*

microprograma *(m)* *n* Es, Pt
De Mikroprogramm *(n)*
En microprogram
Fr microprogramme *(m)*
It microprogramma *(m)*

microprogramação *(f)* *n* Pt
De Mikro-programmierung *(f)*
En microprogramming
Es microprogramación *(f)*
Fr micro-programmation *(f)*
It micro-programmazione *(f)*

microprogramación *(f)* *n* Es
De Mikro-programmierung *(f)*
En microprogramming
Fr micro-programmation *(f)*
It micro-programmazione *(f)*
Pt microprogramação *(f)*

microprogramma *(m)* *n* It
De Mikroprogramm *(n)*
En microprogram
Es microprograma *(m)*
Fr microprogramme *(m)*
Pt microprogramma *(m)*

micro-programmation *(f)* *n* Fr
De Mikro-programmierung *(f)*
En microprogramming
Es microprogramación *(f)*
It micro-programmazione *(f)*
Pt microprogramação *(f)*

microprogrammazione *(f)* *n* It
De Mikro-programmierung *(f)*
En microprogramming
Es microprogramación *(f)*
Fr micro-programmation *(f)*
Pt microprogramação *(f)*

microprogramme *(m)* *n* Fr
De Mikroprogramm *(n)*
En microprogram
Es microprograma *(m)*
It microprogramma *(m)*
Pt microprograma *(m)*

microprogramming *n* En
De Mikro-programmierung *(f)*
Es microprogramación *(f)*
Fr micro-programmation *(f)*
It micro-programmazione *(f)*
Pt microprogramação *(f)*

micro-puce *(f)* *n* Fr
De Mikrochip *(m)*
En microchip
Es microplaqueta *(f)*
It microchip *(m)*
Pt microchip *(m)*

microsecond *n* En
De Mikrosekunde *(f)*
Es microsegundo *(m)*
Fr micro-seconde *(f)*
It microsecondo *(m)*
Pt microsegundo *(m)*

micro-seconde *(f)* *n* Fr
De Mikrosekunde *(f)*
En microsecond
Es microsegundo *(m)*
It microsecondo *(m)*
Pt microsegundo *(m)*

microsecondo *(m)* *n* It
De Mikrosekunde *(f)*
En microsecond
Es microsegundo *(m)*
Fr micro-seconde *(f)*
Pt microsegundo *(m)*

microsegundo *(m)* *n* Es, Pt
De Mikrosekunde *(f)*
En microsecond
Fr micro-seconde *(f)*
It microsecondo *(m)*

microsistema *(m)* *n* Es, It, Pt
De Mikrosystem *(n)*
En microsystem
Fr micro-système *(m)*

microsystem *n* En
De Mikrosystem *(n)*
Es microsistema *(m)*
Fr micro-système *(m)*
It microsistema *(m)*
Pt microsistema *(m)*

micro-système *(m)* *n* Fr
De Mikrosystem *(n)*
En microsystem
Es microsistema *(m)*
It microsistema *(m)*
Pt microsistema *(m)*

Mikro *adj* De
En micro
Es micro
Fr micro
It micro
Pt micro

Mikrobefehl *(m)* *n* De
En microinstruction
Es microinstrucción *(f)*
Fr micro-instructions *(f pl)*
It microistruzione *(f)*
Pt microinstrução *(f)*

Mikrochip *(m)* *n* De
En microchip
Es microplaqueta *(f)*
Fr micro-puce *(f)*

It microchip *(m)*
Pt microchip *(m)*

Mikrocomputer *(m) n* De
En microcomputer
Es microordenador *(m)*
Fr micro-ordinateur *(m)*
It microelaboratore *(m)*
Pt microcomputador *(m)*

Mikroelektronik *(f) n* De
En microelectronics
Es microelectrónica *(f)*
Fr micro-électronique *(f)*
It microelettronica *(f)*
Pt microelectrónica *(f)*

Mikrofiche *(f) n* De
En microfiche
Es microficha *(f)*
Fr micro-fiche *(f)*
It scheda microfilm *(f)*
Pt microficha *(f)*

Mikrofilm *(m) n* De
En microfilm
Es microfilm *(m)*
Fr micro-film *(m)*
It microfilm *(m)*
Pt microfilme *(m)*

Mikroprogramm *(n) n* De
En microprogram
Es microprograma *(m)*
Fr microprogramme *(m)*
It microprogramma *(m)*
Pt microprograma *(m)*

Mikroprogrammierung *(f) n* De
En microprogramming
Es microprogramación *(f)*
Fr micro-programmation *(f)*
It micro-programmazione *(f)*
Pt microprogramação *(f)*

Mikroprozessor *(m) n* De
En microprocessor
Es microprocesador *(m)*
Fr microprocesseur *(m)*
It microelaboratore *(m)*
Pt microprocessador *(m)*

Mikrosekunde *(f) n* De
En microsecond
Es microsegundo *(m)*
Fr micro-seconde *(f)*
It microsecondo *(m)*
Pt microsegundo *(m)*

Mikrosystem *(n) n* De
En microsystem
Es microsistema *(m)*
Fr micro-système *(m)*
It microsistema *(m)*
Pt microsistema *(m)*

mili- Es, Pt
De Milli
En milli-
Fr milli-
It milli

milieu *(m) n* Fr
De Mittel *(n)*
En medium
Es medio *(m)*
It mezzo *(m)*
Pt meio *(m)*

milieux magnétiques *(m pl)* Fr
De magnetisches Aufzeichnungsmittel *(n)*
En magnetic media
Es medios magnéticos *(m pl)*
It mezzi magnetici *(m pl)*
Pt meios magnéticos *(m pl)*

milli It
De Milli
En milli-
Es mili-
Fr milli-
Pt mili-

Milli De
En milli-
Es mili-
Fr milli-
It milli
Pt mili-

milli- En, Fr
De Milli
Es mili-
It milli
Pt mili-

million de bits *(m)* Fr
De Megabit *(m)*
En megabit
Es megabit *(m)*
It megabit *(m)*
Pt megabit *(m)*

million d'octets *(m)* Fr
De Megabyte *(m)*
En megabyte
Es megabyte *(m)*
It megabyte *(m)*
Pt megabyte *(m)*

minicomputador *(m) n* Pt
De Minicomputer *(m)*
En minicomputer
Es miniordenador *(m)*
Fr mini-ordinateur *(m)*
It minielaboratore *(m)*

minicomputer *n* En
De Minicomputer *(m)*
Es miniordenador *(m)*
Fr mini-ordinateur *(m)*
It minielaboratore *(m)*
Pt minicomputador *(m)*

Minicomputer *(m) n* De
En minicomputer
Es miniordenador *(m)*
Fr mini-ordinateur *(m)*
It minielaboratore *(m)*
Pt minicomputador *(m)*

minidisco *(m) n* Es
De Minidiskette *(f)*
En minidiskette
Fr mini-disquette *(f)*
It minidiskette *(m)*
Pt minidisqueta *(f)*

minidisco flexible *(m)* Es
De Mini-Floppy-Disk *(m)*
En minifloppy disk
Fr mini-disque souple *(m)*
It mini floppy disk *(m)*
Pt disco minifloppy *(m)*

minidiskette *n* En, It *(m)*
De Minidiskette *(f)*
Es minidisco *(m)*
Fr mini-disquette *(f)*
Pt minidisqueta *(f)*

Minidiskette *(f) n* De
En minidiskette
Es minidisco *(m)*
Fr mini-disquette *(f)*
It minidiskette *(m)*
Pt minidisqueta *(f)*

minidisque *(m) n* Fr
De Diskette *(f)*
En diskette
Es disco flexible *(m)*
It diskette *(m)*
Pt disqueta *(f)*

mini-disque souple *(m)* Fr
De Mini-Floppy-Disk *(m)*
En minifloppy disk
Es minidisco flexible *(m)*
It mini floppy disk *(m)*
Pt disco minifloppy *(m)*

minidisqueta *(f) n* Pt
De Minidiskette *(f)*
En minidiskette
Es minidisco *(m)*
Fr mini-disquette *(f)*
It minidiskette *(m)*

mini-disquette *(f) n* Fr
De Minidiskette *(f)*
En minidiskette
Es minidisco *(m)*
It minidiskette *(m)*
Pt minidisqueta *(f)*

minielaboratore *(m) n* It
De Minicomputer *(m)*
En minicomputer
Es miniordenador *(m)*
Fr mini-ordinateur *(m)*
Pt minicomputador *(m)*

minifloppy disk En
De Mini-Floppy-Disk *(m)*
Es minidisco flexible *(m)*
Fr mini-disque souple *(m)*
It mini floppy disk *(m)*
Pt disco minifloppy *(m)*

mini floppy disk *(m)* It
De Mini-Floppy-Disk *(m)*
En minifloppy disk
Es minidisco flexible *(m)*
Fr mini-disque souple *(m)*
Pt disco minifloppy *(m)*

Mini-Floppy-Disk *(m) n* De
En minifloppy disk
Es minidisco flexible *(m)*

Fr mini-disque souple *(m)*
It mini floppy disk *(m)*
Pt disco minifloppy *(m)*

minimum-access code En
De Minimum-zugriffscode *(m)*
Es código de mínimo acceso *(m)*
Fr code d'accès minimal *(m)*
It codice di accesso minimo *(m)*
Pt código de acesso mínimo *(m)*

Minimumzugriffscode *(m)* De
En minimum-access code
Es código de mínimo acceso *(m)*
Fr code d'accès minimal *(m)*
It codice di accesso minimo *(m)*
Pt código de acesso mínimo *(m)*

miniordenador *(m) n* Es
De Minicomputer *(m)*
En minicomputer
Fr mini-ordinateur *(m)*
It minielaboratore *(m)*
Pt minicomputador *(m)*

mini-ordinateur *(m) n* Fr
De Minicomputer *(m)*
En minicomputer
Es miniordenador *(m)*
It minielaboratore *(m)*
Pt minicomputador *(m)*

minus zone En
De Minuszone *(f)*
Es zona negativa *(f)*
Fr zone moins *(f)*
It zona meno *(f)*
Pt zona menos *(f)*

Minuszone *(f) n* De
En minus zone
Es zona negativa *(f)*
Fr zone moins *(f)*
It zona meno *(f)*
Pt zona menos *(f)*

Mischdarstellung *(f) n* De
En mixed-base notation
Es notación con base múltiple *(f)*
Fr notation à base multiple *(f)*
It notazione a base mista *(f)*
Pt notação de base mista *(f)*

mise à jour temporisée *(f)* Fr
De verzögerte Aktualisierung *(f)*
En delayed updating
Es actualización diferida *(f)*
It aggiornamento ritardato *(m)*
Pt actualização atrasada *(f)*

mise au point *(f)* Fr
De Abstimmung *(f)*
En tuning
Es sintonización *(f)*
It sintonizzazione *(f)*
Pt afinação *(f)*

mise en application *(f)* Fr
De Durchführung *(f)*
En implementation
Es realización *(f)*
It implementazione *(f)*
Pt implementação *(f)*

mise en file d'attente de message *(f)* Fr
De Nachrichten-schlangestehen *(n)*
En message queuing
Es formación de colas de mensajes *(f)*
It messa in coda dei messaggi *(f)*
Pt bicha de mensagens *(f)*

misturar *vb* Pt
De fusionieren
En merge
Es fusionar
Fr fusionner
It confondere

mitgeschleppter Fehler *(m)* De
En inherited error
Es error arrastrado *(m)*
Fr erreur héritée *(f)*
It errore ereditato *(m)*
Pt erro herdado *(m)*

mitlaufender Fehler *(m)* De
En propagated error
Es error propagado *(m)*
Fr erreur propagée *(f)*
It errore propagato *(m)*
Pt erro propagado *(m)*

Mittel *(n) n* De
En medium
Es medio *(m)*
Fr milieu *(m)*
It mezzo *(m)*
Pt meio *(m)*

mixed-base notation En
De Mischdarstellung *(f)*
Es notación con base múltiple *(f)*
Fr notation à base multiple *(f)*
It notazione a base mista *(f)*
Pt notação de base mista *(f)*

mnemonic *n* En
De Mnemonik *(f)*
Es mnemotécnica *(f)*
Fr mnémonique *(f)*
It mnemonica *(f)*
Pt mnemónica *(f)*

mnemonica *(f) n* It
De Mnemonik *(f)*
En mnemonic
Es mnemotécnica *(f)*
Fr mnémonique *(f)*
Pt mnemónica *(f)*

mnemónica *(f) n* Pt
De Mnemonik *(f)*
En mnemonic
Es mnemotécnica *(f)*
Fr mnémonique *(f)*
It mnemonica *(f)*

mnemónica de instruções *(f)* Pt
De Befehlsmnemonik *(f)*
En instruction mnemonic
Es instrucción mnemotécnica *(f)*
Fr mnémonique d'instruction *(f)*
It mnemonica dell'istruzione *(f)*

mnemonica dell'istruzione *(f)* It
De Befehlsmnemonik *(f)*
En instruction mnemonic
Es instrucción mnemotécnica *(f)*
Fr mnémonique d'instruction *(f)*
Pt mnemónica de instruções *(f)*

mnemonic operation code En
De Mnemonik-Betriebscode *(m)*
Es código de operación mnemotécnico *(m)*
Fr code d'exploitation mnémonique *(m)*
It codice dell'operazione mnemonico *(m)*
Pt código de operação mnemónico *(m)*

Mnemonik *(f) n* De
En mnemonic
Es mnemotécnica *(f)*
Fr mnémonique *(f)*
It mnemonica *(f)*
Pt mnemónica *(f)*

Mnemonik-Betriebscode *(m)* De
En mnemonic operation code
Es código de operación mnemotécnico *(m)*
Fr code d'exploitation mnémonique *(m)*
It codice dell'operazione mnemonico *(m)*
Pt código de operacão mnemónico *(m)*

mnémonique *(f) n* Fr
De Mnemonik *(f)*
En mnemonic
Es mnemotécnica *(f)*
It mnemonica *(f)*
Pt mnemónica *(f)*

mnémonique d'instruction *(f)* Fr
De Befehlsmnemonik *(f)*
En instruction mnemonic
Es instrucción mnemotécnica *(f)*

It mnemonica dell'istruzione *(f)*
Pt mnemónica de instruções *(f)*

mnemotécnica *(f) n* Es
De Mnemonik *(f)*
En mnemonic
Fr mnémonique *(f)*
It mnemonica *(f)*
Pt mnemónica *(f)*

modalità *(f) n* It
De Betriebsart *(f)*
En mode
Es modo *(m)*
Fr mode *(m)*
Pt modo *(m)*

modalità conversazionale *(f)* It
De Dialogbetriebsart *(f)*
En conversational mode
Es modo diálogo *(m)*
Fr mode dialogué *(m)*
Pt modo conversacional *(m)*

modalità interattiva *(f)* It
De interaktive Betriebsart *(f)*
En interactive mode
Es modo interactivo *(m)*
Fr mode interactif *(m)*
Pt modo interactivo *(m)*

modalitá rumorosa *(f)* It
De Rauschbetriebsart *(f)*
En noisy mode
Es modo ruidoso *(m)*
Fr mode bruyant *(m)*
P^ modo ruidoso *(m)*

mode *n* En, Fr *(m)*
De Betriebsart *(f)*
Es modo *(m)*
It modalità *(f)*
Pt modo *(m)*

mode bruyant *(m)* Fr
De Rauschbetriebsart *(f)*
En noisy mode
Es modo ruidoso *(m)*
It modalità rumorosa *(f)*
Pt modo ruidoso *(m)*

mode dialogué *(m)* Fr
De Dialogbetriebsart *(f)*
En conversational mode
Es modo diálogo *(m)*
It modalità conversazionale *(f)*
Pt modo conversacional *(m)*

mode interactif *(m)* Fr
De interaktive Betriebsart *(f)*
En interactive mode
Es modo interactivo *(m)*
It modalità interattiva *(f)*
Pt modo interactivo *(m)*

model *n* En
De Modell *(n)*
Es modelo *(m)*
Fr modèle *(m)*
It modello *(m)*
Pt modelo *(m)*

model *vb* En
De modellieren
Es diseñar
Fr modeler
It modellare
Pt modelar

modelado *(m) n* Es
De Modellierung *(f)*
En modelling
Fr modélisation *(f)*
It modellatura *(f)*
Pt modelagem *(f)*

modelagem *(f) n* Pt
De Modellierung *(f)*
En modelling
Es modelado *(m)*
Fr modélisation *(f)*
It modellatura *(f)*

modelar *vb* Pt
De modellieren
En model
Es diseñar
Fr modeler
It modellare

model building En
De Modellaufbau *(m)*
Es construcción de modelos *(f)*
Fr construction de modèles *(f)*
It costruzione di modelli *(f)*
Pt construção de modelo *(f)*

modèle *(m) n* Fr
De Modell *(n)*
En model
Es modelo *(m)*
It modello *(m)*
Pt modelo *(m)*

modeler *vb* Fr
De modellieren
En model
Es diseñar
It modellare
Pt modelar

modélisation *(f) n* Fr
De Modellierung *(f)*
En modelling
Es modelado *(m)*
It modellatura *(f)*
Pt modelagem *(f)*

Modell *(n) n* De
En model
Es modelo *(m)*
Fr modèle *(m)*
It modello *(m)*
Pt modelo *(m)*

modellare *vb* It
De modellieren
En model
Es diseñar
Fr modeler
Pt modelar

modellatura *(f) n* It
De Modellierung *(f)*
En modelling
Es modelado *(m)*
Fr modélisation *(f)*
Pt modelagem *(f)*

Modellaufbau *(m) n* De
En model building
Es construcción de modelos *(f)*
Fr construction de modèles *(f)*
It costruzione di modelli *(f)*
Pt construção de modelo *(f)*

modellieren *vb* De
En model
Es diseñar
Fr modeler
It modellare
Pt modelar

Modellierung *(f) n* De
En modelling
Es modelado *(m)*
Fr modélisation *(f)*
It modellatura *(f)*
Pt modelagem *(f)*

modelling *n* En
De Modellierung *(f)*
Es modelado *(m)*
Fr modélisation *(f)*
It modellatura *(f)*
Pt modelagem *(f)*

modello *(m) n* It
De Modell *(n)*
En model
Es modelo *(m)*
Fr modèle *(m)*
Pt modelo *(m)*

modelo *(m) n* Es, Pt
De Modell *(n)*
En model
Fr modèle *(m)*
It modello *(m)*

modem *n* En, Fr, It, Pt *(m)*
De Modem *(m)*
Es módem *(m)*

Modem *(m) n* De
En modem
Es módem *(m)*
Fr modem *(m)*
It modem *(m)*
Pt modem *(m)*

módem *(m) n* Es
De Modem *(m)*
En modem
Fr modem *(m)*
It modem *(m)*
Pt modem *(m)*

modificaćão *(f) n* Pt
De Abänderung *(f)*
En modification
Es modificación *(f)*
Fr modification *(f)*
It modificazione *(f)*

modificação do programa *(f)* Pt
De Programmänderung *(f)*
En program modification
Es modificación de programa *(f)*

Fr modification de programme *(f)*
It modificazione di programma *(f)*

modificación *(f) n* Es
De Abänderung *(f)*
En modification
Fr modification *(f)*
It modificazione *(f)*
Pt modificação *(f)*

modificación de programa *(f)* Es
De Programmänderung *(f)*
En program modification
Fr modification de programme *(f)*
It modificazione di programma *(f)*
Pt modificação do programa *(f)*

modificador *(m) n* Es, Pt
De Modifikator *(m)*
En modifier
Fr modificateur *(m)*
It modificatore *(m)*

modificar *vb* Es, Pt
De abändern
En modify
Fr modifier
It modificare

modificare *vb* It
De abändern
En modify
Es modificar
Fr modifier
Pt modificar

modificateur *(m) n* Fr
De Modifikator *(m)*
En modifier
Es modificador *(m)*
It modificatore *(m)*
Pt modificador *(m)*

modification *n* En, Fr *(f)*
De Abänderung *(f)*
Es modificación *(f)*
It modificazione *(f)*
Pt modificação *(f)*

modification de programme *(f)* Fr
De Programmänderung *(f)*
En program modification
Es modificación de programa *(f)*
It modificazione di programma *(f)*
Pt modificação do programa *(f)*

modificatore *(m) n* It
De Modifikator *(m)*
En modifier
Es modificador *(m)*
Fr modificateur *(m)*
Pt modificador *(m)*

modificazione *(f) n* It
De Abänderung *(f)*
En modification
Es modificación *(f)*
Fr modification *(f)*
Pt modificação *(f)*

modificazione di programma *(f)* It
De Programmänderung *(f)*
En program modification
Es modificación de programa *(f)*
Fr modification de programme *(f)*
Pt modificação do programa *(f)*

modifier *n* En
De Modifikator *(m)*
Es modificador *(m)*
Fr modificateur *(m)*
It modificatore *(m)*
Pt modificador *(m)*

modifier *vb* Fr
De abändern
En modify
Es modificar
It modificare
Pt modificar

Modifikator *(m) n* De
En modifier
Es modifacador *(m)*
Fr modificateur *(m)*
It modificatore *(m)*
Pt modificador *(m)*

modify *vb* En
De abändern
Es modificar
Fr modifier
It modificare
Pt modificar

modo *(m) n* Es, Pt
De Betriebsart *(f)*
En mode
Fr mode *(m)*
It modalità *(f)*

modo conversacional *(m)* Pt
De Dialogbetriebsart *(f)*
En conversational mode
Es modo diálogo *(m)*
Fr mode dialogué *(m)*
It modalità conversazionale *(f)*

modo diálogo *(m)* Es
De Dialogbetriebsart *(f)*
En conversational mode
Fr mode dialogué *(m)*
It modalità conversazionale *(f)*
Pt modo conversacional *(m)*

modo interactivo *(m)* Es, Pt
De interaktive Betriebsart *(f)*
En interactive mode
Fr mode interactif *(m)*
It modalità interattiva *(f)*

modo ruidoso *(m)* Es, Pt
De Rauschbetriebsart *(f)*
En noisy mode
Fr mode bruyant *(m)*
It modalità rumorosa *(f)*

Modul *(m) n* De
En module
Es módulo *(m)*
Fr module *(m)*
It modulo *(m)*
Pt módulo *(m)*

modulação *(f) n* Pt
De Modulation *(f)*
En modulation
Es modulación *(f)*
Fr modulation *(f)*
It modulazione *(f)*

modulación *(f) n* Es
De Modulation *(f)*
En modulation
Fr modulation *(f)*
It modulazione *(f)*
Pt modulação *(f)*

modulador *(m) n* Es, Pt
De Modulator *(m)*
En modulator
Fr modulateur *(m)*
It modulatore *(m)*

modulare Programmierung *(f)* De
En modular programming
Es programación modular *(f)*
Fr programmation modulaire *(f)*
It programmazione modulare *(f)*
Pt programação modular *(f)*

modular programming En
De modulare Programmierung *(f)*
Es programación modular *(f)*
Fr programmation modulaire *(f)*
It programmazione modulare *(f)*
Pt programação modular *(f)*

modular system En
De Baukastensystem *(n)*
Es sistema modular *(m)*
Fr système modulaire *(m)*
It sistema modulare *(m)*
Pt sistema modular *(m)*

modulateur *(m) n* Fr
De Modulator *(m)*
En modulator
Es modulador *(m)*
It modulatore *(m)*
Pt modulador *(m)*

modulation *n* En, Fr *(f)*
De Modulation *(f)*
Es modulación *(f)*
It modulazione *(f)*
Pt modulação *(f)*

Modulation *(f) n* De
En modulation
Es modulación *(f)*
Fr modulation *(f)*
It modulazione *(f)*
Pt modulação *(f)*

modulator *n* En
De Modulator *(m)*
Es modulador *(m)*
Fr modulateur *(m)*
It modulatore *(m)*
Pt modulador *(m)*

Modulator *(m) n* De
En modulator
Es modulador *(m)*
Fr modulateur *(m)*
It modulatore *(m)*
Pt modulador *(m)*

modulatore *(m) n* It
De Modulator *(m)*
En modulator
Es modulador *(m)*
Fr modulateur *(m)*
Pt modulador *(m)*

modulazione *(f) n* It
De Modulation *(f)*
En modulation
Es modulación *(f)*
Fr modulation *(f)*
Pt modulação *(f)*

module *n* En, Fr *(m)*
De Modul *(m)*
Es módulo *(m)*
It modulo *(m)*
Pt módulo *(m)*

moduli *(m pl) n* It
De Formulare *(n pl)*
En forms
Es papel *(m)*
Fr formules *(f pl)*
Pt formulários *(m pl)*

moduli a copie multiple *(m pl)* It
De mehrteilige Formulare *(pl)*
En multipart forms
Es paquete de papel continuo *(m)*
Fr liasse *(f)*
Pt formas de partes múltiplas *(f pl)*

modulo *(m) n* It
De Modul *(m)*
En module
Es módulo *(m)*
Fr module *(m)*
Pt módulo *(m)*

modulo-n check En
De Modulo-N-Kontrolle *(f)*
Es verificación de módulo N *(f)*
Fr contrôle module-n *(m)*
It controllo modulo-n *(m)*
Pt verificação modulo-n *(f)*

módulo *(m) n* Es, Pt
De Modul *(m)*
En module
Fr module *(m)*
It modulo *(m)*

Modulo-N-Kontrolle *(f)* De
En modulo-n check
Es verificación de módulo N *(f)*
Fr contrôle module-n *(m)*
It controllo modulo-n *(m)*
Pt verificação modulo-n *(f)*

modulo standard *(m)* It
De Standardform *(f)*
En standard form
Es formato normalizado *(m)*
Fr forme normalisée *(f)*
Pt formulário standard *(m)*

moltiplicatore *(m) n* It
De Multiplizierer *(m)*
En multiplier
Es multiplicador *(m)*
Fr multiplicateur *(m)*
Pt multiplicador *(m)*

monadische Operation *(f)* De
En unary operation
Es operación unaria *(f)*
Fr opération unaire *(f)*
It operazione unaria *(f)*
Pt operação unária *(f)*

moniteur *(m) n* Fr
De Monitor *(m)*
En monitor
Es monitor *(m)*
It monitor *(m)*
Pt monitor *(m)*

monitor *n* En, Es, It, Pt *(m)*
De Monitor *(m)*
Fr moniteur *(m)*

monitor *vb* En
De kontrollieren
Es examinar
Fr surveiller
It esaminare
Pt vigiar

Monitor *(m) n* De
En monitor
Es monitor *(m)*
Fr moniteur *(m)*
It monitor *(m)*
Pt monitor *(m)*

montador *(m) n* Pt
De Assemblierer *(m)*
En assembler
Es ensamblador *(m)*
Fr assembleur *(m)*
It assemblatore *(m)*

montar *vb* Es
De einrichten
En set up
Fr mettre en place
It mettere a punto
Pt instalar

montar *vb* Pt
De assemblieren
En assemble
Es ensamblar
Fr assembler
It assemblare

Monte Carlo method En
De Monte-Carlo-Methode *(f)*
Es método Montecarlo *(m)*
Fr méthode de Monte-Carlo *(f)*
It metodo di Montecarlo *(m)*
Pt método de Monte-Carlo *(m)*

Monte-Carlo-Methode *(f)* De
En Monte Carlo method
Es método Montecarlo *(m)*
Fr méthode de Monte-Carlo *(f)*
It metodo di Montecarlo *(m)*
Pt método de Monte-Carlo *(m)*

MOS complémentaire *(m)* Fr
De komplementäres MOS *(n)*
En complementary MOS
Es MOS suplementario *(m)*
It MOS complementare *(m)*
Pt MOS complementar *(m)*

MOS complementar *(m)* Pt
De komplementäres MOS *(n)*
En complementary MOS
Es MOS suplementario *(m)*
Fr MOS complémentaire *(m)*
It MOS complementare *(m)*

MOS complementare *(m)* It
De komplementäres MOS *(n)*
En complementary MOS
Es MOS suplementario *(m)*
Fr MOS complémentaire *(m)*
Pt MOS complementar *(m)*

MOS field-effect transistor (MOSFET) En
De Metalloxyd-halbleiter-Feldeffekt-transistor *(m)*
Es transistor MOS de efecto de campo *(m)*
Fr transistor à effet de champ à oxydes métalliques *(m)*
It transistore ad effetto di campo MOS *(m)*
Pt transistor de efeito de campo MOS *(m)*

MOS suplementario *(m)* Es
De komplementäres MOS *(n)*
En complementary MOS
Fr MOS complémentaire *(m)*

It MOS complementare *(m)*
Pt MOS complementar *(m)*

mostra di modo punto a punto *(f)* It
De punktweise Darstellung *(f)*
En point-mode display
Es representación de modo puntual *(f)*
Fr affichage mode point par point *(m)*
Pt display de modo pontual *(m)*

mostrar *vb* Pt
De anzeigen
En display
Es presentar
Fr afficher
It visualizzare

mot *(m) n* Fr
De Wort *(n)*
En word
Es palabra *(f)*
It voce *(f)*
Pt palavra *(f)*

mot-clé *(m) n* Fr
De Schlüsselwort *(n)*
En keyword
Es palabra clave *(f)*
It parola chiave *(f)*
Pt palavra chave *(f)*

mot de contrôle *(m)* Fr
De Schablone *(f)*
En control word
Es palabra de control *(f)*
It voce di controllo *(f)*
Pt palavra de controlo *(f)*

mot de passe *(m)* Fr
De Kennwort *(n)*
En password
Es contraseña *(f)*
It parola d'ordine *(f)*
Pt contra-senha *(f)*

mot d'état *(m)* Fr
De Statuswort *(n)*
En status word
Es palabra de estado *(f)*
It voce di stato *(f)*
Pt palavra de status *(f)*

mot machine *(m)* Fr
De Maschinenwort *(n)*
En machine word
Es palabra de máquina *(f)*
It voce macchina *(f)*
Pt palavra da máquina *(f)*

mots par minute (mpm) *(m pl)* Fr
De Worte pro Minute *(pl)*
En words per minute (wpm)
Es palabras por minuto *(f pl)*
It parole al minuto *(f pl)*
Pt palavras por minuto (ppm) *(f pl)*

mouvements *(m pl) n* Fr
De Transaktionsdaten *(pl)*
En transaction data
Es datos de transacciones *(m pl)*
It dati della transazione *(m pl)*
Pt dados de transacção *(m pl)*

moyenne des temps de bon fonctionnement *(f)* Fr
De Effektivzeit zwischen Ausfällen *(f)*
En mean time between failures
Es tiempo medio entre fallos *(m)*
It tempo medio tra i guasti *(m)*
Pt tempo médio entre falhas *(m)*

moyeu porte-bobine *(m)* Fr
De Nabe *(f)*
En hub
Es boca *(f)*
It mozzo *(m)*
Pt cubo *(m)*

mozzo *(m) n* It
De Nabe *(f)*
En hub
Es boca *(f)*
Fr moyeu porte-bobine *(m)*
Pt cubo *(m)*

mudança *(f) n* Pt
De Stellenverschiebung *(f)*
En shift
Es desplazamiento *(m)*
Fr décalage *(m)*
It riporto *(m)*

mudança à direita *(f)* Pt
De Rechtsschiebung *(f)*
En right shift
Es desplazamiento a la derecha *(m)*
Fr décalage à droite *(m)*
It spostamento a destra *(m)*

mudança à esquerda *(f)* Pt
De Linksverschiebung *(f)*
En left shift
Es desplazamiento a la izquierda *(m)*
Fr décalage à gauche *(m)*
It spostamento a sinistra *(m)*

mudança anular *(f)* Pt
De Ringschiebung *(f)*
En ring shift
Es desplazamiento en anillo *(m)*
Fr permutation circulaire *(f)*
It dislocamento ad anello *(m)*

mudança aritmética *(f)* Pt
De arithmetische Stellenverschiebung *(f)*
En arithmetic shift
Es desplazamiento aritmético *(m)*
Fr décalage arithmétique *(m)*
It spostamento aritmetico *(m)*

mudança de páginas *(f)* Pt
De Seitenwechsel *(m)*
En page turning
Es transferencia de página *(f)*
Fr changement de page *(m)*
It trasferimento di pagina *(m)*

mudança de passo *(f)* Pt
De Schrittwechsel *(m)*
En step change
Es cambio de paso *(m)*
Fr changement de phase *(m)*
It cambio di passo *(m)*

mudança lógica *(f)* Pt
De logische Verschiebung *(f)*
En logic(al) shift
Es desplazamiento lógico *(m)*
Fr décalage logique *(m)*
It spostamento logico *(m)*

mudar *vb* Pt
De versetzen
En shift
Es desplazar
Fr décaler
It spostare (dati)

multi-access *adj* En
De Mehrfachzugriff
Es acceso-múltiple
Fr accès-multiples
It accesso-multiplo
Pt multi-acesso

multi-access computing (MAC) En
De Mehrfachzugriffs-rechnen *(n)*
Es cálculo de acceso múltiple *(m)*
Fr traitement à accès multiple (TAM) *(m)*
It calcolo ad accesso multiplo *(m)*
Pt computação de multi-acesso *(f)*

multi-acesso *adj* Pt
De Mehrfachzugriff
En multi-access
Es acceso-múltiple
Fr accès-multiples
It accesso-multiplo

multicalculateur *(m) n* Fr
De Mehrprozessor-system *(n)*
En multiprocessor
Es procesador múltiple *(m)*
It elaboratore multiplo *(m)*
Pt multiprocessador *(m)*

multilayered software En
De mehrschichtige Software *(f)*
Es equipo instruccional multicapas *(m)*
Fr software multi-couche *(m)*
It software a strato multiplo *(m)*
Pt software de camadas múltiplas *(m)*

multipart forms *n pl* En
De mehrteilige Formulare *(pl)*
Es paquete de papel continuo *(m)*
Fr liasse *(f)*
It moduli a copie multiple *(m pl)*
Pt formas de partes múltiplas *(f pl)*

multiple-address instruction En
De Mehrfachadress-befehl *(m)*
Es instrucción de direcciones múltiples *(f)*
Fr instruction multi-adresse *(f)*
It istruzione ad indirizzo multiplo *(f)*
Pt instrução de endereço múltiplo *(f)*

multiple-length arithmetic En
De Arithmetik mit mehrfacher Wortlänge *(f)*
Es aritmética de longitud múltiple *(f)*
Fr calcul à précision multiple *(m)*
It aritmetica a lunghezza multipla *(f)*
Pt aritmética de comprimento múltiplo *(f)*

multiple-length number En
De Zahl mit mehrfacher Wortlänge *(f)*
Es número de longitud múltiple *(m)*
Fr nombre de plusieurs chiffres *(m)*
It numero a lunghezza multipla *(m)*
Pt número de comprimento múltiplo *(m)*

multiplet *(m) n* Fr
De Byte *(m)*
En byte
Es byte *(m)*
It byte *(m)*
Pt byte *(m)*

multiplex *n* En, Fr, It, Pt *(m)*
De Multiplex *(m)*
Es múltiplex *(m)*

Multiplex *(m) n* De
En multiplex
Es múltiplex *(m)*
Fr multiplex *(m)*
It multiplex *(m)*
Pt multiplex *(m)*

múltiplex *(m) n* Es
De Multiplex *(m)*
En multiplex
Fr multiplex *(m)*
It multiplex *(m)*
Pt multiplex *(m)*

multiplexação *(f) n* Pt
De Multiplexen *(n)*
En multiplexing
Es multiplexado *(m)*
Fr multiplexage *(m)*
It multiplexing *(m)*

multiplexado *(m) n* Es
De Multiplexen *(n)*
En multiplexing
Fr multiplexage *(m)*
It multiplexing *(m)*
Pt multiplexação *(f)*

multiplexage *(m) n* Fr
De Multiplexen *(n)*
En multiplexing
Es multiplexado *(m)*
It multiplexing *(m)*
Pt multiplexação *(f)*

Multiplexen *(n) n* De
En multiplexing
Es multiplexado *(m)*
Fr multiplexage *(m)*
It multiplexing *(m)*
Pt multiplexação *(f)*

multiplexing *n* En, It *(m)*
De Multiplexen *(n)*
Es multiplexado *(m)*
Fr multiplexage *(m)*
Pt multiplexação *(f)*

multiplicador *(m) n* Es, Pt
De Multiplizierer *(m)*
En multiplier
Fr multiplicateur *(m)*
It moltiplicatore *(m)*

multiplicateur *(m) n* Fr
De Multiplizierer *(m)*
En multiplier
Es multiplicador *(m)*
It moltiplicatore *(m)*
Pt multiplicador *(m)*

multiplier *n* En
De Multiplizierer *(m)*
Es multiplicador *(m)*
Fr multiplicateur *(m)*
It moltiplicatore *(m)*
Pt multiplicador *(m)*

Multiplizierer *(m) n* De
En multiplier
Es multiplicador *(m)*
Fr multiplicateur *(m)*
It moltiplicatore *(m)*
Pt multiplicador *(m)*

multipoint network En
De Mehrpunktnetz *(n)*
Es red de puntos múltiples *(f)*
Fr réseau multi-point *(m)*
It rete a punti multipli *(f)*
Pt rede de pontos múltiplos *(f)*

multiprocessador *(m) n* Pt
De Mehrprozessor-system *(n)*
En multiprocessor
Es procesador múltiple *(m)*
Fr multicalculateur *(m)*
It elaboratore multiplo *(m)*

multiprocessor *n* En
De Mehrprozessor-system *(n)*
Es procesador múltiple *(m)*
Fr multicalculateur *(m)*
It elaboratore multiplo *(m)*
Pt multiprocessador *(m)*

multiprogramação *(f) n* Pt
De Programm-verzahnung *(f)*
En multiprogramming
Es multiprogramación *(f)*
Fr multi-programmation *(f)*
It programmazione multiple *(f)*

multiprogramación *(f) n* Es
De Programm-verzahnung *(f)*
En multiprogramming
Fr multi-programmation *(f)*
It programmazione multipla *(f)*
Pt multiprogramação *(f)*

multi-programmation *(f) n* Fr
De Programm-verzahnung *(f)*
En multiprogramming
Es multiprogramación *(f)*
It programmazione multipla *(f)*
Pt multiprogramação *(f)*

multiprogramming *n* En
De Programm-verzahnung *(f)*
Es multiprogramación *(f)*
Fr multi-programmation *(f)*
It programmazione multipla *(f)*
Pt multiprogramação *(f)*

multiuser system En
De Mehrfachben-utzersystem *(n)*
Es sistema para usuarios múltiples *(m)*
Fr système à utilisateurs multiples *(m)*
It sistema per utenti multipli *(m)*
Pt sistema de utentes múltiplos *(m)*

N

Nabe *(f)* *n* De
En hub
Es boca *(f)*
Fr moyeu porte-bobine *(m)*
It mozzo *(m)*
Pt cubo *(m)*

Nachahmung *(f)* *n* De
En simulation
Es simulación *(f)*
Fr simulation *(f)*
It simulazione *(f)*
Pt simulação *(f)*

Nachgiebigkeit *(f)* *n* De
En resilience
Es resiliencia *(f)*
Fr résilience *(f)*
It resilienza *(f)*
Pt elasticidade *(f)*

nachredaktieren *vb* De
En post-edit
Es post-editar
Fr post-éditer
It posredigere
Pt pós-editar

Nachrichten-schlangestehen *(n)* *n* De
En message queuing
Es formación de colas de mensajes *(f)*
Fr mise en file d'attente de message *(f)*
It messa in coda dei messaggi *(f)*
Pt bicha de mensagens *(f)*

Nachrichtenvermittlung *(f)* *n* De
En message routing
Es encaminamiento de mensajes *(m)*
Fr acheminement des messages *(m)*
It incanalazione dei messaggi *(f)*
Pt encaminhamento de mensagens *(m)*

Nachrichtenverteilung *(f)* *n* De
En message switching
Es conmutación de mensajes *(f)*
Fr commutation de messages *(f)*
It commutazione di messaggi *(f)*
Pt comutação de mensagem *(f)*

Nachschlagetabelle *(f)* *n* De
En look-up table
Es tabla de consulta *(f)*
Fr table à consulter *(f)*
It tavola di consultazione *(f)*
Pt tabela de consulta *(f)*

NAND-gate *n* En
De NICHT-UND-Schaltung *(f)*
Es puerta NO-Y *(f)*
Fr porte NON-ET *(f)*
It porta NAND *(f)*
Pt porta NAND *(f)*

NAND-operation *n* En
De NAND-Verknüpfung; NICHT-UND-Verknüpfung *(f)*
Es operación NO-Y *(f)*
Fr exploitation NON-ET *(f)*
It operazione NAND; operazione NO-E *(f)*
Pt operação NAND; operação NÃO-E *(f)*

NAND-Verknüpfung *(f)* *n* De
En NAND-operation; NOT-AND operation
Es operación NO-Y *(f)*
Fr exploitation NON-ET *(f)*
It operazione NAND; operazione NO-E *(f)*
Pt operação NAND; operação NÃO-E *(f)*

nastrino di controllo del carrello *(m)* It
De Wagensteuerband *(n)*
En carriage-control tape
Es cinta de control del carro *(f)*
Fr bande pilote *(f)*
Pt fita com controle de carro *(f)*

nastro *(m)* *n* It
De Band *(n)*
En tape
Es cinta *(f)*
Fr bande *(f)*
Pt fita *(f)*

nastro ad alimentazione centrale *(m)* It
Am center-feed tape
De Band mit Zentralvorschub *(n)*
En centre-feed tape
Es cinta de alimentación central *(f)*
Fr bande à entraînement central *(f)*
Pt fita de alimentação central *(f)*

nastro ad inchiostro *(m)* It
De Farbband *(n)*
En ink ribbon
Es cinta entintada *(f)*
Fr ruban à encre *(m)*
Pt fita de tinta *(f)*

nastro con perforazioni totali *(m)* It
De geschuppter Streifen *(m)*
En chadded tape
Es cinta de perforación completa *(f)*
Fr bande à perforations complètes *(f)*
Pt fita recortada *(f)*

nastro dell'istruzioni principali *(m)* It
De Hauptbefehlsband *(n)*
En master-instruction tape (MIT)
Es cinta programa de explotación *(f)*
Fr bande de programme d'exploitation (BPE) *(f)*
Pt fita de instruções principais *(f)*

nastro di carta *(m)* It
De Papierstreifen *(m)*
En paper tape
Es cinta de papel *(f)*
Fr bande de papier *(f)*
Pt fita de papel *(f)*

nastro di lavoro *(m)* It
De Arbeitsband *(n)*
En work tape
Es cinta de maniobra *(f)*
Fr bande de travail *(f)*
Pt fita de trabalho *(f)*

nastro magnetico *(m)* It
De Magnetband *(n)*
En magnetic tape
Es cinta magnética *(f)*
Fr bande magnétique *(f)*
Pt fita magnética *(f)*

nastro nonno *(m)* It
De Erstgenerationsband *(n)*
En grandfather tape
Es cinta primera generación *(f)*
Fr bande première génération *(f)*
Pt fita avó *(f)*

nastro padre *(m)* It
De Urband *n*
En father tape
Es cinta creadora *(f)*
Fr bande créatrice *(f)*
Pt fita pai *(f)*

nastro perforato *(m)* It
De Lochstreifen *(m)*
En perforated tape; punched tape
Es cinta perforada *(f)*
Fr bande perforée *(f)*
Pt fita perfurada *(f)*

nastro principale *(m)* It
De Stammband *(n)*
En master tape
Es bobina emisora *(f)*
Fr bande maîtresse *(f)*
Pt fita principal *(f)*

nastro semiperforato *(m)* It
De Schuppenstreifen *(m)*
En chadless tape
Es cinta semiperforada *(f)*
Fr bande semi-perforée *(f)*
Pt fita sem recorte *(f)*

nastro vergine *(m)* It
De Neuband *(n)*
En virgin tape
Es cint a virgen *(f)*

Fr bande vierge *(f)*
Pt fita virgem *(f)*

Nebenspeicher *(m)* De
En slave store
Es memoria sin parte residente *(f)*
Fr mémoire asservie *(f)*
It memoria satellite *(f)*
Pt armazém escravo *(m)*

Nebensprechen *(n) n* De
En cross talk
Es diafonía *(f)*
Fr diaphonie *(f)*
It diafonia *(f)*
Pt diafonia *(f)*

Nebenzeiten *(pl) n* De
En incidentals time
Es tiempo de actividades anexas *(m)*
Fr temps d'activités annexes *(m)*
It tempo di attività eventuale *(m)*
Pt tempo de incidentes *(m)*

negação *(f) n* Pt
De Negation *(f)*
En negation
Es negación *(f)*
Fr négation *(f)*
It negazione *(f)*

negación *(f) n* Es
De Negation *(f)*
En negation
Fr négation *(f)*
It negazione *(f)*
Pt negação *(f)*

negador *(m) n* Es, Pt
De Negator *(m)*
En negator
Fr négateur *(m)*
It negatore *(m)*

négateur *(m) n* Fr
De Negator *(m)*
En negator
Es negador *(m)*
It negatore *(m)*
Pt negador *(m)*

negation *n* En
De Negation *(f)*
Es negación *(f)*
Fr négation *(f)*
It negazione *(f)*
Pt negação *(f)*

Negation *(f) n* De
En negation
Es negación *(f)*
Fr négation *(f)*
It negazione *(f)*
Pt negação *(f)*

négation *(f) n* Fr
De Negation *(f)*
En negation
Es negación *(f)*
It negazione *(f)*
Pt negação *(f)*

negative acknowledgment En
De negative Rückmeldung *(f)*
Es confirmación negativa *(f)*
Fr accusé de réception négatif *(m)*
It riconoscimento negativo *(m)*
Pt confirmação negativa *(f)*

negative Rückmeldung *(f)* De
En negative acknowledgment
Es confirmación negativa *(f)*
Fr accusé de réception négatif *(m)*
It riconoscimento negativo *(m)*
Pt confirmação negativa *(f)*

negator *n* En
De Negator *(m)*
Es negador *(m)*
Fr négateur *(m)*
It negatore *(m)*
Pt negador *(m)*

Negator *(m) n* De
En negator
Es negador *(m)*
Fr négateur *(m)*
It negatore *(m)*
Pt negador *(m)*

negatore *(m) n* It
De Negator *(m)*
En negator
Es negador *(m)*
Fr négateur *(m)*
Pt negador *(m)*

negazione *(f) n* It
De Negation *(f)*
En negation
Es negación *(f)*
Fr négation *(f)*
Pt negação *(f)*

neither-nor operation En
De NOR-Verknüpfung *(f)*
Es operación ni-no *(f)*
Fr opération NI-NI *(f)*
It operazione nè-nè *(f)*
Pt operação nem-nem *(f)*

nest *vb* En
De schachteln
Es jerarquizar
Fr emboîter
It nidificare
Pt aninhar

nettoyage de données *(f)* Fr
De Datenlöschung *(f)*
En data cleaning
Es limpieza de los datos *(f)*
It pulizia dei dati *(f)*
Pt apagamento de dados *(m)*

network *n* En
De Netz *(n)*
Es red *(f)*
Fr réseau *(m)*
It rete *(f)*
Pt rede *(f)*

network analysis En
De Netzanalyse *(f)*
Es análisis de redes *(m)*
Fr analyse de réseau *(f)*
It analisi delle reti *(f)*
Pt análise de rede *(f)*

network system En
De Netzsystem *(n)*
Es sistema de red *(m)*
Fr système de réseau *(m)*
It sistema di reti *(m)*
Pt sistema de rede *(m)*

Netz *(n) n* De
En network
Es red *(f)*
Fr réseau *(m)*
It rete *(f)*
Pt rede *(f)*

Netzanalyse *(f) n* De
En network analysis
Es análisis de redes *(m)*
Fr analyse de réseau *(f)*
It analisi delle reti *(f)*
Pt análise de rede *(f)*

Netzsystem *(n) n* De
En network system
Es sistema de red *(m)*
Fr système de réseau *(m)*
It sistema di reti *(m)*
Pt sistema de rede *(m)*

Neuband *(n) n* De
En virgin tape
Es cint a virgen *(f)*
Fr bande vierge *(f)*
It nastro vergine *(m)*
Pt fita virgem *(f)*

Neubildung *(f) n* De
En reconstitution
Es reconstitución *(f)*
Fr reconstitution *(f)*
It riconstituzione *(f)*
Pt reconstituição *(f)*

Neunerkomplement *(n) n* De
En nines complement
Es complemento a nueves *(m)*
Fr complément à neuf *(m)*
It complemento al nove *(m)*
Pt complemento de noves *(m)*

nicht lineare Programmierung *(f)* De
En nonlinear programming
Es programación no lineal *(f)*
Fr programmation non linéaire *(f)*
It programmazione non lineare *(f)*
Pt programação não linear *(f)*

nicht löschbarer Speicher *(m)* De
En nonerasable store
Es memoria imborrable *(f)*
Fr mémoire non effaçable *(f)*
It memoria non cancellabile *(f)*
Pt armazém não apagável *(m)*

nicht mechanischer Drucker *(m)* De
En nonimpact printer
Es impresora sin percusión *(f)*
Fr imprimante non à percussion *(f)*
It stampatrice non ad impatto *(f)*
Pt impressora sem impacto *(f)*

NICHT-UND-Schaltung *(f) n* De
En NAND-gate
Es puerta NO-Y *(f)*
Fr porte NON-ET *(f)*
It porta NAND *(f)*
Pt porta NAND *(f)*

NICHT-UND-Verknüpfung *(f)* De
En NAND-operation; NOT-AND operation
Es operación NO-Y *(f)*
Fr exploitation NON-ET *(f)*
It operazione NAND; operazione NO-E *(f)*
Pt operação NAND; operação NÃO-E *(f)*

nicht veränderlicher Speicher *(m)* De
En nonvolatile memory
Es memoria estable *(f)*
Fr mémoire rémanente *(f)*
It memoria non volatile *(f)*
Pt memória não volátil *(f)*

nidificare *vb* It
De schachteln
En nest
Es jerarquizar
Fr emboîter
Pt aninhar

niedriger Grad *(m)* De
En low order
Es orden inferior *(m)*
Fr ordre bas *(m)*
It ordine basso *(m)*
Pt ordem de baixo nível *(f)*

nines complement En
De Neunerkomplement *(n)*
Es complemento a nueves *(m)*
Fr complément à neuf *(m)*
It complemento al nove *(m)*
Pt complemento de noves *(m)*

niveau d'accès *(m)* Fr
De Zugriffsstufe *(f)*
En access level
Es nivel de acceso *(m)*
It livello di accesso *(m)*
Pt nível de acesso *(m)*

nivel de acceso *(m)* Es
De Zugriffsstufe *(f)*
En access level
Fr niveau d'accès *(m)*
It livello di accesso *(m)*
Pt nível de acesso *(m)*

nível de acesso *(m)* Pt
De Zugriffsstufe *(f)*
En access level
Es nivel de acceso *(m)*
Fr niveau d'accès *(m)*
It livello di accesso *(m)*

nó *(m) n* Pt
De Knotenpunkt *(m)*
En node
Es nodo *(m)*
Fr noeud *(m)*
It nodo *(m)*

no-address instruction En
De Kein-Adressenbefehl *(m)*
Es instrucción sin dirección *(f)*
Fr instruction sans adresse *(f)*
It istruzione a non indirizzo *(f)*
Pt instrução de não-endereço *(f)*

node *n* En
De Knotenpunkt *(m)*
Es nodo *(m)*
Fr noeud *(m)*
It nodo *(m)*
Pt nó *(m)*

nodo *(m) n* Es, It
De Knotenpunkt *(m)*
En node
Fr noeud *(m)*
Pt nó *(m)*

noeud *(m) n* Fr
De Knotenpunkt *(m)*
En node
Es nodo *(m)*
It nodo *(m)*
Pt nó *(m)*

noise *n* En
De Rauschen *(n)*
Es ruido *(m)*
Fr bruit *(m)*
It rumore *(m)*
Pt ruído *(m)*

noisy mode En
De Rauschbetriebsart *(f)*
Es modo ruidoso *(m)*
Fr mode bruyant *(m)*
It modalità rumorosa *(f)*
Pt modo ruidoso *(m)*

nombre de datos *(m)* Es
De Datenname *(m)*
En data name
Fr nom des données *(m)*
It nome dei dati *(m)*
Pt nome de dados *(m)*

nombre de plusieurs chiffres *(m)* Fr
De Zahl mit mehrfacher Wortlänge *(f)*
En multiple-length number
Es número de longitud múltiple *(m)*
It numero a lunghezza multipla *(m)*
Pt número de comprimento múltiplo *(m)*

nom des données *(m)* Fr
De Datenname *(m)*
En data name
Es nombre de datos *(m)*
It nome dei dati *(m)*
Pt nome de dados *(m)*

nome de dados *(m)* Pt
De Datenname *(m)*
En data name
Es nombre de datos *(m)*
Fr nom des données *(m)*
It nome dei dati *(m)*

nome dei dati *(m)* It
De Datenname *(m)*
En data name
Es nombre de datos *(m)*
Fr nom des données *(m)*
Pt nome de dados *(m)*

non collegato It
De indirekt
En offline
Es fuera de línea
Fr hors ligne
Pt fora da linha

nondestructive read En
De zerstörungsfreie Auslesung *(f)*
Es lectura no destructiva *(f)*
Fr lecture non destructive *(f)*
It lettura non distruttiva *(f)*
Pt leitura não destrutiva *(f)*

nondestructive read operation (NDRO) En
De zerstörungsfreie Lesefunktion *(f)*
Es operación de lectura no destructiva *(f)*
Fr opération de lecture non destructive (OLND) *(f)*
It operazione di lettura non distruttiva *(f)*
Pt operação de leitura não destrutiva *(f)*

nonerasable store En
De nicht löschbarer Speicher *(m)*
Es memoria imborrable *(f)*
Fr mémoire non effaçable *(f)*
It memoria non cancellabile *(f)*
Pt armazém não apagável *(m)*

nonimpact printer En
De nicht mechanischer Drucker *(m)*
Es impresora sin percusión *(f)*
Fr imprimante non à percussion *(f)*
It stampatrice non ad impatto *(f)*
Pt impressora sem impacto *(f)*

nonlinear programming En
De nicht lineare Programmierung *(f)*
Es programación no lineal *(f)*
Fr programmation non linéaire *(f)*
It programmazione non lineare *(f)*
Pt programação não linear *(f)*

non mouvementé Fr
De unbewegt
En inactive
Es inactivo
It inattivo
Pt inactivo

nonvolatile memory En
De nicht veränderlicher Speicher *(m)*
Es memoria estable *(f)*
Fr mémoire rémanente *(f)*
It memoria non volatile *(f)*
Pt memória não volátil *(f)*

NOR-gate *n* En
De NOR-Schaltung *(f)*
Es puerta NI *(f)*
Fr porte NON-OU *(f)*
It porta NOR *(f)*
Pt porta NOR *(f)*

normaliser *vb* Fr
De normalisieren
En normalize
Es normalizar
It normalizzare
Pt normalizar

normalisieren *vb* De
En normalize
Es normalizar
Fr normaliser
It normalizzare
Pt normalizar

normalización *(f) n* Es
De Normung *(f)*
En standardization
Fr standardisation *(f)*
It standardizzazione *(f)*
Pt standardização *(f)*

normalizar *vb* Es, Pt
De normalisieren
En normalize
Fr normaliser
It normalizzare

normalize *vb* En
De normalisieren
Es normalizar
Fr normaliser
It normalizzare
Pt normalizar

normalizzare *vb* It
De normalisieren
En normalize
Es normalizar
Fr normaliser
Pt normalizar

normen *vb* De
En standardize
Es estandardizar
Fr standardiser
It standardizzare
Pt standardizar

Normung *(f) n* De
En standardization
Es normalización *(f)*
Fr standardisation *(f)*
It standardizzazione *(f)*
Pt standardização *(f)*

NOR-operation *n* En
De NOR-Verknüpfung *(f)*
Es operación NI *(f)*
Fr exploitation NON-OU *(f)*
It operazione NOR *(f)*
Pt operação NOR *(f)*

NOR-Schaltung *(f) n* De
En NOR-gate
Es puerta NI *(f)*
Fr porte NON-OU *(f)*
It porta NOR *(f)*
Pt porta NOR *(f)*

NOR-Verknüpfung *(f) n* De
En neither-nor operation; NOR-operation
Es operación NI; operación ni-no *(f)*
Fr exploitation NON-OU; opération NI-NI *(f)*
It operazione nè-nè; operazione NOR *(f)*
Pt operação nem-nem; operação NOR *(f)*

notação binária *(f)* Pt
De Binärdarstellung *(f)*
En binary notation
Es notación binaria *(f)*
Fr notation binaire *(f)*
It notazione binaria *(f)*

notação de base mista *(f)* Pt
De Mischdarstellung *(f)*
En mixed-base notation
Es notación con base múltiple *(f)*
Fr notation à base multiple *(f)*
It notazione a base mista *(f)*

notação decimal *(f)* Pt
De Dezimaldarstellung *(f)*
En decimal notation
Es notación decimal *(f)*
Fr notation décimale *(f)*
It notazione decimale *(f)*

notação decimal-a-binária *(f)* Pt
De Dezimal-Binärdarstellung *(f)*
En decimal-to-binary notation
Es notación de decimal a binario *(f)*
Fr notation décimale-binaire *(f)*
It notazione da decimale a binario *(f)*

notação de prefixos *(f)* Pt
De Vorsatzdarstellung *(f)*
En prefix notation
Es notación por prefijos *(f)*
Fr notation préfixée *(f)*
It notazione del prefisso *(f)*

notação hexadecimal *(f)* Pt
De hexadezimale Darstellung *(f)*
En hexadecimal notation
Es notación hexadecimal *(f)*
Fr notation hexadécimale *(f)*
It notazione esadecimale *(f)*

notação octal *(f)* Pt
De Oktaldarstellung *(f)*
En octal notation
Es notación octal *(f)*
Fr notation octale *(f)*
It notazione ottale *(f)*

notação polaca *(f)* Pt
De polnische Darstellung *(f)*
En Polish notation
Es notación polaca *(f)*
Fr notation polonaise *(f)*
It notazione polacca *(f)*

notação polaca inversa *(f)*
De umgekehrta polnische Darstellung *(f)*
En reverse Polish notation
Es notación polaca inversa *(f)*
Fr notation polonaise inversée *(f)*
It notazione polacca inversa *(f)*

notação posicional *(f)* Pt
De Stellendarstellung *(f)*
En positional notation
Es notación posicional *(f)*
Fr représentation positionnelle *(f)*
It notazione di posizione *(f)*

notación binaria *(f)* Es
De Binärdarstellung *(f)*
En binary notation
Fr notation binaire *(f)*
It notazione binaria *(f)*
Pt notação binária *(f)*

notación con base múltiple *(f)* Es
De Mischdarstellung *(f)*
En mixed-base notation
Fr notation à base multiple *(f)*
It notazione a base mista *(f)*
Pt notação de base mista *(f)*

notación decimal *(f)* Es
De Dezimaldarstellung *(f)*
En decimal notation
Fr notation décimale *(f)*
It notazione decimale *(f)*
Pt notação decimal *(f)*

notación de decimal a binario *(f)* Es
De Dezimal-Binär-darstellung *(f)*
En decimal-to-binary notation
Fr notation décimale-binaire *(f)*
It notazione da decimale a binario *(f)*
Pt notação decimal-a-binária *(f)*

notación hexadecimal *(f)* Es
De hexadezimale Darstellung *(f)*
En hexadecimal notation
Fr notation hexadécimale *(f)*
It notazione esadecimale *(f)*
Pt notação hexadecimal *(f)*

notación octal *(f)* Es
De Oktaldarstellung *(f)*
En octal notation
Fr notation octale *(f)*
It notazione ottale *(f)*
Pt notação octal *(f)*

notación polaca *(f)* Es
De polnische Darstellung *(f)*
En Polish notation
Fr notation polonaise *(f)*
It notazione polacca *(f)*
Pt notação polaca *(f)*

notación polaca inversa *(f)* Es
De umgekehrte polnische Darstellung *(f)*
En reverse Polish notation
Fr notation polonaise inversée *(f)*
It notazione polacca inversa *(f)*
Pt notação polaca inversa *(f)*

notación por prefijos *(f)* Es
De Vorsatzdarstellung *(f)*
En prefix notation
Fr notation préfixée *(f)*
It notazione del prefisso *(f)*
Pt notação de prefixos *(f)*

notación posicional *(f)* Es
De Stellendarstellung *(f)*
En positional notation
Fr représentation positionnelle *(f)*
It notazione di posizione *(f)*
Pt notação posicional *(f)*

NOT-AND operation En
De NAND-Verknüpfung; NICHT-UND-Verknüpfung *(f)*
Es operación NO-Y *(f)*
Fr exploitation NON-ET *(f)*
It operazione NAND; operazione NO-E *(f)*
Pt operação NAND; operação NÃO-E *(f)*

notation à base multiple *(f)* Fr
De Mischdarstellung *(f)*
En mixed-base notation
Es notación con base múltiple *(f)*
It notazione a base mista *(f)*
Pt notação de base mista *(f)*

notation binaire *(f)* Fr
De Binärdarstellung *(f)*
En binary notation
Es notación binaria *(f)*
It notazione binaria *(f)*
Pt notação binária *(f)*

notation décimale *(f)* Fr
De Dezimaldarstellung *(f)*
En decimal notation
Es notación decimal *(f)*
It notazione decimale *(f)*
Pt notação decimal *(f)*

notation décimale-binaire *(f)* Fr
De Dezimal-Binär-darstellung *(f)*
En decimal-to-binary notation
Es notación de decimal a binario *(f)*
It notazione da decimale a binario *(f)*
Pt notação decimal-a-binária *(f)*

notation hexadécimale *(f)* Fr
De hexadezimale Darstellung *(f)*
En hexadecimal notation
Es notación hexadecimal *(f)*
It notazione esadecimale *(f)*
Pt notação hexadecimal *(f)*

notation octale *(f)* Fr
De Oktaldarstellung *(f)*
En octal notation
Es notación octal *(f)*
It notazione ottale *(f)*
Pt notação octal *(f)*

notation polonaise *(f)* Fr
De polnische Darstellung *(f)*
En Polish notation
Es notación polaca *(f)*
It notazione polacca *(f)*
Pt notação polaca *(f)*

notation polonaise inversée *(f)* Fr
De umgekehrte polnische Darstellung *(f)*
En reverse Polish notation
Es notación polaca inversa *(f)*
It notazione polacca inversa *(f)*
Pt notação polaca inversa *(f)*

notation préfixée *(f)* Fr
De Vorsatzdarstellung *(f)*
En prefix notation
Es notación por prefijos *(f)*
It notazione del prefisso *(f)*
Pt notação de prefixos *(f)*

notazione a base mista *(f)* It
De Mischdarstellung *(f)*
En mixed-base notation
Es notación con base múltiple *(f)*
Fr notation à base multiple *(f)*
Pt notação de base mista *(f)*

notazione binaria *(f)* It
De Binärdarstellung *(f)*
En binary notation
Es notación binaria *(f)*
Fr notation binaire *(f)*
Pt notação binária *(f)*

notazione da decimale a binario *(f)* It
De Dezimal-Binär-darstellung *(f)*
En decimal-to-binary notation
Es notación de decimal a binario *(f)*
Fr notation décimale-binaire *(f)*
Pt notação decimal-a-binária *(f)*

notazione decimale *(f)* It
De Dezimaldarstellung *(f)*
En decimal notation
Es notación decimal *(f)*
Fr notation décimale *(f)*
Pt notação decimal *(f)*

notazione del prefisso *(f)* It
De Vorsatzdarstellung *(f)*
En prefix notation
Es notación por prefijos *(f)*
Fr notation préfixée *(f)*

Pt notação de prefixos *(f)*

notazione di posizione *(f)* It
De Stellendarstellung *(f)*
En positional notation
Es notación posicional *(f)*
Fr représentation positionnelle *(f)*
Pt notação posicional *(f)*

notazione esadecimale *(f)* It
De hexadezimale Darstellung *(f)*
En hexadecimal notation
Es notación hexadecimal *(f)*
Fr notation hexadécimale *(f)*
Pt notação hexadecimal *(f)*

notazione ottale *(f)* It
De Oktaldarstellung *(f)*
En octal notation
Es notación octal *(f)*
Fr notation octale *(f)*
Pt notação octal *(f)*

notazione polacca *(f)* It
De polnische Darstellung *(f)*
En Polish notation
Es notación polaca *(f)*
Fr notation polonaise *(f)*
Pt notação polaca *(f)*

notazione polacca inversa *(f)* It
De umgekehrte polnische Darstellung *(f)*
En reverse Polish notation
Es notación polaca inversa *(f)*
Fr notation polonaise inversée *(f)*
Pt notação polaca inversa *(f)*

NOT-gate *n* En
De NOT-Schaltung *(f)*
Es puerta NO *(f)*
Fr porte NON *(f)*
It porta NO *(f)*
Pt porta NÃO *(f)*

NOT-operation En
De NOT-Verknüpfung *(f)*
Es operación NO *(f)*
Fr exploitation NON *(f)*
It operazione NO *(f)*
Pt operação NÃO *(f)*

NOT-Schaltung *(f) n* De
En NOT-gate
Es puerta NO *(f)*
Fr porte NON *(f)*
It porta NO *(f)*
Pt porta NÃO *(f)*

NOT-Verknüpfung *(f)* De
En NOT-operation
Es operación NO *(f)*
Fr exploitation NON *(f)*
It operazione NO *(f)*
Pt operação NÃO *(f)*

nova passagem *(f)* Pt
De wiederholter Maschinenlauf *(m)*
En rerun
Es repetición de pasada *(f)*
Fr reprise *(f)*
It ripresa *(f)*

novo arranque *(m)* Pt
De Wiederstart *(m)*
En restart
Es reanudación *(f)*
Fr relancement *(m)*
It ricominciamento *(m)*

núcleo *(m) n* Es, Pt
De Kern *(m)*
En core
Fr mémoire centrale *(f)*
It memoria centrale *(f)*

núcleo de ferria *(m)* Es
De Ferritkern *(m)*
En ferrite core
Fr tore de ferrite *(f)*
It memoria di ferrite *(f)*
Pt núcleo de ferrite *(m)*

núcleo de ferrite *(m)* Pt
De Ferritkern *(m)*
En ferrite core
Es núcleo de ferria *(m)*
Fr tore de ferrite *(f)*
It memoria di ferrite *(f)*

nucleo magnetico *(m)* It
De Magnetkern *(m)*
En magnetic core
Es núcleo magnético *(m)*
Fr tore magnétique *(m)*
Pt núcleo magnético *(m)*

núcleo magnético *(m)* Es, Pt
De Magnetkern *(m)*
En magnetic core
Fr tore magnétique *(m)*
It nucleo magnetico *(m)*

Nulladressen-anweisung *(f) n* De
En zero-address instruction
Es instrucción de dirección cero *(f)*
Fr instruction sans adresse *(f)*
It istruzione ad indirizzo zero *(f)*
Pt instrução de endereço zero *(f)*

Nullausgangssignal *(n) n* De
En zero-output signal
Es señal de salida cero *(f)*
Fr signal de sortie zéro *(m)*
It segnale di output zero *(m)*
Pt sinal de output zero *(m)*

Nullunterdrückung *(f) n* De
En zero suppression
Es supresión de ceros *(f)*
Fr élimination des zéros *(f)*
It soppressione di zero *(f)*
Pt supressão zero *(f)*

Nullzustand *(m) n* De
En zero state
Es estado cero *(m)*
Fr état zéro *(m)*
It stato zero *(m)*
Pt estado zero *(m)*

number system En
De Nummernsystem *(n)*
Es sistema de numeración *(m)*
Fr système de numérotation *(m)*
It sistema di numeri *(m)*
Pt sistema numérico *(m)*

numeric *adj* En
De numerisch
Es numérico
Fr numérique
It numerico
Pt numérico

numerical analysis En
De numerische Analyse *(f)*
Es análisis numérico *(m)*
Fr analyse numérique *(f)*
It analisi numerica *(f)*
Pt análise numérica *(f)*

numerical control En
De numerische Steuerung *(f)*
Es control numérico *(m)*
Fr commande numérique *(f)*
It controllo numerico *(m)*
Pt controle numérico *(m)*

numerico *adj* It
De numerisch
En numeric
Es numérico
Fr numérique
Pt numérico

numérico *adj* Es, Pt
De numerisch
En numeric
Fr numérique
It numerico

numérique *adj* Fr
De numerisch
En numeric
Es numérico
It numerico
Pt numérico

numerisch *adj* De
En numeric
Es numérico
Fr numérique
It numerico
Pt numérico

numerische Analyse *(f)* De
En numerical analysis

Es análisis numérico *(m)*
Fr analyse numérique *(f)*
It analisi numerica *(f)*
Pt análise numérica *(f)*

numerische Steuerung *(f)* De
En numerical control
Es control numérico *(m)*
Fr commande numérique *(f)*
It controllo numerico *(m)*
Pt controle numérico *(m)*

numériser *vb* Fr
De verziffern
En digitize
Es digitalizar
It digitalizzare
Pt digitalizar

numériseur *(m) n* Fr
De Verzifferer *(m)*
En digitizer
Es digitalizador *(m)*
It digitalizzatore *(m)*
Pt digitalizador *(m)*

numero a lunghezza multipla *(m)* It
De Zahl mit mehrfacher Wortlänge *(f)*
En multiple-length number
Es número de longitud múltiple *(m)*
Fr nombre de plusieurs chiffres *(m)*
Pt número de comprimento múltiplo *(m)*

numero autocontrollante *(m)* It
De Prüfnummer *(f)*
En self-checking number
Es número autoverificador *(m)*
Fr chiffre d'auto-vérification *(m)*
Pt número autoverificante *(m)*

número autoverificador *(m)* Es
De Prüfnummer *(f)*
En self-checking number
Fr chiffre d'auto-vérification *(m)*
It numero autocontrollante *(m)*
Pt número autoverificante *(m)*

número autoverificante *(m)* Pt
De Prüfnummer *(f)*
En self-checking number
Es número autoverificador *(m)*
Fr chiffre d'auto-vérification *(m)*
It numero autocontrollante *(m)*

numero bobina *(m)* It
De Spulennummer *(f)*
En reel number
Es número de carrete *(m)*
Fr numéro d'ordre de la bobine *(m)*
Pt número de bobina *(m)*

numéro d'appel *(m)* Fr
De Rufnummer *(f)*
En call number
Es número de llamada *(m)*
It numero di richiamo *(m)*
Pt número de chamada *(m)*

número de bobina *(m)* Pt
De Spulennummer *(f)*
En reel number
Es número de carrete *(m)*
Fr numéro d'ordre de la bobine *(m)*
It numero bobina *(m)*

número de carrete *(m)* Es
De Spulennummer *(f)*
En reel number
Fr numéro d'ordre de la bobine *(m)*
It numero bobina *(m)*
Pt número de bobina *(m)*

número de chamada *(m)* Pt
De Rufnummer *(f)*
En call number
Es número de llamada *(m)*
Fr numéro d'appel *(m)*
It numero di richiamo *(m)*

número de comprimento múltiplo *(m)* Pt
De Zahl mit mehrfacher Wortlänge *(f)*
En multiple-length number
Es número de longitud múltiple *(m)*
Fr nombre de plusieurs chiffres *(m)*
It numero a lunghezza multipla *(m)*

número de llamada *(m)* Es
De Rufnummer *(f)*
En call number
Fr numéro d'appel *(m)*
It numero di richiamo *(m)*
Pt número de chamada *(m)*

número de longitud múltiple *(m)* Es
De Zahl mit mehrfacher Wortlänge *(f)*
En multiple-length number
Fr nombre de plusieurs chiffres *(m)*
It numero a lunghezza multipla *(m)*
Pt número de comprimento múltiplo *(m)*

numero di baud *(m)* It
De Baudgeschwindigkeit *(f)*
En baud rate
Es velocidad en baudios *(f)*
Fr débit en bauds *(m)*
Pt taxa de baud *(f)*

número digital *(m)* Pt
De Ziffer *(f)*
En digit
Es dígito *(m)*
Fr chiffre *(m)*
It digit *(m)*

número digital de sinal *(m)* Pt
De Vorzeichenziffer *(f)*
En sign digit
Es dígito de signo *(m)*
Fr caractère de signe *(m)*
It digit del segno *(m)*

número digital de verificação *(m)* Pt
De Prüfziffer *(f)*
En check digit
Es dígito de verificación *(m)*
Fr caractère de contrôle *(m)*
It digit di controllo *(m)*

número digital de zona *(m)* Pt
De Zonenziffer *(f)*
En zone digit
Es dígito de zona *(m)*
Fr chiffre de zone *(m)*
It digit di zonatura *(m)*

numero di guasti *(m)* It
De Ausfallhäufigkeit *(f)*
En failure rate
Es frecuencia de fallos *(f)*
Fr taux de défaillance *(m)*
Pt índice de falhas *(m)*

numero di richiamo *(m)* It
De Rufnummer *(f)*
En call number
Es número de llamada *(m)*
Fr numéro d'appel *(m)*
Pt número de chamada *(m)*

numéro d'ordre de la bobine *(m)* Fr
De Spulennummer *(f)*
En reel number
Es número de carrete *(m)*
It numero bobina *(m)*
Pt número de bobina *(m)*

números digitais binários equivalentes *(m pl)* Pt
De gleichwertige Binärziffern *(pl)*

En equivalent binary digits
Es dígitos binarios equivalentes *(m pl)*
Fr chiffres binaires équivalents *(m pl)*
It digiti binari equivalenti *(m pl)*

números digitais significativos *(m pl)* Pt
De wesentliche Ziffern *(pl)*
En significant digits
Es dígitos significativos *(m pl)*
Fr chiffres significatifs *(m pl)*
It digiti significativi *(m pl)*

Nummernsystem *(n) n* De
En number system
Es sistema de numeración *(m)*
Fr système de numérotation *(m)*
It sistema di numeri *(m)*
Pt sistema numérico *(m)*

O

object code En
De Objektcode *(m)*
Es código objeto *(m)*
Fr code objet *(m)*
It codice oggetto *(m)*
Pt código de objecto *(m)*

object language En
De Objektsprache *(f)*
Es lenguaje objeto *(m)*
Fr langage objet *(m)*
It linguaggio oggetto *(m)*
Pt linguagem de objecto *(f)*

object program En
De Zielprogramm *(n)*
Es programa objeto *(m)*
Fr programme objet *(m)*
It programma oggetto *(m)*
Pt programa de objecto *(m)*

Objektcode *(m) n* De
En object code
Es código objeto *(m)*
Fr code objet *(m)*
It codice oggetto *(m)*
Pt código de objecto *(m)*

Objektsprache *(f) n* De
En object language
Es lenguaje objeto *(m)*
Fr langage objet *(m)*
It linguaggio oggetto *(m)*
Pt linguagem de objecto *(f)*

occhio del carattere *(m)* It
De Schrifttyp *(m)*
En typeface
Es ojo del tipo *(m)*
Fr oeil d'un caractère *(m)*
Pt olho de tipo *(m)*

octal *adj* En, Es, Fr, Pt
De oktal
It ottal

octal notation En
De Oktaldarstellung *(f)*
Es notación octal *(f)*
Fr notation octale *(f)*
It notazione ottale *(f)*
Pt notação octal *(f)*

ocultação *(f) n* Pt
De Maskierung *(f)*
En masking
Es enmascaramiento *(m)*
Fr masquage *(m)*
It mascheratura *(f)*

ocultar *vb* Pt
De maskieren
En mask
Es enmascarar
Fr masquer
It mascherare

odd-even check En
De gerade-ungerade Paritätsprüfung *(f)*
Es control de paridad par-impar *(m)*
Fr contrôle de parité pair-impair *(m)*
It controllo pari-dispari *(m)*
Pt verificação par-impar *(f)*

odd parity En
De ungerade Parität *(f)*
Es imparidad *(f)*
Fr imparité *(f)*
It parità dispari *(f)*
Pt paridade impar *(f)*

ODER-Schaltung *(f) n* De
En OR-gate
Es puerta O *(f)*
Fr porte OU *(f)*
It porta o *(f)*
Pt porta OR *(f)*

ODER-Verknüpfung *(f) n* De
En OR-operation
Es operación O *(f)*
Fr exploitation OU *(f)*
It operazione O *(f)*
Pt operação OR *(f)*

oeil d'un caractère *(m)* Fr
De Schrifttyp *(m)*
En typeface
Es ojo del tipo *(m)*
It occhio del carattere *(m)*
Pt olho de tipo *(m)*

offene Schleife *(f)* De
En open loop
Es circuito abierto *(m)*
Fr boucle ouverte *(f)*
It ciclo aperto *(m)*
Pt circuito aberto *(m)*

offenes Programm *(n)* De
En open routine
Es rutina de apertura *(f)*
Fr programme ouvert *(m)*
It routine aperta *(f)*
Pt rotina aberta *(f)*

offline *adj* En
De indirekt
Es fuera de línea
Fr hors ligne
It non collegato
Pt fora da linha

ojo del tipo *(m)* Es
De Schrifttyp *(m)*
En typeface
Fr oeil d'un caractère *(m)*
It occhio del carattere *(m)*
Pt olho de tipo *(m)*

Ökonometrik *(f) n* De
En econometrics
Es econométrica *(f)*
Fr économétrie *(f)*
It econometria *(f)*
Pt econométrica *(f)*

oktal *adj* De
En octal
Es octal
Fr octal
It ottal
Pt octal

Oktaldarstellung *(f) n* De
En octal notation
Es notación octal *(f)*
Fr notation octale *(f)*
It notazione ottale *(f)*
Pt notação octal *(f)*

olho de tipo *(m)* Pt
De Schrifttyp *(m)*
En typeface
Es ojo del tipo *(m)*
Fr oeil d'un caractère *(m)*
It occhio del carattere *(m)*

omeostasi *(f) n* It
De Homöostase *(f)*
En homeostasis
Es homeostasis *(f)*
Fr homéostasie *(f)*
Pt homeostase *(f)*

omitir *vb* Es, Pt
De überspringen
En skip
Fr sauter
It saltare

one-level store En
De Einstufenspeicher *(m)*
Es memoria de un solo nivel *(f)*
Fr mémoire à un niveau *(f)*
It memoria ad un livello *(f)*
Pt armazém de um só nível *(m)*

one-plus-one address En
De Eins-plus-Eins-Adresse *(f)*
Es dirección uno más uno *(f)*
Fr à une plus une adresse *(f)*
It indirizzo uno-più-uno *(m)*
Pt endereço um mais um *(m)*

ones complement En
De Einerkomplement *(n)*
Es complemento a uno *(m)*
Fr complément à un *(m)*
It complemento all'uno *(m)*
Pt complemento de unidades *(m)*

one state En
De Einzustand *(m)*
Es estado uno *(m)*
Fr état un *(m)*
It stato uno *(m)*
Pt estado de unidade *(m)*

on-line *adj* En
De direkt
Es en línea
Fr direct
It in linea
Pt sobre a linha

on-line data reduction En
De direkte Datenverdichtung *(f)*
Es reducción de datos en línea *(f)*
Fr réduction des données en exploitation continue *(f)*
It riduzione in linea dei dati *(f)*
Pt redução de dados sobre a linha *(f)*

open loop En
De offene Schleife *(f)*
Es circuito abierto *(m)*
Fr boucle ouverte *(f)*
It ciclo aperto *(m)*
Pt circuito aberto *(m)*

open routine En
De offenes Programm *(n)*
Es rutina de apertura *(f)*
Fr programme ouvert *(m)*
It routine aperta *(f)*
Pt rotina aberta *(f)*

operação *(f) n* Pt
De Operation *(f)*
En operation
Es operación *(f)*
Fr exploitation; opération *(f)*
It operazione *(f)*

operação AND *(f)* Pt
De UND-Verknüpfung *(f)*
En AND-operation
Es operación Y *(f)*
Fr opération ET *(f)*
It operazione E *(f)*

operação aritmética *(f)* Pt
De arithmetische Funktion *(f)*
En arithmetic operation
Es operación aritmética *(f)*
Fr opération arithmétique *(f)*
It operazione aritmetica *(f)*

operação binário *(f)* Pt
De Binärfunktion *(f)*
En binary operation
Es operación binaria *(f)*
Fr opération binaire *(f)*
It operazione binaria *(f)*

operação complementar *(f)* Pt
De komplementäre Funktion *(f)*
En complementary operation
Es operación complementaria *(f)*
Fr opération complémentaire *(f)*
It operazione complementare *(f)*

operação condicional *(f)* Pt
De bedingter Betrieb *(m)*
En conditional operation
Es operación condicional *(f)*
Fr opération conditionnelle *(f)*
It operazione condizionale *(f)*

operação de chaves em mão *(f)* Pt
De schlüsselfertiger Betrieb *(m)*
En turnkey operation
Es operación llave en mano *(f)*
Fr opération clé en main *(f)*
It operazione chiavi in mano *(f)*

operação de equivalência *(f)* Pt
De Gleichheitsbetrieb *(m)*
En equivalence operation
Es operación de equivalencia *(f)*
Fr opération d'équivalence *(f)*
It operazione di equivalenza *(f)*

operação de leitura não destrutiva *(f)* Pt
De zerstörungsfreie Lesefunktion *(f)*
En nondestructive read operation (NDRO)
Es operación de lectura no destructiva *(f)*
Fr opération de lecture non destructive (OLND) *(f)*
It operazione di lettura non distruttiva *(f)*

operação de ou-ou *(f)* Pt
De Entweder-oder-Funktion *(f)*
En either-or operation
Es operación ambos o uno *(f)*
Fr opération soit-ou *(f)*
It operazione sia-o *(f)*

operação de uma só fase *(f)* Pt
De Einzelschrittfunktion *(f)*
En single-step operation
Es operación de paso único *(f)*
Fr opération en pas à pas *(f)*
It operazione a fase singola *(f)*

operação diádica *(f)* Pt
De zweistellige Funktion *(f)*
En dyadic operation
Es operación diádica *(f)*
Fr opération dyadique *(f)*
It operazione diadica *(f)*

operação dupla *(f)* Pt
De Doppelbetrieb *(m)*
En dual operation
Es operación dual *(f)*
Fr double opération *(f)*
It operazione duplice *(f)*

operação exclusiva-ou *(f)* Pt
De Antivalenzfunktion *(f)*
En exclusive-or operation
Es operación O exclusivo *(f)*
Fr opération OU exclusif *(f)*
It operazione o-esclusivo *(f)*

operação inclusivé-ou *(f)* Pt
De Inklusiv-ODER-Verknüpfung *(f)*
En disjunction; inclusive-or operation
Es operación O inclusivo *(f)*
Fr opération OU inclusif *(f)*
It operazione inclusivo-o *(f)*

operação lógica *(f)* Pt
De logische Funktion *(f)*
En logic(al) operation
Es operación lógica *(f)*
Fr opération logique *(f)*
It operazione logica *(f)*

operação NAND *(f)* Pt
De NAND-Verknüpfung; NICHT-UND-Verknüpfung *(f)*
En NAND-operation; NOT-AND operation
Es operación NO-Y *(f)*
Fr exploitation NON-ET *(f)*
It operazione NAND; operazione NO-E *(f)*

operação NÃO *(f)* Pt
De NOT-Verknüpfung *(f)*
En NOT-operation
Es operación NO *(f)*
Fr exploitation NON *(f)*
It operazione NO *(f)*

operação NÃO-E *(f)* Pt
De NAND-Verknüpfung; NICHT-UND-Verknüpfung *(f)*
En NAND-operation; NOT-AND operation
Es operación NO-Y *(f)*
Fr exploitation NON-ET *(f)*
It operazione NAND; operazione NO-E *(f)*

operação nem-nem *(f)* Pt
De NOR-Verknüpfung *(f)*
En neither-nor operation
Es operación ni-no *(f)*
Fr opération NI-NI *(f)*
It operazione nè-nè *(f)*

operação NOR *(f)* Pt
De NOR-Verknüpfung *(f)*
En NOR-operation
Es operación NI *(f)*
Fr exploitation NON-OU *(f)*
It operazione NOR *(f)*

operação OR *(f)* Pt
De ODER-Verknüpfung *(f)*
En OR-operation
Es operación O *(f)*
Fr exploitation OU *(f)*
It operazione O *(f)*

operação por partes *(f)* Pt
De Teilbetrieb *(m)*
En part operation
Es operación parcial *(f)*
Fr opération partielle *(f)*
It operazione parziale *(f)*

operação se-então *(f)* Pt
De Implikationsfunktion *(f)*
En if-then operation
Es operación condicional *(f)*
Fr opération conditionnelle *(f)*
It operazione se-allora *(f)*

operação unária *(f)* Pt
De monadische Operation *(f)*
En unary operation
Es operación unaria *(f)*
Fr opération unaire *(f)*
It operazione unaria *(f)*

operación *(f) n* Es
De Operation *(f)*
En operation
Fr exploitation; opération *(f)*
It operazione *(f)*
Pt operação *(f)*

operación ambos o uno *(f)* Es
De Entweder-oder-Funktion *(f)*
En either-or operation
Fr opération soit-ou *(f)*
It operazione sia-o *(f)*
Pt operação de ou-ou *(f)*

operación aritmética *(f)* Es
De arithmetische Funktion *(f)*
En arithmetic operation
Fr opération arithmétique *(f)*
It operazione aritmetica *(f)*
Pt operação aritmética *(f)*

operación binaria *(f)* Es
De Binärfunktion *(f)*
En binary operation
Fr opération binaire *(f)*
It operazione binaria *(f)*
Pt operação binário *(f)*

operación complementaria *(f)* Es
De komplementäre Funktion *(f)*
En complementary operation
Fr opération complémentaire *(f)*
It operazione complementare *(f)*
Pt operação complementar *(f)*

operación condicional *(f)* Es
De bedingter Betrieb; Implikationsfunktion *(m f)*
En conditional operation; if-then operation
Fr opération conditionnelle *(f)*
It operazione condizionale; operazione se-allora *(f)*
Pt operação condicional; operação se-então *(f)*

operación de equivalencia *(f)* Es
De Gleichheitsbetrieb *(m)*
En equivalence operation
Fr opération d'équivalence *(f)*
It operazione di equivalenza *(f)*
Pt operação de equivalência *(f)*

operación de lectura no destructiva *(f)* Es
De zerstörungsfreie Lesefunktion *(f)*
En nondestructive read operation (NDRO)
Fr opération de lecture non destructive (OLND) *(f)*
It operazione di lettura non distruttiva *(f)*
Pt operação de leitura não destrutiva *(f)*

operación de paso único *(f)* Es
De Einzelschrittfunktion *(f)*
En single-step operation
Fr opération en pas à pas *(f)*
It operazione a fase singola *(f)*
Pt operação de uma só fase *(f)*

operación diádica *(f)* Es
De zweistellige Funktion *(f)*
En dyadic operation
Fr opération dyadique *(f)*
It operazione diadica *(f)*
Pt operação diádica *(f)*

operación dual *(f)* Es
De Doppelbetrieb *(m)*
En dual operation
Fr double opération *(f)*
It operazione duplice *(f)*
Pt operação dupla *(f)*

operación llave en mano *(f)* Es
De schlüsselfertiger Betrieb *(m)*
En turnkey operation
Fr opération clé en main *(f)*
It operazione chiavi in mano *(f)*
Pt operação de chaves em mão *(f)*

operación lógica *(f)* Es
De logische Funktion *(f)*
En logic(al) operation
Fr opération logique *(f)*
It operazione logica *(f)*
Pt operação lógica *(f)*

operación NI *(f)* Es
De NOR-Verknüpfung *(f)*
En NOR-operation
Fr exploitation NON-OU *(f)*
It operazione NOR *(f)*
Pt operação NOR *(f)*

operación ni-no *(f)* Es
De NOR-Verknüpfung *(f)*
En neither-nor operation
Fr opération NI-NI *(f)*
It operazione nè-nè *(f)*
Pt operação nem-nem *(f)*

operación NO *(f)* Es
De NOT-Verknüpfung *(f)*
En NOT-operation
Fr exploitation NON *(f)*
It operazione NO *(f)*
Pt operação NÃO *(f)*

operación NO-Y *(f)* Es
De NAND-Verknüpfung; NICHT-UND-Verknüpfung *(f)*
En NAND-operation; NOT-AND operation
Fr exploitation NON-ET *(f)*
It operazione NAND; operazione NO-E *(f)*
Pt operação NAND; operação NÃO-E *(f)*

operación O *(f)* Es
De ODER-Verknüpfung *(f)*
En OR-operation
Fr exploitation OU *(f)*
It operazione O *(f)*
Pt operação OR *(f)*

operación O exclusivo *(f)* Es
De Antivalenzfunktion *(f)*
En exclusive-or operation
Fr opération OU exclusif *(f)*
It operazione o-esclusivo *(f)*
Pt operação exclusiva-ou *(f)*

operación O inclusivo *(f)* Es
De Inklusiv-ODER-Verknüpfung *(f)*
En disjunction; inclusive-or operation
Fr opération OU inclusif *(f)*
It operazione inclusivo-o *(f)*
Pt operação inclusivé-ou *(f)*

operación parcial *(f)* Es
De Teilbetrieb *(m)*
En part operation
Fr opération partielle *(f)*
It operazione parziale *(f)*
Pt operação por partes *(f)*

operación unaria *(f)* Es
De monadische Operation *(f)*
En unary operation
Fr opération unaire *(f)*
It operazione unaria *(f)*
Pt operação unária *(f)*

operación Y *(f)* Es
De UND-Verknüpfung *(f)*
En AND-operation
Fr opération ET *(f)*
It operazione E *(f)*
Pt operação AND *(f)*

operador *(m) n* Es, Pt
De Bediener *(m)*
En operator
Fr opérateur *(m)*
It operatore *(m)*

operador de relación *(m)* Es
De Vergleichsoperator *(m)*
En relational operator
Fr opérateur de relation *(m)*
It operatore relazionale *(m)*
Pt operador relacional *(m)*

operador lógico *(m)* Es, Pt
De Boolescher Operator *(m)*
En logic(al) operator
Fr opérateur logique *(m)*
It operatore logico *(m)*

operador relacional *(m)* Pt
De Vergleichsoperator *(m)*
En relational operator
Es operador de relación *(m)*
Fr opérateur de relation *(m)*
It operatore relazionale *(m)*

opérateur *(m) n* Fr
De Bediener *(m)*
En operator
Es operador *(m)*
It operatore *(m)*
Pt operador *(m)*

opérateur de relation *(m)* Fr
De Vergleichsoperator *(m)*
En relational operator
Es operador de relación *(m)*
It operatore relazionale *(m)*
Pt operador relacional *(m)*

opérateur logique *(m)* Fr
De Boolescher Operator *(m)*
En logic(al) operator
Es operador lógico *(m)*
It operatore logico *(m)*
Pt operador lógico *(m)*

operating ratio En
De Arbeitsverhältnis *(n)*
Es relación de utilización *(f)*
Fr rapport de disponibilité *(m)*
It rapporto di operazione *(m)*
Pt ratio de operação *(f)*

operating station En
De Arbeitsstation *(f)*
Es estación operativa *(f)*
Fr poste d'exploitation *(m)*
It posto funzionante *(m)*
Pt estação de operação *(f)*

operating system (OS) En
De Betriebssystem *(n)*
Es sistema operativo *(m)*
Fr système d'exploitation *(m)*
It sistema operativo *(m)*
Pt sistema de operação *(m)*

operation *n* En
De Operation *(f)*
Es operación *(f)*
Fr exploitation; opération *(f)*
It operazione *(f)*
Pt operação *(f)*

Operation *(f) n* De
En operation
Es operación *(f)*
Fr exploitation; opération *(f)*
It operazione *(f)*
Pt operação *(f)*

operational research (OR) En
De Unternehmungsforschung *(f)*
Es investigación operativa *(f)*
Fr recherche opérationnelle *(f)*
It ricerca operativa *(f)*
Pt investigação operacional *(f)*

opération arithmétique *(f)* Fr
De arithmetische Funktion *(f)*
En arithmetic operation
Es operación aritmética *(f)*
It operazione aritmetica *(f)*
Pt operação aritmética *(f)*

opération binaire *(f)* Fr
De Binärfunktion *(f)*
En binary operation
Es operación binaria *(f)*
It operazione binaria *(f)*
Pt operação binário *(f)*

opération clé en main *(f)* Fr
De schlüsselfertiger Betrieb *(m)*
En turnkey operation
Es operación llave en mano *(f)*
It operazione chiavi in mano *(f)*
Pt operação de chaves em mão *(f)*

opération complémentaire *(f)* Fr
De komplementäre Funktion *(f)*
En complementary operation
Es operación complementaria *(f)*
It operazione complementare *(f)*
Pt operação complementar *(f)*

opération conditionnelle *(f)* Fr
De bedingter Betrieb; Implikationsfunktion *(m f)*
En conditional operation; if-then operation
Es operación condicional *(f)*
It operazione condizionale; operazione se-allora *(f)*
Pt operação condicional; operação se-então *(f)*

opération de lecture non destructive (OLND) *(f)* Fr
De zerstörungsfreie Lesefunktion *(f)*

En nondestructive read operation (NDRO)
Es operación de lectura no destructiva *(f)*
It operazione di lettura non distruttiva *(f)*
Pt operação de leitura não destrutiva *(f)*

opération d'équivalence *(f)* Fr
De Gleichheitsbetrieb *(m)*
En equivalence operation
Es operación de equivalencia *(f)*
It operazione di equivalenza *(f)*
Pt operação de equivalência *(f)*

opération dyadique *(f)* Fr
De zweistellige Funktion *(f)*
En dyadic operation
Es operación diádica *(f)*
It operazione diadica *(f)*
Pt operação diádica *(f)*

opération en pas à pas *(f)* Fr
De Einzelschrittfunktion *(f)*
En single-step operation
Es operación de paso único *(f)*
It operazione a fase singola *(f)*
Pt operação de uma só fase *(f)*

opération ET *(f)* Fr
De UND-Verknüpfung *(f)*
En AND-operation
Es operación Y *(f)*
It operazione E *(f)*
Pt operação AND *(f)*

opération logique *(f)* Fr
De logische Funktion *(f)*
En logic(al) operation
Es operación lógica *(f)*
It operazione logica *(f)*
Pt operação lógica *(f)*

opération NI-NI *(f)* Fr
De NOR-Verknüpfung *(f)*
En neither-nor operation
Es operación ni-no *(f)*
It operazione nè-nè *(f)*
Pt operação nem-nem *(f)*

opération OU exclusif *(f)* Fr
De Antivalenzfunktion *(f)*
En exclusive-or operation
Es operación O exclusivo *(f)*
It operazione o-esclusivo *(f)*
Pt operação exclusiva-ou *(f)*

opération OU inclusif *(f)* Fr
De ODER-Verknüpfung *(f)*
En disjunction; inclusive-or operation
Es operación O inclusivo *(f)*
It operazione inclusivo-o *(f)*
Pt operação inclusivé-ou *(f)*

opération partielle *(f)* Fr
De Teilbetrieb *(m)*
En part operation
Es operación parcial *(f)*
It operazione parziale *(f)*
Pt operação por partes *(f)*

opération soit-ou *(f)* Fr
De Entweder-oder-Funktion *(f)*
En either-or operation
Es operación ambos o uno *(f)*
It operazione sia-o *(f)*
Pt operação de ou-ou *(f)*

opération unaire *(f)* Fr
De monadische Operation *(f)*
En unary operation
Es operación unaria *(f)*
It operazione unaria *(f)*
Pt operação unária *(f)*

operator *n* En
De Bediener *(m)*
Es operador *(m)*
Fr opérateur *(m)*
It operatore *(m)*
Pt operador *(m)*

operatore *(m) n* It
De Bediener *(m)*
En operator
Es operador *(m)*
Fr opérateur *(m)*
Pt operador *(m)*

operatore logico *(m)* It
De Boolescher Operator *(m)*
En logic(al) operator
Es operador lógico *(m)*
Fr opérateur logique *(m)*
Pt operador lógico *(m)*

operatore relazionale *(m)* It
De Vergleichsoperator *(m)*
En relational operator
Es operador de relación *(m)*
Fr opérateur de relation *(m)*
Pt operador relacional *(m)*

operazione *(f) n* It
De Operation *(f)*
En operation
Es operación *(f)*
Fr exploitation; opération *(f)*
Pt operação *(f)*

operazione a fase singola *(f)* It
De Einzelschrittfunktion *(f)*
En single-step operation
Es operación de paso único *(f)*
Fr opération en pas à pas *(f)*
Pt operação de uma só fase *(f)*

operazione aritmetica *(f)* It
De arithmetische Funktion *(f)*
En arithmetic operation
Es operación aritmética *(f)*
Fr opération arithmétique *(f)*
Pt operação aritmética *(f)*

operazione binaria *(f)* It
De Binärfunktion *(f)*
En binary operation
Es operación binaria *(f)*
Fr opération binaire *(f)*
Pt operação binário *(f)*

operazione chiavi in mano *(f)* It
De schlüsselfertiger Betrieb *(m)*
En turnkey operation
Es operación llave en mano *(f)*
Fr opération clé en main *(f)*
Pt operação de chaves em mão *(f)*

operazione complementare *(f)* It
De komplementäre Funktion *(f)*
En complementary operation
Es operación complementaria *(f)*
Fr opération complémentaire *(f)*
Pt operação complementar *(f)*

operazione condizionale *(f)* It
De bedingter Betrieb *(m)*
En conditional operation
Es operación condicional *(f)*
Fr opération conditionnelle *(f)*
Pt operação condicional *(f)*

operazione diadica *(f)* It
De zweistellige Funktion *(f)*
En dyadic operation
Es operación diádica *(f)*
Fr opération dyadique *(f)*
Pt operação diádica *(f)*

operazione di equivalenza *(f)* It
De Gleichheitsbetrieb *(m)*
En equivalence operation
Es operación de equivalencia *(f)*
Fr opération d'équivalence *(f)*
Pt operação de equivalência *(f)*

operazione di lettura non distruttiva *(f)* It
De zerstörungsfreie Lesefunktion *(f)*
En nondestructive read operation (NDRO)
Es operación de lectura no destructiva *(f)*
Fr opération de lecture non destructive (OLND) *(f)*
Pt operação de leitura não destrutiva *(f)*

operazione duplice *(f)* It
De Doppelbetrieb *(m)*
En dual operation
Es operación dual *(f)*
Fr double opération *(f)*
Pt operação dupla *(f)*

operazione E *(f)* It
De UND-Verknüpfung *(f)*
En AND-operation
Es operación Y *(f)*
Fr opération ET *(f)*
Pt operação AND *(f)*

operazione inclusivo-o *(f)* It
De Inklusiv-ODER-Verknüpfung *(f)*
En disjunction; inclusive-or operation
Es operación O inclusivo *(f)*
Fr opération OU inclusif *(f)*
Pt operação inclusivé-ou *(f)*

operazione logica *(f)* It
De logische Funktion *(f)*
En logic(al) operation
Es operación lógica *(f)*
Fr opération logique *(f)*
Pt operação lógica *(f)*

operazione NAND *(f)* It
De NAND-Verknüpfung; NICHT-UND-Verknüpfung *(f)*
En NAND-operation; NOT-AND operation
Es operación NO-Y *(f)*
Fr exploitation NON-ET *(f)*
Pt operação NAND; operação NÃO-E *(f)*

operazione nè-nè *(f)* It
De NOR-Verknüpfung *(f)*
En neither-nor operation
Es operación ni-no *(f)*
Fr opération NI-NI *(f)*
Pt operação nem-nem *(f)*

operazione NO *(f)* It
De NOT-Verknüpfung *(f)*
En NOT-operation
Es operación NO *(f)*
Fr exploitation NON *(f)*
Pt operação NÃO *(f)*

operazione NO-E *(f)* It
De NAND-Verknüpfung; NICHT-UND-Verknüpfung *(f)*
En NAND-operation; NOT-AND operation
Es operación NO-Y *(f)*
Fr exploitation NON-ET *(f)*
Pt operação NAND; operação NÃO-E *(f)*

operazione NOR *(f)* It
De NOR-Verknüpfung *(f)*
En NOR-operation
Es operación NI *(f)*
Fr exploitation NON-OU *(f)*
Pt operação NOR *(f)*

operazione O *(f)* It
De ODER-Verknüpfung *(f)*
En OR-operation
Es operación O *(f)*
Fr exploitation OU *(f)*
Pt operação OR *(f)*

operazione o-esclusivo *(f)* It
De Antivalenzfunktion *(f)*
En exclusive-or operation
Es operación O exclusivo *(f)*
Fr opération OU exclusif *(f)*
Pt operação exclusiva-ou *(f)*

operazione parziale *(f)* It
De Teilbetrieb *(m)*
En part operation
Es operación parcial *(f)*
Fr opération partielle *(f)*
Pt operação por partes *(f)*

operazione se-allora *(f)* It
De Implikationsfunktion *(f)*
En if-then operation
Es operación condicional *(f)*
Fr opération conditionnelle *(f)*
Pt operação se-então *(f)*

operazione sia-o *(f)* It
De Entweder-oder-Funktion *(f)*
En either-or operation
Es operación ambos o uno *(f)*
Fr opération soit-ou *(f)*
Pt operação de ou-ou *(f)*

operazione unaria *(f)* It
De monadische Operation *(f)*
En unary operation
Es operación unaria *(f)*
Fr opération unaire *(f)*
Pt operação unária *(f)*

óptica de fibras *(f)* Pt
Am fiber optics
De Faseroptik *(f)*
En fibre optics
Es óptica de las fibras *(f)*
Fr optique à fibre *(f)*
It fibre ottiche *(f)*

óptica de las fibras *(f)* Es
Am fiber optics
De Faseroptik *(f)*
En fibre optics
Fr optique à fibre *(f)*
It fibre ottiche *(f)*
Pt óptica de fibras *(f)*

optical character reader En
De optischer Zeichenleser *(m)*
Es lectora óptica de caracteres *(f)*
Fr lecteur optique des caractères *(m)*
It lettore di caratteri ottici *(m)*
Pt leitor de caracteres ópticos *(m)*

optical character recognition (OCR) En
De optische Zeichenerkennung *(f)*
Es reconocimiento óptico de caracteres *(m)*
Fr reconnaissance optique des caractères (ROC) *(f)*
It riconoscimento ottico di caratteri *(m)*
Pt reconhecimento óptico de caracteres *(m)*

optical communications En
De optische Fernmeldung *(f)*
Es comunicaciones ópticas *(f)*
Fr transmission optique *(f)*
It comunicazioni ottiche *(f)*
Pt comunicações ópticas *(f)*

optical fiber technology Am
De Faseroptiktechnik *(f)*
En optical fibre technology
Es tecnología de las fibras ópticas *(f)*
Fr technologie des fibres optiques *(f)*
It tecnologia delle fibre ottiche *(f)*
Pt tecnologia de fibras ópticas *(f)*

optical fibre technology En
Am optical fiber technology
De Faseroptiktechnik *(f)*
Es tecnología de las fibras ópticas *(f)*
Fr technologie des fibres optiques *(f)*
It tecnologia delle fibre ottiche *(f)*
Pt tecnologia de fibras ópticas *(f)*

optical mark recognition En
De optische Zeichenerkennung *(f)*
Es reconocimiento óptico de marcas *(m)*
Fr reconnaissance optique de marques *(f)*

It riconoscimento di segni ottici *(m)*
Pt reconhecimento de marcas ópticas *(m)*

optical scanner En
De optischer Abtaster *(m)*
Es explorador óptico *(m)*
Fr lecteur optique *(m)*
It analizzatore per scansione di caratteri ottici *(m)*
Pt explorador óptico *(m)*

optimale Programmierung *(f)* De
En optimum programming
Es programación óptima *(f)*
Fr programmation optimum *(f)*
It programmazione dell'ottimo *(f)*
Pt programação para optimização *(f)*

optimieren *vb* De
En optimize
Es optimizar
Fr optimiser
It ottimizzare
Pt optimisar

Optimierung *(f) n* De
En optimization
Es optimización *(f)*
Fr optimisation *(f)*
It ottimizzazione *(f)*
Pt optimisação *(f)*

optimisação *(f) n* Pt
De Optimierung *(f)*
En optimization
Es optimización *(f)*
Fr optimisation *(f)*
It ottimizzazione *(f)*

optimisar *vb* Pt
De optimieren
En optimize
Es optimizar
Fr optimiser
It ottimizzare

optimisation *(f) n* Fr
De Optimierung *(f)*
En optimization
Es optimización *(f)*
It ottimizzazione *(f)*
Pt optimisação *(f)*

optimiser *vb* Fr
De optimieren
En optimize
Es optimizar
It ottimizzare
Pt optimisar

optimización *(f) n* Es
De Optimierung *(f)*
En optimization
Fr optimisation *(f)*
It ottimizzazione *(f)*
Pt optimisação *(f)*

optimizar *vb* Es
De optimieren
En optimize
Fr optimiser
It ottimizzare
Pt optimisar

optimization *n* En
De Optimierung *(f)*
Es optimización *(f)*
Fr optimisation *(f)*
It ottimizzazione *(f)*
Pt optimisação *(f)*

optimize *vb* En
De optimieren
Es optimizar
Fr optimiser
It ottimizzare
Pt optimisar

optimum programming En
De optimale Programmierung *(f)*
Es programación óptima *(f)*
Fr programmation optimum *(f)*
It programmazione dell'ottimo *(f)*
Pt programação para optimização *(f)*

optique à fibre *(f)* Fr
Am fiber optics
De Faseroptik *(f)*
En fibre optics
Es óptica de las fibras *(f)*
It fibre ottiche *(f)*
Pt óptica de fibras *(f)*

optische Fernmeldung *(f)* De
En optical communications
Es comunicaciones ópticas *(f)*
Fr transmission optique *(f)*
It comunicazioni ottiche *(f)*
Pt comunicações ópticas *(f)*

optischer Abtaster *(m)* De
En optical scanner
Es explorador óptico *(m)*
Fr lecteur optique *(m)*
It analizzatore per scansione di caratteri ottici *(m)*
Pt explorador óptico *(m)*

optischer Zeichenleser *(m)* De
En optical character reader
Es lectora óptica de caracteres *(f)*
Fr lecteur optique des caractères *(m)*
It lettore di caratteri ottici *(m)*
Pt leitor de caracteres ópticos *(m)*

optische Zeichenerkennung *(f)* De
En optical character recognition (OCR); optical mark recognition
Es reconocimiento óptico de caracteres; reconocimiento óptico de marcas *(m)*
Fr reconnaissance optique de marques; reconnaissance optique des caractères (ROC) *(f)*
It riconoscimento di segni ottici; riconoscimento ottico di caratteri *(m)*
Pt reconhecimento de marcas ópticas; reconhecimento óptico de caracteres *(m)*

ordem *(f) n* Pt
De Auftrag; Befehl *(m)*
En command; order
Es orden *(f)*
Fr commande; ordre *(f m)*
It comando; ordine *(m f)*

ordem de baixo nível *(f)* Pt
De niedriger Grad *(m)*
En low order
Es orden inferior *(m)*
Fr ordre bas *(m)*
It ordine basso *(m)*

ordem elevada *(f)* Pt
De hoher Grad *(m)*
En high order
Es orden superior *(m)*
Fr ordre haut *(m)*
It ordine elevato *(m)*

orden *(f) n* Es
De Auftrag; Befehl *(m)*
En command; order
Fr commande; ordre *(f m)*
It comando; ordine *(m f)*
Pt ordem *(f)*

ordenador *(m) n* Es
De Computer; Rechner *(m)*
En computer
Fr ordinateur *(m)*
It elaboratore *(m)*
Pt computador *(m)*

ordenador analógico *(m)* Es
De Analogrechner *(m)*
En analog computer
Fr calculateur analogique *(m)*
It elaboratore analogico *(m)*
Pt computador de analogia *(m)*

ordenador anfitrión *(m)* Es
De Wirtsrechner *(m)*
En host computer
Fr ordinateur central *(m)*
It elaboratore per conto terzi *(m)*
Pt computador hospedeiro *(m)*

ordenador de mesa *(m)* Es
De Tischrechner *(m)*
En desk-top computer
Fr petit ordinateur de bureau *(m)*
It elaboratore da tavolo *(m)*
Pt computador de mesa *(m)*

ordenador digital *(m)* Es
De Digitalrechner *(m)*
En digital computer
Fr calculateur numérique *(m)*
It elaboratore digitale *(m)*
Pt computador digital *(m)*

ordenador en programa almacenado *(m)* Es
De Computer für gespeicherte Programme *(m)*
En stored-program computer
Fr ordinateur à programme enregistré *(m)*
It calcolatore a programmi memorizzati *(m)*
Pt computador com programa armazenado *(m)*

ordenador especializado *(m)* Es
De Spezialrechner *(m)*
En special-purpose computer
Fr calculateur spécialisé *(m)*
It elaboratore a scopo speciale *(m)*
Pt computador para fins especiais *(m)*

ordenador híbrido *(m)* Es
De Hybridrechner *(m)*
En hybrid computer
Fr calculateur hybride *(m)*
It elaboratore ibrido *(m)*
Pt computador híbrido *(m)*

ordenador neumático *(m)* Es
De pneumatischer Computer *(m)*
En pneumatic computer
Fr ordinateur pneumatique *(m)*
It elaboratore pneumatico *(m)*
Pt computador pneumático *(m)*

ordenador personal *(m)* Es
De persönlicher Rechner *(m)*
En personal computer
Fr ordinateur privé *(m)*
It calcolatore personale *(m)*
Pt computador pessoal *(m)*

ordenador portátil *(m)* Es
De tragbarer Computer *(m)*
En portable computer
Fr ordinateur portatif *(m)*
It calcolatore portabile *(m)*
Pt computador portátil *(m)*

ordenador satélite *(m)* Es
De Satellitenrechner *(m)*
En satellite (computer)
Fr calculateur satellite *(m)*
It calcolatore satellite *(m)*
Pt computador satélite *(m)*

ordenador síncrono *(m)* Es
De Synchronisierrechner *(m)*
En synchronous computer
Fr calculateur synchrone *(m)*
It elaboratore sincrono *(m)*
Pt computador sincronizado *(m)*

ordenador universal *(m)* Es
De Allgemeinzweck-computer *(m)*
En general-purpose computer
Fr calculateur universel *(m)*
It elaboratore a scopo generale *(m)*
Pt computador para todos os fins *(m)*

ordenar *vb* Es, Pt
De beauftragen
En order
Fr ordonner
It ordinare

orden inferior *(m)* Es
De niedriger Grad *(m)*
En low order
Fr ordre bas *(m)*
It ordine basso *(m)*
Pt ordem de baixo nível *(f)*

orden superior *(m)* Es
De hoher Grad *(m)*
En high order
Fr ordre haut *(m)*
It ordine elevato *(m)*
Pt ordem elevada *(f)*

order *n* En
De Auftrag *(m)*
Es orden *(f)*
Fr ordre *(m)*
It ordine *(f)*
Pt ordem *(f)*

order *vb* En
De beauftragen
Es ordenar
Fr ordonner
It ordinare
Pt ordenar

order code En
De Anweisungscode *(m)*
Es código de orden *(m)*
Fr code d'ordre *(m)*
It codice di ordine *(m)*
Pt código de ordens *(m)*

ordinare *vb* It
De beauftragen
En order
Es ordenar
Fr ordonner
Pt ordenar

ordinateur *(m) n* Fr
De Computer; Rechner; Verarbeiter *(m)*
En computer; processor
Es ordenador; procesador *(m)*
It elaboratore *(m)*
Pt computador; processor *(m)*

ordinateur à programme enregistré *(m)* Fr
De Computer für gespeicherte Programme *(m)*
En stored-program computer
Es ordenador en programa almacenado *(m)*
It calcolatore a programmi memorizzati *(m)*
Pt computador com programa armazenado *(m)*

ordinateur central *(m)* Fr
De Wirtsrechner *(m)*
En host computer
Es ordenador anfitrión *(m)*
It elaboratore per conto terzi *(m)*
Pt computador hospedeiro *(m)*

ordinateur pneumatique *(m)* Fr
De pneumatischer Computer *(m)*
En pneumatic computer
Es ordenador neumático *(m)*
It elaboratore pneumatico *(m)*
Pt computador pneumático *(m)*

ordinateur portatif *(m)* Fr
De tragbarer Computer *(m)*
En portable computer
Es ordenador portátil *(m)*
It calcolatore portabile *(m)*
Pt computador portátil *(m)*

ordinateur principal *(m)* Fr
De Hauptrechner *(m)*
En mainframe computer
Es computador principal *(m)*
It calcolatore principale *(m)*
Pt computador principal *(m)*

ordinateur privé *(m)* Fr
De persönlicher Rechner *(m)*
En personal computer
Es ordenador personal *(m)*
It calcolatore personale *(m)*
Pt computador pessoal *(m)*

ordinatique *(f) n* Fr
De Computer-wissenschaft *(f)*
En computer science
Es ciencia de ordenador *(f)*
It scienza degli elaboratoria elettronici *(f)*
Pt ciência de computadores *(f)*

ordine *(f) n* It
De Auftrag *(m)*
En order
Es orden *(f)*
Fr ordre *(m)*
Pt ordem *(f)*

ordine basso *(m)* It
De niedriger Grad *(m)*
En low order
Es orden inferior *(m)*
Fr ordre bas *(m)*
Pt ordem de baixo nível *(f)*

ordine elevato *(m)* It
De hoher Grad *(m)*
En high order
Es orden superior *(m)*
Fr ordre haut *(m)*
Pt ordem elevada *(f)*

ordinograma *(m) n* Es
De Flußdiagramm *(n)*
En flowchart
Fr organigramme *(m)*
It diagramma di flusso *(m)*
Pt gráfico de fluxo *(m)*

ordonner *vb* Fr
De beauftragen; folgen
En order; sequence
Es ordenar; secuenciar
It ordinare; sequenziare
Pt formar sequência; ordenar

ordre *(m) n* Fr
De Auftrag *(m)*
En order
Es orden *(f)*
It ordine *(f)*
Pt ordem *(f)*

ordre bas *(m)* Fr
De niedriger Grad *(m)*
En low order
Es orden inferior *(m)*
It ordine basso *(m)*
Pt ordem de baixo nível *(f)*

ordre de contrôle *(m)* Fr
De Steueranweisung *(f)*
En control statement
Es sentencia de control *(f)*
It statement di controllo *(m)*
Pt afirmação de controlo *(f)*

ordre du jour *(m)* Fr
De Agende *(f)*
En agenda
Es agenda *(f)*
It agenda *(f)*
Pt agenda *(f)*

ordre haut *(m)* Fr
De hoher Grad *(m)*
En high order
Es orden superior *(m)*
It ordine elevato *(m)*
Pt ordem elevada *(f)*

organigramme *(m) n* Fr
De Flußdiagramm *(n)*
En flowchart
Es ordinograma *(m)*
It diagramma di flusso *(m)*
Pt gráfico de fluxo *(m)*

organisation et méthodes *(f pl)* Fr
De Organisation und Methoden *(pl)*
En organization and methods (O & M)
Es organización y métodos *(m pl)*
It organizzazione e metodi *(m pl)*
Pt organização e métodos *(m pl)*

Organisation und Methoden *(pl)* De
En organization and methods (O & M)
Es organización y métodos *(m pl)*
Fr organisation et méthodes *(f pl)*
It organizzazione e metodi *(m pl)*
Pt organização e métodos *(m pl)*

organização e métodos *(m pl)* Pt
De Organisation und Methoden *(pl)*
En organization and methods (O & M)
Es organización y métodos *(m pl)*
Fr organisation et méthodes *(f pl)*
It organizzazione e metodi *(m pl)*

organización en páginas *(f)* Es
De Paginierung *(f)*
En paging
Fr pagination *(f)*
It paginatura *(f)*
Pt paginação *(f)*

organización y métodos *(m pl)* Es
De Organisation und Methoden *(pl)*
En organization and methods (O & M)
Fr organisation et méthodes *(f pl)*
It organizzazione e metodi *(m pl)*
Pt organização e métodos *(m pl)*

organization and methods (O & M) En
De Organisation und Methoden *(pl)*
Es organización y métodos *(m pl)*
Fr organisation et méthodes *(f pl)*
It organizzazione e metodi *(m pl)*
Pt organização e métodos *(m pl)*

organizzazione e metodi *(m pl)* It
De Organisation und Methoden *(pl)*
En organization and methods (O & M)
Es organización y métodos *(m pl)*
Fr organisation et méthodes *(f pl)*
Pt organização e métodos *(m pl)*

organo di entrata *(m)* It
De Eingangsvorrichtung *(f)*
En input device
Es dispositivo de entrada *(m)*
Fr périphérique d'entrée *(m)*
Pt dispositivo de entrada *(m)*

organo di entrata-uscita *(m)* It
De Eingangs-Ausgangs-vorrichtung *(f)*
En input-output device
Es dispositivo de entrada-salida *(m)*
Fr périphérique entrée-sortie *(m)*
Pt dispositivo de entrada-sair *(m)*

organo di memoria *(m)* It
De Speichergerät *(n)*
En storage device
Es dispositivo de almacenamiento *(m)*
Fr unité de stockage *(f)*
Pt dispositivo de armazenamento *(m)*

organo di uscita *(m)* It
De Ausgangsvorrichtung *(m)*

En output device
Es dispositivo de salida *(m)*
Fr unité périphérique de sortie *(f)*
Pt dispositivo de output *(m)*

OR-gate *n* En
De ODER-Schaltung *(f)*
Es puerta O *(f)*
Fr porte OU *(f)*
It porta o *(f)*
Pt porta OR *(f)*

orientado a la palabra Es
De wortorientiert
En word-orientated
Fr à mots
It ad orientamento di voce
Pt orientado por palavras

orientado a los caracteres Es
De zeichenmäßig ausgerichtet
En character-orientated
Fr fonctionnement à caractères
It orientato a carattere
Pt orientado por caracteres

orientado por caracteres Pt
De zeichenmäßig ausgerichtet
En character-orientated
Es orientado a los caracteres
Fr fonctionnement à caractères
It orientato a carattere

orientado por palavras Pt
De wortorientiert
En word-orientated
Es orientado a la palabra
Fr à mots
It ad orientamento di voce

orientato a carattere It
De zeichenmäßig ausgerichtet
En character-orientated
Es orientado a los caracteres
Fr fonctionnement à caractères
Pt orientado por caracteres

origem *(f) n* Pt
De Herkunftsort *(m)*
En origin
Es origen *(m)*
Fr origine *(f)*
It origine *(f)*

origen *(m) n* Es
De Herkunftsort *(m)*
En origin
Fr origine *(f)*
It origine *(f)*
Pt origem *(f)*

origin *n* En
De Herkunftsort *(m)*
Es origen *(m)*
Fr origine *(f)*
It origine *(f)*
Pt origem *(f)*

origine *(f) n* Fr, It
De Herkunftsort *(m)*
En origin
Es origen *(m)*
Pt origem *(f)*

orologio *(m) n* It
De Taktgeber *(m)*
En clock
Es reloj *(m)*
Fr horloge *(f)*
Pt relógio *(m)*

orologio digitale *(m)* It
De Digitalzeitgeber *(m)*
En digital clock
Es reloj digital *(m)*
Fr horloge numérique *(f)*
Pt relógio digital *(m)*

orologio di tempo reale *(m)* It
De Uhrzeitgeber *(m)*
En real-time clock
Es reloj binario *(m)*
Fr horloge temps réel *(f)*
Pt relógio de tempo real *(m)*

orologio principale *(m)* It
De Stammzeitgeber *(m)*
En master clock
Es reloj maestro *(m)*
Fr horloge pilote *(f)*
Pt relógio principal *(m)*

OR-operation *n* En
De ODER-Verknüpfung *(f)*
Es operación O *(f)*
Fr exploitation OU *(f)*
It operazione O *(f)*
Pt operação OR *(f)*

ottal *adj* It
De oktal
En octal
Es octal
Fr octal
Pt octal

ottimizzare *vb* It
De optimieren
En optimize
Es optimizar
Fr optimiser
Pt optimisar

ottimizzazione *(f) n* It
De Optimierung *(f)*
En optimization
Es optimización *(f)*
Fr optimisation *(f)*
Pt optimisação *(f)*

outil de mise au point *(m)* Fr
De Fehlersuchhilfe *(f)*
En debugging aid
Es ayuda a la depuración *(f)*
It strumento di messa a punto (di un programma) *(m)*
Pt ajuda de desparasitação *(f)*

output *n* En, Pt *(m)*
De Ausgang *(m)*
Es salida *(f)*
Fr sortie *(f)*
It uscita *(f)*

output *vb* En, It
De ausgeben
Es extraer
Fr sortir
Pt sair

output area En
De Ausgangsbereich *(m)*
Es área de salida *(f)*
Fr zone de sortie *(f)*
It area di uscita *(f)*
Pt área de output *(f)*

output de computador em microfilme *(m)* Pt
De Computerausgang auf Mikrofilm *(m)*
En computer output on microfilm (COM)
Es salida de ordenador en microfilm *(f)*
Fr impression sur microfilm *(f)*
It output del elaboratore su microfilm *(m)*

output del elaboratore su microfilm *(m)* It
De Computerausgang auf Mikrofilm *(m)*
En computer output on microfilm (COM)
Es salida de ordenador en microfilm *(f)*
Fr impression sur microfilm *(f)*
Pt output de computador em microfilme *(m)*

output device En
De Ausgangsvorrichtung *(m)*
Es dispositivo de salida *(m)*
Fr unité périphérique de sortie *(f)*
It organo di uscita *(m)*
Pt dispositivo de output *(m)*

overflow *n* En
De Überlauf *(m)*
Es desbordamiento *(m)*
Fr dépassement de capacité *(m)*
It superamento della capacità di memoria *(m)*
Pt trasbordamento *(m)*

overlap *vb* En
De überlappen
Es solapar
Fr chevaucher
It sovrapporre
Pt sobrepor-se

overwrite *vb* En
De überschreiben
Es recubrir
Fr superposer une écriture
It inscrivere per riempimento
Pt escrever por cima

P

pacco di dischi *(m)* It
De Magnetplatten-installation *(f)*
En disk pack
Es pila de discos *(f)*
Fr dispac *(m)*
Pt pacote de discos *(m)*

pacco di software *(m)* It
De Softwarepaket *(n)*
En software package
Es paqueta de soporte lógico *(m)*
Fr progiciel *(m)*
Pt pacote de software *(m)*

pack *vb* En
De stapeln
Es empaquetar
Fr comprimer
It impaccare
Pt empacotar

packet-switched network En
De Paketschaltennetz *(n)*
Es red de conmutación de paquetes *(f)*
Fr réseau de commutation par paquets *(m)*
It rete di commutazione di pacci *(f)*
Pt rede com comutação de pacotes *(f)*

packet switching En
De Paketschalten *(n)*
Es conmutación de paquetes *(f)*
Fr commutation par paquets *(f)*
It commutazione di pacci *(f)*
Pt comutação de pacotes *(f)*

packing density En
De Fluβwechseldichte *(f)*
Es densidad de empaquetamiento *(f)*
Fr densité d'implantation *(f)*
It densita di compattezza *(f)*
Pt densidade de acumulação *(f)*

pack (of cards) En
Am deck (of cards)
De Kartensatz *(m)*
Es baraja *(f)*
Fr paquet de cartes *(m)*
It mazzo *(m)*
Pt baralho (de cartas) *(m)*

pacote de discos *(m)* Pt
De Magnetplatten-installation *(f)*
En disk pack
Es pila de discos *(f)*
Fr dispac *(m)*
It pacco di dischi *(m)*

pacote de programa *(m)* Pt
De Programmpaket *(n)*
En program package
Es colección de programas *(f)*
Fr programme-produit *(m)*
It serie di programmi *(f)*

pacote de software *(m)* Pt
De Softwarepaket *(n)*
En software package
Es paqueta de soporte lógico *(m)*
Fr progiciel *(m)*
It pacco di software *(m)*

padding *n* En
De Auffüllen *(n)*
Es relleno *(m)*
Fr remplissage *(m)*
It ricaricamento *(m)*
Pt enchimento *(m)*

padrão de bit *(m)* Pt
De Binärzeichenmuster *(n)*
En bit pattern
Es configuración de bits *(f)*
Fr configuration de bits *(f)*
It configurazione dei bit *(f)*

page *n* En; Fr *(f)*
De Seite *(f)*
Es página *(f)*
It pagina *(f)*
Pt página *(f)*

paged memory En
De paginierter Speicher *(m)*
Es memoria organizada en páginas *(f)*
Fr mémoire organisée en pages *(f)*
It memoria per pagine *(f)*
Pt memória com páginas *(f)*

page printer En
De Seitendrucker *(m)*
Es impresora por páginas *(f)*
Fr imprimante page par page *(f)*
It stampatrice di pagina *(f)*
Pt impressora de página *(f)*

page turning En
De Seitenwechsel *(m)*
Es transferencia de página *(f)*
Fr changement de page *(m)*
It trasferimento di pagina *(m)*
Pt mudança de páginas *(f)*

pagina *(f) n* It
De Seite *(f)*
En page
Es página *(f)*
Fr page *(f)*
Pt página *(f)*

página *(f) n* Es, Pt
De Seite *(f)*
En page
Fr page *(f)*
It pagina *(f)*

paginação *(f) n* Pt
De Paginierung *(f)*
En paging
Es organización en páginas *(f)*
Fr pagination *(f)*
It paginatura *(f)*

pagination *(f) n* Fr
De Paginierung *(f)*
En paging
Es organización en páginas *(f)*
It paginatura *(f)*
Pt paginação *(f)*

paginatura *(f) n* It
De Paginierung *(f)*
En paging
Es organización en páginas *(f)*
Fr pagination *(f)*
Pt paginação *(f)*

paging *n* En
De Paginierung *(f)*
Es organización en páginas *(f)*
Fr pagination *(f)*
It paginatura *(f)*
Pt paginação *(f)*

paginierter Speicher *(m)* De
En paged memory
Es memoria organizada en páginas *(f)*
Fr mémoire organisée en pages *(f)*
It memoria per pagine *(f)*
Pt memória com páginas *(f)*

Paginierung *(f) n* De
En paging
Es organización en páginas *(f)*
Fr pagination *(f)*
It paginatura *(f)*
Pt paginação *(f)*

painel de controlo *(m)* Pt
De Steuertafel *(f)*
En control panel
Es panel de control *(m)*
Fr panneau de contrôle *(m)*

It pannello di comando (m)

painel de gráficos *(m)* Pt
De Symboltafel *(f)*
En graphic panel
Es panel gráfico *(m)*
Fr tableau graphique *(m)*
It pannello grafico *(m)*

Paketschalten *(n) n* De
En packet switching
Es conmutación de paquetes *(f)*
Fr commutation par paquets *(f)*
It commutazione di pacci *(f)*
Pt comutação de pacotes *(f)*

Paketschaltennetz *(n) n* De
En packet-switched network
Es red de conmutación de paquetes *(f)*
Fr réseau de commutation par paquets *(m)*
It rete di commutazione di pacci *(f)*
Pt rede com comutação de pacotes *(f)*

palabra *(f) n* Es
De Wort *(n)*
En word
Fr mot *(m)*
It voce *(f)*
Pt palavra *(f)*

palabra clave *(f)* Es
De Schlüsselwort *(n)*
En keyword
Fr mot-clé *(m)*
It parola chiave *(f)*
Pt palavra chave *(f)*

palabra de control *(f)* Es
De Schablone *(f)*
En control word
Fr mot de contrôle *(m)*
It voce di controllo *(f)*
Pt palavra de controlo *(f)*

palabra de estado *(f)* Es
De Statuswort *(n)*
En status word
Fr mot d'état *(m)*
It voce di stato *(f)*
Pt palavra de status *(f)*

palabra de máquina *(f)* Es
De Maschinenwort *(n)*
En machine word
Fr mot machine *(m)*
It voce macchina *(f)*
Pt palavra da máquina *(f)*

palabras por minuto *(f pl)* Es
De Worte pro Minute *(pl)*
En words per minute (wpm)
Fr mots par minute (mpm) *(m pl)*
It parole al minuto *(f pl)*
Pt palavras por minuto (ppm) *(f pl)*

palavra *(f) n* Pt
De Wort *(n)*
En word
Es palabra *(f)*
Fr mot *(m)*
It voce *(f)*

palavra chave *(f)* Pt
De Schlüsselwort *(n)*
En keyword
Es palabra clave *(f)*
Fr mot-clé *(m)*
It parola chiave *(f)*

palavra da máquina *(f)* Pt
De Maschinenwort *(n)*
En machine word
Es palabra de máquina *(f)*
Fr mot machine *(m)*
It voce macchina *(f)*

palavra de controlo *(f)* Pt
De Schablone *(f)*
En control word
Es palabra de control *(f)*
Fr mot de contrôle *(m)*
It voce di controllo *(f)*

palavra de status *(f)* Pt
De Statuswort *(n)*
En status word
Es palabra de estado *(f)*
Fr mot d'état *(m)*
It voce di stato *(f)*

palavras por minuto (ppm) *(f pl)* Pt
De Worte pro Minute *(pl)*
En words per minute (wpm)
Es palabras por minuto *(f pl)*
Fr mots par minute (mpm) *(m pl)*
It parole al minuto *(f pl)*

panel de control *(m)* Es
De Steuertafel *(f)*
En control panel
Fr panneau de contrôle *(m)*
It pannello di comando *(m)*
Pt painel de controlo *(m)*

panel gráfico *(m)* Es
De Symboltafel *(f)*
En graphic panel
Fr tableau graphique *(m)*
It pannello grafico *(m)*
Pt painel de gráficos *(m)*

panne *(f) n* Fr
De Maschinenausfall *(m)*
En equipment failure
Es fallo del equipo *(m)*
It guasto delle apparecchiature *(m)*
Pt falha de equipamento *(f)*

panneau de contrôle *(m)* Fr
De Steuertafel *(f)*
En control panel
Es panel de control *(m)*
It pannello di comando *(m)*
Pt painel de controlo *(m)*

pannello a spine *(m)* It
De Steckplatte *(f)*
En pinboard
Es cuadro de alfileres *(m)*
Fr tableau à aiguilles *(m)*
Pt prancheta de alfinetes *(f)*

pannello di comando *(m)* It
De Steuertafel *(f)*
En control panel
Es panel de control *(m)*
Fr panneau de contrôle *(m)*
Pt painel de controlo *(m)*

pannello di connessione *(m)* It
De Schalttafel *(f)*
En patchboard
Es cuadro de control *(m)*
Fr tableau de connexions *(m)*
Pt placa de concerto *(f)*

pannello di connessioni *(m)* It
De Steckerbrett *(n)*
En plugboard
Es cuadro de conexión *(m)*
Fr tableau de connexions *(m)*
Pt placa de conexões eléctricas *(f)*

pannello grafico *(m)* It
De Symboltafel *(f)*
En graphic panel
Es panel gráfico *(m)*
Fr tableau graphique *(m)*
Pt painel de gráficos *(m)*

pantalla *(f) n* Es
De Schirm *(m)*
En screen
Fr écran *(m)*
It schermo *(m)*
Pt écran *(m)*

papel *(m) n* Es
De Formulare *(n pl)*
En forms
Fr formules *(f pl)*
It moduli *(m pl)*
Pt formulários *(m pl)*

papel continuo *(m)* Es
De Endlosvordrucke *(pl)*
En continuous stationery
Fr papier en continu *(m)*
It carta da tabulati a fisarmonica *(f)*
Pt continuo-estacionário *(m)*

paper tape En
De Papierstreifen *(m)*
Es cinta de papel *(f)*
Fr bande de papier *(f)*

It nastro di carta *(m)*
Pt fita de papel *(f)*

paper-tape punch En
De Lochstreifenlocher *(m)*
Es perforador de cinta *(m)*
Fr perforatrice à papier *(f)*
It perforatrice di nastri di carta *(f)*
Pt perfuradora de fita de papel *(f)*

paper-tape reader En
De Lochstreifenleser *(m)*
Es lectora de cinta de papel *(f)*
Fr lecteur de bande perforée *(m)*
It lettore di nastri di carta *(m)*
Pt leitor de fita de papel *(m)*

paper throw En
De Papiervorschub *(m)*
Es salto del papel *(m)*
Fr saut de papier *(m)*
It salto di pagina (di un modulo) *(m)*
Pt curso do papel *(m)*

papier en continu *(m)* Fr
De Endlosvordrucke *(pl)*
En continuous stationery
Es papel continuo *(m)*
It carta da tabulati a fisarmonica *(f)*
Pt continuo-estacionário *(m)*

Papierstreifen *(m) n* De
En paper tape
Es cinta de papel *(f)*
Fr bande de papier *(f)*
It nastro di carta *(m)*
Pt fita de papel *(f)*

Papiervorschub *(m) n* De
En paper throw
Es salto del papel *(m)*
Fr saut de papier *(m)*
It salto di pagina (di un modulo) *(m)*
Pt curso do papel *(m)*

paqueta de soporte lógico *(m)* Es
De Softwarepaket *(n)*
En software package
Fr progiciel *(m)*
It pacco di software *(m)*
Pt pacote de software *(m)*

paquet de cartes *(m)* Fr
Am deck (of cards)
De Kartensatz *(m)*
En pack (of cards)
Es baraja *(f)*
It mazzo *(m)*
Pt baralho (de cartas) *(m)*

paquete de papel continuo *(m)* Es
De mehrteilige Formulare *(pl)*
En multipart forms
Fr liasse *(f)*
It moduli a copie multiple *(m pl)*
Pt formas de partes múltiplas *(f pl)*

parada *(f) n* Es
De Stopp *(m)*
En halt
Fr arrêt *(m)*
It arresto *(m)*
Pt paragem *(f)*

parada automática *(f)* Es
De automatischer Stopp *(m)*
En automatic stop
Fr arrêt automatique *(m)*
It arresto automatico *(m)*
Pt paragem automática *(f)*

parada del papel *(f)* Es
De Formularanschlag *(m)*
En form stop
Fr arrêt de papier *(m)*
It arresto del modulo *(m)*
Pt paragem de formulários *(f)*

paragem *(f) n* Pt
De Stopp *(m)*
En halt
Es parada *(f)*
Fr arrêt *(m)*
It arresto *(m)*

paragem automática *(f)* Pt
De automatischer Stopp *(m)*
En automatic stop
Es parada automática *(f)*
Fr arrêt automatique *(m)*
It arresto automatico *(m)*

paragem de formulários *(f)* Pt
De Formularanschlag *(m)*
En form stop
Es parada del papel *(f)*
Fr arrêt de papier *(m)*
It arresto del modulo *(m)*

parallel access En
De Parallelzugriff *(m)*
Es acceso en paralelo *(m)*
Fr accès en parallèle *(m)*
It accesso parallelo *(m)*
Pt acesso paralelo *(m)*

Parallelaufzeichnung *(f) n* De
En dual recording
Es registro en paralelo *(m)*
Fr enregistrement double *(m)*
It registrazione duplice *(f)*
Pt registo duplo *(m)*

parallel interface En
De Parallelschnittstelle *(f)*
Es interfase en paralelo *(f)*
Fr interface en parallèle *(f)*
It interfaccia parallela *(f)*
Pt interface paralela *(f)*

Parallellauf *(m) n* De
En parallel running
Es ciclo de funcionamiento en paralelo *(m)*
Fr exploitation en parallèle *(f)*
It esecuzione parallela *(f)*
Pt passagens paralelas *(f)*

parallel processing En
De Parallelsimultan-verarbeitung *(f)*
Es proceso en paralelo *(m)*
Fr traitement en parallèle *(m)*
It elaborazione parallela *(f)*
Pt processamento paralelo *(m)*

parallel running En
De Parallellauf *(m)*
Es ciclo de funcionamiento en paralelo *(m)*
Fr exploitation en parallèle *(f)*
It esecuzione parallela *(f)*
Pt passagens paralelas *(f)*

Parallelschnittstelle *(f) n* De
En parallel interface
Es interfase en paralelo *(f)*
Fr interface en parallèle *(f)*
It interfaccia parallela *(f)*
Pt interface paralela *(f)*

Parallelsimultan-verarbeitung *(f) n* De
En parallel processing
Es proceso en paralelo *(m)*
Fr traitement en parallèle *(m)*
It elaborazione parallela *(f)*
Pt processamento paralelo *(m)*

parallel transfer En
De Parallelübergabe *(f)*
Es transferencia en paralelo *(f)*
Fr transfert en parallèle *(m)*
It trasferimento parallelo *(m)*
Pt transferência paralela *(f)*

Parallelübergabe *(f) n* De
En parallel transfer

Es transferencia en paralelo *(f)*
Fr transfert en parallèle *(m)*
It trasferimento parallelo *(m)*
Pt transferência paralela *(f)*

Parallelverarbeiter *(m) n* De
En dual processor
Es biprocesador *(m)*
Fr biprocesseur *(m)*
It elaboratore duplice *(m)*
Pt processador duplo *(m)*

Parallelzugriff *(m) n* De
En parallel access
Es acceso en paralelo *(m)*
Fr accès en parallèle *(m)*
It accesso parallelo *(m)*
Pt acesso paralelo *(m)*

parameter *n* En
De Parameter *(m)*
Es parámetro *(m)*
Fr paramètre *(m)*
It parametro *(m)*
Pt parâmetro *(m)*

Parameter *(m) n* De
En parameter
Es parámetro *(m)*
Fr paramètre *(m)*
It parametro *(m)*
Pt parâmetro *(m)*

paramètre *(m) n* Fr
De Parameter *(m)*
En parameter
Es parámetro *(m)*
It parametro *(m)*
Pt parâmetro *(m)*

paramètre de programme *(m)* Fr
De Programmparameter *(m)*
En program parameter
Es parámetro de programa *(m)*
It parametro del programma *(m)*
Pt parâmetro de programa *(m)*

paramètre pré-défini *(m)* Fr
De Festparameter *(m)*
En preset parameter
Es parámetro definido previamente *(m)*
It parametro prestabilito *(m)*
Pt parâmetro previamente fixado *(m)*

parametro *(m) n* It
De Parameter *(m)*
En parameter
Es parámetro *(m)*
Fr paramètre *(m)*
Pt parâmetro *(m)*

parámetro *(m) n* Es
De Parameter *(m)*
En parameter
Fr paramètre *(m)*
It parametro *(m)*
Pt parâmetro *(m)*

parâmetro *(m) n* Pt
De Parameter *(m)*
En parameter
Es parámetro *(m)*
Fr paramètre *(m)*
It parametro *(m)*

parámetro definido previamente *(m)* Es
De Festparameter *(m)*
En preset parameter
Fr paramètre pré-défini *(m)*
It parametro prestabilito *(m)*
Pt parâmetro previamente fixado *(m)*

parametro del programma *(m)* It
De Programmparameter *(m)*
En program parameter
Es parámetro de programa *(m)*
Fr paramètre de programme *(m)*
Pt parâmetro de programa *(m)*

parámetro de programa *(m)* Es
De Programmparameter *(m)*
En program parameter
Fr paramètre de programme *(m)*
It parametro del programma *(m)*
Pt parâmetro de programa *(m)*

parâmetro de programa *(m)* Pt
De Programmparameter *(m)*
En program parameter
Es parámetro de programa *(m)*
Fr paramètre de programme *(m)*
It parametro del programma *(m)*

parametro prestabilito *(m)* It
De Festparameter *(m)*
En preset parameter
Es parámetro definido previamente *(m)*
Fr paramètre pré-défini *(m)*
Pt parâmetro previamente fixado *(m)*

parâmetro previamente fixado *(m)* Pt
De Festparameter *(m)*
En preset parameter
Es parámetro definido previamente *(m)*
Fr paramètre pré-défini *(m)*
It parametro prestabilito *(m)*

parche *(m) n* Es
De Korrektur *(f)*
En patch
Fr correction *(f)*
It connessione *(f)*
Pt remendo *(m)*

parchear un programa Es
De korrigieren (ein Programm)
En patch
Fr corriger un programme
It correggere un programma
Pt remendar uma programa

paridad *(f) n* Es
De gerade Bitzahl *(f)*
En even parity
Fr parité *(f)*
It parità pari *(f)*
Pt paridade de igualdade *(f)*

paridade de igualdade *(f)* Pt
De gerade Bitzahl *(f)*
En even parity
Es paridad *(f)*
Fr parité *(f)*
It parità pari *(f)*

paridade impar *(f)* Pt
De ungerade Parität *(f)*
En odd parity
Es imparidad *(f)*
Fr imparité *(f)*
It parità dispari *(f)*

parità dispari *(f)* It
De ungerade Parität *(f)*
En odd parity
Es imparidad *(f)*
Fr imparité *(f)*
Pt paridade impar *(f)*

parità pari *(f)* It
De gerade Bitzahl *(f)*
En even parity
Es paridad *(f)*
Fr parité *(f)*
Pt paridade de igualdade *(f)*

Paritätsbit *(m) n* De
En parity bit
Es bit de paridad *(m)*
Fr bit de parité *(m)*
It bit di parità *(m)*
Pt bit de paridade *(m)*

Paritätsfehler *(m) n* De
En parity error
Es error de paridad *(m)*
Fr erreur de parité *(f)*
It errore di parità *(m)*
Pt erro de paridade *(m)*

Paritätsprüfung *(f) n* De
En parity check
Es control de paridad *(m)*
Fr contrôle de parité *(m)*
It controllo di parità *(m)*
Pt verificação de paridade *(f)*

parité *(f) n* Fr
De gerade Bitzahl *(f)*
En even parity
Es paridad *(f)*
It parità pari *(f)*
Pt paridade de igualdade *(f)*

parity bit En
De Paritätsbit *(m)*
Es bit de paridad *(m)*
Fr bit de parité *(m)*
It bit di parità *(m)*
Pt bit de paridade *(m)*

parity check En
De Paritätsprüfung *(f)*
Es control de paridad *(m)*
Fr contrôle de parité *(m)*
It controllo di parità *(m)*
Pt verificação de paridade *(f)*

parity error En
De Paritätsfehler *(m)*
Es error de paridad *(m)*
Fr erreur de parité *(f)*
It errore di parità *(m)*
Pt erro de paridade *(m)*

parola chiave *(f)* It
De Schlüsselwort *(n)*
En keyword
Es palabra clave *(f)*
Fr mot-clé *(m)*
Pt palavra chave *(f)*

parola d'ordine *(f)* It
De Kennwort *(n)*
En password
Es contraseña *(f)*
Fr mot de passe *(m)*
Pt contra-senha *(f)*

parole al minuto *(f pl)* It
De Worte pro Minute *(pl)*
En words per minute (wpm)
Es palabras por minuto *(f pl)*
Fr mots par minute (mpm) *(m pl)*
Pt palavras por minuto (ppm) *(f pl)*

parte de endereço *(f)* Pt
De Adressenteil *(n)*
En address part
Es parte de la dirección *(f)*
Fr partie d'adresse *(f)*
It indirizzo parziale *(m)*

parte de la dirección *(f)* Es
De Adressenteil *(n)*
En address part
Fr partie d'adresse *(f)*
It indirizzo parziale *(m)*
Pt parte de endereço *(f)*

partial carry En
De Teilübertrag *(m)*
Es arrastre parcial *(m)*
Fr report partiel *(m)*
It riporto parziale *(m)*
Pt transporte parcial *(m)*

partie d'adresse *(f)* Fr
De Adressenteil *(n)*
En address part
Es parte de la dirección *(f)*
It indirizzo parziale *(m)*
Pt parte de endereço *(f)*

part operation En
De Teilbetrieb *(m)*
Es operación parcial *(f)*
Fr opération partielle *(f)*
It operazione parziale *(f)*
Pt operação por partes *(f)*

pasada *(f) n* Es
De Durchlauf *(m)*
En run
Fr passage *(m)*
It esecuzione *(f)*
Pt passagem *(f)*

pasada de ensayo *(f)* Es
De Prüfablauf *(m)*
En test run
Fr passage d'essai *(m)*
It esecuzione di prova *(f)*
Pt passagem de ensaio *(f)*

pasada de máquina *(f)* Es
De Maschinenlauf *(m)*
En machine run
Fr passage en machine *(m)*
It giro della macchina *(m)*
Pt passagem da máquina *(f)*

pasada de ordenador *(f)* Es
De Ablauf *(m)*
En computer run
Fr phase de traitement *(f)*
It esecuzione di elaboratore *(f)*
Pt passagem de computador *(f)*

pasada de producción *(f)* Es
De Fertigungslauf *(m)*
En production run
Fr passage de production *(m)*
It esecuzione di produzione *(f)*
Pt passagem de produção *(f)*

pasada en seco *(f)* Es
De Versuchslauf *(m)*
En dry run
Fr coup d'essai *(m)*
It passo a prova *(m)*
Pt passagem a seco *(f)*

pasar *vb* Es
De durchlaufen
En run
Fr exécuter
It passare
Pt passar

pasar a escala Es
De skalieren
En scale
Fr cadrer
It scalare
Pt fazer concordar com a escala

pas longitudinal *(m)* Fr
De Zeilensprung *(m)*
En row pitch
Es paso entre filas *(m)*
It passo di fila *(m)*
Pt passo de fila *(m)*

paso *(m) n* Es
De Schritt *(m)*
En step
Fr phase *(f)*
It passo *(m)*
Pt passo *(m)*

paso entre filas *(m)* Es
De Zeilensprung *(m)*
En row pitch
Fr pas longitudinal *(m)*
It passo di fila *(m)*
Pt passo de fila *(m)*

passage *(m) n* Fr
De Durchlauf *(m)*
En run
Es pasada *(f)*
It esecuzione *(f)*
Pt passagem *(f)*

passage de production *(m)* Fr
De Fertigungslauf *(m)*
En production run
Es pasada de producción *(f)*
It esecuzione di produzione *(f)*
Pt passagem de produção *(f)*

passage d'essai *(m)* Fr
De Prüfablauf *(m)*
En test run
Es pasada de ensayo *(f)*
It esecuzione di prova *(f)*
Pt passagem de ensaio *(f)*

passage en machine *(m)* Fr
De Maschinenlauf *(m)*
En machine run
Es pasada de máquina *(f)*
It giro della macchina *(m)*
Pt passagem da máquina *(f)*

passagem *(f) n* Pt
De Durchlauf *(m)*
En run
Es pasada *(f)*
Fr passage *(m)*
It esecuzione *(f)*

passagem a seco *(f)* Pt
De Versuchslauf *(m)*
En dry run
Es pasada en seco *(f)*
Fr coup d'essai *(m)*
It passo a prova *(m)*

passagem da máquina *(f)* Pt
De Maschinenlauf *(m)*
En machine run

Es pasada de máquina *(f)*
Fr passage en machine *(m)*
It giro della macchina *(m)*

passagem de computador *(f)* Pt
De Ablauf *(m)*
En computer run
Es pasada de ordenador *(f)*
Fr phase de traitement *(f)*
It esecuzione di elaboratore *(f)*

passagem de ensaio *(f)* Pt
De Prüfablauf *(m)*
En test run
Es pasada de ensayo *(f)*
Fr passage d'essai *(m)*
It esecuzione di prova *(f)*

passagem de produção *(f)* Pt
De Fertigungslauf *(m)*
En production run
Es pasada de producción *(f)*
Fr passage de production *(m)*
It esecuzione di produzione *(f)*

passagens paralelas *(f)* Pt
De Parallellauf *(m)*
En parallel running
Es ciclo de funcionamiento en paralelo *(m)*
Fr exploitation en parallèle *(f)*
It esecuzione parallela *(f)*

passar *vb* Pt
De durchlaufen
En run
Es pasar
Fr exécuter
It passare

passare *vb* It
De durchlaufen
En run
Es pasar
Fr exécuter
Pt passar

passo *(m) n* It, Pt
De Schritt *(m)*
En step
Es paso *(m)*
Fr phase *(f)*

passo a prova *(m)* It
De Versuchslauf *(m)*
En dry run
Es pasada en seco *(f)*
Fr coup d'essai *(m)*
Pt passagem a seco *(f)*

passo de fila *(m)* Pt
De Zeilensprung *(m)*
En row pitch
Es paso entre filas *(m)*
Fr pas longitudinal *(m)*
It passo di fila *(m)*

passo di fila *(m)* It
De Zeilensprung *(m)*
En row pitch
Es paso entre filas *(m)*
Fr pas longitudinal *(m)*
Pt passo de fila *(m)*

password *n* En
De Kennwort *(n)*
Es contraseña *(f)*
Fr mot de passe *(m)*
It parola d'ordine *(f)*
Pt contra-senha *(f)*

patch *n* En
De Korrektur *(f)*
Es parche *(m)*
Fr correction *(f)*
It connessione *(f)*
Pt remendo *(m)*

patch *vb* En
De korrigieren (ein Programm)
Es parchear un programa
Fr corriger un programme
It correggere un programma
Pt remendar uma programa

patchboard *n* En
De Schalttafel *(f)*
Es cuadro de control *(m)*
Fr tableau de connexions *(m)*
It pannello di connessione *(m)*
Pt placa de concerto *(f)*

patchcord *n* En
De Schaltschnur *(f)*
Es cable de conexión *(m)*
Fr fiche de connexion *(f)*
It cordone di connessione *(m)*
Pt cabo de concerto *(m)*

path *n* En
De Zugriffspfad *(m)*
Es curso *(m)*
Fr branchement *(m)*
It percorso *(m)*
Pt caminho *(m)*

Patrone *(f) n* De
En cartridge
Es cartucho *(m)*
Fr cartouche *(f)*
It cartuccia *(f)*
Pt carga *(f)*

Patronenplatte *(f) n* De
En cartridge disk
Es disco de cartucho *(m)*
Fr disque à cartouche *(m)*
It disco a cartuccia *(m)*
Pt disco de carga *(m)*

pattern recognition En
De Strukturerkennung *(f)*
Es reconocimiento de configuraciones *(m)*
Fr reconnaissance des formes *(f)*
It riconoscimento di modelli *(m)*
Pt reconhecimento de padrão *(m)*

penna luminosa *(f)* It
De Lichtschreiber *(m)*
En light pen
Es lápiz fotosensible *(f)*
Fr photo-style *(f)*
Pt caneta de luz *(f)*

percorso *(m) n* It
De Zugriffspfad *(m)*
En path
Es curso *(m)*
Fr branchement *(m)*
Pt caminho *(m)*

perda *(f) n* Pt
De Verlust *(m)*
En loss
Es pérdida *(f)*
Fr perte *(f)*
It perdita *(f)*

pérdida *(f) n* Es
De Verlust *(m)*
En loss
Fr perte *(f)*
It perdita *(f)*
Pt perda *(f)*

perdita *(f) n* It
De Verlust *(m)*
En loss
Es pérdida *(f)*
Fr perte *(f)*
Pt perda *(f)*

perforaciones de alimentación *(f pl)* Es
De Taktlöcher *(n pl)*
En feed holes
Fr trous d'entraînement *(m pl)*
It fori di alimentazione *(m pl)*
Pt furos de alimentação *(m pl)*

perforaciones marginales *(f pl)* Es
De Taktlöcher *(pl)*
En sprocket holes
Fr perforations d'entraînement *(f pl)*
It perforazioni di tabulati *(f pl)*
Pt furos de roda dentada *(m pl)*

perforador *(m) n* Es
De Lochbandlocher *(m)*
En perforator
Fr perforatrice *(f)*
It perforatrice *(f)*
Pt perfuradora *(f)*

perforadora *(f) n* Es
De Locher *(m)*
En punch
Fr perforatrice *(f)*
It perforatrice *(f)*
Pt perfuradora *(f)*

perforadora de cinta *(f)* Es
De Bandlocher *(m)*
En tape punch
Fr perforatrice de bande *(f)*
It perforatrice di nastri *(f)*
Pt perfuradora de fita *(f)*

perforadora de fichas *(f)* Es
De Kartenlocher *(m)*
En card punch
Fr perforatrice de cartes *(f)*
It perforatrice di schede *(f)*
Pt perfuradora de ficha *(f)*

perforadora de tecla *(f)* Es
De Locher mit Tastatur *(m)*
En key punch
Fr perforatrice à clavier *(f)*
It peforatrice a tastiera *(f)*
Pt perfuradora de tecla *(f)*

perforadora impresora *(f)* Es
De Drucklocher *(m)*
En printing punch
Fr perforatrice imprimante *(f)*
It perforatrice di stampa *(f)*
Pt perfuradora de impressão *(f)*

perforador de cinta *(m)* Es
De Lochstreifenlocher *(m)*
En paper-tape punch
Fr perforatrice à papier *(f)*
It perforatrice di nastri di carta *(f)*
Pt perfuradora de fita de papel *(f)*

perforar *vb* Es
De lochen
En punch
Fr perforer
It perforare
Pt perfurar

perforare *vb* It
De lochen
En punch
Es perforar
Fr perforer
Pt perfurar

perforated (or **punched**) **tape** En
De Lochstreifen *(m)*
Es cinta perforada *(f)*
Fr bande perforée *(f)*
It nastro perforato *(m)*
Pt fita perfurada *(f)*

perforation rate En
De Lochungsgeschwindigkeit *(f)*
Es régimen de perforación *(m)*
Fr vitesse de perforation *(f)*
It rapporto di perforazione *(m)*
Pt índice de perfuração *(m)*

perforations d'entraînement *(f pl)* Fr
De Taktlöcher *(pl)*
En sprocket holes
Es perforaciones marginales *(f pl)*
It perforazioni di tabulati *(f pl)*
Pt furos de roda dentada *(m pl)*

perforator *n* En
De Lochbandlocher *(m)*
Es perforador *(m)*
Fr perforatrice *(f)*
It perforatrice *(f)*
Pt perfuradora *(f)*

perforatrice *(f) n* Fr, It
De Lochbandlocher; Locher *(m)*
En perforator; punch
Es perforador; perforadora *(m f)*
Pt perfuradora *(f)*

perforatrice à clavier *(f)* Fr
De Locher mit Tastatur *(m)*
En key punch
Es perforadora de tecla *(f)*
It perforatrice a tastiera *(f)*
Pt perfuradora de tecla *(f)*

perforatrice à papier *(f)* Fr
De Lochstreifenlocher *(m)*
En paper-tape punch
Es perforador de cinta *(m)*
It perforatrice di nastri di carta *(f)*
Pt perfuradora de fita de papel *(f)*

perforatrice a tastiera *(f)* It
De Locher mit Tastatur *(m)*
En key punch
Es perforadora a tecla *(f)*
Fr perforatrice à clavier *(f)*
Pt perfuradora de tecla *(f)*

perforatrice de bande *(f)* Fr
De Bandlocher *(m)*
En tape punch
Es perforadora de cinta *(f)*
It perforatrice di nastri *(f)*
Pt perfuradora de fita *(f)*

perforatrice de cartes *(f)* Fr
De Kartenlocher *(m)*
En card punch
Es perforadora de fichas *(f)*
It perforatrice di schede *(f)*
Pt perfuradora de ficha *(f)*

perforatrice di nastri *(f)* It
De Bandlocher *(m)*
En tape punch
Es perforadora de cinta *(f)*
Fr perforatrice de bande *(f)*
Pt perfuradora de fita *(f)*

perforatrice di nastri di carta *(f)* It
De Lochstreifenlochen *(m)*
En paper-tape punch
Es perforador de cinta *(m)*
Fr perforatrice à papier *(f)*
Pt perfuradora de fita de papel *(f)*

perforatrice di schede *(f)* It
De Kartenlocher *(m)*
En card punch
Es perforadora de fichas *(f)*
Fr perforatrice de cartes *(f)*
Pt perfuradora de ficha *(f)*

perforatrice di stampa *(f)* It
De Drucklocher *(m)*
En printing punch
Es perforadora impresora *(f)*
Fr perforatrice imprimante *(f)*
Pt perfuradora de impressão *(f)*

perforatrice imprimante *(f)* Fr
De Drucklocher *(m)*
En printing punch
Es perforadora impresora *(f)*
It perforatrice di stampa *(f)*
Pt perfuradora de impressão *(f)*

perforazioni di tabulati *(f pl)* It
De Taktlöcher *(pl)*
En sprocket holes
Es perforaciones marginales *(f pl)*
Fr perforations d'entraînement *(f pl)*
Pt furos de roda dentada *(m pl)*

perforer *vb* Fr
De lochen
En punch
Es perforar
It perforare
Pt perfurar

perfuradora *(f) n* Pt
De Lochbandlocher; Locher *(m)*
En perforator; punch
Es perforador; perforadora *(m f)*
Fr perforatrice *(f)*
It perforatrice *(f)*

perfuradora de ficha *(f)* Pt
De Kartenlocher *(m)*
En card punch
Es perforadora de fichas *(f)*
Fr perforatrice de cartes *(f)*
It perforatrice di schede *(f)*

perfuradora de fita *(f)* Pt
De Bandlocher *(m)*
En tape punch
Es perforadora de cinta *(f)*
Fr perforatrice de bande *(f)*
It perforatrice di nastri *(f)*

perfuradora de fita de papel *(f)* Pt
De Lochstreifenlocher *(m)*
En paper-tape punch
Es perforador de cinta *(m)*
Fr perforatrice à papier *(f)*
It perforatrice di nastri di carta *(f)*

perfuradora de impressão *(f)* Pt
De Drucklocher *(m)*
En printing punch
Es perforadora impresora *(f)*
Fr perforatrice imprimante *(f)*
It perforatrice di stampa *(f)*

perfuradora de tecla *(f)* Pt
De Locher mit Tastatur *(m)*
En key punch
Es perforadora de tecla *(f)*
Fr perforatrice à clavier *(f)*
It perforatrice à tastiera *(f)*

perfurar *vb* Pt
De lochen
En punch
Es perforar
Fr perforer
It perforare

perifericamente limitado Pt
De peripherebegrenzt
En peripheral-limited
Es limitado por los periféricos
Fr limité par les périphériques
It limitato per periferichi

période de validité *(f)* Fr
De Verweilzeit *(f)*
En retention period
Es período de retención *(m)*
It tempo di ritenzione *(m)*
Pt periodo de retenção *(m)*

periodo de retenção *(m)* Pt
De Verweilzeit *(f)*
En retention period
Es período de retención *(m)*
Fr période de validité *(f)*
It tempo di ritenzione *(m)*

período de retención *(m)* Es
De Verweilzeit *(f)*
En retention period
Fr période de validité *(f)*
It tempo di ritenzione *(m)*
Pt periodo de retenção *(m)*

peripheral controller En
De peripheres Steuergerät *(n)*
Es controlador periférico *(m)*
Fr contrôleur de périphérique(s) *(m)*
It unità di controllo satellite *(f)*
Pt controlador periférico *(m)*

peripheral-limited *adj* En
De peripherebegrenzt
Es limitado por los periféricos
Fr limité par les périphériques
It limitato per periferichi
Pt perifericamente limitado

peripheral processor En
De peripheres Verarbeitungs- gerät *(n)*
Es procesador periférico *(m)*
Fr unité centrale de périphériques *(f)*
It unità di elaborazione satellite *(f)*
Pt processador periférico *(m)*

peripheral transfer En
De periphere Übergabe *(f)*
Es transferencia periférica *(f)*
Fr transfert entre périphériques *(m)*
It trasferimento periferico *(m)*
Pt transferência periférica *(f)*

peripheral unit En
De periphere Einheit *(f)*
Es unidad periférica *(f)*
Fr unité périphérique *(f)*
It unità periferica *(f)*
Pt unidade periférica *(f)*

peripherebegrenzt *adj* De
En peripheral-limited
Es limitado por los periféricos
Fr limité par les périphériques
It limitato per periferichi
Pt perifericamente limitado

periphere Einheit *(f)* De
En peripheral unit
Es unidad periférica *(f)*
Fr unité périphérique *(f)*
It unità periferica *(f)*
Pt unidade periférica *(f)*

peripheres Steuergerät *(n)* De
En peripheral controller
Es controlador periférico *(m)*
Fr contrôleur de périphérique(s) *(m)*
It unità di controllo satellite *(f)*
Pt controlador periférico *(m)*

peripheres Verarbeitungsgerät *(n)* De
En peripheral processor
Es procesador periférico *(m)*
Fr unité centrale de périphériques *(f)*
It unità di elaborazione satellite *(f)*
Pt processador periférico *(m)*

periphere Übergabe *(f)* De
En peripheral transfer
Es transferencia periférica *(f)*
Fr transfert entre périphériques *(m)*
It trasferimento periferico *(m)*
Pt transferência periférica *(f)*

périphérique d'entrée *(m)* Fr
De Eingangsvorrichtung *(f)*
En input device
Es dispositivo de entrada *(m)*
It organo di entrata *(m)*
Pt dispositivo de entrada *(m)*

périphérique entrée-sortie *(m)* Fr
De Eingangs-Ausgangs-vorrichtung *(f)*
En input-output device
Es dispositivo de entrada-salida *(m)*
It organo di entrata-uscita *(m)*
Pt dispositivo de entrada-sair *(m)*

perla *(f)* *n* Es, It
De Kugel *(f)*
En bead
Fr perle *(f)*
Pt boleado *(m)*

perle *(f)* *n* Fr
De Kugel *(f)*
En bead
Es perla *(f)*
It perla *(f)*
Pt boleado *(m)*

Perlspeicher *(m)* *n* De
En bubble memory
Es memoria de burbuja *(f)*
Fr mémoire à bulles *(f)*
It memoria a bolle *(f)*
Pt memória de bolha *(f)*

permanent memory En
De Dauerspeicher *(m)*
Es memoria permanente *(f)*
Fr mémoire permanente *(f)*
It memoria permanente *(f)*
Pt memória permanente *(f)*

permutation circulaire *(f)* Fr
De Ringschiebung *(f)*
En ring shift
Es desplazamiento en anillo *(m)*
It dislocamento ad anello *(m)*
Pt mudança anular *(f)*

personal computer En
De persönlicher Rechner *(m)*
Es ordenador personal *(m)*
Fr ordinateur privé *(m)*
It calcolatore personale *(m)*
Pt computador pessoal *(m)*

Personal-Maschinen Schnittstelle *(f)* De
En man-machine interface
Es acoplamiento hombre-máquina *(m)*
Fr interface homme-machine *(f)*
It interfaccia uomo-macchina *(f)*
Pt interface homem-máquina *(f)*

Personal-Maschinen Wechselwirkung *(f)* De
En man-machine interaction
Es interacción hombre-máquina *(f)*
Fr interaction homme-machine *(f)*
It interazione uomo-macchina *(f)*
Pt interacção homem-máquina *(f)*

persönlicher Rechner *(m)* De
En personal computer
Es ordenador personal *(m)*
Fr ordinateur privé *(m)*
It calcolatore personale *(m)*
Pt computador pessoal *(m)*

perte *(f)* *n* Fr
De Verlust *(m)*
En loss
Es pérdida *(f)*
It perdita *(f)*
Pt perda *(f)*

perturbação *(f)* *n* Pt
De Defekt *(m)*
En bug
Es defecto *(m)*
Fr défaut *(m)*
It difetto *(m)*

pesquisar *vb* Pt
De fühlen
En sense
Es detectar
Fr détecter
It rilevare

petit ordinateur de bureau *(m)* Fr
De Tischrechner *(m)*
En desk-top computer
Es ordenador de mesa *(m)*
It elaboratore da tavolo *(m)*
Pt computador de mesa *(m)*

Pfeiler *(m)* *n* De
En column
Es columna *(f)*
Fr colonne *(f)*
It colonna *(f)*
Pt coluna *(f)*

phase *(f)* *n* Fr
De Schritt *(m)*
En step
Es paso *(m)*
It passo *(m)*
Pt passo *(m)*

phase de traitement *(f)* Fr
De Ablauf *(m)*
En computer run
Es pasada de ordenador *(f)*
It esecuzione di elaboratore *(f)*
Pt passagem de computador *(f)*

phase opératoire *(f)* Fr
De Aktivierungsphase *(f)*
En execute phase
Es fase de ejecución *(f)*
It fase di esecuzione *(f)*
Pt fase de execução *(f)*

photo-style *(f)* *n* Fr
De Lichtschreiber *(m)*
En light pen
Es lápiz fotosensible *(f)*
It penna luminosa *(f)*
Pt caneta de luz *(f)*

physical file En
De physische Datei *(f)*
Es fichero físico *(m)*
Fr fichier physique *(m)*
It file fisico *(m)*
Pt arquivo físico *(m)*

physische Datei *(f)* De
En physical file
Es fichero físico *(m)*
Fr fichier physique *(m)*
It file fisico *(m)*
Pt arquivo físico *(m)*

pianificatore dei lavoratori *(m)* It
De Jobscheduler *(m)*
En job scheduler
Es planificador de trabajos *(m)*
Fr programmateur des travaux *(m)*
Pt planificador de trabalhos *(m)*

pianificazione *(f)* *n* It
De Arbeitsplanung *(f)*
En scheduling
Es planificación *(f)*
Fr planification *(f)*
Pt planificação *(f)*

piège *(m)* *n* Fr
De Haftstelle *(f)*
En trap
Es trampa *(f)*
It trappola *(f)*
Pt armadilha *(f)*

piéger *vb* Fr
De fangen
En trap
Es entrampar
It intrappolare
Pt apanhar

pila *(f)* *n* Es
De Stapel *(m)*
En stack
Fr pile *(f)*
It armadio *(m)*
Pt pilha *(f)*

pila de discos *(f)* Es
De Magnetplatten-installation *(f)*
En disk pack
Fr dispac *(m)*
It pacco di dischi *(m)*
Pt pacote de discos *(m)*

pile *(f)* *n* Fr
De Stapel *(m)*
En stack
Es pila *(f)*
It armadio *(m)*
Pt pilha *(f)*

pilha *(f)* *n* Pt
De Stapel *(m)*
En stack
Es pila *(f)*
Fr pile *(f)*
It armadio *(m)*

pinboard *n* En
De Steckplatte *(f)*
Es cuadro de alfileres *(m)*
Fr tableau à aiguilles *(m)*
It pannello a spine *(m)*

Pt prancheta de alfinetes *(f)*

pista *(f) n* Es, Pt
De Spur *(f)*
En track
Fr piste *(f)*
It banda *(f)*

pista *(f) n* It
De Leitweg *(m)*
En route
Es ruta *(f)*
Fr itinéraire *(m)*
Pt caminho *(m)*

pista de auditoría *(f)* Es
De Prüfliste *(f)*
En audit trail
Fr vérification à rebours *(f)*
It lista di verifica *(f)*
Pt trilho de verificação *(m)*

piste *(f) n* Fr
De Spur *(f)*
En track
Es pista *(f)*
It banda *(f)*
Pt pista *(f)*

piste d'entraînement de test *(f)* Fr
De Prüfstand *(m)*
En test-bed
Es bancada de prueba *(f)*
It banco di prova *(m)*
Pt mesa de ensaio *(f)*

placa de concerto *(f)* Pt
De Schalttafel *(f)*
En patchboard
Es cuadro de control *(m)*
Fr tableau de connexions *(m)*
It pannello di connessione *(m)*

placa de conexões eléctricas *(f)* Pt
De Steckerbrett *(n)*
En plugboard
Es cuadro de conexión *(m)*
Fr tableau de connexions *(m)*
It pannello di connessioni *(m)*

planificação *(f) n* Pt
De Arbeitsplanung *(f)*
En scheduling
Es planificación *(f)*
Fr planification *(f)*
It pianificazione *(f)*

planificación *(f) n* Es
De Arbeitsplanung *(f)*
En scheduling
Fr planification *(f)*
It pianificazione *(f)*
Pt planificação *(f)*

planificador de trabajos *(m)* Es
De Jobscheduler *(m)*
En job scheduler
Fr programmateur des travaux *(m)*
It pianificatore dei lavoratori *(m)*
Pt planificador de trabalhos *(m)*

planificador de trabalhos *(m)* Pt
De Jobscheduler *(m)*
En job scheduler
Es planificador de trabajos *(m)*
Fr programmateur des travaux *(m)*
It pianificatore dei lavoratori *(m)*

planification *(f) n* Fr
De Arbeitsplanung *(f)*
En scheduling
Es planificación *(f)*
It pianificazione *(f)*
Pt planificação *(f)*

Planzeichner *(m) n* De
En plotter
Es trazadora *(f)*
Fr traceur *(m)*
It tracciatore *(m)*
Pt plotador *(m)*

plaqueta *(f) n* Es
De Chip *(m)*
En chip
Fr puce *(f)*
It chip *(m)*
Pt lasca *(f)*

Platte *(f) n* De
En disc; disk
Es disco *(m)*
Fr disque *(m)*
It disco *(m)*
Pt disco *(m)*

Plattenantrieb *(m) n* De
En disk drive
Es unidad de discos *(f)*
Fr unité de disque(s) *(f)*
It unità a dischi *(f)*
Pt accionamento de disco *(m)*

Plattenbetriebsystem *(n) n* De
En disk-based operating system (DOS)
Es sistema operativo en discos *(m)*
Fr système d'exploitation à disques *(m)*
It sistema operativo su disco *(m)*
Pt sistema de operação baseado em discos *(m)*

Plattendatei *(f) n* De
En disk file
Es fichero de discos *(m)*
Fr fichier sur disque *(m)*
It file su disco *(m)*
Pt arquivo de discos *(m)*

playback head En
De Wiedergabekopf *(m)*
Es cabeza reproductora *(f)*
Fr tête de lecture *(f)*
It testina di lettura *(f)*
Pt cabeça de playback *(f)*

plotador *(m) n* Pt
De Planzeichner *(m)*
En plotter
Es trazadora *(f)*
Fr traceur *(m)*
It tracciatore *(m)*

plotador de gráficos *(m)* Pt
De Kurvenzeichner *(m)*
En graph plotter
Es trazador de curvas *(m)*
Fr traceur de courbes *(m)*
It tracciatore di grafici *(m)*

plotador de leito plano *(m)* Pt
De Flachtisch-kurvenzeichner *(m)*
En flat-bed plotter
Es trazador de base plana *(m)*
Fr traceur à plat *(m)*
It tracciatore in piano *(m)*

plotador de tambor *(m)* Pt
De Trommelkurven-zeichner *(m)*
En drum plotter
Es trazador a tambor *(m)*
Fr traceur à tambour *(m)*
It tracciatore a tamburo *(m)*

plotador incremental *(m)* Pt
De schrittweiser Kurvenzeichner *(m)*
En incremental plotter
Es trazador incremental *(m)*
Fr traceur incrémentiel *(m)*
It tracciatore incrementale *(m)*

plotador X-Y *(m)* Pt
De X-Y-Kurvenzeichner *(m)*
En X-Y plotter
Es trazador X-Y *(m)*
Fr traceur X-Y *(m)*
It tracciatore X-Y *(m)*

plotter *n* En
De Planzeichner *(m)*
Es trazadora *(f)*
Fr traceur *(m)*
It tracciatore *(m)*
Pt plotador *(m)*

plug *n* En
De Stecker *(m)*
Es clavija *(f)*
Fr fiche *(f)*
It spina *(f)*
Pt ficha eléctrica *(f)*

plugboard *n* En
De Steckerbrett *(n)*
Es cuadro de conexión *(m)*
Fr tableau de connexions *(m)*

It pannello di connessioni *(m)*
Pt placa de conexões eléctricas *(f)*

plus zone En
De Pluszone *(f)*
Es zona positiva *(f)*
Fr zone plus *(f)*
It zona più *(f)*
Pt zona mais *(f)*

Pluszone *(f) n* De
En plus zone
Es zona positiva *(f)*
Fr zone plus *(f)*
It zona più *(f)*
Pt zona mais *(f)*

pneumatic computer En
De pneumatischer Computer *(m)*
Es ordenador neumático *(m)*
Fr ordinateur pneumatique *(m)*
It elaboratore pneumatico *(m)*
Pt computador pneumático *(m)*

pneumatischer Computer *(m)* De
En pneumatic computer
Es ordenador neumático *(m)*
Fr ordinateur pneumatique *(m)*
It elaboratore pneumatico *(m)*
Pt computador pneumático *(m)*

point à la base *(m)* Fr
De Basispunkt *(m)*
En radix point
Es coma de la base *(f)*
It punto di base *(m)*
Pt ponto de raiz *(m)*

point d'accès entrée-sortie *(m)* Fr
De Eingangs-Ausgangsanschluβ *(m)*
En input-output port
Es puerta de entrada-salida *(f)*
It porto entrata-uscita *(m)*
Pt abertura de entrada-sair *(f)*

point de chargement *(m)* Fr
De Ladeadresse *(f)*
En load point
Es punto de carga *(m)*
It punto di caricamento *(m)*
Pt ponto de carga *(m)*

point de contrôle *(m)* Fr
De Kontrollpunkt *(m)*
En checkpoint
Es punto de control *(m)*
It punto di controllo *(m)*
Pt ponto de verificação *(m)*

point d'entrée *(m)* Fr
De Eingangspunkt *(m)*
En entry point
Es punto de entrada *(m)*
It punto di entrata *(m)*
Pt ponto de entrada *(m)*

point de reprise *(m)* Fr
De Wiederholungspunkt; Wiederstartspunkt *(m)*
En rerun point; restart point
Es punto de reanudación; punto de reanudación de pasada *(m)*
It punto di riesecuzion; punto di ripartire *(m)*
Pt ponto de nova passagem; ponto de rearranque *(m)*

point de rupture *(m)* Fr
De Ausgleichspunkt *(m)*
En breakpoint
Es punto de interrupción *(m)*
It punto di arresto *(m)*
Pt ponto de rotura *(m)*

point de vidage *(m)* Fr
De Speichauszugspunkt *(m)*
En dump point
Es punto de vaciado *(m)*
It punto di dump *(m)*
Pt ponto de descarga *(m)*

pointer *n* En
De Zeiger *(m)*
Es indicador *(m)*
Fr indicateur *(m)*
It lancetta *(f)*
Pt ponteiro *(m)*

point-mode display En
De punktweise Darstellung *(f)*
Es representación de modo puntual *(f)*
Fr affichage mode point par point *(m)*
It mostra di modo punto a punto *(f)*
Pt display de modo pontual *(m)*

polarisação *(f) n* Pt
De Vorspannung *(f)*
En bias
Es polarización *(f)*
Fr polarisation *(f)*
It polarizzazione *(f)*

polarisation *(f) n* Fr
De Vorspannung *(f)*
En bias
Es polarización *(f)*
It polarizzazione *(f)*
Pt polarisação *(f)*

polariser *vb* Fr
De vorspannen
En bias
Es polarizar
It polarizzare
Pt polarizar

polarización *(f) n* Es
De Vorspannung *(f)*
En bias
Fr polarisation *(f)*
It polarizzazione *(f)*
Pt polarisação *(f)*

polarizar *vb* Es, Pt
De vorspannen
En bias
Fr polariser
It polarizzare

polarizzare *vb* It
De vorspannen
En bias
Es polarizar
Fr polariser
Pt polarizar

polarizzazione *(f) n* It
De Vorspannung *(f)*
En bias
Es polarización *(f)*
Fr polarisation *(f)*
Pt polarisação *(f)*

Polish notation En
De polnische Darstellung *(f)*
Es notación polaca *(f)*
Fr notation polonaise *(f)*
It notazione polacca *(f)*
Pt notação polaca *(f)*

polnische Darstellung *(f)* De
En Polish notation
Es notación polaca *(f)*
Fr notation polonaise *(f)*
It notazione polacca *(f)*
Pt notação polaca *(f)*

polygon clipping En
De Vieleckbegrenzung *(f)*
Es recorte poligonal *(m)*
Fr écrêtage polygone *(m)*
It limitazione poligonale *(f)*
Pt recorte poligonal *(m)*

poner en un índice Es
De indizieren
En index
Fr faire un index
It metter nell'indice
Pt pôr em índex

ponteiro *(m) n* Pt
De Zeiger *(m)*
En pointer
Es indicador *(m)*
Fr indicateur *(m)*
It lancetta *(f)*

ponto de carga *(m)* Pt
De Ladeadresse *(f)*
En load point
Es punto de carga *(m)*
Fr point de chargement *(m)*
It punto di caricamento *(m)*

ponto de descarga *(m)* Pt
De Speichauszugspunkt *(m)*
En dump point
Es punto de vaciado *(m)*
Fr point de vidage *(m)*
It punto di dump *(m)*

ponto de entrada *(m)* Pt
De Eingangspunkt *(m)*
En entry point
Es punto de entrada *(m)*
Fr point d'entrée *(m)*
It punto di entrata *(m)*

ponto de nova passagem *(m)* Pt
De Wiederholungspunkt *(m)*
En rerun point
Es punto de reanudación de pasada *(m)*
Fr point de reprise *(m)*
It punto di riesecuzione *(m)*

ponto de raiz *(m)* Pt
De Basispunkt *(m)*
En radix point
Es coma de la base *(f)*
Fr point à la base *(m)*
It punto di base *(m)*

ponto de rearranque *(m)* Pt
De Wiederstartspunkt *(m)*
En restart point
Es punto de reanudación *(m)*
Fr point de reprise *(m)*
It punto di ripartire *(m)*

ponto de rotura *(m)* Pt
De Ausgleichspunkt *(m)*
En breakpoint
Es punto de interrupción *(m)*
Fr point de rupture *(m)*
It punto di arresto *(m)*

ponto de verificação *(m)* Pt
De Kontrollpunkt *(m)*
En checkpoint
Es punto de control *(m)*
Fr point de contrôle *(m)*
It punto di controllo *(m)*

pôr em índex Pt
De indizieren
En index
Es poner en un índice
Fr faire un index
It metter nell'indice

porta *(f)* *n* It, Pt
De Tor *(n)*
En gate
Es puerta *(f)*
Fr porte *(f)*

porta AND *(f)* Pt
De UND-Schaltung *(f)*
En AND-gate
Es puerta Y *(f)*
Fr porte ET *(f)*
It porta E *(f)*

portabilità *(f)* *n* It
De Datenaustauschbarkeit *(f)*
En portability
Es facultad de ser portátil *(f)*
Fr portabilité *(f)*
Pt portatilidade *(f)*

portabilité *(f)* *n* Fr
De Datenaustauschbarkeit *(f)*
En portability
Es facultad de ser portátil *(f)*
It portabilità *(f)*
Pt portatilidade *(f)*

portability *n* En
De Datenaustauschbarkeit *(f)*
Es facultad de ser portátil *(f)*
Fr portabilité *(f)*
It portabilità *(f)*
Pt portatilidade *(f)*

portable computer En
De tragbarer Computer *(m)*
Es ordenador portátil *(m)*
Fr ordinateur portatif *(m)*
It calcolatore portabile *(m)*
Pt computador portátil *(m)*

porta-cabeças *(m)* *n* Pt
De Kennsatz *(m)*
En header
Es cabecera *(f)*
Fr en-tête *(f)*
It testata *(f)*

porta de anticoincidência *(f)* Pt
De Antizusammentreffensschaltung *(f)*
En anticoincidence gate
Es puerta de anticoincidencia *(f)*
Fr porte anti-coïncidence *(f)*
It porta di anticoincidenza *(f)*

porta de coincidência *(f)* Pt
De Zusammentreffens-Schaltung *(f)*
En coincidence gate
Es puerta de coincidencia *(f)*
Fr porte à coïncidence *(f)*
It porta di coincidenza *(f)*

porta di anticoincidenza *(f)* It
De Antizusammentreffensschaltung *(f)*
En anticoincidence gate
Es puerta de anticoincidencia *(f)*
Fr porte anti-coïncidence *(f)*
Pt porta de anticoincidência *(f)*

porta di coincidenza *(f)* It
De Zusammentreffens-Schaltung *(f)*
En coincidence gate
Es puerta de coincidencia *(f)*
Fr porte à coïncidence *(f)*
Pt porta de coincidência *(f)*

portador *(m)* *n* Es, Pt
De Ladungsträger *(m)*
En carrier
Fr courant porteur *(m)*
It supporto *(m)*

porta E *(f)* It
De UND-Schaltung *(f)*
En AND-gate
Es puerta Y *(f)*
Fr porte ET *(f)*
Pt porta AND *(f)*

porta logica *(f)* It
De Verknüpfungstor *(n)*
En logic gate
Es puerta lógica *(f)*
Fr porte logique *(f)*
Pt porta lógica *(f)*

porta lógica *(f)* Pt
De Verknüpfungstor *(n)*
En logic gate
Es puerta lógica *(f)*
Fr porte logique *(f)*
It porta logica *(f)*

porta NAND *(f)* It, Pt
De NICHT-UND Schaltung *(f)*
En NAND-gate
Es puerta NO-Y *(f)*
Fr porte NON-ET *(f)*

porta NÃO *(f)* Pt
De NOT-Schaltung *(f)*
En NOT-gate
Es puerta NO *(f)*
Fr porte NON *(f)*
It porta NO *(f)*

porta NO *(f)* It
De NOT-Schaltung *(f)*
En NOT-gate
Es puerta NO *(f)*
Fr porte NON *(f)*
Pt porta NÃO *(f)*

porta NOR *(f)* It
De NOR-Schaltung *(f)*
En NOR-gate
Es puerta NI *(f)*
Fr porte NON-OU *(f)*

porta o *(f)* It
De ODER-Schaltung *(f)*
En OR-gate
Es puerta O *(f)*
Fr porte OU *(f)*
Pt porta OR *(f)*

porta OR *(f)* Pt
De ODER-Schaltung *(f)*
En OR-gate
Es puerta O *(f)*
Fr porte OU *(f)*
It porta o *(f)*

portatilidade *(f)* *n* Pt
De Datenaustauschbarkeit *(f)*
En portability

Es facultad de ser portátil *(f)*
Fr portabilité *(f)*
It portabilità *(f)*

porte *(f) n* Fr
De Schaltung *(f)*
En gate
Es puerta *(f)*
It porta *(f)*
Pt porta *(f)*

porte à coïncidence *(f)* Fr
De Zusammentreffens-Schaltung *(f)*
En coincidence gate
Es puerta de coincidencia *(f)*
It porta di coincidenza *(f)*
Pt porta de coincidência *(f)*

porte anti-coïncidence *(f)* Fr
De Antizusammen-treffensschaltung *(f)*
En anticoincidence gate
Es puerta de anticoincidencia *(f)*
It porta di anticoincidenza *(f)*
Pt porta de anticoincidência *(f)*

porte-carte *(m) n* Fr
De Kartenkorb *(m)*
En card cage
Es caja de fichas *(f)*
It scatola schede *(f)*
Pt gaiola de ficha *(f)*

porte ET *(f)* Fr
De UND-Schaltung *(f)*
En AND-gate
Es puerta Y *(f)*
It porta E *(f)*
Pt porta AND *(f)*

porte logique *(f)* Fr
De Verknüpfungstor *(n)*
En logic gate
Es puerta lógica *(f)*
It porta logica *(f)*
Pt porta lógica *(f)*

porte NON *(f)* Fr
De NOT-Schaltung *(f)*
En NOT-gate
Es puerta NO *(f)*
It porta NO *(f)*
Pt porta NÃO *(f)*

porte NON-ET *(f)* Fr
De NICHT-UND-Schaltung *(f)*
En NAND-gate
Es puerta NO-Y *(f)*
It porta NAND *(f)*
Pt porta NAND *(f)*

porte NON-OU *(f)* Fr
De NOR-Schaltung *(f)*
En NOR-gate
Es puerta NI *(f)*
It porta NOR *(f)*
Pt porta NOR *(f)*

porte OU *(f)* Fr
De ODER-Schaltung *(f)*
En OR-gate
Es puerta O *(f)*
It porta o *(f)*
Pt porta OR *(f)*

porto entrata-uscita *(m)* It
De Eingangs-Ausgangsanschluß *(m)*
En input-output port
Es puerta de entrada-salida *(f)*
Fr point d'accès entrée-sortie *(m)*
Pt abertura de entrada-sair *(f)*

pós-editar *vb* Pt
De nachredaktieren
En post-edit
Es post-editar
Fr post-éditer
It posredigere

posição de perfuração *(f)* Pt
De Lochstellung *(f)*
En punching position
Es posición de perforación *(f)*
Fr position de perforation *(f)*
It posizione di perforazione *(f)*

posición *(f) n* Es
De Dateilage *(f)*
En location
Fr emplacement *(m)*
It locazione *(f)*
Pt localização *(f)*

posición de bit *(f)* Es
De Binärzeichenortung *(f)*
En bit location
Fr position de bits *(f)*
It locazione del bit *(f)*
Pt localização de bit *(f)*

posición de perforación *(f)* Es
De Lochstellung *(f)*
En punching position
Fr position de perforation *(f)*
It posizione di perforazione *(f)*
Pt posição de perfuração *(f)*

posición protegida *(f)* Es
De geschützter Ort *(m)*
En protected location
Fr position protégée *(f)*
It locazione protetta *(f)*
Pt localização protegida *(f)*

positional notation En
De Stellendarstellung *(f)*
Es notación posicional *(f)*
Fr représentation positionnelle *(f)*
It notazione di posizione *(f)*
Pt notação posicional *(f)*

position de bits *(f)* Fr
De Binärzeichenortung *(f)*
En bit location
Es posición de bit *(f)*
It locazione del bit *(f)*
Pt localização de bit *(f)*

position de perforation *(f)* Fr
De Lochstellung *(f)*
En punching position
Es posición de perforación *(f)*
It posizione di perforazione *(f)*
Pt posição de perfuração *(f)*

position protégée *(f)* Fr
De geschützter Ort *(m)*
En protected location
Es posición protegida *(f)*
It locazione protetta *(f)*
Pt localização protegida *(f)*

posizione di perforazione *(f)* It
De Lochstellung *(f)*
En punching position
Es posición de perforación *(f)*
Fr position de perforation *(f)*
Pt posição de perfuração *(f)*

posredigere *vb* It
De nachredaktieren
En post-edit
Es post-editar
Fr post-éditer
Pt pós-editar

poste de visualisation *(m)* Fr
De Anzeigestation *(f)*
En display station
Es estación de visualización *(f)*
It posto di visualizzazione *(m)*
Pt estação de visualização *(f)*

poste d'exploitation *(m)* Fr
De Arbeitsstation *(f)*
En operating station
Es estación operativa *(f)*
It posto funzionante *(m)*
Pt estação de operação *(f)*

poste d'interrogation *(m)* Fr
De Abfragestation *(f)*
En inquiry terminal
Es terminal de interrogación *(m)*
It terminale per informazioni *(m)*
Pt terminal de indagação *(m)*

post-edit *vb* En
De nachredaktieren
Es post-editar
Fr post-éditer
It posredigere
Pt pós-editar

post-editar *vb* Es
De nachredaktieren
En post-edit
Fr post-éditer
It posredigere
Pt pós-editar

post-éditer *vb* Fr
De nachredaktieren
En post-edit
Es post-editar
It posredigere
Pt pós-editar

poste du réseau *(m)* Fr
De Teilnehmerstation *(f)*
En subscriber station
Es estación de una red *(f)*
It posto d'abbonato *(m)*
Pt estação de subscritor *(f)*

post-mortem dump En
De Speicherauszug nach dem Tode *(m)*
Es vaciado póstumo *(m)*
Fr vidage d'autopsie *(m)*
It dump di autopsia *(m)*
Pt descarregador de autópsia *(m)*

post-mortem routine En
De Programm nach dem Tode *(n)*
Es rutina póstuma *(f)*
Fr programme d'autopsie *(m)*
It routine di autopsia *(f)*
Pt rotina de autópsia *(f)*

posto d'abbonato *(m)* It
De Teilnehmerstation *(f)*
En subscriber station
Es estación de una red *(f)*
Fr poste du réseau *(m)*
Pt estação de subscritor *(f)*

posto di visualizzazione *(m)* It
De Anzeigestation *(f)*
En display station
Es estación de visualización *(f)*
Fr poste de visualisation *(m)*
Pt estação de visualização *(f)*

posto funzionante *(m)* It
De Arbeitsstation *(f)*
En operating station
Es estación operativa *(f)*
Fr poste d'exploitation *(m)*
Pt estação de operação *(f)*

prancheta de alfinetes *(f)* Pt
De Steckplatte *(f)*
En pinboard
Es cuadro de alfileres *(m)*
Fr tableau à aiguilles *(m)*
It pannello a spine *(m)*

Präzision *(f)* *n* De
En precision
Es precisión *(f)*
Fr précision *(f)*
It precisione *(f)*
Pt precisão *(f)*

pré-amazenar *vb* Pt
De vorspeichern
En pre-store
Es almacenar previamente
Fr pré-enregistrer
It preregistrare

precisão *(f)* *n* Pt
De Präzision *(f)*
En precision
Es precisión *(f)*
Fr précision *(f)*
It precisione *(f)*

precisão dupla *(f)* Pt
De Doppelgenauigkeit *(f)*
En double precision
Es doble precisión *(f)*
Fr double précision *(f)*
It precisione doppia *(f)*

precisão tripla *(f)* Pt
De dreifache Präzision *(f)*
En triple precision
Es precisión triple *(f)*
Fr précision triple *(f)*
It precisione tripla *(f)*

precision *n* En
De Präzision *(f)*
Es precisión *(f)*
Fr précision *(f)*
It precisione *(f)*
Pt precisão *(f)*

précision *(f)* *n* Fr
De Präzision *(f)*
En precision
Es precisión *(f)*
It precisione *(f)*
Pt precisão *(f)*

precisión *(f)* *n* Es
De Präzision *(f)*
En precision
Fr précision *(f)*
It precisione *(f)*
Pt precisão *(f)*

precisione *(f)* *n* It
De Präzision *(f)*
En precision
Es precisión *(f)*
Fr précision *(f)*
Pt precisão *(f)*

precisione doppia *(f)* It
De Doppelgenauigkeit *(f)*
En double precision
Es doble precisión *(f)*
Fr double précision *(f)*
Pt precisão dupla *(f)*

precisione tripla *(f)* It
De dreifache Präzision *(f)*
En triple precision
Es precisión triple *(f)*
Fr précision triple *(f)*
Pt precisão tripla *(f)*

precisión triple *(f)* Es
De dreifache Präzision *(f)*
En triple precision
Fr précision triple *(f)*
It precisione tripla *(f)*
Pt precisão tripla *(f)*

précision triple *(f)* Fr
De dreifache Präzision *(f)*
En triple precision
Es precisión triple *(f)*
It precisione tripla *(f)*
Pt precisão tripla *(f)*

pré-classificação *(f)* *n* Pt
De Vorsortierung *(f)*
En pre-sort
Es creación de monotonías *(f)*
Fr tri préalable *(m)*
It pre-selezione *(f)*

pré-classificado *vb* Pt
De vorsortieren
En pre-sort
Es crear monotonías
Fr trier préalablement
It pre-selezionare

pre-edit *vb* En
De vorredaktieren
Es preeditar
Fr prééditer
It pre-redigere
Pt pré-editar

preeditar *vb* Es
De vorredaktieren
En pre-edit
Fr prééditer
It pre-redigere
Pt pré-editar

pré-editar *vb* Pt
De vorredaktieren
En pre-edit
Es preeditar
Fr prééditer
It pre-redigere

prééditer *vb* Fr
De vorredaktieren
En pre-edit
Es preeditar
It pre-redigere
Pt pré-editar

pré-enregistrer *vb* Fr
De vorspeichern
En pre-store
Es almacenar previamente
It preregistrare
Pt pré-amazenar

prefix notation En
De Vorsatzdarstellung *(f)*
Es notación por prefijos *(f)*
Fr notation préfixée *(f)*
It notazione del prefisso *(f)*
Pt notação de prefixos *(f)*

première-génération *adj* Fr
De erstgeneration
En first-generation
Es primera-generación
It prima-generazione
Pt primeira-geração

premier entré, premier sorti *(m)* Fr
De Prioritätssteuerung *(f)*
En first in, first out (FIFO)
Es primero a llegar, primero que sale *(m)*
It dentro il primo, fuori il primo *(m)*
Pt primeiro a entrar, primeiro a sair *(m)*

prendre le complément de Fr
De ergänzen
En complement
Es complementar
It complementare
Pt complementar

preparação de dados *(f)* Pt
De Datenvorbereitung *(f)*
En data preparation
Es preparación de los datos *(f)*
Fr préparation des données *(f)*
It preparazione dei dati *(f)*

preparación de los datos *(f)* Es
De Datenvorbereitung *(f)*
En data preparation
Fr préparation des données *(f)*
It preparazione dei dati *(f)*
Pt preparação de dados *(f)*

préparation des données *(f)* Fr
De Datenvorbereitung *(f)*
En data preparation
Es preparación de los datos *(f)*
It preparazione dei dati *(f)*
Pt preparação de dados *(f)*

preparazione dei dati *(f)* It
De Datenvorbereitung *(f)*
En data preparation
Es preparación de los datos *(f)*
Fr préparation des données *(f)*
Pt preparação de dados *(f)*

pre-read head En
De Vorlesekopf *(m)*
Es cabeza de lectura previa *(f)*
Fr tête de première lecture *(f)*
It testina di pre-lettura *(f)*
Pt cabeça de pré-leitura *(f)*

pre-redigere *vb* It
De vorredaktieren
En pre-edit
Es preeditar
Fr prééditer
Pt pré-editar

preregistrare *vb* It
De vorspeichern
En pre-store
Es almacenar previamente
Fr pré-enregistrer
Pt pré-amazenar

pre-selezionare *vb* It
De vorsortieren
En pre-sort
Es crear monotonías
Fr trier préalablement
Pt pré-classificado

pre-selezione *(f) n* It
De Vorsortierung *(f)*
En pre-sort
Es creación de monotonías *(f)*
Fr tri préalable *(m)*
Pt pré-classificação *(f)*

presentación de almacenamiento *(f)* Es
De Speicheranzeige *(f)*
En storage display
Fr affichage d'enregistrement *(m)*
It visualizzazione di memoria *(f)*
Pt visualização de armazenamento *(f)*

presentación de trama *(f)* Es
De Rasteranzeige *(f)*
En raster display
Fr affichage tramé *(m)*
It visualizzazione trama *(f)*
Pt apresentação quadriculada *(f)*

presentar *vb* Es
De anzeigen
En display
Fr afficher
It visualizzare
Pt mostrar

présentation de l'impression *(f)* Fr
De Druckformat *(n)*
En print format
Es formato de impresión *(m)*
It formato di stampa *(m)*
Pt formato de impressão *(m)*

preset parameter En
De Festparameter *(m)*
Es parámetro definido previamente *(m)*
Fr paramètre pré-défini *(m)*
It parametro prestabilito *(m)*
Pt parâmetro previamente fixado *(m)*

pre-sort *n* En
De Vorsortierung *(f)*
Es creación de monotonías *(f)*
Fr tri préalable *(m)*
It pre-selezione *(f)*
Pt pré-classificação *(f)*

pre-sort *vb* En
De vorsortieren
Es crear monotonías
Fr trier préalablement
It pre-selezionare
Pt pré-classificado

pre-store *vb* En
De vorspeichern
Es almacenar previamente
Fr pré-enregistrer
It preregistrare
Pt pré-amazenar

preventative maintenance En
De vorbeugende Wartung *(f)*
Es mantenimiento preventivo *(m)*
Fr entretien préventif *(m)*
It manutenzione preventiva *(f)*
Pt manutenção preventiva *(f)*

prima-generazione *adj* It
De erstgeneration
En first-generation
Es primera-generación
Fr première-génération
Pt primeira-geração

Primärspeicher *(m) n* De
En primary store
Es memoria principal *(f)*
Fr mémoire centrale *(f)*
It memoria centrale *(f)*
Pt armazém primária *(m)*

primary store En
De Primärspeicher *(m)*
Es memoria principal *(f)*
Fr mémoire centrale *(f)*
It memoria centrale *(f)*
Pt armazém primária *(m)*

primeira-geração *adj* Pt
De erstgeneration
En first-generation
Es primera-generación
Fr première-génération
It prima-generazione

primeiro a entrar, primeiro a sair *(m)* Pt
De Prioritätssteuerung *(f)*
En first in, first out (FIFO)
Es primero a llegar, primero que sale *(m)*
Fr premier entré, premier sorti *(m)*
It dentro il primo, fuori il primo *(m)*

primera-generación *adj* Es
De erstgeneration
En first-generation
Fr première-génération
It prima-generazione
Pt primeira-geração

primero a llegar, primero que sale *(m)* Es
De Prioritätssteuerung *(f)*
En first in, first out (FIFO)
Fr premier entré, premier sorti *(m)*
It dentro il primo, fuori il primo *(m)*
Pt primeiro a entrar, primeiro a sair *(m)*

primitif *adj Fr*
De primitiv
En primitive
Es primitivo
It primitivo
Pt primitivo

primitiv *adj* De
En primitive
Es primitivo
Fr primitif
It primitivo
Pt primitivo

primitive *adj* En
De primitiv
Es primitivo
Fr primitif
It primitivo
Pt primitivo

primitivo *adj* Es, It, Pt
De primitiv
En primitive
Fr primitif

print barrel En
De Trommeldruckerfaß *(n)*
Es cilindro impresor *(m)*
Fr tambour d'impression *(m)*
It tamburo di stampa *(m)*
Pt cilindro impressor *(m)*

printer *n* En
De Drucker *(m)*
Es impresora *(f)*
Fr imprimante *(f)*
It stampatrice *(f)*
Pt impressora *(f)*

print format En
De Druckformat *(n)*
Es formato de impresión *(m)*
Fr présentation de l'impression *(f)*
It formato di stampa *(m)*
Pt formato de impressão *(m)*

printing punch En
De Drucklocher *(m)*
Es perforadora impresora *(f)*
Fr perforatrice imprimante *(f)*
It perforatrice di stampa *(f)*
Pt perfuradora de impressão *(f)*

printout *n* En
De Ausdruck *(m)*
Es vaciado a la impresora *(m)*
Fr sortie sur imprimante *(f)*
It stampato *(m)*
Pt impressão *(f)*

print wheel En
De Typenrad *(n)*
Es rueda de impresión *(f)*
Fr roue d'impression *(f)*
It ruota di stampa *(f)*
Pt roda impressora *(f)*

prioridad de interrupción *(f)* Es
De Unterbrechungs-priorität *(f)*
En interrupt priority
Fr interruption prioritaire *(f)*
It priorità di interruzione *(f)*
Pt prioridade de interrupção *(f)*

prioridade de interrupção *(f)* Pt
De Unterbrechungs-priorität *(f)*
En interrupt priority
Es prioridad de interrupción *(f)*
Fr interruption prioritaire *(f)*
It priorità di interruzione *(f)*

priorità di interruzione *(f)* It
De Unterbrechungs-priorität *(f)*
En interrupt priority
Es prioridad de interrupción *(f)*
Fr interruption prioritaire *(f)*
Pt prioridade de interrupção *(f)*

Prioritätssteuerung *(f) n* De
En first in, first out (FIFO)
Es primero a llegar, primero que sale *(m)*
Fr premier entré, premier sorti *(m)*
It dentro il primo, fuori il primo *(m)*
Pt primeiro a entrar, primeiro a sair *(m)*

priority indicator En
De Vorranganzeiger *(m)*
Es indicador de prioridad *(m)*
Fr indicateur prioritaire *(m)*
It indicatore di priorità *(m)*
Pt indicador de prioridade *(m)*

priority processing En
De Vorrangverarbeitung *(f)*
Es tratamiento por prioridad *(m)*
Fr traitement par priorités *(m)*
It elaborazione di priorità *(f)*
Pt processamento prioritário *(m)*

privacy *n* En
De Vertraulichkeit *(f)*
Es aspecto confidencial *(m)*
Fr confidentialité *(f)*
It riservatezza *(f)*
Pt aspecto confidencial *(m)*

probabilidad *(f) n* Es
De Wahrscheinlichkeit *(f)*
En probability
Fr probabilité *(f)*
It probabilità *(f)*
Pt probabilidade *(f)*

probabilidade *(f) n* Pt
De Wahrscheinlichkeit *(f)*
En probability
Es probabilidad *(f)*
Fr probabilité *(f)*
It probabilità *(f)*

probabilità *(f) n* It
De Wahrscheinlichkeit *(f)*
En probability
Es probabilidad *(f)*
Fr probabilité *(f)*
Pt probabilidade *(f)*

probabilité *(f) n* Fr
De Wahrscheinlichkeit *(f)*
En probability
Es probabilidad *(f)*
It probabilità *(f)*
Pt probabilidade *(f)*

probability *n* En
De Wahrscheinlichkeit *(f)*
Es probabilidad *(f)*
Fr probabilité *(f)*
It probabilità *(f)*
Pt probabilidade *(f)*

probar *vb* Es
De prüfen
En test
Fr essayer
It provare
Pt ensaiar

problembasierte Sprache *(f)* De
En problem-orientated language
Es lenguaje orientado a los problemas *(m)*
Fr langage orienté aux problèmes *(m)*
It linguaggio orientato alle probleme *(m)*
Pt linguagem orientada peros problemas *(f)*

Problembestimmung *(f) n* De
En problem definition
Es definición del problema *(f)*
Fr définition des problèmes *(f)*
It definizione del problema *(f)*
Pt definição do problema *(f)*

problem definition En
De Problembestimmung *(f)*
Es definición del problema *(f)*
Fr définition des problèmes *(f)*
It definizione del problema *(f)*
Pt definição do problema *(f)*

problem-orientated language En
De problembasierte Sprache *(f)*
Es lenguaje orientado a los problemas *(m)*
Fr langage orienté aux problèmes *(m)*
It linguaggio orientato alle probleme *(m)*
Pt linguagem orientada peros problemas *(f)*

procedimento *(m) n* Pt
De Verfahren *(n)*
En procedure
Es procedimiento *(m)*
Fr procédure *(f)*
It procedura *(f)*

procedimento de reentrância *(m)* Pt
De Wiedereintreter-routine *(f)*
En re-entrant procedure
Es procedimiento reentrable *(m)*
Fr procédure d'invariance *(f)*
It procedimento rientrante *(m)*

procedimento rientrante *(m)* It
De Wiedereintreter-routine *(f)*
En re-entrant procedure
Es procedimiento reentrable *(m)*
Fr procédure d'invariance *(f)*
Pt procedimento de reentrância *(m)*

procedimiento *(m) n* Es
De Verfahren *(n)*
En procedure
Fr procédure *(f)*
It procedura *(f)*
Pt procedimento *(m)*

procedimiento reentrable *(m)* Es
De Wiedereintreter-routine *(f)*
En re-entrant procedure
Fr procédure d'invariance *(f)*
It procedimento rientrante *(m)*
Pt procedimento de reentrância *(m)*

procedura *(f) n* It
De Verfahren *(n)*
En procedure
Es procedimiento *(m)*
Fr procédure *(f)*
Pt procedimento *(m)*

procedure *n* En
De Verfahren *(n)*
Es procedimiento *(m)*
Fr procédure *(f)*
It procedura *(f)*
Pt procedimento *(m)*

procédure *(f) n* Fr
De Verfahren *(n)*
En procedure
Es procedimiento *(m)*
It procedura *(f)*
Pt procedimento *(m)*

procédure d'invariance *(f)* Fr
De Wiedereintreter-routine *(f)*
En re-entrant procedure
Es procedimiento reentrable *(m)*
It procedimento rientrante *(m)*
Pt procedimento de reentrância *(m)*

procedure-orientated language En
De verfahrenbasierte Sprache *(f)*
Es lenguaje orientado a los procedimientos *(m)*
Fr langage orienté à la procédure *(m)*
It linguaggio orientato alla procedura *(m)*
Pt linguagem orientada pelo procedimento *(f)*

procesador *(m) n* Es
De Verarbeiter *(m)*
En processor
Fr ordinateur *(m)*
It elaboratore *(m)*
Pt processor *(m)*

procesador de la palabra *(m)* Es
De Wortverarbeiter *(m)*
En word processor
Fr unité de traitement de textes *(f)*
It processadore di voce *(m)*
Pt processador de palavras *(m)*

procesador múltiple *(m)* Es
De Mehrprozessor-system *(n)*
En multiprocessor
Fr multicalculateur *(m)*
It elaboratore multiplo *(m)*
Pt multiprocessador *(m)*

procesador periférico *(m)* Es
De peripheres Verarbeitungsgerät *(n)*
En peripheral processor
Fr unité centrale de périphériques *(f)*
It unità di elaborazione satellite *(f)*
Pt processador periférico *(m)*

procesar *vb* Es
De bearbeiten
En process
Fr traiter
It elaborare
Pt processar

proceso *(m) n* Es
De Prozeβ *(m)*
En process
Fr processus *(m)*
It processo *(m)*
Pt processo *(m)*

proceso a distancia *(m)* Es
De Fernverarbeitung *(f)*
En remote processing
Fr télétraitement *(m)*
It elaborazione a distanza *(f)*
Pt tele-processamento *(m)*

proceso automático de datos *(m)* Es
De automatische Datenverarbeitung *(f)*
En automatic data processing
Fr traitement automatique de l'information (TAI) *(m)*
It elaborazione automatica dei dati *(f)*
Pt tratamento automático de dados *(m)*

proceso concurrente *(m)* Es
De verzahnt ablaufende Verarbeitung *(f)*
En concurrent processing
Fr traitement en simultané *(m)*
It elaborazione concorrente *(f)*
Pt processamento concorrente *(m)*

proceso de datos *(m)* Es
De Datenverarbeitung *(f)*
En data processing (DP)
Fr traitement de l'information *(m)*
It elaborazione dei dati *(f)*
Pt tratamento de dados *(m)*

proceso de la información *(m)* Es
De Informations-verarbeitung *(f)*
En information processing
Fr traitement de l'information *(m)*
It elaborazione delle informazioni *(f)*
Pt tratamento da informação *(m)*

proceso de programas subordinados *(m)* Es
De Hintergrundver-arbeitung *(f)*
En background processing
Fr traitement non prioritaire *(m)*

It elaborazione non precedenza *(f)*
Pt tratamento de plano de fundo *(m)*

proceso de transacciones *(m)* Es
De Transaktionsverarbeitung *(f)*
En transaction processing
Fr traitement transactionnel *(m)*
It elaborazione delle transazioni *(f)*
Pt processamento de transacções *(m)*

proceso distribuido *(m)* Es
De verteilte Verarbeitung *(f)*
En distributed processing
Fr informatique répartie *(f)*
It elaborazione ripartita *(f)*
Pt tratamento distribuido *(m)*

proceso electrónico de datos *(m)* Es
De elektronische Datenverarbeitung (EDV) *(f)*
En electronic data processing (EDP)
Fr traitement électronique des données (TED) *(m)*
It elaborazione elettronica dei dati *(f)*
Pt tratamento electrónico de dados *(m)*

proceso en paralelo *(m)* Es
De Parallelsimultanverarbeitung *(f)*
En parallel processing
Fr traitement en parallèle *(m)*
It elaborazione parallela *(f)*
Pt processamento paralelo *(m)*

proceso en serie *(m)* Es
De Reihenverarbeitung *(f)*
En serial processing
Fr traitement série *(m)*
It elaborazione in serie *(f)*
Pt processamento em série *(m)*

proceso en tiempo real *(m)* Es
De Uhrzeigverarbeitung *(f)*
En real-time processing
Fr traitement en temps réel *(m)*
It elaborazione in tempo reale *(f)*
Pt processamento de tempo real *(m)*

proceso integrado de datos *(m)* Es
De integrierte Datenverarbeitung *(f)*
En integrated data processing (IDP)
Fr traitement intégré de l'information (TII) *(m)*
It elaborazione integrata dei dati *(f)*
Pt tratamento integrado de dados *(m)*

proceso por lista *(m)* Es
De Listenverarbeitung *(f)*
En list processing
Fr traitement de liste *(m)*
It elaborazione della lista *(f)*
Pt processamento de lista *(m)*

proceso por lotes *(m)* Es
De Stapelverarbeitung *(f)*
En batch processing
Fr traitement par lot *(m)*
It elaborazione a lotti *(f)*
Pt tratamento por lotes *(m)*

proceso preferente *(m)* Es
De Vordergrundverarbeitung *(f)*
En foreground processing
Fr traitement de front *(m)*
It elaborazione di primo piano *(f)*
Pt processamento de primeiro plano *(m)*

proceso secuencial *(m)* Es
De Folgeverarbeitung *(f)*
En sequential processing
Fr traitement séquentiel *(m)*
It elaborazione sequenziale *(f)*
Pt processamento sequencial *(m)*

proceso vectorial *(m)* Es
De Vektorverarbeitung *(f)*
En vector processing
Fr traitement vectoriel *(m)*
It elaborazione di vettori *(f)*
Pt processamento de vectores *(m)*

process *n* En
De Prozeβ *(m)*
Es proceso *(m)*
Fr processus *(m)*
It processo *(m)*
Pt processo *(m)*

process *vb* En
De bearbeiten
Es procesar
Fr traiter
It elaborare
Pt processar

processador de palavras *(m)* Pt
De Wortverarbeiter *(m)*
En word processor
Es procesador de la palabra *(m)*
Fr unité de traitement de textes *(f)*
It processadore di voce *(m)*

processador duplo *(m)* Pt
De Parallelverarbeiter *(m)*
En dual processor
Es biprocesador *(m)*
Fr biprocesseur *(m)*
It elaboratore duplice *(m)*

processadore di voce *(m)* It
De Wortverarbeiter *(m)*
En word processor
Es procesador de la palabra *(m)*
Fr unité de traitement de textes *(f)*
Pt processador de palavras *(m)*

processador periférico *(m)* Pt
De peripheres Verarbeitungsgerät *(n)*
En peripheral processor
Es procesador periférico *(m)*
Fr unité centrale de périphériques *(f)*
It unità di elaborazione satellite *(f)*

processamento *(m) n* Pt
De Verarbeitung *(f)*
En processing
Es tratamiento *(m)*
Fr traitement *(m)*
It elaborazione *(f)*

processamento concorrente *(m)* Pt
De verzahnt ablaufende Verarbeitung *(f)*
En concurrent processing
Es proceso concurrente *(m)*
Fr traitement en simultané *(m)*
It elaborazione concorrente *(f)*

processamento de lista *(m)* Pt
De Listenverarbeitung *(f)*
En list processing
Es proceso por lista *(m)*
Fr traitement de liste *(m)*
It elaborazione della lista *(f)*

processamento de primeiro plano *(m)* Pt
De Vordergrundverarbeitung *(f)*
En foreground processing

Es proceso preferente *(m)*
Fr traitement de front *(m)*
It elaborazione di primo piano *(f)*

processamento de procura *(m)* Pt
De Abrufverarbeitung *(f)*
En demand processing
Es tratamiento inmediato *(m)*
Fr traitement immédiat *(m)*
It elaborazione a domanda *(f)*

processamento de tempo real *(m)* Pt
De Uhrzeigverarbeitung *(f)*
En real-time processing
Es proceso en tiempo real *(m)*
Fr traitement en temps réel *(m)*
It elaborazione in tempo reale *(f)*

processamento de transacções *(m)* Pt
De Transaktions-verarbeitung *(f)*
En transaction processing
Es proceso de transacciones *(m)*
Fr traitement transactionnel *(m)*
It elaborazione delle transazioni *(f)*

processamento de vectores *(m)* Pt
De Vektorverarbeitung *(f)*
En vector processing
Es proceso vectorial *(m)*
Fr traitement vectoriel *(m)*
It elaborazione di vettori *(f)*

processamento em série *(m)* Pt
De Reihenverarbeitung *(f)*
En serial processing
Es proceso en serie *(m)*
Fr traitement série *(m)*
It elaborazione in serie *(f)*

processamento paralelo *(m)* Pt
De Parallelsimultan-verarbeitung *(f)*
En parallel processing
Es proceso en paralelo *(m)*
Fr traitement en parallèle *(m)*
It elaborazione parallela *(f)*

processamento prioritário *(m)* Pt
De Vorrangverarbeitung *(f)*
En priority processing
Es tratamiento por prioridad *(m)*
Fr traitement par priorités *(m)*
It elaborazione di priorità *(f)*

processamento sequencial *(m)* Pt
De Folgeverarbeitung *(f)*
En sequential processing
Es proceso secuencial *(m)*
Fr traitement séquentiel *(m)*
It elaborazione sequenziale *(f)*

processar *vb* Pt
De bearbeiten
En process
Es procesar
Fr traiter
It elaborare

process control En
De Verfahrenssteuerung *(f)*
Es control de procesos *(m)*
Fr commande de processus *(f)*
It controllo di processo *(m)*
Pt controle de processo *(m)*

processing *n* En
De Verarbeitung *(f)*
Es tratamiento *(m)*
Fr traitement *(m)*
It elaborazione *(f)*
Pt processamento *(m)*

processo *(m) n* It, Pt
De Prozeß *(m)*
En process
Es proceso *(m)*
Fr processus *(m)*

processor *n* En; Pt *(m)*
De Verarbeiter *(m)*
Es procesador *(m)*
Fr ordinateur *(m)*
It elaboratore *(m)*

processor-limited *adj* En
De verarbeiter-beschränkt
Es limitado por la procesador
Fr limité par la vitesse de traitement
It limitato per velocitá di elaborazione
Pt limitado ao processor

processus *(m) n* Fr
De Prozeß *(m)*
En process
Es proceso *(m)*
It processo *(m)*
Pt processo *(m)*

procurar *vb* Pt
De suchen
En search
Es investigar
Fr chercher
It ricercare

production run En
De Fertigungslauf *(m)*
Es pasada de producción *(f)*
Fr passage de production *(m)*
It esecuzione di produzione *(f)*
Pt passagem de produção *(f)*

productive time En
De Fertigungszeit *(f)*
Es tiempo do producción *(m)*
Fr temps productif *(m)*
It tempo produttivo *(m)*
Pt tempo produtivo *(m)*

produzione basata sull'elaboratore *(f)* It
De computerunter-stützte Herstellung *(f)*
En computer-aided manufacture (CAM)
Es fabricación con la ayuda de ordenador *(f)*
Fr fabrication assistée par ordinateur (FAO) *(f)*
Pt manufactura com auxílio de computador *(f)*

progettazione automatica del sistema *(f)* It
De automatische Systemkonstruktion *(f)*
En automatic system design
Es diseño automático de sistemas *(m)*
Fr conception de système automatique *(f)*
Pt desenho de sistema automático *(m)*

progettazione basata sull'elaboratore *(f)* It
De computerunter-stützte Konstruktion *(f)*
En computer-aided design (CAD)
Es diseño con la ayuda de ordenador *(m)*
Fr conception assistée par ordinateur (CAO) *(f)*
Pt desenho com auxílio de computador (CAD) *(m)*

progiciel *(m) n* Fr
De Softwarepaket *(n)*
En software package
Es paqueta de soporte lógico *(m)*
It pacco di software *(m)*
Pt pacote de software *(m)*

program *n* En
De Programm *(n)*
Es programa *(m)*
Fr programme *(m)*
It programma *(m)*
Pt programa *(m)*

program *vb* En
De programmieren
Es programar
Fr programmer
It programmare
Pt programar

programa *(m) n* Es, Pt
De Programm *(n)*
En program
Fr programme *(m)*
It programma *(m)*

programa almacenado *(m)* Es
De gespeichertes Programm *(n)*
En stored program
Fr programme enregistré *(m)*
It programma memorizzato *(m)*
Pt programa armazenado *(m)*

programa armazenado *(m)* Pt
De gespeichertes Programm *(n)*
En stored program
Es programa almacenado *(m)*
Fr programme enregistré *(m)*
It programma memorizzato *(m)*

programable *adj* Es
De programmierbar
En programmable
Fr programmable
It programmabile
Pt programável

programação *(f) n* Pt
De Programmieren *(n)*
En programming
Es programación *(f)*
Fr programmation *(f)*
It programmazione *(f)*

programação de sistemas *(f)* Pt
De System-programmierung *(f)*
En systems programming
Es programación de sistemas *(f)*
Fr programmation d'étude *(f)*
It programmazione dei sistemi *(f)*

programação linear *(f)* Pt
De lineare Programmierung *(f)*
En linear programming (LP)
Es programación lineal *(f)*
Fr programmation linéaire (PL) *(f)*
It programmazione lineare *(f)*

programação matemática *(f)* Pt
De mathematische Programmierung *(f)*
En mathematical programming
Es programación matemática *(f)*
Fr programmation mathématique *(f)*
It programmazione matematica *(f)*

programação modular *(f)* Pt
De modulare Programmierung *(f)*
En modular programming
Es programación modular *(f)*
Fr programmation modulaire *(f)*
It programmazione modulare *(f)*

programação não linear *(f)* Pt
De nicht lineare Programmierung *(f)*
En nonlinear programming
Es programación no lineal *(f)*
Fr programmation non linéaire *(f)*
It programmazione non lineare *(f)*

programação para optimização *(f)* Pt
De optimale Programmierung *(f)*
En optimum programming
Es programación óptima *(f)*
Fr programmation optimum *(f)*
It programmazione dell'ottimo *(f)*

programação simbólica *(f)* Pt
De symbolische Programmierung *(f)*
En symbolic programming
Es programación simbólica *(f)*
Fr programmation symbolique *(f)*
It programmazione simbolica *(f)*

programación *(f) n* Es
De Programmieren *(n)*
En programming
Fr programmation *(f)*
It programmazione *(f)*
Pt programação *(f)*

programación de sistemas *(f)* Es
De System-programmierung *(f)*
En systems programming
Fr programmation d'étude *(f)*
It programmazione dei sistemi *(f)*
Pt programação de sistemas *(f)*

programación lineal *(f)* Es
De lineare Programmierung *(f)*
En linear programming (LP)
Fr programmation linéaire (PL) *(f)*
It programmazione lineare *(f)*
Pt programação linear *(f)*

programación matemática *(f)* Es
De mathematische Programmierung *(f)*
En mathematical programming
Fr programmation mathématique *(f)*
It programmazione matematica *(f)*
Pt programação matemática *(f)*

programación modular *(f)* Es
De modulare Programmierung *(f)*
En modular programming
Fr programmation modulaire *(f)*
It programmazione modulare *(f)*
Pt programação modular *(f)*

programación no lineal *(f)* Es
De nicht lineare Programmierung *(f)*
En nonlinear programming
Fr programmation non linéaire *(f)*
It programmazione non lineare *(f)*
Pt programação não linear *(f)*

programación óptima *(f)* Es
De optimale Programmierung *(f)*
En optimum programming
Fr programmation optimum *(f)*
It programmazione dell'ottimo *(f)*
Pt programação para optimização *(f)*

programación simbólica *(f)* Es
De symbolische Programmierung *(f)*
En symbolic programming
Fr programmation symbolique *(f)*
It programmazione simbolica *(f)*
Pt programação simbólica *(f)*

programa de aplicação *(m)* Pt
De Anwendungs-programm *(n)*
En application program
Es programa de aplicación *(m)*

Fr programme d'application *(m)*
It programma applicativo *(m)*

programa de aplicación *(m)* Es
De Anwendungs-programm *(n)*
En application program
Fr programme d'application *(m)*
It programma applicativo *(m)*
Pt programa de aplicação *(m)*

programa de computador *(m)* Pt
De Programm *(n)*
En computer program
Es programa de ordenador *(m)*
Fr programme machine *(m)*
It programma dell'elaboratore *(m)*

programa de edição *(m)* Pt
De Redakteur *(m)*
En editor
Es programa de edición *(m)*
Fr programme d'édition *(m)*
It programma di manipolazione *(m)*

programa de edición *(m)* Es
De Redakteur *(m)*
En editor
Fr programme d'édition *(m)*
It programma di manipolazione *(m)*
Pt programa de edição *(m)*

programa de ensaios *(m)* Pt
De Prüfprogramm *(n)*
En test program
Es programa de ensayo *(m)*
Fr programme d'essai *(m)*
It programma di prova *(m)*

programa de ensayo *(m)* Es
De Prüfprogramm *(n)*
En test program
Fr programme d'essai *(m)*
It programma di prova *(m)*
Pt programa de ensaios *(m)*

programa de execução *(m)* Pt
De Aktivierungs-programm *(n)*
En executive program
Es programa ejecutivo *(m)*
Fr programme superviseur *(m)*
It programma esecutivo *(m)*

programa de informes *(m)* Es
De Listenprogramm *(n)*
En report program
Fr programme des informations *(m)*
It programma di tabulati *(m)*
Pt programa de relatórios *(m)*

programa de objecto *(m)* Pt
De Zielprogramm *(n)*
En object program
Es programa objeto *(m)*
Fr programme objet *(m)*
It programma oggetto *(m)*

programa de ordenador *(m)* Es
De Programm *(n)*
En computer program
Fr programme machine *(m)*
It programma dell'elaboratore *(m)*
Pt programa de computador *(m)*

programa de origem *(m)* Pt
De Quellprogramm *(n)*
En source program
Es programa fuente *(m)*
Fr programme source *(m)*
It programma origine *(m)*

programa de plano de fundo *(m)* Pt
De Hintergrund-programm *(n)*
En background program
Es programa subordinado *(m)*
Fr programme non prioritaire *(m)*
It programma non precedenza *(m)*

programa de relatórios *(m)* Pt
De Listenprogramm *(n)*
En report program
Es programa de informes *(m)*
Fr programme des informations *(m)*
It programma di tabulati *(m)*

programa de supervisão *(m)* Pt
De Überwachungs-programm *(n)*
En supervisory program
Es programa supervisor *(m)*
Fr programme superviseur *(m)*
It programma di supervisione *(m)*

programa de utilidad *(m)* Es
De Hilfsprogramm *(n)*
En utility program
Fr programme utilitaire *(m)*
It programma di utilità *(m)*
Pt programa de utilidade *(m)*

programa de utilidade *(m)* Pt
De Hilfsprogramm *(n)*
En utility program
Es programa de utilidad *(m)*
Fr programme utilitaire *(m)*
It programma di utilità *(m)*

programa de verificação *(m)* Pt
De Prüfprogramm *(n)*
En checking program
Es programa de verificación *(m)*
Fr programme de contrôle *(m)*
It programma di controllo *(m)*

programa de verificación *(m)* Es
De Prüfprogramm *(n)*
En checking program
Fr programme de contrôle *(m)*
It programma di controllo *(m)*
Pt programa de verificação *(m)*

programado *adj* Es, Pt
De programmiert
En programmed
Fr programmé
It programmato

programador *(m) n* Es, Pt
De Programmierer *(m)*
En programmer
Fr programmeur *(m)*
It programmatore *(m)*

programador de computador *(m)* Pt
De Programmierer *(m)*
En computer programmer
Es programador de ordenador *(m)*
Fr programmateur *(m)*
It programmatore di elaboratori *(m)*

programador de ordenador *(m)* Es
De Programmierer *(m)*
En computer programmer
Fr programmateur *(m)*
It programmatore di elaboratori *(m)*
Pt programador de computador *(m)*

programa ejecutivo *(m)* Es
De Aktivierungs-programm *(n)*
En executive program

Fr programme superviseur *(m)*
It programma esecutivo *(m)*
Pt programa de execução *(m)*

programa estructurado *(m)* Es
De gegliedertes Programm *(n)*
En structured program
Fr programme structuré *(m)*
It programma strutturato *(m)*
Pt programa estruturado *(m)*

programa estruturado *(m)* Pt
De gegliedertes Programm *(n)*
En structured program
Es programa estructurado *(m)*
Fr programme structuré *(m)*
It programma strutturato *(m)*

programa fuente *(m)* Es
De Quellprogramm *(n)*
En source program
Fr programme source *(m)*
It programma origine *(m)*
Pt programa de origem *(m)*

programa heurístico *(m)* Es, Pt
De heuristisches Programm *(n)*
En heuristic program
Fr programme heuristique *(m)*
It programma euristico *(m)*

programa objeto *(m)* Es
De Zielprogramm *(n)*
En object program
Fr programme objet *(m)*
It programma oggetto *(m)*
Pt programa de objecto *(m)*

programar *vb* Es, Pt
De programmieren
En program
Fr programmer
It programmare

programa segmentado *(m)* Es, Pt
De segmentiertes Programm *(n)*
En segmented program
Fr programme segmenté *(m)*
It programma segmentato *(m)*

programas em cascada *(m pl)* Pt
De Kaskadenprogramme *(pl)*
En cascaded programs
Es programas en cascada *(m pl)*
Fr programmes en cascade *(m pl)*
It programmi in cascata *(m pl)*

programas en cascada *(m pl)* Es
De Kaskadenprogramme *(pl)*
En cascaded programs
Fr programmes en cascade *(m pl)*
It programmi in cascata *(m pl)*
Pt programas em cascada *(m pl)*

programa subordinado *(m)* Es
De Hintergrund-programm *(n)*
En background program
Fr programme non prioritaire *(m)*
It programma non precedenza *(m)*
Pt programa de plano de fundo *(m)*

programa supervisor *(m)* Es
De Überwachungs-programm *(n)*
En supervisory program
Fr programme superviseur *(m)*
It programma di supervisione *(m)*
Pt programa de supervisão *(m)*

programável *adj* Pt
De programmierbar
En programmable
Es programable
Fr programmable
It programmabile

program compatibility En
De Programm-verträglichkeit *(f)*
Es compatibilidad de programas *(f)*
Fr compatibilité-programme *(f)*
It compatibilità di programma *(f)*
Pt compatibilidade de programas *(f)*

program generator En
De Programmgeber *(m)*
Es generador de programas *(m)*
Fr générateur de programmes *(m)*
It generatore di programmi *(m)*
Pt gerador de programas *(m)*

program library En
De Programmbibliothek *(f)*
Es biblioteca de programas *(f)*
Fr bibliothèque de programmes *(f)*
It libreria dei programmi *(f)*
Pt biblioteca de programas *(f)*

Programm *(n)* *n* De
En computer program; program; routine
Es programa; programa de ordenador; rutina *(m m f)*
Fr programme; programme machine *(m)*
It programma; programma dell'elaboratore; routine *(m m f)*
Pt programa; programa de computador; rotina *(m m f)*

programma *(m)* *n* It
De Programm *(n)*
En program
Es programa *(m)*
Fr programme *(m)*
Pt programa *(m)*

programma applicativo *(m)* It
De Anwendungs-programm *(n)*
En application program
Es programa de aplicación *(m)*
Fr programme d'application *(m)*
Pt programa de aplicação *(m)*

Programmabbruch *(m)* *n* De
En abnormal termination
Es terminación anormal *(f)*
Fr terminaison anormale *(f)*
It conclusione anormale *(f)*
Pt terminação anormal *(f)*

programmabile *adj* It
De programmierbar
En programmable
Es programable
Fr programmable
Pt programável

programmable *adj* En, Fr
De programmierbar
Es programable
It programmabile
Pt programável

programmable read-only memory (PROM) En
De programmierbarer Festspeicher *(m)*
Es memoria fija programable *(f)*
Fr mémoire morte programmable *(f)*
It memoria soltanto di lettura programmabile *(f)*
Pt memória apenas de leitura programável *(f)*

programma dell'elaboratore *(m)* It
De Programm *(n)*
En computer program
Es programa de ordenador *(m)*
Fr programme machine *(m)*
Pt programa de computador *(m)*

programma di controllo *(m)* It
De Prüfprogramm *(n)*
En checking program
Es programa de verificación *(m)*
Fr programme de contrôle *(m)*
Pt programa de verificação *(m)*

programma di manipolazione *(m)* It
De Redakteur *(m)*
En editor
Es programa de edición *(m)*
Fr programme d'édition *(m)*
Pt programa de edição *(m)*

programma di manipolazione di testo *(m)* It
De Textredakteur *(m)*
En text editor
Es editor de texto *(m)*
Fr éditeur de textes *(m)*
Pt editor de textos *(m)*

programma di prova *(m)* It
De Prüfprogramm *(n)*
En test program
Es programa de ensayo *(m)*
Fr programme d'essai *(m)*
Pt programa de ensaios *(m)*

programma di supervisione *(m)* It
De Überwachungsprogramm *(n)*
En supervisory program
Es programa supervisor *(m)*
Fr programme superviseur *(m)*
Pt programa de supervisão *(m)*

programma di tabulati *(m)* It
De Listenprogramm *(n)*
En report program
Es programa de informes *(m)*
Fr programme des informations *(m)*
Pt programa de relatórios *(m)*

programma di utilità *(m)* It
De Hilfsprogramm *(n)*
En utility program
Es programa de utilidad *(m)*
Fr programme utilitaire *(m)*
Pt programa de utilidade *(m)*

programma esecutivo *(m)* It
De Aktivierungsprogramm *(n)*
En executive program
Es programa ejecutivo *(m)*
Fr programme superviseur *(m)*
Pt programa de execução *(m)*

programma euristico *(m)* It
De heuristisches Programm *(n)*
En heuristic program
Es programa heurístico *(m)*
Fr programme heuristique *(m)*
Pt programa heurístico *(m)*

programma memorizzato *(m)* It
De gespeichertes Programm *(n)*
En stored program
Es programa almacenado *(m)*
Fr programme enregistré *(m)*
Pt programa armazenado *(m)*

Programmänderung *(f)* *n* De
En program modification
Es modificación de programa *(f)*
Fr modification de programme *(f)*
It modificazione di programma *(f)*
Pt modificação do programa *(f)*

programma non precedenza *(m)* It
De Hintergrundprogramm *(n)*
En background program
Es programa subordinado *(m)*
Fr programme non prioritaire *(m)*
Pt programa de plano de fundo *(m)*

programma oggetto *(m)* It
De Zielprogramm *(n)*
En object program
Es programa objeto *(m)*
Fr programme objet *(m)*
Pt programa de objecto *(m)*

programma origine *(m)* It
De Quellprogramm *(n)*
En source program
Es programa fuente *(m)*
Fr programme source *(m)*
Pt programa de origem *(m)*

programmare *vb* It
De programmieren
En program
Es programar
Fr programmer
Pt programar

programma segmentato *(m)* It
De segmentiertes Programm *(n)*
En segmented program
Es programa segmentado *(m)*
Fr programme segmenté *(m)*
Pt programa segmentado *(m)*

programma strutturato *(m)* It
De gegliedertes Programm *(n)*
En structured program
Es programa estructurado *(m)*
Fr programme structuré *(m)*
Pt programa estruturado *(m)*

programmateur *(m)* *n* Fr
De Programmierer *(m)*
En computer programmer
Es programador de ordenador *(m)*
It programmatore di elaboratori *(m)*
Pt programador de computador *(m)*

programmateur des travaux *(m)* Fr
De Jobscheduler *(m)*
En job scheduler
Es planificador de trabajos *(m)*
It pianificatore dei lavoratori *(m)*
Pt planificador de trabalhos *(m)*

programmation *(f)* *n* Fr
De Programmieren *(n)*
En programming
Es programación *(f)*
It programmazione *(f)*
Pt programação *(f)*

programmation d'étude *(f)* Fr
De Systemprogrammierung *(f)*
En systems programming
Es programación de sistemas *(f)*
It programmazione dei sistemi *(f)*
Pt programação de sistemas *(f)*

programmation linéaire (PL) *(f)* Fr
De lineare Programmierung *(f)*
En linear programming (LP)
Es programación lineal *(f)*

It programmazione lineare *(f)*
Pt programação linear *(f)*

programmation mathématique *(f)* Fr
De mathematische Programmierung *(f)*
En mathematical programming
Es programación matemática *(f)*
It programmazione matematica *(f)*
Pt programação matemática *(f)*

programmation modulaire *(f)* Fr
De modulare Programmierung *(f)*
En modular programming
Es programación modular *(f)*
It programmazione modulare *(f)*
Pt programação modular *(f)*

programmation non linéaire *(f)* Fr
De nicht lineare Programmierung *(f)*
En nonlinear programming
Es programación no lineal *(f)*
It programmazione non lineare *(f)*
Pt programação não linear *(f)*

programmation optimum *(f)* Fr
De optimale Programmierung *(f)*
En optimum programming
Es programación óptima *(f)*
It programmazione dell'ottimo *(f)*
Pt programação para optimização *(f)*

programmation symbolique *(f)* Fr
De symbolische Programmierung *(f)*
En symbolic programming
Es programación simbólica *(f)*
It programmazione simbolica *(f)*
Pt programação simbólica *(f)*

programmato *adj* It
De programmiert
En programmed
Es programado
Fr programmé
Pt programado

programmatore *(m)* *n* It
De Programmierer *(m)*
En programmer
Es programador *(m)*
Fr programmeur *(m)*
Pt programador *(m)*

programmatore di elaboratori *(m)* It
De Programmierer *(m)*
En computer programmer
Es programador de ordenador *(m)*
Fr programmateur *(m)*
Pt programador de computador *(m)*

Programmausrüstung *(f)* *n* De
En software engineering
Es ingeniería de soportes lógicos *(f)*
Fr technique du logiciel *(f)*
It ingegneria del software *(f)*
Pt engenharia de software *(f)*

Programmausrüstungsgeber *(m)* *n* De
En software generator
Es generador de soportes lógicos *(m)*
Fr générateur de logiciel *(m)*
It generatore di software *(m)*
Pt gerador de software *(m)*

programmazione *(f)* *n* It
De Programmieren *(n)*
En programming
Es programación *(f)*
Fr programmation *(f)*
Pt programação *(f)*

programmazione dei sistemi *(f)* It
De System-programmierung *(f)*
En systems programming
Es programación de sistemas *(f)*
Fr programmation d'étude *(f)*
Pt programação de sistemas *(f)*

programmazione dell'ottimo *(f)* It
De optimale Programmierung *(f)*
En optimum programming
Es programación óptima *(f)*
Fr programmation optimum *(f)*
Pt programação para optimização *(f)*

programmazione lineare *(f)* It
De lineare Programmierung *(f)*
En linear programming (LP)
Es programación lineal *(f)*
Fr programmation linéaire (PL) *(f)*
Pt programação linear *(f)*

programmazione matematica *(f)* It
De mathematische Programmierung *(f)*
En mathematical programming
Es programación matemática *(f)*
Fr programmation mathématique *(f)*
Pt programação matemática *(f)*

programmazione modulare *(f)* It
De modulare Programmierung *(f)*
En modular programming
Es programación modular *(f)*
Fr programmation modulaire *(f)*
Pt programação modular *(f)*

programmazione multipla *(f)* It
De Programm-verzahnung *(f)*
En multiprogramming
Es multiprogramación *(f)*
Fr multi-programmation *(f)*
Pt multiprogramação *(f)*

programmazione non lineare *(f)* It
De nicht lineare Programmierung *(f)*
En nonlinear programming
Es programación no lineal *(f)*
Fr programmation non linéaire *(f)*
Pt programação não linear *(f)*

programmazione simbolica *(f)* It
De symbolische Programmierung *(f)*
En symbolic programming
Es programación simbólica *(f)*
Fr programmation symbolique *(f)*
Pt programação simbólica *(f)*

Programmbibliothek *(f)* *n* De
En program library
Es biblioteca de programas *(f)*
Fr bibliothèque de programmes *(f)*
It libreria dei programmi *(f)*
Pt biblioteca de programas *(f)*

programme *(m)* *n* Fr
De Programm *(n)*
En program; routine
Es programa; rutina *(m f)*
It programma; routine *(m f)*

Pt programa; rotina *(m f)*

programmé *adj* Fr
De programmiert
En programmed
Es programado
It programmato
Pt programado

programmed *adj* En
De programmiert
Es programado
Fr programmé
It programmato
Pt programado

programme d'application *(m)* Fr
De Anwendungs-programm *(n)*
En application program
Es programa de aplicación *(m)*
It programma applicativo *(m)*
Pt programa de aplicação *(m)*

programme d'autopsie *(m)* Fr
De Programm nach dem Tode *(n)*
En post-mortem routine
Es rutina póstuma *(f)*
It routine di autopsia *(f)*
Pt rotina de autópsia *(f)*

programme de chargement *(m)* Fr
De Ladeprogramm *(n)*
En loading routine
Es rutina de carga *(f)*
It routine di caricamento *(f)*
Pt rotina de carga *(f)*

programme de contrôle *(m)* Fr
De Prüfprogramm *(n)*
En checking program
Es programa de verificación *(m)*
It programma di controllo *(m)*
Pt programa de verificação *(m)*

programme de diagnostic *(m)* Fr
De Diagnostikprogramm *(n)*
En diagnostic routine
Es rutina de diagnóstico *(f)*
It routine diagnostica *(f)*
Pt rotina de diagnóstico *(f)*

programme d'édition *(m)* Fr
De Redakteur *(m)*
En editor
Es programa de edición *(m)*
It programma di manipolazione *(m)*
Pt programa de edição *(m)*

programme de service *(m)* Fr
De Dienstprogramm *(n)*
En service routine
Es rutina de servicio *(f)*
It routine di servizio *(f)*
Pt rotina de serviço *(f)*

programme des informations *(m)* Fr
De Listenprogramm *(n)*
En report program
Es programa de informes *(m)*
It programma di tabulati *(m)*
Pt programa de relatórios *(m)*

programme d'essai *(m)* Fr
De Prüfprogramm *(n)*
En test program
Es programa de ensayo *(m)*
It programma di prova *(m)*
Pt programa de ensaios *(m)*

programme de tri *(m)* Fr
De Sortierungs-programm *(n)*
En sorting routine
Es rutina de clasificación *(f)*
It routine di selezione *(f)*
Pt rotina de classificação *(f)*

programme enregistré *(m)* Fr
De gespeichertes Programm *(n)*
En stored program
Es programa almacenado *(m)*
It programma memorizzato *(m)*
Pt programa armazenado *(m)*

programme heuristique *(m)* Fr
De heuristisches Programm *(n)*
En heuristic program
Es programa heurístico *(m)*
It programma euristico *(m)*
Pt programa heurístico *(m)*

programme machine *(m)* Fr
De Programm *(n)*
En computer program
Es programa de ordenador *(m)*
It programma dell'elaboratore *(m)*
Pt programa de computador *(m)*

programme non prioritaire *(m)* Fr
De Hintergrund-programm *(n)*
En background program
Es programa subordinado *(m)*
It programma non precedenza *(m)*
Pt programa de plano de fundo *(m)*

programme objet *(m)* Fr
De Zielprogramm *(n)*
En object program
Es programa objeto *(m)*
It programma oggetto *(m)*
Pt programa de objecto *(m)*

programme ouvert *(m)* Fr
De offenes Programm *(n)*
En open routine
Es rutina de apertura *(f)*
It routine aperta *(f)*
Pt rotina aberta *(f)*

programme permanent *(m)* Fr
De residentes Programm *(n)*
En resident routine
Es rutina residente *(f)*
It routine residente *(f)*
Pt rotina residente *(f)*

programme-produit *(m) n* Fr
De Programmpaket *(n)*
En program package
Es colección de programas *(f)*
It serie di programmi *(f)*
Pt pacote de programa *(m)*

programmer *n* En
De Programmierer *(m)*
Es programador *(m)*
Fr programmeur *(m)*
It programmatore *(m)*
Pt programador *(m)*

programmer *vb* Fr
De programmieren
En program
Es programar
It programmare
Pt programar

programme segmenté *(m)* Fr
De segmentiertes Programm *(n)*
En segmented program
Es programa segmentado *(m)*
It programma segmentato *(m)*
Pt programa segmentado *(m)*

programmes en cascade *(m pl)* Fr
De Kaskadenprogramme *(pl)*
En cascaded programs
Es programas en cascada *(m pl)*
It programmi in cascata *(m pl)*
Pt programas em cascada *(m pl)*

programme source *(m)* Fr
De Quellprogramm *(n)*
En source program
Es programa fuente *(m)*
It programma origine *(m)*
Pt programa de origem *(m)*

programme structuré *(m)* Fr
De gegliedertes Programm *(n)*
En structured program
Es programa estructurado *(m)*
It programma strutturato *(m)*
Pt programa estruturado *(m)*

programme superviseur *(m)* Fr
De Aktivierungsprogramm; Überwachungsprogramm *(n)*
En executive program; supervisory program
Es programa ejecutivo; programa supervisor *(m)*
It programma di supervisione; programma esecutivo *(m)*
Pt programa de execução; programa de supervisão *(m)*

programmeur *(m)* *n* Fr
De Programmierer *(m)*
En programmer
Es programador *(m)*
It programmatore *(m)*
Pt programador *(m)*

programme utilitaire *(m)* Fr
De Hilfsprogramm *(n)*
En utility program
Es programa de utilidad *(m)*
It programma di utilità *(m)*
Pt programa de utilidade *(m)*

Programmgeber *(m)* *n* De
En program generator
Es generador de programas *(m)*
Fr générateur de programmes *(m)*
It generatore di programmi *(m)*
Pt gerador de programas *(m)*

programmierbar *adj* De
En programmable
Es programable
Fr programmable
It programmabile
Pt programável

programmierbarer Festspeicher *(m)* De
En programmable read-only memory (PROM)
Es memoria fija programable *(f)*
Fr mémoire morte programmable *(f)*
It memoria soltanto di lettura programmabile *(f)*
Pt memória apenas de leitura programável *(f)*

programmierbare Station *(f)* De
En intelligent terminal
Es terminal inteligente *(m)*
Fr terminal intelligent *(m)*
It terminale intelligente *(m)*
Pt terminal inteligente *(m)*

programmieren *vb* De
En program
Es programar
Fr programmer
It programmare
Pt programar

Programmieren *(n)* *n* De
En programming
Es programación *(f)*
Fr programmation *(f)*
It programmazione *(f)*
Pt programação *(f)*

Programmierer *(m)* *n* De
En computer programmer; programmer
Es programador; programador de ordenador *(m)*
Fr programmateur; programmeur *(m)*
It programmatore; programmatore di elaboratori *(m)*
Pt programador; programador de computador *(m)*

Programmiersprache *(f)* *n* De
En programming language
Es lenguaje de programación *(m)*
Fr langage de programmation *(m)*
It linguaggio di programmazione *(m)*
Pt linguagem de programação *(f)*

programmiert *adj* De
En programmed
Es programado
Fr programmé
It programmato
Pt programado

programmi in cascata *(m pl)* It
De Kaskadenprogramme *(pl)*
En cascaded programs
Es programas en cascada *(m pl)*
Fr programmes en cascade *(m pl)*
Pt programas em cascada *(m pl)*

programming *n* En
De Programmieren *(n)*
Es programación *(f)*
Fr programmation *(f)*
It programmazione *(f)*
Pt programação *(f)*

programming language En
De Programmiersprache *(f)*
Es lenguaje de programación *(m)*
Fr langage de programmation *(m)*
It linguaggio di programmazione *(m)*
Pt linguagem de programação *(f)*

Programm nach dem Tode *(n)* De
En post-mortem routine
Es rutina póstuma *(f)*
Fr programme d'autopsie *(m)*
It routine di autopsia *(f)*
Pt rotina de autópsia *(f)*

program modification En
De Programmänderung *(f)*
Es modificación de programa *(f)*
Fr modification de programme *(f)*
It modificazione di programma *(f)*
Pt modificação do programa *(f)*

Programmpaket *(n)* *n* De
En program package
Es colección de programas *(f)*
Fr programme-produit *(m)*
It serie di programmi *(f)*
Pt pacote de programa *(m)*

Programmparameter *(m)* *n* De
En program parameter
Es parámetro de programa *(m)*
Fr paramètre de programme *(m)*
It parametro del programma *(m)*
Pt parâmetro de programa *(m)*

Programmprüfung *(f)* *n* De
En program testing
Es ensayo de programa *(m)*
Fr contrôle de programme *(m)*
It collaudo del programma *(m)*
Pt ensaio do programa *(m)*

Programmunterlagen *(pl) n* De
En documentation
Es documentación *(f)*
Fr documentation *(f)*
It documentazione *(f)*
Pt documentação *(f)*

Programm-verträglichkeit *(f) n* De
En program compatibility
Es compatibilidad de programas *(f)*
Fr compatibilité-programme *(f)*
It compatibilità di programma *(f)*
Pt compatibilidade de programas *(f)*

Programmverzahnung *(f) n* De
En multiprogramming
Es multiprogramación *(f)*
Fr multi-programmation *(f)*
It programmazione multipla *(f)*
Pt multiprogramação *(f)*

Programmvorgabe *(f) n* De
En program specification
Es especificación de programa *(f)*
Fr spécification de programme *(f)*
It specificazioni del programma *(f)*
Pt especificação do programa *(f)*

program package En
De Programmpaket *(n)*
Es colección de programas *(f)*
Fr programme-produit *(m)*
It serie di programmi *(f)*
Pt pacote de programa *(m)*

program parameter En
De Programmparameter *(m)*
Es parámetro de programa *(m)*
Fr paramètre de programme *(m)*
It parametro del programma *(m)*
Pt parâmetro de programa *(m)*

program specification En
De Programmvorgabe *(f)*
Es especificación de programa *(f)*
Fr spécification de programme *(f)*
It specificazioni del programma *(f)*
Pt especificação do programa *(f)*

program testing En
De Programmprüfung *(f)*
Es ensayo de programa *(m)*
Fr contrôle de programme *(m)*
It collaudo del programma *(m)*
Pt ensaio do programa *(m)*

project evaluation and review technique (PERT) En
De Projektaus-wertungsund Übersichttechnik *(f)*
Es método de planificación y control de proyectos *(m)*
Fr système d'ordonnancement des opérations et du personnel *(m)*
It tecnica di revisione e valutazione del progetto *(f)*
Pt técnica de avaliação e revisão de projectos *(f)*

Projektaus-wertungsund Übersichttechnik *(f)* De
En project evaluation and review technique (PERT)
Es método de planificación y control de proyectos *(m)*
Fr système d'ordonnancement des opérations et du personnel *(m)*
It tecnica di revisione e valutazione del progetto *(f)*
Pt técnica de avaliação e revisão de projectos *(f)*

PROM apagável *(f)* Pt
De löschbarer PROM *(m)*
En erasable PROM (EPROM)
Es PROM borrable *(f)*
Fr PROM effaçable *(f)*
It PROM cancellabile *(f)*

PROM borrable *(f)* Es
De löschbarer PROM *(m)*
En erasable PROM (EPROM)
Fr PROM effaçable *(f)*
It PROM cancellabile *(f)*
Pt PROM apagável *(f)*

PROM cancellabile *(f)* It
De löschbarer PROM *(m)*
En erasable PROM (EPROM)
Es PROM borrable *(f)*
Fr PROM effaçable *(f)*
Pt PROM apagável *(f)*

PROM effaçable *(f)* Fr
De löschbarer PROM *(m)*
En erasable PROM (EPROM)
Es PROM borrable *(f)*
It PROM cancellabile *(f)*
Pt PROM apagável *(f)*

proof total En
De Kontrollsumme *(f)*
Es total de control *(m)*
Fr total de contrôle *(m)*
It totale di controllo *(m)*
Pt prova total *(f)*

propagated error En
De mitlaufender Fehler *(m)*
Es error propagado *(m)*
Fr erreur propagée *(f)*
It errore propagato *(m)*
Pt erro propagado *(m)*

proportional control En
De Proportional-steuerung *(f)*
Es control proporcional *(m)*
Fr contrôle proportionnel *(m)*
It controllo proporzionale *(m)*
Pt controle proporcional *(m)*

Proportionalsteuerung *(f) n* De
En proportional control
Es control proporcional *(m)*
Fr contrôle proportionnel *(m)*
It controllo proporzionale *(m)*
Pt controle proporcional *(m)*

protecção *(f) n* Pt
De Schutz *(m)*
En protection
Es protección *(f)*
Fr protection *(f)*
It protezione *(f)*

protecção arquitectónica *(f)* Pt
De Aufbauschutz *(m)*
En architectural protection
Es protección estructural *(f)*
Fr protection architecturale *(f)*
It protezione dell'architettura *(f)*

protecção de arquivo *(f)* Pt
De Dateischutz *(m)*
En file protection
Es protección de fichero *(f)*
Fr protection de fichier *(f)*
It protezione del file *(f)*

protecção de dados *(f)* Pt
De Datenschutz *(m)*
En data protection
Es protección de los datos *(f)*
Fr protection des données *(f)*
It protezione dei dati *(f)*

protecção de memória *(f)* Pt
De Speicherschutz *(m)*
En memory protection
Es protección de la memoria *(f)*
Fr protection de la mémoire *(f)*
It protezione della memoria *(f)*

protección *(f)* *n* Es
De Schutz *(m)*
En protection
Fr protection *(f)*
It protezione *(f)*
Pt protecção *(f)*

protección de fichero *(f)* Es
De Dateischutz *(m)*
En file protection
Fr protection de fichier *(f)*
It protezione del file *(f)*
Pt protecção de arquivo *(f)*

protección de la memoria *(f)* Es
De Speicherschutz *(m)*
En memory protection
Fr protection de la mémoire *(f)*
It protezione della memoria *(f)*
Pt protecção de memória *(f)*

protección de los datos *(f)* Es
De Datenschutz *(m)*
En data protection
Fr protection des données *(f)*
It protezione dei dati *(f)*
Pt protecção de dados *(f)*

protección estructural *(f)* Es
De Aufbauschutz *(m)*
En architectural protection
Fr protection architecturale *(f)*
It protezione dell'architettura *(f)*
Pt protecção arquitectónica *(f)*

protected location En
De geschützter Ort *(m)*
Es posición protegida *(f)*
Fr position protégée *(f)*
It locazione protetta *(f)*
Pt localização protegida *(f)*

protected record En
De geschützter Satz *(m)*
Es registro protegido *(m)*
Fr enregistrement protégé *(m)*
It record protetto *(m)*
Pt registo protegido *(m)*

protection *n* En; Fr *(f)*
De Schutz *(m)*
Es protección *(f)*
It protezione *(f)*
Pt protecção *(f)*

protection architecturale *(f)* Fr
De Aufbauschutz *(m)*
En architectural protection
Es protección estructural *(f)*
It protezione dell'architettura *(f)*
Pt protecção arquitectónica *(f)*

protection de fichier *(f)* Fr
De Dateischutz *(m)*
En file protection
Es protección de fichero *(f)*
It protezione del file *(f)*
Pt protecção de arquivo *(f)*

protection de la mémoire *(f)* Fr
De Speicherschutz *(m)*
En memory protection
Es protección de la memoria *(f)*
It protezione della memoria *(f)*
Pt protecção de memória *(f)*

protection des données *(f)* Fr
De Datenschutz *(m)*
En data protection
Es protección de los datos *(f)*
It protezione dei dati *(f)*
Pt protecção de dados *(f)*

protezione *(f)* *n* It
De Schutz *(m)*
En protection
Es protección *(f)*
Fr protection *(f)*
Pt protecção *(f)*

protezione dei dati *(f)* It
De Datenschutz *(m)*
En data protection
Es protección de los datos *(f)*
Fr protection des données *(f)*
Pt protecção de dados *(f)*

protezione del file *(f)* It
De Dateischutz *(m)*
En file protection
Es protección de fichero *(f)*
Fr protection de fichier *(f)*
Pt protecção de arquivo *(f)*

protezione della memoria *(f)* It
De Speicherschutz *(m)*
En memory protection
Es protección de la memoria *(f)*
Fr protection de la mémoire *(f)*
Pt protecção de memória *(f)*

protezione dell'architettura *(f)* It
De Aufbauschutz *(m)*
En architectural protection
Es protección estructural *(f)*
Fr protection architecturale *(f)*
Pt protecção arquitectónica *(f)*

protocol *n* En
De Protokoll *(n)*
Es protocolo *(m)*
Fr protocole *(m)*
It protocollo *(m)*
Pt protocolo *(m)*

protocole *(m)* *n* Fr
De Protokoll *(n)*
En protocol
Es protocolo *(m)*
It protocollo *(m)*
Pt protocolo *(m)*

protocollo *(m)* *n* It
De Protokoll *(n)*
En protocol
Es protocolo *(m)*
Fr protocole *(m)*
Pt protocolo *(m)*

protocolo *(m)* *n* Es, Pt
De Protokoll *(n)*
En protocol
Fr protocole *(m)*
It protocollo *(m)*

Protokoll *(n)* *n* De
En protocol
Es protocolo *(m)*
Fr protocole *(m)*
It protocollo *(m)*
Pt protocolo *(m)*

prova *(f)* *n* It
De Prüfung *(f)*
En test
Es prueba *(f)*
Fr essai *(m)*
Pt ensaio *(m)*

provare *vb* It
De prüfen
En test
Es probar
Fr essayer
Pt ensaiar

prova total *(f)* Pt
De Kontrollsumme *(f)*
En proof total
Es total de control *(m)*
Fr total de contrôle *(m)*
It totale di controllo *(m)*

proving time En
De Kontrollzeit *(f)*
Es tiempo de ensayo *(m)*
Fr durée d'essai de fonctionnement *(f)*
It tempo di prova *(m)*
Pt tempo de prova *(m)*

Prozeduranweisung *(f)* *n* De
En declarative statement

Es sentencia de declaración *(f)*
Fr instruction déclarative *(f)*
It statement di dichiarazione *(m)*
Pt afirmação declarativa *(f)*

Prozeß *(m) n* De
En process
Es proceso *(m)*
Fr processus *(m)*
It processo *(m)*
Pt processo *(m)*

prueba *(f) n* Es
De Prüfung *(f)*
En test
Fr essai *(m)*
It prova *(f)*
Pt ensaio *(m)*

prueba de diagnóstico *(f)* Es
De diagnostische Prüfung *(f)*
En diagnostic test
Fr test de diagnostic *(m)*
It test diagnostico *(m)*
Pt teste de diagnóstico *(m)*

prueba marginal *(f)* Es
De Randwertprüfung *(f)*
En marginal test
Fr épreuve marginale *(f)*
It test marginale *(m)*
Pt teste marginal *(m)*

Prüfablauf *(m) n* De
En test run
Es pasada de ensayo *(f)*
Fr passage d'essai *(m)*
It esecuzione di prova *(f)*
Pt passagem de ensaio *(f)*

Prüfanzeiger *(m) n* De
En check indicator
Es indicador de verificación *(m)*
Fr indicateur de contrôle *(m)*
It indicatore di controllo *(m)*
Pt indicador de verificação *(m)*

Prüfbit *(m) n* De
En check bit
Es bit de verificación *(m)*
Fr bit de contrôle *(m)*
It bit di controllo *(m)*
Pt bit de verificação *(m)*

Prüfdaten *(pl) n* De
En test data
Es datos para ensayo *(m pl)*
Fr donnée d'essai *(f)*
It dati di prova *(m pl)*
Pt dados de ensaio *(m pl)*

prüfen *vb* De
En test; verify
Es probar; verificar
Fr essayer; vérifier
It provare; verificare
Pt ensaiar; verificar

Prüfliste *(f) n* De
En audit trail
Es pista de auditoría *(f)*
Fr vérification à rebours *(f)*
It lista di verifica *(f)*
Pt trilho de verificação *(m)*

Prüfnummer *(f) n* De
En self-checking number
Es número autoverificador *(m)*
Fr chiffre d'auto-vérification *(m)*
It numero autocontrollante *(m)*
Pt número autoverificante *(m)*

Prüfprogramm *(n) n* De
En checking program; test program
Es programa de ensayo; programa de verificación *(m)*
Fr programme de contrôle; programme d'essai *(m)*
It programma di controllo; programma di prova *(m)*
Pt programa de ensaios; programa de verificação *(m)*

Prüfstand *(m) n* De
En test-bed
Es bancada de prueba *(f)*
Fr piste d'entraînement de test *(f)*
It banco di prova *(m)*
Pt mesa de ensaio *(f)*

Prüfung *(f) n* De
En check; test; verification
Es prueba; verificación *(f)*
Fr contrôle; essai; vérification *(m m f)*
It controllo; prova; verifica *(m f f)*
Pt ensaio; verificação *(m f)*

Prüfziffer *(f) n* De
En check digit
Es dígito de verificación *(m)*
Fr caractère de contrôle *(m)*
It digit di controllo *(m)*
Pt número digital de verificação *(m)*

pseudo-aléatoire *adj* Fr
De pseudozufällig
En pseudo-random
Es pseudoaleatorio
It pseudo casuale
Pt pseudo-aleatório

pseudoaleatorio *adj* Es
De pseudozufällig
En pseudo-random
Fr pseudo-aléatoire
It pseudo casuale
Pt pseudo-aleatório

pseudo-aleatório *adj* Pt
De pseudozufällig
En pseudo-random
Es pseudoaleatorio
Fr pseudo-aléatoire
It pseudo casuale

Pseudoanweisung *(f) n* De
En pseudo instruction
Es pseudoinstrucción *(f)*
Fr pseudoinstruction *(f)*
It pseudo istruzione *(f)*
Pt pseudo-instrução *(f)*

Pseudobetrieb *(m) n* De
En pseudo operation
Es pseudo-operación *(f)*
Fr pseudo-opération *(f)*
It pseudo operazione *(f)*
Pt pseudo-operação *(f)*

pseudo casuale It
De pseudozufällig
En pseudo-random
Es pseudoaleatorio
Fr pseudo-aléatoire
Pt pseudo-aleatório

pseudocode *n* En
De Pseudocode *(m)*
Es pseudocódigo *(m)*
Fr pseudo-code *(m)*
It pseudo codice *(m)*
Pt pseudocódigo *(m)*

pseudo-code *(m) n* Fr
De Pseudocode *(m)*
En pseudocode
Es pseudocódigo *(m)*
It pseudo codice *(m)*
Pt pseudocódigo *(m)*

Pseudocode *(m) n* De
En pseudocode
Es pseudocódigo *(m)*
Fr pseudo-code *(m)*
It pseudo codice *(m)*
Pt pseudocódigo *(m)*

pseudo codice *(m)* It
De Pseudocode *(m)*
En pseudocode
Es pseudocódigo *(m)*
Fr pseudo-code *(m)*
Pt pseudocódigo *(m)*

pseudocódigo *(m) n* Es, Pt
De Pseudocode *(m)*
En pseudocode
Fr pseudo-code *(m)*
It pseudo codice *(m)*

pseudo-instrução *(f) n* Pt
De Pseudoanweisung *(f)*
En pseudo instruction
Es pseudoinstrucción *(f)*
Fr pseudo-instruction *(f)*
It pseudo istruzione *(f)*

pseudoinstrucción *(f) n* Es
De Pseudoanweisung *(f)*
En pseudo instruction

Fr pseudo-instruction *(f)*
It pseudo istruzione *(f)*
Pt pseudo-instrução *(f)*

pseudo instruction En
De Pseudoanweisung *(f)*
Es pseudoinstrucción *(f)*
Fr pseudo-instruction *(f)*
It pseudo istruzione *(f)*
Pt pseudo-instrução *(f)*

pseudo-instruction *(f) n* Fr
De Pseudoanweisung *(f)*
En pseudo instruction
Es pseudoinstrucción *(f)*
It pseudo istruzione *(f)*
Pt pseudo-instrução *(f)*

pseudo istruzione *(f)* It
De Pseudoanweisung *(f)*
En pseudo instruction
Es pseudoinstrucción *(f)*
Fr pseudo-instruction *(f)*
Pt pseudo-instrução *(f)*

pseudo-operação *(f) n* Pt
De Pseudobetrieb *(m)*
En pseudo operation
Es pseudo-operación *(f)*
Fr pseudo-opération *(f)*
It pseudo operazione *(f)*

pseudo-operación *(f) n* Es
De Pseudobetrieb *(m)*
En pseudo operation
Fr pseudo-opération *(f)*
It pseudo operazione *(f)*
Pt pseudo-operação *(f)*

pseudo operation En
De Pseudobetrieb *(m)*
Es pseudo-operación *(f)*
Fr pseudo-opération *(f)*
It pseudo operazione *(f)*
Pt pseudo-operação *(f)*

pseudo-opération *(f) n* Fr
De Pseudobetrieb *(m)*
En pseudo operation
Es pseudo-operación *(f)*
It pseudo operazione *(f)*
Pt pseudo-operação *(f)*

pseudo operazione *(f)* It
De Pseudobetrieb *(m)*
En pseudo operation
Es pseudo-operación *(f)*
Fr pseudo-opération *(f)*
Pt pseudo-operação *(f)*

pseudo-random *adj* En
De pseudozufällig
Es pseudoaleatorio
Fr pseudo-aléatoire
It pseudo casuale
Pt pseudo-aleatório

pseudozufällig *adj* De
En pseudo-random
Es pseudoaleatorio
Fr pseudo-aléatoire
It pseudo casuale
Pt pseudo-aleatório

puce *(f) n* Fr
De Chip *(m)*
En chip
Es plaqueta *(f)*
It chip *(m)*
Pt lasca *(f)*

puce au silicium *(f)* Fr
De Silikonchip *(m)*
En silicon chip
Es microplaqueta de silicio *(f)*
It scheggia di silicone *(f)*
Pt ficha de silício *(f)*

puerta *(f) n* Es
De Tor *(n)*
En gate
Fr porte *(f)*
It porta *(f)*
Pt porta *(f)*

puerta de anticoincidencia *(f)* Es
De Antizusammen-treffensschaltung *(f)*
En anticoincidence gate
Fr porte anti-coïncidence *(f)*
It porta di anticoincidenza *(f)*
Pt porta de anticoincidência *(f)*

puerta de coincidencia *(f)* Es
De Zusammentreffens-Schaltung *(f)*
En coincidence gate
Fr porte à coïncidence *(f)*
It porta di coincidenza *(f)*
Pt porta de coincidência *(f)*

puerta de entrada-salida *(f)* Es
De Eingangs-Ausgangsanschluβ *(m)*
En input-output port
Fr point d'accès entrée-sortie *(m)*
It porto entrata-uscita *(m)*
Pt abertura de entrada-sair *(f)*

puerta lógica *(f)* Es
De Verknüpfungstor *(n)*
En logic gate
Fr porte logique *(f)*
It porta logica *(f)*
Pt porta lógica *(f)*

puerta NI *(f)* Es
De NOR-Schaltung *(f)*
En NOR-gate
Fr porte NON-OU *(f)*
It porta NOR *(f)*
Pt porta NOR *(f)*

puerta NO *(f)* Es
De NOT-Schaltung *(f)*
En NOT-gate
Fr porte NON *(f)*
It porta NO *(f)*
Pt porta NÃO *(f)*

puerta NO-Y *(f)* Es
De NICHT-UND-Schaltung *(f)*
En NAND-gate
Fr porte NON-ET *(f)*
It porta NAND *(f)*
Pt porta NAND *(f)*

puerta O *(f)* Es
De ODER-Schaltung *(f)*
En OR-gate
Fr porte OU *(f)*
It porta o *(f)*
Pt porta OR *(f)*

puerta Y *(f)* Es
De UND-Schaltung *(f)*
En AND-gate
Fr porte ET *(f)*
It porta E *(f)*
Pt porta AND *(f)*

Pufferspeicher *(m)* De
En buffer store
Es registro intermedio *(m)*
Fr mémoire tampon *(f)*
It memoria di transito *(f)*
Pt memória buffer *(f)*

pulizia dei dati *(f)* It
De Datenlöschung *(f)*
En data cleaning
Es limpieza de los datos *(f)*
Fr nettoyage de données *(f)*
Pt apagamento de dados *(m)*

pulse *n* En
De Impuls *(m)*
Es impulso *(m)*
Fr impulsion *(f)*
It impulso *(m)*
Pt impulso *(m)*

pulse repetition frequency (prf) En
De Impulsfolgefrequenz *(f)*
Es frecuencia de repetición de impulsos *(f)*
Fr fréquence par récurrence des impulsions *(f)*
It frequenza a ripetizione di impulsi *(f)*
Pt frequência de repetição de impulsos *(f)*

pulse train En
De Impulsfolge *(f)*
Es tren de impulsos *(m)*
Fr train d'impulsions *(m)*
It treno d'impulsi *(m)*
Pt trem de impulsos *(m)*

punch *n* En
De Locher *(m)*
Es perforadora *(f)*
Fr perforatrice *(f)*
It perforatrice *(f)*
Pt perfuradora *(f)*

punch *vb* En
De lochen
Es perforar
Fr perforer

It perforare
Pt perfurar

punch card Am
De Lochkarte *(f)*
En punched card
Es ficha perforada *(f)*
Fr carte mécanographique *(f)*
It scheda perforata *(f)*
Pt ficha perfurada *(f)*

punched card En
Am punch card
De Lochkarte *(f)*
Es ficha perforada *(f)*
Fr carte mécanographique *(f)*
It scheda perforata *(f)*
Pt ficha perfurada *(f)*

punching position En
De Lochstellung *(f)*
Es posición de perforación *(f)*
Fr position de perforation *(f)*
It posizione di perforazione *(f)*
Pt posição de perfuração *(f)*

punching rate En
De Lochungs-geschwindigkeit *(f)*
Es velocidad de perforación *(f)*
Fr vitesse de perforation *(f)*
It volume di perforazione *(m)*
Pt índice de perfuração *(m)*

punch verifier En
De Lochungsprüfer *(m)*
Es verificador de perforación *(m)*
Fr vérificatrice de perforations *(f)*
It verificatrice della perforazione *(f)*
Pt verificador de perfuração *(m)*

Punktdrucker *(m) n* De
En dot printer
Es impresora por puntos *(f)*
Fr imprimante par points *(f)*
It stampatrice a punti *(f)*
Pt impressora de pontos *(f)*

Punktmatrix *(f) n* De
En dot matrix
Es matriz de puntos *(f)*
Fr matrice par points *(f)*
It matrice di punti *(f)*
Pt matriz de pontos *(f)*

punktweise Darstellung *(f)* De
En point-mode display
Es representación de modo puntual *(f)*
Fr affichage mode point par point *(m)*
It mostra di modo punto a punto *(f)*
Pt display de modo pontual *(m)*

punto de carga *(m)* Es
De Ladeadresse *(f)*
En load point
Fr point de chargement *(m)*
It punto di caricamento *(m)*
Pt ponto de carga *(m)*

punto de control *(m)* Es
De Kontrollpunkt *(m)*
En checkpoint
Fr point de contrôle *(m)*
It punto di controllo *(m)*
Pt ponto de verificação *(m)*

punto de entrada *(m)* Es
De Eingangspunkt *(m)*
En entry point
Fr point d'entrée *(m)*
It punto di entrata *(m)*
Pt ponto de entrada *(m)*

punto de interrupción *(m)* Es
De Ausgleichspunkt *(m)*
En breakpoint
Fr point de rupture *(m)*
It punto di arresto *(m)*
Pt ponto de rotura *(m)*

punto de reanudación *(m)* Es
De Wiederstartspunkt *(m)*
En restart point
Fr point de reprise *(m)*
It punto di ripartire *(m)*
Pt ponto de rearranque *(m)*

punto de reanudación de pasada *(m)* Es
De Wiederholungspunkt *(m)*
En rerun point
Fr point de reprise *(m)*
It punto di riesecuzione *(m)*
Pt ponto de nova passagem *(m)*

punto de vaciado *(m)* Es
De Speichauszugspunkt *(m)*
En dump point
Fr point de vidage *(m)*
It punto di dump *(m)*
Pt ponto de descarga *(m)*

punto di arresto *(m)* It
De Ausgleichspunkt *(m)*
En breakpoint
Es punto de interrupción *(m)*
Fr point de rupture *(m)*
Pt ponto de rotura *(m)*

punto di base *(m)* It
De Basispunkt *(m)*
En radix point
Es coma de la base *(f)*
Fr point à la base *(m)*
Pt ponto de raiz *(m)*

punto di caricamento *(m)* It
De Ladeadresse *(f)*
En load point
Es punto de carga *(m)*
Fr point de chargement *(m)*
Pt ponto de carga *(m)*

punto di controllo *(m)* It
De Kontrollpunkt *(m)*
En checkpoint
Es punto de control *(m)*
Fr point de contrôle *(m)*
Pt ponto de verificação *(m)*

punto di dump *(m)* It
De Speichauszugspunkt *(m)*
En dump point
Es punto de vaciado *(m)*
Fr point de vidage *(m)*
Pt ponto de descarga *(m)*

punto di entrata *(m)* It
De Eingangspunkt *(m)*
En entry point
Es punto de entrada *(m)*
Fr point d'entrée *(m)*
Pt ponto de entrada *(m)*

punto di riesecuzione *(m)* It
De Wiederholungspunkt *(m)*
En rerun point
Es punto de reanudación de pasada *(m)*
Fr point de reprise *(m)*
Pt ponto de nova passagem *(m)*

punto di ripartire *(m)* It
De Wiederstartspunkt *(m)*
En restart point
Es punto de reanudación *(m)*
Fr point de reprise *(m)*
Pt ponto de rearranque *(m)*

pupitre à distance *(m)* Fr
De Außenkonsole *(f)*
En remote console
Es consola remota *(f)*
It console a distanza *(f)*
Pt consola remota *(f)*

pupitre de commande *(m)* Fr
De Systemkonsole *(f)*
En console
Es consola *(f)*
It console *(f)*
Pt consola *(f)*

Q

quadro *(m) n* Pt
De Rahmen *(m)*
En frame
Es encuadre *(m)*
Fr cadre *(m)*
It telaio *(m)*

quantificateur *(m) n* Fr
De Quantisierer *(m)*
En quantizer
Es cuantificador *(m)*
It quantizzatore *(f)*
Pt quantizador *(m)*

quantification *(f) n* Fr
De Quantisierung *(f)*
En quantization
Es cuantificación *(f)*
It quantizzazione *(f)*
Pt quantização *(f)*

Quantisierer *(m) n* De
En quantizer
Es cuantificador *(m)*
Fr quantificateur *(m)*
It quantizzatore *(f)*
Pt quantizador *(m)*

Quantisierung *(f) n* De
En quantization
Es cuantificación *(f)*
Fr quantification *(f)*
It quantizzazione *(f)*
Pt quantização *(f)*

quantização *(f) n* Pt
De Quantisierung *(f)*
En quantization
Es cuantificación *(f)*
Fr quantification *(f)*
It quantizzazione *(f)*

quantizador *(m) n* Pt
De Quantisierer *(m)*
En quantizer
Es cuantificador *(m)*
Fr quantificateur *(m)*
It quantizzatore *(f)*

quantization *n* En
De Quantisierung *(f)*
Es cuantificación *(f)*
Fr quantification *(f)*
It quantizzazione *(f)*
Pt quantização *(f)*

quantizer *n* En
De Quantisierer *(m)*
Es cuantificador *(m)*
Fr quantificateur *(m)*
It quantizzatore *(f)*
Pt quantizador *(m)*

quantizzatore *(f) n* It
De Quantisierer *(m)*
En quantizer
Es cuantificador *(m)*
Fr quantificateur *(m)*
Pt quantizador *(m)*

quantizzazione *(f) n* It
De Quantisierung *(f)*
En quantization
Es cuantificación *(f)*
Fr quantification *(f)*
Pt quantização *(f)*

quarta-generazione *adj* It
De viertgeneration
En fourth-generation
Es cuarta-generación
Fr quatrième-génération
Pt quarta-geração

quarta-geração *adj* Pt
De viertgeneration
En fourth-generation
Es cuarta-generación
Fr quatrième-génération
It quarta-generazione

quase-instrução *(f) n* Pt
De Quasianweisung *(f)*
En quasi instruction
Es cuasi-instrucción *(f)*
Fr quasi-instruction *(f)*
It quasi istruzione *(f)*

Quasianweisung *(f) n* De
En quasi instruction
Es cuasi-instrucción *(f)*
Fr quasi-instruction *(f)*
It quasi istruzione *(f)*
Pt quase-instrução *(f)*

quasi instruction En
De Quasianweisung *(f)*
Es cuasi-instrucción *(f)*
Fr quasi-instruction *(f)*
It quasi istruzione *(f)*
Pt quase-instrução *(f)*

quasi-instruction *(f) n* Fr
De Quasianweisung *(f)*
En quasi instruction
Es cuasi-instrucción *(f)*
It quasi istruzione *(f)*
Pt quase-instrução *(f)*

quasi istruzione *(f)* It
De Quasianweisung *(f)*
En quasi instruction
Es cuasi-instrucción *(f)*
Fr quasi-instruction *(f)*
Pt quase-instrução *(f)*

quatrième-génération *adj* Fr
De viertgeneration
En fourth-generation
Es cuarta-generación
It quarta-generazione
Pt quarta-geração

quebrar *vb* Es
De durchschlagen
En crash
Fr accélérer
It urtare
Pt colidir

Quellcode *(m) n* De
En source code
Es código fuente *(m)*
Fr séquence en langage source *(f)*
It codice origine *(m)*
Pt código de origem *(m)*

Quelldatenfang *(m) n* De
En source data capture
Es captura de datos fuente *(f)*
Fr saisie des données à la source *(f)*
It cattura di dati all'origine *(f)*
Pt captação de dados de origem *(f)*

Quelldokument *(n) n* De
En source document
Es documento fuente *(m)*
Fr document de base *(m)*
It documento origine *(m)*
Pt documento de origem *(m)*

Quellprogramm *(n) n* De
En source program
Es programa fuente *(m)*
Fr programme source *(m)*
It programma origine *(m)*
Pt programa de origem *(m)*

Quellsprache *(f) n* De
En source language
Es lenguaje fuente *(m)*
Fr langage source *(m)*
It linguaggio origine *(m)*
Pt linguagem de origem *(f)*

queuing theory En
De Warteschlangen-theorie *(f)*
Es teoría de colas *(f)*
Fr théorie des files d'attente *(f)*
It teoria delle code *(f)*
Pt teoria de colocação em fila *(f)*

R

raccolta dei dati *(f)* It
De Datenerfassung *(f)*
En data collection
Es recopilación de datos *(f)*
Fr collecte de données *(f)*
Pt colecção de dados *(f)*

radix *n* En
De Basis *(f)*
Es base *(f)*
Fr base *(f)*
It base *(f)*
Pt raiz *(f)*

radix complement En
De Basiskomplement *(n)*
Es complemento de la base *(m)*
Fr complément à la base *(m)*
It complemento di base *(m)*
Pt complemento de raiz *(m)*

radix point En
De Basispunkt *(m)*
Es coma de la base *(f)*
Fr point à la base *(m)*
It punto di base *(m)*
Pt ponto de raiz *(m)*

Rahmen *(m) n* De
En frame
Es encuadre *(m)*
Fr cadre *(m)*
It telaio *(m)*
Pt quadro *(m)*

raiz *(f) n* Pt
De Basis *(f)*
En radix
Es base *(f)*
Fr base *(f)*
It base *(f)*

ramo *(m) n* Pt
De Zweig *(m)*
En branch
Es bifurcación *(f)*
Fr branchement *(m)*
It diramazione *(f)*

random access En
De direkter Zugriff *(m)*
Es acceso al azar *(m)*
Fr accès sélectif *(m)*
It accesso casuale *(m)*
Pt acesso aleatório *(m)*

random-access memory (RAM) En
De Direktzugriffsspeicher *(m)*
Es memoria de acceso al azar *(f)*
Fr mémoire à accès sélectif *(f)*
It memoria ad accesso casuale *(f)*
Pt memória de acesso aleatório *(f)*

random-number generator En
De Zufallsnummerngeber *(m)*
Es generador de números aleatorios *(m)*
Fr générateur de nombres aléatoires *(m)*
It generatore di numeri casuali *(m)*
Pt gerador de números aleatórios *(m)*

Randwertprüfung *(f) n* De
En marginal test
Es prueba marginal *(f)*
Fr épreuve marginale *(f)*
It test marginale *(m)*
Pt teste marginal *(m)*

range *n* En
De Bereich *(m)*
Es margen *(m)*
Fr gamme *(f)*
It gamma *(f)*
Pt alcance *(m)*

range independence En
De Bereichsunabhängigkeit *(f)*
Es independencia del margen *(f)*
Fr indépendance de gamme *(f)*
It indipendenza di gamma *(f)*
Pt independência do alcance *(f)*

rapid-access loop En
De Schnellzugriffsschleife *(f)*
Es bucle de acceso rápido *(m)*
Fr boucle d'accès rapide *(f)*
It ciclo ad accesso rapido *(m)*
Pt circuito de acesso rápido *(m)*

rappeler le chariot Fr
De rückwärtsschreiten
En backspace
Es retroceder
It tornare indietro
Pt retroceder

rapport de disponibilité *(m)* Fr
De Arbeitsverhältnis *(n)*
En operating ratio
Es relación de utilización *(f)*
It rapporto di operazione *(m)*
Pt ratio de operação *(f)*

rapport de pliage *(m)* Fr
De Faltverhältnis *(n)*
En folding ratio
Es relación de plegado *(f)*
It rapporto pieghevole *(m)*
Pt ratio de dobragem *(f)*

rapporto di operazione *(m)* It
De Arbeitsverhältnis *(n)*
En operating ratio
Es relación de utilización *(f)*
Fr rapport de disponibilité *(m)*
Pt ratio de operação *(f)*

rapport d'utilisation *(m)* Fr
De Benutzungsverhältnis *(n)*
En utilization ratio
Es relación de utilización *(f)*
It rapporto di utilizzazione *(m)*
Pt ratio de utilização *(f)*

rapporto di utilizzazione *(m)* It
De Benutzungsverhältnis *(n)*
En utilization ratio
Es relación de utilización *(f)*
Fr rapport d'utilisation *(m)*
Pt ratio de utilização *(f)*

rapporto pieghevole *(m)* It
De Faltverhältnis *(n)*
En folding ratio
Es relación de plegado *(f)*
Fr rapport de pliage *(m)*
Pt ratio de dobragem *(f)*

rapporto segnale-rumore *(m)* It
De Rauschverhältnis *(n)*
En signal-to-noise ratio
Es relación señal-ruido *(f)*
Fr rapport signal-bruit *(m)*
Pt ratio entre sinal e ruído *(f)*

rapport signal-bruit *(m)* Fr
De Rauschverhältnis *(n)*
En signal-to-noise ratio
Es relación señal-ruido *(f)*
It rapporto segnale-rumore *(m)*
Pt ratio entre sinal e ruído *(f)*

rappresentazione incrementale *(f)* It
De schrittweise Darstellung *(f)*
En incremental representation
Es representación incremental *(f)*
Fr représentation incrémentielle *(f)*
Pt representação incremental *(f)*

Rasteranzeige *(f) n* De
En raster display
Es presentación de trama *(f)*
Fr affichage tramé *(m)*
It visualizzazione trama *(f)*
Pt apresentação quadriculada *(f)*

raster display En
De Rasteranzeige *(f)*
Es presentación de trama *(f)*
Fr affichage tramé *(m)*
It visualizzazione trama *(f)*
Pt apresentação quadriculada *(f)*

ratio de dobragem *(f)* Pt
De Faltverhältnis *(n)*
En folding ratio
Es relación de plegado *(f)*
Fr rapport de pliage *(m)*
It rapporto pieghevole *(m)*

ratio de operação *(f)* Pt
De Arbeitsverhältnis *(n)*
En operating ratio
Es relación de utilización *(f)*
Fr rapport de disponibilité *(m)*
It rapporto di operazione *(m)*

ratio de utilização *(f)* Pt
De Benutzungsverhältnis *(n)*

En utilization ratio
Es relación de utilización *(f)*
Fr rapport d'utilisation *(m)*
It rapporto di utilizzazione *(m)*

ratio entre sinal e ruído *(f)* Pt
De Rauschverhältnis *(n)*
En signal-to-noise ratio
Es relación señal-ruido *(f)*
Fr rapport signal-bruit *(m)*
It rapporto segnale-rumore *(m)*

Rauschbetriebsart *(f) n* De
En noisy mode
Es modo ruidoso *(m)*
Fr mode bruyant *(m)*
It modalità rumorosa *(f)*
Pt modo ruidoso *(m)*

Rauschen *(n) n* De
En noise
Es ruido *(m)*
Fr bruit *(m)*
It rumore *(m)*
Pt ruído *(m)*

Rauschverhältnis *(n) n* De
En signal-to-noise ratio
Es relación señal-ruido *(f)*
Fr rapport signal-bruit *(m)*
It rapporto segnale-rumore *(m)*
Pt ratio entre sinal e ruído *(f)*

raw data En
De Ursprungsdaten *(pl)*
Es datos sin procesar *(m pl)*
Fr données brutes *(f pl)*
It dati crudi *(m pl)*
Pt dados em bruto *(m pl)*

réacheminer *vb* Fr
De wiederführen
En reroute
Es reencaminar
It dirottare
Pt reencaminhar

read *vb* En
De lesen
Es leer
Fr lire
It leggere
Pt ler

read *n* En
De Lesung *(f)*
Es lectura *(f)*
Fr lecture *(f)*
It lettura *(f)*
Pt leitura *(f)*

reader *n* En
De Leser *(m)*
Es lectora *(f)*
Fr lecteur *(m)*
It lettore *(m)*
Pt leitor *(m)*

read head En
De Lesekopf *(m)*
Es cabeza de lectura *(f)*
Fr tête de lecture *(f)*
It testina di lettura *(f)*
Pt cabeça leitora *(f)*

read-only memory (ROM) En
De Festspeicher *(m)*
Es memoria fija *(f)*
Fr mémoire fixe *(f)*
It memoria soltanto di lettura *(f)*
Pt memória apenas de leitura *(f)*

read out En
De auslesen
Es leer en salida
Fr extraire de la memoire
It leggere dalla memoria
Pt ler em saida

read-out *n* En
De Ausleser *(m)*
Es lectura de salida *(f)*
Fr sortie de lecture *(f)*
It lettura dalla memoria *(f)*
Pt leitura de saida *(f)*

read rate En
De Auslese-geschwindigkeit *(f)*
Es velocidad de lectura *(f)*
Fr vitesse de lecture *(f)*
It volume di lettura *(m)*
Pt velocidade de leitura *(f)*

read time En
De Auslesezeit *(f)*
Es tiempo de lectura *(m)*
Fr durée de lecture *(f)*
It tempo di lettura *(m)*
Pt tempo de leitura *(m)*

read-write channel En
De Lesen-Schreiben-Kanal *(m)*
Es canal de lectura-escritura *(m)*
Fr voie lecture-écriture *(f)*
It canale di lettura-scrittura *(m)*
Pt canal de leitura-escrita *(m)*

read-write head En
De Les-Schreibkopf *(m)*
Es cabeza de lectura-escritura *(f)*
Fr tête lecture-écriture *(f)*
It testina di lettura-scrittura *(f)*
Pt cabeça de leitura-escrita *(f)*

reajustar *vb* Es
De rückstellen
En reset
Fr mettre à zéro
It riazzerare
Pt tornar a acertar

realimentação *(f) n* Pt
De Rückkopplung *(f)*
En feedback
Es realimentación *(f)*
Fr rétroaction *(f)*
It retroazione *(f)*

realimentación *(f) n* Es
De Rückkopplung *(f)*
En feedback
Fr rétroaction *(f)*
It retroazione *(f)*
Pt realimentação *(f)*

realización *(f) n* Es
De Durchführung *(f)*
En implementation
Fr mise en application *(f)*
It implementazione *(f)*
Pt implementação *(f)*

Realspeicher *(m) n* De
En real store
Es memoria real *(f)*
Fr mémoire réelle *(f)*
It memoria reale *(f)*
Pt armazém real *(m)*

real store En
De Realspeicher *(m)*
Es memoria real *(f)*
Fr mémoire réelle *(f)*
It memoria reale *(f)*
Pt armazém real *(m)*

real time En
De Echtzeit *(f)*
Es tiempo real *(m)*
Fr temps réel *(m)*
It tempo reale *(m)*
Pt tempo real *(m)*

real-time clock En
De Uhrzeitgeber *(m)*
Es reloj binario *(m)*
Fr horloge temps réel *(f)*
It orologio di tempo reale *(m)*
Pt relógio de tempo real *(m)*

real-time processing En
De Uhrzeigverarbeitung *(f)*
Es proceso en tiempo real *(m)*
Fr traitement en temps réel *(m)*
It elaborazione in tempo reale *(f)*
Pt processamento de tempo real *(m)*

reanudación *(f) n* Es
De Wiederstart *(m)*
En restart
Fr relancement *(m)*
It ricominciamento *(m)*
Pt novo arranque *(m)*

reanudar *vb* Es
De wiederstarten
En restart
Fr relancer
It ripartire
Pt rearrancar

rearmazenar *vb* Pt
De in Ausgangsstellung bringen
En restore
Es restaurar
Fr rétablir
It ripristinare

rearrancar *vb* Pt
De wiederstarten
En restart
Es reanudar
Fr relancer
It ripartire

rebobinar *vb* Es
De wiederaufwickeln
En rewind
Fr rebobiner
It riavvolgere
Pt tornar a enrolar

rebobiner *vb* Fr
De wiederaufwickeln
En rewind
Es rebobinar
It riavvolgere
Pt tornar a enrolar

recargar *vb* Es
De wiederladen
En reload
Fr recharger
It ricaricare
Pt recarregar

recarregar *vb* Pt
De wiederladen
En reload
Es recargar
Fr recharger
It ricaricare

recharger *vb* Fr
De wiederladen
En reload
Es recargar
It ricaricare
Pt recarregar

Rechenwerk *(n) n* De
En arithmetic unit (AU)
Es unidad aritmética (UA) *(f)*
Fr unité de calcul (UC) *(f)*
It unità aritmetica *(f)*
Pt unidade aritmética *(f)*

recherche *(f) n* Fr
De Suche *(f)*
En search
Es búsqueda sistemática *(f)*
It ricerca *(f)*
Pt busca *(f)*

recherche dichotomique *(f)* Fr
De binäres Suchen; dichotomizierendes Suchen *(n)*
En binary search; dichotomizing search
Es búsqueda binaria; búsqueda dicotómica *(f)*
It ricerca binaria; ricerca dicotoma *(f)*
Pt busca binária; busca dicotomizante *(f)*

recherche documentaire *(f)* Fr
De Wiederauffinden von Informationen *(n)*
En information retrieval
Es recuperación de la información *(f)*
It reperimento delle informazioni *(m)*
Pt recuperação da informação *(f)*

recherche opérationnelle *(f)* Fr
De Unternehmungs-forschung *(f)*
En operational research (OR)
Es investigación operativa *(f)*
It ricerca operativa *(f)*
Pt investigação operacional *(f)*

recherche par chaînage *(f)* Fr
De Kettensuche *(f)*
En chaining search
Es búsqueda de la cadena *(f)*
It ricerca concatenata *(f)*
Pt busca de cadeia *(f)*

Rechner *(m) n* De
En calculator
Es calculadora *(f)*
Fr calculateur *(m)*
It calcolatore *(m)*
Pt calculador *(m)*

rechtsbündig *adj* De
En right-justified
Es justificado a la derecha
Fr cadré à droite
It giustificato a destra
Pt justificado à direita

Rechtsschiebung *(f) n* De
En right shift
Es desplazamiento a la derecha *(m)*
Fr décalage à droite *(m)*
It spostamento a destra *(m)*
Pt mudança à direita *(f)*

recompilar *vb* Es, Pt
De wiederkompilieren
En recompile
Fr recompiler
It ricompilare

recompile *vb* En
De wiederkompilieren
Es recompilar
Fr recompiler
It ricompilare
Pt recompilar

recompiler *vb* Fr
De wiederkompilieren
En recompile
Es recompilar
It ricompilare
Pt recompilar

reconfiguração *(f) n* Pt
De Rekonfiguration *(f)*
En reconfiguration
Es reconfiguración *(f)*
Fr reconfiguration *(f)*
It riconfigurazione *(f)*

reconfiguración *(f) n* Es
De Rekonfiguration *(f)*
En reconfiguration
Fr reconfiguration *(f)*
It riconfigurazione *(f)*
Pt reconfiguração *(f)*

reconfiguration *n* En; Fr *(f)*
De Rekonfiguration *(f)*
Es reconfiguración *(f)*
It riconfigurazione *(f)*
Pt reconfiguração *(f)*

reconhecimento de caracteres *(m)* Pt
De Zeichenerkennung *(f)*
En character recognition
Es reconocimiento de caracteres *(m)*
Fr reconnaissance de caractères *(f)*
It riconoscimento di carattere *(m)*

reconhecimento de caracteres de tinta magnética *(m)* Pt
De Erkennung von Magnettintenzeichen *(f)*
En magnetic-ink character recognition
Es reconocimiento de caracteres de tinta magnética *(m)*
Fr reconnaissance magnétique de caractères *(f)*
It riconoscimento di caratteri di inchiostro magnetico *(m)*

reconhecimento de marcas ópticas *(m)* Pt
De optische Zeichenerkennung *(f)*
En optical mark recognition
Es reconocimiento óptico de marcas *(m)*
Fr reconnaissance optique de marques *(f)*
It riconoscimento di segni ottici *(m)*

reconhecimento de padrão *(m)* Pt
De Strukturerkennung *(f)*
En pattern recognition
Es reconocimiento de configuraciones *(m)*
Fr reconnaissance des formes *(f)*
It riconoscimento di modelli *(m)*

reconhecimento óptico de caracteres *(m)* Pt

De optische Zeichenerkennung *(f)*
En optical character recognition (OCR)
Es reconocimiento óptico de caracteres *(m)*
Fr reconnaissance optique des caractères (ROC) *(f)*
It riconoscimento ottico di caratteri *(m)*

reconnaissance de caractères *(f)* Fr
De Zeichenerkennung *(f)*
En character recognition
Es reconocimiento de caracteres *(m)*
It riconoscimento di carattere *(m)*
Pt reconhecimento de caracteres *(m)*

reconnaissance des formes *(f)* Fr
De Strukturerkennung *(f)*
En pattern recognition
Es reconocimiento de configuraciones *(m)*
It riconoscimento di modelli *(m)*
Pt reconhecimento de padrão *(m)*

reconnaissance magnétique de caractères *(f)* Fr
De Erkennung von Magnettintenzeichen *(f)*
En magnetic-ink character recognition
Es reconocimiento de caracteres de tinta magnética *(m)*
It riconoscimento di caratteri di inchiostro magnetico *(m)*
Pt reconhecimento de caracteres de tinta magnética *(m)*

reconnaissance optique de marques *(f)* Fr
De optische Zeichenerkennung *(f)*
En optical mark recognition
Es reconocimiento óptico de marcas *(m)*
It riconoscimento di segni ottici *(m)*
Pt reconhecimento de marcas ópticas *(m)*

reconnaissance optique des caractères (ROC) *(f)* Fr
De optische Zeichenerkennung *(f)*
En optical character recognition (OCR)
Es reconocimiento óptico de caracteres *(m)*
It riconoscimento ottico di caratteri *(m)*
Pt reconhecimento óptico de caracteres *(m)*

reconocimiento de caracteres *(m)* Es
De Zeichenerkennung *(f)*
En character recognition
Fr reconnaissance de caractères *(f)*
It riconoscimento di carattere *(m)*
Pt reconhecimento de caracteres *(m)*

reconocimiento de caracteres de tinta magnética *(m)* Es
De Erkennung von Magnettintenzeichen *(f)*
En magnetic-ink character recognition
Fr reconnaissance magnétique de caractères *(f)*
It riconoscimento di caratteri di inchiostro magnetico *(m)*
Pt reconhecimento de caracteres de tinta magnética *(m)*

reconocimiento de configuraciones *(m)* Es
De Strukturerkennung *(f)*
En pattern recognition
Fr reconnaissance des formes *(f)*
It riconoscimento di modelli *(m)*
Pt reconhecimento de padrão *(m)*

reconocimiento óptico de caracteres *(m)* Es
De optische Zeichenerkennung *(f)*
En optical character recognition (OCR)
Fr reconnaissance optique des caractères (ROC) *(f)*
It riconoscimento ottico di caratteri *(m)*
Pt reconhecimento óptico de caracteres *(m)*

reconocimiento óptico de marcas *(m)* Es
De optische Zeichenerkennung *(f)*
En optical mark recognition
Fr reconnaissance optique de marques *(f)*
It riconoscimento di segni ottici *(m)*
Pt reconhecimento de marcas ópticas *(m)*

reconstitución *(f)* *n* Es
De Neubildung *(f)*
En reconstitution
Fr reconstitution *(f)*
It riconstituzione *(f)*
Pt reconstituição *(f)*

reconstituição *(f)* *n* Pt
De Neubildung *(f)*
En reconstitution
Es reconstitución *(f)*
Fr reconstitution *(f)*
It riconstituzione *(f)*

reconstitution *n* En; Fr *(f)*
De Neubildung *(f)*
Es reconstitución *(f)*
It riconstituzione *(f)*
Pt reconstituição *(f)*

recopilación de datos *(f)* Es
De Datenerfassung *(f)*
En data collection
Fr collecte de données *(f)*
It raccolta dei dati *(f)*
Pt colecção de dados *(f)*

record *n* En; It *(m)*
De Satz *(m)*
Es registro *(m)*
Fr enregistrement *(m)*
Pt registo *(m)*

record *vb* En
De aufzeichnen
Es registrar
Fr enregistrer
It registrare
Pt registar

record blocking En
De Satzblockierung *(f)*
Es bloqueo de registro *(m)*
Fr groupage enregistrement *(m)*
It bloccaggio di record *(m)*
Pt bloqueio de registo *(m)*

record concatenato *(m)* It
De Kettensatz *(m)*
En chained record
Es registro en cadena *(m)*
Fr enregistrement en chaîne *(m)*
Pt registo com cadeia *(m)*

record de modification *(m)* Fr
De Änderungssatz *(m)*
En change record
Es registro de cambio *(m)*
It record di cambiamento *(m)*
Pt registo de mudança *(m)*

record di cambiamento *(m)* It
De Änderungssatz *(m)*
En change record
Es registro de cambio *(m)*
Fr record de modification *(m)*
Pt registo de mudança *(m)*

record di cancellazione *(m)* It
De Löschungssatz *(m)*
En deletion record

Es registro de eliminación *(m)*
Fr enregistrement d'effacement *(m)*
Pt registo de apagamento *(m)*

record di fine *(m)* It
De Beisatz *(m)*
En trailer record
Es registro de cola *(m)*
Fr article fin *(m)*
Pt registo de trailer *(m)*

record di unità *(m)* It
De Einheitssatz *(m)*
En unit record
Es registro unitario *(m)*
Fr enregistrement unitaire *(m)*
Pt registo de unidades *(m)*

record head En
De Aufzeichnungskopf *(m)*
Es cabeza de registro *(f)*
Fr tête d'enregistrement *(f)*
It testina del record *(f)*
Pt cabeça de registo *(f)*

recording density En
De Schreibdichte *(f)*
Es densidad de registro *(f)*
Fr densité d'enregistrement *(f)*
It densità di registrazione *(f)*
Pt densidade de registo *(f)*

record length En
De Satzlänge *(f)*
Es longitud de registro *(f)*
Fr longueur d'enregistrement *(f)*
It lunghezza del record *(f)*
Pt comprimento de registo *(m)*

record principale *(m)* It
De Hauptsatz *(m)*
En master record
Es registro maestro *(m)*
Fr article du fichier permanent *(m)*
Pt registo principal *(m)*

record protetto *(m)* It
De geschützter Satz *(m)*
En protected record
Es registro protegido *(m)*
Fr enregistrement protégé *(m)*
Pt registo protegido *(m)*

recorrência *(f) n* Pt
De Rekursion *(f)*
En recursion
Es recursión *(f)*
Fr récurrence *(f)*
It ricorrenza *(f)*

recorrente *adj* Pt
De rekursiv
En recursive
Es recursivo
Fr récurrent
It ricorrente

recorte *(m) n* Pt
De Stanzrückstand *(m)*
En chad
Es confeti *(m)*
Fr confetti *(m)*
It coriandoli di perforazione *(m)*

recorte poligonal *(m)* Es, Pt
De Vieleckbegrenzung *(f)*
En polygon clipping
Fr écrêtage polygone *(m)*
It limitazione poligonale *(f)*

recovery *n* En
De Wiederherstellung *(f)*
Es reparación *(f)*
Fr récupération *(f)*
It recupero *(m)*
Pt recuperação *(f)*

récrire *vb* Fr
De wiederschreiben
En rewrite
Es reescribir
It riscrivere
Pt tornar a escrever

recubrir *vb* Es
De überschreiben
En overwrite
Fr superposer une écriture
It inscrivere per riempimento
Pt escrever por cima

recuperação *(f) n* Pt
De Wiederauffinden; Wiederherstellung *(n f)*
En recovery; retrieval
Es reparación *(f)*
Fr extraction; récupération *(f)*
It recupero; reperimento *(m)*

recuperação da informação *(f)* Pt
De Wiederauffinden von Informationen *(n)*
En information retrieval
Es recuperación de la información *(f)*
Fr recherche documentaire *(f)*
It reperimento delle informazioni *(m)*

recuperação de alto nível *(f)* Pt
De Wiederherstellung der höheren Übermittlungsstufe *(f)*
En high-level recovery
Es recuperación de alto nivel *(f)*
Fr redressement évolué *(m)*
It ricupero di alto livello *(m)*

recuperação de falha *(f)* Pt
De Ausfallrückgängigkeit *(f)*
En failure recovery
Es reparación de fallo *(f)*
Fr redressement de défaillance *(m)*
It recupero di fallimento *(m)*

recuperação falsa *(f)* Pt
De unechtes Wiederauffinden *(n)*
En false retrieval
Es falsa recuperación *(f)*
Fr référence non pertinente *(f)*
It falso reperimento *(m)*

recuperación *(f) n* Es
De Wiederauffinden *(n)*
En retrieval
Fr extraction *(f)*
It reperimento *(m)*
Pt recuperação *(f)*

recuperación de alto nivel *(f)* Es
De Wiederherstellung der höheren Übermittlungsstufe *(f)*
En high-level recovery
Fr redressement évolué *(m)*
It ricupero di alto livello *(m)*
Pt recuperação de alto nível *(f)*

recuperación de la información *(f)* Es
De Wiederauffinden von Informationen *(n)*
En information retrieval
Fr recherche documentaire *(f)*
It reperimento delle informazioni *(m)*
Pt recuperação da informação *(f)*

récupération *(f) n* Fr
De Wiederherstellung *(f)*
En recovery
Es reparación *(f)*
It recupero *(m)*
Pt recuperação *(f)*

recupero *(m) n* It
De Wiederherstellung *(f)*
En recovery
Es reparación *(f)*
Fr récupération *(f)*
Pt recuperação *(f)*

recupero di fallimento *(m) n* It
De Ausfallrückgängigkeit *(f)*
En failure recovery
Es reparación de fallo *(f)*
Fr redressement de défaillance *(m)*
Pt recuperação de falha *(f)*

récurrence *(f) n* Fr
De Rekursion *(f)*
En recursion
Es recursión *(f)*

It ricorrenza *(f)*
Pt recorrência *(f)*

récurrent *adj* Fr
De rekursiv
En recursive
Es recursivo
It ricorrente
Pt recorrente

recursion *n* En
De Rekursion *(f)*
Es recursión *(f)*
Fr récurrence *(f)*
It ricorrenza *(f)*
Pt recorrência *(f)*

recursión *(f) n* Es
De Rekursion *(f)*
En recursion
Fr récurrence *(f)*
It ricorrenza *(f)*
Pt recorrência *(f)*

recursive *adj* En
De rekursiv
Es recursivo
Fr récurrent
It ricorrente
Pt recorrente

recursivo *adj* Es
De rekursiv
En recursive
Fr récurrent
It ricorrente
Pt recorrente

recurso *(m) n* Es
De Betriebsmittel *(n)*
En resource
Fr ressource *(f)*
It risorsa *(f)*
Pt recurso *(m)*

recurso *(m) n* Pt
De Betriebsmittel *(n)*
En resource
Es recurso *(m)*
Fr ressource *(f)*
It risorsa *(f)*

red *(f) n* Es
De Netz *(n)*
En network
Fr réseau *(m)*
It rete *(f)*
Pt rede *(f)*

Redakteur *(m) n* De
En editor
Es programa de edición *(m)*
Fr programme d'édition *(m)*
It programma di manipolazione *(m)*
Pt programa de edição *(m)*

red de comunicaciones *(f)* Es
De Kommunikationsnetz *(n)*
En communication network
Fr réseau de communication *(m)*
It rete di comunicazione *(f)*
Pt rede de comunicação *(f)*

red de conmutación de mensajes *(f)* Es
De geschaltetes Nachrichtennetz *(n)*
En switched-message network
Fr réseau de messages commutés *(m)*
It rete di messaggi commutati *(f)*
Pt rede de mensagens comutadas *(f)*

red de conmutación de paquetes *(f)* Es
De Paketschaltennetz *(n)*
En packet-switched network
Fr réseau de commutation par paquets *(m)*
It rete di commutazione di pacci *(f)*
Pt rede com comutação de pacotes *(f)*

red de puntos múltiples *(f)* Es
De Mehrpunktnetz *(n)*
En multipoint network
Fr réseau multi-point *(m)*
It rete a punti multipli *(f)*
Pt rede de pontos múltiplos *(f)*

red digital *(f)* Es
De Digitalnetz *(n)*
En digital network
Fr réseau numérique *(m)*
It rete digitale *(f)*
Pt rede digital *(f)*

rede *(f) n* Pt
De Netz *(n)*
En network
Es red *(f)*
Fr réseau *(m)*
It rete *(f)*

rede com comutação de pacotes *(f)* Pt
De Paketschaltennetz *(n)*
En packet-switched network
Es red de conmutación de paquetes *(f)*
Fr réseau de commutation par paquets *(m)*
It rete di commutazione di pacci *(f)*

rede de comunicação *(f)* Pt
De Kommunikationsnetz *(n)*
En communication network
Es red de comunicaciones *(f)*
Fr réseau de communication *(m)*
It rete di comunicazione *(f)*

rede de dados *(f)* Pt
De Datennetz *(n)*
En data network
Es red para transmisión de datos *(f)*
Fr réseau de transmission de données *(m)*
It rete di dati *(f)*

rede de mensagens comutadas *(f)* Pt
De geschaltetes Nachrichtennetz *(n)*
En switched-message network
Es red de conmutación de mensajes *(f)*
Fr réseau de messages commutés *(m)*
It rete di messaggi commutati *(f)*

rede de pontos múltiplos *(f)* Pt
De Mehrpunktnetz *(n)*
En multipoint network
Es red de puntos múltiples *(f)*
Fr réseau multi-point *(m)*
It rete a punti multipli *(f)*

rede digital *(f)* Pt
De Digitalnetz *(n)*
En digital network
Es red digital *(f)*
Fr réseau numérique *(m)*
It rete digitale *(f)*

redondance *(f) n* Fr
De Redundanz *(f)*
En redundancy
Es redundancia *(f)*
It ridondanza *(f)*
Pt redundância *(f)*

redondear *vb* Es
De runden
En round off
Fr arrondir
It arrotondare
Pt arredondar

red para transmisión de datos *(f)* Es
De Datennetz *(n)*
En data network
Fr réseau de transmission de données *(m)*
It rete di dati *(f)*
Pt rede de dados *(f)*

redressement de défaillance *(m)* Fr
De Ausfallrückgängigkeit *(f)*
En failure recovery
Es reparación de fallo *(f)*
It recupero di fallimento *(m)*
Pt recuperação de falha *(f)*

redressement évolué *(m)* Fr
De Wiederherstellung der höheren

Übermittlungsstufe *(f)*
En high-level recovery
Es recuperación de alto nivel *(f)*
It ricupero di alto livello *(m)*
Pt recuperação de alto nível *(f)*

redução de dados *(f)* Pt
De Datenverdichtung *(f)*
En data reduction
Es reducción de datos *(f)*
Fr réduction de données *(f)*
It riduzione dei dati *(f)*

redução de dados sobre a linha *(f)* Pt
De direkte Datenverdichtung *(f)*
En on-line data reduction
Es reducción de datos en línea *(f)*
Fr réduction des données en exploitation continue *(f)*
It riduzione in linea dei dati *(f)*

reducción de datos *(f)* Es
De Datenverdichtung *(f)*
En data reduction
Fr réduction de données *(f)*
It riduzione dei dati *(f)*
Pt redução de dados *(f)*

reducción de datos en línea *(f)* Es
De direkte Datenverdichtung *(f)*
En on-line data reduction
Fr réduction des données en exploitation continue *(f)*
It riduzione in linea dei dati *(f)*
Pt redução de dados sobre a linha *(f)*

reduced format En
De verdichtetes Format *(n)*
Es formato reducido *(m)*
Fr structure réduite *(f)*
It formato ridotto *(m)*
Pt formato reduzido *(m)*

réduction de données *(f)* Fr
De Datenverdichtung *(f)*
En data reduction
Es reducción de datos *(f)*
It riduzione dei dati *(f)*
Pt redução de dados *(f)*

réduction des données en exploitation continue *(f)* Fr
De direkte Datenverdichtung *(f)*
En on-line data reduction
Es reducción de datos en línea *(f)*
It riduzione in linea dei dati *(f)*
Pt redução de dados sobre a linha *(f)*

redundancia *(f) n* Es
De Redundanz *(f)*
En redundancy
Fr redondance *(f)*
It ridondanza *(f)*
Pt redundância *(f)*

redundância *(f) n* Pt
De Redundanz *(f)*
En redundancy
Es redundancia *(f)*
Fr redondance *(f)*
It ridondanza *(f)*

redundancy *n* En
De Redundanz *(f)*
Es redundancia *(f)*
Fr redondance *(f)*
It ridondanza *(f)*
Pt redundância *(f)*

redundancy check En
De Redundanzkontrolle *(f)*
Es verificación por redundancia *(f)*
Fr contrôle par redondance *(m)*
It controllo di ridondanza *(m)*
Pt verificação de redundância *(f)*

redundant code En
De redundanter Code *(m)*
Es código redundante *(m)*
Fr code redondant *(m)*
It codice ridondante *(m)*
Pt código redundante *(m)*

redundanter Code *(m)* De
En redundant code
Es código redundante *(m)*
Fr code redondant *(m)*
It codice ridondante *(m)*
Pt código redundante *(m)*

Redundanz *(f) n* De
En redundancy
Es redundancia *(f)*
Fr redondance *(f)*
It ridondanza *(f)*
Pt redundância *(f)*

Redundanzkontrolle *(f) n* De
En redundancy check
Es verificación por redundancia *(f)*
Fr contrôle par redondance *(m)*
It controllo di ridondanza *(m)*
Pt verificação de redundância *(f)*

reel *n* En
De Spule *(f)*
Es carrete *(m)*
Fr bobine *(f)*
It bobina *(f)*
Pt bobina *(f)*

reel number En
De Spulennummer *(f)*
Es número de carrete *(m)*
Fr numéro d'ordre de la bobine *(m)*
It numero bobina *(m)*
Pt número de bobina *(m)*

reemisor *(m) n* Es
De Relaiszentrale *(f)*
En relay centre
Fr centre de commutation *(m)*
It centro di relè *(m)*
Pt centro de relé *(m)*

reencaminar *vb* Es
De wiederführen
En reroute
Fr réacheminer
It dirottare
Pt reencaminhar

reencaminhar *vb* Pt
De wiederführen
En reroute
Es reencaminar
Fr réacheminer
It dirottare

re-entrant procedure En
De Wiedereintreter-routine *(f)*
Es procedimiento reentrable *(m)*
Fr procédure d'invariance *(f)*
It procedimento rientrante *(m)*
Pt procedimento de reentrância *(m)*

reescribir *vb* Es
De wiederschreiben
En rewrite
Fr récrire
It riscrivere
Pt tornar a escrever

réexécuter *vb* Fr
De wiederholen
En rerun
Es repetir la pasada
It riprendere
Pt tornar a passar

reference address En
De Bezugsadresse *(f)*
Es dirección de referencia *(f)*
Fr adresse primitive *(f)*
It indirizzo di riferimento *(m)*
Pt endereço de referência *(m)*

reference listing En
De Bezugsliste *(f)*
Es lista de referencias *(f)*
Fr listage primitif *(m)*
It listato di riferimento *(m)*

Pt listagem de referência *(f)*

référence non pertinente *(f)* Fr
De unechtes Wiederauffinden *(n)*
En false retrieval
Es falsa recuperación *(f)*
It falso reperimento *(m)*
Pt recuperação falsa *(f)*

referencia *(f) n* Es
De Fixpunkt *(m)*
En benchmark
Fr repère *(m)*
It riferimento *(m)*
Pt referência de nível *(f)*

referência de nível *(f)* Pt
De Fixpunkt *(m)*
En benchmark
Es referencia *(f)*
Fr repère *(m)*
It riferimento *(m)*

refrescar *vb* Pt
De auffrischen
En refresh
Es regenerar
Fr régénérer
It rinfrescare

refresh *vb* En
De auffrischen
Es regenerar
Fr régénérer
It rinfrescare
Pt refrescar

refresh display En
De Auffrischungsanzeige *(f)*
Es representación regenerada *(f)*
Fr affichagerégénération *(m)*
It visualizzazione di aggiornamento *(f)*
Pt apresentação de refrescamento *(f)*

refugo *(m) n* Pt
De Schund *(m)*
En garbage
Es información parásita *(f)*
Fr informations parasites *(f pl)*
It rifiuti *(m pl)*

regelmäßige Wartung *(f)* De
En routine maintenance
Es mantenimiento de rutina *(m)*
Fr entretien de routine *(m)*
It manutenzione ordinaria *(f)*
Pt manutenção de rotina *(f)*

regeneração *(f) n* Pt
De Regenerierung *(f)*
En regeneration
Es regeneración *(f)*
Fr régénération *(f)*
It rigenerazione *(f)*

regeneración *(f) n* Es
De Regenerierung *(f)*
En regeneration
Fr régénération *(f)*
It rigenerazione *(f)*
Pt regeneração *(f)*

regenerar *vb* Es
De auffrischen
En refresh
Fr régénérer
It rinfrescare
Pt refrescar

regeneration *n* En
De Regenerierung *(f)*
Es regeneración *(f)*
Fr régénération *(f)*
It rigenerazione *(f)*
Pt regeneração *(f)*

régénération *(f) n* Fr
De Regenerierung *(f)*
En regeneration
Es regeneración *(f)*
It rigenerazione *(f)*
Pt regeneração *(f)*

regenerative Auslesung *(f)* De
En regenerative read
Es lectura regenerativa *(f)*
Fr lecture régénératrice *(f)*
It lettura rigenerativa *(f)*
Pt leitura regenerativa *(f)*

regenerative read En
De regenerative Auslesung *(f)*
Es lectura regenerativa *(f)*
Fr lecture régénératrice *(f)*
It lettura rigenerativa *(f)*
Pt leitura regenerativa *(f)*

regenerativer Speicher *(m)* De
En regenerative store
Es memoria regenerativa *(f)*
Fr mémoire à régénération *(f)*
It memoria rigenerativa *(f)*
Pt armazém regenerativo *(m)*

regenerative store En
De regenerativer Speicher *(m)*
Es memoria regenerativa *(f)*
Fr mémoire à régénération *(f)*
It memoria rigenerativa *(f)*
Pt armazém regenerativo *(m)*

régénérer *vb* Fr
De auffrischen
En refresh
Es regenerar
It rinfrescare
Pt refrescar

Regenerierung *(f) n* De
En regeneration
Es regeneración *(f)*
Fr régénération *(f)*
It rigenerazione *(f)*
Pt regeneração *(f)*

registador automático *(m)* Pt
De Schreibgerät *(n)*
En logger
Es registrador automático *(m)*
Fr enregistreur automatique *(m)*
It registratore automatico *(m)*

registador de películas *(m)* Pt
De Filmaufzeichner *(m)*
En film recorder
Es registrador de películas *(m)*
Fr unité d'enregistrement sur film *(f)*
It registratore di pellicole *(m)*

registar *vb* Pt
De aufzeichnen
En record
Es registrar
Fr enregistrer
It registrare

registar em diário Pt
De senden
En log
Es registrar
Fr consigner
It registrare

register *n* En
De Register *(n)*
Es registro *(m)*
Fr registre *(m)*
It registro *(m)*
Pt registo *(m)*

Register *(n) n* De
En register
Es registro *(m)*
Fr registre *(m)*
It registro *(m)*
Pt registo *(m)*

registo *(m) n* Pt
De Register; Satz *(n m)*
En record; register
Es registro *(m)*
Fr enregistrement; registre *(m)*
It record; registro *(m)*

registo com cadeia *(m)* Pt
De Kettensatz *(m)*
En chained record
Es registro en cadena *(m)*
Fr enregistrement en chaîne *(m)*
It record concatenato *(m)*

registo de apagamento *(m)* Pt
De Löschungssatz *(m)*
En deletion record
Es registro de eliminación *(m)*

Fr enregistrement d'effacement *(m)*
It record di cancellazione *(m)*

registo de base *(m)* Pt
De Basisregister *(n)*
En base register
Es registro de base *(m)*
Fr registre de base *(m)*
It registro base *(m)*

registo de circulação *(m)* Pt
De Umlaufregister *(n)*
En circulating register
Es registro circulante *(m)*
Fr registre circulant *(m)*
It registro circolante *(m)*

registo de controlo *(m)* Pt
De Steuerregister *(n)*
En control register
Es registro de control *(m)*
Fr registre de contrôle *(m)*
It registro di controllo *(m)*

registo de deslocamento *(m)* Pt
De Schieberegister *(n)*
En shift register
Es registro de desplazamiento *(m)*
Fr registre à décalage *(m)*
It registro per operazioni di spostamento dati *(m)*

registo de endereço de instrução *(m)* Pt
De Befehlsadressen-register *(n)*
En instruction-address register
Es registro de instrucción-dirección *(m)*
Fr registre d'adresse de l'instruction *(m)*
It registro dell'indirizzo dell'istruzione *(m)*

registo de feixe de electrões *(m)* Pt
De Elektronstrahl-aufzeichnung *(f)*
En electron beam recording (EBR)
Es registro por haz de electrones *(m)*
Fr enregistrement à faisceau électronique *(m)*
It registrazione a fascio di elettroni *(f)*

registo de mudança *(m)* Pt
De Änderungssatz *(m)*
En change record
Es registro de cambio *(m)*
Fr record de modification *(m)*
It record di cambiamento *(m)*

registo de trailer *(m)* Pt
De Beisatz *(m)*
En trailer record
Es registro de cola *(m)*
Fr article fin *(m)*
It record di fine *(m)*

registo de unidades *(m)* Pt
De Einheitssatz *(m)*
En unit record
Es registro unitario *(m)*
Fr enregistrement unitaire *(m)*
It record di unità *(m)*

registo duplo *(m)* Pt
De Parallelaufzeichnung *(f)*
En dual recording
Es registro en paralelo *(m)*
Fr enregistrement double *(m)*
It registrazione duplice *(f)*

registo principal *(m)* Pt
De Hauptsatz *(m)*
En master record
Es registro maestro *(m)*
Fr article du fichier permanent *(m)*
It record principale *(m)*

registo protegido *(m)* Pt
De geschützter Satz *(m)*
En protected record
Es registro protegido *(m)*
Fr enregistrement protégé *(m)*
It record protetto *(m)*

registrador automático *(m)* Es
De Schreibgerät *(n)*
En logger
Fr enregistreur automatique *(m)*
It registratore automatico *(m)*
Pt registador automático *(m)*

registrador de películas *(m)* Es
De Filmaufzeichner *(m)*
En film recorder
Fr unité d'enregistrement sur film *(f)*
It registratore di pellicole *(m)*
Pt registador de películas *(m)*

registrar *vb* Es
De aufzeichnen; senden
En log; record
Fr consigner; enregistrer
It registrare
Pt registar; registar em diário

registrare *vb* It
De aufzeichnen; senden
En log; record
Es registrar
Fr consigner; enregistrer
Pt registar; registar em diário

registratore automatico *(m)* It
De Schreibgerät *(n)*
En logger
Es registrador automático *(m)*
Fr enregistreur automatique *(m)*
Pt registador automático *(m)*

registratore di pellicole *(m)* It
De Filmaufzeichner *(m)*
En film recorder
Es registrador de películas *(m)*
Fr unité d'enregistrement sur film *(f)*
Pt registador de películas *(m)*

registrazione a fascio di elettroni *(f)* It
De Elektronstrahl-aufzeichnung *(f)*
En electron beam recording (EBR)
Es registro por haz de electrones *(m)*
Fr enregistrement à faisceau électronique *(m)*
Pt registo de feixe de electrões *(m)*

registrazione duplice *(f)* It
De Parallelaufzeichnung *(f)*
En dual recording
Es registro en paralelo *(m)*
Fr enregistrement double *(m)*
Pt registo duplo *(m)*

registrazione su disco It
De Taste auf Platte
En key-to-disk
Es registro sobre disco
Fr enregistrement sur disque
Pt tecla-ao-disco

registrazione su nastro magnetico It
De Taste auf Band
En key-to-tape
Es registro sobre cinta
Fr enregistrement sur bande
Pt tecla-à-fita

registre *(m)* *n* Fr
De Register *(n)*
En register
Es registro *(m)*
It registro *(m)*
Pt registo *(m)*

registre à décalage *(m)* Fr
De Schieberegister *(n)*
En shift register
Es registro de desplazamiento *(m)*
It registro per operazioni di spostamento dati *(m)*
Pt registo de deslocamento *(m)*

registre circulant *(m)* Fr
De Umlaufregister *(n)*
En circulating register
Es registro circulante *(m)*
It registro circolante *(m)*
Pt registo de circulação *(m)*

registre d'adresse de l'instruction *(m)* Fr
De Befehlsadressen-register *(n)*
En instruction-address register
Es registro de instrucción- dirección *(m)*
It registro dell'indirizzo dell'istruzione *(m)*
Pt registo de endereço de instrução *(m)*

registre de base *(m)* Fr
De Basisregister *(n)*
En base register
Es registro de base *(m)*
It registro base *(m)*
Pt registo de base *(m)*

registre de contrôle *(m)* Fr
De Steuerregister *(n)*
En control register
Es registro de control *(m)*
It registro di controllo *(m)*
Pt registo de controlo *(m)*

registro *(m) n* Es, It
De Journal; Register; Satz *(n n m)*
En log; record; register
Fr consignation; enregistrement; registre *(f m m)*
Pt diário; registo *(m)*

registro base *(m)* It
De Basisregister *(n)*
En base register
Es registro de base *(m)*
Fr registre de base *(m)*
Pt registo de base *(m)*

registro circolante *(m)* It
De Umlaufregister *(n)*
En circulating register
Es registro circulante *(m)*
Fr registre circulant *(m)*
Pt registo de circulação *(m)*

registro circulante *(m)* Es
De Umlaufregister *(n)*
En circulating register
Fr registre circulant *(m)*
It registro circolante *(m)*
Pt registo de circulação *(m)*

registro de base *(m)* Es
De Basisregister *(n)*
En base register
Fr registre de base *(m)*
It registro base *(m)*
Pt registo de base *(m)*

registro de cambio *(m)* Es
De Änderungssatz *(m)*
En change record
Fr record de modification *(m)*
It record di cambiamento *(m)*
Pt registo de mudança *(m)*

registro de cola *(m)* Es
De Beisatz *(m)*
En trailer record
Fr article fin *(m)*
It record di fine *(m)*
Pt registo de trailer *(m)*

registro de control *(m)* Es
De Steuerregister *(n)*
En control register
Fr registre de contrôle *(m)*
It registro di controllo *(m)*
Pt registo de controlo *(m)*

registro de desplazamiento *(m)* Es
De Schieberegister *(n)*
En shift register
Fr registre à décalage *(m)*
It registro per operazioni di spostamento dati *(m)*
Pt registo de deslocamento *(m)*

registro de eliminación *(m)* Es
De Löschungssatz *(m)*
En deletion record
Fr enregistrement d'effacement *(m)*
It record di cancellazione *(m)*
Pt registo de apagamento *(m)*

registro de instrucción-dirección *(m)* Es
De Befehlsadressen-register *(n)*
En instruction-address register
Fr registre d'adresse de l'instruction *(m)*
It registro dell'indirizzo dell'istruzione *(m)*
Pt registo de endereço de instrução *(m)*

registro dell'indirizzo dell'istruzione *(m)* It
De Befehlsadressen-register *(n)*
En instruction-address register
Es registro de instrucción- dirección *(m)*
Fr registre d'adresse de l'instruction *(m)*
Pt registo de endereço de instrução *(m)*

registro di controllo *(m)* It
De Steuerregister *(n)*
En control register
Es registro de control *(m)*
Fr registre de contrôle *(m)*
Pt registo de controlo *(m)*

registro en cadena *(m)* Es
De Kettensatz *(m)*
En chained record
Fr enregistrement en chaîne *(m)*
It record concatenato *(m)*
Pt registo com cadeia *(m)*

registro en paralelo *(m)* Es
De Parallelaufzeichnung *(f)*
En dual recording
Fr enregistrement double *(m)*
It registrazione duplice *(f)*
Pt registo duplo *(m)*

registro intermedio *(m)* Es
De Pufferspeicher *(m)*
En buffer store
Fr mémoire tampon *(f)*
It memoria di transito *(f)*
Pt memória buffer *(f)*

registro maestro *(m)* Es
De Hauptsatz *(m)*
En master record
Fr article du fichier permanent *(m)*
It record principale *(m)*
Pt registo principal *(m)*

registro per operazioni di spostamento dati *(m)* It
De Schieberegister *(n)*
En shift register
Es registro de desplazamiento *(m)*
Fr registre à décalage *(m)*
Pt registo de deslocamento *(m)*

registro por haz de electrones *(m)* Es
De Elektronstrahl-aufzeichnung *(f)*
En electron beam recording (EBR)
Fr enregistrement à faisceau électronique *(m)*
It registrazione a fascio di elettroni *(f)*

Pt registo de feixe de electrões *(m)*

registro protegido *(m)* Es
De geschützter Satz *(m)*
En protected record
Fr enregistrement protégé *(m)*
It record protetto *(m)*
Pt registo protegido *(m)*

registro sobre cinta Es
De Taste auf Band
En key-to-tape
Fr enregistrement sur bande
It registrazione su nastro magnetico
Pt tecla-à-fita

registro sobre disco Es
De Taste auf Platte
En key-to-disk
Fr enregistrement sur disque
It registrazione su disco
Pt tecla-ao-disco

registro unitario *(m)* Es
De Einheitssatz *(m)*
En unit record
Fr enregistrement unitaire *(m)*
It record di unità *(m)*
Pt registo de unidades *(m)*

régler *vb* Fr
De setzen
En set
Es ajustar
It disporre
Pt colocar

regressar *vb* Pt
De rücklaufen
En return
Es retornar
Fr renvoyer à
It ritornare

regresso *(m) n* Pt
De Rücklauf *(m)*
En return
Es retorno *(m)*
Fr retour *(m)*
It ritorno *(m)*

Reihendrucker *(m) n* De
En serial printer
Es impresora en serie *(f)*
Fr imprimante série *(f)*
It stampatrice in serie *(f)*
Pt impressora em série *(f)*

Reihen-Parallelumwandler *(m)* De
En serial-parallel converter
Es convertidor serie-paralelo *(m)*
Fr convertisseur série-parallèle *(m)*
It convertitore serie-parallelo *(m)*
Pt conversor de série em paralelo *(m)*

Reihenübergabe *(f) n* De
En serial transfer
Es transferencia en serie *(f)*
Fr transfert en série *(m)*
It trasferimento in serie *(m)*
Pt transferência em série *(f)*

Reihenverarbeitung *(f) n* De
En serial processing
Es proceso en serie *(m)*
Fr traitement série *(m)*
It elaborazione in serie *(f)*
Pt processamento em série *(m)*

Reißer *(m) n* De
En burster
Es separadora de hojas *(f)*
Fr rupteuse *(f)*
It impulsore *(m)*
Pt separador de folha *(m)*

Rekonfiguration *(f) n* De
En reconfiguration
Es reconfiguración *(f)*
Fr reconfiguration *(f)*
It riconfigurazione *(f)*
Pt reconfiguração *(f)*

Rekursion *(f) n* De
En recursion
Es recursión *(f)*
Fr récurrence *(f)*
It ricorrenza *(f)*
Pt recorrência *(f)*

rekursiv *adj* De
En recursive
Es recursivo
Fr récurrent
It ricorrente
Pt recorrente

relación de plegado *(f)* Es
De Faltverhältnis *(n)*
En folding ratio
Fr rapport de pliage *(m)*
It rapporto pieghevole *(m)*
Pt ratio de dobragem *(f)*

relación de utilización *(f)* Es
De Arbeitsverhältnis; Benutzungsverhältnis *(n)*
En operating ratio; utilization ratio
Fr rapport de disponibilité; rapport d'utilisation *(m)*
It rapporto di operazione; rapporto di utilizzazione *(m)*
Pt ratio de operação; ratio de utilização *(f)*

relación señal-ruido *(f)* Es
De Rauschverhältnis *(n)*
En signal-to-noise ratio
Fr rapport signal-bruit *(m)*
It rapporto segnale-rumore *(m)*
Pt ratio entre sinal e ruído *(f)*

Relaiszentrale *(f) n* De
En relay centre
Es reemisor *(m)*
Fr centre de commutation *(m)*
It centro di relè *(m)*
Pt centro de relé *(m)*

relancement *(m) n* Fr
De Wiederstart *(m)*
En restart
Es reanudación *(f)*
It ricominciamento *(m)*
Pt novo arranque *(m)*

relancer *vb* Fr
De wiederstarten
En restart
Es reanudar
It ripartire
Pt rearrancar

relational operator Er.
De Vergleichsoperator *(m)*
Es operador de relación *(m)*
Fr opérateur de relation *(m)*
It operatore relazionale *(m)*
Pt operador relacional *(m)*

relative address En
De relative Adresse *(f)*
Es dirección relativa *(f)*
Fr adresse relative *(f)*
It indirizzo relativo *(m)*
Pt endereço relativo *(m)*

relative addressing En
De relative Adressierung *(f)*
Es direccionado relativo *(m)*
Fr adressage relatif *(m)*
It indirizzamento relativo *(m)*
Pt endereçamento relativo *(m)*

relative Adresse *(f)* De
En relative address
Es dirección relativa *(f)*
Fr adresse relative *(f)*
It indirizzo relativo *(m)*
Pt endereço relativo *(m)*

relative Adressierung *(f)* De
En relative addressing
Es direccionado relativo *(m)*
Fr adressage relatif *(m)*
It indirizzamento relativo *(m)*
Pt endereçamento relativo *(m)*

relative code En
De relativer Code *(m)*
Es código relativo *(m)*
Fr code relative *(m)*
It codice relativo *(m)*
Pt código relativo *(m)*

relativer Code *(m)* De
En relative code
Es código relativo *(m)*
Fr code relative *(m)*
It codice relativo *(m)*
Pt código relativo *(m)*

relatório de erros *(m)* Pt
De Fehlerbericht *(m)*
En error report
Es informe de errores *(m)*
Fr état sélectif *(m)*
It tabulato errori *(m)*

relay centre En
De Relaiszentrale *(f)*
Es reemisor *(m)*
Fr centre de commutation *(m)*
It centro di relè *(m)*
Pt centro de relé *(m)*

release *vb* En
De auslösen
Es liberar
Fr libérer
It rilasciare
Pt libertar

reliability *n* En
De Zuverlässigkeit *(f)*
Es fiabilidad *(f)*
Fr fiabilité *(f)*
It affidabilita *(f)*
Pt confiança *(f)*

relleno *(m) n* Es
De Auffüllen *(n)*
En padding
Fr remplissage *(m)*
It ricaricamento *(m)*
Pt enchimento *(m)*

reload *vb* En
De wiederladen
Es recargar
Fr recharger
It ricaricare
Pt recarregar

relocalizar Pt
De verschieben
En relocate
Es reubicar
Fr translater
It rilocare

relocatable address En
De verschiebliche Adresse *(f)*
Es dirección reubicable *(f)*
Fr adresse translatable *(f)*
It indirizzo rilocabile *(m)*
Pt endereço relocalizável *(m)*

relocatable code En
De verschieblicher Code *(m)*
Es código reubicable *(m)*
Fr code translatable *(m)*
It codice rilocabile *(m)*
Pt código relocalizável *(m)*

relocate En
De verschieben
Es reubicar
Fr translater
It rilocare
Pt relocalizar

relógio *(m) n* Pt
De Taktgeber *(m)*
En clock
Es reloj *(m)*
Fr horloge *(f)*
It orologio *(m)*

relógio de tempo real *(m)* Pt
De Uhrzeitgeber *(m)*
En real-time clock
Es reloj binario *(m)*
Fr horloge temps réel *(f)*
It orologio di tempo reale *(m)*

relógio digital *(m)* Pt
De Digitalzeitgeber *(m)*
En digital clock
Es reloj digital *(m)*
Fr horloge numérique *(f)*
It orologio digitale *(m)*

relógio marcador de tempos *(m)* Pt
De Zeituhr *(f)*
En timer; timer clock
Es temporizador *(m)*
Fr rythmeur *(m)*
It temporizzatore *(m)*

relógio principal *(m)* Pt
De Stammzeitgeber *(m)*
En master clock
Es reloj maestro *(m)*
Fr horloge pilote *(f)*
It orologio principale *(m)*

reloj *(m) n* Es
De Taktgeber *(m)*
En clock
Fr horloge *(f)*
It orologio *(m)*
Pt relógio *(m)*

reloj binario *(m)* Es
De Uhrzeitgeber *(m)*
En real-time clock
Fr horloge temps réel *(f)*
It orologio di tempo reale *(m)*
Pt relógio de tempo real *(m)*

reloj digital *(m)* Es
De Digitalzeitgeber *(m)*
En digital clock
Fr horloge numérique *(f)*
It orologio digitale *(m)*
Pt relógio digital *(m)*

reloj maestro *(m)* Es
De Stammzeitgeber *(m)*
En master clock
Fr horloge pilote *(f)*
It orologio principale *(m)*
Pt relógio principal *(m)*

remendar uma programa Pt
De korrigieren (ein Programm)
En patch
Es parchear un programa
Fr corriger un programme
It correggere un programma

remendo *(m) n* Pt
De Korrektur *(f)*
En patch
Es parche *(m)*
Fr correction *(f)*
It connessione *(f)*

remettre à zéro Fr
De löschen
En clear
Es despejar
It rimettere a zero
Pt limpar

remote computing system En
De Fernrechensystem *(n)*
Es sistema de cálculo a distancia *(m)*
Fr système de traitement à distance *(m)*
It sistema di elaborazione a distanza *(m)*
Pt sistema de tele-computador *(m)*

remote console En
De Außenkonsole *(f)*
Es consola remota *(f)*
Fr pupitre à distance *(m)*
It console a distanza *(f)*
Pt consola remota *(f)*

remote job entry En
De Jobfernverarbeitung *(f)*
Es entrada de trabajos a distancia *(f)*
Fr télésoumission de travaux *(f)*
It entrata del lavoro a distanza *(f)*
Pt entrada de trabalho remota *(f)*

remote processing En
De Fernverarbeitung *(f)*
Es proceso a distancia *(m)*
Fr télétraitement *(m)*
It elaborazione a distanza *(f)*
Pt tele-processamento *(m)*

remote testing En
De Fernprüfung *(f)*
Es ensayo a distancia *(m)*
Fr contrôle à distance *(m)*
It collaudo a distanza *(m)*
Pt tele-ensaio *(m)*

remplissage *(m) n* Fr
De Auffüllen *(n)*
En padding

Es relleno *(m)*
It ricaricamento *(m)*
Pt enchimento *(m)*

renvoyer à Fr
De rücklaufen
En return
Es retornar
It ritornare
Pt regressar

reorganisieren *vb* De
En reorganize
Es reorganizar
Fr restructurer
It riorganizzare
Pt reorganizar

reorganizar *vb* Es, Pt
De reorganisieren
En reorganize
Fr restructurer
It riorganizzare

reorganize *vb* En
De reorganisieren
Es reorganizar
Fr restructurer
It riorganizzare
Pt reorganizar

repair time En
De Reparaturzeit *(f)*
Es tiempo de reparación *(m)*
Fr temps de réparation *(m)*
It tempo di riparazione *(m)*
Pt tempo de reparação *(m)*

reparación *(f) n* Es
De Wiederherstellung *(f)*
En recovery
Fr récupération *(f)*
It recupero *(m)*
Pt recuperação *(f)*

reparación de fallo *(f)* Es
De Ausfallrückgängigkeit *(f)*
En failure recovery
Fr redressement de défaillance *(m)*
It recupero di fallimento *(m)*
Pt recuperação de falha *(f)*

Reparaturzeit *(f) n* De
En repair time
Es tiempo de reparación *(m)*
Fr temps de réparation *(m)*
It tempo di riparazione *(m)*
Pt tempo de reparação *(m)*

repère *(m) n* Fr
De Fixpunkt; Kennzeichner *(m)*
En benchmark; marker
Es marcador; referencia *(m f)*
It identificativo riferimento *(m)*
Pt marcador; referência de nivel *(m f)*

reperimento *(m) n* It
De Wiederauffinden *(n)*
En retrieval
Es recuperación *(f)*
Fr extraction *(f)*
Pt recuperação *(f)*

reperimento delle informazioni *(m)* It
De Wiederauffinden von Informationen *(n)*
En information retrieval
Es recuperación de la información *(f)*
Fr recherche documentaire *(f)*
Pt recuperação da informação *(f)*

repertoire *n* En
De Vorrat *(m)*
Es repertorio de la instrucción *(m)*
Fr répertoire *(m)*
It repertorio *(m)*
Pt repertório *(m)*

répertoire *(m) n* Fr
De Vorrat *(m)*
En repertoire
Es repertorio de la instrucción *(m)*
It repertorio *(m)*
Pt repertório *(m)*

répertoire d'adresses *(m) n* Fr
De Inhaltsverzeichnis *(n)*
En directory
Es directorio *(m)*
It elenco *(m)*
Pt anuário *(m)*

répertoire d'instructions *(m)* Fr
De Wiederholungsbefehl *(m)*
En repetition instruction
Es instrucción de repetición *(f)*
It istruzione di ripetizione *(f)*
Pt instrução de repetição *(f)*

repertorio *(m) n* It
De Vorrat *(m)*
En repertoire
Es repertorio de la instrucción *(m)*
Fr répertoire *(m)*
Pt repertório *(m)*

repertório *(m) n* Pt
De Vorrat *(m)*
En repertoire
Es repertorio de la instrucción *(m)*
Fr répertoire *(m)*
It repertorio *(m)*

repertorio de la instrucción *(m)* Es
De Vorrat *(m)*
En repertoire
Fr répertoire *(m)*
It repertorio *(m)*
Pt repertório *(m)*

repetición de pasada *(f)* Es
De wiederholter Maschinenlauf *(m)*
En rerun
Fr reprise *(f)*
It ripresa *(f)*
Pt nova passagem *(f)*

repetir la pasada Es
De wiederholen
En rerun
Fr réexécuter
It riprendere
Pt tornar a passar

repetition instruction En
De Wiederholungsbefehl *(m)*
Es instrucción de repetición *(f)*
Fr répertoire d'instructions *(m)*
It istruzione di ripetizione *(f)*
Pt instrução de repetição *(f)*

repetitive addressing En
De wiederholte Adressierung *(f)*
Es direccionado repetitivo *(m)*
Fr adressage sous-entendu *(m)*
It indirizzamento ripetitivo *(m)*
Pt endereçamento repetitivo *(m)*

replication *n* En
De Replikation *(f)*
Es respuesta *(f)*
Fr copiage *(m)*
It ripetizione *(f)*
Pt resposta *(f)*

Replikation *(f) n* De
En replication
Es respuesta *(f)*
Fr copiage *(m)*
It ripetizione *(f)*
Pt resposta *(f)*

répondeur vocal *(m)* Fr
De Sprachausgabe *(f)*
En audio response unit
Es unidad de respuesta de audio *(f)*
It unità della risposta audio *(f)*
Pt unidade de audio-resposta *(f)*

report generator En
De Listengeber *(m)*
Es generador de informes *(m)*
Fr générateur d'édition *(m)*
It generatore di tabulati *(m)*
Pt gerador de relatório *(m)*

report partiel *(m)* Fr
De Teilübertrag *(m)*
En partial carry
Es arrastre parcial *(m)*
It riporto parziale *(m)*
Pt transporte parcial *(m)*

report program En
De Listenprogramm *(n)*
Es programa de informes *(m)*
Fr programme des informations *(m)*
It programma di tabulati *(m)*
Pt programa de relatórios *(m)*

representação gráfica *(f)* Pt
De Zeichenanzeige *(f)*
En graphics display
Es representación gráfica *(f)*
Fr visualisation graphique *(f)*
It visualizzatore grafico *(m)*

representação incremental *(f)* Pt
De schrittweise Darstellung *(f)*
En incremental representation
Es representación incremental *(f)*
Fr représentation incrémentielle *(f)*
It rappresentazione incrementale *(f)*

representação visual *(f)* Pt
De Anzeige *(f)*
En display
Es representación visual *(f)*
Fr affichage *(m)*
It visualizzatore *(m)*

representación de modo puntual *(f)* Es
De punktweise Darstellung *(f)*
En point-mode display
Fr affichage mode point par point *(m)*
It mostra di modo punto a punto *(f)*
Pt display de modo pontual *(m)*

representación en modo vectorial *(f)* Es
De Vektorbetriebs-artanzeige *(f)*
En vector-mode display
Fr affichage mode vectoriel *(m)*
It visualizzazione di modo vettore *(f)*
Pt visualização de modo vector *(f)*

representación gráfica *(f)* Es
De Zeichenanzeige *(f)*
En graphics display
Fr visualisation graphique *(f)*
It visualizzatore grafico *(m)*
Pt representação gráfica *(f)*

representación incremental *(f)* Es
De schrittweise Darstellung *(f)*
En incremental representation
Fr représentation incrémentielle *(f)*
It rappresentazione incrementale *(f)*
Pt representação incremental *(f)*

representación interactiva *(f)* Es
De Dialoganzeige *(f)*
En interactive display
Fr visualisation interactive *(f)*
It visualizzatore interattivo *(m)*
Pt visualização interactiva *(f)*

representación regenerada *(f)* Es
De Auffrischungsanzeige *(f)*
En refresh display
Fr affichageré-génération *(m)*
It visualizzazione di aggiornamento *(f)*
Pt apresentação de refrescamento *(f)*

representación tabular *(f)* Es
De tabellarische Anzeige *(f)*
En tabular display
Fr affichage tabulaire *(m)*
It visualizzazione tabulare *(f)*
Pt visualização tabelar *(f)*

representación visual *(f)* Es
De Anzeige *(f)*
En display
Fr affichage *(m)*
It visualizzatore *(m)*
Pt representação visual *(f)*

représentation incrémentielle *(f)* Fr
De schrittweise Darstellung *(f)*
En incremental representation
Es representación incremental *(f)*
It rappresentazione incrementale *(f)*
Pt representação incremental *(f)*

représentation positionnelle *(f)* Fr
De Stellendarstellung *(f)*
En positional notation
Es notación posicional *(f)*
It notazione di posizione *(f)*
Pt notação posicional *(f)*

reprise *(f)* *n* Fr
De wiederholter Maschinenlauf *(m)*
En rerun
Es repetición de pasada *(f)*
It ripresa *(f)*
Pt nova passagem *(f)*

reproducer *n* En
De Kopierer *(m)*
Es reproductor *(m)*
Fr reproductrice *(f)*
It riproduttore *(m)*
Pt reprodutor *(m)*

reproductor *(m)* *n* Es
De Kopierer *(m)*
En reproducer
Fr reproductrice *(f)*
It riproduttore *(m)*
Pt reprodutor *(m)*

reproductrice *(f)* *n* Fr
De Kopierer *(m)*
En reproducer
Es reproductor *(m)*
It riproduttore *(m)*
Pt reprodutor *(m)*

reprodutor *(m)* *n* Pt
De Kopierer *(m)*
En reproducer
Es reproductor *(m)*
Fr reproductrice *(f)*
It riproduttore *(m)*

reroute *vb* En
De wiederführen
Es reencaminar
Fr réacheminer
It dirottare
Pt reencaminhar

rerun *n* En
De wiederholter Maschinenlauf *(m)*
Es repetición de pasada *(f)*
Fr reprise *(f)*
It ripresa *(f)*
Pt nova passagem *(f)*

rerun *vb* En
De wiederholen
Es repetir la pasada
Fr réexécuter
It riprendere
Pt tornar a passar

rerun point En
De Wiederholungspunkt *(m)*
Es punto de reanudación de pasada *(m)*
Fr point de reprise *(m)*
It punto di riesecuzione *(m)*
Pt ponto de nova passagem *(m)*

rescue dump En
De Wiedereinstiegs-speicherauszug *(m)*
Es vaciado de rescate *(m)*
Fr vidage de secours *(m)*
It dump di salvataggio *(m)*
Pt armazém de emergência *(m)*

réseau *(m) n* Fr
De Netz *(n)*
En network
Es red *(f)*
It rete *(f)*
Pt rede *(f)*

réseau de communication *(m)* Fr
De Kommunikationsnetz *(n)*
En communication network
Es red de comunicaciones *(f)*
It rete di comunicazione *(f)*
Pt rede de comunicação *(f)*

réseau de commutation par paquets *(m)* Fr
De Paketschaltennetz *(n)*
En packet-switched network
Es red de conmutación de paquetes *(f)*
It rete di commutazione di pacci *(f)*
Pt rede com comutação de pacotes *(f)*

réseau de messages commutés *(m)* Fr
De geschaltetes Nachrichtennetz *(n)*
En switched-message network
Es red de conmutación de mensajes *(f)*
It rete di messaggi commutati *(f)*
Pt rede de mensagens comutadas *(f)*

réseau de transmission de données *(m)* Fr
De Datennetz *(n)*
En data network
Es red para transmisión de datos *(f)*
It rete di dati *(f)*
Pt rede de dados *(f)*

réseau multi-point *(m)* Fr
De Mehrpunktnetz *(n)*
En multipoint network
Es red de puntos múltiples *(f)*
It rete a punti multipli *(f)*
Pt rede de pontos múltiplos *(f)*

réseau numérique *(m)* Fr
De Digitalnetz *(n)*
En digital network
Es red digital *(f)*
It rete digitale *(f)*
Pt rede digital *(f)*

reserva *(f) n* Es
De Ausweichbetrieb *(m)*
En backup
Fr sauvegarde *(f)*
It riserva *(f)*
Pt apoio *(m)*

reservar *vb* Es, Pt
De reservieren
En reserve
Fr réserver
It riservare

reserve *vb* En
De reservieren
Es reservar
Fr réserver
It riservare
Pt reservar

réserver *vb* Fr
De reservieren
En reserve
Es reservar
It riservare
Pt reservar

reservieren *vb* De
En reserve
Es reservar
Fr réserver
It riservare
Pt reservar

reset *vb* En
De rückstellen
Es reajustar
Fr mettre à zéro
It riazzerare
Pt tornar a acertar

reset pulse En
De Rückstellenpuls *(m)*
Es impulso de reposición *(m)*
Fr impulsion RAZ *(f)*
It impulso di riazzeramento *(m)*
Pt impulso de reacerto *(m)*

residentes Programm *(n)* De
En resident routine
Es rutina residente *(f)*
Fr programme permanent *(m)*
It routine residente *(f)*
Pt rotina residente *(f)*

resident routine En
De residentes Programm *(n)*
Es rutina residente *(f)*
Fr programme permanent *(m)*
It routine residente *(f)*
Pt rotina residente *(f)*

residual error En
De Restfehler *(m)*
Es error residual *(m)*
Fr erreur résiduelle *(f)*
It errore residuo *(m)*
Pt erro residual *(m)*

residue check En
De Restprüfung *(f)*
Es verificación por residuo *(f)*
Fr contrôle de résidu *(m)*
It controllo residuo *(m)*
Pt verificação de resíduos *(f)*

resilience *n* En
De Nachgiebigkeit *(f)*
Es resiliencia *(f)*
Fr résilience *(f)*
It resilienza *(f)*
Pt elasticidade *(f)*

résilience *(f) n* Fr
De Nachgiebigkeit *(f)*
En resilience
Es resiliencia *(f)*
It resilienza *(f)*
Pt elasticidade *(f)*

resiliencia *(f) n* Es
De Nachgiebigkeit *(f)*
En resilience
Fr résilience *(f)*
It resilienza *(f)*
Pt elasticidade *(f)*

resilienza *(f) n* It
De Nachgiebigkeit *(f)*
En resilience
Es resiliencia *(f)*
Fr résilience *(f)*
Pt elasticidade *(f)*

resistor-transistor logic (RTL) En
De Widerstand-Transistor-verknüpfung *(f)*
Es lógica de resistencia-transistor *(f)*
Fr logique résistance-transistor *(f)*
It logica resistore-transistore *(f)*
Pt lógica de resistor-transistor *(f)*

resource *n* En
De Betriebsmittel *(n)*
Es recurso *(m)*
Fr ressource *(f)*
It risorsa *(f)*
Pt recurso *(m)*

resource allocation En
De Betriebsmittel-zuweisung *(f)*
Es asignación de recursos *(f)*
Fr affectation des ressources *(f)*
It allocazione delle risorse *(f)*
Pt atribuição de recursos *(f)*

response time En
De Ansprechzeit *(f)*
Es tiempo de respuesta *(m)*
Fr temps de réponse *(m)*
It tempo di risposta *(m)*
Pt tempo de resposta *(m)*

resposta *(f) n* Pt
De Replikation *(f)*
En replication
Es respuesta *(f)*
Fr copiage *(m)*
It ripetizione *(f)*

respuesta *(f) n* Es
De Replikation *(f)*
En replication
Fr copiage *(m)*
It ripetizione *(f)*
Pt resposta *(f)*

ressource *(f) n* Fr
De Betriebsmittel *(n)*
En resource
Es recurso *(m)*
It risorsa *(f)*
Pt recurso *(m)*

restart *n* En
De Wiederstart *(m)*
Es reanudación *(f)*
Fr relancement *(m)*
It ricominciamento *(m)*
Pt novo arranque *(m)*

restart *vb* En
De wiederstarten
Es reanudar
Fr relancer
It ripartire
Pt rearrancar

restart point En
De Wiederstartspunkt *(m)*
Es punto de reanudación *(m)*
Fr point de reprise *(m)*
It punto di ripartire *(m)*
Pt ponto de rearranque *(m)*

restaurar *vb* Es
De in Ausgangsstellung bringen
En restore
Fr rétablir
It ripristinare
Pt rearmazenar

Restfehler *(m) n* De
En residual error
Es error residual *(m)*
Fr erreur résiduelle *(f)*
It errore residuo *(m)*
Pt erro residual *(m)*

restore *vb* En
De in Ausgangsstellung bringen
Es restaurar
Fr rétablir
It ripristinare
Pt rearmazenar

Restprüfung *(f) n* De
En residue check
Es verificación por residuo *(f)*
Fr contrôle de résidu *(m)*
It controllo residuo *(m)*
Pt verificação de resíduos *(f)*

restructurer *vb* Fr
De reorganisieren
En reorganize
Es reorganizar
It riorganizzare
Pt reorganizar

rétablir *vb* Fr
De in Ausgangsstellung bringen
En restore
Es restaurar
It ripristinare
Pt rearmazenar

rete *(f) n* It
De Netz *(n)*
En network
Es red *(f)*
Fr réseau *(m)*
Pt rede *(f)*

rete a punti multipli *(f)* It
De Mehrpunktnetz *(n)*
En multipoint network
Es red de puntos múltiples *(f)*
Fr réseau multi-point *(m)*
Pt rede de pontos múltiplos *(f)*

rete di commutazione di pacci *(f)* It
De Paketschaltennetz *(n)*
En packet-switched network
Es red de conmutación de paquetes *(f)*
Fr réseau de commutation par paquets *(m)*
Pt rede com comutação de pacotes *(f)*

rete di comunicazione *(f)* It
De Kommunikationsnetz *(n)*
En communication network
Es red de comunicaciones *(f)*
Fr réseau de communication *(m)*
Pt rede de comunicação *(f)*

rete di dati *(f)* It
De Datennetz *(n)*
En data network
Es red para transmisión de datos *(f)*
Fr réseau de transmission de données *(m)*
Pt rede de dados *(f)*

rete digitale *(f)* It
De Digitalnetz *(n)*
En digital network
Es red digital *(f)*
Fr réseau numérique *(m)*
Pt rede digital *(f)*

rete di messaggi commutati *(f)* It
De geschaltetes Nachrichtennetz *(n)*
En switched-message network
Es red de conmutación de mensajes *(f)*
Fr réseau de messages commutés *(m)*
Pt rede de mensagens comutadas *(f)*

rete interurbana *(f)* It
De Sammelschaltung *(f)*
En trunk circuit
Es circuito común *(m)*
Fr circuit interurbain *(m)*
Pt circuito principal *(m)*

retention period En
De Verweilzeit *(f)*
Es período de retención *(m)*
Fr période de validité *(f)*
It tempo di ritenzione *(m)*
Pt periodo de retenção *(m)*

rete semiconduttori *(f)* It
De Halbleiterfeld *(n)*
En semiconductor array
Es matriz de semiconductores *(f)*
Fr ensemble à semiconducteurs *(m)*
Pt disposição semicondutora *(f)*

retornar *vb* Es
De rücklaufen
En return
Fr renvoyer à
It ritornare
Pt regressar

retorno *(m) n* Es
De Rücklauf *(m)*
En return
Fr retour *(m)*
It ritorno *(m)*
Pt regresso *(m)*

retorno del carro *(m)* Es
De Wagenrücklauf *(m)*
En carriage return
Fr retour chariot *(m)*
It ritorno del carrello *(m)*
Pt retrocesso do carro *(m)*

retour *(m) n* Fr
De Rücklauf *(m)*
En return
Es retorno *(m)*
It ritorno *(m)*
Pt regresso *(m)*

retour chariot *(m)* Fr
De Wagenrücklauf *(m)*
En carriage return
Es retorno del carro *(m)*
It ritorno del carrello *(m)*
Pt retrocesso do carro *(m)*

retraso rotacional *(m)* Es
De Umdrehungs-wartezeit *(f)*
En rotational delay
Fr délai d'attente *(m)*
It ritardo rotazionale *(m)*
Pt atraso rotacional *(m)*

retrieval *n* En
De Wiederauffinden *(n)*
Es recuperación *(f)*
Fr extraction *(f)*
It reperimento *(m)*
Pt recuperação *(f)*

rétroaction *(f) n* Fr
De Rückkopplung *(f)*
En feedback
Es realimentación *(f)*
It retroazione *(f)*
Pt realimentação *(f)*

retroazione *(f) n* It
De Rückkopplung *(f)*
En feedback
Es realimentación *(f)*
Fr rétroaction *(f)*
Pt realimentação *(f)*

retroceder *vb* Es
De rückwärtsschreiten
En backspace
Fr rappeler le chariot
It tornare indietro
Pt retroceder

retroceder *vb* Pt
De rückwärtsschreiten
En backspace
Es retroceder
Fr rappeler le chariot
It tornare indietro

retrocesso do carro *(m)* Pt
De Wagenrücklauf *(m)*
En carriage return
Es retorno del carro *(m)*
Fr retour chariot *(m)*
It ritorno del carrello *(m)*

return *n* En
De Rücklauf *(m)*
Es retorno *(m)*
Fr retour *(m)*
It ritorno *(m)*
Pt regresso *(m)*

return *vb* En
De rücklaufen
Es retornar
Fr renvoyer à
It ritornare
Pt regressar

return instruction En
De Rücklaufanweisung *(f)*
Es instrucción de retorno *(f)*
Fr instruction de retour *(f)*
It istruzione di ritorno *(f)*
Pt instrução de regresso *(f)*

reubicar Es
De verschieben
En relocate
Fr translater
It rilocare
Pt relocalizar

reverse Polish notation En
De umgekehrte polnische Darstellung *(f)*
Es notación polaca inversa *(f)*
Fr notation polonaise inversée *(f)*
It notazione polacca inversa *(f)*
Pt notação polaca inversa *(f)*

reversible counter En
De umkehrbarer Zähler *(m)*
Es contador reversible *(m)*
Fr compteur-décompteur *(m)*
It contatore reversibile *(m)*
Pt contador reversível *(m)*

rewind *vb* En
De wiederaufwickeln
Es rebobinar
Fr rebobiner
It riavvolgere
Pt tornar a enrolar

rewrite *vb* En
De wiederschreiben
Es reescribir
Fr récrire
It riscrivere
Pt tornar a escrever

riavvolgere *vb* It
De wiederaufwickeln
En rewind
Es rebobinar
Fr rebobiner
Pt tornar a enrolar

riazzerare *vb* It
De rückstellen
En reset
Es reajustar
Fr mettre à zéro
Pt tornar a acertar

ricaricamento *(m) n* It
De Auffüllen *(n)*
En padding
Es relleno *(m)*
Fr remplissage *(m)*
Pt enchimento *(m)*

ricaricare *vb* It
De wiederladen
En reload
Es recargar
Fr recharger
Pt recarregar

ricerca *(f) n* It
De Suche *(f)*
En search
Es búsqueda sistemática *(f)*
Fr recherche *(f)*
Pt busca *(f)*

ricerca binaria *(f)* It
De binäres Suchen *(n)*
En binary search
Es búsqueda binaria *(f)*
Fr recherche dichotomique *(f)*
Pt busca binária *(f)*

ricerca concatenata *(f)* It
De Kettensuche *(f)*
En chaining search
Es búsqueda de la cadena *(f)*
Fr recherche par chaînage *(f)*
Pt busca de cadeia *(f)*

ricerca dicotoma *(f)* It
De dichotomizierendes Suchen *(n)*
En dichotomizing search
Es búsqueda dicotómica *(f)*
Fr recherche dichotomique *(f)*
Pt busca dicotomizante *(f)*

ricerca operativa *(f)* It
De Unternehmungs-forschung *(f)*
En operational research (OR)
Es investigación operativa *(f)*
Fr recherche opérationnelle *(f)*
Pt investigação operacional *(f)*

ricercare *vb* It
De suchen
En search
Es investigar
Fr chercher
Pt procurar

ricetrasmettitore *(m) n* It
De Senderempfänger *(m)*
En transceiver
Es transceptor *(m)*
Fr émetteurrécepteur *(m)*
Pt transreceptor *(m)*

ricominciamento *(m) n* It
De Wiederstart *(m)*
En restart
Es reanudación *(f)*
Fr relancement *(m)*
Pt novo arranque *(m)*

ricompilare *vb* It
De wiederkompilieren
En recompile
Es recompilar
Fr recompiler
Pt recompilar

riconfigurazione *(f) n* It
De Rekonfiguration *(f)*
En reconfiguration
Es reconfiguración *(f)*
Fr reconfiguration *(f)*
Pt reconfiguração *(f)*

riconoscimento *(m) n* It
De Rückmeldung *(f)*
En acknowledgment
Es admisión confirmación *(f)*
Fr accusé de réception *(m)*
Pt confirmação de recepção *(f)*

riconoscimento di carattere *(m)* It
De Zeichenerkennung *(f)*
En character recognition
Es reconocimiento de caracteres *(m)*
Fr reconnaissance de caractères *(f)*
Pt reconhecimento de caracteres *(m)*

riconoscimento di caratteri di inchiostro magnetico *(m)* It
De Erkennung von

Magnettintenzeichen *(f)*
En magnetic-ink character recognition
Es reconocimiento de caracteres de tinta magnética *(m)*
Fr reconnaissance magnétique de caractères *(f)*
Pt reconhecimento de caracteres de tinta magnética *(m)*

riconoscimento di modelli *(m)* It
De Strukturerkennung *(f)*
En pattern recognition
Es reconocimiento de configuraciones *(m)*
Fr reconnaissance des formes *(f)*
Pt reconhecimento de padrão *(m)*

riconoscimento di segni ottici *(m)* It
De optische Zeichenerkennung *(f)*
En optical mark recognition
Es reconocimiento óptico de marcas *(m)*
Fr reconnaissance optique de marques *(f)*
Pt reconhecimento de marcas ópticas *(m)*

riconoscimento negativo *(m)* It
De negative Rückmeldung *(f)*
En negative acknowledgment
Es confirmación negativa *(f)*
Fr accusé de réception négatif *(m)*
Pt confirmação negativa *(f)*

riconoscimento ottico di caratteri *(m)* It
De optische Zeichenerkennung *(f)*
En optical character recognition (OCR)
Es reconocimiento óptico de caracteres *(m)*
Fr reconnaissance optique des caractères (ROC) *(f)*
Pt reconhecimento óptico de caracteres *(m)*

ricostituzione *(f) n* It
De Neubildung *(f)*
En reconstitution
Es reconstitución *(f)*
Fr reconstitution *(f)*
Pt reconstituição *(f)*

ricorrente *adj* It
De rekursiv
En recursive
Es recursivo
Fr récurrent
Pt recorrente

ricorrenza *(f) n* It
De Rekursion *(f)*
En recursion
Es recursión *(f)*
Fr récurrence *(f)*
Pt recorrência *(f)*

ricupero di alto livello *(m)* It
De Wiederherstellung der höheren Übermittlungsstufe *(f)*
En high-level recovery
Es recuperación de alto nivel *(f)*
Fr redressement évolué *(m)*
Pt recuperação de alto nível *(f)*

ridondanza *(f) n* It
De Redundanz *(f)*
En redundancy
Es redundancia *(f)*
Fr redondance *(f)*
Pt redundância *(f)*

riduzione dei dati *(f)* It
De Datenverdichtung *(f)*
En data reduction
Es reducción de datos *(f)*
Fr réduction de données *(f)*
Pt redução de dados *(f)*

riduzione in linea dei dati *(f)* It
De direkte Datenverdichtung *(f)*
En on-line data reduction
Es reducción de datos en línea *(f)*
Fr réduction des données en exploitation continue *(f)*
Pt redução de dados sobre a linha *(f)*

riferimento *(m) n* It
De Fixpunkt *(m)*
En benchmark
Es referencia *(f)*
Fr repère *(m)*
Pt referência de nível *(f)*

rifiuti *(m pl) n* It
De Schund *(m)*
En garbage
Es información parásita *(f)*
Fr informations parasites *(f pl)*
Pt refugo *(m)*

rigenerazione *(f) n* It
De Regenerierung *(f)*
En regeneration
Es regeneración *(f)*
Fr régénération *(f)*
Pt regeneração *(f)*

right-justified *adj* En
De rechtsbündig
Es justificado a la derecha
Fr cadré à droite
It giustificato a destra
Pt justificado à direita

right shift En
De Rechtsschiebung *(f)*
Es desplazamiento a la derecha *(m)*
Fr décalage à droite *(m)*
It spostamento a destra *(m)*
Pt mudança à direita *(f)*

rilasciare *vb* It
De auslösen
En release
Es liberar
Fr libérer
Pt libertar

rilevare *vb* It
De fühlen
En sense
Es detectar
Fr détecter
Pt pesquisar

rilocare It
De verschieben
En relocate
Es reubicar
Fr translater
Pt relocalizar

rimettere a zero It
De löschen
En clear
Es despejar
Fr remettre à zéro
Pt limpar

rinfrescare *vb* It
De auffrischen
En refresh
Es regenerar
Fr régénérer
Pt refrescar

ring counter En
De Ringzähler *(m)*
Es contador en anillo *(m)*
Fr compteur annulaire *(m)*
It contatore ad anello *(m)*
Pt contador anular *(m)*

Ringschiebung *(f) n* De
En ring shift
Es desplazamiento en anillo *(m)*
Fr permutation circulaire *(f)*
It dislocamento ad anello *(m)*
Pt mudança anular *(f)*

ring shift En
De Ringschiebung *(f)*
Es desplazamiento en anillo *(m)*
Fr permutation circulaire *(f)*
It dislocamento ad anello *(m)*
Pt mudança anular *(f)*

Ringzähler *(m) n* De
En ring counter
Es contador en anillo *(m)*
Fr compteur annulaire *(m)*

It contatore ad anello *(m)*
Pt contador anular *(m)*

riorganizzare *vb* It
De reorganisieren
En reorganize
Es reorganizar
Fr restructurer
Pt reorganizar

ripartire *vb* It
De wiederstarten
En restart
Es reanudar
Fr relancer
Pt rearrancar

ripartizione di tempo *(f)* It
De Zeitscheiben-verfahren *(n)*
En time slice
Es fracción de tiempo *(f)*
Fr découpage du temps *(m)*
Pt fatia de tempo *(f)*

ripetizione *(f) n* It
De Replikation *(f)*
En replication
Es respuesta *(f)*
Fr copiage *(m)*
Pt resposta *(f)*

riporto *(m) n* It
De Stellenverschiebung *(f)*
En shift
Es desplazamiento *(m)*
Fr décalage *(m)*
Pt mudança *(f)*

riporto parziale *(m)* It
De Teilübertrag *(m)*
En partial carry
Es arrastre parcial *(m)*
Fr report partiel *(m)*
Pt transporte parcial *(m)*

riprendere *vb* It
De wiederholen
En rerun
Es repetir la pasada
Fr réexécuter
Pt tornar a passar

ripresa *(f) n* It
De wiederholter Maschinenlauf *(m)*
En rerun
Es repetición de pasada *(f)*
Fr reprise *(f)*
Pt nova passagem *(f)*

ripristinare *vb* It
De in Ausgangsstellung bringen
En restore
Es restaurar
Fr rétablir
Pt rearmazenar

riproduttore *(m) n* It
De Kopierer *(m)*
En reproducer
Es reproductor *(m)*
Fr reproductrice *(f)*
Pt reprodutor *(m)*

riscrivere *vb* It
De wiederschreiben
En rewrite
Es reescribir
Fr récrire
Pt tornar a escrever

riserva *(f) n* It
De Ausweichbetrieb *(m)*
En backup
Es reserva *(f)*
Fr sauvegarde *(f)*
Pt apoio *(m)*

riservare *vb* It
De reservieren
En reserve
Es reservar
Fr réserver
Pt reservar

riservatezza *(f) n* It
De Vertraulichkeit *(f)*
En privacy
Es aspecto confidencial *(m)*
Fr confidentialité *(f)*
Pt aspecto confidencial *(m)*

risoluzione dei problemi organizzativi *(f)* It
De Fehlersuchen *(n)*
En trouble shooting
Es localización de errores *(f)*
Fr dépannage *(m)*
Pt detecção de avarias *(f)*

risorsa *(f) n* It
De Betriebsmittel *(n)*
En resource
Es recurso *(m)*
Fr ressource *(f)*
Pt recurso *(m)*

ritardo rotazionale *(m)* It
De Umdrehungs-wartezeit *(f)*
En rotational delay
Es retraso rotacional *(m)*
Fr délai d'attente *(m)*
Pt atraso rotacional *(m)*

ritornare *vb* It
De rücklaufen
En return
Es retornar
Fr renvoyer à
Pt regressar

ritorno *(m) n* It
De Rücklauf *(m)*
En return
Es retorno *(m)*
Fr retour *(m)*
Pt regresso *(m)*

ritorno del carrello *(m)* It
De Wagenrücklauf *(m)*
En carriage return
Es retorno del carro *(m)*
Fr retour chariot *(m)*
Pt retrocesso do carro *(m)*

roda impressora *(f)* Pt
De Typenrad *(n)*
En print wheel
Es rueda de impresión *(f)*
Fr roue d'impression *(f)*
It ruota di stampa *(f)*

Röhre *(f) n* De
En tube
Es tubo *(m)*
Fr tube *(m)*
It tubo *(m)*
Pt válvula *(f)*

rotational delay En
De Umdrehungs-wartezeit *(f)*
Es retraso rotacional *(m)*
Fr délai d'attente *(m)*
It ritardo rotazionale *(m)*
Pt atraso rotacional *(m)*

rotina *(f) n* Pt
De Programm *(n)*
En routine
Es rutina *(f)*
Fr programme *(m)*
It routine *(f)*

rotina aberta *(f)* Pt
De offenes Programm *(n)*
En open routine
Es rutina de apertura *(f)*
Fr programme ouvert *(m)*
It routine aperta *(f)*

rotina de autópsia *(f)* Pt
De Programm nach dem Tode *(n)*
En post-mortem routine
Es rutina póstuma *(f)*
Fr programme d'autopsie *(m)*
It routine di autopsia *(f)*

rotina de carga *(f)* Pt
De Ladeprogramm *(n)*
En loading routine
Es rutina de carga *(f)*
Fr programme de chargement *(m)*
It routine di caricamento *(f)*

rotina de classificação *(f)* Pt
De Sortierungs-programm *(n)*
En sorting routine
Es rutina de clasificación *(f)*
Fr programme de tri *(m)*
It routine di selezione *(f)*

rotina de diagnóstico *(f)* Pt
De Diagnostikprogramm *(n)*
En diagnostic routine
Es rutina de diagnóstico *(f)*
Fr programme de diagnostic *(m)*
It routine diagnostica *(f)*

rotina de erros *(f)* Pt
De Fehlerprogramm *(n)*
En error routine
Es rutina de errores *(f)*

Fr routine de détection d'erreurs *(f)*
It routine errori *(f)*

rotina de serviço *(f)* Pt
De Dienstprogramm *(n)*
En service routine
Es rutina de servicio *(f)*
Fr programme de service *(m)*
It routine di servizio *(f)*

rotina fechada *(f)* Pt
De abgeschlossenes Programm *(n)*
En closed routine
Es rutina cerrada *(f)*
Fr routine fermée *(f)*
It routine chiusa *(f)*

rotina residente *(f)* Pt
De residentes Programm *(n)*
En resident routine
Es rutina residente *(f)*
Fr programme permanent *(m)*
It routine residente *(f)*

rótulo *(m) n* Pt
De Schildchen *(n)*
En label
Es marbete *(m)*
Fr label *(m)*
It etichetta *(f)*

rótulo de arquivo *(m)* Pt
De Dateikennsatz *(m)*
En file label
Es etiqueta de fichero *(f)*
Fr étiquette de fichier *(f)*
It etichetta del file *(f)*

rótulo de pista *(m)* Pt
De Spurkennzeichen *(n)*
En track label
Es etiqueta de pista *(f)*
Fr label piste *(m)*
It etichetta di pista *(f)*

rótulo de porta-cabeças *(m)* Pt
De Anfangskennsatz *(m)*
En header label
Es etiqueta de cabecera *(f)*
Fr label début *(m)*
It etichetta della testata *(f)*

rótulo de trailer *(m)* Pt
De Beisatzkennzeichen *(n)*
En trailer label
Es etiqueta de cola *(f)*
Fr label fin *(m)*
It etichetta di fine *(f)*

roue d'impression *(f)* Fr
De Typenrad *(n)*
En print wheel
Es rueda de impresión *(f)*
It ruota di stampa *(f)*
Pt roda impressora *(f)*

rounding error En
De Rundungsfehler *(m)*
Es error de redondeo *(m)*
Fr erreur d'arrondi *(f)*
It errore di arrotondamento *(m)*
Pt erro de arredondamento *(m)*

round off En
De runden
Es redondear
Fr arrondir
It arrotondare
Pt arredondar

route *n* En
De Leitweg *(m)*
Es ruta *(f)*
Fr itinéraire *(m)*
It pista *(f)*
Pt caminho *(m)*

route *vb* En
De führen
Es encaminar
Fr acheminar
It incanalare
Pt encaminhar

routine *n* En; It *(f)*
De Programm *(n)*
Es rutina *(f)*
Fr programme *(m)*
Pt rotina *(f)*

routine aperta *(f)* It
De offenes Programm *(n)*
En open routine
Es rutina de apertura *(f)*
Fr programme ouvert *(m)*
Pt rotina aberta *(f)*

routine chiusa *(f)* It
De abgeschlossenes Programm *(n)*
En closed routine
Es rutina cerrada *(f)*
Fr routine fermée *(f)*
Pt rotina fechada *(f)*

routine de détection d'erreurs *(f)* Fr
De Fehlerprogramm *(n)*
En error routine
Es rutina de errores *(f)*
It routine errori *(f)*
Pt rotina de erros *(f)*

routine diagnostica *(f)* It
De Diagnostikprogramm *(n)*
En diagnostic routine
Es rutina de diagnóstico *(f)*
Fr programme de diagnostic *(m)*
Pt rotina de diagnóstico *(f)*

routine di autopsia *(f)* It
De Programm nach dem Tode *(n)*
En post-mortem routine
Es rutina póstuma *(f)*
Fr programme d'autopsie *(m)*
Pt rotina de autópsia *(f)*

routine di caricamento *(f)* It
De Ladeprogramm *(n)*
En loading routine
Es rutina de carga *(f)*
Fr programme de chargement *(m)*
Pt rotina de carga *(f)*

routine di selezione *(f)* It
De Sortierungs-programm *(n)*
En sorting routine
Es rutina de clasificación *(f)*
Fr programme de tri *(m)*
Pt rotina de classificação *(f)*

routine di servizio *(f)* It
De Dienstprogramm *(n)*
En service routine
Es rutina de servicio *(f)*
Fr programme de service *(m)*
Pt rotina de serviço *(f)*

routine errori *(f)* It
De Fehlerprogramm *(n)*
En error routine
Es rutina de errores *(f)*
Fr routine de détection d'erreurs *(f)*
Pt rotina de erros *(f)*

routine fermée *(f)* Fr
De abgeschlossenes Programm *(n)*
En closed routine
Es rutina cerrada *(f)*
It routine chiusa *(f)*
Pt rotina fechada *(f)*

routine maintenance En
De regelmäßige Wartung *(f)*
Es mantenimiento de rutina *(m)*
Fr entretien de routine *(m)*
It manutenzione ordinaria *(f)*
Pt manutenção de rotina *(f)*

routine residente *(f)* It
De residentes Programm *(n)*
En resident routine
Es rutina residente *(f)*
Fr programme permanent *(m)*
Pt rotina residente *(f)*

row *n* En
De Zeile *(f)*
Es fila *(f)*
Fr ligne *(f)*
It fila *(f)*
Pt fila *(f)*

row pitch En
De Zeilensprung *(m)*
Es paso entre filas *(m)*
Fr pas longitudinal *(m)*
It passo di fila *(m)*
Pt passo de fila *(m)*

ruban à encre *(m)* Fr
De Farbband *(n)*
En ink ribbon
Es cinta entintada *(f)*
It nastro ad inchiostro *(m)*
Pt fita de tinta *(f)*

rückgekoppeltes Regelungssystem *(n)* De
En feedback control
Es control de realimentación *(m)*
Fr commande de rétroaction *(f)*
It controllo di retroazione *(m)*
Pt controle de realimentação *(m)*

Rückkopplung *(f) n* De
En feedback
Es realimentación *(f)*
Fr rétroaction *(f)*
It retroazione *(f)*
Pt realimentação *(f)*

Rücklauf *(m) n* De
En return
Es retorno *(m)*
Fr retour *(m)*
It ritorno *(m)*
Pt regresso *(m)*

Rücklaufanweisung *(f) n* De
En return instruction
Es instrucción de retorno *(f)*
Fr instruction de retour *(f)*
It istruzione di ritorno *(f)*
Pt instrução de regresso *(f)*

rücklaufen *vb* De
En return
Es retornar
Fr renvoyer à
It ritornare
Pt regressar

Rückmeldung *(f) n* De
En acknowledgment
Es admisión confirmación *(f)*
Fr accusé de réception *(m)*
It riconoscimento *(m)*
Pt confirmação de recepção *(f)*

rückstellen *vb* De
En reset
Es reajustar
Fr mettre à zéro
It riazzerare
Pt tornar a acertar

Rückstellenpuls *(m) n* De
En reset pulse
Es impulso de reposición *(m)*
Fr impulsion RAZ *(f)*
It impulso di riazzeramento *(m)*
Pt impulso de reacerto *(m)*

rückwärtsschreiten *vb* De
En backspace
Es retroceder
Fr rappeler le chariot
It tornare indietro
Pt retroceder

rueda de impresión *(f)* Es
De Typenrad *(n)*
En print wheel
Fr roue d'impression *(f)*
It ruota di stampa *(f)*
Pt roda impressora *(f)*

Rufnummer *(f) n* De
En call number
Es número de llamada *(m)*
Fr numéro d'appel *(m)*
It numero di richiamo *(m)*
Pt número de chamada *(m)*

Ruhezeit *(f) n* De
En unattended time
Es tiempo sin personal *(m)*
Fr temps de fonctionnement sans surveillance *(m)*
It tempo uncustodita *(m)*
Pt tempo de abandono *(m)*

ruido *(m) n* Es
De Rauschen *(n)*
En noise
Fr bruit *(m)*
It rumore *(m)*
Pt ruído *(m)*

ruído *(m) n* Pt
De Rauschen *(n)*
En noise
Es ruido *(m)*
Fr bruit *(m)*
It rumore *(m)*

rumore *(m) n* It
De Rauschen *(n)*
En noise
Es ruido *(m)*
Fr bruit *(m)*
Pt ruído *(m)*

run *n* En
De Durchlauf *(m)*
Es pasada *(f)*
Fr passage *(m)*
It esecuzione *(f)*
Pt passagem *(f)*

run *vb* En
De durchlaufen
Es pasar
Fr exécuter
It passare
Pt passar

runden *vb* De
En round off
Es redondear
Fr arrondir
It arrotondare
Pt arredondar

Rundungsfehler *(m) n* De
En rounding error
Es error de redondeo *(m)*
Fr erreur d'arrondi *(f)*
It errore di arrotondamento *(m)*
Pt erro de arredondamento *(m)*

run time En
De Durchlaufzeit *(f)*
Es tiempo de pasada *(m)*
Fr temps d'exécution *(m)*
It tempo di esecuzione *(m)*
Pt tempo de passagem *(m)*

ruota di stampa *(f)* It
De Typenrad *(n)*
En print wheel
Es rueda de impresión *(f)*
Fr roue d'impression *(f)*
Pt roda impressora *(f)*

rupteuse *(f) n* Fr
De Reißer *(m)*
En burster
Es separadora de hojas *(f)*
It impulsore *(m)*
Pt separador de folha *(m)*

ruta *(f) n* Es
De Leitweg *(m)*
En route
Fr itinéraire *(m)*
It pista *(f)*
Pt caminho *(m)*

rutina *(f) n* Es
De Programm *(n)*
En routine
Fr programme *(m)*
It routine *(f)*
Pt rotina *(f)*

rutina cerrada *(f)* Es
De abgeschlossenes Programm *(n)*
En closed routine
Fr routine fermée *(f)*
It routine chiusa *(f)*
Pt rotina fechada *(f)*

rutina de apertura *(f)* Es
De offenes Programm *(n)*
En open routine
Fr programme ouvert *(m)*
It routine aperta *(f)*
Pt rotina aberta *(f)*

rutina de carga *(f)* Es
De Ladeprogramm *(n)*
En loading routine
Fr programme de chargement *(m)*
It routine di caricamento *(f)*
Pt rotina de carga *(f)*

rutina de clasificación *(f)* Es
De Sortierungs-programm *(n)*
En sorting routine
Fr programme de tri *(m)*
It routine di selezione *(f)*
Pt rotina de classificação *(f)*

rutina de diagnóstico *(f)* Es
De Diagnostikprogramm *(n)*
En diagnostic routine

Fr programme de diagnostic *(m)*
It routine diagnostica *(f)*
Pt rotina de diagnóstico *(f)*

rutina de errores *(f)* Es
De Fehlerprogramm *(n)*
En error routine
Fr routine de détection d'erreurs *(f)*
It routine errori *(f)*
Pt rotina de erros *(f)*

rutina de servicio *(f)* Es
De Dienstprogramm *(n)*
En service routine
Fr programme de service *(m)*
It routine di servizio *(f)*
Pt rotina de serviço *(f)*

rutina póstuma *(f)* Es
De Programm nach dem Tode *(n)*
En post-mortem routine
Fr programme d'autopsie *(m)*
It routine di autopsia *(f)*
Pt rotina de autópsia *(f)*

rutina residente *(f)* Es
De residentes Programm *(n)*
En resident routine
Fr programme permanent *(m)*
It routine residente *(f)*
Pt rotina residente *(f)*

rythmeur *(m)* Fr
De Zeituhr *(f)*
En timer; timer clock
Es temporizador *(m)*
It temporizzatore *(m)*
Pt relógio marcador de tempos *(m)*

S

Sachwörterverzeichnis *(n) n* De
En index
Es índice *(m)*
Fr index *(m)*
It indice *(m)*
Pt índex *(m)*

saída *(f) n* Pt
De Ausgang *(m)*
En exit
Es salida *(f)*
Fr sortie *(f)*
It uscita *(f)*

sair *vb* Pt
De ausgehen
En exit; output
Es extraer; salir
Fr sortir
It output; uscire

saisie de données *(f)* Fr
De Dateneingabe *(f)*
En data entry
Es entrada de datos *(f)*
It ingresso dei dati *(m)*
Pt entrada de dados *(f)*

saisie de donneés automatique *(f)* Fr
De automatische Datenerwerbung *(f)*
En automatic data acquisition (ADA)
Es adquisición automatica de datos *(f)*
It acquisto automatico dei dati *(m)*
Pt adquisição automática de dados *(f)*

saisie des données à la source *(f)* Fr
De Quelldatenfang *(m)*
En source data capture
Es captura de datos fuente *(f)*
It cattura di dati all'origine *(f)*
Pt captação de dados de origem *(f)*

sala de máquinas *(f)* Es, Pt
De Maschinenraum *(m)*
En machine room
Fr salle des machines *(f)*
It sala macchine *(f)*

sala macchine *(f)* It
De Maschinenraum *(m)*
En machine room
Es sala de máquinas *(f)*
Fr salle des machines *(f)*
Pt sala de máquinas *(f)*

salida *(f) n* Es
De Ausgang *(m)*
En exit; output
Fr sortie *(f)*
It uscita *(f)*
Pt output; saída *(m f)*

salida de ordenador en microfilm *(f)* Es
De Computerausgang auf Mikrofilm *(m)*
En computer output on microfilm (COM)
Fr impression sur microfilm *(f)*
It output del elaboratore su microfilm *(m)*
Pt output de computador em microfilme *(m)*

salida impresa *(f)* Es
De dauerhafter Text *(m)*
En hard copy
Fr document en clair *(m)*
It copia stampata *(f)*
Pt cópia dura *(f)*

salir *vb* Es
De ausgehen
En exit
Fr sortir
It uscire
Pt sair

salle des machines *(f)* Fr
De Maschinenraum *(m)*
En machine room
Es sala de máquinas *(f)*
It sala macchine *(f)*
Pt sala de máquinas *(f)*

saltar *vb* Es, Pt
De überspringen
En jump
Fr sauter
It saltare

saltare *vb* It
De überspringen
En jump; skip
Es omitir; saltar
Fr sauter
Pt omitir; saltar

salto *(m) n* Es, It, Pt
De Sprung *(m)*
En jump
Fr saut *(m)*

salto del papel *(m)* Es
De Papiervorschub *(m)*
En paper throw
Fr saut de papier *(m)*
It salto di pagina (di un modulo) *(m)*
Pt curso do papel *(m)*

salto di pagina (di un modulo) *(m)* It
De Papiervorschub *(m)*
En paper throw
Es salto del papel *(m)*
Fr saut de papier *(m)*
Pt curso do papel *(m)*

sammelnbeschreiben *vb* De
En gather write
Es escribir agrupada
Fr écrire en regroupant
It scrivere di raccolta
Pt escrever em condensado

Sammelschaltung *(f) n* De
En trunk circuit
Es circuito común *(m)*
Fr circuit interurbain *(m)*
It rete interurbana *(f)*
Pt circuito principal *(m)*

Sammelverbindung *(f) n* De
En trunk link
Es enlace común *(m)*
Fr liaison interurbaine *(f)*
It linea principale *(f)*
Pt linha principal *(f)*

sampling rate En
De Abtastfrequenz *(f)*
Es frecuencia de muestreo *(f)*

Fr vitesse d'échantillonnage *(f)*
It volume di campionamento *(m)*
Pt índice de amostragem *(m)*

satellite (computer) *n* En
De Satellitenrechner *(m)*
Es ordenador satélite *(m)*
Fr calculateur satellite *(m)*
It calcolatore satellite *(m)*
Pt computador satélite *(m)*

Satellitenrechner *(m) n* De
En satellite (computer)
Es ordenador satélite *(m)*
Fr calculateur satellite *(m)*
It calcolatore satellite *(m)*
Pt computador satélite *(m)*

Satz *(m) n* De
En record
Es registro *(m)*
Fr enregistrement *(m)*
It record *(m)*
Pt registo *(m)*

Satzblockierung *(f) n* De
En record blocking
Es bloqueo de registro *(m)*
Fr groupage enregistrement *(m)*
It bloccaggio di record *(m)*
Pt bloqueio de registo *(m)*

Satzlänge *(f) n* De
En record length
Es longitud de registro *(f)*
Fr longueur d'enregistrement *(f)*
It lunghezza del record *(f)*
Pt comprimento de registo *(m)*

Satzwischenraum *(m) n* De
En inter-record gap
Es separación entre registros *(f)*
Fr espace interbloc *(m)*
It distanza tra i record *(f)*
Pt intervalo entre registos *(m)*

saut *(m) n* Fr
De Sprung *(m)*
En jump
Es salto *(m)*
It salto *(m)*
Pt salto *(m)*

saut de papier *(m)* Fr
De Papiervorschub *(m)*
En paper throw
Es salto del papel *(m)*
It salto di pagina (di un modulo) *(m)*
Pt curso do papel *(m)*

sauter *vb* Fr
De überspringen
En jump; skip
Es omitir; saltar
It saltare
Pt omitir; saltar

sauvegarde *(f) n* Fr
De Ausweichbetrieb *(m)*
En backup
Es reserva *(f)*
It riserva *(f)*
Pt apoio *(m)*

sbarra di caratteri *(f)* It
De Typenstange *(f)*
En type bar
Es barra de tipos *(f)*
Fr barre d'impression *(f)*
Pt barra de tipos *(f)*

scala *(f) n* It
De Skala *(f)*
En scale
Es escala *(f)*
Fr échelle *(f)*
Pt escala *(f)*

scala di tempo *(f)* It
De Zeitskala *(f)*
En time scale
Es escala de tiempos *(f)*
Fr échelle des temps *(f)*
Pt escala de tempo *(f)*

scalare *vb* It
De skalieren
En scale
Es pasar a escala
Fr cadrer
Pt fazer concordar com a escala

scale *n* En
De Skala *(f)*
Es escala *(f)*
Fr échelle *(f)*
It scala *(f)*
Pt escala *(f)*

scale *vb* En
De skalieren
Es pasar a escala
Fr cadrer
It scalare
Pt fazer concordar com a escala

scale factor En
De Skalierfaktor *(m)*
Es factor escalar *(m)*
Fr facteur de cadrage *(m)*
It fattore di scala *(m)*
Pt factor de escala *(m)*

scambiare *vb* It
De vermitteln
En exchange
Es cambiar
Fr intervenir
Pt intercambiar

scambio *(m) n* It
De Vermittlung *(f)*
En exchange
Es intercambio *(m)*
Fr échange *(m)*
Pt intercâmbio *(m)*

scan *n* En
De Abtastung *(f)*
Es exploración *(f)*
Fr exploration *(f)*
It esplorazione *(f)*
Pt exploracão *(f)*

scan *vb* En
De abtasten
Es explorar
Fr explorer
It scrutare
Pt explorar

scanner *n* En
De Abtaster *(m)*
Es explorador *(m)*
Fr explorateur *(m)*
It analizzatore per scansione *(m)*
Pt dispositivo de exploração *(m)*

scansione di marcature *(f)* It
De Kennzeichen-abtastung *(f)*
En mark scanning
Es exploración de marcas *(f)*
Fr lecture optique de marques *(f)*
Pt exploração de marca *(f)*

scatola schede *(f)* It
De Kartenkorb *(m)*
En card cage
Es caja de fichas *(f)*
Fr porte-carte *(m)*
Pt gaiola de ficha *(f)*

scatto *(m) n* It
De Trigger *(m)*
En trigger
Es disparador *(m)*
Fr détente *(f)*
Pt gatilho *(m)*

Schablone *(f) n* De
En control word
Es palabra de control *(f)*
Fr mot de contrôle *(m)*
It voce di controllo *(f)*
Pt palavra de controlo *(f)*

schachteln *vb* De
En nest
Es jerarquizar
Fr emboîter
It nidificare
Pt aninhar

schalten *vb* De
En switch
Es conmutar
Fr commuter
It commutare
Pt comutar

Schalter *(m) n* De
En switch
Es conmutador *(m)*
Fr interrupteur *(m)*

It interruttore *(m)*
Pt comutador *(m)*

Schaltschnur *(f)* *n* De
En patchcord
Es cable de conexión *(m)*
Fr fiche de connexion *(f)*
It cordone di connessione *(m)*
Pt cabo de concerto *(m)*

Schalttafel *(f)* *n* De
En patchboard
Es cuadro de control *(m)*
Fr tableau de connexions *(m)*
It pannello di connessione *(m)*
Pt placa de concerto *(f)*

Schaltung *(f)* *n* De
En circuit
Es circuito *(m)*
Fr circuit *(m)*
It circuito *(m)*
Pt circuito *(m)*

Schaltzentrum *(n)* *n* De
En switching centre
Es centro de conmutación *(m)*
Fr centre de commutation *(m)*
It centro di commutazione *(m)*
Pt centro de comutação *(m)*

scheda *(f)* *n* It
De Karte *(f)*
En card
Es ficha *(f)*
Fr carte *(f)*
Pt ficha *(f)*

scheda ad ottanta colonne *(f)* It
De achtzig-Spalten-Karte *(f)*
En eighty-column card
Es tarjeta de ochenta columnas *(f)*
Fr carte de quatre-vingt colonnes *(f)*
Pt ficha de oitenta colunas *(f)*

scheda magnetica *(f)* It
De Magnetkarte *(f)*
En magnetic card
Es ficha magnética *(f)*
Fr carte magnétique *(f)*
Pt ficha magnética *(f)*

scheda microfilm *(f)* It
De Mikrofiche *(f)*
En microfiche
Es microficha *(f)*
Fr micro-fiche *(f)*
Pt microficha *(f)*

scheda perforata *(f)* It
Am punch card
De Lochkarte *(f)*
En punched card
Es ficha perforada *(f)*
Fr carte mécanographique *(f)*
Pt ficha perfurada *(f)*

scheduled maintenance En
De Terminwartung *(f)*
Es mantenimiento programado *(m)*
Fr entretien périodique *(m)*
It manutenzione programmata *(f)*
Pt manutenção planificada *(f)*

scheduling *n* En
De Arbeitsplanung *(f)*
Es planificación *(f)*
Fr planification *(f)*
It pianificazione *(f)*
Pt planificação *(f)*

scheggia di silicone *(f)* It
De Silikonchip *(m)*
En silicon chip
Es microplaqueta de silicio *(f)*
Fr puce au silicium *(f)*
Pt ficha de silício *(f)*

Schein- *adj* De
En dummy
Es ficticio
Fr fictif
It fittizio
Pt simulado

Scheinvariable *(f)* *n* De
En dummy variable
Es variable ficticia *(f)*
Fr variable fictive *(f)*
It variabile fittizia *(f)*
Pt variável simulada *(f)*

schema *n* En; It *(m)*
De Schema *(n)*
Es esquema *(m)*
Fr schéma *(m)*
Pt esquema *(m)*

Schema *(n)* *n* De
En schema
Es esquema *(m)*
Fr schéma *(m)*
It schema *(m)*
Pt esquema *(m)*

schéma *(m)* *n* Fr
De Schema *(n)*
En schema
Es esquema *(m)*
It schema *(m)*
Pt esquema *(m)*

schéma fonctionnel *(m)* Fr
De Blockschaltung *(f)*
En block diagram
Es diagrama por bloques *(m)*
It diagramma a blocchi *(m)*
Pt diagrama de bloco *(m)*

schéma logique *(m)* Fr
De Verknüpfungs-diagramm *(n)*
En logic diagram
Es diagrama lógico *(m)*
It diagramma logico *(m)*
Pt diagrama lógico *(m)*

schermare *vb* It
De schirmen
En screen
Es cribar
Fr sélectionner
Pt mascarar

schermo *(m)* *n* It
De Schirm *(m)*
En screen
Es pantalla *(f)*
Fr écran *(m)*
Pt écran *(m)*

Schieberegister *(n)* *n* De
En shift register
Es registro de desplazamiento *(m)*
Fr registre à décalage *(m)*
It registro per operazioni di spostamento dati *(m)*
Pt registo de deslocamento *(m)*

Schildchen *(n)* *n* De
En label
Es marbete *(m)*
Fr label *(m)*
It etichetta *(f)*
Pt rótulo *(m)*

Schirm *(m)* *n* De
En screen
Es pantalla *(f)*
Fr écran *(m)*
It schermo *(m)*
Pt écran *(m)*

schirmen *vb* De
En screen
Es cribar
Fr sélectionner
It schermare
Pt mascarar

Schleife *(f)* *n* De
En loop
Es bucle *(m)*
Fr boucle *(f)*
It ciclo *(m)*
Pt circuito *(m)*

Schlüssel *(m)* *n* De
En key
Es tecla *(f)*
Fr touche *(f)*
It tasto *(m)*
Pt tecla *(f)*

schlüsselfertiger Betrieb *(m)* De
En turnkey operation
Es operación llave en mano *(f)*
Fr opération clé en main *(f)*
It operazione chiavi in mano *(f)*
Pt operação de chaves em mão *(f)*

Schlüsselwort *(n)* *n* De
En keyword
Es palabra clave *(f)*
Fr mot-clé *(m)*
It parola chiave *(f)*
Pt palavra chave *(f)*

Schnellzugriffsschleife *(f)* *n* De
En rapid-access loop
Es bucle de acceso rápido *(m)*
Fr boucle d'accès rapide *(f)*
It ciclo ad accesso rapido *(m)*
Pt circuito de acesso rápido *(m)*

Schnittstelle *(f)* *n* De
En interface
Es acoplamiento mutuo *(m)*
Fr interface *(f)*
It interfaccia *(f)*
Pt interface *(f)*

Schreibdichte *(f)* *n* De
En recording density
Es densidad de registro *(f)*
Fr densité d'enregistrement *(f)*
It densità di registrazione *(f)*
Pt densidade de registo *(f)*

schreiben *vb* De
En write
Es escribir
Fr écrire
It scrivere
Pt escrever

Schreibgerät *(n)* *n* De
En logger
Es registrador automático *(m)*
Fr enregistreur automatique *(m)*
It registratore automatico *(m)*
Pt registador automático *(m)*

Schreibkopf *(m)* *n* De
En write head
Es cabeza de excritura *(f)*
Fr tête d'écriture *(f)*
It testina di scrittura *(f)*
Pt cabeça escritora *(f)*

Schreibmaschine *(f)* *n* De
En typewriter
Es máquina de escribir *(f)*
Fr machine à écrire *(f)*
It macchina da scrivere *(f)*
Pt máquina de escrever *(f)*

Schreibmaschine-station *(f)* *n* De
En typewriter terminal
Es terminal con teclado *(m)*
Fr terminal équipé d'un clavier *(m)*
It terminale a macchina da scrivere *(m)*
Pt terminal de máquina de escrever *(m)*

Schreibzeit *(f)* *n* De
En write time
Es tiempo de escritura *(m)*
Fr temps d'écriture *(m)*
It tempo di scrittura *(m)*
Pt tempo de escrita *(m)*

Schriftstück *(m)* *n* De
En document
Es documento *(m)*
Fr document *(m)*
It documento *(m)*
Pt documento *(m)*

Schriftstücksortierer *(m)* *n* De
En document sorter
Es clasificadora de documentos *(f)*
Fr trieuse de documents *(f)*
It selezionatrice di documenti *(f)*
Pt classificador de documentação *(m)*

Schrifttyp *(m)* *n* De
En typeface
Es ojo del tipo *(m)*
Fr oeil d'un caractère *(m)*
It occhio del carattere *(m)*
Pt olho de tipo *(m)*

Schriftzeichen *(n)* *n* De
En character
Es carácter *(m)*
Fr caractère *(m)*
It carattere *(m)*
Pt carácter *(m)*

Schritt *(m)* *n* De
En step
Es paso *(m)*
Fr phase *(f)*
It passo *(m)*
Pt passo *(m)*

Schrittwechsel *(m)* *n* De
En step change
Es cambio de paso *(m)*
Fr changement de phase *(m)*
It cambio di passo *(m)*
Pt mudança de passo *(f)*

schrittweise Darstellung *(f)* De
En incremental representation
Es representación incremental *(f)*
Fr représentation incrémentielle *(f)*
It rappresentazione incrementale *(f)*
Pt representação incremental *(f)*

schrittweiser Kurvenzeichner *(m)* De
En incremental plotter
Es trazador incremental *(m)*
Fr traceur incrémentiel *(m)*
It tracciatore incrementale *(m)*
Pt plotador incremental *(m)*

Schund *(m)* *n* De
En garbage
Es información parásita *(f)*
Fr informations parasites *(f pl)*
It rifiuti *(m pl)*
Pt refugo *(m)*

Schuppenstreifen *(m)* *n* De
En chadless tape
Es cinta semiperforada *(f)*
Fr bande semi-perforée *(f)*
It nastro semiperforato *(m)*
Pt fita semi recorte *(f)*

Schutz *(m)* *n* De
En protection
Es protección *(f)*
Fr protection *(f)*
It protezione *(f)*
Pt protecção *(f)*

Schutzband *(n)* *n* De
En guard band
Es banda de guardia *(f)*
Fr bande protection *(f)*
It banda di guardia *(f)*
Pt banda de protecção *(f)*

Schwebungsfrequenz *(f)* De
En beat frequency
Es frecuencia de pulsación *(f)*
Fr fréquence de battement *(f)*
It frequenza di battimento *(f)*
Pt frequência de pulso *(f)*

Schwellwertdaten-element *(n)* *n* De
En threshold element
Es elemento de umbral *(m)*
Fr élément à seuil *(m)*
It elemento di soglia *(m)*
Pt elemento de limiar *(m)*

scienza degli elaboratoria elettronici *(f)* It
De Computer-wissenschaft *(f)*
En computer science
Es ciencia de ordenador *(f)*
Fr ordinatique *(f)*
Pt ciência de computadores *(f)*

scratch pad En
De Arbeitspuffer *(m)*
Es bloc de notas *(m)*
Fr mémoire de travail *(f)*
It bloc-notes *(m)*
Pt almofada de raspar *(f)*

screen *n* En
De Schirm *(m)*
Es pantalla *(f)*
Fr écran *(m)*

It schermo *(m)*
Pt écran *(m)*

screen *vb* En
De schirmen
Es cribar
Fr sélectionner
It schermare
Pt mascarar

scrittura a domanda *(f)* It
De Abrufschreiben *(n)*
En demand writing
Es escritura inmediata *(f)*
Fr écriture immédiate *(f)*
Pt escrita de procura *(f)*

scrivere *vb* It
De schreiben
En write
Es escribir
Fr écrire
Pt escrever

scrivere a macchina It
De maschinenschreiben
En type
Es escribir a máquina
Fr écrire à la machine
Pt escrever à máquina

scrivere di raccolta It
De sammelnbeschreiben
En gather write
Es escribir agrupada
Fr écrire en regroupant
Pt escrever em condensado

scrutare *vb* It
De abtasten
En scan
Es explorar
Fr explorer
Pt explorar

search *n* En
De Suche *(f)*
Es búsqueda sistemática *(f)*
Fr recherche *(f)*
It ricerca *(f)*
Pt busca *(f)*

search *vb* En
De suchen
Es investigar
Fr chercher
It ricercare
Pt procurar

search time En
De Suchzeit *(f)*
Es tiempo de búsqueda *(m)*
Fr temps de recherche *(m)*
It tempo di ricerca *(m)*
Pt tempo de busca *(m)*

seconda-generazione *adj* It
De zweitgeneration
En second-generation
Es segunda-generación
Fr deuxième-génération
Pt segunda-geração

second-generation *adj* En
De zweitgeneration
Es segunda-generación
Fr deuxième-génération
It seconda-generazione
Pt segunda-geração

second-level address En
De Adresse der zweiten Stufe *(f)*
Es dirección de segundo nivel *(f)*
Fr adresse à deuxième niveau *(f)*
It indirizzo del secondo livello *(m)*
Pt endereço de segundo nível *(m)*

secuencia *(f) n* Es
De Folge *(f)*
En sequence
Fr séquence *(f)*
It sequenza *(f)*
Pt sequência *(f)*

secuencia de control *(f)* Es
De Steuerfolge *(f)*
En control sequence
Fr séquence de contrôle *(f)*
It sequenza di controllo *(f)*
Pt sequência de controlo *(f)*

secuencia de llamada *(f)* Es
De Aufruffolge *(f)*
En calling sequence
Fr séquence d'appel *(f)*
It sequenza di richiamo *(f)*
Pt sequência de chamada *(f)*

secuenciar *vb* Es
De folgen
En sequence
Fr ordonner
It sequenziare
Pt formar sequência

segment *n* En; Fr *(m)*
De Segment *(n)*
Es segmento *(m)*
Fr segment *(m)*
It segmento *(m)*
Pt segmento *(m)*

segment *vb* En
De segmentieren
Es segmentar
Fr segmenter
It segmentare
Pt segmentar

Segment *(n) n* De
En segment
Es segmento *(m)*
Fr segment *(m)*
It segmento *(m)*
Pt segmento *(m)*

segmentar *vb* Es, Pt
De segmentieren
En segment
Fr segmenter
It segmentare

segmentare *vb* It
De segmentieren
En segment
Es segmentar
Fr segmenter
Pt segmentar

segmented program En
De segmentiertes Programm *(n)*
Es programa segmentado *(m)*
Fr programme segmenté *(m)*
It programma segmentato *(m)*
Pt programa segmentado *(m)*

segmenter *vb* Fr
De segmentieren
En segment
Es segmentar
It segmentare
Pt segmentar

segmentieren *vb* De
En segment
Es segmentar
Fr segmenter
It segmentare
Pt segmentar

segmentiertes Programm *(n)* De
En segmented program
Es programa segmentado *(m)*
Fr programme segmenté *(m)*
It programma segmentato *(m)*
Pt programa segmentado *(m)*

segment mark En
De Segmentmarke *(f)*
Es marca de segmento *(f)*
Fr marque de segment *(f)*
It marca di segmento *(f)*
Pt marca de segmento *(f)*

Segmentmarke *(f) n* De
En segment mark
Es marca de segmento *(f)*
Fr marque de segment *(f)*
It marca di segmento *(f)*
Pt marca de segmento *(f)*

segment non organisé en pages *(m)* Fr
De ungepacktes Segment *(n)*
En unpaged segment
Es segmento no paginado *(m)*
It segmento non impaginato *(m)*
Pt segmento sem páginação *(m)*

segmento *(m) n* Es, It, Pt
De Segment *(n)*
En segment
Fr segment *(m)*

segmento non impaginato *(m)* It
De ungepacktes Segment *(n)*
En unpaged segment
Es segmento no paginado *(m)*
Fr segment non organisé en pages *(m)*
Pt segmento sem páginação *(m)*

segmento no paginado *(m)* Es
De ungepacktes Segment *(n)*
En unpaged segment
Fr segment non organisé en pages *(m)*
It segmento non impaginato *(m)*
Pt segmento sem páginação *(m)*

segmento sem páginação *(m)* Pt
De ungepacktes Segment *(n)*
En unpaged segment
Es segmento no paginado *(m)*
Fr segment non organisé en pages *(m)*
It segmento non impaginato *(m)*

segnale *(m) n* It
De Signal *(n)*
En signal
Es señal *(f)*
Fr signal *(m)*
Pt sinal *(m)*

segnale di abilitazione *(m)* It
De Aktiviersignal *(n)*
En enabling signal
Es señal de activación *(f)*
Fr signal de validation *(m)*
Pt sinal de capacitação *(m)*

segnale di output non disturbato *(m)* It
De ungestörtes Ausgangssignal *(n)*
En undisturbed output signal
Es señal de salida no cambiada *(f)*
Fr signal de sortie non perturbé *(m)*
Pt sinal de output não perturbado *(m)*

segnale di output zero *(m)* It
De Nullausgangssignal *(n)*
En zero-output signal
Es señal de salida cero *(f)*
Fr signal de sortie zéro *(m)*
Pt sinal de output zero *(m)*

segnale inibitore *(m)* It
De Sperrsignal *(n)*
En inhibiting signal
Es señal inhibidora *(f)*
Fr signal d'interdiction *(m)*
Pt sinal de inibição *(m)*

segno *(m) n* It
De Vorzeichen *(n)*
En sign
Es signo *(m)*
Fr signe *(m)*
Pt indicação *(f)*

segno del nastro *(m)* It
De Bandkennzeichen *(n)*
En tape mark
Es marca de cinta *(f)*
Fr marque de bande *(f)*
Pt marca de fita *(f)*

segno di gruppo *(m)* It
De Trennmarke *(f)*
En group mark
Es marca de grupo *(f)*
Fr drapeau groupe *(m)*
Pt marca de grupo *(f)*

segunda-generación *adj* Es
De zweitgeneration
En second-generation
Fr deuxième-génération
It seconda-generazione
Pt segunda-geração

segunda-geração *adj* Pt
De zweitgeneration
En second-generation
Es segunda-generación
Fr deuxième-génération
It seconda-generazione

seguro contra falhas Pt
De eigensicher
En fail-safe
Es sin riesgo de fallo
Fr à sécurité intégrée
It sicuro contro guasti

Seite *(f) n* De
En page
Es página *(f)*
Fr page *(f)*
It pagina *(f)*
Pt página *(f)*

Seitendrucker *(m) n* De
En page printer
Es impresora por páginas *(f)*
Fr imprimante page par page *(f)*
It stampatrice di pagina *(f)*
Pt impressora de página *(f)*

Seitenwechsel *(m) n* De
En page turning
Es transferencia de página *(f)*
Fr changement de page *(m)*
It trasferimento di pagina *(m)*
Pt mudança de páginas *(f)*

selbstorganisierend *adj* De
En self-organizing
Es autoestructurador
Fr auto-organisant
It auto-organizzante
Pt auto-organizante

seleccionar *vb* Es, Pt
De auswählen
En select
Fr sélectionner
It selezionare

select *vb* En
De auswählen
Es seleccionar
Fr sélectionner
It selezionare
Pt seleccionar

sélecteur *(m) n* Fr
De Wähler *(m)*
En selector
Es selector *(m)*
It selettore *(m)*
Pt selector *(m)*

sélectionner *vb* Fr
De auswählen; schirmen
En screen; select Es cribar; seleccionar
It schermare; selezionare
Pt mascarar; seleccionar

selector *n* En; Es, Pt *(m)*
De Wähler *(m)*
Fr sélecteur *(m)*
It selettore *(m)*

selector channel En
De Wählkanal *(m)*
Es canal selector *(m)*
Fr canal sélecteur *(m)*
It canale del selettore *(m)*
Pt canal selector *(m)*

selettore *(m) n* It
De Wähler *(m)*
En selector
Es selector *(m)*
Fr sélecteur *(m)*
Pt selector *(m)*

selezionare *vb* It
De auswählen
En select
Es seleccionar
Fr sélectionner
Pt seleccionar

selezionatrice *(f) n* It
De Sortierer *(m)*
En sorter
Es clasificadora *(f)*
Fr trieuse *(f)*
Pt classificador *(m)*

selezionatrice di documenti *(f)* It
De Schriftstücksortierer *(m)*
En document sorter
Es clasificadora de documentos *(f)*

Fr trieuse de documents *(f)*
Pt classificador de documentação *(m)*

selezione *(f) n* It
De Sortierung *(f)*
En sort
Es clasificación *(f)*
Fr tri *(m)*
Pt espécie *(f)*

selezione-inserimento *(f) n* It
De Sortierungfusion *(f)*
En sort-merge
Es clasificación-fusión *(f)*
Fr tri-fusion *(m)*
Pt classificaçãofusão *(f)*

self-checking number En
De Prüfnummer *(f)*
Es número autoverificador *(m)*
Fr chiffre d'auto-vérification *(m)*
It numero autocontrollante *(m)*
Pt número autoverificante *(m)*

self-organizing *adj* En
De selbstorganisierend
Es autoestructurador
Fr auto-organisant
It auto-organizzante
Pt auto-organizante

semaforo *(m) n* It
De Semaphor *(m)*
En semaphore
Es semáforo *(m)*
Fr sémaphore *(m)*
Pt semáforo *(m)*

semáforo *(m) n* Es, Pt
De Semaphor *(m)*
En semaphore
Fr sémaphore *(m)*
It semaforo *(m)*

semantic *adj* En
De semantisch
Es semántico
Fr sémantique
It semantico
Pt semântico

semantico *adj* It
De semantisch
En semantic
Es semántico
Fr sémantique
Pt semântico

semántico *adj* Es
De semantisch
En semantic
Fr sémantique
It semantico
Pt semântico

semântico *adj* Pt
De semantisch
En semantic
Es semántico
Fr sémantique
It semantico

sémantique *adj* Fr
De semantisch
En semantic
Es semántico
It semantico
Pt semântico

semantisch *adj* De
En semantic
Es semántico
Fr sémantique
It semantico
Pt semântico

Semaphor *(m) n* De
En semaphore
Es semáforo *(m)*
Fr sémaphore *(m)*
It semaforo *(m)*
Pt semáforo *(m)*

semaphore *n* En
De Semaphor *(m)*
Es semáforo *(m)*
Fr sémaphore *(m)*
It semaforo *(m)*
Pt semáforo *(m)*

sémaphore *(m) n* Fr
De Semaphor *(m)*
En semaphore
Es semáforo *(m)*
It semaforo *(m)*
Pt semáforo *(m)*

semi-automatic *adj* En
De halbautomatisch
Es semiautomático
Fr semiautomatique
It semiautomatico
Pt semiautomático

semiautomatico *adj* It
De halbautomatisch
En semi-automatic
Es semiautomático
Fr semiautomatique
Pt semiautomático

semiautomático *adj* Es, Pt
De halbautomatisch
En semi-automatic
Fr semiautomatique
It semiautomatico

semiautomatique *adj* Fr
De halbautomatisch
En semi-automatic
Es semiautomático
It semiautomatico
Pt semiautomático

semiconducteur *(m) n* Fr
De Halbleiter *(m)*
En semiconductor
Es semiconductor *(m)*
It semiconduttore *(m)*
Pt semicondutor *(m)*

semiconducteur à oxyde métallique *(m)* Fr
De Metalloxydhalbleiter *(m)*
En metal-oxide semiconductor (MOS)
Es semiconductor de óxido metálico *(m)*
It semiconduttore ad ossidi metallici *(m)*
Pt semi-condutor de óxido de metal *(m)*

semiconductor *n* En; Es *(m)*
De Halbleiter *(m)*
Fr semiconducteur *(m)*
It semiconduttore *(m)*
Pt semicondutor *(m)*

semiconductor array En
De Halbleiterfeld *(n)*
Es matriz de semiconductores *(f)*
Fr ensemble à semiconducteurs *(m)*
It rete semiconduttori *(f)*
Pt disposição semicondutora *(f)*

semiconductor de óxido metálico *(m)* Es
De Metalloxydhalbleiter *(m)*
En metal-oxide semiconductor (MOS)
Fr semiconducteur à oxyde métallique *(m)*
It semiconduttore ad ossidi metallici *(m)*
Pt semi-condutor de óxido de metal *(m)*

semiconductor memory En
De Halbleiterspeicher *(m)*
Es memoria de semiconductores *(f)*
Fr mémoire à semiconducteurs *(f)*
It memoria a semiconduttori *(f)*
Pt memória semi-condutora *(f)*

semicondutor *(m) n* Pt
De Halbleiter *(m)*
En semiconductor
Es semiconductor *(m)*
Fr semiconducteur *(m)*
It semiconduttore *(m)*

semi-condutor de óxido de metal *(m)* Pt
De Metalloxydhalbleiter *(m)*
En metal-oxide semiconductor (MOS)
Es semiconductor de óxido metálico *(m)*
Fr semiconducteur à oxyde métallique *(m)*
It semiconduttore ad ossidi metallici *(m)*

semiconduttore *(m) n* It
De Halbleiter *(m)*
En semiconductor
Es semiconductor *(m)*
Fr semiconducteur *(m)*
Pt semicondutor *(m)*

semiconduttore ad ossidi metallici *(m)* It

De Metalloxydhalbleiter *(m)*
En metal-oxide semiconductor (MOS)
Es semiconductor de óxido metálico *(m)*
Fr semiconducteur à oxyde métallique *(m)*
Pt semi-condutor de óxido de metal *(m)*

semiduplex *(m) n* Es
De Halbduplex *(m)*
En half duplex
Fr semi-duplex *(m)*
It metà duplex *(m)*
Pt semi-duplex *(m)*

semi-duplex *(m) n* Fr, Pt
De Halbduplex *(m)*
En half duplex
Es semiduplex *(m)*
It metà duplex *(m)*

semi-somador *(m) n* Pt
De Halbaddierglied *(n)*
En half adder
Es semi-sumador *(m)*
Fr demi-additionneur *(m)*
It metà addizionatore *(m)*

semi-soustracteur *(m) n* Fr
De Halbsubtrahierer *(m)*
En half subtractor
Es semi-sustractor *(m)*
It metà sottrattore *(m)*
Pt semi-subtractor *(m)*

semi-subtractor *(m) n* Pt
De Halbsubtrahierer *(m)*
En half subtractor
Es semi-sustractor *(m)*
Fr semi-soustracteur *(m)*
It metà sottrattore *(m)*

semi-sumador *(m) n* Es
De Halbaddierglied *(n)*
En half adder
Fr demi-additionneur *(m)*
It metà addizionatore *(m)*
Pt semi-somador *(m)*

semi-sustractor *(m) n* Es
De Halbsubtrahierer *(m)*
En half subtractor
Fr semi-soustracteur *(m)*
It metà sottrattore *(m)*
Pt semi-subtractor *(m)*

señal *(f) n* Es
De Signal *(n)*
En signal
Fr signal *(m)*
It segnale *(m)*
Pt sinal *(m)*

señal de activación *(f)* Es
De Aktiviersignal *(n)*
En enabling signal
Fr signal de validation *(m)*
It segnale di abilitazione *(m)*
Pt sinal de capacitação *(m)*

señal de salida cero *(f)* Es
De Nullausgangssignal *(n)*
En zero-output signal
Fr signal de sortie zéro *(m)*
It segnale di output zero *(m)*
Pt sinal de output zero *(m)*

señal de salida no cambiada *(f)* Es
De ungestörtes Ausgangssignal *(n)*
En undisturbed output signal
Fr signal de sortie non perturbé *(m)*
It segnale di output non disturbato *(m)*
Pt sinal de output não perturbado *(m)*

señal inhibidora *(f)* Es
De Sperrsignal *(n)*
En inhibiting signal
Fr signal d'interdiction *(m)*
It segnale inibitore *(m)*
Pt sinal de inibição *(m)*

señalizador *(m) n* Es
De Markierung *(f)*
En flag
Fr drapeau *(m)*
It indicatore *(m)*
Pt bandeira *(f)*

senden *vb* De
En log
Es registrar
Fr consigner
It registrare
Pt registar em diário

Senderempfänger *(m) n* De
En transceiver
Es transceptor *(m)*
Fr émetteur-récepteur *(m)*
It ricetrasmettitore *(m)*
Pt transreceptor *(m)*

sense *vb* En
De fühlen
Es detectar
Fr détecter
It rilevare
Pt pesquisar

sentencia *(f) n* Es
De Anweisung *(f)*
En statement
Fr instructions *(f pl)*
It statement *(m)*
Pt afirmação *(f)*

sentencia de control *(f)* Es
De Steueranweisung *(f)*
En control statement
Fr ordre de contrôle *(m)*
It statement di controllo *(m)*
Pt afirmação de controlo *(f)*

sentencia de declaración *(f)* Es
De Prozeduranweisung *(f)*
En declarative statement
Fr instruction déclarative *(f)*
It statement di dichiarazione *(m)*
Pt afirmação declarativa *(f)*

separación entre registros *(f)* Es
De Satzzwischenraum *(m)*
En inter-record gap
Fr espace interbloc *(m)*
It distanza tra i record *(f)*
Pt intervalo entre registos *(m)*

separador *(m) n* Es, Pt
De Separator *(m)*
En separator
Fr séparateur *(m)*
It separatore *(m)*

separadora de hojas *(f)* Es
De Reißer *(m)*
En burster
Fr rupteuse *(f)*
It impulsore *(m)*
Pt separador de folha *(m)*

separador de entrada *(m)* Pt
De Eingangspuffer *(m)*
En input buffer
Es memoria intermedia de entrada *(f)*
Fr tampon d'entrée *(m)*
It memoria di transito dell'entrata *(f)*

separador de entrada-sair *(m)* Pt
De Eingangs-Ausgangspuffer *(m)*
En input-output buffer
Es memoria intermedia de entrada-salida *(f)*
Fr tampon entrée-sortie *(m)*
It memoria di transito entrata-uscita *(f)*

separador de folha *(m)* Pt
De Reißer *(m)*
En burster
Es separadora de hojas *(f)*
Fr rupteuse *(f)*
It impulsore *(m)*

separare *vb* It
De auspacken
En unpack
Es desempaquetar
Fr décondenser
Pt desembalar

séparateur *(m) n* Fr
De Separator *(m)*
En separator

Es separador *(m)*
It separatore *(m)*
Pt separador *(m)*

separator *n* En
De Separator *(m)*
Es separador *(m)*
Fr séparateur *(m)*
It separatore *(m)*
Pt separador *(m)*

Separator *(m) n* De
En separator
Es separador *(m)*
Fr séparateur *(m)*
It separatore *(m)*
Pt separador *(m)*

separatore *(m) n* It
De Separator *(m)*
En separator
Es separador *(m)*
Fr séparateur *(m)*
Pt separador *(m)*

sequence *n* En
De Folge *(f)*
Es secuencia *(f)*
Fr séquence *(f)*
It sequenza *(f)*
Pt sequência *(f)*

sequence *vb* En
De folgen
Es secuenciar
Fr ordonner
It sequenziare
Pt formar sequência

séquence *(f) n* Fr
De Folge *(f)*
En sequence
Es secuencia *(f)*
It sequenza *(f)*
Pt sequência *(f)*

sequence check En
De Folgeprüfung *(f)*
Es verificación de secuencia *(f)*
Fr contrôle de séquence *(m)*
It controllo di sequenza *(m)*
Pt verificação de sequência *(f)*

séquence d'appel *(f)* Fr
De Aufruffolge *(f)*
En calling sequence
Es secuencia de llamada *(f)*
It sequenza di richiamo *(f)*
Pt sequência de chamada *(f)*

séquence de contrôle *(f)* Fr
De Steuerfolge *(f)*
En control sequence
Es secuencia de control *(f)*
It sequenza di controllo *(f)*
Pt sequência de controlo *(f)*

séquence en langage source *(f)* Fr
De Quellcode *(m)*
En source code
Es código fuente *(m)*
It codice origine *(m)*
Pt código de origem *(m)*

séquence paramétrable *(f)* Fr
De Skelettcode *(m)*
En skeletal code
Es código esquemático *(m)*
It codice schematico *(m)*
Pt código reduzido *(m)*

sequência *(f) n* Pt
De Folge *(f)*
En sequence
Es secuencia *(f)*
Fr séquence *(f)*
It sequenza *(f)*

sequência de chamada *(f)* Pt
De Aufruffolge *(f)*
En calling sequence
Es secuencia de llamada *(f)*
Fr séquence d'appel *(f)*
It sequenza di richiamo *(f)*

sequência de controlo *(f)* Pt
De Steuerfolge *(f)*
En control sequence
Es secuencia de control *(f)*
Fr séquence de contrôle *(f)*
It sequenza di controllo *(f)*

sequential access En
De Folgezugriff *(m)*
Es acceso secuencial *(m)*
Fr accès séquentiel *(m)*
It accesso sequenziale *(m)*
Pt acesso sequencial *(m)*

sequential file En
De Folgedatei *(f)*
Es fichero secuencial *(m)*
Fr fichier séquentiel *(m)*
It file sequenziale *(m)*
Pt arquivo sequencial *(f)*

sequential processing En
De Folgeverarbeitung *(f)*
Es proceso secuencial *(m)*
Fr traitement séquentiel *(m)*
It elaborazione sequenziale *(f)*
Pt processamento sequencial *(m)*

sequenza *(f) n* It
De Folge *(f)*
En sequence
Es secuencia *(f)*
Fr séquence *(f)*
Pt sequência *(f)*

sequenza di controllo *(f)* It
De Steuerfolge *(f)*
En control sequence
Es secuencia de control *(f)*
Fr séquence de contrôle *(f)*
Pt sequência de controlo *(f)*

sequenza di richiamo *(f)* It
De Aufruffolge *(f)*
En calling sequence
Es secuencia de llamada *(f)*
Fr séquence d'appel *(f)*
Pt sequência de chamada *(f)*

sequenziare *vb* It
De folgen
En sequence
Es secuenciar
Fr ordonner
Pt formar sequência

sequenzieller Zugriff *(m)* De
En serial access
Es acceso en serie *(m)*
Fr accès en série *(m)*
It accesso in serie *(m)*
Pt acesso em série *(m)*

serbatoio di alimentazione (schede) *(m)* It
De Magazin *(n)*
En hopper
Es depósito de alimentación *(m)*
Fr magasin d'alimentation *(m)*
Pt tremonha *(f)*

serial access En
De sequenzieller Zugriff *(m)*
Es acceso en serie *(m)*
Fr accès en série *(m)*
It accesso in serie *(m)*
Pt acesso em série *(m)*

serial-parallel converter En
De Reihen-Parallelumwandler *(m)*
Es convertidor serie-paralelo *(m)*
Fr convertisseur série-parallèle *(m)*
It convertitore serie-parallelo *(m)*
Pt conversor de série em paralelo *(m)*

serial printer En
De Reihendrucker *(m)*
Es impresora en serie *(f)*
Fr imprimante série *(f)*
It stampatrice in serie *(f)*
Pt impressora em série *(f)*

serial processing En
De Reihenverarbeitung *(f)*
Es proceso en serie *(m)*
Fr traitement série *(m)*

It elaborazione in serie *(f)*
Pt processamento em série *(m)*

serial transfer En
De Reihenübergabe *(f)*
Es transferencia en serie *(f)*
Fr transfert en série *(m)*
It trasferimento in serie *(m)*
Pt transferência em série *(f)*

serie *(f) n* Es
De Folge *(f)*
En string
Fr chaîne *(f)*
It stringa *(f)*
Pt fileira *(f)*

serie de bits *(f)* Es
De Binärzeichenfolge *(f)*
En bit string
Fr chaîne de bits *(f)*
It stringa di bit *(f)*
Pt fila de bits *(f)*

serie di programmi *(f)* It
De Programmpaket *(n)*
En program package
Es colección de programas *(f)*
Fr programme-produit *(m)*
Pt pacote de programa *(m)*

serviceability *n* En
De Betriebsfähigkeit *(f)*
Es utilidad *(f)*
Fr aptitude au service *(f)*
It utilità *(f)*
Pt aptidão a ser utilizado *(f)*

service bit En
De Dienstbit *(m)*
Es bit de servicio *(m)*
Fr bit de service *(m)*
It bit di servizio *(m)*
Pt bit de serviço *(m)*

service des transports *(m)* Fr
De Transportdienst *(m)*
En transport service
Es servicio de transporte *(m)*
It servizio di trasporto *(m)*
Pt serviço de transporte *(m)*

service routine En
De Dienstprogramm *(n)*
Es rutina de servicio *(f)*
Fr programme de service *(m)*
It routine di servizio *(f)*
Pt rotina de serviço *(f)*

servicio de transporte *(m)* Es
De Transportdienst *(m)*
En transport service
Fr service des transports *(m)*
It servizio di trasporto *(m)*
Pt serviço de transporte *(m)*

serviço de transporte *(m)* Pt
De Transportdienst *(m)*
En transport service
Es servicio de transporte *(m)*
Fr service des transports *(m)*
It servizio di trasporto *(m)*

servizio di trasporto *(m)* It
De Transportdienst *(m)*
En transport service
Es servicio de transporte *(m)*
Fr service des transports *(m)*
Pt serviço de transporte *(m)*

set *n* En
De Menge *(f)*
Es conjunto *(m)*
Fr ensemble *(m)*
It insieme *(m)*
Pt conjunto *(m)*

set *vb* En
De setzen
Es ajustar
Fr régler
It disporre
Pt colocar

set up En
De einrichten
Es montar
Fr mettre en place
It mettere a punto
Pt instalar

set-up time En
De Einrichtezeit *(f)*
Es tiempo de preparación *(m)*
Fr temps de préparation *(m)*
It tempo messa a punto *(m)*
Pt tempo de instalação *(m)*

setzen *vb* De
En set
Es ajustar
Fr régler
It disporre
Pt colocar

shared files *n pl* En
De gemeinsam benutzte Datei *(f)*
Es ficheros compartidos *(m pl)*
Fr fichiers partagés *(m pl)*
It file in comune *(f pl)*
Pt arquivos compartidos *(m pl)*

shift *n* En
De Stellenverschiebung *(f)*
Es desplazamiento *(m)*
Fr décalage *(m)*
It riporto *(m)*
Pt mudança *(f)*

shift *vb* En
De versetzen
Es desplazar
Fr décaler
It spostare (dati)
Pt mudar

shift register En
De Schieberegister *(n)*
Es registro de desplazamiento *(m)*
Fr registre à décalage *(m)*
It registro per operazioni di spostamento dati *(m)*
Pt registo de deslocamento *(m)*

Sicherheit *(f) n* De
En integrity
Es integridad *(f)*
Fr intégrité *(f)*
It integrità *(f)*
Pt integridade *(f)*

Sichtgerät *(n) n* De
En visual-display unit (VDU)
Es unidad de visualización *(f)*
Fr appareil de visualisation (AV) *(m)*
It unitá di visualizzazione *(f)*
Pt unidade de visualização *(f)*

sicronizzatore *(m) n* It
De Synchronisiergerät *(n)*
En synchronizer
Es sincronizador *(m)*
Fr synchroniseur *(m)*
Pt sincronizador *(m)*

sicuro contro guasti It
De eigensicher
En fail-safe
Es sin riesgo de fallo
Fr à sécurité intégrée
Pt seguro contra falhas

sign *n* En
De Vorzeichen *(n)*
Es signo *(m)*
Fr signe *(m)*
It segno *(m)*
Pt indicação *(f)*

signal *n* En; Fr *(m)*
De Signal *(n)*
Es señal *(f)*
It segnale *(m)*
Pt sinal *(m)*

Signal *(n) n* De
En signal
Es señal *(f)*
Fr signal *(m)*
It segnale *(m)*
Pt sinal *(m)*

Signalabstand *(m) n* De
En signal distance
Es distancia de señal *(f)*
Fr distance de signalisation *(f)*

It distanza del segnale *(f)*
Pt distância de sinal *(f)*

signal de sortie non perturbé *(m)* Fr
De ungestörtes Ausgangssignal *(n)*
En undisturbed output signal
Es señal de salida no cambiada *(f)*
It segnale di output non disturbato *(m)*
Pt sinal de output não perturbado *(m)*

signal de sortie zéro *(m)* Fr
De Nullausgangssignal *(n)*
En zero-output signal
Es señal de salida cero *(f)*
It segnale di output zero *(m)*
Pt sinal de output zero *(m)*

signal de validation *(m)* Fr
De Aktiviersignal *(n)*
En enabling signal
Es señal de activación *(f)*
It segnale di abilitazione *(m)*
Pt sinal de capacitação *(m)*

signal d'interdiction *(m)* Fr
De Sperrsignal *(n)*
En inhibiting signal
Es señal inhibidora *(f)*
It segnale inibitore *(m)*
Pt sinal de inibição *(m)*

signal distance En
De Signalabstand *(m)*
Es distancia de señal *(f)*
Fr distance de signalisation *(f)*
It distanza del segnale *(f)*
Pt distância de sinal *(f)*

Signalisiergeschwindigkeit *(f)* *n* De
En signalling rate
Es velocidad de transmisión de señal *(f)*
Fr vitesse de signalisation *(f)*
It velocità dai segnali *(f)*
Pt índice de sinalização *(m)*

signalling rate En
De Signalisiergeschwindigkeit *(f)*
Es velocidad de transmisión de señal *(f)*
Fr vitesse de signalisation *(f)*
It velocità dai segnali *(f)*
Pt índice de sinalização *(m)*

signal-to-noise ratio En
De Rauschverhältnis *(n)*
Es relación señal-ruido *(f)*
Fr rapport signal-bruit *(m)*
It rapporto segnale-rumore *(m)*
Pt ratio entre sinal e ruído *(f)*

sign bit En
De Vorzeichenbit *(m)*
Es bit de signo *(m)*
Fr bit de signe *(m)*
It bit del segno *(m)*
Pt bit de sinal *(m)*

sign-check indicator En
De Vorzeichenprüfanzeiger *(m)*
Es indicador de verificación de signo *(m)*
Fr indicateur de contrôle de signes *(m)*
It indicatore del controllo di segno *(m)*
Pt indicador de verificação de sinal *(m)*

sign digit En
De Vorzeichenziffer *(f)*
Es dígito de signo *(m)*
Fr caractère de signe *(m)*
It digit del segno *(m)*
Pt número digital de sinal *(m)*

signe *(m)* *n* Fr
De Vorzeichen *(n)*
En sign
Es signo *(m)*
It segno *(m)*
Pt indicação *(f)*

significant digits *n pl* En
De wesentliche Ziffern *(pl)*
Es dígitos significativos *(m pl)*
Fr chiffres significatifs *(m pl)*
It digiti significativi *(m pl)*
Pt números digitais significativos *(m pl)*

signo *(m)* *n* Es
De Vorzeichen *(n)*
En sign
Fr signe *(m)*
It segno *(m)*
Pt indicação *(f)*

silicio *(m)* *n* Es, It
De Silikon *(n)*
En silicon
Fr silicium *(m)*
Pt silício *(m)*

silício *(m)* *n* Pt
De Silikon *(n)*
En silicon
Es silicio *(m)*
Fr silicium *(m)*
It silicio *(m)*

silicium *(m)* *n* Fr
De Silikon *(n)*
En silicon
Es silicio *(m)*
It silicio *(m)*
Pt silício *(m)*

silicon *n* En
De Silikon *(n)*
Es silicio *(m)*
Fr silicium *(m)*
It silicio *(m)*
Pt silício *(m)*

silicon chip En
De Silikonchip *(m)*
Es microplaqueta de silicio *(f)*
Fr puce au silicium *(f)*
It scheggia di silicone *(f)*
Pt ficha de silício *(f)*

Silikon *(n)* *n* De
En silicon
Es silicio *(m)*
Fr silicium *(m)*
It silicio *(m)*
Pt silício *(m)*

Silikonchip *(m)* *n* De
En silicon chip
Es microplaqueta de silicio *(f)*
Fr puce au silicium *(f)*
It scheggia di silicone *(f)*
Pt ficha de silício *(f)*

simbolo *(m)* *n* It
De Symbol *(n)*
En symbol
Es símbolo *(m)*
Fr symbole *(m)*
Pt símbolo *(m)*

símbolo *(m)* *n* Es, Pt
De Symbol *(n)*
En symbol
Fr symbole *(m)*
It simbolo *(m)*

símbolo de decisión *(m)* Es
De Blockdiagrammsymbol-Entscheidung *(f)*
En decision box
Fr symbole de décision *(m)*
It casella di decisione *(f)*
Pt caixa de decisão *(f)*

simbolo logico *(m)* It
De logisches Symbol *(n)*
En logic symbol
Es símbolo lógico *(m)*
Fr symbole logique *(m)*
Pt símbolo lógico *(m)*

símbolo lógico *(m)* Es, Pt
De logisches Symbol *(n)*
En logic symbol
Fr symbole logique *(m)*
It simbolo logico *(m)*

simplesso *(m)* *n* It
De Simplex *(n)*
En simplex
Es simplex *(m)*
Fr simplex *(m)*
Pt simplex *(m)*

simplex *n* En; Es, Fr, Pt *(m)*
De Simplex *(n)*
It simplesso *(m)*

Simplex *(n) n* De
En simplex
Es simplex *(m)*
Fr simplex *(m)*
It simplesso *(m)*
Pt simplex *(m)*

simulação *(f) n* Pt
De Nachahmung *(f)*
En simulation
Es simulación *(f)*
Fr simulation *(f)*
It simulazione *(f)*

simulación *(f) n* Es
De Nachahmung *(f)*
En simulation
Fr simulation *(f)*
It simulazione *(f)*
Pt simulação *(f)*

simulado *adj* Pt
De Schein-
En dummy
Es ficticio
Fr fictif
It fittizio

simulador *(m) n* Es, Pt
De Simulator *(m)*
En simulator
Fr simulateur *(m)*
It simulatore *(m)*

simulateur *(m) n* Fr
De Simulator *(m)*
En simulator
Es simulador *(m)*
It simulatore *(m)*
Pt simulador *(m)*

simulation *n* En; Fr *(f)*
De Nachahmung *(f)*
Es simulación *(f)*
It simulazione *(f)*
Pt simulação *(f)*

simulator *n* En
De Simulator *(m)*
Es simulador *(m)*
Fr simulateur *(m)*
It simulatore *(m)*
Pt simulador *(m)*

Simulator *(m) n* De
En simulator
Es simulador *(m)*
Fr simulateur *(m)*
It simulatore *(m)*
Pt simulador *(m)*

simulatore *(m) n* It
De Simulator *(m)*
En simulator
Es simulador *(m)*
Fr simulateur *(m)*
Pt simulador *(m)*

simulazione *(f) n* It
De Nachahmung *(f)*
En simulation
Es simulación *(f)*
Fr simulation *(f)*
Pt simulação *(f)*

simultaneous access En
De gleichzeitiger Zugriff *(m)*
Es acceso simultáneo *(m)*
Fr accès simultané *(m)*
It accesso simultaneo *(m)*
Pt acesso simultâneo *(m)*

sinal *(m) n* Pt
De Signal *(n)*
En signal
Es señal *(f)*
Fr signal *(m)*
It segnale *(m)*

sinal de capacitação *(m)* Pt
De Aktiviersignal *(n)*
En enabling signal
Es señal de activación *(f)*
Fr signal de validation *(m)*
It segnale di abilitazione *(m)*

sinal de inibição *(m)* Pt
De Sperrsignal *(n)*
En inhibiting signal
Es señal inhibidora *(f)*
Fr signal d'interdiction *(m)*
It segnale inibitore *(m)*

sinal de output não perturbado *(m)* Pt
De ungestörtes Ausgangssignal *(n)*
En undisturbed output signal
Es señal de salida no cambiada *(f)*
Fr signal de sortie non perturbé *(m)*
It segnale di output non disturbato *(m)*

sinal de output zero *(m)* Pt
De Nullausgangssignal *(n)*
En zero-output signal
Es señal de salida cero *(f)*
Fr signal de sortie zéro *(m)*
It segnale di output zero *(m)*

sincronizador *(m) n* Es, Pt
De Synchronisiergerät *(n)*
En synchronizer
Fr synchroniseur *(m)*
It sicronizzatore *(m)*

single-address instruction En
De Einzeladress-anweisung *(f)*
Es instrucción de una sola dirección *(f)*
Fr instruction à une adresse *(f)*
It istruzione ad indirizzo singolo *(f)*
Pt instrução de endereço único *(f)*

single-step operation En
De Einzelschrittfunktion *(f)*
Es operación de paso único *(f)*
Fr opération en pas à pas *(f)*
It operazione a fase singola *(f)*
Pt operação de uma só fase *(f)*

sin riesgo de fallo Es
De eigensicher
En fail-safe
Fr à sécurité intégrée
It sicuro contro guasti
Pt seguro contra falhas

sintassi *(f) n* It
De Syntax *(f)*
En syntax
Es sintaxis *(f)*
Fr syntaxe *(f)*
Pt sintaxe *(f)*

sintaxe *(f) n* Pt
De Syntax *(f)*
En syntax
Es sintaxis *(f)*
Fr syntaxe *(f)*
It sintassi *(f)*

sintaxis *(f) n* Es
De Syntax *(f)*
En syntax
Fr syntaxe *(f)*
It sintassi *(f)*
Pt sintaxe *(f)*

sintonización *(f) n* Es
De Abstimmung *(f)*
En tuning
Fr mise au point *(f)*
It sintonizzazione *(f)*
Pt afinação *(f)*

sintonizzazione *(f) n* It
De Abstimmung *(f)*
En tuning
Es sintonización *(f)*
Fr mise au point *(f)*
Pt afinação *(f)*

sistema *(m) n* Es, It, Pt
De System *(n)*
En system
Fr système *(m)*

sistema abbinato *(m)* It
De Anschlußsystem *(n)*
En tandem system
Es sistema en tandem *(m)*
Fr système en tandem *(m)*
Pt sistema em tandem *(m)*

sistema a controllo adattivo *(m)* It
De adaptives Steuersystem *(n)*
En adaptive-control system
Es sistema de control autoadaptable *(m)*
Fr système de commande adaptatif *(m)*

Pt sistema de controlo adaptável *(m)*

sistema a principio di eccezione *(m)* It
De Ausnahmeprinzip-system *(n)*
En exception principle system
Es control por excepción *(m)*
Fr gestion par exception *(f)*
Pt sistema de princípio de excepção *(m)*

sistema combinado maestro-satélite *(m)* Es
De Master-Slave-Anordnung *(f)*
En master-slave system
Fr système pilote-asservi *(m)*
It sistema maestro-schiavo *(m)*
Pt sistema mestre-escravo *(m)*

sistema de cálculo a distancia *(m)* Es
De Fernrechensystem *(n)*
En remote computing system
Fr système de traitement à distance *(m)*
It sistema di elaborazione a distanza *(m)*
Pt sistema de tele-computador *(m)*

sistema de computador duplex *(m)* Pt
De Duplex-Rechnersystem *(n)*
En duplex computer system
Es sistema de ordenador duplex *(m)*
Fr système informatique en duplex *(m)*
It sistema di calcolatore doppio *(m)*

sistema de comunicação *(m)* Pt
De Kommunikations-system *(n)*
En communication system
Es sistema de comunicaciones *(m)*
Fr système de communication *(m)*
It sistema di comunicazione *(m)*

sistema de comunicaciones *(m)* Es
De Kommunikations-system *(n)*
En communication system
Fr système de communication *(m)*
It sistema di comunicazione *(m)*
Pt sistema de comunicação *(m)*

sistema de control autoadaptable *(m)* Es
De adaptives Steuersystem *(n)*
En adaptive-control system
Fr système de commande adaptatif *(m)*
It sistema a controllo adattivo *(m)*
Pt sistema de controlo adaptável *(m)*

sistema de control de trabajos *(m)* Es
De Jobkontrollsystem *(n)*
En job control system
Fr système de contrôle des travaux *(m)*
It sistema di controllo olei lavori *(m)*
Pt sistema de controle de trabalho *(m)*

sistema de controle de trabalho *(m)* Pt
De Jobkontrollsystem *(n)*
En job control system
Es sistema de control de trabajos *(m)*
Fr système de contrôle des travaux *(m)*
It sistema di controllo olei lavori *(m)*

sistema de controlo adaptável *(m)* Pt
De adaptives Steuersystem *(n)*
En adaptive-control system
Es sistema de control autoadaptable *(m)*
Fr système de commande adaptatif *(m)*
It sistema a controllo adattivo *(m)*

sistema de gestión del banco de datos *(m)* Es
De Datenverwaltungs-system *(n)*
En database management system (DBMS)
Fr système de gestion de base de données (SGBD) *(m)*
It sistema di gestione della banca dei dati *(m)*
Pt sistema de management de base de dados *(m)*

sistema de informação *(m)* Pt
De Informationssystem *(n)*
En information system
Es sistema de información *(m)*
Fr système informatique *(m)*
It sistema di informazioni *(m)*

sistema de información *(m)* Es
De Informationssystem *(n)*
En information system
Fr système informatique *(m)*
It sistema di informazioni *(m)*
Pt sistema de informação *(m)*

sistema de management de base de dados *(m)* Pt
De Datenverwaltungs-system *(n)*
En database management system (DBMS)
Es sistema de gestión del banco de datos *(m)*
Fr système de gestion de base de données (SGBD) *(m)*
It sistema di gestione della banca dei dati *(m)*

sistema de numeración *(m)* Es
De Nummernsystem *(n)*
En number system
Fr système de numérotation *(m)*
It sistema di numeri *(m)*
Pt sistema numérico *(m)*

sistema de operação *(m)* Pt
De Betriebssystem *(n)*
En operating system (OS)
Es sistema operativo *(m)*
Fr système d'exploitation *(m)*
It sistema operativo *(m)*

sistema de operação baseado em discos *(m)* Pt
De Plattenbetriebsystem *(n)*
En disk-based operating system (DOS)
Es sistema operativo en discos *(m)*
Fr système d'exploitation à disques *(m)*
It sistema operativo su disco *(m)*

sistema de ordenador duplex *(m)* Es
De Duplex-Rechnersystem *(n)*
En duplex computer system
Fr système informatique en duplex *(m)*
It sistema di calcolatore doppio *(m)*
Pt sistema de computador duplex *(m)*

sistema de princípio de excepção *(m)* Pt
De Ausnahmeprinzip-system *(n)*
En exception principle system
Es control por excepción *(m)*
Fr gestion par exception *(f)*
It sistema a principio di eccezione *(m)*

sistema de red *(m)* Es
De Netzsystem *(n)*
En network system
Fr système de réseau *(m)*
It sistema di reti *(m)*
Pt sistema de rede *(m)*

sistema de rede *(m)* Pt
De Netzsystem *(n)*
En network system
Es sistema de red *(m)*
Fr système de réseau *(m)*
It sistema di reti *(m)*

sistema de tele-computador *(m)* Pt
De Fernrechensystem *(n)*
En remote computing system
Es sistema de cálculo a distancia *(m)*
Fr système de traitement à distance *(m)*
It sistema di elaborazione a distanza *(m)*

sistema de utentes múltiplos *(m)* Pt
De Mehrfachbenutzer-system *(n)*
En multiuser system
Es sistema para usuarios múltiples *(m)*
Fr système à utilisateurs multiples *(m)*
It sistema per utenti multipli *(m)*

sistema di calcolatore doppio *(m)* It
De Duplex-Rechnersystem *(n)*
En duplex computer system
Es sistema de ordenador duplex *(m)*
Fr système informatique en duplex *(m)*
Pt sistema de computador duplex *(m)*

sistema di comunicazione *(m)* It
De Kommunikations-system *(n)*
En communication system
Es sistema de comunicaciones *(m)*
Fr système de communication *(m)*
Pt sistema de comunicação *(m)*

sistema di controllo olei lavori *(m)* It
De Jobkontrollsystem *(n)*
En job control system
Es sistema de control de trabajos *(m)*
Fr système de contrôle des travaux *(m)*
Pt sistema de controle de trabalho *(m)*

sistema di elaborazione a distanza *(m)* It
De Fernrechensystem *(n)*
En remote computing system
Es sistema de cálculo a distancia *(m)*
Fr système de traitement à distance *(m)*
Pt sistema de tele-computador *(m)*

sistema di gestione della banca dei dati *(m)* It
De Datenverwaltungs-system *(n)*
En database management system (DBMS)
Es sistema de gestión del banco de datos *(m)*
Fr système de gestion de base de données (SGBD) *(m)*
Pt sistema de management de base de dados *(m)*

sistema di informazioni *(m)* It
De Informationssystem *(n)*
En information system
Es sistema de información *(m)*
Fr système informatique *(m)*
Pt sistema de informação *(m)*

sistema di numeri *(m)* It
De Nummernsystem *(n)*
En number system
Es sistema de numeración *(m)*
Fr système de numérotation *(m)*
Pt sistema numérico *(m)*

sistema di reti *(m)* It
De Netzsystem *(n)*
En network system
Es sistema de red *(m)*
Fr système de réseau *(m)*
Pt sistema de rede *(m)*

sistema em tandem *(m)* Pt
De Anschlußsystem *(n)*
En tandem system
Es sistema en tandem *(m)*
Fr système en tandem *(m)*
It sistema abbinato *(m)*

sistema en tandem *(m)* Es
De Anschlußsystem *(n)*
En tandem system
Fr système en tandem *(m)*
It sistema abbinato *(m)*
Pt sistema em tandem *(m)*

sistema maestro-schiavo *(m)* It
De Master-Slave-Anordnung *(f)*
En master-slave system
Es sistema combinado maestro-satélite *(m)*
Fr système pilote-asservi *(m)*
Pt sistema mestre-escravo *(m)*

sistema mestre-escravo *(m)* Pt
De Master-Slave-Anordnung *(f)*
En master-slave system
Es sistema combinado maestro-satélite *(m)*
Fr système pilote-asservi *(m)*
It sistema maestro-schiavo *(m)*

sistema modular *(m)* Es, Pt
De Baukastensystem *(n)*
En modular system
Fr système modulaire *(m)*
It sistema modulare *(m)*

sistema modulare *(m)* It
De Baukastensystem *(n)*
En modular system
Es sistema modular *(m)*
Fr système modulaire *(m)*
Pt sistema modular *(m)*

sistema numérico *(m)* Pt
De Nummernsystem *(n)*
En number system
Es sistema de numeración *(m)*
Fr système de numérotation *(m)*
It sistema di numeri *(m)*

sistema operativo *(m)* Es
De Betriebssystem *(n)*
En operating system (OS)
Fr système d'exploitation *(m)*
It sistema operativo *(m)*
Pt sistema de operação *(m)*

sistema operativo *(m)* It
De Betriebssystem *(n)*
En operating system (OS)
Es sistema operativo *(m)*
Fr système d'exploitation *(m)*
Pt sistema de operação *(m)*

sistema operativo en discos *(m)* Es
De Plattenbetriebsystem *(n)*
En disk-based operating system (DOS)
Fr système d'exploitation à disques *(m)*
It sistema operativo su disco *(m)*
Pt sistema de operação baseado em discos *(m)*

sistema operativo su disco *(m)* It
De Plattenbetriebsystem *(n)*
En disk-based operating system (DOS)
Es sistema operativo en discos *(m)*
Fr système d'exploitation à disques *(m)*
Pt sistema de operação baseado em discos *(m)*

sistema para usuarios múltiples *(m)* Es
De Mehrfachbenutzer-system *(n)*
En multiuser system
Fr système à utilisateurs multiples *(m)*
It sistema per utenti multipli *(m)*
Pt sistema de utentes múltiplos *(m)*

sistema per utenti multipli *(m)* It
De Mehrfachbenutzer-system *(n)*
En multiuser system
Es sistema para usuarios múltiples *(m)*
Fr système à utilisateurs multiples *(m)*
Pt sistema de utentes múltiplos *(m)*

Skala *(f) n* De
En scale
Es escala *(f)*
Fr échelle *(f)*
It scala *(f)*
Pt escala *(f)*

skalieren *vb* De
En scale
Es pasar a escala
Fr cadrer
It scalare
Pt fazer concordar com a escala

Skalierfaktor *(m) n* De
En scale factor
Es factor escalar *(m)*
Fr facteur de cadrage *(m)*
It fattore di scala *(m)*
Pt factor de escala *(m)*

skeletal code En
De Skelettcode *(m)*
Es código esquemático *(m)*
Fr séquence paramétrable *(f)*
It codice schematico *(m)*
Pt código reduzido *(m)*

Skelettcode *(m) n* De
En skeletal code
Es código esquemático *(m)*
Fr séquence paramétrable *(f)*
It codice schematico *(m)*
Pt código reduzido *(m)*

skip *vb* En
De überspringen
Es omitir
Fr sauter
It saltare
Pt omitir

slave store En
De Nebenspeicher *(m)*
Es memoria sin parte residente *(f)*
Fr mémoire asservie *(f)*
It memoria satellite *(f)*
Pt armazém escravo *(m)*

smorzamento *(m) n* It
De Dämpfung *(f)*
En damping
Es amortiguamiento *(m)*
Fr amortissement *(m)*
Pt amortecimento *(m)*

sobre a linha Pt
De direkt
En on-line
Es en línea
Fr direct
It in linea

sobrepor-se *vb* Pt
De überlappen
En overlap
Es solapar
Fr chevaucher
It sovrapporre

sociedad especializada en programación *(f)* Es
De Softwarehaus *(n)*
En software house
Fr société de services et de conseils en informatique (SSCI) *(f)*
It ditta specializzata nel fare programmi per conto terzi *(f)*
Pt casa de software *(f)*

société de services et de conseils en informatique (SSCI) *(f)* Fr
De Softwarehaus *(n)*
Es sociedad especializada en programación *(f)*
En software house
It ditta specializzata nel fare programmi per conto terzi *(f)*
Pt casa de software *(f)*

software *n* En; It, Pt *(m)*
De Software *(f)*
Es soporte lógico *(m)*
Fr logiciel *(m)*

Software *(f) n* De
En software
Es soporte lógico *(m)*
Fr logiciel *(m)*
It software *(m)*
Pt software *(m)*

software a strato multiplo *(m)* It
De mehrschichtige Software *(f)*
En multilayered software
Es equipo instruccional multicapas *(m)*
Fr software multi-couche *(m)*
Pt software de camadas múltiplas *(m)*

software de camadas múltiplas *(m)* Pt
De mehrschichtige Software *(f)*
En multilayered software
Es equipo instruccional multicapas *(m)*
Fr software multi-couche *(m)*
It software a strato multiplo *(m)*

software engineering En
De Programm-ausrüstung *(f)*
Es ingeniería de soportes lógicos *(f)*
Fr technique du logiciel *(f)*
It ingegneria del software *(f)*
Pt engenharia de software *(f)*

software generator En
De Programm-ausrüstungsgeber *(m)*
Es generador de soportes lógicos *(m)*
Fr générateur de logiciel *(m)*
It generatore di software *(m)*
Pt gerador de software *(m)*

Softwarehaus *(n) n* De
Es sociedad especializada en programación *(f)*
En software house
Fr société de services et de conseils en informatique (SSCI) *(f)*
It ditta specializzata nel fare programmi per conto terzi *(f)*
Pt casa de software *(f)*

software house En
De Softwarehaus *(n)*
Es sociedad especializada en programación *(f)*
Fr société de services et de conseils en informatique (SSCI) *(f)*
It ditta specializzata nel

fare programmi per conto terzi *(f)*
Pt casa de software *(f)*

software multi-couche *(m)* Fr
De mehrschichtige Software *(f)*
En multilayered software
Es equipo instruccional multicapas *(m)*
It software a strato multiplo *(m)*
Pt software de camadas múltiplas *(m)*

software package En
De Softwarepaket *(n)*
Es paqueta de soporte lógico *(m)*
Fr progiciel *(m)*
It pacco di software *(m)*
Pt pacote de software *(m)*

Softwarepaket *(n) n* De
En software package
Es paqueta de soporte lógico *(m)*
Fr progiciel *(m)*
It pacco di software *(m)*
Pt pacote de software *(m)*

solapar *vb* Es
De überlappen
En overlap
Fr chevaucher
It sovrapporre
Pt sobrepor-se

solid-state memory En
De Festschaltungs-speicher *(m)*
Es memoria de estado sólido *(f)*
Fr mémoire en état solide *(f)*
It memoria a stato solido *(f)*
Pt memória solid-state *(f)*

soma de verificação *(f)* Pt
De Summenprüfung *(f)*
En check sum
Es suma de verificación *(f)*
Fr somme de contrôle *(f)*
It somma di controllo *(f)*

somador *(m) n* Pt
De Addierglied *(n)*
En adder
Es sumador *(m)*
Fr additionneur *(m)*
It addizionatore *(m)*

somador-subtractor *(m) n* Pt
De Addier-Subtrahierglied *(n)*
En adder-subtracter
Es sumador-sustractor *(m)*
Fr additionneur-soustracteur *(m)*
It addizionatore-sottrattore *(m)*

somador total *(m)* Pt
De Feldaddierer *(m)*
En full adder
Es adicionador completo *(m)*
Fr additionneur complet *(m)*
It addizionatore totale *(m)*

somma di controllo *(f)* It
De Summenprüfung *(f)*
En check sum
Es suma de verificación *(f)*
Fr somme de contrôle *(f)*
Pt soma de verificação *(f)*

somme de contrôle *(f)* Fr
De Summenprüfung *(f)*
En check sum
Es suma de verificación *(f)*
It somma di controllo *(f)*
Pt soma de verificação *(f)*

Sonderzeichen *(n) n* De
En special character
Es carácter especial *(m)*
Fr caractère spécial *(m)*
It carattere speciale *(m)*
Pt carácter especial *(m)*

soporte lógico *(m)* Es
De Software *(f)*
En software
Fr logiciel *(m)*
It software *(m)*
Pt software *(m)*

soppressione *(f) n* It
De Unterdrückung *(f)*
En suppression
Es supresión *(f)*
Fr suppression *(f)*
Pt supressão *(f)*

soppressione di zero *(f)* It
De Nullunterdrückung *(f)*
En zero suppression
Es supresión de ceros *(f)*
Fr élimination des zéros *(f)*
Pt supressão zero *(f)*

sort *n* En
De Sortierung *(f)*
Es clasificación *(f)*
Fr tri *(m)*
It selezione *(f)*
Pt espécie *(f)*

sort *vb* En
De sortieren
Es clasificar
Fr trier
It classificare
Pt classificar

sorter *n* En
De Sortierer *(m)*
Es clasificadora *(f)*
Fr trieuse *(f)*
It selezionatrice *(f)*
Pt classificador *(m)*

sortie *(f) n* Fr
De Ausgang *(m)*
En exit; output
Es salida *(f)*
It uscita *(f)*
Pt output; saída *(m f)*

sortie de lecture *(f)* Fr
De Ausleser *(m)*
En read-out
Es lectura de salida *(f)*
It lettura dalla memoria *(f)*
Pt leitura de saida *(f)*

sortieren *vb* De
En sort
Es clasificar
Fr trier
It classificare
Pt classificar

Sortierer *(m) n* De
En sorter
Es clasificadora *(f)*
Fr trieuse *(f)*
It selezionatrice *(f)*
Pt classificador *(m)*

Sortierung *(f) n* De
En sort
Es clasificación *(f)*
Fr tri *(m)*
It selezione *(f)*
Pt espécie *(f)*

Sortierungfusion *(f) n* De
En sort-merge
Es clasificación-fusión *(f)*
Fr tri-fusion *(m)*
It selezione-inserimento *(f)*
Pt classificação-fusão *(f)*

Sortierungsprogramm *(n) n* De
En sorting routine
Es rutina de clasificación *(f)*
Fr programme de tri *(m)*
It routine di selezione *(f)*
Pt rotina de classificação *(f)*

sortie sur imprimante *(f)* Fr
De Ausdruck *(m)*
En printout
Es vaciado a la impresora *(m)*
It stampato *(m)*
Pt impressão *(f)*

sorting routine En
De Sortierungs-programm *(n)*
Es rutina de clasificación *(f)*
Fr programme de tri *(m)*
It routine di selezione *(f)*
Pt rotina de classificação *(f)*

sortir *vb* Fr
De ausgehen
En exit
Es salir
It uscire
Pt sair

sortir *vb* Fr
De ausgeben
En output
Es extraer
It output
Pt sair

sort-merge *n* En
De Sortierungfusion *(f)*
Es clasificación-fusión *(f)*
Fr tri-fusion *(m)*
It selezione-inserimento *(f)*
Pt classificação-fusão *(f)*

sottoflusso *(m) n* It
De Unterlauf *(m)*
En underflow
Es subdesbordamiento *(m)*
Fr dépassement de capacité inférieur *(m)*
Pt subfluxo *(m)*

sottogruppo *(m) n* It
De Untermenge *(f)*
En subset
Es subgrupo *(m)*
Fr sous-ensemble *(m)*
Pt sub-conjunto *(m)*

sottoprogramma *(m) n* It
De Unterprogramm *(n)*
En subprogram
Es subprograma *(m)*
Fr sous-programme *(m)*
Pt subprograma *(m)*

sottosopra *adj* It
De kieloben
En bottom-up
Es boca-abajo
Fr ascendant
Pt fundo para cima

sottrattore *(m) n* It
De Subtrahierer *(m)*
En subtracter
Es sustractor *(m)*
Fr soustracteur *(m)*
Pt subtracctor *(m)*

source code En
De Quellcode *(m)*
Es código fuente *(m)*
Fr séquence en langage source *(f)*
It codice origine *(m)*
Pt código de origem *(m)*

source data capture En
De Quelldatenfang *(m)*
Es captura de datos fuente *(f)*
Fr saisie des données à la source *(f)*
It cattura di dati all'origine *(f)*
Pt captação de dados de origem *(f)*

source document En
De Quelldokument *(n)*
Es documento fuente *(m)*
Fr document de base *(m)*
It documento origine *(m)*
Pt documento de origem *(m)*

source language En
De Quellsprache *(f)*
Es lenguaje fuente *(m)*
Fr langage source *(m)*
It linguaggio origine *(m)*
Pt linguagem de origem *(f)*

source program En
De Quellprogramm *(n)*
Es programa fuente *(m)*
Fr programme source *(m)*
It programma origine *(m)*
Pt programa de origem *(m)*

sous-ensemble *(m) n* Fr
De Untermenge *(f)*
En subset
Es subgrupo *(m)*
It sottogruppo *(m)*
Pt sub-conjunto *(m)*

sous-programme *(m) n* Fr
De Unterprogramm *(n)*
En subprogram
Es subprograma *(m)*
It sottoprogramma *(m)*
Pt subprograma *(m)*

sous-programme standard *(m)* Fr
De Standardunterprogramm *(n)*
En standard subroutine
Es subrutina estándar *(f)*
It subroutine standard *(f)*
Pt subrotina standard *(f)*

sous-programme statique *(m)* Fr
De statisches Unterprogramm *(n)*
En static subroutine
Es subrutina estática *(f)*
It subroutine statica *(f)*
Pt subrotina estática *(f)*

sous-routine *(f) n* Fr
De Unterroutine *(f)*
En subroutine
Es subrutina *(f)*
It subroutine *(f)*
Pt subrotina *(f)*

soustracteur *(m) n* Fr
De Subtrahierer *(m)*
En subtracter
Es sustractor *(m)*
It sottrattore *(m)*
Pt subtracctor *(m)*

sovrapporre *vb* It
De überlappen
En overlap
Es solapar
Fr chevaucher
Pt sobrepor-se

space character En
De Leerstellenzeichen *(n)*
Es carácter blanco *(m)*
Fr caractère blanc *(m)*
It carattere di spazio *(m)*
Pt carácter de espaço *(m)*

Spalte *(f) n* De
En gap
Es intervalo *(m)*
Fr intervalle *(m)*
It intervallo *(m)*
Pt intervalo *(m)*

special character En
De Sonderzeichen *(n)*
Es carácter especial *(m)*
Fr caractère spécial *(m)*
It carattere speciale *(m)*
Pt carácter especial *(m)*

spécialisé *adj* Fr
De ausschließlich zugeordnet
En dedicated
Es dedicado
It dedicato
Pt dedicado

special-purpose computer En
De Spezialrechner *(m)*
Es ordenador especializado *(m)*
Fr calculateur spécialisé *(m)*
It elaboratore a scopo speciale *(m)*
Pt computador para fins especiais *(m)*

specification *n* En
De Spezifikation *(f)*
Es especificación *(f)*
Fr spécification *(f)*
It specificazione *(f)*
Pt especificação *(f)*

spécification *(f) n* Fr
De Spezifikation *(f)*
En specification
Es especificación *(f)*
It specificazione *(f)*
Pt especificação *(f)*

spécification de programme *(f)* Fr
De Programmvorgabe *(f)*
En program specification
Es especificación de programa *(f)*
It specificazioni del programma *(f)*
Pt especificação do programa *(f)*

specificazione *(f) n* It
De Spezifikation *(f)*
En specification
Es especificación *(f)*
Fr spécification *(f)*
Pt especificação *(f)*

specificazioni del programma *(f)* It
De Programmvorgabe *(f)*
En program specification
Es especificación de programa *(f)*
Fr spécification de programme *(f)*
Pt especificação do programa *(f)*

Speichauszugspunkt *(m) n* De
En dump point
Es punto de vaciado *(m)*
Fr point de vidage *(m)*
It punto di dump *(m)*
Pt ponto de descarga *(m)*

Speicher *(m) n* De
En memory; store
Es memoria *(f)*
Fr mémoire *(f)*
It memoria *(f)*
Pt armazém; memória *(m f)*

Speicheranzeige *(f) n* De
En storage display
Es presentación de almacenamiento *(f)*
Fr affichage d'enregistrement *(m)*
It visualizzazione di memoria *(f)*
Pt visualização de armazenamento *(f)*

speicherausziehen *vb* De
En dump
Es volcar
Fr vider
It fare un dump
Pt descarregar

Speicherauszug *(m) n* De
En dump; memory dump
Es vuelco de la memoria *(m)*
Fr vidage; vidage de la mémoire *(m)*
It dump; dump della memoria *(m)*
Pt descarregador; descarregador de memória *(m)*

Speicherauszug nach dem Tode *(m)* De
En post-mortem dump
Es vaciado póstumo *(m)*
Fr vidage d'autopsie *(m)*
It dump di autopsia *(m)*
Pt descarregador de autópsia *(m)*

Speicherauszugsprüfung *(f) n* De
En dump check
Es control por vaciado *(m)*
Fr contrôle par vidage *(m)*
It controllo del dump *(m)*
Pt verificação de descarga *(f)*

Speicherdichte *(f) n* De
En storage density
Es densidad de almacenamiento *(f)*
Fr densité de stockage *(f)*
It densità di memoria *(f)*
Pt densidade de armazenamento *(f)*

Speichergerät *(n) n* De
En storage device
Es dispositivo de almacenamiento *(m)*
Fr unité de stockage *(f)*
It organo di memoria *(m)*
Pt dispositivo de armazenamento *(m)*

Speicherkapazität *(f) n* De
En storage capacity
Es capacidad de almacenamiento *(f)*
Fr capacité de mémoire *(f)*
It capacità di memoria *(f)*
Pt capacidade de armazenamento *(f)*

speichern *vb* De
En store
Es almacenar
Fr mémoriser
It memorizzare
Pt armazenar

Speicherröhre *(f) n* De
En storage tube
Es tubo de almacenamiento *(m)*
Fr tube à mémoire *(m)*
It tubo di memoria *(m)*
Pt válvula de armazenamento *(f)*

Speicherschutz *(m) n* De
En memory protection
Es protección de la memoria *(f)*
Fr protection de la mémoire *(f)*
It protezione della memoria *(f)*
Pt protecção de memória *(f)*

Speicherung *(f) n* De
En storage
Es almacenamiento *(m)*
Fr stockage *(m)*
It immagazzinamento *(m)*
Pt armazenamento *(m)*

Speicherzuweisung *(f) n* De
En storage allocation
Es asignación de almacenamiento *(f)*
Fr affectation de la mémoire *(f)*
It assegnazione in memoria *(f)*
Pt atribuição de armazenamento *(f)*

sperren *vb* De
En inhibit; lock out
Es bloquear; inhibir
Fr bloquer; inhiber
It chiudere fuori; inibire
Pt bloquear; inibir

Sperrimpuls *(m) n* De
En inhibit pulse
Es impulso de bloqueo *(m)*
Fr impulsion d'interdiction *(f)*
It impulso inibitore *(m)*
Pt impulso de inibição *(m)*

Sperrsignal *(n) n* De
En inhibiting signal
Es señal inhibidora *(f)*
Fr signal d'interdiction *(m)*
It segnale inibitore *(m)*
Pt sinal de inibição *(m)*

Spezialrechner *(m) n* De
En special-purpose computer
Es ordenador especializado *(m)*
Fr calculateur spécialisé *(m)*
It elaboratore a scopo speciale *(m)*
Pt computador para fins especiais *(m)*

Spezifikation *(f) n* De
En specification
Es especificación *(f)*
Fr spécification *(f)*
It specificazione *(f)*
Pt especificação *(f)*

spina *(f) n* It
De Stecker *(m)*
En plug
Es clavija *(f)*
Fr fiche *(f)*
Pt ficha eléctrica *(f)*

splicer *n* En
De Klebegerät *(n)*
Es empalmadora *(f)*
Fr colleuse de bandes *(f)*
It incollatrice *(f)*
Pt emendador *(m)*

spool *n* En
De Spule *(f)*
Es bobina *(f)*
Fr bobine *(f)*
It bobina *(f)*
Pt bobina *(f)*

spool *vb* En
De spulen
Es bobinar
Fr bobiner
It bobinare
Pt embobinar

spooler *n* En
De Aufspulgerät *(n)*
Es bobinadora *(f)*
Fr enrouleur *(m)*
It avvolgitore *(m)*
Pt embobinador *(m)*

spooling *n* En
De Aufspulen *(n)*
Es bobinado *(m)*
Fr bobinage *(m)*
It bobinaggio *(m)*
Pt embobinagem *(f)*

spostamento a destra *(m)* It
De Rechtsschiebung *(f)*
En right shift
Es desplazamiento a la derecha *(m)*
Fr décalage à droite *(m)*
Pt mudança à direita *(f)*

spostamento aritmetico *(m)* It
De arithmetische Stellenverschiebung *(f)*
En arithmetic shift
Es desplazamiento aritmético *(m)*
Fr décalage arithmétique *(m)*
Pt mudança aritmética *(f)*

spostamento a sinistra *(m)* It
De Linksverschiebung *(f)*
En left shift
Es desplazamiento a la izquierda *(m)*
Fr décalage à gauche *(m)*
Pt mudança à esquerda *(f)*

spostamento logico *(m)* It
De logische Verschiebung *(f)*
En logic(al) shift
Es desplazamiento lógico *(m)*
Fr décalage logique *(m)*
Pt mudança lógica *(f)*

spostare (dati) It
De versetzen
En shift
Es desplazar
Fr décaler
Pt mudar

Sprachausgabe *(f) n* De
En audio response unit
Es unidad de respuesta de audio *(f)*
Fr répondeur vocal *(m)*
It unità della risposta audio *(f)*
Pt unidade de audio-resposta *(f)*

Sprache *(f) n* De
En language
Es lenguaje *(m)*
Fr langage *(m)*
It linguaggio *(m)*
Pt linguagem *(f)*

sprocket holes *n pl* En
De Taktlöcher *(pl)*
Es perforaciones marginales *(f pl)*
Fr perforations d'entraînement *(f pl)*
It perforazioni di tabulati *(f pl)*
Pt furos de roda dentada *(m pl)*

sprocket pulse En
De Taktpulse *(pl)*
Es impulso de sincronización *(m)*
Fr impulsion de synchronisation *(f)*
It impulso del rocchetto *(m)*
Pt impulso de roda dentada *(m)*

Sprung *(m) n* De
En jump
Es salto *(m)*
Fr saut *(m)*
It salto *(m)*
Pt salto *(m)*

Spule *(f) n* De
En reel; spool
Es bobina; carrete *(f m)*
Fr bobine *(f)*
It bobina *(f)*
Pt bobina *(f)*

spulen *vb* De
En spool
Es bobinar
Fr bobiner
It bobinare
Pt embobinar

Spulennummer *(f) n* De
En reel number
Es número de carrete *(m)*
Fr numéro d'ordre de la bobine *(m)*
It numero bobina *(m)*
Pt número de bobina *(m)*

Spur *(f) n* De
En track
Es pista *(f)*
Fr piste *(f)*
It banda *(f)*
Pt pista *(f)*

Spurkennzeichen *(n) n* De
En track label
Es etiqueta de pista *(f)*
Fr label piste *(m)*
It etichetta di pista *(f)*
Pt rótulo de pista *(m)*

stack *n* En
De Stapel *(m)*
Es pila *(f)*
Fr pile *(f)*
It armadio *(m)*
Pt pilha *(f)*

stacker *n* En
De Stapler *(m)*
Es casillero receptor *(m)*
Fr case de réception *(f)*
It carrello elevatore *(m)*
Pt empilhadora *(f)*

Stammband *(n) n* De
En master tape
Es bobina emisora *(f)*
Fr bande maîtresse *(f)*
It nastro principale *(m)*
Pt fita principal *(f)*

Stammdatei *(f) n* De
En master file
Es fichero maestro *(m)*
Fr fichier principal *(m)*
It file principale *(m)*
Pt arquivo principal *(m)*

Stammzeitgeber *(m) n* De
En master clock
Es reloj maestro *(m)*
Fr horloge pilote *(f)*
It orologio principale *(m)*
Pt relógio principal *(m)*

stampato *(m) n* It
De Ausdruck *(m)*
En printout
Es vaciado a la impresora *(m)*
Fr sortie sur imprimante *(f)*
Pt impressão *(f)*

stampatrice *(f) n* It
De Drucker *(m)*
En printer
Es impresora *(f)*
Fr imprimante *(f)*
Pt impressora *(f)*

stampatrice a catena *(f)* It
De Kettendrucker *(m)*
En chain printer
Es impresora de cadena *(f)*
Fr imprimante à chaîne *(f)*
Pt impressora de cadeia *(f)*

stampatrice ad impatto *(f)* It
De mechanischer Drucker *(m)*
En impact printer
Es impresora a percusión *(f)*
Fr imprimante à percussion *(f)*
Pt impressora de impacto *(f)*

stampatrice a laser *(f)* It
De Laserdrucker *(m)*
En laser printer
Es impresora de laser *(f)*
Fr imprimante à laser *(f)*
Pt impressora laser *(f)*

stampatrice a linea *(f)* It
De Zeilendrucker *(m)*
En line printer
Es impresora de líneas *(f)*
Fr imprimante ligne par ligne *(f)*
Pt impressora de linha *(f)*

stampatrice a matrice *(f)* It
De Matrizendrucker *(m)*
En matrix printer
Es impresora de matriz *(f)*
Fr imprimante matricielle *(f)*

Pt impressora de matriz *(f)*

stampatrice a pallina *(f)* It
De Kugelkopfdrucker *(m)*
En golfball printer
Es impresora de esfera *(f)*
Fr imprimante à sphère *(f)*
Pt impressora de bola de golf *(f)*

stampatrice a punti *(f)* It
De Punktdrucker *(m)*
En dot printer
Es impresora por puntos *(f)*
Fr imprimante par points *(f)*
Pt impressora de pontos *(f)*

stampatrice a tamburo *(f)* It
De Trommeldrucker *(m)*
En barrel printer; drum printer
Es impresora a tambor; impresora de rodillo *(f)*
Fr imprimante à tambour *(f)*
Pt impressora de tambor *(f)*

stampatrice a treno di caratteri *(f)* It
De Gliederdrucker *(m)*
En train printer
Es impresora de cadena *(f)*
Fr imprimante à train de caractères *(f)*
Pt impressora de trem *(f)*

stampatrice daisywheel *(f)* It
De Gänseblümchen-Typenraddrucker *(m)*
En daisywheel printer
Es impresora de ruedas de mariposa *(f)*
Fr imprimante à marguerite *(f)*
Pt impressora margarida *(f)*

stampatrice di pagina *(f)* It
De Seitendrucker *(m)*
En page printer
Es impresora por páginas *(f)*
Fr imprimante page par page *(f)*
Pt impressora de página *(f)*

stampatrice di ruota *(f)* It
De Typenraddrucker *(m)*
En wheel printer
Es impresora de ruedas *(f)*
Fr imprimante à roues *(f)*
Pt impressora de roda *(f)*

stampatrice elettrostatica *(f)* It
De elektrostatischer Drucker *(m)*
En electrostatic printer
Es impresora electrostática *(f)*
Fr imprimante électrostatique *(f)*
Pt impressora electrostática *(f)*

stampatrice grafica *(f)* It
De Zeichendrucker *(m)*
En graphics printer
Es impresora gráfica *(f)*
Fr imprimante graphique *(f)*
Pt impressora gráfica *(f)*

stampatrice in serie *(f)* It
De Reihendrucker *(m)*
En serial printer
Es impresora en serie *(f)*
Fr imprimante série *(f)*
Pt impressora em série *(f)*

stampatrice non ad impatto *(f)* It
De nicht mechanischer Drucker *(m)*
En nonimpact printer
Es impresora sin percusión *(f)*
Fr imprimante non à percussion *(f)*
Pt impressora sem impacto *(f)*

stampatrice xerografica *(f)* It
De xerographischer Drucker *(m)*
En xerographic printer
Es impresora xerográfica *(f)*
Fr imprimante xérographique *(f)*
Pt impressora xerográfica *(f)*

standard form En
De Standardform *(f)*
Es formato normalizado *(m)*
Fr forme normalisée *(f)*
It modulo standard *(m)*
Pt formulário standard *(m)*

Standardform *(f) n* De
En standard form
Es formato normalizado *(m)*
Fr forme normalisée *(f)*
It modulo standard *(m)*
Pt formulário standard *(m)*

standard interface En
De Standardschnittstelle *(f)*
Es interfase normalizada *(f)*
Fr interface normalisée *(f)*
It interfaccia standard *(f)*
Pt interface standard *(f)*

standardisation *(f) n* Fr
De Normung *(f)*
En standardization
Es normalización *(f)*
It standardizzazione *(f)*
Pt standardização *(f)*

standardiser *vb* Fr
De normen
En standardize
Es estandardizar
It standardizzare
Pt standardizar

standardização *(f) n* Pt
De Normung *(f)*
En standardization
Es normalización *(f)*
Fr standardisation *(f)*
It standardizzazione *(f)*

standardizar *vb* Pt
De normen
En standardize
Es estandardizar
Fr standardiser
It standardizzare

standardization *n* En
De Normung *(f)*
Es normalización *(f)*
Fr standardisation *(f)*
It standardizzazione *(f)*
Pt standardização *(f)*

standardize *vb* En
De normen
Es estandardizar
Fr standardiser
It standardizzare
Pt standardizar

standardizzare *vb* It
De normen
En standardize
Es estandardizar
Fr standardiser
Pt standardizar

standardizzazione *(f) n* It
De Normung *(f)*
En standardization
Es normalización *(f)*
Fr standardisation *(f)*
Pt standardização *(f)*

Standardschnittstelle *(f) n* De
En standard interface
Es interfase normalizada *(f)*
Fr interface normalisée *(f)*
It interfaccia standard *(f)*
Pt interface standard *(f)*

standard subroutine En
De Standardunter-programm *(n)*
Es subrutina estándar *(f)*
Fr sous-programme standard *(m)*
It subroutine standard *(f)*
Pt subrotina standard *(f)*

Standardunter-programm *(n) n* De
En standard subroutine
Es subrutina estándar *(f)*

Fr sous-programme standard *(m)*
It subroutine standard *(f)*
Pt subrotina standard *(f)*

Stanzrückstand *(m) n* De
En chad
Es confeti *(m)*
Fr confetti *(m)*
It coriandoli di perforazione *(m)*
Pt recorte *(m)*

Stapel *(m) n* De
En stack
Es pila *(f)*
Fr pile *(f)*
It armadio *(m)*
Pt pilha *(f)*

Stapelarbeit *(f) n* De
En batch job
Es trabajo por lotes *(m)*
Fr travail en traitement par lots *(m)*
It lavoro a lotti *(m)*
Pt trabalho por lotes *(m)*

stapeln *vb* De
En pack
Es empaquetar
Fr comprimer
It impaccare
Pt empacotar

Stapelverarbeitung *(f) n* De
En batch processing
Es proceso por lotes *(m)*
Fr traitement par lot *(m)*
It elaborazione a lotti *(f)*
Pt tratamento por lotes *(m)*

Stapler *(m) n* De
En stacker
Es casillero receptor *(m)*
Fr case de réception *(f)*
It carrello elevatore *(m)*
Pt empilhadora *(f)*

Startroutine *(f) n* De
En bootstrap
Es autocargador *(m)*
Fr amorce *(f)*
It istruzioni di avviamento *(f)*
Pt bootstrap *(m)*

Start-Stopp-Steuerung *(f)* De
En asynchronous communication
Es comunicación asíncrona *(f)*
Fr transmission asynchrone *(f)*
It comunicazione asincrona *(f)*
Pt comunicação assíncrona *(f)*

Start-Stopp-Zeit *(f) n* De
En start-stop time
Es tiempo de arranque-espera *(m)*
Fr temps de démarrage-arrêt *(m)*
It tempo inizio-arresto *(m)*
Pt tempo de arranque-paragem *(m)*

start-stop time En
De Start-Stopp-Zeit *(f)*
Es tiempo de arranque-espera *(m)*
Fr temps de démarrage-arrêt *(m)*
It tempo inizio-arresto *(m)*
Pt tempo de arranque-paragem *(m)*

start time En
De Start-Zeit *(f)*
Es tiempo de arranque *(m)*
Fr temps de démarrage *(m)*
It tempo di salita in regime *(m)*
Pt tempo de arranque *(m)*

Start-Zeit *(f) n* De
En start time
Es tiempo de arranque *(m)*
Fr temps de démarrage *(m)*
It tempo di salita in regime *(m)*
Pt tempo de arranque *(m)*

statement *n* En; It *(m)*
De Anweisung *(f)*
Es sentencia *(f)*
Fr instructions *(f pl)*
Pt afirmação *(f)*

statement di controllo *(m)* It
De Steueranweisung *(f)*
En control statement
Es sentencia de control *(f)*
Fr ordre de contrôle *(m)*
Pt afirmação de controlo *(f)*

statement di dichiarazione *(m)* It
De Prozeduranweisung *(f)*
En declarative statement
Es sentencia de declaración *(f)*
Fr instruction déclarative *(f)*
Pt afirmação declarativa *(f)*

static dump En
De statischer Speicherauszug *(m)*
Es vuelco estático de la memoria *(m)*
Fr vidage en un point fixe du programme *(m)*
It dump statico *(m)*
Pt descarregador estático *(m)*

static store En
De statischer Speicher *(m)*
Es memoria estática *(f)*
Fr mémoire statique *(f)*
It memoria statica *(f)*
Pt armazém estático *(m)*

static subroutine En
De statisches Unterprogramm *(n)*
Es subrutina estática *(f)*
Fr sous-programme statique *(m)*
It subroutine statica *(f)*
Pt subrotina estática *(f)*

statischer Speicher *(m)* De
En static store
Es memoria estática *(f)*
Fr mémoire statique *(f)*
It memoria statica *(f)*
Pt armazém estático *(m)*

statischer Speicherauszug *(m)* De
En static dump
Es vuelco estático de la memoria *(m)*
Fr vidage en un point fixe du programme *(m)*
It dump statico *(m)*
Pt descarregador estático *(m)*

statisches Unterprogramm *(n)* De
En static subroutine
Es subrutina estática *(f)*
Fr sous-programme statique *(m)*
It subroutine statica *(f)*
Pt subrotina estática *(f)*

stato uno *(m)* It
De Einzustand *(m)*
En one state
Es estado uno *(m)*
Fr état un *(m)*
Pt estado de unidade *(m)*

stato zero *(m)* It
De Nullzustand *(m)*
En zero state
Es estado cero *(m)*
Fr état zéro *(m)*
Pt estado zero *(m)*

status word En
De Statuswort *(n)*
Es palabra de estado *(f)*
Fr mot d´état *(m)*
It voce di stato *(f)*
Pt palavra de status *(f)*

Statuswort *(n) n* De
En status word
Es palabra de estado *(f)*
Fr mot d´état *(m)*
It voce di stato *(f)*
Pt palavra de status *(f)*

Stecker *(m) n* De
En plug
Es clavija *(f)*
Fr fiche *(f)*
It spina *(f)*
Pt ficha eléctrica *(f)*

Steckerbrett *(n) n* De
En plugboard
Es cuadro de conexión *(m)*
Fr tableau de connexions *(m)*
It pannello di connessioni *(m)*
Pt placa de conexões eléctricas *(f)*

Steckplatte *(f) n* De
En pinboard
Es cuadro de alfileres *(m)*
Fr tableau à aiguilles *(m)*
It pannello a spine *(m)*
Pt prancheta de alfinetes *(f)*

Stellendarstellung *(f) n* De
En positional notation
Es notación posicional *(f)*
Fr représentation positionnelle *(f)*
It notazione di posizione *(f)*
Pt notação posicional *(f)*

Stellenverschiebung *(f) n* De
En shift
Es desplazamiento *(m)*
Fr décalage *(m)*
It riporto *(m)*
Pt mudança *(f)*

Stellgröße *(f) n* De
En manipulated variable
Es variable manipulada *(f)*
Fr variable manipulée *(f)*
It variabile manipolata *(f)*
Pt variável manipulada *(f)*

step *n* En
De Schritt *(m)*
Es paso *(m)*
Fr phase *(f)*
It passo *(m)*
Pt passo *(m)*

step change En
De Schrittwechsel *(m)*
Es cambio de paso *(m)*
Fr changement de phase *(m)*
It cambio di passo *(m)*
Pt mudança de passo *(f)*

Steueranweisung *(f) n* De
En control statement
Es sentencia de control *(f)*
Fr ordre de contrôle *(m)*
It statement di controllo *(m)*
Pt afirmação de controlo *(f)*

Steuerfolge *(f) n* De
En control sequence
Es secuencia de control *(f)*
Fr séquence de contrôle *(f)*
It sequenza di controllo *(f)*
Pt sequência de controlo *(f)*

steuern *vb* De
En control
Es controlar
Fr contrôler
It controllare
Pt controlar

Steuerregister *(n) n* De
En control register
Es registro de control *(m)*
Fr registre de contrôle *(m)*
It registro di controllo *(m)*
Pt registo de controlo *(m)*

Steuersprache *(f) n* De
En control language
Es lenguaje de control *(m)*
Fr langage de contrôle *(m)*
It linguaggio di controllo *(m)*
Pt linguagem de controlo *(f)*

Steuertafel *(f) n* De
En control panel
Es panel de control *(m)*
Fr panneau de contrôle *(m)*
It pannello di comando *(m)*
Pt painel de controlo *(m)*

Steuertheorie *(f) n* De
En control theory
Es teoría de control *(f)*
Fr théorie de contrôle *(f)*
It teoria del controllo *(f)*
Pt teoria de controlo *(f)*

Steuerübertragung *(f) n* De
En control transfer; transfer of control
Es transferencia de control *(f)*
Fr transfert de contrôle *(m)*
It trasferimento di controllo *(m)*
Pt transferência de controlo *(f)*

Steuerung *(f) n* De
En control
Es control *(m)*
Fr contrôle *(m)*
It controllo *(m)*
Pt controlo *(m)*

Steurungsdaten *(pl)* De
En control data
Es datos de control *(m pl)*
Fr données de contrôle *(f pl)*
It dati di controllo *(m pl)*
Pt dados de controlo *(m pl)*

stockage *(m) n* Fr
De Speicherung *(f)*
En storage
Es almacenamiento *(m)*
It immagazzinamento *(m)*
Pt armazenamento *(m)*

stockage à double entrée *(m)* Fr
De zweidimensionale Speicherung *(f)*
En two-dimensional storage
Es memoria bidimensional *(f)*
It memoria bidimensionale *(f)*
Pt armazenamento bidimensional *(m)*

stockage central *(m)* Fr
De Hauptspeicherung *(f)*
En main storage
Es almacenamiento principal *(m)*
It immagazzinamento principale *(m)*
Pt armazenagem principal *(f)*

Stopp *(m) n* De
En halt
Es parada *(f)*
Fr arrêt *(m)*
It arresto *(m)*
Pt paragem *(f)*

storage *n* En
De Speicherung *(f)*
Es almacenamiento *(m)*
Fr stockage *(m)*
It immagazzinamento *(m)*
Pt armazenamento *(m)*

storage allocation En
De Speicherzuweisung *(f)*
Es asignación de almacenamiento *(f)*
Fr affectation de la mémoire *(f)*
It assegnazione in memoria *(f)*
Pt atribuição de armazenamento *(f)*

storage capacity En
De Speicherkapazität *(f)*
Es capacidad de almacenamiento *(f)*
Fr capacité de mémoire *(f)*
It capacità di memoria *(f)*
Pt capacidade de armazenamento *(f)*

storage density En
De Speicherdichte *(f)*
Es densidad de almacenamiento *(f)*
Fr densité de stockage *(f)*
It densità di memoria *(f)*
Pt densidade de armazenamento *(f)*

storage device En
De Speichergerät *(n)*

Es dispositivo de almacenamiento *(m)*
Fr unité de stockage *(f)*
It organo di memoria *(m)*
Pt dispositivo de armazenamento *(m)*

storage display En
De Speicheranzeige *(f)*
Es presentación de almacenamiento *(f)*
Fr affichage d'enregistrement *(m)*
It visualizzazione di memoria *(f)*
Pt visualização de armazenamento *(f)*

storage tube En
De Speicherröhre *(f)*
Es tubo de almacenamiento *(m)*
Fr tube à mémoire *(m)*
It tubo di memoria *(m)*
Pt válvula de armazenamento *(f)*

store *n* En
De Speicher *(m)*
Es memoria *(f)*
Fr mémoire *(f)*
It memoria *(f)*
Pt armazém *(m)*

store *vb* En
De speichern
Es almacenar
Fr mémoriser
It memorizzare
Pt armazenar

stored program En
De gespeichertes Programm *(n)*
Es programa almacenado *(m)*
Fr programme enregistré *(m)*
It programma memorizzato *(m)*
Pt programa armazenado *(m)*

stored-program computer En
De Computer für gespeicherte Programme *(m)*
Es ordenador en programa almacenado *(m)*
Fr ordinateur à programme enregistré *(m)*
It calcolatore a programmi memorizzati *(m)*
Pt computador com programa armazenado *(m)*

Strahlenspeicher *(m) n* De
En beam store
Es memoria a rayos *(f)*
Fr mémoire à faisceau *(f)*
It memoria a fascio *(f)*
Pt armazém de raio *(m)*

string *n* En
De Folge *(f)*
Es serie *(f)*
Fr chaîne *(f)*
It stringa *(f)*
Pt fileira *(f)*

stringa *(f) n* It
De Folge *(f)*
En string
Es serie *(f)*
Fr chaîne *(f)*
Pt fileira *(f)*

stringa di bit *(f)* It
De Binärzeichenfolge *(f)*
En bit string
Es serie de bits *(f)*
Fr chaîne de bits *(f)*
Pt fila de bits *(f)*

string manipulation En
De Folgebearbeitung *(f)*
Es manipulación de series *(f)*
Fr manipulation de chaîne *(f)*
It manipolazione di stringa *(f)*
Pt manipulação de fileira *(f)*

Stromschleifen-Schnittstelle *(f)* De
En current-loop interface
Es acoplamiento mutuo por bucle de corriente *(m)*
Fr interface boucle courant *(f)*
It interfaccia del ciclo corrente *(f)*
Pt interface de circuito de corrente *(f)*

structure de l'instruction *(f)* Fr
De Befehlsformat *(n)*
En instruction format
Es formato de la instrucción *(m)*
It formato dell'istruzione *(m)*
Pt formato de instruções *(m)*

structured program En
De gegliedertes Programm *(n)*
Es programa estructurado *(m)*
Fr programme structuré *(m)*
It programma strutturato *(m)*
Pt programa estruturado *(m)*

structure réduite *(f)* Fr
De verdichtetes Format *(n)*
En reduced format
Es formato reducido *(m)*
It formato ridotto *(m)*
Pt formato reduzido *(m)*

Strukturerkennung *(f) n* De
En pattern recognition
Es reconocimiento de configuraciones *(m)*
Fr reconnaissance des formes *(f)*
It riconoscimento di modelli *(m)*
Pt reconhecimento de padrão *(m)*

strumenti programmati automaticamente *(m pl)* It
De automatisch programmierte Werkzeuge *(pl)*
En automatically programmed tools (APT)
Es herramientas programadas automáticamente *(f pl)*
Fr machines-outils programmées automatiquement *(f pl)*
Pt ferramentas programadas automaticamente *(f pl)*

strumento di messa a punto (di un programma) *(m)* It
De Fehlersuchhilfe *(f)*
En debugging aid
Es ayuda a la depuración *(f)*
Fr outil de mise au point *(m)*
Pt ajuda de desparasitação *(f)*

studio di fattibilità *(m)* It
De Wirklichkeits-untersuchung *(f)*
En feasibility study
Es estudio de posibilidades *(m)*
Fr étude de faisabilité *(f)*
Pt estudo de viabilidade *(m)*

sub-conjunto *(m) n* Pt
De Untermenge *(f)*
En subset
Es subgrupo *(m)*
Fr sous-ensemble *(m)*
It sottogruppo *(m)*

subdesbordamiento *(m) n* Es
De Unterlauf *(m)*
En underflow
Fr dépassement de capacité inférieur *(m)*
It sottoflusso *(m)*
Pt subfluxo *(m)*

subfluxo *(m) n* Pt
De Unterlauf *(m)*
En underflow
Es subdesbordamiento *(m)*
Fr dépassement de capacité inférieur *(m)*
It sottoflusso *(m)*

subgrupo *(m) n* Es
De Untermenge *(f)*
En subset
Fr sous-ensemble *(m)*
It sottogruppo *(m)*
Pt sub-conjunto *(m)*

subprogram *n* En
De Unterprogramm *(n)*
Es subprograma *(m)*
Fr sous-programme *(m)*
It sottoprogramma *(m)*
Pt subprograma *(m)*

subprograma *(m) n* Es, Pt
De Unterprogramm *(n)*
En subprogram
Fr sous-programme *(m)*
It sottoprogramma *(m)*

subrotina *(f) n* Pt
De Unterroutine *(f)*
En subroutine
Es subrutina *(f)*
Fr sous-routine *(f)*
It subroutine *(f)*

subrotina estática *(f)* Pt
De statisches Unterprogramm *(n)*
En static subroutine
Es subrutina estática *(f)*
Fr sous-programme statique *(m)*
It subroutine statica *(f)*

subrotina standard *(f)* Pt
De Standardunter-programm *(n)*
En standard subroutine
Es subrutina estándar *(f)*
Fr sous-programme standard *(m)*
It subroutine standard *(f)*

subroutine *n* En; It *(f)*
De Unterroutine *(f)*
Es subrutina *(f)*
Fr sous-routine *(f)*
Pt subrotina *(f)*

subroutine standard *(f)* It
De Standardunter-programm *(n)*
En standard subroutine
Es subrutina estándar *(f)*
Fr sous-programme standard *(m)*
Pt subrotina standard *(f)*

subroutine statica *(f)* It
De statisches Unterprogramm *(n)*
En static subroutine
Es subrutina estática *(f)*
Fr sous-programme statique *(m)*
Pt subrotina estática *(f)*

subrutina *(f) n* Es
De Unterroutine *(f)*
En subroutine
Fr sous-routine *(f)*
It subroutine *(f)*
Pt subrotina *(f)*

subrutina estándar *(f)* Es
De Standardunter-programm *(n)*
En standard subroutine
Fr sous-programme standard *(m)*
It subroutine standard *(f)*
Pt subrotina standard *(f)*

subrutina estática *(f)* Es
De statisches Unterprogramm *(n)*
En static subroutine
Fr sous-programme statique *(m)*
It subroutine statica *(f)*
Pt subrotina estática *(f)*

subscriber station En
De Teilnehmerstation *(f)*
Es estación de una red *(f)*
Fr poste du réseau *(m)*
It posto d'abbonato *(m)*
Pt estação de subscritor *(f)*

subset *n* En
De Untermenge *(f)*
Es subgrupo *(m)*
Fr sous-ensemble *(m)*
It sottogruppo *(m)*
Pt sub-conjunto *(m)*

subtracctor *(m) n* Pt
De Subtrahierer *(m)*
En subtracter
Es sustractor *(m)*
Fr soustracteur *(m)*
It sottrattore *(m)*

subtracter *n* En
De Subtrahierer *(m)*
Es sustractor *(m)*
Fr soustracteur *(m)*
It sottrattore *(m)*
Pt subtracctor *(m)*

Subtrahierer *(m) n* De
En subtracter
Es sustractor *(m)*
Fr soustracteur *(m)*
It sottrattore *(m)*
Pt subtracctor *(m)*

Suche *(f) n* De
En search
Es búsqueda sistemática *(f)*
Fr recherche *(f)*
It ricerca *(f)*
Pt busca *(f)*

suchen *vb* De
En search
Es investigar
Fr chercher
It ricercare
Pt procurar

Suchzeit *(f) n* De
En search time
Es tiempo de búsqueda *(m)*
Fr temps de recherche *(m)*
It tempo di ricerca *(m)*
Pt tempo de busca *(m)*

suma destructiva *(f)* Es
De Löschen der Addition *(n)*
En destructive addition
Fr addition destructive *(f)*
It addizione distruttiva *(f)*
Pt adição destrutiva *(f)*

suma de verificación *(f)* Es
De Summenprüfung *(f)*
En check sum
Fr somme de contrôle *(f)*
It somma di controllo *(f)*
Pt soma de verificação *(f)*

sumador *(m) n* Es
De Addierglied *(n)*
En adder
Fr additionneur *(m)*
It addizionatore *(m)*
Pt somador *(m)*

sumador-sustractor *(m) n* Es
De Addier-Subtrahierglied *(n)*
En adder-subtracter
Fr additionneur-soustracteur *(m)*
It addizionatore-sottrattore *(m)*
Pt somador-subtractor *(m)*

summation check En
De Summenprüfung *(f)*
Es comprobación de suma *(f)*
Fr contrôle par totalisation *(m)*
It controllo di addizione *(m)*
Pt verificação de soma *(f)*

Summenprüfung *(f) n* De
En check sum; summation check
Es comprobación de suma; suma de verificación *(f)*
Fr contrôle par totalisation; somme de contrôle *(m f)*
It controllo di addizione; somma di controllo *(m f)*
Pt soma de verificação; verificação de soma *(f)*

superamento della capacità di memoria *(m)* It
De Überlauf *(m)*
En overflow
Es desbordamiento *(m)*
Fr dépassement de capacité *(m)*
Pt trasbordamento *(m)*

superposer une écriture Fr
De überschreiben
En overwrite
Es recubrir
It inscrivere per riempimento
Pt escrever por cima

superviseur *(m) n* Fr
De Überwacher *(m)*
En supervisor
Es supervisor *(m)*

It supervisore *(m)*
Pt supervisor *(m)*

supervisor *n* En; Es, Pt *(m)*
De Überwacher *(m)*
Fr superviseur *(m)*
It supervisore *(m)*

supervisore *(m) n* It
De Überwacher *(m)*
En supervisor
Es supervisor *(m)*
Fr superviseur *(m)*
Pt supervisor *(m)*

supervisory control En
De Überwachungs-steuerung *(f)*
Es control supervisor *(m)*
Fr commande de superviseur *(f)*
It controllo di supervisione *(m)*
Pt controle de supervisão *(m)*

supervisory program En
De Überwachungs-programm *(n)*
Es programa supervisor *(m)*
Fr programme superviseur *(m)*
It programma di supervisione *(m)*
Pt programa de supervisão *(m)*

supplementary maintenance En
De Zusatzwartung *(f)*
Es mantenimiento suplementario *(m)*
Fr maintenance supplémentaire *(f)*
It manutenzione supplementare *(f)*
Pt manutenção suplementária *(f)*

supporto *(m) n* It
De Ladungsträger *(m)*
En carrier
Es portador *(m)*
Fr courant porteur *(m)*
Pt portador *(m)*

suppression *n* En; Fr *(f)*
De Unterdrückung *(f)*
Es supresión *(f)*
It soppressione *(f)*
Pt supressão *(f)*

supresión *(f) n* Es
De Unterdrückung *(f)*
En suppression
Fr suppression *(f)*
It soppressione *(f)*
Pt supressão *(f)*

supresión de ceros *(f)* Es
De Nullunterdrückung *(f)*
En zero suppression
Fr élimination des zéros *(f)*
It soppressione di zero *(f)*
Pt supressão zero *(f)*

supressão *(f) n* Pt
De Unterdrückung *(f)*
En suppression
Es supresión *(f)*
Fr suppression *(f)*
It soppressione *(f)*

supressão zero *(f)* Pt
De Nullunterdrückung *(f)*
En zero suppression
Es supresión de ceros *(f)*
Fr élimination des zéros *(f)*
It soppressione di zero *(f)*

suprimir *vb* Es
De löschen
En delete
Fr éliminer
It cancellare
Pt apagar

surveiller *vb* Fr
De kontrollieren
En monitor
Es examinar
It esaminare
Pt vigiar

suspendre *vb* Fr
De abbrechen
En abort
Es malograrse
It abortire
Pt abortar

suspensión *(f) n* Es
De Blockabbruch *(m)*
En abort
Fr suspension d'exécution *(f)*
It insuccesso *(m)*
Pt aborto *(m)*

suspension d'exécution *(f)* Fr
De Blockabbruch *(m)*
En abort
Es suspensión *(f)*
It insuccesso *(m)*
Pt aborto *(m)*

sustractor *(m) n* Es
De Subtrahierer *(m)*
En subtracter
Fr soustracteur *(m)*
It sottrattore *(m)*
Pt subtracctor *(m)*

svolgere *vb* It
De abwickeln
En unwind
Es desovillar
Fr dérouler
Pt desenrolar

switch *n* En
De Schalter *(m)*
Es conmutador *(m)*
Fr interrupteur *(m)*
It interruttore *(m)*
Pt comutador *(m)*

switch *vb* En
De schalten
Es conmutar
Fr commuter
It commutare
Pt comutar

switched-message network En
De geschaltetes Nachrichtennetz *(n)*
Es red de conmutación de mensajes *(f)*
Fr réseau de messages commutés *(m)*
It rete di messaggi commutati *(f)*
Pt rede de mensagens comutadas *(f)*

switching centre En
De Schaltzentrum *(n)*
Es centro de conmutación *(m)*
Fr centre de commutation *(m)*
It centro di commutazione *(m)*
Pt centro de comutação *(m)*

symbol *n* En
De Symbol *(n)*
Es símbolo *(m)*
Fr symbole *(m)*
It simbolo *(m)*
Pt símbolo *(m)*

Symbol *(n) n* De
En symbol
Es símbolo *(m)*
Fr symbole *(m)*
It simbolo *(m)*
Pt símbolo *(m)*

symbole *(m) n* Fr
De Symbol *(n)*
En symbol
Es símbolo *(m)*
It simbolo *(m)*
Pt símbolo *(m)*

symbole de décision *(m)* Fr
De Blockdiagramm-symbol-Entscheidung *(f)*
En decision box
Es símbolo de decisión *(m)*
It casella di decisione *(f)*
Pt caixa de decisão *(f)*

symbole logique *(m)* Fr
De logisches Symbol *(n)*
En logic symbol
Es símbolo lógico *(m)*
It simbolo logico *(m)*
Pt símbolo lógico *(m)*

symbolic address En
De symbolische Adresse *(f)*
Es dirección simbólica *(f)*
Fr adresse symbolique *(f)*
It indirizzo simbolico *(m)*
Pt endereço simbólico *(m)*

symbolic language En
De symbolische Sprache *(f)*
Es lenguaje simbólico *(m)*
Fr langage symbolique *(m)*
It linguaggio simbolico *(m)*
Pt linguagem simbólica *(f)*

symbolic logic En
De symbolische Verknüpfung *(f)*
Es lógica simbólica *(f)*
Fr logique symbolique *(f)*
It logica simbolica *(f)*
Pt lógica simbólica *(f)*

symbolic programming En
De symbolische Programmierung *(f)*
Es programación simbólica *(f)*
Fr programmation symbolique *(f)*
It programmazione simbolica *(f)*
Pt programação simbólica *(f)*

symbolische Adresse *(f)* De
En symbolic address
Es dirección simbólica *(f)*
Fr adresse symbolique *(f)*
It indirizzo simbolico *(m)*
Pt endereço simbólico *(m)*

symbolische Programmierung *(f)* De
En symbolic programming
Es programación simbólica *(f)*
Fr programmation symbolique *(f)*
It programmazione simbolica *(f)*
Pt programação simbólica *(f)*

symbolische Sprache *(f)* De
En symbolic language
Es lenguaje simbólico *(m)*
Fr langage symbolique *(m)*
It linguaggio simbolico *(m)*
Pt linguagem simbólica *(f)*

symbolische Verknüpfung *(f)* De
En symbolic logic
Es lógica simbólica *(f)*
Fr logique symbolique *(f)*
It logica simbolica *(f)*
Pt lógica simbólica *(f)*

Symboltafel *(f) n* De
En graphic panel
Es panel gráfico *(m)*
Fr tableau graphique *(m)*
It pannello grafico *(m)*
Pt painel de gráficos *(m)*

synchroniseur *(m) n* Fr
De Synchronisiergerät *(n)*
En synchronizer
Es sincronizador *(m)*
It sicronizzatore *(m)*
Pt sincronizador *(m)*

Synchronisiergerät *(n) n* De
En synchronizer
Es sincronizador *(m)*
Fr synchroniseur *(m)*
It sicronizzatore *(m)*
Pt sincronizador *(m)*

Synchronisierrechner *(m) n* De
En synchronous computer
Es ordenador síncrono *(m)*
Fr calculateur synchrone *(m)*
It elaboratore sincrono *(m)*
Pt computador sincronizado *(m)*

synchronizer *n* En
De Synchronisiergerät *(n)*
Es sincronizador *(m)*
Fr synchroniseur *(m)*
It sicronizzatore *(m)*
Pt sincronizador *(m)*

synchronous computer En
De Synchronisierrechner *(m)*
Es ordenador síncrono *(m)*
Fr calculateur synchrone *(m)*
It elaboratore sincrono *(m)*
Pt computador sincronizado *(m)*

syntax *n* En
De Syntax *(f)*
Es sintaxis *(f)*
Fr syntaxe *(f)*
It sintassi *(f)*
Pt sintaxe *(f)*

Syntax *(f) n* De
En syntax
Es sintaxis *(f)*
Fr syntaxe *(f)*
It sintassi *(f)*
Pt sintaxe *(f)*

syntaxe *(f) n* Fr
De Syntax *(f)*
En syntax
Es sintaxis *(f)*
It sintassi *(f)*
Pt sintaxe *(f)*

synthetic language En
De künstliche Sprache *(f)*
Es lenguaje sintético *(m)*
Fr langage synthétique *(m)*
It linguaggio sintetico *(m)*
Pt linguagem sintética *(f)*

system *n* En
De System *(n)*
Es sistema *(m)*
Fr système *(m)*
It sistema *(m)*
Pt sistema *(m)*

System *(n) n* De
En system
Es sistema *(m)*
Fr système *(m)*
It sistema *(m)*
Pt sistema *(m)*

Systemanalyse *(f) n* De
En systems analysis
Es análisis de sistemas *(m)*
Fr analyse fonctionnelle *(f)*
It analisi dei sistemi *(f)*
Pt análise de sistemas *(f)*

Systemanalyst *(m) n* De
En systems analyst
Es analista de sistemas *(m)*
Fr analyste fonctionnel *(m)*
It analista di sistemi *(m)*
Pt analista de sistemas *(m)*

système *(m) n* Fr
De System *(n)*
En system
Es sistema *(m)*
It sistema *(m)*
Pt sistema *(m)*

système à utilisateurs multiples *(m)* Fr
De Mehrfachbenutzer-system *(n)*
En multiuser system
Es sistema para usuarios múltiples *(m)*
It sistema per utenti multipli *(m)*
Pt sistema de utentes múltiplos *(m)*

système de commande adaptatif *(m)* Fr
De adaptives Steuersystem *(n)*
En adaptive-control system
Es sistema de control autoadaptable *(m)*
It sistema a controllo adattivo *(m)*
Pt sistema de controlo adaptável *(m)*

système de communication *(m)* Fr
De Kommunikations-system *(n)*
En communication system
Es sistema de comunicaciones *(m)*

It sistema di comunicazione *(m)*
Pt sistema de comunicação *(m)*

système de contrôle des travaux *(m)* Fr
De Jobkontrollsystem *(n)*
En job control system
Es sistema de control de trabajos *(m)*
It sistema di controllo olei lavori *(m)*
Pt sistema de controle de trabalho *(m)*

système de gestion de base de données (SGBD) *(m)* Fr
De Datenverwaltungs-system *(n)*
En database management system (DBMS)
Es sistema de gestión del banco de datos *(m)*
It sistema di gestione della banca dei dati *(m)*
Pt sistema de management de base de dados *(m)*

système de numérotation *(m)* Fr
De Nummernsystem *(n)*
En number system
Es sistema de numeración *(m)*
It sistema di numeri *(m)*
Pt sistema numérico *(m)*

système de réseau *(m)* Fr
De Netzsystem *(n)*
En network system
Es sistema de red *(m)*
It sistema di reti *(m)*
Pt sistema de rede *(m)*

système de traitement à distance *(m)* Fr
De Fernrechensystem *(n)*
En remote computing system
Es sistema de cálculo a distancia *(m)*
It sistema di elaborazione a distanza *(m)*
Pt sistema de tele-computador *(m)*

système d'exploitation *(m)* Fr
De Betriebssystem *(n)*
En operating system (OS)
Es sistema operativo *(m)*
It sistema operativo *(m)*
Pt sistema de operação *(m)*

système d'exploitation à disques *(m)* Fr
De Plattenbetriebsystem *(n)*
En disk-based operating system (DOS)
Es sistema operativo en discos *(m)*
It sistema operativo su disco *(m)*
Pt sistema de operação baseado em discos *(m)*

système d'ordonnancement des opérations et du personnel *(m)* Fr
De Projekt-auswertungs- und Übersichttechnik *(f)*
En project evaluation and review technique (PERT)
Es método de planificación y control de proyectos *(m)*
It tecnica di revisione e valutazione del progetto *(f)*
Pt técnica de avaliação e revisão de projectos *(f)*

système en tandem *(m)* Fr
De Anschlußsystem *(n)*
En tandem system
Es sistema en tandem *(m)*
It sistema abbinato *(m)*
Pt sistema em tandem *(m)*

système informatique *(m)* Fr
De Informationssystem *(n)*
En information system
Es sistema de información *(m)*
It sistema di informazioni *(m)*
Pt sistema de informação *(m)*

système informatique en duplex *(m)* Fr
De Duplex-Rechnersystem *(n)*
En duplex computer system
Es sistema de ordenador duplex *(m)*
It sistema di calcolatore doppio *(m)*
Pt sistema de computador duplex *(m)*

système modulaire *(m)* Fr
De Baukastensystem *(n)*
En modular system
Es sistema modular *(m)*
It sistema modulare *(m)*
Pt sistema modular *(m)*

système pilote-asservi *(m)* Fr
De Master-Slave-Anordnung *(f)*
En master-slave system
Es sistema combinado maestro-satélite *(m)*
It sistema maestro-schiavo *(m)*
Pt sistema mestre-escravo *(m)*

system generation En
De Systemgenerierung *(f)*
Es generación del sistema *(f)*
Fr génération d'un système *(f)*
It generazione di sistemi *(f)*
Pt geração de sistemas *(f)*

Systemgenerierung *(f) n* De
En system generation
Es generación del sistema *(f)*
Fr génération d'un système *(f)*
It generazione di sistemi *(f)*
Pt geração de sistemas *(f)*

Systemkonsole *(f) n* De
En console
Es consola *(f)*
Fr pupitre de commande *(m)*
It console *(f)*
Pt consola *(f)*

Systemnetzaufbau *(m) n* De
En systems network architecture (SNA)
Es estructura de redes de sistemas *(f)*
Fr architecture unifiée de réseau (AUR) *(f)*
It architettura della rete di sistemi *(f)*
Pt arquitectura de rede de sistemas *(f)*

System-programmierung *(f) n* De
En systems programming
Es programación de sistemas *(f)*
Fr programmation d'étude *(f)*
It programmazione dei sistemi *(f)*
Pt programação de sistemas *(f)*

systems analysis En
De Systemanalyse *(f)*
Es análisis de sistemas *(m)*
Fr analyse fonctionnelle *(f)*
It analisi dei sistemi *(f)*
Pt análise de sistemas *(f)*

systems analyst En
De Systemanalyst *(m)*
Es analista de sistemas *(m)*

Fr analyste fonctionnel *(m)*
It analista di sistemi *(m)*
Pt analista de sistemas *(m)*

systems network architecture (SNA) En
De Systemnetzaufbau *(m)*
Es estructura de redes de sistemas *(f)*
Fr architecture unifiée de réseau (AUR) *(f)*
It architettura della rete di sistemi *(f)*
Pt arquitectura de rede de sistemas *(f)*

systems programming En
De System-programmierung *(f)*
Es programación de sistemas *(f)*
Fr programmation d'étude *(f)*
It programmazione dei sistemi *(f)*
Pt programação de sistemas *(f)*

T

tabela *(f) n* Pt
De Tabelle *(f)*
En table
Es tabla *(f)*
Fr table *(f)*
It tavola *(f)*

tabela de consulta *(f)* Pt
De Nachschlagetabelle *(f)*
En look-up table
Es tabla de consulta *(f)*
Fr table à consulter *(f)*
It tavola di consultazione *(f)*

tabela de decisão *(f)* Pt
De Entscheidungstabelle *(f)*
En decision table
Es tabla de decisión *(f)*
Fr table de décision *(f)*
It tavola di decisione *(f)*

tabela de valores verdadeiros *(f)* Pt
De Echtheitstabelle *(f)*
En truth table
Es tabla de decisión lógica *(f)*
Fr table de vérité *(f)*
It tavola della verità *(f)*

tabellarische Anzeige *(f)* De
En tabular display
Es representación tabular *(f)*
Fr affichage tabulaire *(m)*
It visualizzazione tabulare *(f)*
Pt visualização tabelar *(f)*

tabellarische Sprache *(f)* De
En tabular language
Es lenguaje tabular *(m)*
Fr langage tabulaire *(m)*
It linguaggio tabulare *(m)*
Pt linguagem tabelar *(f)*

Tabelle *(f) n* De
En table
Es tabla *(f)*
Fr table *(f)*
It tavola *(f)*
Pt tabela *(f)*

Tabellenaufsuchung *(f) n* De
En table look up (TLU)
Es consulta de tablas *(f)*
Fr consultation de table *(f)*
It consulta di tavola *(f)*
Pt consulta de tabela *(f)*

tabellieren *vb* De
En tabulate
Es tabular
Fr tabuler
It tabulare
Pt tabular

tabla *(f) n* Es
De Tabelle *(f)*
En table
Fr table *(f)*
It tavola *(f)*
Pt tabela *(f)*

tabla de consulta *(f)* Es
De Nachschlagetabelle *(f)*
En look-up table
Fr table à consulter *(f)*
It tavola di consultazione *(f)*
Pt tabela de consulta *(f)*

tabla de decisión *(f)* Es
De Entscheidungs tabelle *(f)*
En decision table
Fr table de décision *(f)*
It tavola di decisione *(f)*
Pt tabela de decisão *(f)*

tabla de decisión lógica *(f)* Es
De Echtheitstabelle *(f)*
En truth table
Fr table de vérité *(f)*
It tavola della verità *(f)*
Pt tabela de valores verdadeiros *(f)*

table *n* En; Fr *(f)*
De Tabelle *(f)*
Es tabla *(f)*
It tavola *(f)*
Pt tabela *(f)*

table à consulter *(f)* Fr
De Nachschlagetabelle *(f)*
En look-up table
Es tabla de consulta *(f)*
It tavola di consultazione *(f)*
Pt tabela de consulta *(f)*

tableau à aiguilles *(m)* Fr
De Steckplatte *(f)*
En pinboard
Es cuadro de alfileres *(m)*
It pannello a spine *(m)*
Pt prancheta de alfinetes *(f)*

tableau de connexions *(m)* Fr
De Schalttafel; Steckerbrett *(f n)*
En patchboard; plugboard
Es cuadro de conexio; cuadro de control *(m)*
It pannello di connessione *(m)*
Pt placa de concerto; place de conexões eléctricas *(f)*

tableau graphique *(m)* Fr
De Symboltafel *(f)*
En graphic panel
Es panel gráfico *(m)*
It pannello grafico *(m)*
Pt painel de gráficos *(m)*

table de décision *(f)* Fr
De Entscheidungstabelle *(f)*
En decision table
Es tabla de decisión *(f)*
It tavola di decisione *(f)*
Pt tabela de decisão *(f)*

table de vérité *(f)* Fr
De Echtheitstabelle *(f)*
En truth table
Es tabla de decisión lógica *(f)*
It tavola della verità *(f)*
Pt tabela de valores verdadeiros *(f)*

table look up (TLU) En
De Tabellenaufsuchung *(f)*
Es consulta de tablas *(f)*
Fr consultation de table *(f)*
It consulta di tavola *(f)*
Pt consulta de tabela *(f)*

tablet *n* En
De Block *(m)*
Es tableta *(f)*
Fr tablette *(f)*
It tavoletta *(f)*
Pt bloco *(m)*

tableta *(f) n* Es
De Block *(m)*
En tablet
Fr tablette *(f)*
It tavoletta *(f)*
Pt bloco *(m)*

tablette *(f) n* Fr
De Block *(m)*
En tablet
Es tableta *(f)*
It tavoletta *(f)*
Pt bloco *(m)*

tabulação *(f)* *n* Pt
De Tabulation *(f)*
En tabulation
Es tabulación *(f)*
Fr tabulation *(f)*
It tabulazione *(f)*

tabulación *(f)* *n* Es
De Tabulation *(f)*
En tabulation
Fr tabulation *(f)*
It tabulazione *(f)*
Pt tabulação *(f)*

tabulador *(m)* *n* Pt
De Tabulator *(m)*
En tabulator
Es tabuladora *(f)*
Fr tabulatrice *(f)*
It tabulatore *(m)*

tabuladora *(f)* *n* Es
De Tabulator *(m)*
En tabulator
Fr tabulatrice *(f)*
It tabulatore *(m)*
Pt tabulador *(m)*

tabular *vb* Es, Pt
De tabellieren
En tabulate
Fr tabuler
It tabulare

tabular display En
De tabellarische Anzeige *(f)*
Es representación tabular *(f)*
Fr affichage tabulaire *(m)*
It visualizzazione tabulare *(f)*
Pt visualização tabelar *(f)*

tabulare *vb* It
De tabellieren
En tabulate
Es tabular
Fr tabuler
Pt tabular

tabular language En
De tabellarische Sprache *(f)*
Es lenguaje tabular *(m)*
Fr langage tabulaire *(m)*
It linguaggio tabulare *(m)*
Pt linguagem tabelar *(f)*

tabulate *vb* En
De tabellieren
Es tabular
Fr tabuler
It tabulare
Pt tabular

tabulation *n* En; Fr *(f)*
De Tabulation *(f)*
Es tabulación *(f)*
It tabulazione *(f)*
Pt tabulação *(f)*

Tabulation *(f)* *n* De
En tabulation
Es tabulación *(f)*
Fr tabulation *(f)*
It tabulazione *(f)*
Pt tabulação *(f)*

tabulato errori *(m)* It
De Fehlerbericht *(m)*
En error report
Es informe de errores *(m)*
Fr état sélectif *(m)*
Pt relatório de erros *(m)*

tabulator *n* En
De Tabulator *(m)*
Es tabuladora *(f)*
Fr tabulatrice *(f)*
It tabulatore *(m)*
Pt tabulador *(m)*

Tabulator *(m)* *n* De
En tabulator
Es tabuladora *(f)*
Fr tabulatrice *(f)*
It tabulatore *(m)*
Pt tabulador *(m)*

tabulatore *(m)* *n* It
De Tabulator *(m)*
En tabulator
Es tabuladora *(f)*
Fr tabulatrice *(f)*
Pt tabulador *(m)*

tabulatrice *(f)* *n* Fr
De Tabulator *(m)*
En tabulator
Es tabuladora *(f)*
It tabulatore *(m)*
Pt tabulador *(m)*

tabulazione *(f)* *n* It
De Tabulation *(f)*
En tabulation
Es tabulación *(f)*
Fr tabulation *(f)*
Pt tabulação *(f)*

tabuler *vb* Fr
De tabellieren
En tabulate
Es tabular
It tabulare
Pt tabular

tâche *(f)* *n* Fr
De Aufgabe *(f)*
En task
Es tarea *(f)*
It compito *(m)*
Pt tarefa *(f)*

tag *n* En
De Etikett *(n)*
Es etiqueta *(f)*
Fr étiquette *(f)*
It identificatore *(m)*
Pt etiqueta *(f)*

Taktgeber *(m)* *n* De
En clock
Es reloj *(m)*
Fr horloge *(f)*
It orologio *(m)*
Pt relógio *(m)*

Taktgeschwindigkeit *(f)* *n* De
En clock rate
Es velocidad de impulsos de reloj *(f)*
Fr fréquence des impulsions d'horloge *(f)*
It frequenza degli impulsi dell'orologio *(f)*
Pt taxa de impulsos de relógio *(f)*

Taktimpulse *(pl)* *n* De
En clock pulses
Es impulsos de reloj *(m pl)*
Fr impulsions d'horloge *(f pl)*
It impulsi dell'orologio *(m pl)*
Pt impulsos de relógio *(m pl)*

Taktlöcher *(pl)* *n* De
En feed holes; sprocket holes
Es perforaciones de alimentación; perforaciones marginales *(f pl)*
Fr perforations d'entraînement; trous d'entraînement *(f pl m pl)*
It fori di alimentazione; perforazioni di tabulati *(m pl f pl)*
Pt furos de alimentação; furos de roda dentada *(m pl)*

Taktpulse *(pl)* *n* De
En sprocket pulse
Es impulso de sincronización *(m)*
Fr impulsion de synchronisation *(f)*
It impulso del rocchetto *(m)*
Pt impulso de roda dentada *(m)*

tambor *(m)* *n* Es, Pt
De Trommel *(f)*
En drum
Fr tambour *(m)*
It tamburo *(m)*

tambor de tipos *(m)* Es, Pt
De Typentrommel *(f)*
En type drum
Fr tambour à caractères *(m)*
It tamburo di caratteri *(m)*

tambor magnético *(m)* Es, Pt
De Magnettrommel *(f)*
En magnetic drum
Fr tambour magnétique *(m)*
It tamburo magnetico *(m)*

tambour *(m)* *n* Fr
De Trommel *(f)*
En drum
Es tambor *(m)*
It tamburo *(m)*
Pt tambor *(m)*

tambour à caractères *(m)* Fr
De Typentrommel *(f)*
En type drum
Es tambor de tipos *(m)*

It tamburo di caratteri *(m)*
Pt tambor de tipos *(m)*

tambour d'impression *(m)* Fr
De Trommeldruckerfaß *(n)*
En print barrel
Es cilindro impresor *(m)*
It tamburo di stampa *(m)*
Pt cilindro impressor *(m)*

tambour magnétique *(m)* Fr
De Magnettrommel *(f)*
En magnetic drum
Es tambor magnético *(m)*
It tamburo magnetico *(m)*
Pt tambor magnético *(m)*

tamburo *(m) n* It
De Trommel *(f)*
En drum
Es tambor *(m)*
Fr tambour *(m)*
Pt tambor *(m)*

tamburo di caratteri *(m)* It
De Typentrommel *(f)*
En type drum
Es tambor de tipos *(m)*
Fr tambour à caractères *(m)*
Pt tambor de tipos *(m)*

tamburo di stampa *(m)* It
De Trommeldruckerfaß *(n)*
En print barrel
Es cilindro impresor *(m)*
Fr tambour d'impression *(m)*
Pt cilindro impressor *(m)*

tamburo magnetico *(m)* It
De Magnettrommel *(f)*
En magnetic drum
Es tambor magnético *(m)*
Fr tambour magnétique *(m)*
Pt tambor magnético *(m)*

tampon d'entrée *(m)* Fr
De Eingangspuffer *(m)*
En input buffer
Es memoria intermedia de entrada *(f)*
It memoria di transito dell'entrata *(f)*
Pt separador de entrada *(m)*

tampon entrée-sortie *(m)* Fr
De Eingangs-Ausgangspuffer *(m)*
En input-output buffer
Es memoria intermedia de entrada-salida *(f)*
It memoria di transito entrata-uscita *(f)*
Pt separador de entrada-sair *(m)*

tandem system En
De Anschlußsystem *(n)*
Es sistema en tandem *(m)*
Fr système en tandem *(m)*
It sistema abbinato *(m)*
Pt sistema em tandem *(m)*

tape *n* En
De Band *(n)*
Es cinta *(f)*
Fr bande *(f)*
It nastro *(m)*
Pt fita *(f)*

tape drive En
De Bandantrieb *(m)*
Es impulsor de cinta *(m)*
Fr dérouleur de bande *(m)*
It guida del nastro *(f)*
Pt accionamento da fita *(m)*

tape feed En
De Bandvorschub *(m)*
Es alimentador de cinta *(m)*
Fr entraînement du ruban *(m)*
It alimentazione del nastro *(f)*
Pt alimentação de fita *(f)*

tape library En
De Bandbibliothek *(f)*
Es biblioteca de cintas *(f)*
Fr bandothèque *(f)*
It libreria dei nastri *(f)*
Pt biblioteca de fitas *(f)*

tape mark En
De Bandkennzeichen *(n)*
Es marca de cinta *(f)*
Fr marque de bande *(f)*
It segno del nastro *(m)*
Pt marca de fita *(f)*

tape punch En
De Bandlocher *(m)*
Es perforadora de cinta *(f)*
Fr perforatrice de bande *(f)*
It perforatrice di nastri *(f)*
Pt perfuradora de fita *(f)*

tape reader En
De Bandleser *(m)*
Es lectora de cinta *(f)*
Fr lecteur de bande *(m)*
It lettore di nastri *(m)*
Pt leitor de fita *(m)*

tape transport En
De Bandtransport *(m)*
Es transporte de cinta *(m)*
Fr transport de la bande *(m)*
It trasporto del nastro *(m)*
Pt transporte de fita *(m)*

tape unit En
De Bandgerät *(n)*
Es unidad de cinta *(f)*
Fr unité de ruban magnétique *(f)*
It unità a nastri *(f)*
Pt unidade de fita *(f)*

tape verifier En
De Bandprüfgerät *(n)*
Es verificadora de cinta *(f)*
Fr vérificatrice de bande *(f)*
It verificatrice di nastri *(f)*
Pt verificador de fita *(m)*

tarea *(f) n* Es
De Aufgabe *(f)*
En task
Fr tâche *(f)*
It compito *(m)*
Pt tarefa *(f)*

tarefa *(f) n* Pt
De Aufgabe *(f)*
En task
Es tarea *(f)*
Fr tâche *(f)*
It compito *(m)*

target language En
De Zielsprache *(f)*
Es lenguaje resultante *(m)*
Fr langage généré *(m)*
It linguaggio risultante *(m)*
Pt linguagem de objectivo *(f)*

tarjeta de ochenta columnas *(f)* Es
De achtzig-Spalten-Karte *(f)*
En eighty-column card
Fr carte de quatre-vingt colonnes *(f)*
It scheda ad ottanta colonne *(f)*
Pt ficha de oitenta colunas *(f)*

tasa en bits *(f)* Es
De Binärzeichen-geschwindigkeit *(f)*
En bit rate
Fr débit de bits *(m)*
It volume di bit *(m)*
Pt taxa de bit *(f)*

task *n* En
De Aufgabe *(f)*
Es tarea *(f)*
Fr tâche *(f)*
It compito *(m)*
Pt tarefa *(f)*

tasso di errori *(m)* It
De Fehlerhäufigkeit *(f)*
En error rate
Es coeficiente de errores *(m)*
Fr taux d'erreurs *(m)*
Pt índice de erros *(m)*

Tastatur *(m) n* De
En keyboard
Es teclado *(m)*
Fr clavier *(m)*
It tastiera *(f)*
Pt teclado *(m)*

Taste auf Band De
En key-to-tape
Es registro sobre cinta
Fr enregistrement sur bande
It registrazione su nastro magnetico
Pt tecla-à-fita

Taste auf Platte De
En key-to-disk
Es registro sobre disco
Fr enregistrement sur disque
It registrazione su disco
Pt tecla-ao-disco

tastiera *(f) n* It
De Tastatur *(m)*
En keyboard
Es teclado *(m)*
Fr clavier *(m)*
Pt teclado *(m)*

tasto *(m) n* It
De Schlüssel *(m)*
En key
Es tecla *(f)*
Fr touche *(f)*
Pt tecla *(f)*

tasto di funzione *(m)* It
De Funktionsschlüssel *(m)*
En function key
Es tecla de función *(f)*
Fr touche de fonction *(f)*
Pt tecla de funções *(f)*

taux de défaillance *(m)* Fr
De Ausfallhäufigkeit *(f)*
En failure rate
Es frecuencia de fallos *(f)*
It numero di guasti *(m)*
Pt índice de falhas *(m)*

taux d'erreurs *(m)* Fr
De Fehlerhäufigkeit *(f)*
En error rate
Es coeficiente de errores *(m)*
It tasso di errori *(m)*
Pt índice de erros *(m)*

tavola *(f) n* It
De Tabelle *(f)*
En table
Es tabla *(f)*
Fr table *(f)*
Pt tabela *(f)*

tavola della verità *(f)* It
De Echtheitstabelle *(f)*
En truth table
Es tabla de decisión lógica *(f)*
Fr table de vérité *(f)*
Pt tabela de valores verdadeiros *(f)*

tavola di consultazione *(f)* It
De Nachschlagetabelle *(f)*
En look-up table
Es tabla de consulta *(f)*
Fr table à consulter *(f)*
Pt tabela de consulta *(f)*

tavola di decisione *(f)* It
De Entscheidungstabelle *(f)*
En decision table
Es tabla de decisión *(f)*
Fr table de décision *(f)*
Pt tabela de decisão *(f)*

tavoletta *(f) n* It
De Block *(m)*
En tablet
Es tableta *(f)*
Fr tablette *(f)*
Pt bloco *(m)*

taxa de baud *(f)* Pt
De Baudgeschwindigkeit *(f)*
En baud rate
Es velocidad en baudios *(f)*
Fr débit en bauds *(m)*
It numero di baud *(m)*

taxa de bit *(f)* Pt
De Binärzeichen-geschwindigkeit *(f)*
En bit rate
Es tasa en bits *(f)*
Fr débit de bits *(m)*
It volume di bit *(m)*

taxa de impulsos de relógio *(f)* Pt
De Taktgeschwindigkeit *(f)*
En clock rate
Es velocidad de impulsos de reloj *(f)*
Fr fréquence des impulsions d'horloge *(f)*
It frequenza degli impulsi dell'orologio *(f)*

technique de mise au point dynamique *(f)* Fr
De dynamische Fehlerbeseitigung *(f)*
En dynamic debugging technique (DDT)
Es técnica dinámica de depuración *(f)*
It tecnica di messa a punto di un programma dinamica *(f)*
Pt técnica de desparatização dinâmica *(f)*

technique du logiciel *(f)* Fr
De Programm-ausrüstung *(f)*
En software engineering
Es ingeniería de soportes lógicos *(f)*
It ingegneria del software *(f)*
Pt engenharia de software *(f)*

technologie des fibres optiques *(f)* Fr
Am optical fiber technology
De Faseroptiktechnik *(f)*
En optical fibre technology
Es tecnología de las fibras ópticas *(f)*
It tecnologia delle fibre ottiche *(f)*
Pt tecnologia de fibras ópticas *(f)*

tecla *(f) n* Es, Pt
De Schlüssel *(m)*
En key
Fr touche *(f)*
It tasto *(m)*

tecla-à-fita Pt
De Taste auf Band
En key-to-tape
Es registro sobre cinta
Fr enregistrement sur bande
It registrazione su nastro magnetico

tecla-ao-disco Pt
De Taste auf Platte
En key-to-disk
Es registro sobre disco
Fr enregistrement sur disque
It registrazione su disco

tecla de función *(f)* Es
De Funktionsschlüssel *(m)*
En function key
Fr touche de fonction *(f)*
It tasto di funzione *(m)*
Pt tecla de funções *(f)*

tecla de funções *(f)* Pt
De Funktionsschlüssel *(m)*
En function key
Es tecla de función *(f)*
Fr touche de fonction *(f)*
It tasto di funzione *(m)*

teclado *(m) n* Es
De Tastatur *(m)*
En keyboard
Fr clavier *(m)*
It tastiera *(f)*

técnica de avaliação e revisão de projectos *(f)* Pt
De Projekt-auswertungs- und Übersichttechnik *(f)*
En project evaluation and review technique (PERT)
Es método de planificación y control de proyectos *(m)*
Fr système d'ordonnancement des opérations et du personnel *(m)*
It tecnica di revisione e valutazione del progetto *(f)*

técnica de desparatização dinâmica *(f)* Pt
De dynamische Fehlerbeseitigung *(f)*
En dynamic debugging technique (DDT)

Es técnica dinámica de depuración *(f)*
Fr technique de mise au point dynamique *(f)*
It tecnica di messa a punto di un programma dinamica *(f)*

tecnica di messa a punto di un programma dinamica *(f)* It
De dynamische Fehlerbeseitigung *(f)*
En dynamic debugging technique (DDT)
Es técnica dinámica de depuración *(f)*
Fr technique de mise au point dynamique *(f)*
Pt técnica de desparatização dinâmica *(f)*

técnica dinámica de depuración *(f)* Es
De dynamische Fehlerbeseitigung *(f)*
En dynamic debugging technique (DDT)
Fr technique de mise au point dynamique *(f)*
It tecnica di messa a punto di un programma dinamica *(f)*
Pt técnica de desparatização dinâmica *(f)*

tecnica di revisione e valutazione del progetto *(f)* It
De Projekt-auswertungs- und Übersichttechnik *(f)*
En project evaluation and review technique (PERT)
Es método de planificación y control de proyectos *(m)*
Fr système d'ordonnancement des opérations et du personnel *(m)*
Pt técnica de avaliação e revisão de projectos *(f)*

tecnologia de fibras ópticas *(f)* Pt
Am optical fiber technology
De Faseroptiktechnik *(f)*
En optical fibre technology
Es tecnología de las fibras ópticas *(f)*
Fr technologie des fibres optiques *(f)*
It tecnologia delle fibre ottiche *(f)*

tecnología de las fibras ópticas *(f)* Es
Am optical fiber technology
De Faseroptiktechnik *(f)*
En optical fibre technology
Fr technologie des fibres optiques *(f)*
It tecnologia delle fibre ottiche *(f)*
Pt tecnologia de fibras ópticas *(f)*

tecnologia delle fibre ottiche *(f)* It
Am optical fiber technology
De Faseroptiktechnik *(f)*
En optical fibre technology
Es tecnología de las fibras ópticas *(f)*
Fr technologie des fibres optiques *(f)*
Pt tecnologia de fibras ópticas *(f)*

Teilbetrieb *(m) n* De
En part operation
Es operación parcial *(f)*
Fr opération partielle *(f)*
It operazione parziale *(f)*
Pt operação por partes *(f)*

Teiler *(m) n* De
En divider
Es divisor *(m)*
Fr diviseur *(m)*
It divisore *(m)*
Pt divisor *(m)*

Teilnehmerstation *(f) n* De
En subscriber station
Es estación de una red *(f)*
Fr poste du réseau *(m)*
It posto d'abbonato *(m)*
Pt estação de subscritor *(f)*

Teilübertrag *(m) n* De
En partial carry
Es arrastre parcial *(m)*
Fr report partiel *(m)*
It riporto parziale *(m)*
Pt transporte parcial *(m)*

telaio *(m) n* It
De Rahmen *(m)*
En frame
Es encuadre *(m)*
Fr cadre *(m)*
Pt quadro *(m)*

telecommunication *n* En
De Fernmeldung *(f)*
Es telecomunicación *(f)*
Fr télécommunication *(f)*
It telecomunicazione *(f)*
Pt telecomunicação *(f)*

télécommunication *(f) n* Fr
De Fernmeldung *(f)*
En telecommunication
Es telecomunicación *(f)*
It telecomunicazione *(f)*
Pt telecomunicação *(f)*

telecomunicação *(f) n* Pt
De Fernmeldung *(f)*
En telecommunication
Es telecomunicación *(f)*
Fr télécommunication *(f)*
It telecomunicazione *(f)*

telecomunicación *(f) n* Es
De Fernmeldung *(f)*
En telecommunication
Fr télécommunication *(f)*
It telecomunicazione *(f)*
Pt telecomunicação *(f)*

telecomunicazione *(f) n* It
De Fernmeldung *(f)*
En telecommunication
Es telecomunicación *(f)*
Fr télécommunication *(f)*
Pt telecomunicação *(f)*

tele-elaborazione *(f) n* It
De Fernverarbeitung *(f)*
En teleprocessing
Es teleproceso *(m)*
Fr télétraitement *(m)*
Pt tele-processamento *(m)*

tele-ensaio *(m) n* Pt
De Fernprüfung *(f)*
En remote testing
Es ensayo a distancia *(m)*
Fr contrôle à distance *(m)*
It collaudo a distanza *(m)*

Telefondatensatz *(m) n* De
En telephone data set
Es equipo de datos telefónicos *(m)*
Fr ensemble de données téléphoniques *(m)*
It gruppo di dati telefonici *(m)*
Pt conjunto de dados telefónicos *(m)*

telefonische Verbindung *(f)* De
En telephonic communication
Es comunicación telefónica *(f)*
Fr communication téléphonique *(f)*
It comunicazione telefonica *(f)*
Pt comunicação telefónica *(f)*

telefonische Vermittlung *(f)* De
En telephone switching
Es conmutación telefónica *(f)*
Fr commutation téléphonique *(f)*
It commutazione telefonica *(f)*
Pt comutação telefónica *(f)*

Telefonleitung *(f) n* De
En voice-grade channel
Es canal de rango vocal *(m)*
Fr voie téléphonique *(f)*

It canale a frequenze vocali *(m)*
Pt canal para fonia *(m)*

teleimpresor *(m) n* Es
De Fernschreiber *(m)*
En teleprinter
Fr téléimprimeur *(m)*
It telestampatrice *(f)*
Pt tele-impressor *(m)*

tele-impressor *(m) n* Pt
De Fernschreiber *(m)*
En teleprinter
Es teleimpresor *(m)*
Fr téléimprimeur *(m)*
It telestampatrice *(f)*

téléimprimeur *(m) n* Fr
De Fernschreiber *(m)*
En teleprinter
Es teleimpresor *(m)*
It telestampatrice *(f)*
Pt tele-impressor *(m)*

télémesure *(f) n* Fr
De Fernmessung *(f)*
En telemetry
Es telemetría *(f)*
It telemetria *(f)*
Pt telemetria *(f)*

telemetria *(f) n* It, Pt
De Fernmessung *(f)*
En telemetry
Es telemetría *(f)*
Fr télémesure *(f)*

telemetría *(f) n* Es
De Fernmessung *(f)*
En telemetry
Fr télémesure *(f)*
It telemetria *(f)*
Pt telemetria *(f)*

telemetry *n* En
De Fernmessung *(f)*
Es telemetría *(f)*
Fr télémesure *(f)*
It telemetria *(f)*
Pt telemetria *(f)*

telephone data set En
De Telefondatensatz *(m)*
Es equipo de datos telefónicos *(m)*
Fr ensemble de données téléphoniques *(m)*
It gruppo di dati telefonici *(m)*
Pt conjunto de dados telefónicos *(m)*

telephone switching En
De telefonische Vermittlung *(f)*
Es conmutación telefónica *(f)*
Fr commutation téléphonique *(f)*
It commutazione telefonica *(f)*
Pt comutação telefónica *(f)*

telephonic communication En
De telefonische Verbindung *(f)*
Es comunicación telefónica *(f)*
Fr communication téléphonique *(f)*
It comunicazione telefonica *(f)*
Pt comunicação telefónica *(f)*

teleprinter *n* En
De Fernschreiber *(m)*
Es teleimpresor *(m)*
Fr téléimprimeur *(m)*
It telestampatrice *(f)*
Pt tele-impressor *(m)*

teleproceso *(m) n* Es
De Fernverarbeitung *(f)*
En teleprocessing
Fr télétraitement *(m)*
It tele-elaborazione *(f)*
Pt tele-processamento *(m)*

tele-processamento *(m)* Pt
De Fernverarbeitung *(f)*
En remote processing; teleprocessing
Es proceso a distancia; teleproceso *(m)*
Fr télétraitement *(m)*
It elaborazione a distanza; tele-elaborazione *(f)*

teleprocessing *n* En
De Fernverarbeitung *(f)*
Es teleproceso *(m)*
Fr télétraitement *(m)*
It tele-elaborazione *(f)*
Pt tele-processamento *(m)*

télésoumission de travaux *(f)* Fr
De Jobfernverarbeitung *(f)*
En remote job entry
Es entrada de trabajos a distancia *(f)*
It entrata del lavoro a distanza *(f)*
Pt entrada de trabalho remota *(f)*

telestampatrice *(f) n* It
De Fernschreiber *(m)*
En teleprinter
Es teleimpresor *(m)*
Fr téléimprimeur *(m)*
Pt tele-impressor *(m)*

teletesto *(m) n* It
De Ferntext *(m)*
En teletext
Es teletexto *(m)*
Fr télétexte *(m)*
Pt teletexto *(m)*

teletext *n* En
De Ferntext *(m)*
Es teletexto *(m)*
Fr télétexte *(m)*
It teletesto *(m)*
Pt teletexto *(m)*

télétexte *(m) n* Fr
De Ferntext *(m)*
En teletext
Es teletexto *(m)*
It teletesto *(m)*
Pt teletexto *(m)*

teletexto *(m) n* Es, Pt
De Ferntext *(m)*
En teletext
Fr télétexte *(m)*
It teletesto *(m)*

télétraitement *(m) n* Fr
De Fernverarbeitung *(f)*
En remote processing; teleprocessing
Es proceso a distancia; teleproceso *(m)*
It elaborazione a distanza; tele-elaborazione *(f)*
Pt tele-processamento *(m)*

tempo de abandono *(m)* Pt
De Ruhezeit *(f)*
En unattended time
Es tiempo sin personal *(m)*
Fr temps de fonctionnement sans surveillance *(m)*
It tempo uncustodita *(m)*

tempo de aceleração *(m)* Pt
De Beschleunigungszeit *(f)*
En acceleration time
Es tiempo de aceleración *(m)*
Fr temps d'accélération *(m)*
It tempo di accelerazione *(m)*

tempo de acesso *(m)* Pt
De Zugriffszeit *(f)*
En access time
Es tiempo de acceso *(m)*
Fr temps d'accès *(m)*
It tempo di accesso *(m)*

tempo de arranque *(m)* Pt
De Start-Zeit *(f)*
En start time
Es tiempo de arranque *(m)*
Fr temps de démarrage *(m)*
It tempo di salita in regime *(m)*

tempo de arranque-paragem *(m)* Pt
De Start-Stopp-Zeit *(f)*
En start-stop time
Es tiempo de arranque-espera *(m)*
Fr temps de démarrage-arrêt *(m)*
It tempo inizio-arresto *(m)*

tempo de busca *(m)* Pt
De Suchzeit *(f)*
En search time
Es tiempo de búsqueda *(m)*
Fr temps de recherche *(m)*
It tempo di ricerca *(m)*

tempo decorrido *(m)* Pt
De verstrichene Zeit *(f)*
En elapsed time
Es tiempo transcurrido *(m)*
Fr temps écoulé *(m)*
It tempo trascorso *(m)*

tempo de desaceleração *(m)* Pt
De Verzögerungszeit *(f)*
En deceleration time
Es tiempo de deceleración *(m)*
Fr temps de décélération *(m)*
It tempo di decelerazione *(m)*

tempo de engenharia *(m)* Pt
De Zeit für technische Arbeiten *(f)*
En engineering time
Es tiempo de inmovilización *(m)*
Fr temps d'immobilisation *(m)*
It tempo di immobilizzazione *(m)*

tempo de escrita *(m)* Pt
De Schreibzeit *(f)*
En write time
Es tiempo de escritura *(m)*
Fr temps d'écriture *(m)*
It tempo di scrittura *(m)*

tempo de espera *(m)* Pt
De Wartezeit *(f)*
En waiting time
Es tiempo de espera *(m)*
Fr temps d'attente *(m)*
It tempo di attesa *(m)*

tempo de execução *(m)* Pt
De Aktivierungszeit *(f)*
En execution time
Es tiempo de ejecución *(m)*
Fr durée d'exécution *(f)*
It tempo di esecuzione *(m)*

tempo de functionamento em vazio *(m)* Pt
De Leerlaufzeit *(f)*
En idle time
Es tiempo pasivo *(m)*
Fr temps en chômage *(m)*
It tempo passivo *(m)*

tempo de incidentes *(m)* Pt
De Nebenzeiten *(pl)*
En incidentals time
Es tiempo de actividades anexas *(m)*
Fr temps d'activités annexes *(m)*
It tempo di attività eventuale *(m)*

tempo de instalação *(m)* Pt
De Einrichtezeit *(f)*
En set-up time
Es tiempo de preparación *(m)*
Fr temps de préparation *(m)*
It tempo messa a punto *(m)*

tempo de instruções *(m)* Pt
De Befehlszeit *(f)*
En instruction time
Es tiempo de una instrucción *(m)*
Fr temps d'exécution d'une instruction *(m)*
It tempo per l'istruzione *(m)*

tempo de leitura *(m)* Pt
De Auslesezeit *(f)*
En read time
Es tiempo de lectura *(m)*
Fr durée de lecture *(f)*
It tempo di lettura *(m)*

tempo de paragem *(m)* Pt
De Ausfallzeit *(f)*
En downtime
Es tiempo de pana *(m)*
Fr temps de panne *(m)*
It tempo di panna *(m)*

tempo de passagem *(m)* Pt
De Durchlaufzeit *(f)*
En run time
Es tiempo de pasada *(m)*
Fr temps d'exécution *(m)*
It tempo di esecuzione *(m)*

tempo de prova *(m)* Pt
De Kontrollzeit *(f)*
En proving time
Es tiempo de ensayo *(m)*
Fr durée d'essai de fonctionnement *(f)*
It tempo di prova *(m)*

tempo de reparação *(m)* Pt
De Reparaturzeit *(f)*
En repair time
Es tiempo de reparación *(m)*
Fr temps de réparation *(m)*
It tempo di riparazione *(m)*

tempo de resposta *(m)* Pt
De Ansprechzeit *(f)*
En response time
Es tiempo de respuesta *(m)*
Fr temps de réponse *(m)*
It tempo di risposta *(m)*

tempo de soma-subtracção *(m)* Pt
De Addier-Subtrahierzeit *(f)*
En add-subtract time
Es tiempo de suma-resta *(m)*
Fr temps d'addition-soustraction *(m)*
It tempo di addizione-sottrazione *(m)*

tempo di accelerazione *(m)* It
De Beschleunigungszeit *(f)*
En acceleration time
Es tiempo de aceleración *(m)*
Fr temps d'accélération *(m)*
Pt tempo de aceleração *(m)*

tempo di accesso *(m)* It
De Zugriffszeit *(f)*
En access time
Es tiempo de acceso *(m)*
Fr temps d'accès *(m)*
Pt tempo de acesso *(m)*

tempo di addizione-sottrazione *(m)* It
De Addier-Subtrahierzeit *(f)*
En add-subtract time
Es tiempo de suma-resta *(m)*
Fr temps d'addition-soustraction *(m)*
Pt tempo de soma-subtracção *(m)*

tempo di attesa *(m)* It
De Wartezeit *(f)*
En waiting time
Es tiempo de espera *(m)*
Fr temps d'attente *(m)*
Pt tempo de espera *(m)*

tempo di attività eventuale *(m)* It
De Nebenzeiten *(pl)*
En incidentals time
Es tiempo de actividades anexas *(m)*
Fr temps d'activités annexes *(m)*
Pt tempo de incidentes *(m)*

tempo di decelerazione *(m)* It
De Verzögerungszeit *(f)*
En deceleration time
Es tiempo de deceleración *(m)*
Fr temps de décélération *(m)*
Pt tempo de desaceleração *(m)*

tempo di esecuzione *(m)* It
De Aktivierungszeit; Durchlaufzeit *(f)*
En execution time; run time
Es tiempo de ejecución; tiempo de pasada *(m)*
Fr durée d'exécution; temps d'exécution *(f m)*
Pt tempo de execução; tempo de passagem *(m)*

tempo di immobilizzazione *(m)* It
De Zeit für technische Arbeiten *(f)*
En engineering time
Es tiempo de inmovilización *(m)*
Fr temps d'immobilisation *(m)*
Pt tempo de engenharia *(m)*

tempo di lettura *(m)* It
De Auslesezeit *(f)*
En read time
Es tiempo de lectura *(m)*
Fr durée de lecture *(f)*
Pt tempo de leitura *(m)*

tempo di panna *(m)* It
De Ausfallzeit *(f)*
En downtime
Es tiempo de pana *(m)*
Fr temps de panne *(m)*
Pt tempo de paragem *(m)*

tempo di prova *(m)* It
De Kontrollzeit *(f)*
En proving time
Es tiempo de ensayo *(m)*
Fr durée d'essai de fonctionnement *(f)*
Pt tempo de prova *(m)*

tempo di ricerca *(m)* It
De Suchzeit *(f)*
En search time
Es tiempo de búsqueda *(m)*
Fr temps de recherche *(m)*
Pt tempo de busca *(m)*

tempo di riparazione *(m)* It
De Reparaturzeit *(f)*
En repair time
Es tiempo de reparación *(m)*
Fr temps de réparation *(m)*
Pt tempo de reparação *(m)*

tempo di riparazione medio *(m)* It
De effektive Reparaturzeit *(f)*
En mean repair time
Es tiempo medio para reparación *(m)*
Fr temps moyen de réparation *(m)*
Pt tempo médio de reparação *(m)*

tempo di risposta *(m)* It
De Ansprechzeit *(f)*
En response time
Es tiempo de respuesta *(m)*
Fr temps de réponse *(m)*
Pt tempo de resposta *(m)*

tempo di ritenzione *(m)* It
De Verweilzeit *(f)*
En retention period
Es período de retención *(m)*
Fr période de validité *(f)*
Pt periodo de retenção *(m)*

tempo di salita in regime *(m)* It
De Start-Zeit *(f)*
En start time
Es tiempo de arranque *(m)*
Fr temps de démarrage *(m)*
Pt tempo de arranque *(m)*

tempo di scrittura *(m)* It
De Schreibzeit *(f)*
En write time
Es tiempo de escritura *(m)*
Fr temps d'écriture *(m)*
Pt tempo de escrita *(m)*

tempo disponibile *(m)* It
De verfügbare Zeit *(f)*
En available time
Es tiempo disponible *(m)*
Fr temps disponible *(m)*
Pt tempo disponível *(m)*

tempo disponível *(m)* Pt
De verfügbare Zeit *(f)*
En available time
Es tiempo disponible *(m)*
Fr temps disponible *(m)*
It tempo disponibile *(m)*

tempo di utilizzazione *(m)* It
De Benutzerzeit *(f)*
En uptime
Es tiempo productivo *(m)*
Fr temps de bon fonctionnement *(m)*
Pt tempo terminado *(m)*

tempo efectivo *(m)* Pt
De effektive Zeit *(f)*
En effective time
Es tiempo efectivo *(m)*
Fr temps utile *(m)*
It tempo efficace *(m)*

tempo efficace *(m)* It
De effektive Zeit *(f)*
En effective time
Es tiempo efectivo *(m)*
Fr temps utile *(m)*
Pt tempo efectivo *(m)*

tempo inefficace *(m)* It
De unwirksame Zeit *(f)*
En ineffective time
Es tiempo ineficaz *(m)*
Fr temps ineffectif *(m)*
Pt tempo irreal *(m)*

tempo inizio-arresto *(m)* It
De Start-Stopp-Zeit *(f)*
En start-stop time
Es tiempo de arranque-espera *(m)*
Fr temps de démarrage-arrêt *(m)*
Pt tempo de arranque-paragem *(m)*

tempo inutilizzato *(m)* It
De unbenutzte Zeit *(f)*
En unused time
Es tiempo de inutilización *(m)*
Fr temps d'inutilisation *(m)*
Pt tempo não utilizado *(m)*

tempo irreal *(m)* Pt
De unwirksame Zeit *(f)*
En ineffective time
Es tiempo ineficaz *(m)*
Fr temps ineffectif *(m)*
It tempo inefficace *(m)*

tempo justificável *(m)* Pt
De abrechenbare Zeit *(f)*
En accountable time
Es tiempo contable *(m)*
Fr temps comptable *(m)*
It tempo responsabile *(m)*

tempo médio de reparação *(m)* Pt
De effektive Reparaturzeit *(f)*
En mean repair time
Es tiempo medio para reparación *(m)*
Fr temps moyen de réparation *(m)*
It tempo di riparazione medio *(m)*

tempo médio entre falhas *(m)* Pt
De Effektivzeit zwischen Ausfällen *(f)*
En mean time between failures
Es tiempo medio entre fallos *(m)*
Fr moyenne des temps de bon fonctionnement *(f)*
It tempo medio tra i guasti *(m)*

tempo medio tra i guasti *(m)* It
De Effektivzeit zwischen Ausfällen *(f)*
En mean time between failures
Es tiempo medio entre fallos *(m)*
Fr moyenne des temps de bon fonctionnement *(f)*
Pt tempo médio entre falhas *(m)*

tempo messa a punto *(m)* It
De Einrichtezeit *(f)*
En set-up time
Es tiempo de preparación *(m)*
Fr temps de préparation *(m)*
Pt tempo de instalação *(m)*

tempo morto *(m)* It, Pt
De Totzeit *(f)*
En dead time

Es tiempo muerto *(m)*
Fr temps mort *(m)*

tempo não utilizado *(m)* Pt
De unbenutzte Zeit *(f)*
En unused time
Es tiempo de inutilización *(m)*
Fr temps d'inutilisation *(m)*
It tempo inutilizzato *(m)*

tempo passivo *(m)* It
De Leerlaufzeit *(f)*
En idle time
Es tiempo pasivo *(m)*
Fr temps en chômage *(m)*
Pt tempo de functionamento em vazio *(m)*

tempo per l'istruzione *(m)* It
De Befehlszeit *(f)*
En instruction time
Es tiempo de una instrucción *(m)*
Fr temps d'exécution d'une instruction *(m)*
Pt tempo de instruções *(m)*

tempo produtivo *(m)* Pt
De Fertigungszeit *(f)*
En productive time
Es tiempo do producción *(m)*
Fr temps productif *(m)*
It tempo produttivo *(m)*

tempo produttivo *(m)* It
De Fertigungszeit *(f)*
En productive time
Es tiempo do producción *(m)*
Fr temps productif *(m)*
Pt tempo produtivo *(m)*

temporary storage En
De vorübergehende Speicherung *(f)*
Es memoria temporal *(f)*
Fr mémoire intermédiaire *(f)*
It memoria temporanea *(f)*
Pt armazenamento temporário *(m)*

tempo real *(m)* Pt
De Echtzeit *(f)*
En real time
Es tiempo real *(m)*
Fr temps réel *(m)*
It tempo reale *(m)*

tempo reale *(m)* It
De Echtzeit *(f)*
En real time
Es tiempo real *(m)*
Fr temps réel *(m)*
Pt tempo real *(m)*

tempo responsabile *(m)* It
De abrechenbare Zeit *(f)*
En accountable time
Es tiempo contable *(m)*
Fr temps comptable *(m)*
Pt tempo justificável *(m)*

temporizador *(m)* *n* Es
De Zeituhr *(f)*
En timer; timer clock
Fr rythmeur *(m)*
It temporizzatore *(m)*
Pt relógio marcador de tempos *(m)*

temporizzatore *(m)* *n* It
De Zeituhr *(f)*
En timer; timer clock
Es temporizador *(m)*
Fr rythmeur *(m)*
Pt relógio marcador de tempos *(m)*

tempo terminado *(m)* Pt
De Benutzerzeit *(f)*
En uptime
Es tiempo productivo *(m)*
Fr temps de bon fonctionnement *(m)*
It tempo di utilizzazione *(m)*

tempo trascorso *(m)* It
De verstrichene Zeit *(f)*
En elapsed time
Es tiempo transcurrido *(m)*
Fr temps écoulé *(m)*
Pt tempo decorrido *(m)*

tempo uncustodita *(m)* It
De Ruhezeit *(f)*
En unattended time
Es tiempo sin personal *(m)*
Fr temps de fonctionnement sans surveillance *(m)*
Pt tempo de abandono *(m)*

temps comptable *(m)* Fr
De abrechenbare Zeit *(f)*
En accountable time
Es tiempo contable *(m)*
It tempo responsabile *(m)*
Pt tempo justificável *(m)*

temps d'accélération *(m)* Fr
De Beschleunigungszeit *(f)*
En acceleration time
Es tiempo de aceleración *(m)*
It tempo di accelerazione *(m)*
Pt tempo de aceleração *(m)*

temps d'accès *(m)* Fr
De Zugriffszeit *(f)*
En access time
Es tiempo de acceso *(m)*
It tempo di accesso *(m)*
Pt tempo de acesso *(m)*

temps d'activités annexes *(m)* Fr
De Nebenzeiten *(pl)*
En incidentals time
Es tiempo de actividades anexas *(m)*
It tempo di attività eventuale *(m)*
Pt tempo de incidentes *(m)*

temps d'addition-soustraction *(m)* Fr
De Addier-Subtrahierzeit *(f)*
En add-subtract time
Es tiempo de suma-resta *(m)*
It tempo di addizione-sottrazione *(m)*
Pt tempo de soma-subtracção *(m)*

temps d'attente *(m)* Fr
De Wartezeit *(f)*
En waiting time
Es tiempo de espera *(m)*
It tempo di attesa *(m)*
Pt tempo de espera *(m)*

temps de bon fonctionnement *(m)* Fr
De Benutzerzeit *(f)*
En uptime
Es tiempo productivo *(m)*
It tempo di utilizzazione *(m)*
Pt tempo terminado *(m)*

temps d'écriture *(m)* Fr
De Schreibzeit *(f)*
En write time
Es tiempo de escritura *(m)*
It tempo di scrittura *(m)*
Pt tempo de escrita *(m)*

temps de décélération *(m)* Fr
De Verzögerungszeit *(f)*
En deceleration time
Es tiempo de deceleración *(m)*
It tempo di decelerazione *(m)*
Pt tempo de desaceleração *(m)*

temps de démarrage *(m)* Fr
De Start-Zeit *(f)*
En start time
Es tiempo de arranque *(m)*
It tempo di salita in regime *(m)*
Pt tempo de arranque *(m)*

temps de démarrage-arrêt *(m)* Fr
De Start-Stopp-Zeit *(f)*
En start-stop time
Es tiempo de arranque-espera *(m)*
It tempo inizio-arresto *(m)*
Pt tempo de arranque-paragem *(m)*

temps de fonctionnement sans surveillance *(m)* Fr
- De Ruhezeit *(f)*
- En unattended time
- Es tiempo sin personal *(m)*
- It tempo uncustodita *(m)*
- Pt tempo de abandono *(m)*

temps de panne *(m)* Fr
- De Ausfallzeit *(f)*
- En downtime
- Es tiempo de pana *(m)*
- It tempo di panna *(m)*
- Pt tempo de paragem *(m)*

temps de préparation *(m)* Fr
- De Einrichtezeit *(f)*
- En set-up time
- Es tiempo de preparación *(m)*
- It tempo messa a punto *(m)*
- Pt tempo de instalação *(m)*

temps de recherche *(m)* Fr
- De Suchzeit *(f)*
- En search time
- Es tiempo de búsqueda *(m)*
- It tempo di ricerca *(m)*
- Pt tempo de busca *(m)*

temps de réparation *(m)* Fr
- De Reparaturzeit *(f)*
- En repair time
- Es tiempo de reparación *(m)*
- It tempo di riparazione *(m)*
- Pt tempo de reparação *(m)*

temps de réponse *(m)* Fr
- De Ansprechzeit *(f)*
- En response time
- Es tiempo de respuesta *(m)*
- It tempo di risposta *(m)*
- Pt tempo de resposta *(m)*

temps d'exécution *(m)* Fr
- De Durchlaufzeit *(f)*
- En run time
- Es tiempo de pasada *(m)*
- It tempo di esecuzione *(m)*
- Pt tempo de passagem *(m)*

temps d'exécution d'une instruction *(m)* Fr
- De Befehlszeit *(f)*
- En instruction time
- Es tiempo de una instrucción *(m)*
- It tempo per l'istruzione *(m)*
- Pt tempo de instruções *(m)*

temps d'immobilisation *(m)* Fr
- De Zeit für technische Arbeiten *(f)*
- En engineering time
- Es tiempo de inmovilización *(m)*
- It tempo di immobilizzazione *(m)*
- Pt tempo de engenharia *(m)*

temps d'inutilisation *(m)* Fr
- De unbenutzte Zeit *(f)*
- En unused time
- Es tiempo de inutilización *(m)*
- It tempo inutilizzato *(m)*
- Pt tempo não utilizado *(m)*

temps disponible *(m)* Fr
- De verfügbare Zeit *(f)*
- En available time
- Es tiempo disponible *(m)*
- It tempo disponibile *(m)*
- Pt tempo disponível *(m)*

temps écoulé *(m)* Fr
- De verstrichene Zeit *(f)*
- En elapsed time
- Es tiempo transcurrido *(m)*
- It tempo trascorso *(m)*
- Pt tempo decorrido *(m)*

temps en chômage *(m)* Fr
- De Leerlaufzeit *(f)*
- En idle time
- Es tiempo pasivo *(m)*
- It tempo passivo *(m)*
- Pt tempo de functionamento em vazio *(m)*

temps ineffectif *(m)* Fr
- De unwirksame Zeit *(f)*
- En ineffective time
- Es tiempo ineficaz *(m)*
- It tempo inefficace *(m)*
- Pt tempo irreal *(m)*

temps mort *(m)* Fr
- De Totzeit *(f)*
- En dead time
- Es tiempo muerto *(m)*
- It tempo morto *(m)*
- Pt tempo morto *(m)*

temps moyen de réparation *(m)* Fr
- De effektive Reparaturzeit *(f)*
- En mean repair time
- Es tiempo medio para reparación *(m)*
- It tempo di riparazione medio *(m)*
- Pt tempo médio de reparação *(m)*

temps productif *(m)* Fr
- De Fertigungszeit *(f)*
- En productive time
- Es tiempo do producción *(m)*
- It tempo produttivo *(m)*
- Pt tempo produtivo *(m)*

temps réel *(m)* Fr
- De Echtzeit *(f)*
- En real time
- Es tiempo real *(m)*
- It tempo reale *(m)*
- Pt tempo real *(m)*

temps utile *(m)* Fr
- De effektive Zeit *(f)*
- En effective time
- Es tiempo efectivo *(m)*
- It tempo efficace *(m)*
- Pt tempo efectivo *(m)*

tener una avería Es
- De abgehen
- En go down
- Fr tomber en panne
- It avere una panna
- Pt avariar

tenir *vb* Fr
- De anhalten
- En hold
- Es mantener
- It mantenere
- Pt manter

tens complement En
- De Zehnerkomplement *(n)*
- Es complemento a diez *(m)*
- Fr complément à dix *(m)*
- It complemento di decine *(m)*
- Pt complemento de dezenas *(m)*

tenue à jour de fichier *(f)* Fr
- De Dateiwartung *(f)*
- En file maintenance
- Es mantenimiento de ficheros *(m)*
- It manutenzione del file *(f)*
- Pt manutenção de arquivo *(f)*

teoría de colas *(f)* Es
- De Warteschlangen-theorie *(f)*
- En queuing theory
- Fr théorie des files d'attente *(f)*
- It teoria delle code *(f)*
- Pt teoria de colocação em fila *(f)*

teoria de colocação em fila *(f)* Pt
- De Warteschlangen-theorie *(f)*
- En queuing theory
- Es teoría de colas *(f)*
- Fr théorie des files d'attente *(f)*
- It teoria delle code *(f)*

teoría de control *(f)* Es
- De Steuertheorie *(f)*
- En control theory
- Fr théorie de contrôle *(f)*
- It teoria del controllo *(f)*
- Pt teoria de controlo *(f)*

teoria de controlo *(f)* Pt
De Steuertheorie *(f)*
En control theory
Es teoría de control *(f)*
Fr théorie de contrôle *(f)*
It teoria del controllo *(f)*

teoria de informação *(f)* Pt
De Informationstheorie *(f)*
En information theory
Es teoría de la información *(f)*
Fr théorie de l'information *(f)*
It teoria delle informazioni *(f)*

teoría de la información *(f)* Es
De Informationstheorie *(f)*
En information theory
Fr théorie de l'information *(f)*
It teoria delle informazioni *(f)*
Pt teoria de informação *(f)*

teoria del controllo *(f)* It
De Steuertheorie *(f)*
En control theory
Es teoría de control *(f)*
Fr théorie de contrôle *(f)*
Pt teoria de controlo *(f)*

teoria delle code *(f)* It
De Warteschlangentheorie *(f)*
En queuing theory
Es teoría de colas *(f)*
Fr théorie des files d'attente *(f)*
Pt teoria de colocação em fila *(f)*

teoria delle informazioni *(f)* It
De Informationstheorie *(f)*
En information theory
Es teoría de la información *(f)*
Fr théorie de l'information *(f)*
Pt teoria de informação *(f)*

terceira-geração *adj* Pt
De drittgeneration
En third-generation
Es tercera-generación
Fr troisième-génération
It terza-generazione

tercera-generación *adj* Es
De drittgeneration
En third-generation
Fr troisième-génération
It terza-generazione
Pt terceira-geração

terminação *(f) n* Pt
De Endstelle *(f)*
En termination
Es terminación *(f)*
Fr fin *(f)*
It conclusione *(f)*

terminação anormal *(f)* Pt
De Programmabbruch *(m)*
En abnormal termination
Es terminación anormal *(f)*
Fr terminaison anormale *(f)*
It conclusione anormale *(f)*

terminación *(f) n* Es
De Endstelle *(f)*
En termination
Fr fin *(f)*
It conclusione *(f)*
Pt terminação *(f)*

terminación anormal *(f)* Es
De Programmabbruch *(m)*
En abnormal termination
Fr terminaison anormale *(f)*
It conclusione anormale *(f)*
Pt terminação anormal *(f)*

terminaison anormale *(f)* Fr
De Programmabbruch *(m)*
En abnormal termination
Es terminación anormal *(f)*
It conclusione anormale *(f)*
Pt terminação anormal *(f)*

terminal *n* En; Es, Fr, Pt *(m)*
De Endstation *(f)*
It terminale *(m)*

terminal à écran de visualisation *(m)* Fr
De Anzeigeendstation *(f)*
En display terminal
Es terminal de visualización *(m)*
It terminale di visualizzazione *(m)*
Pt terminal de visualização *(m)*

terminal con teclado *(m)* Es
De Schreibmaschinestation *(f)*
En typewriter terminal
Fr terminal équipé d'un clavier *(m)*
It terminale a macchina da scrivere *(m)*
Pt terminal de máquina de escrever *(m)*

terminal de indagação *(m)* Pt
De Abfragestation *(f)*
En inquiry terminal
Es terminal de interrogación *(m)*
Fr poste d'interrogation *(m)*
It terminale per informazioni *(m)*

terminal de interrogación *(m)* Es
De Abfragestation *(f)*
En inquiry terminal
Fr poste d'interrogation *(m)*
It terminale per informazioni *(m)*
Pt terminal de indagação *(m)*

terminal de máquina de escrever *(m)* Pt
De Schreibmaschinestation *(f)*
En typewriter terminal
Es terminal con teclado *(m)*
Fr terminal équipé d'un clavier *(m)*
It terminale a macchina da scrivere *(m)*

terminal de video *(m)* Es
De Videostation *(f)*
En video terminal
Fr terminal vidéo *(m)*
It terminale video *(m)*
Pt terminal video *(m)*

terminal de visualização *(m)* Pt
De Anzeigeendstation *(f)*
En display terminal
Es terminal de visualización *(m)*
Fr terminal à écran de visualisation *(m)*
It terminale di visualizzazione *(m)*

terminal de visualización *(m)* Es
De Anzeigeendstation *(f)*
En display terminal
Fr terminal à écran de visualisation *(m)*
It terminale di visualizzazione *(m)*
Pt terminal de visualização *(m)*

terminale *(m) n* It
De Endstation *(f)*
En terminal
Es terminal *(m)*
Fr terminal *(m)*
Pt terminal *(m)*

terminale a macchina da scrivere *(m)* It
De Schreibmaschinestation *(f)*
En typewriter terminal
Es terminal con teclado *(m)*
Fr terminal équipé d'un clavier *(m)*
Pt terminal de máquina de escrever *(m)*

terminale di visualizzazione *(m)* It
De Anzeigeendstation *(f)*
En display terminal
Es terminal de visualización *(m)*
Fr terminal à écran de visualisation *(m)*

Pt terminal de visualização *(m)*

terminale grafico *(m)* It
De Zeichenstation *(f)*
En graphics terminal
Es terminal gráfico *(m)*
Fr terminal graphique *(m)*
Pt terminal gráfico *(m)*

terminale intelligente *(m)* It
De programmierbare Station *(f)*
En intelligent terminal
Es terminal inteligente *(m)*
Fr terminal intelligent *(m)*
Pt terminal inteligente *(m)*

terminale interattivo *(m)* It
De Dialogdatenstation *(f)*
En interactive terminal
Es terminal interactivo *(m)*
Fr terminal interactif *(m)*
Pt terminal interactivo *(m)*

terminale per informazioni *(m)* It
De Abfragestation *(f)*
En inquiry terminal
Es terminal de interrogación *(m)*
Fr poste d'interrogation *(m)*
Pt terminal de indagação *(m)*

terminal équipé d'un clavier *(m)* Fr
De Schreibmaschinestation *(f)*
En typewriter terminal
Es terminal con teclado *(m)*
It terminale a macchina da scrivere *(m)*
Pt terminal de máquina de escrever *(m)*

terminale video *(m)* It
De Videostation *(f)*
En video terminal
Es terminal de video *(m)*
Fr terminal vidéo *(m)*
Pt terminal video *(m)*

terminal gráfico *(m)* Es
De Zeichenstation *(f)*
En graphics terminal
Fr terminal graphique *(m)*
It terminale grafico *(m)*
Pt terminal gráfico *(m)*

terminal gráfico *(m)* Pt
De Zeichenstation *(f)*
En graphics terminal
Es terminal gráfico *(m)*
Fr terminal graphique *(m)*
It terminale grafico *(m)*

terminal graphique *(m)* Fr
De Zeichenstation *(f)*
En graphics terminal
Es terminal gráfico *(m)*
It terminale grafico *(m)*
Pt terminal gráfico *(m)*

terminal inteligente *(m)* Es, Pt
De programmierbare Station *(f)*
En intelligent terminal
Fr terminal intelligent *(m)*
It terminale intelligente *(m)*

terminal intelligent *(m)* Fr
De programmierbare Station *(f)*
En intelligent terminal
Es terminal inteligente *(m)*
It terminale intelligente *(m)*
Pt terminal inteligente *(m)*

terminal interactif *(m)* Fr
De Dialogdatenstation *(f)*
En interactive terminal
Es terminal interactivo *(m)*
It terminale interattivo *(m)*
Pt terminal interactivo *(m)*

terminal interactivo *(m)* Es, Pt
De Dialogdatenstation *(f)*
En interactive terminal
Fr terminal interactif *(m)*
It terminale interattivo *(m)*

terminal video *(m)* Pt
De Videostation *(f)*
En video terminal
Es terminal de video *(m)*
Fr terminal vidéo *(m)*
It terminale video *(m)*

terminal vidéo *(m)* Fr
De Videostation *(f)*
En video terminal
Es terminal de video *(m)*
It terminale video *(m)*
Pt terminal video *(m)*

termination *n* En
De Endstelle *(f)*
Es terminación *(f)*
Fr fin *(f)*
It conclusione *(f)*
Pt terminação *(f)*

Terminwartung *(f) n* De
En scheduled maintenance
Es mantenimiento programado *(m)*
Fr entretien périodique *(m)*
It manutenzione programmata *(f)*
Pt manutenção planificada *(f)*

terza-generazione *adj* It
De drittgeneration
En third-generation
Es tercera-generación
Fr troisième-génération
Pt terceira-geração

test *n* En
De Prüfung *(f)*
Es prueba *(f)*
Fr essai *(m)*
It prova *(f)*
Pt ensaio *(m)*

test *vb* En
De prüfen
Es probar
Fr essayer
It provare
Pt ensaiar

testata *(f) n* It
De Kennsatz *(m)*
En header
Es cabecera *(f)*
Fr en-tête *(f)*
Pt porta-cabeças *(m)*

testbed *n* En
De Prüfstand *(m)*
Es bancada de prueba *(f)*
Fr piste d'entraînement de test *(f)*
It banco di prova *(m)*
Pt mesa de ensaio *(f)*

test data En
De Prüfdaten *(pl)*
Es datos para ensayo *(m pl)*
Fr donnée d'essai *(f)*
It dati di prova *(m pl)*
Pt dados de ensaio *(m pl)*

test de diagnostic *(m)* Fr
De diagnostische Prüfung *(f)*
En diagnostic test
Es prueba de diagnóstico *(f)*
It test diagnostico *(m)*
Pt teste de diagnóstico *(m)*

test de réception en clientèle *(m)* Fr
De Kundenabnahmeprüfung *(f)*
En customer-acceptance test
Es ensayo de aceptación por el cliente *(m)*
It controllo accettazione clienti *(m)*
Pt teste de aceitação de cliente *(m)*

test di accettazione *(m)* It
De Abnahmeprüfung *(f)*
En acceptance test
Es ensayo de aceptación *(m)*
Fr essai de réception *(m)*
Pt teste de aceitação *(m)*

test diagnostico *(m)* It
De diagnostische Prüfung *(f)*
En diagnostic test

Es prueba de diagnóstico *(f)*
Fr test de diagnostic *(m)*
Pt teste de diagnóstico *(m)*

teste de aceitação *(m)* Pt
De Abnahmeprüfung *(f)*
En acceptance test
Es ensayo de aceptación *(m)*
Fr essai de réception *(m)*
It test di accettazione *(m)*

teste de aceitação de cliente *(m)* Pt
De Kundenabnahme-prüfung *(f)*
En customer-acceptance test
Es ensayo de aceptación por el cliente *(m)*
Fr test de réception en clientèle *(m)*
It controllo accettazione clienti *(m)*

teste de diagnóstico *(m)* Pt
De diagnostische Prüfung *(f)*
En diagnostic test
Es prueba de diagnóstico *(f)*
Fr test de diagnostic *(m)*
It test diagnostico *(m)*

teste marginal *(m)* Pt
De Randwertprüfung *(f)*
En marginal test
Es prueba marginal *(f)*
Fr épreuve marginale *(f)*
It test marginale *(m)*

testina *(f) n* It
De Magnetkopf *(m)*
En head
Es cabeza *(f)*
Fr tête *(f)*
Pt cabeça *(f)*

testina del record *(f)* It
De Aufzeichnungskopf *(m)*
En record head
Es cabeza de registro *(f)*
Fr tête d'enregistrement *(f)*
Pt cabeça de registo *(f)*

testina di cancellazione *(f)* It
De Löschkopf *(m)*
En erase head
Es cabeza de borrado *(f)*
Fr tête d'effacement *(f)*
Pt cabeça apagadora *(f)*

testina di lettura *(f)* It
De Wiedergabekopf *(m)*
En playback head
Es cabeza reproductora *(f)*
Fr tête de lecture *(f)*
Pt cabeça de playback *(f)*

testina di lettura *(f)* It
De Lesekopf *(m)*
En read head
Es cabeza de lectura *(f)*
Fr tête de lecture *(f)*
Pt cabeça leitora *(f)*

testina di lettura-scrittura *(f)* It
De Les-Schreibkopf *(m)*
En read-write head
Es cabeza de lectura-escritura *(f)*
Fr tête lecture-écriture *(f)*
Pt cabeça de leitura-escrita *(f)*

testina di pre-lettura *(f)* It
De Vorlesekopf *(m)*
En pre-read head
Es cabeza de lectura previa *(f)*
Fr tête de première lecture *(f)*
Pt cabeça de pré-leitura *(f)*

testina di scrittura *(f)* It
De Schreibkopf *(m)*
En write head
Es cabeza de excritura *(f)*
Fr tête d'écriture *(f)*
Pt cabeça escritora *(f)*

test marginale *(m)* It
De Randwertprüfung *(f)*
En marginal test
Es prueba marginal *(f)*
Fr épreuve marginale *(f)*
Pt teste marginal *(m)*

testo *(m) n* It
De Text *(m)*
En text
Es texto *(m)*
Fr texte *(m)*
Pt texto *(m)*

test program En
De Prüfprogramm *(n)*
Es programa de ensayo *(m)*
Fr programme d'essai *(m)*
It programma di prova *(m)*
Pt programa de ensaios *(m)*

test run En
De Prüfablauf *(m)*
Es pasada de ensayo *(f)*
Fr passage d'essai *(m)*
It esecuzione di prova *(f)*
Pt passagem de ensaio *(f)*

tête *(f) n* Fr
De Magnetkopf *(m)*
En head
Es cabeza *(f)*
It testina *(f)*
Pt cabeça *(f)*

tête d'écriture *(f)* Fr
De Schreibkopf *(m)*
En write head
Es cabeza de excritura *(f)*
It testina di scrittura *(f)*
Pt cabeça escritora *(f)*

tête d'effacement *(f)* Fr
De Löschkopf *(m)*
En erase head
Es cabeza de borrado *(f)*
It testina di cancellazione *(f)*
Pt cabeça apagadora *(f)*

tête de lecture *(f)* Fr
De Wiedergabekopf *(m)*
En playback head
Es cabeza reproductora *(f)*
It testina di lettura *(f)*
Pt cabeça de playback *(f)*

tête de lecture *(f)* Fr
De Lesekopf *(m)*
En read head
Es cabeza de lectura *(f)*
It testina di lettura *(f)*
Pt cabeça leitora *(f)*

tête d'enregistrement *(f)* Fr
De Aufzeichnungskopf *(m)*
En record head
Es cabeza de registro *(f)*
It testina del record *(f)*
Pt cabeça de registo *(f)*

tête de première lecture *(f)* Fr
De Vorlesekopf *(m)*
En pre-read head
Es cabeza de lectura previa *(f)*
It testina di pre-lettura *(f)*
Pt cabeça de pré-leitura *(f)*

tête lecture-écriture *(f)* Fr
De Les-Schreibkopf *(m)*
En read-write head
Es cabeza de lectura-escritura *(f)*
It testina di lettura-scrittura *(f)*
Pt cabeça de leitura-escrita *(f)*

text *n* En
De Text *(m)*
Es texto *(m)*
Fr texte *(m)*
It testo *(m)*
Pt texto *(m)*

Text *(m) n* De
En text
Es texto *(m)*
Fr texte *(m)*
It testo *(m)*
Pt texto *(m)*

texte *(m) n* Fr
De Text *(m)*
En text
Es texto *(m)*
It testo *(m)*
Pt texto *(m)*

text editor En
De Textredakteur *(m)*
Es editor de texto *(m)*
Fr éditeur de textes *(m)*
It programma di manipolazione di testo *(m)*
Pt editor de textos *(m)*

texto *(m) n* Es, Pt
De Text *(m)*
En text
Fr texte *(m)*
It testo *(m)*

Textredakteur *(m) n* De
En text editor
Es editor de texto *(m)*
Fr éditeur de textes *(m)*
It programma di manipolazione di testo *(m)*
Pt editor de textos *(m)*

théorie de contrôle *(f)* Fr
De Steuertheorie *(f)*
En control theory
Es teoría de control *(f)*
It teoria del controllo *(f)*
Pt teoria de controlo *(f)*

théorie de l'information *(f)* Fr
De Informationstheorie *(f)*
En information theory
Es teoría de la información *(f)*
It teoria delle informazioni *(f)*
Pt teoria de informação *(f)*

théorie des files d'attente *(f)* Fr
De Warteschlangentheorie *(f)*
En queuing theory
Es teoría de colas *(f)*
It teoria delle code *(f)*
Pt teoria de colocação em fila *(f)*

thin-film memory En
De Dünnfilmspeicher *(m)*
Es memoria de película delgada *(f)*
Fr mémoire à couche mince *(f)*
It memoria a pellicola sottile *(f)*
Pt memória de película fina *(f)*

third-generation *adj* En
De drittgeneration
Es tercera-generación
Fr troisième-génération
It terza-generazione
Pt terceira-geração

three-address instruction En
De Dreiadressenanweisung *(f)*
Es instrucción con tres direcciones *(f)*
Fr instruction à trois adresses *(f)*
It istruzione a tre indirizzi *(f)*
Pt instrução de três endereços *(f)*

three-input element En
De Dreieingangsdatenelement *(n)*
Es elemento con tres entradas *(m)*
Fr élément à trois entrées *(m)*
It elemento a tre entrati *(m)*
Pt elemento de três entradas *(m)*

threshold element En
De Schwellwertdatenelement *(n)*
Es elemento de umbral *(m)*
Fr élément à seuil *(m)*
It elemento di soglia *(m)*
Pt elemento de limiar *(m)*

throughput *n* En
De Durchfluß *(m)*
Es capacidad de tratamiento *(f)*
Fr débit *(m)*
It capacità di trattamento *(f)*
Pt capacidade de tratamento *(f)*

tiempo compartido *(m)* Es
De Zeitteilung *(f)*
En time sharing
Fr utilisation en temps partagé *(f)*
It lavoro di multiprogrammazione *(m)*
Pt compartido tempo *(m)*

tiempo contable *(m)* Es
De abrechenbare Zeit *(f)*
En accountable time
Fr temps comptable *(m)*
It tempo responsabile *(m)*
Pt tempo justificável *(m)*

tiempo de acceso *(m)* Es
De Zugriffszeit *(f)*
En access time
Fr temps d'accès *(m)*
It tempo di accesso *(m)*
Pt tempo de acesso *(m)*

tiempo de aceleración *(m)* Es
De Beschleunigungszeit *(f)*
En acceleration time
Fr temps d'accélération *(m)*
It tempo di accelerazione *(m)*
Pt tempo de aceleração *(m)*

tiempo de actividades anexas *(m)* Es
De Nebenzeiten *(pl)*
En incidentals time
Fr temps d'activités annexes *(m)*
It tempo di attività eventuale *(m)*
Pt tempo de incidentes *(m)*

tiempo de arranque *(m)* Es
De Start-Zeit *(f)*
En start time
Fr temps de démarrage *(m)*
It tempo di salita in regime *(m)*
Pt tempo de arranque *(m)*

tiempo de arranque-espera *(m)* Es
De Start-Stopp-Zeit *(f)*
En start-stop time
Fr temps de démarrage-arrêt *(m)*
It tempo inizio-arresto *(m)*
Pt tempo de arranque-paragem *(m)*

tiempo de búsqueda *(m)* Es
De Suchzeit *(f)*
En search time
Fr temps de recherche *(m)*
It tempo di ricerca *(m)*
Pt tempo de busca *(m)*

tiempo de deceleración *(m)* Es
De Verzögerungszeit *(f)*
En deceleration time
Fr temps de décélération *(m)*
It tempo di decelerazione *(m)*
Pt tempo de desaceleração *(m)*

tiempo de ejecución *(m)* Es
De Aktivierungszeit *(f)*
En execution time
Fr durée d'exécution *(f)*
It tempo di esecuzione *(m)*
Pt tempo de execução *(m)*

tiempo de ensayo *(m)* Es
De Kontrollzeit *(f)*
En proving time
Fr durée d'essai de fonctionnement *(f)*
It tempo di prova *(m)*
Pt tempo de prova *(m)*

tiempo de escritura *(m)* Es
De Schreibzeit *(f)*
En write time
Fr temps d'écriture *(m)*
It tempo di scrittura *(m)*
Pt tempo de escrita *(m)*

tiempo de espera *(m)* Es
De Wartezeit *(f)*
En waiting time
Fr temps d'attente *(m)*
It tempo di attesa *(m)*
Pt tempo de espera *(m)*

tiempo de inmovilización *(m)* Es
De Zeit für technische Arbeiten *(f)*
En engineering time
Fr temps d'immobilisation *(m)*
It tempo di immobilizzazione *(m)*
Pt tempo de engenharia *(m)*

tiempo de inutilización *(m)* Es
De unbenutzte Zeit *(f)*
En unused time
Fr temps d'inutilisation *(m)*
It tempo inutilizzato *(m)*
Pt tempo não utilizado *(m)*

tiempo de lectura *(m)* Es
De Auslesezeit *(f)*
En read time
Fr durée de lecture *(f)*
It tempo di lettura *(m)*
Pt tempo de leitura *(m)*

tiempo de pana *(m)* Es
De Ausfallzeit *(f)*
En downtime
Fr temps de panne *(m)*
It tempo di panna *(m)*
Pt tempo de paragem *(m)*

tiempo de pasada *(m)* Es
De Durchlaufzeit *(f)*
En run time
Fr temps d'exécution *(m)*
It tempo di esecuzione *(m)*
Pt tempo de passagem *(m)*

tiempo de preparación *(m)* Es
De Einrichtezeit *(f)*
En set-up time
Fr temps de préparation *(m)*
It tempo messa a punto *(m)*
Pt tempo de instalação *(m)*

tiempo de reparación *(m)* Es
De Reparaturzeit *(f)*
En repair time
Fr temps de réparation *(m)*
It tempo di riparazione *(m)*
Pt tempo de reparação *(m)*

tiempo de respuesta *(m)* Es
De Ansprechzeit *(f)*
En response time
Fr temps de réponse *(m)*
It tempo di risposta *(m)*
Pt tempo de resposta *(m)*

tiempo de suma-resta *(m)* Es
De Addier-Subtrahierzeit *(f)*
En add-subtract time
Fr temps d'addition-soustraction *(m)*
It tempo di addizione-sottrazione *(m)*
Pt tempo de soma-subtracção *(m)*

tiempo de una instrucción *(m)* Es
De Befehlszeit *(f)*
En instruction time
Fr temps d'exécution d'une instruction *(m)*
It tempo per l'istruzione *(m)*
Pt tempo de instruções *(m)*

tiempo disponible *(m)* Es
De verfügbare Zeit *(f)*
En available time
Fr temps disponible *(m)*
It tempo disponibile *(m)*
Pt tempo disponível *(m)*

tiempo do producción *(m)* Es
De Fertigungszeit *(f)*
En productive time
Fr temps productif *(m)*
It tempo produttivo *(m)*
Pt tempo produtivo *(m)*

tiempo efectivo *(m)* Es
De effektive Zeit *(f)*
En effective time
Fr temps utile *(m)*
It tempo efficace *(m)*
Pt tempo efectivo *(m)*

tiempo ineficaz *(m)* Es
De unwirksame Zeit *(f)*
En ineffective time
Fr temps ineffectif *(m)*
It tempo inefficace *(m)*
Pt tempo irreal *(m)*

tiempo medio entre fallos *(m)* Es
De Effektivzeit zwischen Ausfällen *(f)*
En mean time between failures
Fr moyenne des temps de bon fonctionnement *(f)*
It tempo medio tra i guasti *(m)*
Pt tempo médio entre falhas *(m)*

tiempo medio para reparación *(m)* Es
De effektive Reparaturzeit *(f)*
En mean repair time
Fr temps moyen de réparation *(m)*
It tempo di riparazione medio *(m)*
Pt tempo médio de reparação *(m)*

tiempo muerto *(m)* Es
De Totzeit *(f)*
En dead time
Fr temps mort *(m)*
It tempo morto *(m)*
Pt tempo morto *(m)*

tiempo pasivo *(m)* Es
De Leerlaufzeit *(f)*
En idle time
Fr temps en chômage *(m)*
It tempo passivo *(m)*
Pt tempo de functionamento em vazio *(m)*

tiempo productivo *(m)* Es
De Benutzerzeit *(f)*
En uptime
Fr temps de bon fonctionnement *(m)*
It tempo di utilizzazione *(m)*
Pt tempo terminado *(m)*

tiempo real *(m)* Es
De Echtzeit *(f)*
En real time
Fr temps réel *(m)*
It tempo reale *(m)*
Pt tempo real *(m)*

tiempo sin personal *(m)* Es
De Ruhezeit *(f)*
En unattended time
Fr temps de fonctionnement sans surveillance *(m)*
It tempo uncustodita *(m)*
Pt tempo de abandono *(m)*

tiempo transcurrido *(m)* Es
De verstrichene Zeit *(f)*
En elapsed time
Fr temps écoulé *(m)*
It tempo trascorso *(m)*
Pt tempo decorrido *(m)*

tightly coupled En
De eng gekoppelt
Es fuertemente acoplado
Fr à couplage serré
It accoppiado fortemente
Pt firmemente acoplado

timer (or **timer clock**) *n* En
De Zeituhr *(f)*
Es temporizador *(m)*
Fr rythmeur *(m)*
It temporizzatore *(m)*
Pt relógio marcador de tempos *(m)*

time scale En
De Zeitskala *(f)*
Es escala de tiempos *(f)*
Fr échelle des temps *(f)*
It scala di tempo *(f)*
Pt escala de tempo *(f)*

time sharing En
De Zeitteilung *(f)*
Es tiempo compartido *(m)*
Fr utilisation en temps partagé *(f)*
It lavoro di multi-programmazione *(m)*
Pt compartido tempo *(m)*

time slice En
De Zeitscheiben-verfahren *(n)*
Es fracción de tiempo *(f)*
Fr découpage du temps *(m)*
It ripartizione di tempo *(f)*
Pt fatia de tempo *(f)*

tinta magnética *(f)* Es, Pt
De Magnettinte *(f)*
En magnetic ink
Fr encre magnétique *(f)*
It inchiostro magnetico *(m)*

Tischrechner *(m) n* De
En desk-top computer
Es ordenador de mesa *(m)*
Fr petit ordinateur de bureau *(m)*
It elaboratore da tavolo *(m)*
Pt computador de mesa *(m)*

tolerante con las averías Es
De defekttolerant
En fault-tolerant
Fr insensible aux défaillances
It tollerante di guasto
Pt tolerante relativamente a erros

tolerante relativamente a erros Pt
De defekttolerant
En fault-tolerant
Es tolerante con las averías
Fr insensible aux défaillances
It tollerante di guasto

tollerante di guasto It
De defekttolerant
En fault-tolerant
Es tolerante con las averías
Fr insensible aux défaillances
Pt tolerante relativamente a erros

tomber en panne Fr
De abgehen
En go down
Es tener una avería
It avere una panna
Pt avariar

Tor *(n) n* De
En gate
Es puerta *(f)*
Fr porte *(f)*
It porta *(f)*
Pt porta *(f)*

tore de ferrite *(f)* Fr
De Ferritkern *(m)*
En ferrite core
Es núcleo de ferria *(m)*
It memoria di ferrite *(f)*
Pt núcleo de ferrite *(m)*

tore magnétique *(m)* Fr
De Magnetkern *(m)*
En magnetic core
Es núcleo magnético *(m)*
It nucleo magnetico *(m)*
Pt núcleo magnético *(m)*

tornar a acertar Pt
De rückstellen
En reset
Es restaurar
Fr mettre à zéro
It riazzerare

tornar a enrolar Pt
De wiederaufwickeln
En rewind
Es rebobinar
Fr rebobiner
It riavvolgere

tornar a escrever Pt
De wiederschreiben
En rewrite
Es reescribir
Fr récrire
It riscrivere

tornar a passar Pt
De wiederholen
En rerun
Es repetir la pasada
Fr réexécuter
It riprendere

tornare indietro It
De rückwärtsschreiten
En backspace
Es retroceder
Fr rappeler le chariot
Pt retroceder

total de control *(m)* Es
De Kontrollsumme *(f)*
En control total; proof total
Fr total de contrôle *(m)*
It totale di controllo *(m)*
Pt total de controlo *(m)*

total de contrôle *(m)* Fr
De Kontrollsumme *(f)*
En control total; proof total
Es total de control *(m)*
It totale di controllo *(m)*
Pt total de controlo *(m)*

total de controlo *(m)* Pt
De Kontrollsumme *(f)*
En control total; proof total
Es total de control *(m)*
Fr total de contrôle *(m)*
It totale di controllo *(m)*

totale di controllo *(m)* It
De Kontrollsumme *(f)*
En control total; proof total
Es total de control *(m)*
Fr total de contrôle *(m)*
Pt total de controlo *(m)*

Totzeit *(f) n* De
En dead time
Es tiempo muerto *(m)*
Fr temps mort *(m)*
It tempo morto *(m)*
Pt tempo morto *(m)*

touche *(f) n* Fr
De Schlüssel *(m)*
En key
Es tecla *(f)*
It tasto *(m)*
Pt tecla *(f)*

touche de fonction *(f)* Fr
De Funktionsschlüssel *(m)*
En function key
Es tecla de función *(f)*
It tasto di funzione *(m)*
Pt tecla de funções *(f)*

trabajo *(m) n* Es
De Job *(m)*
En job
Fr travail *(m)*
It lavoro *(m)*
Pt trabalho *(m)*

trabajo por lotes *(m)* Es
De Stapelarbeit *(f)*
En batch job
Fr travail en traitement par lots *(m)*
It lavoro a lotti *(m)*
Pt trabalho por lotes *(m)*

trabalho *(m) n* Pt
De Job *(m)*
En job
Es trabajo *(m)*
Fr travail *(m)*
It lavoro *(m)*

trabalho por lotes *(m)* Pt
De Stapelarbeit *(f)*
En batch job
Es trabajo por lotes *(m)*
Fr travail en traitement par lots *(m)*
It lavoro a lotti *(m)*

traccia *(f) n* It
De Aufzeichnungslinie *(f)*
En trace
Es traza *(f)*
Fr trace *(f)*
Pt decalque *(m)*

tracciatore *(m) n* It
De Planzeichner *(m)*
En plotter
Es trazadora *(f)*
Fr traceur *(m)*
Pt plotador *(m)*

tracciatore a tamburo *(m)* It
De Trommelkurven-zeichner *(m)*
En drum plotter
Es trazador a tambor *(m)*
Fr traceur à tambour *(m)*
Pt plotador de tambor *(m)*

tracciatore di grafici *(m)* It
De Kurvenzeichner *(m)*
En graph plotter
Es trazador de curvas *(m)*
Fr traceur de courbes *(m)*

Pt plotador de gráficos *(m)*

tracciatore incrementale *(m)* It
De schrittweiser Kurvenzeichner *(m)*
En incremental plotter
Es trazador incremental *(m)*
Fr traceur incrémentiel *(m)*
Pt plotador incremental *(m)*

tracciatore in piano *(m)* It
De Flachtischkurven-zeichner *(m)*
En flat-bed plotter
Es trazador de base plana *(m)*
Fr traceur à plat *(m)*
Pt plotador de leito plano *(m)*

tracciatore X-Y *(m)* It
De X-Y-Kurvenzeichner *(m)*
En X-Y plotter
Es trazador X-Y *(m)*
Fr traceur X-Y *(m)*
Pt plotador X-Y *(m)*

trace *n* En; Fr *(f)*
De Aufzeichnungslinie *(f)*
Es traza *(f)*
It traccia *(f)*
Pt decalque *(m)*

traceur *(m) n* Fr
De Planzeichner *(m)*
En plotter
Es trazadora *(f)*
It tracciatore *(m)*
Pt plotador *(m)*

traceur à plat *(m)* Fr
De Flachtischkurven-zeichner *(m)*
En flat-bed plotter
Es trazador de base plana *(m)*
It tracciatore in piano *(m)*
Pt plotador de leito plano *(m)*

traceur à tambour *(m)* Fr
De Trommelkurven-zeichner *(m)*
En drum plotter
Es trazador a tambor *(m)*
It tracciatore a tamburo *(m)*
Pt plotador de tambor *(m)*

traceur de courbes *(m)* Fr
De Kurvenzeichner *(m)*
En graph plotter
Es trazador de curvas *(m)*
It tracciatore di grafici *(m)*
Pt plotador de gráficos *(m)*

traceur incrémentiel *(m)* Fr
De schrittweiser Kurvenzeichner *(m)*
En incremental plotter
Es trazador incremental *(m)*
It tracciatore incrementale *(m)*
Pt plotador incremental *(m)*

traceur X-Y *(m)* Fr
De X-Y-Kurvenzeichner *(m)*
En X-Y plotter
Es trazador X-Y *(m)*
It tracciatore X-Y *(m)*
Pt plotador X-Y *(m)*

track *n* En
De Spur *(f)*
Es pista *(f)*
Fr piste *(f)*
It banda *(f)*
Pt pista *(f)*

track label En
De Spurkennzeichen *(n)*
Es etiqueta de pista *(f)*
Fr label piste *(m)*
It etichetta di pista *(f)*
Pt rótulo de pista *(m)*

tractor de arrastre del papel *(m)* Es
De Formulartraktor *(m)*
En forms tractor
Fr entraîneur de papier *(m)*
It trattore di moduli *(m)*
Pt tractor de formulários *(m)*

tractor de formulários *(m)* Pt
De Formulartraktor *(m)*
En forms tractor
Es tractor de arrastre del papel *(m)*
Fr entraîneur de papier *(m)*
It trattore di moduli *(m)*

traducir *vb* Es
De übersetzen
En translate
Fr traduire
It tradurre
Pt traduzir

traducteur *(m) n* Fr
De Übersetzer *(m)*
En translator
Es traductor *(m)*
It traduttore *(m)*
Pt tradutor *(m)*

traductor *(m) n* Es
De Übersetzer *(m)*
En translator
Fr traducteur *(m)*
It traduttore *(m)*
Pt tradutor *(m)*

traductrice *(f) n* Fr
De Lochschrift-übersetzer *(m)*
En interpreter
Es interpretadora *(f)*
It interprete *(m)*
Pt intérprete *(m)*

traduire *vb* Fr
De übersetzen
En translate
Es traducir
It tradurre
Pt traduzir

tradurre *vb* It
De übersetzen
En translate
Es traducir
Fr traduire
Pt traduzir

tradutor *(m) n* Pt
De Übersetzer *(m)*
En translator
Es traductor *(m)*
Fr traducteur *(m)*
It traduttore *(m)*

traduttore *(m) n* It
De Übersetzer *(m)*
En translator
Es traductor *(m)*
Fr traducteur *(m)*
Pt tradutor *(m)*

traduzir *vb* Pt
De übersetzen
En translate
Es traducir
Fr traduire
It tradurre

tragbarer Computer *(m)* De
En portable computer
Es ordenador portátil *(m)*
Fr ordinateur portatif *(m)*
It calcolatore portabile *(m)*
Pt computador portátil *(m)*

trailer label En
De Beisatzkennzeichen *(n)*
Es etiqueta de cola *(f)*
Fr label fin *(m)*
It etichetta di fine *(f)*
Pt rótulo de trailer *(m)*

trailer record En
De Beisatz *(m)*
Es registro de cola *(m)*
Fr article fin *(m)*
It record di fine *(m)*
Pt registo de trailer *(m)*

train d'impulsions *(m)* Fr
De Impulsfolge *(f)*
En pulse train
Es tren de impulsos *(m)*
It treno d'impulsi *(m)*
Pt trem de impulsos *(m)*

train printer En
De Gliederdrucker *(m)*
Es impresora de cadena *(f)*
Fr imprimante à train de caractères *(f)*
It stampatrice a treno di caratteri *(f)*
Pt impressora de trem *(f)*

traitement *(m)* *n* Fr
De Verarbeitung *(f)*
En processing
Es tratamiento *(m)*
It elaborazione *(f)*
Pt processamento *(m)*

traitement à accès multiple (TAM) *(m)* Fr
De Mehrfachzugriffsrechnen *(n)*
En multi-access computing (MAC)
Es cálculo de acceso múltiple *(m)*
It calcolo ad accesso multiplo *(m)*
Pt computação de multi-acesso *(f)*

traitement automatique de l'information (TAI) *(m)* Fr
De automatische Datenverarbeitung *(f)*
En automatic data processing
Es proceso automático de datos *(m)*
It elaborazione automatica dei dati *(f)*
Pt tratamento automático de dados *(m)*

traitement de front *(m)* Fr
De Vordergrundverarbeitung *(f)*
En foreground processing
Es proceso preferente *(m)*
It elaborazione di primo piano *(f)*
Pt processamento de primeiro plano *(m)*

traitement de l'information *(m)* Fr
De Datenverarbeitung *(f)*
En data processing (DP)
Es proceso de datos *(m)*
It elaborazione dei dati *(f)*
Pt tratamento de dados *(m)*

traitement de liste *(m)* Fr
De Listenverarbeitung *(f)*
En list processing
Es proceso por lista *(m)*
It elaborazione della lista *(f)*
Pt processamento de lista *(m)*

traitement des données *(m)* Fr
De Datenverarbeitung *(f)*
En data processing
Es proceso de datos *(m)*
It elaborazione dei dati *(f)*
Pt tratamento de dados *(m)*

traitement domestique *(m)* Fr
De Lokalrechnung *(f)*
En home computing
Es cálculo inicial *(m)*
It elaborazione in proprio *(f)*
Pt computação doméstica *(f)*

traitement électronique des données (TED) *(m)* Fr
De elektronische Datenverarbeitung (EDV) *(f)*
En electronic data processing (EDP)
Es proceso electrónico de datos *(m)*
It elaborazione elettronica dei dati *(f)*
Pt tratamento electrónico de dados *(m)*

traitement en parallèle *(m)* Fr
De Parallelsimultanverarbeitung *(f)*
En parallel processing
Es proceso en paralelo *(m)*
It elaborazione parallela *(f)*
Pt processamento paralelo *(m)*

traitement en simultané *(m)* Fr
De verzahnt ablaufende Verarbeitung *(f)*
En concurrent processing
Es proceso concurrente *(m)*
It elaborazione concorrente *(f)*
Pt processamento concorrente *(m)*

traitement en temps réel *(m)* Fr
De Uhrzeigverarbeitung *(f)*
En real-time processing
Es proceso en tiempo real *(m)*
It elaborazione in tempo reale *(f)*
Pt processamento de tempo real *(m)*

traitement immédiat *(m)* Fr
De Abrufverarbeitung *(f)*
En demand processing
Es tratamiento inmediato *(m)*
It elaborazione a domanda *(f)*
Pt processamento de procura *(m)*

traitement intégré de l'information (TII) *(m)* Fr
De integrierte Datenverarbeitung *(f)*
En integrated data processing (IDP)
Es proceso integrado de datos *(m)*
It elaborazione integrata dei dati *(f)*
Pt tratamento integrado de dados *(m)*

traitement interactif *(m)* Fr
De Dialogbetrieb *(m)*
En interactive computing
Es cálculo interactivo *(m)*
It calcoli interattivi *(m)*
Pt computação interactiva *(f)*

traitement non prioritaire *(m)* Fr
De Hintergrundverarbeitung *(f)*
En background processing
Es proceso de programas subordinados *(m)*
It elaborazione non precedenza *(f)*
Pt tratamento de plano de fundo *(m)*

traitement par lot *(m)* Fr
De Stapelverarbeitung *(f)*
En batch processing
Es proceso por lotes *(m)*
It elaborazione a lotti *(f)*
Pt tratamento por lotes *(m)*

traitement par priorités *(m)* Fr
De Vorrangverarbeitung *(f)*
En priority processing
Es tratamiento por prioridad *(m)*
It elaborazione di priorità *(f)*
Pt processamento prioritário *(m)*

traitement séquentiel *(m)* Fr
De Folgeverarbeitung *(f)*
En sequential processing
Es proceso secuencial *(m)*
It elaborazione sequenziale *(f)*
Pt processamento sequencial *(m)*

traitement série *(m)* Fr
De Reihenverarbeitung *(f)*
En serial processing
Es proceso en serie *(m)*
It elaborazione in serie *(f)*
Pt processamento em série *(m)*

traitement transactionnel *(m)* Fr
De Transaktionsverarbeitung *(f)*
En transaction processing
Es proceso de transacciones *(m)*

It elaborazione delle transazioni *(f)*
Pt processamento de transacções *(m)*

traitement vectoriel *(m)* Fr
De Vektorverarbeitung *(f)*
En vector processing
Es proceso vectorial *(m)*
It elaborazione di vettori *(f)*
Pt processamento de vectores *(m)*

traiter *vb* Fr
De bearbeiten
En process
Es procesar
It elaborare
Pt processar

trampa *(f) n* Es
De Haftstelle *(f)*
En trap
Fr piège *(m)*
It trappola *(f)*
Pt armadilha *(f)*

transacção *(f) n* Pt
De Vorgang *(m)*
En transaction
Es transacción *(f)*
Fr transaction *(f)*
It transazione *(f)*

transacción *(f) n* Es
De Vorgang *(m)*
En transaction
Fr transaction *(f)*
It transazione *(f)*
Pt transacção *(f)*

transaction *n* En; Fr *(f)*
De Vorgang *(m)*
Es transacción *(f)*
It transazione *(f)*
Pt transacção *(f)*

transaction data En
De Transaktionsdaten *(pl)*
Es datos de transacciones *(m pl)*
Fr mouvements *(m pl)*
It dati della transazione *(m pl)*
Pt dados de transacção *(m pl)*

transaction processing En
De Transaktions-verarbeitung *(f)*
Es proceso de transacciones *(m)*
Fr traitement transactionnel *(m)*
It elaborazione delle transazioni *(f)*
Pt processamento de transacções *(m)*

Transaktionsdaten *(pl) n* De
En transaction data
Es datos de transacciones *(m pl)*
Fr mouvements *(m pl)*
It dati della transazione *(m pl)*
Pt dados de transacção *(m pl)*

Transaktions-verarbeitung *(f) n* De
En transaction processing
Es proceso de transacciones *(m)*
Fr traitement transactionnel *(m)*
It elaborazione delle transazioni *(f)*
Pt processamento de transacções *(m)*

transazione *(f) n* It
De Vorgang *(m)*
En transaction
Es transacción *(f)*
Fr transaction *(f)*
Pt transacção *(f)*

transceiver *n* En
De Senderempfänger *(m)*
Es transceptor *(m)*
Fr émetteur-récepteur *(m)*
It ricetrasmettitore *(m)*
Pt transreceptor *(m)*

transceptor *(m) n* Es
De Senderempfänger *(m)*
En transceiver
Fr émetteur-récepteur *(m)*
It ricetrasmettitore *(m)*
Pt transreceptor *(m)*

transcrever *vb* Pt
De abschreiben
En transcribe
Es transcribir
Fr transcrire
It trascrivere

transcribe *vb* En
De abschreiben
Es transcribir
Fr transcrire
It trascrivere
Pt transcrever

transcribir *vb* Es
De abschreiben
En transcribe
Fr transcrire
It trascrivere
Pt transcrever

transcrire *vb* Fr
De abschreiben
En transcribe
Es transcribir
It trascrivere
Pt transcrever

transfer *n* En
De Übergabe *(f)*
Es transferencia *(f)*
Fr transfert *(m)*
It trasferimento *(m)*
Pt transferência *(f)*

transfer *vb* En
De übergeben
Es transferir
Fr transférer
It trasferire
Pt transferir

transfer check En
De Übertragungs-prüfung *(f)*
Es verificación de transferencia *(f)*
Fr contrôle par répétition *(m)*
It controllo di trasferimento *(m)*
Pt verificação de transferência *(f)*

transferencia *(f) n* Es
De Übergabe *(f)*
En transfer
Fr transfert *(m)*
It trasferimento *(m)*
Pt transferência *(f)*

transferência *(f) n* Pt
De Übergabe *(f)*
En transfer
Es transferencia *(f)*
Fr transfert *(m)*
It trasferimento *(m)*

transferencia condicional *(f)* Es
De bedingte Übergabe *(f)*
En conditional transfer
Fr transfert conditionnel *(m)*
It trasferimento condizionale *(m)*
Pt transferência condicional *(f)*

transferência condicional *(f)* Pt
De bedingte Übergabe *(f)*
En conditional transfer
Es transferencia condicional *(f)*
Fr transfert conditionnel *(m)*
It trasferimento condizionale *(m)*

transferência de bloco *(f)* Pt
De Blockübergabe *(f)*
En block transfer
Es transferencia del bloque *(f)*
Fr transfert par blocs *(m)*
It trasferimento di blocco *(m)*

transferencia de control *(f)* Es
De Steuerübertragung *(f)*
En control transfer; transfer of control
Fr transfert de contrôle *(m)*
It trasferimento di controllo *(m)*
Pt transferência de controlo *(f)*

transferência de controlo *(f)* Pt
De Steuerübertragung *(f)*
En control transfer; transfer of control
Es transferencia de control *(f)*

Fr transfert de contrôle *(m)*
It trasferimento di controllo *(m)*

transferencia del bloque *(f)* Es
De Blockübergabe *(f)*
En block transfer
Fr transfert par blocs *(m)*
It trasferimento di blocco *(m)*
Pt transferência de bloco *(f)*

transferencia de página *(f)* Es
De Seitenwechsel *(m)*
En page turning
Fr changement de page *(m)*
It trasferimento di pagina *(m)*
Pt mudança de páginas *(f)*

transferência em série *(f)* Pt
De Reihenübergabe *(f)*
En serial transfer
Es transferencia en serie *(f)*
Fr transfert en série *(m)*
It trasferimento in serie *(m)*

transferencia en paralelo *(f)* Es
De Parallelübergabe *(f)*
En parallel transfer
Fr transfert en parallèle *(m)*
It trasferimento parallelo *(m)*
Pt transferência paralela *(f)*

transferencia en serie *(f)* Es
De Reihenübergabe *(f)*
En serial transfer
Fr transfert en série *(m)*
It trasferimento in serie *(m)*
Pt transferência em série *(f)*

transferencia incondicional *(f)* Es
De unbedingte Übergabe *(f)*
En unconditional transfer
Fr transfert inconditionnel *(m)*
It trasferimento non condizionale *(m)*
Pt transferência incondicional *(f)*

transferência incondicional *(f)* Pt
De unbedingte Übergabe *(f)*
En unconditional transfer
Es transferencia incondicional *(f)*
Fr transfert inconditionnel *(m)*
It trasferimento non condizionale *(m)*

transferência paralela *(f)* Pt
De Parallelübergabe *(f)*
En parallel transfer
Es transferencia en paralelo *(f)*
Fr transfert en parallèle *(m)*
It trasferimento parallelo *(m)*

transferencia periférica *(f)* Es
De periphere Übergabe *(f)*
En peripheral transfer
Fr transfert entre périphériques *(m)*
It trasferimento periferico *(m)*
Pt transferência periférica *(f)*

transferência periférica *(f)* Pt
De periphere Übergabe *(f)*
En peripheral transfer
Es transferencia periférica *(f)*
Fr transfert entre périphériques *(m)*
It trasferimento periferico *(m)*

transférer *vb* Fr
De übergeben
En transfer
Es transferir
It trasferire
Pt transferir

transfer function En
De Übertragungsfunktion *(f)*
Es función de transferencia *(f)*
Fr fonction de transfert *(f)*
It funzione di trasferimento *(f)*
Pt função de transferência *(f)*

transfer instruction En
De Übertragungsanweisung *(f)*
Es instrucción de transferencia *(f)*
Fr instruction de branchement *(f)*
It istruzione di trasferimento *(f)*
Pt instrução de transferência *(f)*

transferir *vb* Es, Pt
De übergeben
En transfer
Fr transférer
It trasferire

transfer of control (or **control transfer**) En
De Steuerübertragung *(f)*
Es transferencia de control *(f)*
Fr transfert de contrôle *(m)*
It trasferimento di controllo *(m)*
Pt transferência de controlo *(f)*

transfer rate En
De Übertragungsfrequenz *(f)*
Es indice de transferencia *(m)*
Fr vitesse de transfert *(f)*
It volume di trasferimento *(m)*
Pt índice de transferência *(m)*

transfert *(m) n* Fr
De Übergabe *(f)*
En transfer
Es transferencia *(f)*
It trasferimento *(m)*
Pt transferência *(f)*

transfert conditionnel *(m)* Fr
De bedingte Übergabe *(f)*
En conditional transfer
Es transferencia condicional *(f)*
It trasferimento condizionale *(m)*
Pt transferência condicional *(f)*

transfert de contrôle *(m)* Fr
De Steuerübertragung *(f)*
En control transfer; transfer of control
Es transferencia de control *(f)*
It trasferimento di controllo *(m)*
Pt transferência de controlo *(f)*

transfert en parallèle *(m)* Fr
De Parallelübergabe *(f)*
En parallel transfer
Es transferencia en paralelo *(f)*
It trasferimento parallelo *(m)*
Pt transferência paralela *(f)*

transfert en série *(m)* Fr
De Reihenübergabe *(f)*
En serial transfer
Es transferencia en serie *(f)*
It trasferimento in serie *(m)*
Pt transferência em série *(f)*

transfert entre périphériques *(m)* Fr
De periphere Übergabe *(f)*
En peripheral transfer
Es transferencia periférica *(f)*
It trasferimento periferico *(m)*
Pt transferência periférica *(f)*

transfert inconditionnel *(m)* Fr
De unbedingte Übergabe *(f)*

En unconditional transfer
Es transferencia incondicional *(f)*
It trasferimento non condizionale *(m)*
Pt transferência incondicional *(f)*

transfert par blocs *(m)* Fr
De Blockübergabe *(f)*
En block transfer
Es transferencia del bloque *(f)*
It trasferimento di blocco *(m)*
Pt transferência de bloco *(f)*

transform *vb* En
De umformen
Es transformar
Fr transformer
It trasformare
Pt transformar

transformar *vb* Es
De umformen
En transform
Fr transformer
It trasformare
Pt transformar

transformar *vb* Pt
De umformen
En transform
Es transformar
Fr transformer
It trasformare

transformer *vb* Fr
De umformen
En transform
Es transformar
It trasformare
Pt transformar

transição *(f) n* Pt
De Übergang *(m)*
En transition
Es transicion *(f)*
Fr transition *(f)*
It transizione *(f)*

transicion *(f) n* Es
De Übergang *(m)*
En transition
Fr transition *(f)*
It transizione *(f)*
Pt transição *(f)*

transient *adj* En
De flüchtig
Es transitorio
Fr transitoire
It transitorio
Pt transitório

transistor *n* En; Es, Fr, Pt *(m)*
De Transistor *(m)*
It transistore *(m)*

Transistor *(m) n* De
En transistor
Es transistor *(m)*
Fr transistor *(m)*
It transistore *(m)*
Pt transistor *(m)*

transistor à effet de champ à oxydes métalliques *(m)* Fr
De Metalloxyd-halbleiter- Feldeffekt-transistor *(m)*
En MOS field-effect transistor (MOSFET)
Es transistor MOS de efecto de campo *(m)*
It transistore ad effetto di campo MOS *(m)*
Pt transistor de efeito de campo MOS *(m)*

transistor à effet de champ (TEC) *(m)* Fr
De Feldeffekttransistor *(m)*
En field-effect transistor (FET)
Es transistor de efecto de campo *(m)*
It transistore ad effetto di campo *(m)*
Pt transistor de efeito de campo *(m)*

transistor de efecto de campo *(m)* Es
De Feldeffekttransistor *(m)*
En field-effect transistor (FET)
Fr transistor à effet de champ (TEC) *(m)*
It transistore ad effetto di campo *(m)*
Pt transistor de efeito de campo *(m)*

transistor de efeito de campo *(m)* Pt
De Feldeffekttransistor *(m)*
En field-effect transistor (FET)
Es transistor de efecto de campo *(m)*
Fr transistor à effet de champ (TEC) *(m)*
It transistore ad effetto di campo *(m)*

transistor de efeito de campo MOS *(m)* Pt
De Metalloxyd-halbleiter- Feldeffekt-transistor *(m)*
En MOS field-effect transistor (MOSFET)
Es transistor MOS de efecto de campo *(m)*
Fr transistor à effet de champ à oxydes métalliques *(m)*
It transistore ad effetto di campo MOS *(m)*

transistore *(m) n* It
De Transistor *(m)*
En transistor
Es transistor *(m)*
Fr transistor *(m)*
Pt transistor *(m)*

transistore ad effetto di campo *(m)* It
De Feldeffekttransistor *(m)*
En field-effect transistor (FET)
Es transistor de efecto de campo *(m)*
Fr transistor à effet de champ (TEC) *(m)*
Pt transistor de efeito de campo *(m)*

transistore ad effetto di campo MOS *(m)* It
De Metalloxyd-halbleiter- Feldeffekt-transistor *(m)*
En MOS field-effect transistor (MOSFET)
Es transistor MOS de efecto de campo *(m)*
Fr transistor à effet de champ à oxydes métalliques *(m)*
Pt transistor de efeito de campo MOS *(m)*

transistor MOS de efecto de campo *(m)* Es
De Metalloxyd-halbleiter- Feldeffekt-transistor *(m)*
En MOS field-effect transistor (MOSFET)
Fr transistor à effet de champ à oxydes métalliques *(m)*
It transistore ad effetto di campo MOS *(m)*
Pt transistor de efeito de campo MOS *(m)*

transistor-transistor logic (TTL) En
De Transistor-Transistor-Verknüpfung *(f)*
Es lógica de transistor-transistor *(f)*
Fr logique transistor-transistor *(f)*
It logica transistore-transistore *(f)*
Pt lógica transistor-transistor *(f)*

Transistor-Transistor-Verknüpfung *(f)* De
En transistor-transistor logic (TTL)
Es lógica de transistor-transistor *(f)*
Fr logique transistor-transistor *(f)*
It logica transistore-transistore *(f)*
Pt lógica transistor-transistor *(f)*

transition *n* En; Fr *(f)*
De Übergang *(m)*
Es transicion *(f)*
It transizione *(f)*
Pt transição *(f)*

transitoire *adj* Fr
De flüchtig
En transient
Es transitorio

It transitorio
Pt transitório

transitorio *adj* Es, It
De flüchtig
En transient
Fr transitoire
Pt transitório

transitório *adj* Pt
De flüchtig
En transient
Es transitorio
Fr transitoire
It transitorio

transizione *(f) n* It
De Übergang *(m)*
En transition
Es transicion *(f)*
Fr transition *(f)*
Pt transição *(f)*

translate *vb* En
De übersetzen
Es traducir
Fr traduire
It tradurre
Pt traduzir

translater Fr
De verschieben
En relocate
Es reubicar
It rilocare
Pt relocalizar

translator *n* En
De Übersetzer *(m)*
Es traductor *(m)*
Fr traducteur *(m)*
It traduttore *(m)*
Pt tradutor *(m)*

transliterar *vb* Es, Pt
De wortwörtlich übersetzen
En transliterate
Fr translitérer
It traslitterare

transliterate *vb* En
De wortwörtlich übersetzen
Es transliterar
Fr translitérer
It traslitterare
Pt transliterar

translitérer *vb* Fr
De wortwörtlich übersetzen
En transliterate
Es transliterar
It traslitterare
Pt transliterar

transmettre *vb* Fr
De übertragen
En transmit
Es transmitir
It trasmettere
Pt transmitir

transmisión *(f) n* Es
De Übertragung *(f)*
En transmission
Fr transmission *(f)*
It trasmissione *(f)*
Pt transmissão *(f)*

transmisión de datos *(f)* Es
De Datenübertragung *(f)*
En data transmission
Fr transmission de données *(f)*
It trasmissione dei dati *(f)*
Pt transmissão de dados *(f)*

transmisión digital *(f)* Es
De digitale Übertragung *(f)*
En digital transmission
Fr transmission numérique *(f)*
It trasmissione digitale *(f)*
Pt transmissão digital *(f)*

transmisión en banda ancha *(f)* Es
De Breitband-übertragung *(f)*
En broadband transmission
Fr transmission bande large *(f)*
It trasmissione a banda larga *(f)*
Pt transmissão de banda larga *(f)*

transmissão *(f) n* Pt
De Übertragung *(f)*
En transmission
Es transmisión *(f)*
Fr transmission *(f)*
It trasmissione *(f)*

transmissão de banda larga *(f)* Pt
De Breitband-übertragung *(f)*
En broadband transmission
Es transmisión en banda ancha *(f)*
Fr transmission bande large *(f)*
It trasmissione a banda larga *(f)*

transmissão de dados *(f)* Pt
De Datenübertragung *(f)*
En data transmission
Es transmisión de datos *(f)*
Fr transmission de données *(f)*
It trasmissione dei dati *(f)*

transmissão digital *(f)* Pt
De digitale Übertragung *(f)*
En digital transmission
Es transmisión digital *(f)*
Fr transmission numérique *(f)*
It trasmissione digitale *(f)*

transmission *n* En; Fr *(f)*
De Übertragung *(f)*
Es transmisión *(f)*
It trasmissione *(f)*
Pt transmissão *(f)*

transmission asynchrone *(f)* Fr
De Start-Stopp-Steuerung *(f)*
En asynchronous communication
Es comunicación asíncrona *(f)*
It comunicazione asincrona *(f)*
Pt comunicação assíncrona *(f)*

transmission bande large *(f)* Fr
De Breitband-übertragung *(f)*
En broadband transmission
Es transmisión en banda ancha *(f)*
It trasmissione a banda larga *(f)*
Pt transmissão de banda larga *(f)*

transmission de données *(f)* Fr
De Datenübertragung *(f)*
En data transmission
Es transmisión de datos *(f)*
It trasmissione dei dati *(f)*
Pt transmissão de dados *(f)*

transmission interface En
De Übertragungs-schnittstelle *(f)*
Es interfase de transmisión *(f)*
Fr interface de transmission *(f)*
It interfaccia di trasmissione *(f)*
Pt interface de transmissão *(f)*

transmission inter-système *(f)* Fr
De Zwischensystem-Verbindungswege *(pl)*
En intersystem communications
Es comunicaciones entre sistemas *(f pl)*
It comunicazioni tra sistemi *(f pl)*
Pt comunicações entre sistemas *(f pl)*

transmission numérique *(f)* Fr
De digitale Übertragung *(f)*
En digital transmission
Es transmisión digital *(f)*
It trasmissione digitale *(f)*
Pt transmissão digital *(f)*

transmission optique *(f)* Fr
De optische Fernmeldung *(f)*

En optical communications
Es comunicaciones ópticas *(f)*
It comunicazioni ottiche *(f)*
Pt comunicações ópticas *(f)*

transmission speed En
De Übertragungs-geschwindigkeit *(f)*
Es velocidad de transmisión *(f)*
Fr vitesse de transmission *(f)*
It velocità di trasmissione *(f)*
Pt velocidade de transmissão *(f)*

transmit *vb* En
De übertragen
Es transmitir
Fr transmettre
It trasmettere
Pt transmitir

transmitir *vb* Es, Pt
De übertragen
En transmit
Fr transmettre
It trasmettere

transparence *(f) n* Fr
De Durchsichtigkeit *(f)*
En transparency
Es transparencia *(f)*
It trasparenza *(f)*
Pt transparência *(f)*

transparencia *(f) n* Es
De Durchsichtigkeit *(f)*
En transparency
Fr transparence *(f)*
It trasparenza *(f)*
Pt transparência *(f)*

transparência *(f) n* Pt
De Durchsichtigkeit *(f)*
En transparency
Es transparencia *(f)*
Fr transparence *(f)*
It trasparenza *(f)*

transparency *n* En
De Durchsichtigkeit *(f)*
Es transparencia *(f)*
Fr transparence *(f)*
It trasparenza *(f)*
Pt transparência *(f)*

transparent *adj* En, Fr
De durchsichtig
Es transparente
It trasparente
Pt transparente

transparente *adj* Es, Pt
De durchsichtig
En transparent
Fr transparent
It trasparente

transport de la bande *(m)* Fr
De Bandtransport *(m)*
En tape transport
Es transporte de cinta *(m)*
It trasporto del nastro *(m)*
Pt transporte de fita *(m)*

Transportdienst *(m) n* De
En transport service
Es servicio de transporte *(m)*
Fr service des transports *(m)*
It servizio di trasporto *(m)*
Pt serviço de transporte *(m)*

transporte de cinta *(m)* Es
De Bandtransport *(m)*
En tape transport
Fr transport de la bande *(m)*
It trasporto del nastro *(m)*
Pt transporte de fita *(m)*

transporte de fita *(m)* Pt
De Bandtransport *(m)*
En tape transport
Es transporte de cinta *(m)*
Fr transport de la bande *(m)*
It trasporto del nastro *(m)*

transporte parcial *(m)* Pt
De Teilübertrag *(m)*
En partial carry
Es arrastre parcial *(m)*
Fr report partiel *(m)*
It riporto parziale *(m)*

transport service En
De Transportdienst *(m)*
Es servicio de transporte *(m)*
Fr service des transports *(m)*
It servizio di trasporto *(m)*
Pt serviço de transporte *(m)*

transreceptor *(m) n* Pt
De Senderempfänger *(m)*
En transceiver
Es transceptor *(m)*
Fr émetteur-récepteur *(m)*
It ricetrasmettitore *(m)*

trap *n* En
De Haftstelle *(f)*
Es trampa *(f)*
Fr piège *(m)*
It trappola *(f)*
Pt armadilha *(f)*

trap *vb* En
De fangen
Es entrampar
Fr piéger
It intrappolare
Pt apanhar

trappola *(f) n* It
De Haftstelle *(f)*
En trap
Es trampa *(f)*
Fr piège *(m)*
Pt armadilha *(f)*

trasbordamento *(m) n* Pt
De Überlauf *(m)*
En overflow
Es desbordamiento *(m)*
Fr dépassement de capacité *(m)*
It superamento della capacità di memoria *(m)*

trascrivere *vb* It
De abschreiben
En transcribe
Es transcribir
Fr transcrire
Pt transcrever

trasferimento *(m) n* It
De Übergabe *(f)*
En transfer
Es transferencia *(f)*
Fr transfert *(m)*
Pt transferência *(f)*

trasferimento condizionale *(m)* It
De bedingte Übergabe *(f)*
En conditional transfer
Es transferencia condicional *(f)*
Fr transfert conditionnel *(m)*
Pt transferência condicional *(f)*

trasferimento di blocco *(m)* It
De Blockübergabe *(f)*
En block transfer
Es transferencia del bloque *(f)*
Fr transfert par blocs *(m)*
Pt transferência de bloco *(f)*

trasferimento di controllo *(m)* It
De Steuerübertragung *(f)*
En control transfer; transfer of control
Es transferencia de control *(f)*
Fr transfert de contrôle *(m)*
Pt transferência de controlo *(f)*

trasferimento di pagina *(m)* It
De Seitenwechsel *(m)*
En page turning
Es transferencia de página *(f)*
Fr changement de page *(m)*
Pt mudança de páginas *(f)*

trasferimento in serie *(m)* It
De Reihenübergabe *(f)*
En serial transfer
Es transferencia en serie *(f)*
Fr transfert en série *(m)*
Pt transferência em série *(f)*

trasferimento non condizionale *(m)* It
De unbedingte Übergabe *(f)*
En unconditional transfer
Es transferencia incondicional *(f)*
Fr transfert inconditionnel *(m)*
Pt transferência incondicional *(f)*

trasferimento parallelo *(m)* It
De Parallelübergabe *(f)*
En parallel transfer
Es transferencia en paralelo *(f)*
Fr transfert en parallèle *(m)*
Pt transferência paralela *(f)*

trasferimento periferico *(m)* It
De periphere Übergabe *(f)*
En peripheral transfer
Es transferencia periférica *(f)*
Fr transfert entre périphériques *(m)*
Pt transferência periférica *(f)*

trasferire *vb* It
De übergeben
En transfer
Es transferir
Fr transférer
Pt transferir

trasformare *vb* It
De umformen
En transform
Es transformar
Fr transformer
Pt transformar

traslitterare *vb* It
De wortwörtlich übersetzen
En transliterate
Es transliterar
Fr translitérer
Pt transliterar

trasmettere *vb* It
De übertragen
En transmit
Es transmitir
Fr transmettre
Pt transmitir

trasmissione *(f) n* It
De Übertragung *(f)*
En transmission
Es transmisión *(f)*
Fr transmission *(f)*
Pt transmissão *(f)*

trasmissione a banda larga *(f)* It
De Breitband-übertragung *(f)*
En broadband transmission
Es transmisión en banda ancha *(f)*
Fr transmission bande large *(f)*
Pt transmissão de banda larga *(f)*

trasmissione dei dati *(f)* It
De Datenübertragung *(f)*
En data transmission
Es transmisión de datos *(f)*
Fr transmission de données *(f)*
Pt transmissão de dados *(f)*

trasmissione digitale *(f)* It
De digitale Übertragung *(f)*
En digital transmission
Es transmisión digital *(f)*
Fr transmission numérique *(f)*
Pt transmissão digital *(f)*

trasparente *adj* It
De durchsichtig
En transparent
Es transparente
Fr transparent
Pt transparente

trasparenza *(f) n* It
De Durchsichtigkeit *(f)*
En transparency
Es transparencia *(f)*
Fr transparence *(f)*
Pt transparência *(f)*

trasporto del nastro *(m)* It
De Bandtransport *(m)*
En tape transport
Es transporte de cinta *(m)*
Fr transport de la bande *(m)*
Pt transporte de fita *(m)*

tratamento automático de dados *(m)* Pt
De automatische Datenverarbeitung *(f)*
En automatic data processing
Es proceso automático de datos *(m)*
Fr traitement automatique de l'information (TAI) *(m)*
It elaborazione automatica dei dati *(f)*

tratamento da informação *(m)* Pt
De Informations-verarbeitung *(f)*
En information processing
Es proceso de la información *(m)*
Fr traitement de l'information *(m)*
It elaborazione delle informazioni *(f)*

tratamento de dados *(m)* Pt
De Datenverarbeitung *(f)*
En data processing (DP)
Es proceso de datos *(m)*
Fr traitement de l'information *(m)*
It elaborazione dei dati *(f)*

tratamento de plano de fundo *(m)* Pt
De Hintergrund-verarbeitung *(f)*
En background processing
Es proceso de programas subordinados *(m)*
Fr traitement non prioritaire *(m)*
It elaborazione non precedenza *(f)*

tratamento distribuido *(m)* Pt
De verteilte Verarbeitung *(f)*
En distributed processing
Es proceso distribuido *(m)*
Fr informatique répartie *(f)*
It elaborazione ripartita *(f)*

tratamento electrónico de dados *(m)* Pt
De elektronische Datenverarbeitung (EDV) *(f)*
En electronic data processing (EDP)
Es proceso electrónico de datos *(m)*
Fr traitement électronique des données (TED) *(m)*
It elaborazione elettronica dei dati *(f)*

tratamento integrado de dados *(m)* Pt
De integrierte Datenverarbeitung *(f)*
En integrated data processing (IDP)
Es proceso integrado de datos *(m)*
Fr traitement intégré de l'information (TII) *(m)*
It elaborazione integrata dei dati *(f)*

tratamento por lotes *(m)* Pt
De Stapelverarbeitung *(f)*
En batch processing
Es proceso por lotes *(m)*
Fr traitement par lot *(m)*
It elaborazione a lotti *(f)*

tratamiento *(m) n* Es
De Verarbeitung *(f)*
En processing
Fr traitement *(m)*
It elaborazione *(f)*
Pt processamento *(m)*

tratamiento inmediato *(m)* Es
De Abrufverarbeitung *(f)*
En demand processing
Fr traitement immédiat *(m)*

It elaborazione a domanda *(f)*
Pt processamento de procura *(m)*

tratamiento por prioridad *(m)* Es
De Vorrangverarbeitung *(f)*
En priority processing
Fr traitement par priorités *(m)*
It elaborazione di priorità *(f)*
Pt processamento prioritário *(m)*

trattore di moduli *(m)* It
De Formulartraktor *(m)*
En forms tractor
Es tractor de arrastre del papel *(m)*
Fr entraîneur de papier *(m)*
Pt tractor de formulários *(m)*

travail *(m) n* Fr
De Job *(m)*
En job
Es trabajo *(m)*
It lavoro *(m)*
Pt trabalho *(m)*

travail en traitement par lots *(m)* Fr
De Stapelarbeit *(f)*
En batch job
Es trabajo por lotes *(m)*
It lavoro a lotti *(m)*
Pt trabalho por lotes *(m)*

traza *(f) n* Es
De Aufzeichnungslinie *(f)*
En trace
Fr trace *(f)*
It traccia *(f)*
Pt decalque *(m)*

trazadora *(f)* Es
De Planzeichner *(m)*
En plotter
Fr traceur *(m)*
It tracciatore *(m)*
Pt plotador *(m)*

trazador a tambor *(m)* Es
De Trommelkurvenzeichner *(m)*
En drum plotter
Fr traceur à tambour *(m)*
It tracciatore a tamburo *(m)*
Pt plotador de tambor *(m)*

trazador de base plana *(m)* Es
De Flachtischkurvenzeichner *(m)*
En flat-bed plotter
Fr traceur à plat *(m)*
It tracciatore in piano *(m)*
Pt plotador de leito plano *(m)*

trazador de curvas *(m)* Es
De Kurvenzeichner *(m)*
En graph plotter
Fr traceur de courbes *(m)*
It tracciatore di grafici *(m)*
Pt plotador de gráficos *(m)*

trazador incremental *(m)* Es
De schrittweiser Kurvenzeichner *(m)*
En incremental plotter
Fr traceur incrémentiel *(m)*
It tracciatore incrementale *(m)*
Pt plotador incremental *(m)*

trazador X-Y *(m)* Es
De X-Y-Kurvenzeichner *(m)*
En X-Y plotter
Fr traceur X-Y *(m)*
It tracciatore X-Y *(m)*
Pt plotador X-Y *(m)*

tre di eccesso *(m)* It
De Drei-Überschuß *(m)*
En excess three
Es tres excedente *(m)*
Fr code plus trois *(m)*
Pt três em excesso *(m)*

tree *n* En
De Überlagerungsbaum *(m)*
Es árbol *(m)*
Fr arbre *(m)*
It albero *(m)*
Pt árvore *(f)*

trem de impulsos *(m)* Pt
De Impulsfolge *(f)*
En pulse train
Es tren de impulsos *(m)*
Fr train d'impulsions *(m)*
It treno d'impulsi *(m)*

tremonha *(f) n* Pt
De Magazin *(n)*
En hopper
Es depósito de alimentación *(m)*
Fr magasin d'alimentation *(m)*
It serbatoio di alimentazione (schede) *(m)*

tren de impulsos *(m)* Es
De Impulsfolge *(f)*
En pulse train
Fr train d'impulsions *(m)*
It treno d'impulsi *(m)*
Pt trem de impulsos *(m)*

Trennmarke *(f) n* De
En group mark
Es marca de grupo *(f)*
Fr drapeau groupe *(m)*
It segno di gruppo *(m)*
Pt marca de grupo *(f)*

treno d'impulsi *(m)* It
De Impulsfolge *(f)*
En pulse train
Es tren de impulsos *(m)*
Fr train d'impulsions *(m)*
Pt trem de impulsos *(m)*

três em excesso *(m)* Pt
De Drei-Überschuß *(m)*
En excess three
Es tres excedente *(m)*
Fr code plus trois *(m)*
It tre di eccesso *(m)*

tres excedente *(m)* Es
De Drei-Überschuß *(m)*
En excess three
Fr code plus trois *(m)*
It tre di eccesso *(m)*
Pt três em excesso *(m)*

tri *(m) n* Fr
De Sortierung *(f)*
En sort
Es clasificación *(f)*
It selezione *(f)*
Pt espécie *(f)*

trier *vb* Fr
De sortieren
En sort
Es clasificar
It classificare
Pt classificar

trier préalablement Fr
De vorsortieren
En pre-sort
Es crear monotonías
It pre-selezionare
Pt pré-classificado

trieuse *(f) n* Fr
De Sortierer *(m)*
En sorter
Es clasificadora *(f)*
It selezionatrice *(f)*
Pt classificador *(m)*

trieuse de documents *(f)* Fr
De Schriftstücksortierer *(m)*
En document sorter
Es clasificadora de documentos *(f)*
It selezionatrice di documenti *(f)*
Pt classificador de documentação *(m)*

tri-fusion *(m) n* Fr
De Sortierungfusion *(f)*
En sort-merge
Es clasificación-fusión *(f)*
It selezione-inserimento *(f)*
Pt classificação-fusão *(f)*

trigger *n* En
De Trigger *(m)*
Es disparador *(m)*
Fr détente *(f)*
It scatto *(m)*
Pt gatilho *(m)*

trigger *vb* En
De triggern
Es disparar
Fr declencher
It innescare
Pt disparar

Trigger *(m) n* De
En trigger
Es disparador *(m)*
Fr détente *(f)*
It scatto *(m)*
Pt gatilho *(m)*

trigger circuit En
De Triggerschaltung *(f)*
Es circuito de disparo *(m)*
Fr circuit de déclenchement *(m)*
It circuito di scatto *(m)*
Pt circuito de disparo *(m)*

triggern *vb* De
En trigger
Es disparar
Fr declencher
It innescare
Pt disparar

Triggerschaltung *(f) n* De
En trigger circuit
Es circuito de disparo *(m)*
Fr circuit de déclenchement *(m)*
It circuito di scatto *(m)*
Pt circuito de disparo *(m)*

trilho de verificação *(m)* Pt
De Prüfliste *(f)*
En audit trail
Es pista de auditoría *(f)*
Fr vérification à rebours *(f)*
It lista di verifica *(f)*

triple precision En
De dreifache Präzision *(f)*
Es precisión triple *(f)*
Fr précision triple *(f)*
It precisione tripla *(f)*
Pt precisão tripla *(f)*

tri préalable *(m)* Fr
De Vorsortierung *(f)*
En pre-sort
Es creación de monotonías *(f)*
It pre-selezione *(f)*
Pt pré-classificação *(f)*

troisième-génération *adj* Fr
De drittgeneration
En third-generation
Es tercera-generación
It terza-generazione
Pt terceira-geração

Trommel *(f) n* De
En drum
Es tambor *(m)*
Fr tambour *(m)*
It tamburo *(m)*
Pt tambor *(m)*

Trommeldrucker *(m) n* De
En barrel printer; drum printer
Es impresora a tambor; impresora de rodillo *(f)*
Fr imprimante à tambour *(f)*
It stampatrice a tamburo *(f)*
Pt impressora de tambor *(f)*

Trommeldruckerfaβ *(n) n* De
En print barrel
Es cilindro impresor *(m)*
Fr tambour d'impression *(m)*
It tamburo di stampa *(m)*
Pt cilindro impressor *(m)*

Trommelkurvenzëichner *(m) n* De
En drum plotter
Es trazador a tambor *(m)*
Fr traceur à tambour *(m)*
It tracciatore a tamburo *(m)*
Pt plotador de tambor *(m)*

troncare *vb* It
De abschneiden
En truncate
Es truncar
Fr tronquer
Pt truncar

tronquer *vb* Fr
De abschneiden
En truncate
Es truncar
It troncare
Pt truncar

trouble shooting En
De Fehlersuchen *(n)*
Es localización de errores *(f)*
Fr dépannage *(m)*
It risoluzione dei problemi organizzativi *(f)*
Pt detecção de avarias *(f)*

trous d'entraînement *(m pl)* Fr
De Taktlöcher *(n pl)*
En feed holes
Es perforaciones de alimentación *(f pl)*
It fori di alimentazione *(m pl)*
Pt furos de alimentação *(m pl)*

truncar *vb* Es, Pt
De abschneiden
En truncate
Fr tronquer
It troncare

truncate *vb* En
De abschneiden
Es truncar
Fr tronquer
It troncare
Pt truncar

truncation error En
De Abschneidefehler *(m)*
Es error de truncamiento *(m)*
Fr erreur par troncation *(f)*
It errore di troncamento *(m)*
Pt erro de truncamento *(m)*

trunk circuit En
De Sammelschaltung *(f)*
Es circuito común *(m)*
Fr circuit interurbain *(m)*
It rete interurbana *(f)*
Pt circuito principal *(m)*

trunk link En
De Sammelverbindung *(f)*
Es enlace común *(m)*
Fr liaison interurbaine *(f)*
It linea principale *(f)*
Pt linha principal *(f)*

truth table En
De Echtheitstabelle *(f)*
Es tabla de decisión lógica *(f)*
Fr table de vérité *(f)*
It tavola della verità *(f)*
Pt tabela de valores verdadeiros *(f)*

tube *n* En; Fr *(m)*
De Röhre *(f)*
Es tubo *(m)*
It tubo *(m)*
Pt válvula *(f)*

tube à mémoire *(m)* Fr
De Speicherröhre *(f)*
En storage tube
Es tubo de almacenamiento *(m)*
It tubo di memoria *(m)*
Pt válvula de armazenamento *(f)*

tube à rayons cathodiques *(m)* Fr
De Kathodenstrahlröhre *(f)*
En cathode-ray tube (CRT)
Es tubo de rayos catódicos (TRC) *(m)*
It tubo a raggi catodici *(m)*
Pt válvula catódica *(f)*

tube cathodique de visualisation *(m)* Fr
De Anzeigeröhre *(f)*
En display tube
Es tubo de representación visual *(m)*
It tubo visualizzatore *(m)*
Pt válvula de visualização *(f)*

tubo *(m) n* Es, It
De Röhre *(f)*
En tube
Fr tube *(m)*
Pt válvula *(f)*

tubo a raggi catodici *(m)* It
De Kathodenstrahlröhre *(f)*

En cathode-ray tube (CRT)
Es tubo de rayos catódicos (TRC) *(m)*
Fr tube à rayons cathodiques *(m)*
Pt válvula catódica *(f)*

tubo de almacenamiento *(m)* Es
De Speicherröhre *(f)*
En storage tube
Fr tube à mémoire *(m)*
It tubo di memoria *(m)*
Pt válvula de armazenamento *(f)*

tubo de rayos catódicos (TRC) *(m)* Es
De Kathodenstrahlröhre *(f)*
En cathode-ray tube (CRT)
Fr tube à rayons cathodiques *(m)*
It tubo a raggi catodici *(m)*
Pt válvula catódica *(f)*

tubo de representación visual *(m)* Es
De Anzeigeröhre *(f)*
En display tube
Fr tube cathodique de visualisation *(m)*
It tubo visualizzatore *(m)*
Pt válvula de visualização *(f)*

tubo di memoria *(m)* It
De Speicherröhre *(f)*
En storage tube
Es tubo de almacenamiento *(m)*
Fr tube à mémoire *(m)*
Pt válvula de armazenamento *(f)*

tubo visualizzatore *(m)* It
De Anzeigeröhre *(f)*
En display tube
Es tubo de representación visual *(m)*
Fr tube cathodique de visualisation *(m)*
Pt válvula de visualização *(f)*

tuning *n* En
De Abstimmung *(f)*
Es sintonización *(f)*
Fr mise au point *(f)*
It sintonizzazione *(f)*
Pt afinação *(f)*

Turings-Universalmaschine *(f)* De
En universal Turing machine
Es máquina de Turing universal *(f)*
Fr machine de Turing universelle *(f)*
It macchina di Turing universale *(f)*
Pt máquina Turing universal *(f)*

turnkey operation En
De schlüsselfertiger Betrieb *(m)*
Es operación llave en mano *(f)*
Fr opération clé en main *(f)*
It operazione chiavi in mano *(f)*
Pt operação de chaves em mão *(f)*

twin check En
De Doppelprüfung *(f)*
Es doble control *(m)*
Fr double contrôle *(m)*
It doppio controllo *(m)*
Pt verificação dupla paralela *(f)*

two-address instruction En
De Zweiadressen-anweisung *(f)*
Es instrucción con dos direcciones *(f)*
Fr instruction à deux adresses *(f)*
It istruzione a due indirizzi *(f)*
Pt instrução de dois endereços *(f)*

two-dimensional storage En
De zweidimensionale Speicherung *(f)*
Es memoria bidimensional *(f)*
Fr stockage à double entrée *(m)*
It memoria bidimensionale *(f)*
Pt armazenamento bidimensional *(m)*

twos complement En
De Zweierkomplement *(n)*
Es complemento a dos *(m)*
Fr complément deux *(m)*
It complemento al due *(m)*
Pt complemento de dois *(m)*

type *vb* En
De maschinenschreiben
Es escribir a máquina
Fr écrire à la machine
It scrivere a macchina
Pt escrever à máquina

type bar En
De Typenstange *(f)*
Es barra de tipos *(f)*
Fr barre d'impression *(f)*
It sbarra di caratteri *(f)*
Pt barra de tipos *(f)*

type drum En
De Typentrommel *(f)*
Es tambor de tipos *(m)*
Fr tambour à caractères *(m)*
It tamburo di caratteri *(m)*
Pt tambor de tipos *(m)*

typeface *n* En
De Schrifttyp *(m)*
Es ojo del tipo *(m)*
Fr oeil d'un caractère *(m)*
It occhio del carattere *(m)*
Pt olho de tipo *(m)*

Typenrad *(n) n* De
En print wheel
Es rueda de impresión *(f)*
Fr roue d'impression *(f)*
It ruota di stampa *(f)*
Pt roda impressora *(f)*

Typenraddrucker *(m) n* De
En wheel printer
Es impresora de ruedas *(f)*
Fr imprimante à roues *(f)*
It stampatrice di ruota *(f)*
Pt impressora de roda *(f)*

Typenstange *(f) n* De
En type bar
Es barra de tipos *(f)*
Fr barre d'impression *(f)*
It sbarra di caratteri *(f)*
Pt barra de tipos *(f)*

Typentrommel *(f) n* De
En type drum
Es tambor de tipos *(m)*
Fr tambour à caractères *(m)*
It tamburo di caratteri *(m)*
Pt tambor de tipos *(m)*

typewriter *n* En
De Schreibmaschine *(f)*
Es máquina de escribir *(f)*
Fr machine à écrire *(f)*
It macchina da scrivere *(f)*
Pt máquina de escrever *(f)*

typewriter terminal En
De Schreibmaschine-station *(f)*
Es terminal con teclado *(m)*
Fr terminal équipé d'un clavier *(m)*
It terminale a macchina da scrivere *(m)*
Pt terminal de máquina de escrever *(m)*

U

Übereinstimmung *(f) n* De
En match
Es correspondencia *(f)*
Fr assortiment *(m)*

It accoppiamento *(m)*
Pt equiparação *(f)*

Übergabe *(f) n* De
En transfer
Es transferencia *(f)*
Fr transfert *(m)*
It trasferimento *(m)*
Pt transferência *(f)*

Übergang *(m) n* De
En transition
Es transicion *(f)*
Fr transition *(f)*
It transizione *(f)*
Pt transição *(f)*

übergeben *vb* De
En transfer
Es transferir
Fr transférer
It trasferire
Pt transferir

Übergehenzeichen *(n) n* De
En ignore character
Es carácter de supresión *(m)*
Fr caractère d'omission *(m)*
It carattere di ignorare *(m)*
Pt carácter ignore *(m)*

Überlagerungsbaum *(m) n* De
En tree
Es árbol *(m)*
Fr arbre *(m)*
It albero *(m)*
Pt árvore *(f)*

überlappen *vb* De
En overlap
Es solapar
Fr chevaucher
It sovrapporre
Pt sobrepor-se

Überlauf *(m) n* De
En overflow
Es desbordamiento *(m)*
Fr dépassement de capacité *(m)*
It superamento della capacità di memoria *(m)*
Pt trasbordamento *(m)*

überschreiben *vb* De
En overwrite
Es recubrir
Fr superposer une écriture
It inscrivere per riempimento
Pt escrever por cima

übersetzen *vb* De
En translate
Es traducir
Fr traduire
It tradurre
Pt traduzir

Übersetzer *(m) n* De
En translator
Es traductor *(m)*
Fr traducteur *(m)*
It traduttore *(m)*
Pt tradutor *(m)*

überspringen *vb* De
En jump; skip
Es omitir; saltar
Fr sauter
It saltare
Pt saltar

übertragen *vb* De
En transmit
Es transmitir
Fr transmettre
It trasmettere
Pt transmitir

Übertragung *(f) n* De
En transmission
Es transmisión *(f)*
Fr transmission *(f)*
It trasmissione *(f)*
Pt transmissão *(f)*

Übertragungsanweisung *(f) n* De
En transfer instruction
Es instrucción de transferencia *(f)*
Fr instruction de branchement *(f)*
It istruzione di trasferimento *(f)*
Pt instrução de transferência *(f)*

Übertragungsfrequenz *(f) n* De
En transfer rate
Es indice de transferencia *(m)*
Fr vitesse de transfert *(f)*
It volume di trasferimento *(m)*
Pt índice de transferência *(m)*

Übertragungsfunktion *(f) n* De
En transfer function
Es función de transferencia *(f)*
Fr fonction de transfert *(f)*
It funzione di trasferimento *(f)*
Pt função de transferência *(f)*

Übertragungsgeschwindigkeit *(f) n* De
En transmission speed
Es velocidad de transmisión *(f)*
Fr vitesse de transmission *(f)*
It velocità di trasmissione *(f)*
Pt velocidade de transmissão *(f)*

Übertragungsprüfung *(f) n* De
En transfer check
Es verificación de transferencia *(f)*
Fr contrôle par répétition *(m)*
It controllo di trasferimento *(m)*
Pt verificação de transferência *(f)*

Übertragungsschnittstelle *(f) n* De
En transmission interface
Es interfase de transmisión *(f)*
Fr interface de transmission *(f)*
It interfaccia di trasmissione *(f)*
Pt interface de transmissão *(f)*

Überwacher *(m) n* De
En supervisor
Es supervisor *(m)*
Fr superviseur *(m)*
It supervisore *(m)*
Pt supervisor *(m)*

Überwachungsprogramm *(n) n* De
En supervisory program
Es programa supervisor *(m)*
Fr programme superviseur *(m)*
It programma di supervisione *(m)*
Pt programa de supervisão *(m)*

Überwachungssteuerung *(f) n* De
En supervisory control
Es control supervisor *(m)*
Fr commande de superviseur *(f)*
It controllo di supervisione *(m)*
Pt controle de supervisão *(m)*

Uhrzeigverarbeitung *(f) n* De
En real-time processing
Es proceso en tiempo real *(m)*
Fr traitement en temps réel *(m)*
It elaborazione in tempo reale *(f)*
Pt processamento de tempo real *(m)*

Uhrzeitgeber *(m) n* De
En real-time clock
Es reloj binario *(m)*
Fr horloge temps réel *(f)*
It orologio di tempo reale *(m)*
Pt relógio de tempo real *(m)*

Umdrehungswartezeit *(f) n* De
En rotational delay
Es retraso rotacional *(m)*
Fr délai d'attente *(m)*
It ritardo rotazionale *(m)*
Pt atraso rotacional *(m)*

umformen *vb* De
En transform
Es transformar
Fr transformer

It trasformare
Pt transformar

Umgebung *(f) n* De
En environment
Es ambiente *(m)*
Fr ambiance *(f)*
It ambiente *(m)*
Pt ambiente *(m)*

umgekehrte polnische Darstellung *(f)* De
En reverse Polish notation
Es notación polaca inversa *(f)*
Fr notation polonaise inversée *(f)*
It notazione polacca inversa *(f)*
Pt notação polaca inversa *(f)*

umkehrbarer Zähler *(m)* De
En reversible counter
Es contador reversible *(m)*
Fr compteur-décompteur *(m)*
It contatore reversibile *(m)*
Pt contador reversível *(m)*

Umlaufregister *(n) n* De
En circulating register
Es registro circulante *(m)*
Fr registre circulant *(m)*
It registro circolante *(m)*
Pt registo de circulação *(m)*

umwandeln *vb* De
En convert
Es convertir
Fr convertir
It convertire
Pt converter

umwandeln und ausführen De
En load and go
Es cargar y ejecutar
Fr charger et exécuter
It caricare e eseguire
Pt carregar e seguir

Umwandler *(m) n* De
En converter
Es convertidor *(m)*
Fr convertisseur *(m)*
It convertitore *(m)*
Pt conversor *(m)*

Umwandlung *(f) n* De
En conversion
Es conversión *(f)*
Fr conversion *(f)*
It conversione *(f)*
Pt conversão *(f)*

unary operation En
De monadische Operation *(f)*
Es operación unaria *(f)*
Fr opération unaire *(f)*
It operazione unaria *(f)*
Pt operação unária *(f)*

unattended time En
De Ruhezeit *(f)*
Es tiempo sin personal *(m)*
Fr temps de fonctionnement sans surveillance *(m)*
It tempo uncustodita *(m)*
Pt tempo de abandono *(m)*

unbedingte Übergabe *(f)* De
En unconditional transfer
Es transferencia incondicional *(f)*
Fr transfert inconditionnel *(m)*
It trasferimento non condizionale *(m)*
Pt transferência incondicional *(f)*

unbedingte Verzweigungs-anweisung *(f)* De
En unconditional branch instruction
Es instrucción de bifurcación incondicional *(f)*
Fr instruction de branchement inconditionnel *(f)*
It istruzione di diramazione non condizionale *(f)*
Pt instrução de ramo incondicional *(f)*

unbenutzte Zeit *(f)* De
En unused time
Es tiempo de inutilización *(m)*
Fr temps d'inutilisation *(m)*
It tempo inutilizzato *(m)*
Pt tempo não utilizado *(m)*

unbewegt *adj* De
En inactive
Es inactivo
Fr non mouvementé
It inattivo
Pt inactivo

unconditional branch instruction En
De unbedingte Verzweigungs-anweisung *(f)*
Es instrucción de bifurcación incondicional *(f)*
Fr instruction de branchement inconditionnel *(f)*
It istruzione di diramazione non condizionale *(f)*
Pt instrução de ramo incondicional *(f)*

unconditional transfer En
De unbedingte Übergabe *(f)*
Es transferencia incondicional *(f)*
Fr transfert inconditionnel *(m)*
It trasferimento non condizionale *(m)*
Pt transferência incondicional *(f)*

underflow *n* En
De Unterlauf *(m)*
Es subdesbordamiento *(m)*
Fr dépassement de capacité inférieur *(m)*
It sottoflusso *(m)*
Pt subfluxo *(m)*

undisturbed output signal En
De ungestörtes Ausgangssignal *(n)*
Es señal de salida no cambiada *(f)*
Fr signal de sortie non perturbé *(m)*
It segnale di output non disturbato *(m)*
Pt sinal de output não perturbado *(m)*

UND-Schaltung *(f) n* De
En AND-gate
Es puerta Y *(f)*
Fr porte ET *(f)*
It porta E *(f)*
Pt porta AND *(f)*

UND-Verknüpfung *(f) n* De
En AND-operation
Es operación Y *(f)*
Fr opération ET *(f)*
It operazione E *(f)*
Pt operação AND *(f)*

unechtes Wiederauffinden *(n)* De
En false retrieval
Es falsa recuperación *(f)*
Fr référence non pertinente *(f)*
It falso reperimento *(m)*
Pt recuperação falsa *(f)*

ungepacktes Segment *(n)* De
En unpaged segment
Es segmento no paginado *(m)*
Fr segment non organisé en pages *(m)*
It segmento non impaginato *(m)*
Pt segmento sem páginação *(m)*

ungerade Parität *(f)* De
En odd parity
Es imparidad *(f)*
Fr imparité *(f)*
It parità dispari *(f)*
Pt paridade impar *(f)*

ungestörtes Ausgangssignal *(n)* De
En undisturbed output signal

Es señal de salida no cambiada *(f)*
Fr signal de sortie non perturbé *(m)*
It segnale di output non disturbato *(m)*
Pt sinal de output não perturbado *(m)*

unidad *(f) n* Es
De Einheit *(f)*
En unit
Fr unité *(f)*
It unità *(f)*
Pt unidade *(f)*

unidad aritmética (UA) *(f)* Es
De Rechenwerk *(n)*
En arithmetic unit (AU)
Fr unité de calcul (UC) *(f)*
It unità aritmetica *(f)*
Pt unidade aritmética *(f)*

unidad aritmética y lógica (UAL) *(f)* Es
De arithmetische und logische Einheit *(f)*
En arithmetic and logic unit (ALU)
Fr unité arithmétique et logique (UAL) *(f)*
It unità logica ed aritmetica *(f)*
Pt unidade aritmética e lógica *(f)*

unidad central de proceso *(f)* Es
De Zentraleinheit *(f)*
En central processing unit
Fr unité de traitement centrale *(f)*
It unità centrale di elaborazione *(f)*
Pt unidade de processamento central *(f)*

unidad de cinta *(f)* Es
De Bandgerät *(n)*
En tape unit
Fr unité de ruban magnétique *(f)*
It unità a nastri *(f)*
Pt unidade de fita *(f)*

unidad de control *(f)* Es
De Leitwerk *(n)*
En control unit
Fr unité de contrôle *(f)*
It unità di controllo *(f)*
Pt unidade de controlo *(f)*

unidad de discos *(f)* Es
De Plattenantrieb *(m)*
En disk drive
Fr unité de disque(s) *(f)*
It unità a dischi *(f)*
Pt accionamento de disco *(m)*

unidad de discos flexibles *(f)* Es
De Floppy-Disk-Antrieb *(m)*
En floppy-disk drive
Fr unité de disque souple *(f)*
It unità floppy disk *(f)*
Pt accionamento do disco floppy *(m)*

unidad de discos móviles *(f)* Es
De auswechselbarer Plattenspeicher *(m)*
En exchangeable disk store (EDS)
Fr unité de disques à chargeur (UTC) *(f)*
It memoria a dischi inseribili *(f)*
Pt armazém de discos intercambiáveis *(m)*

unidad de doble acceso *(f)* Es
De Doppelzugriffsantrieb *(m)*
En dual-access drive
Fr entraînement d'accès double *(m)*
It unità ad accesso duplice *(f)*
Pt accionamento de acesso duplo *(m)*

unidad de identidad *(f)* Es
De Einzeleinheit *(f)*
En identity unit
Fr unité d'identification *(f)*
It unità di identità *(f)*
Pt unidade de identidade *(f)*

unidad de igualdad *(f)* Es
De Äquivalenzschaltung *(f)*
En equality unit
Fr unité d'égalité *(f)*
It unità di uguaglianza *(f)*
Pt unidade de igualdade *(f)*

unidad de información *(f)* Es
De Datenfeld *(n)*
En data item
Fr donnée élémentaire *(f)*
It voce di dato *(f)*
Pt item de dados *(m)*

unidad de respuesta de audio *(f)* Es
De Sprachausgabe *(f)*
En audio response unit
Fr répondeur vocal *(m)*
It unità della risposta audio *(f)*
Pt unidade de audio-resposta *(f)*

unidad de visualización *(f)* Es
De Sichtgerät *(n)*
En visual-display unit (VDU)
Fr appareil de visualisation (AV) *(m)*
It unitá di visualizzazione *(f)*
Pt unidade de visualização *(f)*

unidade *(f) n* Pt
De Einheit *(f)*
En unit
Es unidad *(f)*
Fr unité *(f)*
It unità *(f)*

unidade aritmética *(f)* Pt
De Rechenwerk *(n)*
En arithmetic unit (AU)
Es unidad aritmética (UA) *(f)*
Fr unité de calcul (UC) *(f)*
It unità aritmetica *(f)*

unidade aritmética e lógica *(f)* Pt
De arithmetische und logische Einheit *(f)*
En arithmetic and logic unit (ALU)
Es unidad aritmética y lógica (UAL) *(f)*
Fr unité arithmétique et logique (UAL) *(f)*
It unità logica ed aritmetica *(f)*

unidade de audio-resposta *(f)* Pt
De Sprachausgabe *(f)*
En audio response unit
Es unidad de respuesta de audio *(f)*
Fr répondeur vocal *(m)*
It unità della risposta audio *(f)*

unidade de controlo *(f)* Pt
De Leitwerk *(n)*
En control unit
Es unidad de control *(f)*
Fr unité de contrôle *(f)*
It unità di controllo *(f)*

unidade de fita *(f)* Pt
De Bandgerät *(n)*
En tape unit
Es unidad de cinta *(f)*
Fr unité de ruban magnétique *(f)*
It unità a nastri *(f)*

unidade de identidade *(f)* Pt
De Einzeleinheit *(f)*
En identity unit
Es unidad de identidad *(f)*
Fr unité d'identification *(f)*
It unità di identità *(f)*

unidade de igualdade *(f)* Pt
De Äquivalenzschaltung *(f)*
En equality unit
Es unidad de igualdad *(f)*
Fr unité d'égalité *(f)*
It unità di uguaglianza *(f)*

unidade de processamento central *(f)* Pt
De Zentraleinheit *(f)*
En central processing unit
Es unidad central de proceso *(f)*
Fr unité de traitement centrale *(f)*

It unità centrale di elaborazione *(f)*

unidade de visualização *(f)* Pt
De Sichtgerät *(n)*
En visual-display unit (VDU)
Es unidad de visualización *(f)*
Fr appareil de visualisation (AV) *(m)*
It unitá di visualizzazione *(f)*

unidade lógica *(f)* Pt
De logische Einheit *(f)*
En logic(al) unit (LU)
Es unidad lógica *(f)*
Fr unité logique *(f)*
It unità logica *(f)*

unidade periférica *(f)* Pt
De periphere Einheit *(f)*
En peripheral unit
Es unidad periférica *(f)*
Fr unité périphérique *(f)*
It unità periferica *(f)*

unidad lógica *(f)* Es
De logische Einheit *(f)*
En logic(al) unit (LU)
Fr unité logique *(f)*
It unità logica *(f)*
Pt unidade lógica *(f)*

unidad periférica *(f)* Es
De periphere Einheit *(f)*
En peripheral unit
Fr unité périphérique *(f)*
It unità periferica *(f)*
Pt unidade periférica *(f)*

unipolaire *adj* Fr
De unipolar
En unipolar
Es unipolar
It unipolare
Pt unipolar

unipolar *adj* En, De, Es, Pt
Fr unipolaire
It unipolare

unipolare *adj* It
De unipolar
En unipolar
Es unipolar
Fr unipolaire
Pt unipolar

unir *vb* Es, Pt
De zusammenfügen
En join
Fr grouper
It unire

unire *vb* It
De zusammenfügen
En join
Es unir
Fr grouper
Pt unir

unit *n* En
De Einheit *(f)*
Es unidad *(f)*
Fr unité *(f)*
It unità *(f)*
Pt unidade *(f)*

unità *(f) n* It
De Einheit *(f)*
En unit
Es unidad *(f)*
Fr unité *(f)*
Pt unidade *(f)*

unità ad accesso duplice *(f)* It
De Doppelzugriffsantrieb *(m)*
En dual-access drive
Es unidad de doble acceso *(f)*
Fr entraînement d'accès double *(m)*
Pt accionamento de acesso duplo *(m)*

unità a dischi *(f)* It
De Plattenantrieb *(m)*
En disk drive
Es unidad de discos *(f)*
Fr unité de disque(s) *(f)*
Pt accionamento de disco *(m)*

unità a nastri *(f)* It
De Bandgerät *(n)*
En tape unit
Es unidad de cinta *(f)*
Fr unité de ruban magnétique *(f)*
Pt unidade de fita *(f)*

unità aritmetica *(f)* It
De Rechenwerk *(n)*
En arithmetic unit (AU)
Es unidad aritmética (UA) *(f)*
Fr unité de calcul (UC) *(f)*
Pt unidade aritmética *(f)*

unità centrale di elaborazione *(f)* It
De Zentraleinheit *(f)*
En central processing unit
Es unidad central de proceso *(f)*
Fr unité de traitement centrale *(f)*
Pt unidade de processamento central *(f)*

unità della risposta audio *(f)* It
De Sprachausgabe *(f)*
En audio response unit
Es unidad de respuesta de audio *(f)*
Fr répondeur vocal *(m)*
Pt unidade de audio-resposta *(f)*

unità di controllo *(f)* It
De Leitwerk *(n)*
En control unit
Es unidad de control *(f)*
Fr unité de contrôle *(f)*
Pt unidade de controlo *(f)*

unità di controllo satellite *(f)* It
De peripheres Steuergerät *(n)*
En peripheral controller
Es controlador periférico *(m)*
Fr contrôleur de périphérique(s) *(m)*
Pt controlador periférico *(m)*

unità di elaborazione satellite *(f)* It
De peripheres Verarbeitungsgerät *(n)*
En peripheral processor
Es procesador periférico *(m)*
Fr unité centrale de périphériques *(f)*
Pt processador periférico *(m)*

unità di identità *(f)* It
De Einzeleinheit *(f)*
En identity unit
Es unidad de identidad *(f)*
Fr unité d'identification *(f)*
Pt unidade de identidade *(f)*

unità di uguaglianza *(f)* It
De Äquivalenzschaltung *(f)*
En equality unit
Es unidad de igualdad *(f)*
Fr unité d'égalité *(f)*
Pt unidade de igualdade *(f)*

unitá di visualizzazione *(f)* It
De Sichtgerät *(n)*
En visual-display unit (VDU)
Es unidad de visualización *(f)*
Fr appareil de visualisation (AV) *(m)*
Pt unidade de visualização *(f)*

unità floppy disk *(f)* It
De Floppy-Disk-Antrieb *(m)*
En floppy-disk drive
Es unidad de discos flexibles *(f)*
Fr unité de disque souple *(f)*
Pt accionamento do disco floppy *(m)*

unità logica *(f)* It
De logische Einheit *(f)*
En logic(al) unit (LU)
Es unidad lógica *(f)*
Fr unité logique *(f)*
Pt unidade lógica *(f)*

unità logica ed aritmetica *(f)* It
De arithmetische und logische Einheit *(f)*
En arithmetic and logic unit (ALU)
Es unidad aritmética y lógica (UAL) *(f)*

Fr unité arithmétique et logique (UAL) *(f)*
Pt unidade aritmética e lógica *(f)*

unità periferica *(f)* It
De periphere Einheit *(f)*
En peripheral unit
Es unidad periférica *(f)*
Fr unité périphérique *(f)*
Pt unidade periférica *(f)*

unité *(f) n* Fr
De Einheit *(f)*
En unit
Es unidad *(f)*
It unità *(f)*
Pt unidade *(f)*

unité à mémoire à accès direct *(f)* Fr
De Direktzugriffsspeicher *(m)*
En direct-access storage device (DASD)
Es dispositivo de almacenamiento de acceso directo *(m)*
It dispositivo con memoria ad accesso diretto *(m)*
Pt dispositivo de armazenagem de acesso directo *(m)*

unité arithmétique et logique (UAL) *(f)* Fr
De arithmetische und logische Einheit *(f)*
En arithmetic and logic unit (ALU)
Es unidad aritmética y lógica (UAL) *(f)*
It unità logica ed aritmetica *(f)*
Pt unidade aritmética e lógica *(f)*

unité centrale de périphériques *(f)* Fr
De peripheres Verarbeitungsgerät *(n)*
En peripheral processor
Es procesador periférico *(m)*
It unità di elaborazione satellite *(f)*
Pt processador periférico *(m)*

unité de calcul (UC) *(f)* Fr
De Rechenwerk *(n)*
En arithmetic unit (AU)
Es unidad aritmética (UA) *(f)*
It unità aritmetica *(f)*
Pt unidade aritmética *(f)*

unité de contrôle *(f)* Fr
De Leitwerk *(n)*
En control unit
Es unidad de control *(f)*
It unità di controllo *(f)*
Pt unidade de controlo *(f)*

unité de disque(s) *(f)* Fr
De Plattenantrieb *(m)*
En disk drive
Es unidad de discos *(f)*
It unità a dischi *(f)*
Pt accionamento de disco *(m)*

unité de disques à chargeur (UTC) *(f)* Fr
De auswechselbarer Plattenspeicher *(m)*
En exchangeable disk store (EDS)
Es unidad de discos móviles *(f)*
It memoria a dischi inseribili *(f)*
Pt armazém de discos intercambiáveis *(m)*

unité de disque souple *(f)* Fr
De Floppy-Disk-Antrieb *(m)*
En floppy-disk drive
Es unidad de discos flexibles *(f)*
It unità floppy disk *(f)*
Pt accionamento do disco floppy *(m)*

unité d'égalité *(f)* Fr
De Äquivalenzschaltung *(f)*
En equality unit
Es unidad de igualdad *(f)*
It unità di uguaglianza *(f)*
Pt unidade de igualdade *(f)*

unité d'enregistrement sur film *(f)* Fr
De Filmaufzeichner *(m)*
En film recorder
Es registrador de películas *(m)*
It registratore di pellicole *(m)*
Pt registador de películas *(m)*

unité de ruban magnétique *(f)* Fr
De Bandgerät *(n)*
En tape unit
Es unidad de cinta *(f)*
It unità a nastri *(f)*
Pt unidade de fita *(f)*

unité de stockage *(f)* Fr
De Speichergerät *(n)*
En storage device
Es dispositivo de almacenamiento *(m)*
It organo di memoria *(m)*
Pt dispositivo de armazenamento *(m)*

unité de traitement centrale *(f)* Fr
De Zentraleinheit *(f)*
En central processing unit
Es unidad central de proceso *(f)*
It unità centrale di elaborazione *(f)*
Pt unidade de processamento central *(f)*

unité de traitement de textes *(f)* Fr
De Wortverarbeiter *(m)*
En word processor
Es procesador de la palabra *(m)*
It processadore di voce *(m)*
Pt processador de palavras *(m)*

unité d'identification *(f)* Fr
De Einzeleinheit *(f)*
En identity unit
Es unidad de identidad *(f)*
It unità di identità *(f)*
Pt unidade de identidade *(f)*

unité logique *(f)* Fr
De logische Einheit *(f)*
En logic(al) unit (LU)
Es unidad lógica *(f)*
It unità logica *(f)*
Pt unidade lógica *(f)*

unité périphérique *(f)* Fr
De periphere Einheit *(f)*
En peripheral unit
Es unidad periférica *(f)*
It unità periferica *(f)*
Pt unidade periférica *(f)*

unité périphérique de sortie *(f)* Fr
De Ausgangsvorrichtung *(m)*
En output device
Es dispositivo de salida *(m)*
It organo di uscita *(m)*
Pt dispositivo de output *(m)*

unit record En
De Einheitssatz *(m)*
Es registro unitario *(m)*
Fr enregistrement unitaire *(m)*
It record di unità *(m)*
Pt registo de unidades *(m)*

universal Turing machine En
De Turings-Universalmaschine *(f)*
Es máquina de Turing universal *(f)*
Fr machine de Turing universelle *(f)*
It macchina di Turing universale *(f)*
Pt máquina Turing universal *(f)*

unmittelbare Adresse *(f)* De
En immediate address
Es dirección inmediata *(f)*
Fr adresse immédiate *(f)*
It indirizzo immediato *(m)*
Pt endereço imediato *(m)*

unmittelbarer Zugriff *(m)* De
En immediate access
Es acceso inmediato *(m)*

Fr accès immédiat *(m)*
It accesso immediato *(m)*
Pt acesso imediato *(m)*

unpack *vb* En
De auspacken
Es desempaquetar
Fr décondenser
It separare
Pt desembalar

unpaged segment En
De ungepacktes Segment *(n)*
Es segmento no paginado *(m)*
Fr segment non organisé en pages *(m)*
It segmento non impaginato *(m)*
Pt segmento sem páginação *(m)*

unterbrechen *vb* De
En interrupt
Es interrumpir
Fr interrompre
It interrompere
Pt interromper

Unterbrechung *(f) n* De
En interrupt
Es interrupción *(f)*
Fr interruption *(f)*
It interruzione *(f)*
Pt interrupção *(f)*

Unterbrechungs-priorität *(f) n* De
En interrupt priority
Es prioridad de interrupción *(f)*
Fr interruption prioritaire *(f)*
It priorità di interruzione *(f)*
Pt prioridade de interrupção *(f)*

Unterdrückung *(f) n* De
En suppression
Es supresión *(f)*
Fr suppression *(f)*
It soppressione *(f)*
Pt supressão *(f)*

Unterlauf *(m) n* De
En underflow
Es subdesbordamiento *(m)*
Fr dépassement de capacité inférieur *(m)*
It sottoflusso *(m)*
Pt subfluxo *(m)*

Untermenge *(f) n* De
En subset
Es subgrupo *(m)*
Fr sous-ensemble *(m)*
It sottogruppo *(m)*
Pt sub-conjunto *(m)*

Unternehmungs-forschung *(f) n* De
En operational research (OR)
Es investigación operativa *(f)*
Fr recherche opérationnelle *(f)*
It ricerca operativa *(f)*
Pt investigação operacional *(f)*

Unterprogramm *(n) n* De
En subprogram
Es subprograma *(m)*
Fr sous-programme *(m)*
It sottoprogramma *(m)*
Pt subprograma *(m)*

Unterroutine *(f) n* De
En subroutine
Es subrutina *(f)*
Fr sous-routine *(f)*
It subroutine *(f)*
Pt subrotina *(f)*

unused time En
De unbenutzte Zeit *(f)*
Es tiempo de inutilización *(m)*
Fr temps d'inutilisation *(m)*
It tempo inutilizzato *(m)*
Pt tempo não utilizado *(m)*

unwind *vb* En
De abwickeln
Es desovillar
Fr dérouler
It svolgere
Pt desenrolar

unwirksame Zeit *(f)* De
En ineffective time
Es tiempo ineficaz *(m)*
Fr temps ineffectif *(m)*
It tempo inefficace *(m)*
Pt tempo irreal *(m)*

unzulässiges Zeichen *(n)* De
En illegal character
Es carácter no válido *(m)*
Fr caractère interdit *(m)*
It carattere illegale *(m)*
Pt carácter ilegal *(m)*

update *vb* En
De auf den neuesten Stand bringen
Es actualizar
Fr mettre à jour
It aggiornare
Pt actualizar

uptime *n* En
De Benutzerzeit *(f)*
Es tiempo productivo *(m)*
Fr temps de bon fonctionnement *(m)*
It tempo di utilizzazione *(m)*
Pt tempo terminado *(m)*

Urband *n* De
En father tape
Es cinta creadora *(f)*
Fr bande créatrice *(f)*
It nastro padre *(m)*
Pt fita pai *(f)*

Ursprungsdaten *(pl) n* De
En raw data
Es datos sin procesar *(m pl)*
Fr données brutes *(f pl)*
It dati crudi *(m pl)*
Pt dados em bruto *(m pl)*

urtare *vb* It
De durchschlagen
En crash
Es quebrar
Fr accélérer
Pt colidir

urto *(m) n* It
De Durchschlag *(m)*
En crash
Es choque *(m)*
Fr accélération *(f)*
Pt colisão *(f)*

uscire *vb* It
De ausgehen
En exit
Es salir
Fr sortir
Pt sair

uscita *(f) n* It
De Ausgang *(m)*
En exit; output
Es salida *(f)*
Fr sortie *(f)*
Pt output; saída *(m f)*

user *n* En
De Benutzer *(m)*
Es usuario *(m)*
Fr utilisateur *(m)*
It utente *(m)*
Pt utente *(m)*

user group En
De Benutzergruppe *(f)*
Es grupo de usuarios *(m)*
Fr groupement d'utilisateurs *(m)*
It gruppo di utenti *(m)*
Pt group utente *(m)*

usuario *(m) n* Es
De Benutzer *(m)*
En user
Fr utilisateur *(m)*
It utente *(m)*
Pt utente *(m)*

utente *(m) n* It, Pt
De Benutzer *(m)*
En user
Es usuario *(m)*
Fr utilisateur *(m)*

utilidad *(f) n* Es
De Betriebsfähigkeit *(f)*
En serviceability
Fr aptitude au service *(f)*
It utilità *(f)*
Pt aptidão a ser utilizado *(f)*

utilisateur *(m) n* Fr
De Benutzer *(m)*
En user
Es usuario *(m)*
It utente *(m)*
Pt utente *(m)*

utilisation en temps partagé *(f)* Fr
De Zeitteilung *(f)*
En time sharing
Es tiempo compartido *(m)*
It lavoro di multiprogrammazione *(m)*
Pt compartido tempo *(m)*

utilità *(f) n* It
De Betriebsfähigkeit *(f)*
En serviceability
Es utilidad *(f)*
Fr aptitude au service *(f)*
Pt aptidão a ser utilizado *(f)*

utility program En
De Hilfsprogramm *(n)*
Es programa de utilidad *(m)*
Fr programme utilitaire *(m)*
It programma di utilità *(m)*
Pt programa de utilidade *(m)*

utilization ratio En
De Benutzungsverhältnis *(n)*
Es relación de utilización *(f)*
Fr rapport d'utilisation *(m)*
It rapporto di utilizzazione *(m)*
Pt ratio de utilização *(f)*

V

vaciado a la impresora *(m)* Es
De Ausdruck *(m)*
En printout
Fr sortie sur imprimante *(f)*
It stampato *(m)*
Pt impressão *(f)*

vaciado de rescate *(m)* Es
De Wiedereinstiegs-speicherauszug *(m)*
En rescue dump
Fr vidage de secours *(m)*
It dump di salvataggio *(m)*
Pt armazém de emergência *(m)*

vaciado póstumo *(m)* Es
De Speicherauszug nach dem Tode *(m)*
En post-mortem dump
Fr vidage d'autopsie *(m)*
It dump di autopsia *(m)*
Pt descarregador de autópsia *(m)*

validity check En
De Gültigkeitsprüfung *(f)*
Es verificación de validez *(f)*
Fr contrôle de vraisemblance *(m)*
It controllo di validità *(m)*
Pt verificação de validez *(f)*

válvula *(f) n* Pt
De Röhre *(f)*
En tube
Es tubo *(m)*
Fr tube *(m)*
It tubo *(m)*

válvula catódica *(f)* Pt
De Kathodenstrahlröhre *(f)*
En cathode-ray tube (CRT)
Es tubo de rayos catódicos (TRC) *(m)*
Fr tube à rayons cathodiques *(m)*
It tubo a raggi catodici *(m)*

válvula de armazenamento *(f)* Pt
De Speicherröhre *(f)*
En storage tube
Es tubo de almacenamiento *(m)*
Fr tube à mémoire *(m)*
It tubo di memoria *(m)*

válvula de visualização *(f)* Pt
De Anzeigeröhre *(f)*
En display tube
Es tubo de representación visual *(m)*
Fr tube cathodique de visualisation *(m)*
It tubo visualizzatore *(m)*

variabile *adj* It
De veränderlich
En variable
Es variable
Fr variable
Pt variável

variabile *(f) n* It
De veränderliche Größe *(f)*
En variable
Es variable *(f)*
Fr variable *(f)*
Pt variável *(f)*

variabile fittizia *(f)* It
De Scheinvariable *(f)*
En dummy variable
Es variable ficticia *(f)*
Fr variable fictive *(f)*
Pt variável simulada *(f)*

variabile manipolata *(f)* It
De Stellgröße *(f)*
En manipulated variable
Es variable manipulada *(f)*
Fr variable manipulée *(f)*
Pt variável manipulada *(f)*

variable *adj* En, Es, Fr
De veränderlich
It variabile
Pt variável

variable *n* En, Es, Fr *(f)*
De veränderliche Größe *(f)*
It variabile *(f)*
Pt variável *(f)*

variable ficticia *(f)* Es
De Scheinvariable *(f)*
En dummy variable
Fr variable fictive *(f)*
It variabile fittizia *(f)*
Pt variável simulada *(f)*

variable fictive *(f)* Fr
De Scheinvariable *(f)*
En dummy variable
Es variable ficticia *(f)*
It variabile fittizia *(f)*
Pt variável simulada *(f)*

variable field En
De veränderliches Feld *(n)*
Es campo variable *(m)*
Fr champ variable *(m)*
It campo variabile *(m)*
Pt campo variável *(m)*

variable manipulada *(f)* Es
De Stellgröße *(f)*
En manipulated variable
Fr variable manipulée *(f)*
It variabile manipolata *(f)*
Pt variável manipulada *(f)*

variable manipulée *(f)* Fr
De Stellgröße *(f)*
En manipulated variable
Es variable manipulada *(f)*
It variabile manipolata *(f)*
Pt variável manipulada *(f)*

variável *adj* Pt
De veränderlich
En variable
Es variable
Fr variable
It variabile

variável *(f) n* Pt
De veränderliche Größe *(f)*
En variable
Es variable *(f)*
Fr variable *(f)*
It variabile *(f)*

variável manipulada *(f)* Pt
De Stellgröße *(f)*
En manipulated variable
Es variable manipulada *(f)*
Fr variable manipulée *(f)*
It variabile manipolata *(f)*

variável simulada *(f)* Pt
De Scheinvariable *(f)*
En dummy variable
Es variable ficticia *(f)*
Fr variable fictive *(f)*
It variabile fittizia *(f)*

vector arithmetic En
De Vektorarithmetik *(f)*
Es aritmética vectorial *(f)*
Fr arithmétique vectorielle *(f)*
It aritmetica dei vettori *(f)*
Pt aritmética de vectores *(f)*

vector-mode display En
De Vektorbetriebs-artanzeige *(f)*
Es representación en modo vectorial *(f)*
Fr affichage mode vectoriel *(m)*
It visualizzazione di modo vettore *(f)*
Pt visualização de modo vector *(f)*

vector processing En
De Vektorverarbeitung *(f)*
Es proceso vectorial *(m)*
Fr traitement vectoriel *(m)*
It elaborazione di vettori *(f)*
Pt processamento de vectores *(m)*

Vektorarithmetik *(f) n* De
En vector arithmetic
Es aritmética vectorial *(f)*
Fr arithmétique vectorielle *(f)*
It aritmetica dei vettori *(f)*
Pt aritmética de vectores *(f)*

Vektorbetriebs-artanzeige *(f) n* De
En vector-mode display
Es representación en modo vectorial *(f)*
Fr affichage mode vectoriel *(m)*
It visualizzazione di modo vettore *(f)*
Pt visualização de modo vector *(f)*

Vektorverarbeitung *(f) n* De
En vector processing
Es proceso vectorial *(m)*
Fr traitement vectoriel *(m)*
It elaborazione di vettori *(f)*
Pt processamento de vectores *(m)*

velocidad de impulsos de reloj *(f)* Es
De Taktgeschwindigkeit *(f)*
En clock rate
Fr fréquence des impulsions d'horloge *(f)*
It frequenza degli impulsi dell'orologio *(f)*
Pt taxa de impulsos de relógio *(f)*

velocidad de lectura *(f)* Es
De Auslese-geschwindigkeit *(f)*
En read rate
Fr vitesse de lecture *(f)*
It volume di lettura *(m)*
Pt velocidade de leitura *(f)*

velocidad de perforación *(f)* Es
De Lochungs-geschwindigkeit *(f)*
En perforation rate; punching rate
Fr vitesse de perforation *(f)*
It volume di perforazione *(m)*
Pt índice de perfuração *(m)*

velocidad de transmisión *(f)* Es
De Übertragungs-geschwindigkeit *(f)*
En transmission speed
Fr vitesse de transmission *(f)*
It velocità di trasmissione *(f)*
Pt velocidade de transmissão *(f)*

velocidad de transmisión de señal *(f)* Es
De Signalisier-geschwindigkeit *(f)*
En signalling rate
Fr vitesse de signalisation *(f)*
It velocità dai segnali *(f)*
Pt índice de sinalização *(m)*

velocidade de leitura *(f)* Pt
De Auslese-geschwindigkeit *(f)*
En read rate
Es velocidad de lectura *(f)*
Fr vitesse de lecture *(f)*
It volume di lettura *(m)*

velocidade de transmissão *(f)* Pt
De Übertragungs-geschwindigkeit *(f)*
En transmission speed
Es velocidad de transmisión *(f)*
Fr vitesse de transmission *(f)*
It velocità di trasmissione *(f)*

velocidad en baudios *(f)* Es
De Baudgeschwindigkeit *(f)*
En baud rate
Fr débit en bauds *(m)*
It numero di baud *(m)*
Pt taxa de baud *(f)*

velocità dai segnali *(f)* It
De Signalisier-geschwindigkeit *(f)*
En signalling rate
Es velocidad de transmisión de señal *(f)*
Fr vitesse de signalisation *(f)*
Pt índice de sinalização *(m)*

velocità di trasmissione *(f)* It
De Übertragungs-geschwindigkeit *(f)*
En transmission speed
Es velocidad de transmisión *(f)*
Fr vitesse de transmission *(f)*
Pt velocidade de transmissão *(f)*

veränderlich *adj* De
En variable
Es variable
Fr variable
It variabile
Pt variável

veränderliche Größe *(f)* De
En variable
Es variable *(f)*
Fr variable *(f)*
It variabile *(f)*
Pt variável *(f)*

veränderliches Feld *(n)* De
En variable field
Es campo variable *(m)*
Fr champ variable *(m)*
It campo variabile *(m)*
Pt campo variável *(m)*

Verarbeiter *(m) n* De
En processor
Es procesador *(m)*
Fr ordinateur *(m)*
It elaboratore *(m)*
Pt processor *(m)*

verarbeiterbeschränkt *adj* De
En processor-limited
Es limitado por la procesador
Fr limité par la vitesse de traitement
It limitato per velocitá di elaborazione
Pt limitado ao processor

Verarbeitung *(f) n* De
En processing
Es tratamiento *(m)*
Fr traitement *(m)*
It elaborazione *(f)*
Pt processamento *(m)*

Verbesserungswartung *(f) n* De
En corrective maintenance
Es mantenimiento correctivo *(m)*
Fr entretien correctif *(m)*

It manutenzione correttiva *(f)*
Pt manutenção correctiva *(f)*

Verbinder *(m) n* De
En connector
Es conector *(m)*
Fr connecteur *(m)*
It connettore *(m)*
Pt conector *(m)*

Verbindung *(f) n* De
En linkage
Es enlace *(m)*
Fr lien *(m)*
It interconnessione *(f)*
Pt ligação *(f)*

verdichtetes Format *(n)* De
En reduced format
Es formato reducido *(m)*
Fr structure réduite *(f)*
It formato ridotto *(m)*
Pt formato reduzido *(m)*

Verdopplung *(f) n* De
En duplication
Es duplicación *(f)*
Fr duplication *(f)*
It duplicazione *(f)*
Pt duplicação *(f)*

Vereinbarung *(f) n* De
En directive
Es directiva *(f)*
Fr directive *(f)*
It direttiva *(f)*
Pt directiva *(f)*

Verfahren *(n) n* De
En procedure
Es procedimiento *(m)*
Fr procédure *(f)*
It procedura *(f)*
Pt procedimento *(m)*

verfahrenbasierte Sprache *(f)* De
En procedure-orientated language
Es lenguaje orientado a los procedimientos *(m)*
Fr langage orienté à la procédure *(m)*
It linguaggio orientato alla procedura *(m)*
Pt linguagem orientada pelo procedimento *(f)*

Verfahrenssteuerung *(f) n* De
En process control
Es control de procesos *(m)*
Fr commande de processus *(f)*
It controllo di processo *(m)*
Pt controle de processo *(m)*

verfügbare Zeit *(f)* De
En available time
Es tiempo disponible *(m)*
Fr temps disponible *(m)*
It tempo disponibile *(m)*
Pt tempo disponível *(m)*

vergleichen *vb* De
En compare
Es comparar
Fr comparer
It comparare
Pt comparar

Vergleichsoperator *(m) n* De
En relational operator
Es operador de relación *(m)*
Fr opérateur de relation *(m)*
It operatore relazionale *(m)*
Pt operador relacional *(m)*

verifica *(f) n* It
De Prüfung *(f)*
En verification
Es verificación *(f)*
Fr vérification *(f)*
Pt verificação *(f)*

verificação *(f) n* Pt
De Prüfung *(f)*
En check; verification
Es verificación *(f)*
Fr contrôle; vérification *(m f)*
It controllo; verifica *(m f)*

verificação automática *(f)* Pt
De automatische Prüfung *(f)*
En automatic check
Es verificación automática *(f)*
Fr contrôle automatique *(m)*
It controllo automatico *(m)*

verificação cruzada *(f)* Pt
De Gegenprüfung *(f)*
En cross check
Es verificación cruzada *(f)*
Fr contre-vérification *(f)*
It verifica generale completa *(f)*

verificação de codificação *(f)* Pt
De Kodierungsprüfung *(f)*
En coding check
Es verificación de la codificación *(f)*
Fr contrôle de codage *(m)*
It controllo di codificazione *(m)*

verificação de congruência *(f)* Pt
De Kontrolle der Konsistenz *(f)*
En consistency check
Es control de uniformidad *(m)*
Fr contrôle de cohérence *(m)*
It controllo di consistenza *(m)*

verificação de descarga *(f)* Pt
De Speicherauszugs-prüfung *(f)*
En dump check
Es control por vaciado *(m)*
Fr contrôle par vidage *(m)*
It controllo del dump *(m)*

verificação de eco *(f)* Pt
De Echoprüfung *(f)*
En echo check
Es verificación por eco *(f)*
Fr contrôle par écho *(m)*
It controllo dell'eco *(m)*

verificação de fichas *(f)* Pt
De Kartenprüfung *(f)*
En card verifying
Es verificación de fichas *(f)*
Fr vérification de cartes *(f)*
It verifica delle schede *(f)*

verificação de paridade *(f)* Pt
De Paritätsprüfung *(f)*
En parity check
Es control de paridad *(m)*
Fr contrôle de parité *(m)*
It controllo di parità *(m)*

verificação de redundância *(f)* Pt
De Redundanzkontrolle *(f)*
En redundancy check
Es verificación por redundancia *(f)*
Fr contrôle par redondance *(m)*
It controllo di ridondanza *(m)*

verificação de resíduos *(f)* Pt
De Restprüfung *(f)*
En residue check
Es verificación por residuo *(f)*
Fr contrôle de résidu *(m)*
It controllo residuo *(m)*

verificação de sequência *(f)* Pt
De Folgeprüfung *(f)*
En sequence check
Es verificación de secuencia *(f)*
Fr contrôle de séquence *(m)*
It controllo di sequenza *(m)*

verificação de soma *(f)* Pt
De Summenprüfung *(f)*
En summation check
Es comprobación de suma *(f)*
Fr contrôle par totalisation *(m)*

It controllo di addizione *(m)*

verificação de transferência *(f)* Pt
De Übertragungsprüfung *(f)*
En transfer check
Es verificación de transferencia *(f)*
Fr contrôle par répétition *(m)*
It controllo di trasferimento *(m)*

verificação de validez *(f)* Pt
De Gültigkeitsprüfung *(f)*
En validity check
Es verificación de validez *(f)*
Fr contrôle de vraisemblance *(m)*
It controllo di validità *(m)*

verificação dupla paralela *(f)* Pt
De Doppelprüfung *(f)*
En twin check
Es doble control *(m)*
Fr double contrôle *(m)*
It doppio controllo *(m)*

verificação modulo-n *(f)* Pt
De Modulo-N-Kontrolle *(f)*
En modulo-n check
Es verificación de módulo N *(f)*
Fr contrôle module-n *(m)*
It controllo modulo-n *(m)*

verificação par-impar *(f)* Pt
De gerade-ungerade Paritätsprüfung *(f)*
En odd-even check
Es control de paridad par-impar *(m)*
Fr contrôle de parité pair-impair *(m)*
It controllo pari-dispari *(m)*

verificación *(f)* *n* Es
De Prüfung *(f)*
En check; verification
Fr contrôle; vérification *(m f)*
It controllo; verifica *(m f)*
Pt verificação *(f)*

verificación automática *(f)* Es
De automatische Prüfung *(f)*
En automatic check
Fr contrôle automatique *(m)*
It controllo automatico *(m)*
Pt verificação automática *(f)*

verificación cruzada *(f)* Es
De Gegenprüfung *(f)*
En cross check
Fr contre-vérification *(f)*
It verifica generale completa *(f)*
Pt verificação cruzada *(f)*

verificación de fichas *(f)* Es
De Kartenprüfung *(f)*
En card verifying
Fr vérification de cartes *(f)*
It verifica delle schede *(f)*
Pt verificação de fichas *(f)*

verificación de la codificación *(f)* Es
De Kodierungsprüfung *(f)*
En coding check
Fr contrôle de codage *(m)*
It controllo di codificazione *(m)*
Pt verificação de codificação *(f)*

verificación de módulo N *(f)* Es
De Modulo-N-Kontrolle *(f)*
En modulo-n check
Fr contrôle module-n *(m)*
It controllo modulo-n *(m)*
Pt verificação modulo-n *(f)*

verificación de secuencia *(f)* Es
De Folgeprüfung *(f)*
En sequence check
Fr contrôle de séquence *(m)*
It controllo di sequenza *(m)*
Pt verificação de sequência *(f)*

verificación de transferencia *(f)* Es
De Übertragungsprüfung *(f)*
En transfer check
Fr contrôle par répétition *(m)*
It controllo di trasferimento *(m)*
Pt verificação de transferência *(f)*

verificación de validez *(f)* Es
De Gültigkeitsprüfung *(f)*
En validity check
Fr contrôle de vraisemblance *(m)*
It controllo di validità *(m)*
Pt verificação de validez *(f)*

verificación por eco *(f)* Es
De Echoprüfung *(f)*
En echo check
Fr contrôle par écho *(m)*
It controllo dell'eco *(m)*
Pt verificação de eco *(f)*

verificación por redundancia *(f)* Es
De Redundanzkontrolle *(f)*
En redundancy check
Fr contrôle par redondance *(m)*
It controllo di ridondanza *(m)*
Pt verificação de redundância *(f)*

verificación por residuo *(f)* Es
De Restprüfung *(f)*
En residue check
Fr contrôle de résidu *(m)*
It controllo residuo *(m)*
Pt verificação de resíduos *(f)*

verifica delle schede *(f)* It
De Kartenprüfung *(f)*
En card verifying
Es verificación de fichas *(f)*
Fr vérification de cartes *(f)*
Pt verificação de fichas *(f)*

verificadora de cinta *(f)* Es
De Bandprüfgerät *(n)*
En tape verifier
Fr vérificatrice de bande *(f)*
It verificatrice di nastri *(f)*
Pt verificador de fita *(m)*

verificador de fita *(m)* Pt
De Bandprüfgerät *(n)*
En tape verifier
Es verificadora de cinta *(f)*
Fr vérificatrice de bande *(f)*
It verificatrice di nastri *(f)*

verificador de perforación *(m)* Es
De Lochungsprüfer *(m)*
En punch verifier
Fr vérificatrice de perforations *(f)*
It verificatrice della perforazione *(f)*
Pt verificador de perfuração *(m)*

verificador de perfuração *(m)* Pt
De Lochungsprüfer *(m)*
En punch verifier
Es verificador de perforación *(m)*
Fr vérificatrice de perforations *(f)*
It verificatrice della perforazione *(f)*

verifica generale completa *(f)* It
De Gegenprüfung *(f)*
En cross check
Es verificación cruzada *(f)*

Fr contre-vérification *(f)*
Pt verificação cruzada *(f)*

verificar *vb* Es, Pt
De prüfen
En verify
Fr vérifier
It verificare

verificare *vb* It
De prüfen
En verify
Es verificar
Fr vérifier
Pt verificar

verificar por comparación Es
De gegenprüfen
En cross check
Fr contre-vérifier
It contra-verificare
Pt contra-verificar

verification *n* En
De Prüfung *(f)*
Es verificación *(f)*
Fr vérification *(f)*
It verifica *(f)*
Pt verificação *(f)*

vérification *(f) n* Fr
De Prüfung *(f)*
En verification
Es verificación *(f)*
It verifica *(f)*
Pt verificação *(f)*

vérification à rebours *(f)* Fr
De Prüfliste *(f)*
En audit trail
Es pista de auditoría *(f)*
It lista di verifica *(f)*
Pt trilho de verificação *(m)*

vérification de cartes *(f)* Fr
De Kartenprüfung *(f)*
En card verifying
Es verificación de fichas *(f)*
It verifica delle schede *(f)*
Pt verificação de fichas *(f)*

vérificatrice de bande *(f)* Fr
De Bandprüfgerät *(n)*
En tape verifier
Es verificadora de cinta *(f)*
It verificatrice di nastri *(f)*
Pt verificador de fita *(m)*

verificatrice della perforazione *(f)* It
De Lochungsprüfer *(m)*
En punch verifier
Es verificador de perforación *(m)*
Fr vérificatrice de perforations *(f)*
Pt verificador de perfuração *(m)*

vérificatrice de perforations *(f)* Fr
De Lochungsprüfer *(m)*
En punch verifier
Es verificador de perforación *(m)*
It verificatrice della perforazione *(f)*
Pt verificador de perfuração *(m)*

verificatrice di nastri *(f)* It
De Bandprüfgerät *(n)*
En tape verifier
Es verificadora de cinta *(f)*
Fr vérificatrice de bande *(f)*
Pt verificador de fita *(m)*

vérifier *vb* Fr
De prüfen
En verify
Es verificar
It verificare
Pt verificar

verify *vb* En
De prüfen
Es verificar
Fr vérifier
It verificare
Pt verificar

Verklemmung *(f) n* De
En jam
Es atascamiento *(m)*
Fr bourrage *(m)*
It inceppamento *(m)*
Pt congestionamento *(m)*

Verknüpfung *(f) n* De
En logic
Es lógica *(f)*
Fr logique *(f)*
It logica *(f)*
Pt lógica *(f)*

Verknüpfungs-diagramm *(n) n* De
En logic diagram
Es diagrama lógico *(m)*
Fr schéma logique *(m)*
It diagramma logico *(m)*
Pt diagrama lógico *(m)*

Verknüpfungstor *(n) n* De
En logic gate
Es puerta lógica *(f)*
Fr porte logique *(f)*
It porta logica *(f)*
Pt porta lógica *(f)*

Verknüpfungs-schaltung *(f) n* De
En logic circuit
Es circuito lógico *(m)*
Fr circuit logique *(m)*
It circuito logico *(m)*
Pt circuito lógico *(m)*

Verlust *(m) n* De
En loss
Es pérdida *(f)*
Fr perte *(f)*
It perdita *(f)*
Pt perda *(f)*

vermitteln *vb* De
En exchange
Es cambiar
Fr intervenir
It scambiare
Pt intercambiar

Vermittlung *(f) n* De
En exchange
Es intercambio *(m)*
Fr échange *(m)*
It scambio *(m)*
Pt intercâmbio *(m)*

verriegeln *vb* De
En interlock
Es interbloquear
Fr verrouiller
It interbloccare
Pt engrenar

verrouiller *vb* Fr
De verriegeln
En interlock
Es interbloquear
It interbloccare
Pt engrenar

verschieben De
En relocate
Es reubicar
Fr translater
It rilocare
Pt relocalizar

verschiebliche Adresse *(f)* De
En relocatable address
Es dirección reubicable *(f)*
Fr adresse translatable *(f)*
It indirizzo rilocabile *(m)*
Pt endereço relocalizável *(m)*

verschieblicher Code *(m)* De
En relocatable code
Es código reubicable *(m)*
Fr code translatable *(m)*
It codice rilocabile *(m)*
Pt código relocalizável *(m)*

Verschlüssler *(m) n* De
En encoder
Es codificador *(m)*
Fr codeur *(m)*
It codificatore *(m)*
Pt codificador *(m)*

versetzen *vb* De
En shift
Es desplazar
Fr décaler
It spostare (dati)
Pt mudar

Versteckzeilen-algorithmus *(m) n* De
En hidden-line algorithm
Es algoritmo de línea oculta *(m)*
Fr algorithme ligne cachée *(m)*

It algoritmo a linea nascosta *(m)*
Pt algoritmo de linha oculta *(m)*

verstrichene Zeit *(f)* De
En elapsed time
Es tiempo transcurrido *(m)*
Fr temps écoulé *(m)*
It tempo trascorso *(m)*
Pt tempo decorrido *(m)*

Versuchslauf *(m)* *n* De
En dry run
Es pasada en seco *(f)*
Fr coup d'essai *(m)*
It passo a prova *(m)*
Pt passagem a seco *(f)*

verteilte Verarbeitung *(f)* De
En distributed processing
Es proceso distribuido *(m)*
Fr informatique répartie *(f)*
It elaborazione ripartita *(f)*
Pt tratamento distribuido *(m)*

Verträglichkeit *(f)* *n* De
En compatibility
Es compatibilidad *(f)*
Fr compatibilité *(f)*
It compatibilità *(f)*
Pt compatibilidade *(f)*

Vertraulichkeit *(f)* *n* De
En privacy
Es aspecto confidencial *(m)*
Fr confidentialité *(f)*
It riservatezza *(f)*
Pt aspecto confidencial *(m)*

Verweilzeit *(f)* *n* De
En retention period
Es período de retención *(m)*
Fr période de validité *(f)*
It tempo di ritenzione *(m)*
Pt periodo de retenção *(m)*

verzahnt ablaufende Verarbeitung *(f)* De
En concurrent processing
Es proceso concurrente *(m)*
Fr traitement en simultané *(m)*
It elaborazione concorrente *(f)*
Pt processamento concorrente *(m)*

Verzahnung *(f)* *n* De
En interleaving
Es interfolición *(f)*
Fr interfoliage *(m)*
It interfogliare *(m)*
Pt interfolição *(f)*

Verzifferer *(m)* *n* De
En digitizer
Es digitalizador *(m)*
Fr numériseur *(m)*
It digitalizzatore *(m)*
Pt digitalizador *(m)*

verziffern *vb* De
En digitize
Es digitalizar
Fr numériser
It digitalizzare
Pt digitalizar

verzögerte Aktualisierung *(f)* De
En delayed updating
Es actualización diferida *(f)*
Fr mise à jour temporisée *(f)*
It aggiornamento ritardato *(m)*
Pt actualização atrasada *(f)*

Verzögerungsleitung *(f)* *n* De
En delay line
Es línea de retardo *(f)*
Fr ligne à retard *(f)*
It linea di ritardo *(f)*
Pt linha de atraso *(f)*

Verzögerungszeit *(f)* *n* De
En deceleration time
Es tiempo de deceleración *(m)*
Fr temps de décélération *(m)*
It tempo di decelerazione *(m)*
Pt tempo de desaceleração *(m)*

Verzweigungsbefehl *(m)* *n* De
En branch instruction
Es instrucción de bifurcación *(f)*
Fr instruction de branchement *(f)*
It istruzione di diramazione *(f)*
Pt instruções para ligar *(f)*

vidage *(m)* *n* Fr
De Speicherauszug *(m)*
En dump
Es vuelco de la memoria *(m)*
It dump *(m)*
Pt descarregador *(m)*

vidage d'autopsie *(m)* Fr
De Speicherauszug nach dem Tode *(m)*
En post-mortem dump
Es vaciado póstumo *(m)*
It dump di autopsia *(m)*
Pt descarregador de autópsia *(m)*

vidage de la mémoire *(m)* Fr
De Speicherauszug *(m)*
En memory dump
Es vuelco de la memoria *(m)*
It dump della memoria *(m)*
Pt descarregador de memória *(m)*

vidage de secours *(m)* Fr
De Wiedereinstiegs-speicherauszug *(m)*
En rescue dump
Es vaciado de rescate *(m)*
It dump di salvataggio *(m)*
Pt armazém de emergência *(m)*

vidage en un point fixe du programme *(m)* Fr
De statischer Speicherauszug *(m)*
En static dump
Es vuelco estático de la memoria *(m)*
It dump statico *(m)*
Pt descarregador estático *(m)*

video *n* En, Es, It, Pt
De Video *(n)*
Fr vidéo *(m)*

Video *(n)* *n* De
En video
Es video *(m)*
Fr vidéo *(m)*
It video *(m)*
Pt video *(m)*

vidéo *(m)* *n* Fr
De Video *(n)*
En video
Es video *(m)*
It video *(m)*
Pt video *(m)*

Videostation *(f)* *n* De
En video terminal
Es terminal de video *(m)*
Fr terminal vidéo *(m)*
It terminale video *(m)*
Pt terminal video *(m)*

video terminal En
De Videostation *(f)*
Es terminal de video *(m)*
Fr terminal vidéo *(m)*
It terminale video *(m)*
Pt terminal video *(m)*

vider *vb* Fr
De speicherausziehen
En dump
Es volcar
It fare un dump
Pt descarregar

Vieleckbegrenzung *(f)* *n* De
En polygon clipping
Es recorte poligonal *(m)*
Fr écrêtage polygone *(m)*
It limitazione poligonale *(f)*
Pt recorte poligonal *(m)*

Vierdrahtschaltung *(f)* *n* De
En four-wire circuit
Es circuito de cuatro hilos *(m)*

Fr circuit quatre fils *(m)*
It circuito a quattro fili *(m)*
Pt circuito de quatro fios *(m)*

viertgeneration *adj* De
En fourth-generation
Es cuarta-generación
Fr quatrième-génération
It quarta-generazione
Pt quarta-geração

vigiar *vb* Pt
De kontrollieren
En monitor
Es examinar
Fr surveiller
It esaminare

virgin tape En
De Neuband *(n)*
Es cint a virgen *(f)*
Fr bande vierge *(f)*
It nastro vergine *(m)*
Pt fita virgem *(f)*

virtual address En
De virtuelle Adresse *(f)*
Es dirección virtual *(f)*
Fr adresse virtuelle *(f)*
It indirizzo virtuale *(m)*
Pt endereço virtual *(m)*

virtual machine En
De virtuelle Maschine *(f)*
Es máquina virtual *(f)*
Fr machine virtuelle *(f)*
It macchina virtuale *(f)*
Pt máquina virtual *(f)*

virtual store (VS) En
De virtueller Speicher *(m)*
Es memoria virtual *(f)*
Fr mémoire virtuelle *(f)*
It memoria virtuale *(f)*
Pt memória virtual *(f)*

virtuelle Adresse *(f)* De
En virtual address
Es dirección virtual *(f)*
Fr adresse virtuelle *(f)*
It indirizzo virtuale *(m)*
Pt endereço virtual *(m)*

virtuelle Maschine *(f)* De
En virtual machine
Es máquina virtual *(f)*
Fr machine virtuelle *(f)*
It macchina virtuale *(f)*
Pt máquina virtual *(f)*

virtueller Speicher *(m)* De
En virtual store (VS)
Es memoria virtual *(f)*
Fr mémoire virtuelle *(f)*
It memoria virtuale *(f)*
Pt memória virtual *(f)*

visual-display unit (VDU) En
De Sichtgerät *(n)*
Es unidad de visualización *(f)*
Fr appareil de visualisation (AV) *(m)*
It unitá di visualizzazione *(f)*
Pt unidade de visualização *(f)*

visualisation graphique *(f)* Fr
De Zeichenanzeige *(f)*
En graphics display
Es representación gráfica *(f)*
It visualizzatore grafico *(m)*
Pt representação gráfica *(f)*

visualisation interactive *(f)* Fr
De Dialoganzeige *(f)*
En interactive display
Es representación interactiva *(f)*
It visualizzatore interattivo *(m)*
Pt visualização interactiva *(f)*

visualização de armazenamento *(f)* Pt
De Speicheranzeige *(f)*
En storage display
Es presentación de almacenamiento *(f)*
Fr affichage d'enregistrement *(m)*
It visualizzazione di memoria *(f)*

visualização de modo vector *(f)* Pt
De Vektorbetriebs-artanzeige *(f)*
En vector-mode display
Es representación en modo vectorial *(f)*
Fr affichage mode vectoriel *(m)*
It visualizzazione di modo vettore *(f)*

visualização interactiva *(f)* Pt
De Dialoganzeige *(f)*
En interactive display
Es representación interactiva *(f)*
Fr visualisation interactive *(f)*
It visualizzatore interattivo *(m)*

visualização tabelar *(f)* Pt
De tabellarische Anzeige *(f)*
En tabular display
Es representación tabular *(f)*
Fr affichage tabulaire *(m)*
It visualizzazione tabulare *(f)*

visualizzare *vb* It
De anzeigen
En display
Es presentar
Fr afficher
Pt mostrar

visualizzatore *(m) n* It
De Anzeige *(f)*
En display
Es representación visual *(f)*
Fr affichage *(m)*
Pt representação visual *(f)*

visualizzatore grafico *(m)* It
De Zeichenanzeige *(f)*
En graphics display
Es representación gráfica *(f)*
Fr visualisation graphique *(f)*
Pt representação gráfica *(f)*

visualizzatore interattivo *(m)* It
De Dialoganzeige *(f)*
En interactive display
Es representación interactiva *(f)*
Fr visualisation interactive *(f)*
Pt visualização interactiva *(f)*

visualizzazione di aggiornamento *(f)* It
De Auffrischungsanzeige *(f)*
En refresh display
Es representación regenerada *(f)*
Fr affichage-régénération *(m)*
Pt apresentação de refrescamento *(f)*

visualizzazione di memoria *(f)* It
De Speicheranzeige *(f)*
En storage display
Es presentación de almacenamiento *(f)*
Fr affichage d'enregistrement *(m)*
Pt visualização de armazenamento *(f)*

visualizzazione di modo vettore *(f)* It
De Vektorbetriebs-artanzeige *(f)*
En vector-mode display
Es representación en modo vectorial *(f)*
Fr affichage mode vectoriel *(m)*
Pt visualização de modo vector *(f)*

visualizzazione tabulare *(f)* It
De tabellarische Anzeige *(f)*
En tabular display
Es representación tabular *(f)*
Fr affichage tabulaire *(m)*
Pt visualização tabelar *(f)*

visualizzazione trama *(f)* It
De Rasteranzeige *(f)*
En raster display
Es presentación de trama *(f)*
Fr affichage tramé *(m)*

Pt apresentação quadriculada *(f)*

vitesse d'échantillonnage *(f)* Fr
De Abtastfrequenz *(f)*
En sampling rate
Es frecuencia de muestreo *(f)*
It volume di campionamento *(m)*
Pt índice de amostragem *(m)*

vitesse de lecture *(f)* Fr
De Auslese-geschwindigkeit *(f)*
En read rate
Es velocidad de lectura *(f)*
It volume di lettura *(m)*
Pt velocidade de leitura *(f)*

vitesse de perforation *(f)* Fr
De Lochungs-geschwindigkeit *(f)*
En perforation rate; punching rate
Es velocidad de perforación *(f)*
It volume di perforazione *(m)*
Pt índice de perfuração *(m)*

vitesse de signalisation *(f)* Fr
De Signalisier-geschwindigkeit *(f)*
En signalling rate
Es velocidad de transmisión de señal *(f)*
It velocità dai segnali *(f)*
Pt índice de sinalização *(m)*

vitesse de transfert *(f)* Fr
De Übertragungs-frequenz *(f)*
En transfer rate
Es indice de transferencia *(m)*
It volume di trasferimento *(m)*
Pt índice de transferência *(m)*

vitesse de transmission *(f)* Fr
De Übertragungs-geschwindigkeit *(f)*
En transmission speed
Es velocidad de transmisión *(f)*
It velocità di trasmissione *(f)*
Pt velocidade de transmissão *(f)*

vocabolario *(m)* *n* It
De Wörterbuch *(n)*
En vocabulary
Es vocabulario *(m)*
Fr vocabulaire *(m)*
Pt vocabulário *(m)*

vocabulaire *(m)* *n* Fr
De Wörterbuch *(n)*
En vocabulary
Es vocabulario *(m)*
It vocabolario *(m)*
Pt vocabulário *(m)*

vocabulario *(m)* *n* Es
De Wörterbuch *(n)*
En vocabulary
Fr vocabulaire *(m)*
It vocabolario *(m)*
Pt vocabulário *(m)*

vocabulário *(m)* *n* Pt
De Wörterbuch *(n)*
En vocabulary
Es vocabulario *(m)*
Fr vocabulaire *(m)*
It vocabolario *(m)*

vocabulary *n* En
De Wörterbuch *(n)*
Es vocabulario *(m)*
Fr vocabulaire *(m)*
It vocabolario *(m)*
Pt vocabulário *(m)*

voce *(f)* *n* It
De Wort *(n)*
En word
Es palabra *(f)*
Fr mot *(m)*
Pt palavra *(f)*

voce di controllo *(f)* It
De Schablone *(f)*
En control word
Es palabra de control *(f)*
Fr mot de contrôle *(m)*
Pt palavra de controlo *(f)*

voce di dato *(f)* It
De Datenfeld *(n)*
En data item
Es unidad de información *(f)*
Fr donnée élémentaire *(f)*
Pt item de dados *(m)*

voce di stato *(f)* It
De Statuswort *(n)*
En status word
Es palabra de estado *(f)*
Fr mot d'état *(m)*
Pt palavra de status *(f)*

voce macchina *(f)* It
De Maschinenwort *(n)*
En machine word
Es palabra de máquina *(f)*
Fr mot machine *(m)*
Pt palavra da máquina *(f)*

voice-grade channel En
De Telefonleitung *(f)*
Es canal de rango vocal *(m)*
Fr voie téléphonique *(f)*
It canale a frequenze vocali *(m)*
Pt canal para fonia *(m)*

voie de communication *(f)* Fr
De Kommunikations-kanal *(m)*
En communication channel
Es canal de comunicación *(m)*
It canale di comunicazione *(m)*
Pt canal de comunicação *(m)*

voie lecture-écriture *(f)* Fr
De Lesen-Schreiben-Kanal *(m)*
En read-write channel
Es canal de lectura-escritura *(m)*
It canale di lettura-scrittura *(m)*
Pt canal de leitura-escrita *(m)*

voie téléphonique *(f)* Fr
De Telefonleitung *(f)*
En voice-grade channel
Es canal de rango vocal *(m)*
It canale a frequenze vocali *(m)*
Pt canal para fonia *(m)*

volatile memory En
De energieabhängiger Speicher *(m)*
Es memoria volátil *(f)*
Fr mémoire non rémanente *(f)*
It memoria volatile *(f)*
Pt memória volátil *(f)*

volcar *vb* Es
De speicherausziehen
En dump
Fr vider
It fare un dump
Pt descarregar

volume *n* En; Fr, It, Pt *(m)*
De Volumen *(n)*
Es volumen *(m)*

volume di bit *(m)* It
De Binärzeichen-geschwindigkeit *(f)*
En bit rate
Es tasa en bits *(f)*
Fr débit de bits *(m)*
Pt taxa de bit *(f)*

volume di campionamento *(m)* It
De Abtastfrequenz *(f)*
En sampling rate
Es frecuencia de muestreo *(f)*
Fr vitesse d'échantillonnage *(f)*
Pt índice de amostragem *(m)*

volume di lettura *(m)* It
De Auslese-geschwindigkeit *(f)*
En read rate
Es velocidad de lectura *(f)*
Fr vitesse de lecture *(f)*
Pt velocidade de leitura *(f)*

volume di perforazione *(m)* It
De Lochungs-geschwindigkeit *(f)*

En perforation rate; punching rate
Es velocidad de perforación *(f)*
Fr vitesse de perforation *(f)*
Pt índice de perfuração *(m)*

volume di trasferimento *(m)* It
De Übertragungsfrequenz *(f)*
En transfer rate
Es indice de transferencia *(m)*
Fr vitesse de transfert *(f)*
Pt índice de transferência *(m)*

volumen *(m) n* Es
De Volumen *(n)*
En volume
Fr volume *(m)*
It volume *(m)*
Pt volume *(m)*

Volumen *(n) n* De
En volume
Es volumen *(m)*
Fr volume *(m)*
It volume *(m)*
Pt volume *(m)*

vorbeugende Wartung *(f)* De
En preventative maintenance
Es mantenimiento preventivo *(m)*
Fr entretien préventif *(m)*
It manutenzione preventiva *(f)*
Pt manutenção preventiva *(f)*

Vordergrundverarbeitung *(f) n* De
En foreground processing
Es proceso preferente *(m)*
Fr traitement de front *(m)*
It elaborazione di primo piano *(f)*
Pt processamento de primeiro plano *(m)*

Vorgang *(m) n* De
En transaction
Es transacción *(f)*
Fr transaction *(f)*
It transazione *(f)*
Pt transacção *(f)*

Vorlesekopf *(m) n* De
En pre-read head
Es cabeza de lectura previa *(f)*
Fr tête de première lecture *(f)*
It testina di pre-lettura *(f)*
Pt cabeça de pré-leitura *(f)*

Vorranganzeiger *(m) n* De
En priority indicator
Es indicador de prioridad *(m)*
Fr indicateur prioritaire *(m)*
It indicatore di priorità *(m)*
Pt indicador de prioridade *(m)*

Vorrangverarbeitung *(f) n* De
En priority processing
Es tratamiento por prioridad *(m)*
Fr traitement par priorités *(m)*
It elaborazione di priorità *(f)*
Pt processamento prioritário *(m)*

Vorrat *(m) n* De
En repertoire
Es repertorio de la instrucción *(m)*
Fr répertoire *(m)*
It repertorio *(m)*
Pt repertório *(m)*

vorredaktieren *vb* De
En pre-edit
Es preeditar
Fr prééditer
It pre-redigere
Pt pré-editar

Vorsatzdarstellung *(f)* De
En prefix notation
Es notación por prefijos *(f)*
Fr notation préfixée *(f)*
It notazione del prefisso *(f)*
Pt notação de prefixos *(f)*

vorschieben *vb* De
En feed
Es alimentar
Fr faire avancer
It alimentare
Pt alimentar

Vorschub *(m) n* De
En feed
Es alimentación *(f)*
Fr avance *(f)*
It alimentazione *(f)*
Pt alimentação *(f)*

vorsortieren *vb* De
En pre-sort
Es crear monotonías
Fr trier préalablement
It pre-selezionare
Pt pré-classificado

Vorsortierung *(f) n* De
En pre-sort
Es creación de monotonías *(f)*
Fr tri préalable *(m)*
It pre-selezione *(f)*
Pt pré-classificação *(f)*

vorspannen *vb* De
En bias
Es polarizar
Fr polariser
It polarizzare
Pt polarizar

Vorspannung *(f) n* De
En bias
Es polarización *(f)*
Fr polarisation *(f)*
It polarizzazione *(f)*
Pt polarisação *(f)*

vorspeichern *vb* De
En pre-store
Es almacenar previamente
Fr pré-enregistrer
It preregistrare
Pt pré-amazenar

vorübergehende Speicherung *(f)* De
En temporary storage
Es memoria temporal *(f)*
Fr mémoire intermédiaire *(f)*
It memoria temporanea *(f)*
Pt armazenamento temporário *(m)*

Vorzeichen *(n) n* De
En sign
Es signo *(m)*
Fr signe *(m)*
It segno *(m)*
Pt indicação *(f)*

Vorzeichenbit *(m) n* De
En sign bit
Es bit de signo *(m)*
Fr bit de signe *(m)*
It bit del segno *(m)*
Pt bit de sinal *(m)*

Vorzeichenprüfanzeiger *(m) n* De
En sign-check indicator
Es indicador de verificación de signo *(m)*
Fr indicateur de contrôle de signes *(m)*
It indicatore del controllo di segno *(m)*
Pt indicador de verificação de sinal *(m)*

Vorzeichenziffer *(f) n* De
En sign digit
Es dígito de signo *(m)*
Fr caractère de signe *(m)*
It digit del segno *(m)*
Pt número digital de sinal *(m)*

vuelco de la memoria *(m)* Es
De Speicherauszug *(m)*
En dump; memory dump
Fr vidage; vidage de la mémoire *(m)*
It dump; dump della memoria *(m)*
Pt descarregador; descarregador de memória *(m)*

vuelco estático de la memoria *(m)* Es
De statischer Speicherauszug *(m)*
En static dump
Fr vidage en un point fixe du programme *(m)*
It dump statico *(m)*
Pt descarregador estático *(m)*

W

Wagenrücklauf *(m) n* De
En carriage return
Es retorno del carro *(m)*
Fr retour chariot *(m)*
It ritorno del carrello *(m)*
Pt retrocesso do carro *(m)*

Wagensteuerband *(n) n* De
En carriage-control tape
Es cinta de control del carro *(f)*
Fr bande pilote *(f)*
It nastrino di controllo del carrello *(m)*
Pt fita com controle de carro *(f)*

Wähler *(m) n* De
En selector
Es selector *(m)*
Fr sélecteur *(m)*
It selettore *(m)*
Pt selector *(m)*

Wählkanal *(m) n* De
En selector channel
Es canal selector *(m)*
Fr canal sélecteur *(m)*
It canale del selettore *(m)*
Pt canal selector *(m)*

Wahrscheinlichkeit *(f) n* De
En probability
Es probabilidad *(f)*
Fr probabilité *(f)*
It probabilità *(f)*
Pt probabilidade *(f)*

waiting time En
De Wartezeit *(f)*
Es tiempo de espera *(m)*
Fr temps d'attente *(m)*
It tempo di attesa *(m)*
Pt tempo de espera *(m)*

Warteschlangentheorie *(f) n* De
En queuing theory
Es teoría de colas *(f)*
Fr théorie des files d'attente *(f)*
It teoria delle code *(f)*
Pt teoria de colocação em fila *(f)*

Wartezeit *(f) n* De
En waiting time
Es tiempo de espera *(m)*
Fr temps d'attente *(m)*
It tempo di attesa *(m)*
Pt tempo de espera *(m)*

Wartung *(f) n* De
En maintenance
Es mantenimiento *(m)*
Fr maintenance *(f)*
It manutenzione *(f)*
Pt manutenção *(f)*

wesentliche Ziffern *(pl)* De
En significant digits
Es dígitos significativos *(m pl)*
Fr chiffres significatifs *(m pl)*
It digiti significativi *(m pl)*
Pt números digitais significativos *(m pl)*

wheel printer En
De Typenraddrucker *(m)*
Es impresora de ruedas *(f)*
Fr imprimante à roues *(f)*
It stampatrice di ruota *(f)*
Pt impressora de roda *(f)*

Widerstand-Transistor-verknüpfung *(f)* De
En resistor-transistor logic (RTL)
Es lógica de resistencia-transistor *(f)*
Fr logique résistance-transistor *(f)*
It logica resistore-transistore *(f)*
Pt lógica de resistor-transistor *(f)*

Wiederauffinden *(n) n* De
En retrieval
Es recuperación *(f)*
Fr extraction *(f)*
It reperimento *(m)*
Pt recuperação *(f)*

Wiederauffinden von Informationen *(n)* De
En information retrieval
Es recuperación de la información *(f)*
Fr recherche documentaire *(f)*
It reperimento delle informazioni *(m)*
Pt recuperação da informação *(f)*

wiederaufwickeln *vb* De
En rewind
Es rebobinar
Fr rebobiner
It riavvolgere
Pt tornar a enrolar

Wiedereinstiegs-speicherauszug *(m) n* De
En rescue dump
Es vaciado de rescate *(m)*
Fr vidage de secours *(m)*
It dump di salvataggio *(m)*
Pt armazém de emergência *(m)*

Wiedereintreterroutine *(f)* De
En re-entrant procedure
Es procedimiento reentrable *(m)*
Fr procédure d'invariance *(f)*
It procedimento rientrante *(m)*
Pt procedimento de reentrância *(m)*

wiederführen *vb* De
En reroute
Es reencaminar
Fr réacheminer
It dirottare
Pt reencaminhar

Wiedergabe *(f) n* De
En image
Es imagen *(f)*
Fr image *(f)*
It immagine *(f)*
Pt imagem *(f)*

Wiedergabekopf *(m) n* De
En playback head
Es cabeza reproductora *(f)*
Fr tête de lecture *(f)*
It testina di lettura *(f)*
Pt cabeça de playback *(f)*

Wiederherstellung *(f) n* De
En recovery
Es reparación *(f)*
Fr récupération *(f)*
It recupero *(m)*
Pt recuperação *(f)*

Wiederherstellung der höheren Übermittlungs-stufe *(f)* De
En high-level recovery
Es recuperación de alto nivel *(f)*
Fr redressement évolué *(m)*
It ricupero di alto livello *(m)*
Pt recuperação de alto nível *(f)*

wiederholen *vb* De
En rerun
Es repetir la pasada
Fr réexécuter
It riprendere
Pt tornar a passar

wiederholend *adj* De
En iterative
Es iterativo
Fr itératif

It iterativo
Pt iterativo

wiederholte Adressierung *(f)* De
En repetitive addressing
Es direccionado repetitivo *(m)*
Fr adressage sous-entendu *(m)*
It indirizzamento ripetitivo *(m)*
Pt endereçamento repetitivo *(m)*

wiederholter Maschinenlauf *(m)* De
En rerun
Es repetición de pasada *(f)*
Fr reprise *(f)*
It ripresa *(f)*
Pt nova passagem *(f)*

Wiederholung *(f) n* De
En iteration
Es iteración *(f)*
Fr itération *(f)*
It iterazione *(f)*
Pt iteração *(f)*

Wiederholungsbefehl *(m) n* De
En repetition instruction
Es instrucción de repetición *(f)*
Fr répertoire d'instructions *(m)*
It istruzione di ripetizione *(f)*
Pt instrução de repetição *(f)*

Wiederholungspunkt *(m) n* De
En rerun point
Es punto de reanudación de pasada *(m)*
Fr point de reprise *(m)*
It punto di riesecuzione *(m)*
Pt ponto de nova passagem *(m)*

wiederkompilieren *vb* De
En recompile
Es recompilar
Fr recompiler
It ricompilare
Pt recompilar

wiederladen *vb* De
En reload
Es recargar
Fr recharger
It ricaricare
Pt recarregar

wiederschreiben *vb* De
En rewrite
Es reescribir
Fr récrire
It riscrivere
Pt tornar a escrever

Wiederstart *(m) n* De
En restart
Es reanudación *(f)*
Fr relancement *(m)*
It ricominciamento *(m)*
Pt novo arranque *(m)*

wiederstarten *vb* De
En restart
Es reanudar
Fr relancer
It ripartire
Pt rearrancar

Wiederstartspunkt *(m) n* De
En restart point
Es punto de reanudación *(m)*
Fr point de reprise *(m)*
It punto di ripartire *(m)*
Pt ponto de rearranque *(m)*

Wirklichkeits-untersuchung *(f) n* De
En feasibility study
Es estudio de posibilidades *(m)*
Fr étude de faisabilité *(f)*
It studio di fattibilità *(m)*
Pt estudo de viabilidade *(m)*

Wirtsrechner *(m) n* De
En host computer
Es ordenador anfitrión *(m)*
Fr ordinateur central *(m)*
It elaboratore per conto terzi *(m)*
Pt computador hospedeiro *(m)*

word *n* En
De Wort *(n)*
Es palabra *(f)*
Fr mot *(m)*
It voce *(f)*
Pt palavra *(f)*

word length En
De Wortlänge *(f)*
Es longitud de palabra *(f)*
Fr longueur de mot *(f)*
It lunghezza della voce *(f)*
Pt comprimento de palavra *(m)*

word-orientated *adj* En
De wortorientiert
Es orientado a la palabra
Fr à mots
It ad orientamento di voce
Pt orientado por palavras

word processor En
De Wortverarbeiter *(m)*
Es procesador de la palabra *(m)*
Fr unité de traitement de textes *(f)*
It processadore di voce *(m)*
Pt processador de palavras *(m)*

words per minute (wpm) En
De Worte pro Minute *(pl)*
Es palabras por minuto *(f pl)*
Fr mots par minute (mpm) *(m pl)*
It parole al minuto *(f pl)*
Pt palavras por minuto (ppm) *(f pl)*

work area En
De Arbeitsbereich *(m)*
Es zona de maniobra *(f)*
Fr zone de travail *(f)*
It area di lavoro *(f)*
Pt área de trabalho *(f)*

work tape En
De Arbeitsband *(n)*
Es cinta de maniobra *(f)*
Fr bande de travail *(f)*
It nastro di lavoro *(m)*
Pt fita de trabalho *(f)*

Wort *(n) n* De
En word
Es palabra *(f)*
Fr mot *(m)*
It voce *(f)*
Pt palavra *(f)*

Worte pro Minute *(pl)* De
En words per minute (wpm)
Es palabras por minuto *(f pl)*
Fr mots par minute (mpm) *(m pl)*
It parole al minuto *(f pl)*
Pt palavras por minuto (ppm) *(f pl)*

Wörterbuch *(n) n* De
En dictionary; vocabulary
Es diccionario; vocabulario *(m)*
Fr dictionnaire; vocabulaire *(m)*
It dizionario; vocabolario *(m)*
Pt dicionário; vocabulário *(m)*

Wortlänge *(f) n* De
En word length
Es longitud de palabra *(f)*
Fr longueur de mot *(f)*
It lunghezza della voce *(f)*
Pt comprimento de palavra *(m)*

wortorientiert *adj* De
En word-orientated
Es orientado a la palabra
Fr à mots
It ad orientamento di voce
Pt orientado por palavras

Wortverarbeiter *(m) n* De
En word processor
Es procesador de la palabra *(m)*
Fr unité de traitement de textes *(f)*

It processadore di voce (m)
Pt processador de palavras (m)

wortwörtlich übersetzen De
En transliterate
Es transliterar
Fr translitérer
It traslitterare
Pt transliterar

write *vb* En
De schreiben
Es escribir
Fr écrire
It scrivere
Pt escrever

write head En
De Schreibkopf *(m)*
Es cabeza de excritura *(f)*
Fr tête d'écriture *(f)*
It testina di scrittura *(f)*
Pt cabeça escritora *(f)*

write time En
De Schreibzeit *(f)*
Es tiempo de escritura *(m)*
Fr temps d'écriture *(m)*
It tempo di scrittura *(m)*
Pt tempo de escrita *(m)*

X

xerographic printer En
De xerographischer Drucker *(m)*
Es impresora xerográfica *(f)*
Fr imprimante xérographique *(f)*
It stampatrice xerografica *(f)*
Pt impressora xerográfica *(f)*

xerographischer Drucker *(m)* De
En xerographic printer
Es impresora xerográfica *(f)*
Fr imprimante xérographique *(f)*
It stampatrice xerografica *(f)*
Pt impressora xerográfica *(f)*

X-Y-Kurvenzeichner *(m)* De
En X-Y plotter
Es trazador X-Y *(m)*
Fr traceur X-Y *(m)*
It tracciatore X-Y *(m)*
Pt plotador X-Y *(m)*

X-Y plotter En
De X-Y-Kurvenzeichner *(m)*
Es trazador X-Y *(m)*
Fr traceur X-Y *(m)*
It tracciatore X-Y *(m)*
Pt plotador X-Y *(m)*

Z

Zähler *(m) n* De
En counter
Es contador *(m)*
Fr compteur *(m)*
It contatore *(m)*
Pt contador *(m)*

Zahl mit mehrfacher Wortlänge *(f)* De
En multiple-length number
Es número de longitud múltiple *(m)*
Fr nombre de plusieurs chiffres *(m)*
It numero a lunghezza multipla *(m)*
Pt número de comprimento múltiplo *(m)*

Zehnerkomplement *(n) n* De
En tens complement
Es complemento a diez *(m)*
Fr complément à dix *(m)*
It complemento di decine *(m)*
Pt complemento de dezenas *(m)*

Zeichen *(n) n* De
En graphics
Es gráfica *(f)*
Fr graphisme *(m)*
It grafica *(f)*
Pt gráfica *(f)*

Zeichenanzeige *(f) n* De
En graphics display
Es representación gráfica *(f)*
Fr visualisation graphique *(f)*
It visualizzatore grafico *(m)*
Pt representação gráfica *(f)*

Zeichencode *(m) n* De
En character code
Es código de caracteres *(m)*
Fr code de caractère *(m)*
It codice del carattere *(m)*
Pt código de caracteres *(m)*

Zeichendichte *(f) n* De
En character density
Es densidad de caracteres *(f)*
Fr densité de caractères *(f)*
It densità di caratteri *(f)*
Pt densidade de caracteres *(f)*

Zeichendrucker *(m) n* De
En graphics printer
Es impresora gráfica *(f)*
Fr imprimante graphique *(f)*
It stampatrice grafica *(f)*
Pt impressora gráfica *(f)*

Zeichenerkennung *(f) n* De
En character recognition
Es reconocimiento de caracteres *(m)*
Fr reconnaissance de caractères *(f)*
It riconoscimento di carattere *(m)*
Pt reconhecimento de caracteres *(m)*

Zeichenleser *(m) n* De
En character reader
Es lectora de caracteres *(f)*
Fr lecteur de caractères *(m)*
It lettore di caratteri *(m)*
Pt leitor de caracteres *(m)*

zeichenmäβig ausgerichtet De
En character-orientated
Es orientado a los caracteres
Fr fonctionnement à caractères
It orientato a carattere
Pt orientado por caracteres

Zeichen pro Sekunde *(pl)* De
En characters per second (cps)
Es caracteres por segundo *(m pl)*
Fr caractères par seconde *(m pl)*
It caratteri al secondo *(m pl)*
Pt caracteres por segundo *(m pl)*

Zeichensatz *(m) n* De
En character set
Es juego de caracteres *(m)*
Fr jeu de caractères *(m)*
It gruppo di caratteri *(m)*
Pt jogo de caracteres *(m)*

Zeichenstation *(f) n* De
En graphics terminal
Es terminal gráfico *(m)*
Fr terminal graphique *(m)*
It terminale grafico *(m)*
Pt terminal gráfico *(m)*

Zeiger *(m) n* De
En pointer
Es indicador *(m)*
Fr indicateur *(m)*
It lancetta *(f)*
Pt ponteiro *(m)*

Zeile *(f) n* De
En row
Es fila *(f)*
Fr ligne *(f)*
It fila *(f)*
Pt fila *(f)*

Zeilendrucker *(m) n* De
En line printer
Es impresora de líneas *(f)*
Fr imprimante ligne par ligne *(f)*
It stampatrice a linea *(f)*
Pt impressora de linha *(f)*

Zeilen pro Minute *(pl)* De
En lines per minute (lpm)
Es líneas por minuto *(f pl)*
Fr lignes par minute *(f pl)*
It linee al minuto *(f pl)*
Pt linhas por minuto *(f pl)*

Zeilensprung *(m) n* De
En row pitch
Es paso entre filas *(m)*
Fr pas longitudinal *(m)*
It passo di fila *(m)*
Pt passo de fila *(m)*

Zeit für technische Arbeiten *(f)* De
En engineering time
Es tiempo de inmovilización *(m)*
Fr temps d'immobilisation *(m)*
It tempo di immobilizzazione *(m)*
Pt tempo de engenharia *(m)*

Zeitscheibenverfahren *(n) n* De
En time slice
Es fracción de tiempo *(f)*
Fr découpage du temps *(m)*
It ripartizione di tempo *(f)*
Pt fatia de tempo *(f)*

Zeitskala *(f) n* De
En time scale
Es escala de tiempos *(f)*
Fr échelle des temps *(f)*
It scala di tempo *(f)*
Pt escala de tempo *(f)*

Zeitteilung *(f) n* De
En time sharing
Es tiempo compartido *(m)*
Fr utilisation en temps partagé *(f)*
It lavoro di multi-programmazione *(f)*
Pt compartido tempo *(m)*

Zeituhr *(f) n* De
En timer; timer clock
Es temporizador *(m)*
Fr rythmeur *(m)*
It temporizzatore *(m)*
Pt relógio marcador de tempos *(m)*

Zelle *(f) n* De
En cell
Es célula *(f)*
Fr cellule *(f)*
It cellula *(f)*
Pt célula *(f)*

Zentraleinheit *(f) n* De
En central processing unit
Es unidad central de proceso *(f)*
Fr unité de traitement centrale *(f)*
It unità centrale di elaborazione *(f)*
Pt unidade de processamento central *(f)*

zero-address instruction En
De Nulladressen-anweisung *(f)*
Es instrucción de dirección cero *(f)*
Fr instruction sans adresse *(f)*
It istruzione ad indirizzo zero *(f)*
Pt instrução de endereço zero *(f)*

zero-output signal En
De Nullausgangssignal *(n)*
Es señal de salida cero *(f)*
Fr signal de sortie zéro *(m)*
It segnale di output zero *(m)*
Pt sinal de output zero *(m)*

zero state En
De Nullzustand *(m)*
Es estado cero *(m)*
Fr état zéro *(m)*
It stato zero *(m)*
Pt estado zero *(m)*

zero suppression En
De Nullunterdrückung *(f)*
Es supresión de ceros *(f)*
Fr élimination des zéros *(f)*
It soppressione di zero *(f)*
Pt supressão zero *(f)*

zerstörungsfreie Auslesung *(f)* De
En nondestructive read
Es lectura no destructiva *(f)*
Fr lecture non destructive *(f)*
It lettura non distruttiva *(f)*
Pt leitura não destrutiva *(f)*

zerstörungsfreie Lesefunktion *(f)* De
En nondestructive read operation (NDRO)
Es operación de lectura no destructiva *(f)*
Fr opération de lecture non destructive (OLND) *(f)*
It operazione di lettura non distruttiva *(f)*
Pt operação de leitura não destrutiva *(f)*

Zielprogramm *(n) n* De
En object program
Es programa objeto *(m)*
Fr programme objet *(m)*
It programma oggetto *(m)*
Pt programa de objecto *(m)*

Zielsprache *(f) n* De
En target language
Es lenguaje resultante *(m)*
Fr langage généré *(m)*
It linguaggio risultante *(m)*
Pt linguagem de objectivo *(f)*

Ziffer *(f) n* De
En digit
Es dígito *(m)*
Fr chiffre *(m)*
It digit *(m)*
Pt número digital *(m)*

zona *(f) n* Es, Pt
De Zone *(f)*
En zone
Fr zone *(f)*
It zonatura *(f)*

zona de maniobra *(f)* Es
De Arbeitsbereich *(m)*
En work area
Fr zone de travail *(f)*
It area di lavoro *(f)*
Pt área de trabalho *(f)*

zona mais *(f)* Pt
De Pluszone *(f)*
En plus zone
Es zona positiva *(f)*
Fr zone plus *(f)*
It zona più *(f)*

zona meno *(f)* It
De Minuszone *(f)*
En minus zone
Es zona negativa *(f)*
Fr zone moins *(f)*
Pt zona menos *(f)*

zona menos *(f)* Pt
De Minuszone *(f)*
En minus zone
Es zona negativa *(f)*
Fr zone moins *(f)*
It zona meno *(f)*

zona negativa *(f)* Es
De Minuszone *(f)*
En minus zone
Fr zone moins *(f)*
It zona meno *(f)*
Pt zona menos *(f)*

zona più *(f)* It
De Pluszone *(f)*
En plus zone
Es zona positiva *(f)*
Fr zone plus *(f)*
Pt zona mais *(f)*

zona positiva *(f)* Es
De Pluszone *(f)*
En plus zone
Fr zone plus *(f)*
It zona più *(f)*
Pt zona mais *(f)*

zonatura *(f) n* It
De Zone *(f)*
En zone
Es zona *(f)*
Fr zone *(f)*
Pt zona *(f)*

zone *n* En; Fr *(f)*
De Zone *(f)*
Es zona *(f)*
It zonatura *(f)*
Pt zona *(f)*

Zone *(f) n* De
En zone
Es zona *(f)*
Fr zone *(f)*
It zonatura *(f)*
Pt zona *(f)*

zone bit En
De Zonenbit *(m)*
Es bit de zona *(m)*
Fr bit de zone *(m)*
It bit di zonatura *(m)*
Pt bit de zona *(m)*

zone de sortie *(f)* Fr
De Ausgangsbereich *(m)*
En output area
Es área de salida *(f)*
It area di uscita *(f)*
Pt área de output *(f)*

zone de travail *(f)* Fr
De Arbeitsbereich *(m)*
En work area
Es zona de maniobra *(f)*
It area di lavoro *(f)*
Pt área de trabalho *(f)*

zone digit En
De Zonenziffer *(f)*
Es dígito de zona *(m)*
Fr chiffre de zone *(m)*
It digit di zonatura *(m)*
Pt número digital de zona *(m)*

zone fixe *(f)* Fr
De festes Feld *(n)*
En fixed field
Es campo fijo *(m)*
It campo fisso *(m)*
Pt campo fixo *(m)*

zone moins *(f)* Fr
De Minuszone *(f)*
En minus zone
Es zona negativa *(f)*
It zona meno *(f)*
Pt zona menos *(f)*

Zonenbit *(m) n* De
En zone bit
Es bit de zona *(m)*
Fr bit de zone *(m)*
It bit di zonatura *(m)*
Pt bit de zona *(m)*

Zonenziffer *(f) n* De
En zone digit
Es dígito de zona *(m)*
Fr chiffre de zone *(m)*
It digit di zonatura *(m)*
Pt número digital de zona *(m)*

zone plus *(f)* Fr
De Pluszone *(f)*
En plus zone
Es zona positiva *(f)*
It zona più *(f)*
Pt zona mais *(f)*

Zufallsnummerngeber *(m) n* De
En random-number generator
Es generador de números aleatorios *(m)*
Fr générateur de nombres aléatoires *(m)*
It generatore di numeri casuali *(m)*
Pt gerador de números aleatórios *(m)*

zugreifen *vb* De
En access
Es acceder
Fr accéder
It accedere
Pt aceder

Zugriff *(m) n* De
En access
Es acceso *(m)*
Fr accès *(m)*
It accesso *(m)*
Pt acesso *(m)*

Zugriffspfad *(m) n* De
En path
Es curso *(m)*
Fr branchement *(m)*
It percorso *(m)*
Pt caminho *(m)*

Zugriffsstufe *(f) n* De
En access level
Es nivel de acceso *(m)*
Fr niveau d'accès *(m)*
It livello di accesso *(m)*
Pt nível de acesso *(m)*

Zugriffsverzögerung *(f)* De
En latency
Es latencia *(f)*
Fr latence *(f)*
It latenza *(f)*
Pt latência *(f)*

Zugriffszeit *(f) n* De
En access time
Es tiempo de acceso *(m)*
Fr temps d'accès *(m)*
It tempo di accesso *(m)*
Pt tempo de acesso *(m)*

zusammenfügen *vb* De
En join
Es unir
Fr grouper
It unire
Pt unir

Zusammentreffens-Schaltung *(f)* De
En coincidence gate
Es puerta de coincidencia *(f)*
Fr porte à coïncidence *(f)*
It porta di coincidenza *(f)*
Pt porta de coincidência *(f)*

Zusatzwartung *(f) n* De
En supplementary maintenance
Es mantenimiento suplementario *(m)*
Fr maintenance supplémentaire *(f)*
It manutenzione supplementare *(f)*
Pt manutenção suplementária *(f)*

Zuverlässigkeit *(f) n* De
En reliability
Es fiabilidad *(f)*
Fr fiabilité *(f)*
It affidabilita *(f)*
Pt confiança *(f)*

zuweisen *vb* De
En allocate
Es asignar
Fr affecter
It allocare
Pt atribuir

Zuweisung *(f) n* De
En allocation
Es asignación *(f)*
Fr affectation *(f)*
It allocazione *(f)*
Pt atribuição *(f)*

Zweiadressen-anweisung *(f) n* De
En two-address instruction
Es instrucción con dos direcciones *(f)*
Fr instruction à deux adresses *(f)*
It istruzione a due indirizzi *(f)*
Pt instrução de dois endereços *(f)*

Zweideutigkeitsfehler *(m)* De
En ambiguity error
Es error de ambigüedad *(m)*
Fr erreur d'ambiguité *(f)*
It errore di ambiguità *(m)*
Pt erro de ambiguidade *(m)*

zweidimensionale Speicherung *(f)* De
En two-dimensional storage
Es memoria bidimensional *(f)*
Fr stockage à double entrée *(m)*
It memoria bidimensionale *(f)*
Pt armazenamento bidimensional *(m)*

Zweierkomplement *(n) n* De
En twos complement

Es complemento a dos *(m)*
Fr complément deux *(m)*
It complemento al due *(m)*
Pt complemento de dois *(m)*

Zweig *(m)* *n* De
En branch
Es bifurcación *(f)*
Fr branchement *(m)*
It diramazione *(f)*
Pt ramo *(m)*

zweistellige Funktion *(f)* De
En dyadic operation
Es operación diádica *(f)*
Fr opération dyadique *(f)*
It operazione diadica *(f)*
Pt operação diádica *(f)*

zweitgeneration *adj* De
En second-generation
Es segunda-generación
Fr deuxième-génération
It seconda-generazione
Pt segunda-geração

zwingen *vb* De
En force
Es forzar
Fr forcer
It forzare
Pt forçar

Zwischenspeicherung *(f)* *n* De
En intermediate storage
Es memoria intermedia *(f)*
Fr mémoire intermédiaire *(f)*
It memoria intermedia *(f)*
Pt armazenagem intermediária *(m)*

Zwischensystem-Verbindungswege *(pl)* De
En intersystem communications
Es comunicaciones entre sistemas *(f pl)*
Fr transmission inter-système *(f)*
It comunicazioni tra sistemi *(f pl)*
Pt comunicações entre sistemas *(f pl)*

zyklischer Code *(m)* De
En cyclic code
Es código cíclico *(m)*
Fr code cyclique *(m)*
It codice ciclico *(m)*
Pt código cíclico *(m)*

Zylinder *(m)* *n* De
En cylinder
Es cilindro *(m)*
Fr cylindre *(m)*
It cilindro *(m)*
Pt cilindro *(m)*